Truman & MacArthur

Truman &

Policy, Politics, and the Hunger
for Honor and Renown

MacArthur

Michael D. Pearlman

INDIANA UNIVERSITY PRESS ✪ BLOOMINGTON AND INDIANAPOLIS

This book is a publication of

Indiana University Press
601 North Morton Street
Bloomington, IN 47404-3797 USA

http://iupress.indiana.edu

Telephone orders   800-842-6796
Fax orders   812-855-7931
Orders by e-mail   iuporder@indiana.edu

The paper used in this publication meets the minimum requirements of American National
Standard for Information Sciences—Permanence of Paper for Printed Library Materials,
ANSI Z39.48-1984.

Manufactured in the United States of America
Library of Congress Cataloging-in-Publication Data

Pearlman, Michael D., date
    Truman and MacArthur : policy, politics, and the hunger for honor and renown / Michael
D. Pearlman.
        p. cm.
    Includes bibliographical references and index.
    ISBN-13: 978-0-253-35066-4 (cloth : alk. paper)   1. Korean War, 1950–1953—United
States. 2. Truman, Harry S., 1884–1972. 3. MacArthur, Douglas, 1880–1964. 4. Civil-mili-
tary relations—United States—History—20th century. 5. Executive power—United States—
History—20th century. 6. United States—Politics and government—1945–1953.   I. Title.
    DS919.P43 2008
    951.904'24092273—dc22

                                    2007030658

1   2   3   4   5   13   12   11   10   09   08

To family, friends, and memories, as well as to the future

Of all the passions that inspire men in battle, none, we have to admit, is so powerful and so constant as the hunger for honor and renown.

KARL VON CLAUSEWITZ, 1832

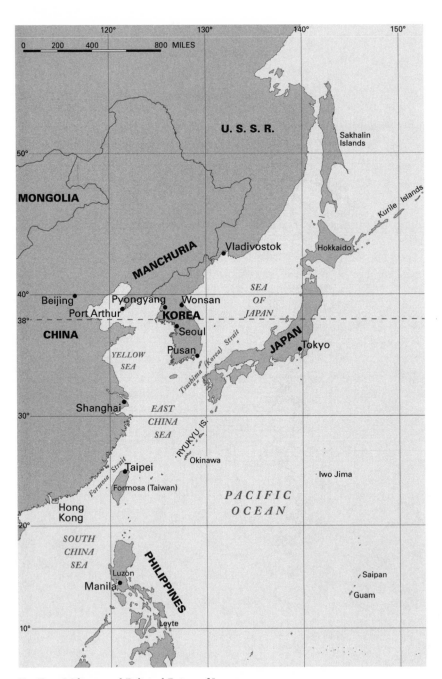

Far East: Military and Political Points of Interest

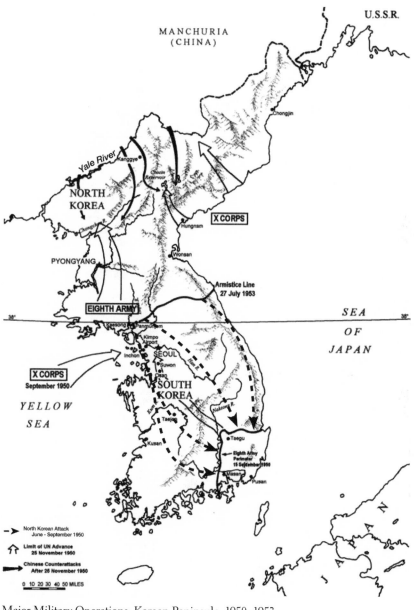

Major Military Operations; Korean Peninsula, 1950–1953

Contents

Acknowledgments

Several people deserve lots of the credit and none of the blame this book may or may not garner. Colonel (Ret.) Rick Swain and Pat Roe, author and Marine veteran of Korea, read what I wrote about military operations and saved me from some bad mistakes. Bob Ferrell, Dennis Giangreco, and Ed Drea, true experts on Truman or MacArthur, read drafts and tried to educate me about this president and that general. Paul Edwards, founder of the Center for the Study of the Korean War, shared his extraordinary knowledge of that conflict. Jim Schneider, John Braeman, and Don Gilmore read the entire manuscript and improved the writing substantially, although subsequent readers might wonder where. The staff of the Indiana University Press and freelance copy editor Carol Kennedy have been very helpful, patient, and understanding. At the MacArthur and Truman libraries, Jim Zobel, Liz Safly, Dennis Bilger, Randy Sowell, and Pauline Testerman were invaluable. If Truman and MacArthur had been nearly that helpful to one another, I would have had no story to tell.

Introduction

Notwithstanding movies such as *Seven Days in May* and *JFK*, the American officer corps has been remarkably compliant to the civilian head of state, although generals have disagreed with government policy, as has everyone else. Winfield Scott, the commander of the expeditionary army occupying Mexico in 1847, was deeply aggrieved at President James K. Polk's policy of conquest. George B. McClellan, the commander of the Army of the Potomac, despised Abraham Lincoln's Emancipation Proclamation, September 1862. John J. Pershing, commander of American Expeditionary Forces, lamented Woodrow Wilson's cease-fire with Germany, November 1918. William C. Westmoreland, army commander in Vietnam, regretted Lyndon Johnson's refusal to take the ground war into enemy sanctuaries, 1967 and 1968. Wesley Clark, supreme allied commander, Europe, tried to push Bill Clinton toward committing ground troops against Serbia in 1998. The Korean War, the context of this particular book, was no exception, even after Harry S. Truman relieved Douglas MacArthur from military command in 1951. General Mark W. Clark, a successor in the Far East, signed an armistice with tears in his eyes in 1953, evidence of deep disappointment that Truman's successor, Dwight Eisenhower, would not listen to Clark's plans for victory, although they had been friends since they were cadets at West Point forty years before. In each case, what really mattered was that personal preferences did not affect professional behavior. They all obeyed their orders as good soldiers, although three sought subsequent redress through constitutional means. Scott ran against Polk's party in 1852; McClellan ran against Lincoln in 1864. Wes Clark sought the Democratic nomination in 2004 as vindication after involuntary retirement.[1]

The great exception to deference to presidential policy is the case of MacArthur during Korea, an incident that still stirs passion on both sides of the issue. Many feel the general was an egomaniac who threatened the survival of the U.S. Constitution, let alone humankind. Others I met while a historian for the army think Truman a political "hack." My job, writing some fifty years after the fact, is not to produce another partisan polemic for one individual or the other, something not endearing to those who have told me "well, I like MacArthur" or "you should see things Truman's way." Let me come to my own defense, a lonely job that befalls writers on controversial topics. I no longer have certain opinions held when beginning my research several years ago. Truman, despite his reputation for decisiveness, often deferred to MacArthur. MacArthur, while often reckless, made a reasonable case that his policy would not lead to world war with the Soviet Union, the purported reason for his dismissal. I therefore trust I am better prepared to give an objective and comprehensive account of events through everyone's—and hence no one's—point of view. This precludes a rush to bestow blame or acclaim. It also draws this book beyond the territorial confines of Korea into partisan competition for control of Washington and the political power of military officers in an administration too weak to carry national policy on its own accord. America's alliance with European nations was another important factor. So was the government's position toward Formosa (now known as Taiwan), which was the long-standing root of the dispute between Truman and MacArthur. The president first discussed relieving the general in August 1950, after the latter wrote a letter to the Veterans of Foreign War about defense policy concerning that island. He dismissed him in April 1951, after MacArthur wrote a letter to a Republican congressman about using Formosa in the war against China.

Neither Truman nor MacArthur fully met his objectives during the Korean War. The president ended up with something much more than a "police action" conducted to forestall a major conflict. The general did not inflict on communist China a defeat so catastrophic that it collapsed the regime. Both men were out of power by 1953, after the country placed the war in the hands of a replacement neither favored, Dwight D. Eisenhower. This crisis in U.S. civil-military relations affected him and he affected it, as did other prominent people discussed in this book: Dean Acheson, Dean Rusk, Averell Harriman, George Kennan, George Marshall, Omar Bradley, Matt Ridgway, J. Lawton Collins, Robert Taft, Tom Dewey, Richard Russell, and Lyndon Johnson. The same was true of other military and civilian figures less-remembered now: Joe Martin, Louis Johnson, George Reedy, Frank Lowe, Harry Vaughan, Ned Almond, Charles Willoughby, and Courtney Whitney. Foreign figures also played prominent roles, particularly Clement Attlee, Chiang Kai-shek, Mao Tse-tung, Kim Il-sung, and Joseph Stalin. Archival material opened since the fall of the Soviet Union helps clarify the international setting for the conflict between Truman and MacArthur.[2]

Accomplished historians have written some excellent studies about or pertaining to the war in Korea. My footnotes demonstrate my debt to Robert Ferrell, D. Clayton James, William Stueck, Roy Appleman, Kathryn Weathersby, Alan Millett, Chen Jian, and others. My own work is a hybrid: part military and political analysis, part diplomatic history, and part collective biography overlapping in the same narrative. Most writers usually give most attention to policies, politics, or personalities in a relatively concise period. I hope to shed some fresh light on an old topic by focusing on the interaction of all three before, during, and after the Korean War. The central issue in the story has long been known: the general would attack China; the president would not. A synthesis that reconsiders the effects of interpersonal relations, as well as institutions, may strengthen the explanation as to how, when, and why the impasse came to be.

Truman and MacArthur—and virtually every other American in authority—opposed communism, feared displaying weakness, and took assurance from military strength. Critics of this cold war consensus see little substantive difference between these men, whom they reproach for unwarranted intervention in Korea on behalf of a right-wing regime. Other academics may simply discount another look at Truman and MacArthur at a time when current scholarship is more concerned with common people and their place in social history. Neither point of view is completely valid when it comes to the general and the president. The common people of the body politic are not absent since they played an important role, rarely off the mind of either man. Their preference would determine who prevailed: actually Eisenhower by 1952. As for the cold war consensus, it determined events when Truman and MacArthur cooperated but cannot explain their ultimate conflict. National interests such as security and prosperity did not implement themselves. They lay in the hands of complex individuals with motives beyond plain affairs of state. Government policy and power were at stake; so were personal reputation, honor, and renown.

As to policy, in broad brush, Truman preferred prudence to direct confrontation with the Soviet Union or communist China, at least when military push came to shove. MacArthur, on the other hand, held to his maxim "there is no substitute for victory." The president, from mid to late 1950, gave him latitude to escalate the war against North Korea, lest weakness encourage communist expansion and therefore the major conflict Truman wished to preclude. Ironically, the strength demonstrated in pushing North Korea's army back to its border precipitated war with China and tense deliberations about using the atomic bomb to prevent potential Soviet deployment of air and submarine forces in the Far East theater.

Policy might have never faced this predicament were it not for politics. Truman's partisan opponents, searching for issues to end Democratic rule in Washington, were happy to make use of MacArthur, a military hero with a seductive platform of victory over communism. The general, well informed about political currents, used this leverage to loosen executive branch controls on his command. His sympathies were certainly with Republicans, but he did not personally enter the partisan debate as long as Truman allowed him to fight North Korea as he wished. Truman, once China entered the war, had to make the fateful choice he long tried to avoid: limit his theater commander or risk World War III. When MacArthur subsequently endorsed a sharp Republican attack on administration policy, the president relieved the general for reasons not solely policy or politics.

Deeply personal feelings also drove Truman, whether abiding MacArthur in 1950 or relieving him in 1951. A fervent reader of history, the president felt the record of great generals taught a basic rule: politicians have no business interfering with military operations. This belief staid Truman's hand even after China's intervention forced him to stay MacArthur's hand. The general retained his posting, although openly critical of presidential policy, until he endorsed a Republican broadsheet. He thereby lost the aura soldiers could have in Truman's mind. However, by relieving MacArthur once he seemed a political operative, the president gave the political opposition exactly what it wanted, the chance to pin on Truman the onus of a politician interfering with a commander in the midst of war.

Policy, politics, and personality are the themes and thesis of this book. They interweave throughout this narrative about Truman, MacArthur, and the supplementary characters collectively creating the most dramatic crisis in U.S. civil-military relations. One factor blended into another; they interacted to produce a dynamic stronger than policy, politics, or personality acting by itself. This created, through combination, a stream of themes not bound exclusively to the Korean War. Perceptions as of 1905 foretell events in 1951. Subsequent incidents from the mid-1950s to the national election of 2004 provide context for what had transpired when the United States waged war in northeast Asia. Less clarity, of course, existed for people having to cope with contingencies once the North Korean army crossed the 38th parallel on 25 June 1950.

Abbreviations

AAA	antiaircraft artillery
AEF	American Expeditionary Force (World War I)
CCP	Chinese Communist Party
CCF	Chinese communist (military) forces
CIA	(United States government) Central Intelligence Agency
CINCFE	(military) commander in chief, Far East
CNO	chief of naval operation
CP	(military) command post
CWIHPB	Cold War International History Project Bulletin
DA	Department of the (United States) Army
DOD	(United States government) Department of Defense
EPL	(Dwight D.) Eisenhower Presidential Library, Abilene, Kansas
FRUS	(State Department) Foreign Relations of the United States
GHQ	general headquarters
JCS	(United States Armed Forces) Joint Chiefs of Staff
JCS, CF	Joint Chiefs of Staff, Chairman's File (in Record Group 218, National Archives)
JCS, GF	Joint Chiefs of Staff, Geographical File (in Record Group 218, National Archives)
JPL	(Lyndon B.) Johnson Presidential Library, Austin, Texas
KMT	Kuomintang
KPA	(North) Korean People's Army
MMFL	(Douglas) MacArthur Memorial Foundation Library, Norfolk, Virginia
NA	National Archives and Records Administration, College Park, Maryland

NATO	North Atlantic Treaty Organization
n.d.	no date
NYHT	*New York Herald Tribune*
NYT	*New York Times*
PLA	(Chinese communist) People's Liberation Army
POW	prisoner of war
PPOPE	*Public Papers of President Eisenhower*
PPOPT	*Public Papers of President Truman*
PRC	(Communist) People's Republic of China
PSB	Psychological Strategy Board
PSF	President's Secretary's File (Truman Library)
PSYOPS	psychological operations
RG	record group (National Archives and MacArthur Library)
ROK	Republic of (South) Korea, government or armed forces
SCAP	Supreme Commander Allied Powers (occupied Japan)
SWPA	Southwest Pacific Area (of World War II military operations)
TPL	(Harry S.) Truman Presidential Library, Independence, Missouri
USMHI	United States Military History Institute, Army War College, Carlisle Barracks, Pennsylvania
USSR	Union of Soviet Socialist Republics
WP	*Washington Post*

Truman & MacArthur

Truman and MacArthur, before Korea

1 2 3 4 5 6 7 8 9

What is past is prologue.

WILLIAM SHAKESPEARE AND UNITED STATES NATIONAL ARCHIVES

Hostility toward a president did not suddenly emerge in Douglas MacArthur in the midst of the Korean War. It had roots in the parents who raised him to believe he had a special destiny, an outgrowth of his father's own conflicts with officialdom. It also lay in MacArthur's experience in the Philippines, the place he thought destined to determine global supremacy. He would become a public icon in the futile attempt to protect those islands from Japan, all the while raging at Washington for not sending resources adequate to execute this mission he craved. The result was a national hero with a festering resentment, later to be focused on the Truman administration when MacArthur shifted propositions and proposals first formed about the Philippine Islands to the island of Formosa, from which he hoped to shape great events in Asia. The president, not inclined to handle him firmly, let a combustible combination of anger, ambition, and opportunity gather critical momentum. The real story is not that Harry Truman ever fired Douglas MacArthur; it is how long it took him to make that move. His reluctance to face up to the problem had a pedigree apart from the common American belief that politicians should not interfere in military operations. It lay in Truman's ambivalence about professional soldiers and the books he read growing up in the 1890s, a personal experience profoundly affecting presidential policy.

Douglas MacArthur: His Career in Brief

He has imagination, self-confidence, physical courage and charm but no humor about himself, no regard for truth, and is unaware of these defects. He mistakes his emotions and ambitions for principles. With moral depth he would be a great man; as it is he is a near-miss, which may be worse than a mile.

BRITISH ARMY LIAISON OFFICER, MACARTHUR HEADQUARTERS, 15 OCT. 1943[1]

Douglas MacArthur was seventy years old when the Korean War began. No one can give a full but brief account of a span this long in anyone's life, let alone an army chief of staff, World War II theater commander, and proconsul of occupied Japan. Because the focus of this study is his conflict with President Truman, these topics will only be discussed in relation to problems with government authorities. Even here, caveats are required. All human beings are complex and inconsistent: part admirable, part petty. However, whereas most people are moderately good or relatively bad, MacArthur played at the edges. "The best and the worst things you hear about him," said one allied general, "are both true."[2]

This Dr. Jekyll–Mr. Hyde syndrome, for want of a better term, was one striking factor in MacArthur's makeup. So were rapid mood swings between excessive optimism and equal pessimism, in Korea as in World War II. These characteristics may well have been related to the general's baffling states of physical health, apt to exaggerate his paradoxical traits. He could wear out men less than half his age when trampling through tropical jungles or riding on rocky Korean roads in an open jeep facing a cold wind. Yet within a few weeks, he could look like a "querulous old man with the shakes," often thought to be a sign of Parkinson's disease. He had no such illness, said physicians who served with the general or attended his deathbed. He had a very mild tremor, barely perceptible except when under extreme stress associated with major points of transition: immediately before and after World War II, near the end of his civil mission in Japan, and after China's intervention in the Korean War.[3]

How this sporadic change in MacArthur's physiology relates to his behavior—cause, effect, or symptom—remains something of a mystery. So does the man himself. Many people who worked with the general, from headquarters stenographer up to assistant chiefs of staff, testify that MacArthur "in the ordinary routine of the day was the epitome of courtesy, consideration, and sympathetic understanding"; he "never showed the little human failures that most people have, neither on the personal or official side." They did not see the general shed the role he played with the "grace and charm of a stage hero," to quote a prominent newspaperman. MacArthur actually was an introvert, attests his devoted wife. He spent hours in solitude at the West Point cemetery in the late 1950s: "I want to be with my friends."[4]

Even when a Dr. Jekyll seemed present, a Mr. Hyde lurked behind MacArthur's curtain. Certain observers got a glance on particular occasions, such as a private meeting on joint military command in 1945, when the U.S. Air Force chief of staff noted that MacArthur "gets excited and walks the floor, raises his voice," obviously discharging anger while retaining some semblance of self-control. Dr. Roger Egeberg, the physician cum confessor in MacArthur headquarters, saw the general with his veil of propriety completely off, no outsider present, such as the staff assistant who "never heard him use any profanity, even 'hell' or 'damn.'" He could actually "let loose with a flow of invectives welling up from deep distress," what Egeberg called a "vocabulary any Missouri mule skinner would have envied."[5]

When searching for something of relative assurance in the midst of MacArthur's inconsistencies, one can fall back on the fact that his parents were striking figures with enormous drive and ambition. His mother's brothers were officers in the Army of Northern Virginia, of more than antiquarian interest. Its commander, Robert E. Lee, set the standard MacArthur was supposed to meet, thanks to his mother, "Pinky," instilling goals befitting some kind of superman. This may have been the root of MacArthur's least admirable traits: hypersensitivity to criticism and hostility toward potential competitors. If not supreme and ideal, might he be rejected—by his mother and the world at large? As for his father, Lieutenant General Arthur MacArthur, he too was a legendary figure: "Of all the men I have ever known, he was the one I most respected and admired." The Yankee war hero was also the person he most resembled, even if "the rebel yell and the sound of 'Dixie' have been in my ears since birth." Arthur was exceptionally brave and articulate, as well as charming when it served his purpose. He was also rebellious and resentful when it came to anything that slighted his honor and authority, real or just perceived.[6]

At seventeen, Arthur MacArthur enlisted in the Civil War against the wishes of his own father. One year later, he led a renowned charge at the Battle of Chattanooga, where he exceeded instructions to attack no further than the first line of Confederates at the base of a substantial hill. He broke through these enemy positions onto higher ground, the rare occasion when a frontal assault carried a prepared defense. This would contain a lesson for his impressionable son, whose "vivid imagination," said a West Point classmate, "made him feel that he had gone up Missionary Ridge with his father's regiment." Disregard orthodox directives, run substantial risk, and win substantial reward: in this case promotion to brevet colonel at the age of twenty and the Congressional Medal of Honor, although bestowed belatedly. "It's the orders you disobey that make you famous," Douglas MacArthur subsequently said.[7]

Arthur MacArthur's career came up short, despite its spectacular start, insofar as failing to reach his goal, that of army chief of staff. He clashed with civilian authorities such as William Howard Taft, colonial governor of the Philippines in the early 1900s, especially when the general failed to support the Republican Party line that U.S. forces had broken the back of the local insurgency. His position, right or wrong, was of use to Democrats, who held that America was stuck in military stalemate. The general, certainly no anti-imperialist, was not lining up directly with the political opposition in 1901, as his son did fifty years later. However, MacArthur so seriously alienated the War Department and the White House that they were ready to strike when the occasion arrived in 1904. He made some comments that were discovered by a reporter, getting Washington's attention with a screeching headline: "GENERAL MACARTHUR WARNS HAWAII OF A COMING WAR WITH GERMANY." President Theodore Roosevelt then filed a rebuke: "Our army and navy officers must not comment about foreign power in a way that will cause trouble."[8]

Taft, now secretary of war, stepped in to send MacArthur on a so-called reconnaissance mission in the Far East, a patent move to get rid of an embarrassing figure. His family accompanied the general on what became his son's seminal education about issues of the Orient, of less importance to Washington than to young Lieutenant Douglas MacArthur. The government did not even ask the general to file a trip report, although he had plenty of time on his hands while waiting in Milwaukee for a next assignment that never arrived. His son, detailed to river and harbor duty there, lived at home with a man so embittered at the White House, the War Department, and their underlings on the general staff that by Arthur's decree no uniforms were to be worn at his funeral in 1912. Douglas, who kept his father's picture by his bedside until he too passed away, not only told people "I really feel Dad's presence." He wrote that he took responsibilities he did not relish because his mother said that "my father would be ashamed if I showed timidity." When he became army chief of staff in 1930, his mother whispered in his ear, "If only your father could see you now Douglas, you're everything he wanted to be."[9]

This appointment did not settle all contention between the MacArthur family and the U.S. government, particularly whether Europe was more important than Asia. Douglas thought the former "a dying system . . . worn out and run down," but one cannot be sure about motivation. Did the MacArthurs seek postings along the western Pacific because they deemed them crucial, or did they think the region crucial because they sought postings deemed a stairway for their personal ascent? Either way, in 1882 Arthur requested assignment as military attaché in China, a country he studied extensively. He wrote a forty-four-page manuscript about its civilization and institutions to establish his expertise. Washington, however, paid it little heed, even when referred by Ulysses S. Grant, commanding general when MacArthur charged up Missionary Ridge. The War Department sent attaches to Europe, not the Far East, despite MacArthur's emphatic opinion that "the American Republic can never acquire its full complement of riches and power if it permits itself to be excluded from the field of Asiatic commerce."[10]

The acquisition of the Philippines in 1898 renewed debates about international priorities that eventually evolved into the Pacific defense perimeter of islands off the coast of mainland Asia that America held on the eve of the Korean War. Arthur MacArthur proposed much the same thing in 1902, when testifying that the Philippine archipelago constituted a "strategic position unexcelled by that of any other position on the globe." Douglas, raised on such propositions about "the stepping stone to commanding influence" in "all future contests for supremacy," repeated them virtually verbatim, particularly about the destiny of the Philippines to attain "a universal influence upon the prosperity and welfare of all civilized peoples." In 1935, he went to Manila with the encouragement of Franklin Roosevelt, as eager as Taft to get a MacArthur out of the United States. FDR dangled in front of the general's face a joint civil-military appointment, that of senior armed forces officer and high commissioner to the Philippines. To MacArthur, this would be a position of "high glamour and potential political possibilities," especially inviting when he was facing the fate of his father: no suitable position left for the highest-ranking officer in the army. The president promised to extend his lapsing appointment as chief of staff to mid-December so that MacArthur could arrive on the islands with the institutional leverage to jump-start his mission of building an effective Filipino military force. He could raid instructors, cadre, and equipment from the American garrison on Luzon—that is, until he reached Wyoming en route by train to his ship sailing out of San Francisco. On 1 October, MacArthur got a War Department wire informing him that, as of that day, he was no longer chief of staff: the result of a plot hatched within the government, "strictly confidential," instructed FDR. MacArthur exploded, recalled an aide named Dwight Eisenhower. He denounced: "politics, bad manners, bad judgment, broken promises, arrogance, unconstitutionality, insensitivity, and the way the world had gone to hell."[11]

MacArthur retired from the army in 1937 to complete his work of "transcendent importance," that of defending the Philippines, now as an employee of the government of the commonwealth. He was uniquely qualified, at least in spirit and ambition, since hardly any other officer in any U.S. military service seemed to think the islands defensible at all. MacArthur, while never cowed by this consensus, agreed that the current plan was "completely useless," one of falling back to redoubts on Bataan and Corregidor while awaiting rescue from a fleet out of Hawaii. Far better, he felt, "to defend every inch of the possession," eventually with a Filipino army of forty divisions. This was supposed to provide an impenetrable shield for U.S. air and naval bases on Luzon, able to ensure America's geopolitical position in the western Pacific on a permanent basis.[12]

In 1945, on a road back to recapture Manila, MacArthur stopped to look at a location where his father once planted his tactical headquarters. He spoke, said an aide, with "a certain wistfulness, as though he wished that the famous general could see what his son was doing now." Neither generation would have taken much comfort in the disaster that occurred before the belated return to

Luzon. The War Department had been loath to waste more capital on a bad strategic investment in the defense of the islands. MacArthur cursed "every prominent officer in the U.S. army and officials in Washington"; so reads the diary, 8 October 1937, of Lieutenant Colonel Eisenhower, the general's chief of staff. He once was the recipient of substantial praise: "Much better than I could have done. I am grateful. MacArthur." In turn, Eisenhower had thought the world of his "extremely likeable" boss who hated "favoritism and special privilege . . . I doubt he has any real political ambition." Their subsequent ordeal over the defense of the Philippines drove Eisenhower to think the worst of Mac-Arthur, hanging on in Manila "to draw his munificent salary" while "damning everybody who disagrees with him over any detail, in extravagant, sometimes almost hysterical fashion." "He seemed particularly bitter toward me," now a symbol of the "technicians and small-minded people" who questioned the feasibility of stopping an invasion of the islands in its tracks.[13]

Eisenhower later testified that MacArthur could project "amazing determination and optimism." In 1940, MacArthur looked out over Manila Bay, "the key that turns the lock that opens the door to the mastery of the Pacific." "By God," he told a magazine reporter, "it is destiny that brings me here now," although some men quite familiar with the general thought him not so cocksure. One aide said MacArthur doubted he could live up to his daunting responsibilities but could not think of how to relinquish the burden. "I used to think that I had a mission, that I would be spared," the general once divulged to another confidant, "but I don't believe it anymore."[14]

This tension between responsibility and capability can explain the frenetic quality in the general's behavior under daunting conditions that would have forced others to back down. He even profusely praised Franklin Roosevelt, whom he privately despised for assorted lies and slights, particularly about the Philippines. MacArthur called his reelection in 1940 the worst disaster that could befall the world. Yet when seeking reactivation to command the defense of the Philippines, he wrote Stephen Early, the White House press secretary, "how much I admire the magnificent conception and grasp of the world situation the president has exhibited. He has proved himself not only our greatest statesman but what to me is even more thrilling, our greatest strategist. Let me know, Steve, if the President can utilize me."[15]

Those who might think this nothing more than unctuous flattery worthy of Uriah Heep might reconsider the responsibility for which MacArthur pleaded: what he called the "exposed outpost [constituting] the weakest link in our defense system." MacArthur had assumed the post of "field marshall," commonwealth armed forces, as if the title would generate an army commensurate with his rank. Soldiers in the American garrison, of their own opinion, snickered at "the Napoleon of Luzon." Eisenhower meanwhile did what he could to cut plans down to force structure: "I was the only one who argued with him on official matters but he kept me with him," probably because he

General Douglas MacArthur, reviewing a parade upon arriving in Manila, October 1935. Directly to his right is (then) Major Dwight D. Eisenhower, his chief of staff. Their subsequent conflict about the military defense of the Philippines embittered each man toward the other. Eisenhower in 1952 preempted MacArthur's chance to become president of the United States: "My God anything would be better than that!" *U.S. Army Signal Corps, courtesy of the MacArthur Memorial Library.*

was then trusted to be a sounding board and emotional vent. MacArthur was letting down his self-control through "regular shouting tirades," as Eisenhower described behavior unknown to those who testify that MacArthur "was never aggressive in his dealings with anybody, including his staff." He remained in the special place by MacArthur's side until 1938, when he was punished for so-called secret meetings with the president of the Philippines, who consulted the lieutenant colonel because the senior officer on the island carried little weight in Washington.[16]

MacArthur, taking out his frustration on Eisenhower, turned toward replacing him with Major Richard Sutherland, a recent arrival in Manila, whom he thought "a real find: concise, energetic, and able." What happened next is a matter of dispute. MacArthur's retinue said Eisenhower was depressed by these events that seem to have ruined his career. Eisenhower claimed that he relished the opportunity to relinquish administrative work and get a troop command. One thing is certain in life, war, and politics: success is the ultimate revenge.

MacArthur would repeatedly speak of "that traitor," exposing a broken bond of special trust with an old protégé harboring his own grudge about the way he had been used, abused, and discarded. In mid-1943, after clearing the Axis from North Africa, Eisenhower expressed concern to his own aide that MacArthur might not have noticed. He need not have worried; MacArthur was exceedingly attentive. He thought Eisenhower's whole campaign a "cabal" to deprive him of equipment badly needed in the Pacific and launched veiled barbs through favored newspapermen about "faceless staff officers" who had let the Philippines die on the vine. These comments "practically gave me indigestion," Eisenhower said at the time. By 1944, he was firmly on the ladder from which he would snatch MacArthur's chance to be president of the United States in 1953. For want of a nail—or a staff officer—the kingdom would be lost, meaning the great opportunity to trump Harry Truman.[17]

Back in 1938, when Eisenhower shipped back to the States, no one could foresee his ascent beginning with a posting to Washington in late 1941 to see what could be done about saving the Philippines. In the meantime, MacArthur's own plans did not completely contravene national policy. He could have said on the eve of World War II what he said in the early 1950s: the "sorry truth is that we have no [Far East] policy," meaning a clear and coherent set of ends, ways, and means. The War Department was the foremost proponent of fighting in Europe while holding a defensive perimeter anchored in Midway and the Aleutians. It also wanted the navy to sail posthaste to rescue soldiers responsible for the land defense of the Philippines. The navy, while resisting the attempt to make the Pacific a secondary theater, planned a cautious, three-year progression from Hawaii to Luzon, lest its capital ships be destroyed in exposed positions far from their main base of reinforcement, supply, and repair. As for President Roosevelt, he acted in his normal fashion, declining to choose between opposing points of view until the last moment, in this case when Japan took the grim decision off his hands by sinking the battleships berthed at Pearl Harbor on 7 December 1941.[18]

MacArthur attempted to fill this vacuum with a policy of his own making: "The man in command at the time will be the man who will determine the main features of the campaign." He held this tenet in Korea as well as the Philippines, where the general now planned to defend all of Luzon by crushing an invasion force "where he is weakest, namely at the beach." Eisenhower thought this a fantasy. On occasion, MacArthur seemed prone to agree, although still likely to wire the War Department about preparedness "progressing by leaps and bounds." He privately concurred about facing "an almost insurmountable task," that is until America got a so-called wonder weapon that suddenly gave hope in a grim situation to MacArthur, Roosevelt, and George C. Marshall, the U.S. Army chief of staff.[19]

In late 1941, the Philippines suddenly became valuable as a platform for the B-17 heavy bomber, supposedly able to devastate Japan, as well as to sink its invasion fleet. Because Tokyo also threatened to attack the Soviet Union, at war with Germany since late June, the Far East became an important factor in the struggle for Europe, always Washington's primary concern. The administration therefore reversed policy "not to reinforce the Philippines except in minor particulars" and adopted MacArthur's preference for a forward defense based on eleven to thirteen Filipino divisions to be ready by April 1942, along with coastal artillery. If MacArthur had not been willing to promise that he would hold all the "land and sea areas necessary for the defense of the Philippine Archipelago," Washington might not have committed the airplanes thought to make the islands impervious to invasion. In summary, the Philippines must be safe to justify the weapon that was supposed to make it safe, 165 B-17s scheduled by March to supplement reinforcements "dispatched as fast as availability or shipping of units permit." A man less emotionally involved might have noted the provisos and planned for the worst. MacArthur, according to the man who hand-delivered this message from Marshall on October 18th, "acted like a small boy who had been told that he is going to get a holiday from school." He exclaimed to Sutherland: "Dick, they are going to give us everything we have asked for."[20]

It soon proved too late to do much more than fixate on fruitless promises impossible to fulfill that left MacArthur's force awaiting modern rifles, machine guns, and mortars, let alone radar for air defense. Nine hours after Japan struck Pearl Harbor its planes destroyed the B-17s on the ground. Several participants in this long-debated military mishap say that MacArthur was asleep at the switch from conviction that the Philippines would not be attacked before he was ready to defend, as one might think if blessed with a special destiny. Whoever bears the blame, the B-17 debacle was not decisive, since this remarkably durable bomber in the European theater would compile a dismal record as a ship-killer: eighty planes, 350 missions, two vessels sunk in the Pacific. On December 23rd, after the Japanese invasion force crushed whatever resistance MacArthur could mount near the beaches, he had to adopt the old defense plan he once called bankrupt. He ordered a retreat to Bataan and Corregidor, where his soldiers were to be reinforced—or so he wished to believe.[21]

No one can know what Roosevelt would have done if Japan had done what Washington expected, attack the Philippines but not Pearl Harbor. In Hawaii, dive and torpedo bombers, true ship-killers, sank all feasible options "for a long time," to quote Eisenhower, now on the War Department staff to construct a reasonable plan for rescue of the archipelago, not militarily reasonable at all. A commitment of assets large enough to matter was thought "an entirely unjustifiable diversion from the principal theater—the Atlantic," the preference that plagued MacArthur until dismissed in Korea by those he thought "blind to anything but the small portion of the globe comprising western and central Europe." MacArthur was bitter but not incorrect about priorities, even for Henry Stimson, the World War II secretary of war who had his own emotional commitment to the Philippines, since he had been governor general in the late 1920s. Stimson long concluded that U.S. troops would "be merely a pawn to fall into the hands of Japan and force the naval issue, perhaps in an unfavorable way" by luring the fleet to its precipitous destruction in a decisive battle for the far Pacific. In 1941, he succumbed temporarily to the B-17 panacea, but fell back to reality by 5 January 1942, when he confessed to his diary that "everybody knows the chances are against our getting relief to [the Philippines] but there is no use in saying so before hand."[22]

Stimson would have the army conduct what he later called "a glorious but hopeless defense," especially after the navy pulled its Far East fleet: "we could not give up the Philippines in that way." He and Marshall were honorable men who would not tell a bald-faced lie. Nor did they tell MacArthur the unvarnished truth when relaying that "the President has seen all your messages [for help] and directs the Navy to give you every possible support in your splendid fight." In theory, Franklin Roosevelt could have leveled with MacArthur from the day the Japanese attacked Pearl Harbor. This would have been out of character for someone said to be "tricky for fun." There was far more incentive than personal amusement in late 1941, when Washington held out hope to sustain morale in the American solider not raised in the Bushido code of honorable death in hopeless circumstances. The president felt the U.S. public needed an example of prolonged combat to make it understand the grim responsibilities it now had. He also wanted to show resolve to Britain and the Soviet Union, so heavily engaged with Germany that they might capitulate if the United States did not flash a sign that it would fight to the finish. As Roosevelt wired MacArthur in a moment of candor when defeatism began to surface within the general's command: "It is mandatory that there be established once and for all in the minds of all peoples complete evidence [of] the American determination and indomitable will to win."[23]

Most messages from Washington "could be interpreted two ways," MacArthur later admitted. "I can see now that I may have deluded myself"—and other people too, one might add. He requested morale-boosting communiqués to counter Japanese promises to protect those who surrendered. The War Department told him of landing heavy bombers in Australia, "three a day since Sunday." He passed on to his soldiers "help is on the way . . . thousands of troops and hundreds of planes are being dispatched." Indeed, the messages he sent Washington were as misleading as what he received, apparently hoping to get reinforcements if the battle were not foredoomed. "There are indications," MacArthur wrote the War Department on 22 February 1942, "that the enemy has been so badly mauled during the Bataan fighting that he is unable to set up with his present forces the attack necessary to destroy me."[24]

The Japanese actually were settling down to a siege that would starve the American garrison into surrender in the next three months. Washington was aware of the real situation, no matter what MacArthur said or did, as he had lost his credibility with prior predictions about throwing back a Japanese invasion. The White House certainly did not increase its troop commitment. Neither did it censor dissemination of MacArthur's message traffic that trumpeted America would fight, at least with MacArthur in command, until he was ordered to Australia in early April. Roosevelt subsequently gave his successor, Jonathan Wainwright, leeway to give up if he felt this in the "best interests" of "your magnificent troops." They had fulfilled their real mission, becoming "living symbols of our war aims and the guarantee of victory."[25]

The U.S. body politic tends to personalize collective events. It blamed the Great Depression on Herbert Hoover. MacArthur was much better off insofar as getting credit for Bataan, partly thanks to communiqués from "MacArthur headquarters" filled with references to "MacArthur's men" and "MacArthur's flanks." Roosevelt had a direct role, as seen in his nationwide radio address, 27 February: "The defense put up by General MacArthur has magnificently exceeded the previous estimates of endurance." By then, the front page of the *Washington Post* read: "There was no way yet for millions of humble Americans to tell General MacArthur fighting his last ditch fight in the bamboo jungles of Bataan of the hope and pride he has fanned to flame in their hearts." Eisenhower, of a different opinion, noted: "Poor Wainwright! He did the fighting another got such glory as the public could find in the operation." However, as a newly minted two-star general (still lieutenant colonel, permanent rank) he was in no position to decide the future of "the acknowledged king on the spot." That fell to Roosevelt and Marshall, who thought MacArthur's performance close to "criminal" negligence, especially the destruction of the B-17s. Still, no one drummed him out of the service, as happened to the senior command at Pearl Harbor. MacArthur received the Medal of Honor he felt he had earned back in 1916 on scouting operations in the Mexican Expedition, which had been denied, in part, for exceeding the directives of his superior, as his father did at Missionary Ridge.[26]

The White House press office had helped create the problem the president now had to face. Roosevelt, although sending MacArthur to the Philippines in 1935, could not leave him there lest critics accuse FDR of wasting a military treasure. Meanwhile, as MacArthur vowed, "I shall return," the Bataan force with its "flickering, forlorn hope" acquired martyrdom in his consciousness: "The sacrifice and halo of Jesus of Nazareth has descended and God will take them unto Himself." His words were far less sacred after hearing of European-first policy decisions: "Never before in history was so large and gallant an army written off so callously." "I could have held Bataan," the general exclaimed in mid-1943, "if I had not been so completely deserted," by the likes of George Marshall, in charge of the Washington end of the communication line. The army chief of staff was a man of strong rectitude and, one suspects, a nagging conscience for never delivering the reinforcements to which he alluded in late 1941. He later claimed that he "supported [MacArthur] through thick and thin"—unfortunately true in late 1950, when Marshall upheld MacArthur's ill-conceived plunge toward the Yalu River in the Korean War.[27]

MacArthur, despite all his grace and charm, could be worse than unpleasant when lashing out at Roosevelt and Marshall—and later, Harry Truman. Statements spewed in World War II reveal how he personalized issues of national security that transcended personalities to most other people. The issue was always "the enemy and I," reported one newspaperman, nor was Japan the only enemy judging by statements from the general about "some people in Washington who would rather see [me] MacArthur lose a battle than America win a war." As in Korea, this anger crept into the press, particularly when planted by MacArthur or his staff. In 1951, the object of his ire would be limited war. In 1942, it was the European Theater and the U.S. Navy, which had failed to cut through the "lightly-held" blockade around the Philippines. The president, not one to appreciate this position, complained about "a good deal of loose newspaper talk coming out of Australia" soon after MacArthur arrived to set up command for the Southwest Pacific Area (SWPA). Articles citing "authoritative military and civilian circles" alleged a lack of support from the government, an embarrassment Marshall tried to finesse. In August, he wired SWPA that although publications "create the impression that you are objecting to our strategy by indirection, I assume this to be an erroneous impression" because they must be aware of the "exceedingly difficult and complex" pressures the government was facing in this global war. MacArthur, not politically deaf, got the velvet-coated hint from someone always sensitive to MacArthur's sensibilities. "You are," he wired Marshall, "entirely correct in your assumption."[28]

Newspaper stories temporarily abated but reemerged that fall when demands by the navy for men and equipment sent to Guadalcanal made SWPA the secondary front in the secondary theater of the Second World War. Henry Stimson, by October, had enough. This East Coast establishment Republican, brought into the administration for bipartisan footing, chafed once copy circulated that Washington feared MacArthur capturing the White House if he ever got the wherewithal to beat Japan. The secretary of war, who still liked to be called colonel, must have thought he had a solemn military duty to tackle the task of warning a "prima donna" to stop publicizing his complaints, particularly about the lack of shipping for his effort in New Guinea. This could not "go on without damaging the united war effort"—reason to send Eddie Rickenbacker to deliver in December what this World War I ace flyer called "a message of such sensitivity that it could not be put on paper." It had particular credibility because the recipient already feared the worst: "If anything goes wrong [I] MacArthur will be sent home." Hence Stimson, blunt but private, could keep the general within broad limits of propriety—at least for the time being.[29]

MacArthur remained very critical of the navy, but not for attribution, even by Roy Howard, one of his closest friends. To the head of the Scripps-Howard newspaper chain, "it was all off the record," explains entries in a headquarters diary: "W[ar] D[epartment] would not permit [the] latitude he had taken." Actually, Washington could get no more than literal compliance with the strict letter of its directives. A willing spirit of agreement was another matter, as demonstrated in June 1945 when "MacA. blew up" at a Marshall-forwarded suggestion that he move his headquarters to Guam in order to facilitate coordination with the navy. "He resented the letter and did not propose to obey it," a pointed reaction that concluded this particular issue as far as one can tell, aside from portending MacArthur's relationship with Washington during the Korean War.[30]

Harry Truman was also no great fan of "Mr. Prima Donna, Brass Hat Five Star MacArthur." However, he was less demanding and hence less effective than Henry Stimson, who was freer to take action because less burdened by personal interest in the next election. In mid-1950, Truman sent his own special emissary, in this case Averell Harriman, when the general said things about Formosa unacceptable to the White House. Rather than carry a message that minced no words, ala Rickenbacker, Harriman essentially offered a deal, to be discussed in chapter 3. That tactic for reconciling differences fell short of success after the Chinese intervention in late 1950. The Truman administration, through George Marshall, then secretary of defense, issued its own version of a gag order, somewhat reminiscent of Stimson, but too tepid and equivocal to bring MacArthur under control. Little that happened in Korea was unprecedented for the National Command Authority or the theater commander.[31]

MacArthur said of Franklin Roosevelt, after his death in April 1945: "He never resorted to the truth when a lie would suffice." That September, the general told one member of the executive branch: "I have absolutely no use for the people in Washington, including the [new] President." In October, Truman passed a message through Marshall informing MacArthur "that he wishes you to understand that he would like you to make a trip home" to be honored by the government, as were the other senior commanders. MacArthur, while "deeply grateful and most appreciative," had to decline because of the "inflammable situation" supposedly existing in Japan. To a confidant, he said out of pique or defiance, "there has been a joint resolution in Congress inviting me to appear. . . . I intend to be the first man in our history to refuse."[32]

Despite hate for FDR, MacArthur said of Harry Truman "we're even worse off with that Jew in the White House." ("You can tell by his name. Look at his face.") Washington was not wrong to think "an acute persecution complex at work," although the government was not immune to tales of its own. MacArthur "was accused of a lot of things very falsely," said one person on his staff not uncritical of the general. Consider Dean Acheson, acting secretary of state in the fall of 1945. He blamed MacArthur for undermining the effort to retain conscription by unauthorized talk of cutting the garrison in Japan 60 percent: "The occupation forces are the instruments . . . not the determinants of policy." This was the first exchange in their long-term conflict but was no spiteful act of sabotage for the general's personal advantage. Halfway through World War

II land-based aircraft had become MacArthur's major combat arm. He firmly held that "as the power and force of weapons increase, the need for masses of men will sharply decrease . . . in almost geometrical ratio." Thus MacArthur told assistants that "the infantry won't be slogging to the front—there probably will be no front," one reason he was lax in preparing his garrison troops for linear combat in Korea.[33]

MacArthur held that Acheson "would never come out with that attack on me unless it had been directed by the President," who "evidently is starting out to fool the people just like FDR did." Truman was equally wary of MacArthur, despite statements to a mutual acquaintance assured of getting back to the general that he "did not mind MacArthur politically," unlike Roosevelt, who "hated and feared him" with such passion that "his statements against MacArthur may have influenced me some." The president told a different story to Harold Ickes, the secretary of interior responsible for the Commonwealth of the Philippines. "Politically he couldn't do anything else" in 1945 but appoint MacArthur to military commander in chief, Far East (CINCFE).[34]

One way or the other, when it came to demobilization, Truman felt topped on a topic of utmost importance to the electorate. He had bawled out newspaper columnist Drew Pearson, "as if I were a private," for bringing a petition from GIs in the Philippines wanting to get out of the army. ("You are upsetting my foreign policy.") Could Douglas MacArthur, his military subordinate, expect more tactful treatment from his commander in chief? Truman, fed up with the idea that the general could manage Japan with minimal manpower, declared on September 18th that he was "tired of fooling around" and would "do something with that fellow who had been balling things up." Assistant Secretary of War John J. McCloy thereupon set out "to muzzle" the CINCFE, having done similar duties in World War II when McCloy told George Patton, direct from Eisenhower, "to keep his God damn mouth shut."[35]

MacArthur was a different case, doing most of the talking when he met McCloy at headquarters, Tokyo. The envoy "swallowed hard several times," according to one observer. Then, "by sheer might and main," McCloy "succeeded to get my words in," although compromising as to whether Washington could govern MacArthur. They discussed the wisdom of granting the Soviet Union a rather meaningless place on the allied control commission for Japan theoretically guiding MacArthur as Supreme Commander Allied Powers (SCAP). Washington thought this useful in the grand scheme of global diplomacy, when seeking membership on boards influencing Red Army–occupied Europe and Soviet policy in Northeast Asia. "If the Russians decide to give active support to the Chinese communists then we are in a real mess," McCloy was about to report. As for MacArthur, "I finally got him to state what he would do and what he did not want to do"—words like "orders" and "obedience" were conspicuously absent. When McCloy returned to America, he told government agencies to "avoid invidious detail in the directives that are sent," what he also assured the general he had done. "MacArthur was the only important American official," wrote the Tokyo bureau chief of the Associated Press, "who could make policy statements without prior consultation with the State Department."[36]

Joseph Stalin was hardly satisfied with·MacArthur's concession to him and Washington, membership in a meaningless commission that made the premier of the Soviet Union feel "like a piece of furniture." He had hoped that Red Army occupation would ensure the perpetual subservience of Japan, for which he had been willing to make a territorial trade: the southern half of Korea for Hokkaido, the northern island of the archipelago. Dean Rusk, War Department staff officer and future State Department official, was surprised to be able to draw the demarcation at the 38th Parallel: the Soviets "might insist upon a line further south in view of our respective military positions." Truman then ordered to the peninsula what was left of the XXIV Corps after 20,000 casualties on Okinawa. One week later he let Stalin know that General MacArthur, in his SCAP responsibilities, would employ only "Allied token forces" in Japan, if and when needed in emergencies. Stalin replied: "I and my colleagues did not expect such an answer from you."[37]

Stalin's mood did not improve in the next four years as Japan went through a postwar recovery. In April 1950, he approved North Korea's invasion of the South in order to ensure that the peninsula would not revert to its old role as a beachhead in the hands of a Japanese army, this time allied with the United States. The Truman administration could not fathom this line of thinking about South Korea, hardly a pawn of Japan. Washington, in the meantime, had its own problems, at least with the Tokyo command. Harold Ickes, a bit naïve, told Acheson "how much I thought of him for setting Gen. MacArthur back on his heels." This was not the first—or the last—time the government spun a fantasy about taking firm control. Washington sent MacArthur numerous directives in the next few years, usually in his SCAP capacity. Often ignored, they left the president saying that if that "so-and-so hesitated one [more] minute," he personally would "bust him to a corporal," After this self-applied psychotherapy whereby Truman let off steam, he turned to other problems on the presidential plate: production shortages, inflation, labor strikes, Europe, the Middle East, Congress, and Roosevelt appointees such as Harold Ickes, who was handled with a much stronger hand than was MacArthur.[38]

The general not only had a higher stature than Ickes, forced to resign after criticizing a White House "crony" before a Senate committee in February 1946. Truman had appointed MacArthur to the new command he now held. This meant he was no FDR holdover to a president proud of saying "sometimes people quit me but I never quit people when I start to back them up." That May he sent MacArthur a personal message via Eisenhower, the new army chief of staff. He conveyed his "great satisfaction that you personally were in good health and spirits" as he renewed his futile request for political assistance with conscription. After that, the closest thing to concrete action on the MacArthur front came in late 1948, when the administration offered the command in Japan to the military governor of Germany, to take effect "when General MacArthur retires," presumably in the near future.[39]

Washington might have grasped at news of decline in MacArthur's physical condition: thinness in his hands and nervousness evident to a reporter who had seventeen different meetings with the general. In one, he said of Napoleon before Waterloo, "the drive that kept him going was wearing out." That comment may have been autobiographical, but MacArthur would not retire, nor would the administration press the issue. It apparently decided to wait things out and gradually shift more authority for occupation policy from Tokyo to Washington, a situation reminiscent of the marginal position MacArthur occupied in the Philippines before reactivated into the American army, mid-1941. Barely remembered, at least for the time being, was a message George Marshall sent him back in September 1945, two months before the army chief of staff retired. He instructed MacArthur, on behalf of the War Department, to make no more statements about demobilization without prior "coordination" with Washington. This foreshadowed the December 1950 "gag order" in which the Marshall-led Pentagon told MacArthur not to make statements about military policy, particularly in regard to China, another futile directive to a man mixing ambition, apprehension, and calculation with self-absorbed bravado.[40]

Harry S. Truman:
Soldier, Senator, and Commander-in-Chief

> I have been with the president on occasions when he had what appeared to me to be a perfectly normal and amiable conversation with a caller. After the caller left, he would say to me "I certainly set him straight" or "I let him have it." The president's remarks seemed to me to have no conceivable relation to the conversation I had just heard. He may have been commenting on what he wished he had said.
>
> ADMIRAL ROBERT DENNISON, WHITE HOUSE
> ASSISTANT TO PRESIDENT TRUMAN, 1948–1953[41]

Harry Truman, like most other people, was subject to conflicting impulses. He once told Dean Acheson that he liked "being a nose buster and an ass kicker much better" than a statesman. Actually, talk like this to the contrary, Truman was too nice a man to be the man he dreamed of being, except in rare moments when his temper took complete control. He usually avoided personal confrontation, being a modest, considerate person who hated flamboyance, one reason he disliked Douglas MacArthur. Truman could call the presidency "the most powerful and greatest office in the history of the world" but spent his time "at the President's desk talking to people and kissing them on both cheeks trying to get them to do what they ought to do without getting kissed." This fell short of his hero, Andrew Jackson, but was a reason Truman once worked so well on Capitol Hill, where the upper house functions by compromise and conciliation. He enjoyed his reputation as "the nicest man in the Senate," where he spent "the happiest time of my life."[42]

Truman's views toward military officers were also complex and ambivalent. He had been raised on heroic stories of battlefield commanders, particularly Hannibal, Robert E. Lee, and "Stonewall" Jackson, compiled in *Great Men and Famous Women*, a Victorian anthology of biographical portraits received from his mother at age ten and kept until he died. His understanding of their careers would affect decisions made throughout his life, whether dealing with MacArthur or courting Bess Wallace, the childhood sweetheart whom Truman later wed. He tried to enter West Point because her family was far more prominent than his. "I studied the career of great men to be worthy of her. I found that most of them came from the army." This plan failed to make provision for eyes not able to read the examination chart for the Academy. The rejected applicant subsequently harbored mixed feelings of anger, envy, and inferiority toward its graduates, "trained to think they are gods in uniform." Still, while expressing populist resentment at the military elite, Truman thought their code of honor superior to what he saw in business, politics, and everyday life, all in need of a revolution or "reformation of the heart."[43]

Truman, no doubt recalling his own disappointment, appointed the underprivileged to West Point, as in one application sent to his Senate office made in pencil on a rough sheet of paper, with no recommendations from people of power. He later favored a school system along martial curriculum lines but minus the "class distinctions and cliques which now exist through the snobbery created by the academies." Truman would "teach our kids honor, kill a few sex psychologists, [and] put boys in high schools to themselves with men teachers (not sissies)." Then universal military training would commence for three successive summers beginning at age seventeen, a proposal that got no further than a futile address to Congress in March 1948. Presumably, in March 1918, there were no sex psychologists affecting the atmosphere of Battery D, 129th Field Artillery, 35th Division, Missouri National Guard. Truman could recall his World War I experience in extraordinary detail, evidence of its importance to his sense of self-worth. More than thirty years after the fact, he corrected a comrade in arms about the exact day they shipped out from Kansas City: 25 September 1917, not September 28th. On Armistice Day 1954 he could recall "my last shot was fired at 10:45." By contrast, he could fail to remember important facts having to do with a major political controversy a year or two after they occurred. He jotted down that he met MacArthur at Wake Island in 1951, instead of 1950, and that the secretary of defense advocated the general's dismissal, but it was really the secretary of state.[44]

A Truman entry in *Who's Who* gave his presidency two lines; his military service got five. The fact that he could favor the role of soldier over that of policy maker was of importance in contacts with MacArthur. It was also important to spend two weeks each summer in National Guard training, at least as long as Senator Truman could wrangle a special exemption from the policy excusing all reservists in Congress. The War Department concluded "it was to the advantage of everyone to keep Colonel Truman on good terms," a response to his protest that "it has given me more pleasure to train second lieutenants to shoot than anything I have done since the war." Ten years later his White House military staff were also reservists, for example Frank Lowe, later sent to report from Korea, although just another "National Guard windbag" to one senior officer there. Other guardsmen, Harry Vaughan and Louis Renfrow, were Truman's main and assistant military aides, positions professional soldiers heretofore held.[45]

The president said Vaughan, a fellow battery commander from Missouri, had a "military record beyond comparison," rather hyperbolic notwithstanding a Silver Star with Oak Leaves and Croix de Guerre. Truman was utterly loyal to loyal friends, especially under fire, as was Vaughan, who was widely said to be an influence peddler running a "friendship racket" out of the White House. Even there, people thought his improprieties "entirely to blame for his troubles and the troubles he has brought on the president." The president himself took a different stance, particularly in public, nor did he seem concerned that many military men disliked his National Guard cronies, as a slap at the profession of arms. These reservists responded in kind, a common cause for close liaison at MacArthur headquarters with Courtney Whitney and Charles Willoughby, the general's military secretary and his chief of intelligence. They felt Vaughan was their "friend at court," as was Frank Lowe, all sharing a dislike for "the boys in the Pentagon who take particular delight in scuttling everyone who is not on their own individual private team."[46]

Being more ecumenical than Vaughan, Truman did not feel outsiders monopolized military virtue. He wondered how the U.S. Army could "produce such men as Robert E. Lee, John J. Pershing, Eisenhower, and Bradley and at the same time produce Custers, Pattons, and MacArthur." This dichotomy, known in psychology as "splitting," said nearly as much about Truman as about the military men he discussed. A person with strong feelings can handle ambivalence about a group by attributing all bad qualities to some of its members, all good qualities to others. In the case of Truman on professional soldiers, MacArthur could be a lightening rod for resentment. Other officers got the adoration, particularly George Marshall, as Louis Renfrow would attest: Truman thought more of him "than he did anybody else, except Mrs. Truman and [his daughter] Margaret."[47]

Unlike professional soldiers, politicians were mixtures of good and bad according to Truman. He could see the good side of a Tom Pendergast, the boss

Missouri National Guard Colonel (and United States Senator) Harry S. Truman thoroughly enjoying military training in 1936. He used his political position to continue this experience, from which members of Congress were automatically exempt. *Courtesy of the Harry S. Truman Library.*

of Kansas City who used him to give his urban machine a veneer of honesty. Truman even thought well of Joe Stalin at their first meeting: "Straightforward. Knows what he wants and will compromise when he can't get it." None of this meant political men were qualified to oversee military operations, as revealed the day Truman made "the most momentous announcement of my life," that of

Major General Harry Vaughan, Truman's military aide from the Missouri National Guard, testifying on 30 August 1949 before a Senate committee investigating influence peddling. Despite widespread calls for Vaughan's removal, Truman never relieved his personal friend (and incidentally, friend of officers at MacArthur's headquarters). *Harris and Ewing, courtesy of the Harry S. Truman Library.*

leaving local office, where he once expected to retire, to run for the U.S. Senate. He got his bearings by recapping his life in his diary, 14 May 1934, wherein he jotted: "Of all the military heroes Hannibal and Lee were to my mind the best . . . they won every battle [but] lost the war due to crazy politicians."[48]

Great Men and Famous Women held that Hannibal's "niggardly, shortsighted countrymen denied him the support without which success was impossible." *Makers of History: Hannibal* also lay on Truman's bookshelf but had less impact on the future president. In this volume, published in 1906, the Carthaginian commander comes off as a MacArthur-like figure whose "reckless ambition" and obsession to conquer Rome leads to his obliteration. Truman still held that Hannibal "fought in Italy without home support for sixteen years and he never lost a battle. . . . The merchants of Carthage caused their own destruction because they would not support him." An offhand phrase or two may well have tainted Truman's mind irrevocably. *Makers of History* describes the civil authorities as "a small body of wealthy and aristocratic families." Truman's hero, on the other hand, "dressed plainly; he assumed no airs; he sought no pleasures or indulgences, nor any exemption from the dangers and privations which the common soldier had to endure." Case closed for Harry Truman. One could hardly think of a depiction more likely to appeal to a Jacksonian populist whose own political oratory, described in chapter 2, attacked the elite as the enemy.[49]

Whatever one might think of the government of Carthage, the head of state in the Confederacy performed monumental service for Robert E. Lee, during and after the Civil War. Jefferson Davis preferred to fight on the strategic defensive but stripped his capitol barricades to fill requisitions when Lee moved into enemy territory. Lincoln never went quite so far, even for Grant, whose name was oddly absent from Truman's list of great West Point graduates. Different from Hannibal or Lee, he was what Truman aspired to be: a self-made man and soldier. Grant was "very familiar with defeat, with failing at things, and," as Truman later said, "he knew about being poor." Truman still thought his fame ultimately derived from "being in at the death of one of the really great," much like Scipio Africanus against Hannibal. Notions like this stripped Grant of credit for victory and preserved the culpability of Jeff Davis as a scapegoat for Lee's defeat. Balanced assessments had not entered the Truman household. Lee was the immaculate hero of his mother, as he was for "Pinky" MacArthur.[50]

Truman said that he would have liked to be a history teacher, less troublesome than president of the United States. His favorite book bar none, when an older man, was Douglas Southall Freeman's *R. E. Lee*, his guide on terrain walks such as the one he made to Gettysburg in 1937. *Lee* is a four-volume literary masterpiece. It could also morph into an adult rendition of *Great Men and Famous Women* iconography. "No enigma" was present in the protagonist, someone of "simplicity and spirituality," although a more recent school of history, quite distasteful to Truman, finds that portrait simplistic itself. Revisionists now paint Lee planning to win the war on enemy soil, across the 38th parallel so to speak. Invasions of Maryland and Pennsylvania were faits accomplis for President Davis. Still, suspicion of noncompliance never crossed Truman's mind, as he was a deacon of the congregation wherein "Lee is God and Freeman is his prophet," to paraphrase one revisionist.[51]

The Lee-Davis model for civil-military relations had a hold on Truman, conscious or not. Davis would disregard protocols of office by traveling to consult Lee—shades of Truman's trip to see MacArthur at Wake Island during the Korean War. If Truman had to go about "soothing the sensitivities of the people he wanted to get to work for him," well better that of a theater commander during an armed conflict than a member of the Cabinet or the Congress. Union politicians often affronted their military officers, disgraceful behavior that Truman rejected despite strong temptation from his experience in World War I. An officious West Point colonel "shamefully" insulted Captain Truman, who was later threatened with court-martial for firing outside his sector, although necessary to suppress enemy artillery. ("No gentleman would say what he said. Damn him.") Higher headquarters subsequently criticized his whole division for insufficient progress against machine-gun fire and inattention to saluting, not much reward for suffering over 7,000 casualties in four days during the Meuse-Argonne offensive, 1918.[52]

John Pershing on a visit to the 35th Division ridiculed the sector-fire rule Truman violated, probably a reason why the commander of the AEF became one of Truman's West Point good guys. That incident could not extinguish the indignation of this impatient guardsman awaiting return to civilian life. Truman fantasized about giving "my right arm" to wreak revenge on "this man's Army" by taking a congressional seat on the Military Affairs Committee. In World War II, he had ample opportunity to strike back at the brass when chairing the Senate Special Committee to Investigate the National Defense Program, commonly called the Truman Committee. He still focused his ire on contractors and contracting, foretelling fiscal policy in his presidency when holding down military spending before the Korean War. Truman then displayed "the most rocklike example of civilian control the world has ever witnessed," at least according to James Forrestal, his first secretary of defense. Truman was always less comfortable in control of military operations, partly due to Douglas Southall Freeman, whom he met while observing army maneuvers in March 1944.[53]

Civil War biography was Freeman's higher calling; his day job was that of newspaper editor attentive to contemporary affairs. His own testimony and speeches to the Truman Committee pushed its chairman toward keeping generalship and war-fighting off the agenda, lest the body that bore his name take its place in history beside the Joint Committee on the Conduct of the [Civil] War. Freeman and the other leading lights of historiography blamed that group of partisan politicians for gross interference with the prosecution of the conflict. To an acolyte such as Truman, those politicos were the mid-nineteenth-century embodiment of the Carthaginian Senate, whose meddling with military initiative "kept Hannibal from winning the Second Punic War." Right-wing Republicans gunning for Franklin Roosevelt were the latest incarnation. "They tried to get me to make a Committee on the Conduct of the War out of my committee," said Truman. "Thank goodness I knew my history and I wouldn't do it."[54]

Such thoughts were also present in 1951, two weeks after Truman "found [himself] compelled to take this distressing action" of relieving Douglas MacArthur. He had no such qualms about attacking the "most unpatriotic" activities of the Committee on the Conduct of the [Civil] War: "They abused General Meade like a pickpocket—you read that." As regards his own behavior despite what MacArthur forced him to do, the president liked to think and persistently proclaim: "The commanders in the field have absolute control of the tactics and the strategy, and they always have." Other politicians were not so deferential. Take Franklin Roosevelt when insisting on invading North Africa in 1942, "the blackest day in history," according to General Eisenhower. However, when Truman's predecessor managed military strategy he did it so subtly that he misled serious students of civil-military relations, let alone common citizens more concerned with mundane issues of work, health, and family. Compare the comment of John Spanier, author of *The Truman-MacArthur Controversy*, with that of Admiral William Leahy, White House military chief of staff. The historian wrote: "Roosevelt recognized his lack of expertise in military matters and relied almost wholly upon the advice of his Chiefs of Staff." Leahy said the Anglo-American high command "were just artisans building definite patterns of strategy from the rough blueprints handed us by our respective Commanders-in-Chief."[55]

Truman was not as shrewd as Roosevelt, who only pretended to defer to the prevailing opinion that presidents should not overrule officers practicing their profession in military campaigns. Roosevelt's successor really believed in this tenet of American culture that draws a clear distinction between political and military endeavors. The CINCFE was another story, at least according to Eisenhower: "If General MacArthur ever recognized the existence of that line he usually chose to ignore it"—or exploit it, one could add. That did not insulate Truman from political damage when the commander in chief reluctantly relieved his theater commander for "insubordination." Then, Truman cited precedents in James K. Polk, his fellow Jacksonian Democrat, and Abraham Lincoln, another great president, even if a Republican. Neither case was quite analogous. Polk did not relieve General Winfield Scott until the latter defeated the Mexican army, which had no prospect for foreign support, unlike North Korea, which was backed by the Soviet Union and the People's Republic of China in mid-1951. Truman's own policy resembled that of Scott, not Polk, insofar as the military man sought armistice, negotiations, and compromise, rather than pursue total victory. As for Lincoln and George McClellan during the Civil War, a president then relieved his field commander for reluctance to engage the enemy, certainly not MacArthur's own shortcoming.[56]

One might argue that when it came to MacArthur, Truman never should have felt any need to avoid any tint of the Committee on the Conduct of the War since his Far East commander was no Robert E. Lee, no matter what Mac-Arthur's mother believed. True, when the president reached for negative similes in mid-1951, MacArthur, finally stripped of the martial residue he once shared with Lee, morphed into McClellan. However, until then, the administration usually gave him the deference traditionally granted to someone considered a military genius. MacArthur "was a great American," declared Averell Harriman, Truman's senior White House assistant. "Very few others in either the Army or the Navy possessed his sense of strategy and tactics or his capacity for leadership," said Paul Nitze, head of the State Department's policy planning staff; "he had done tremendous things in World War II." This being the opinion of sophisticated insiders, one need not wonder why so many people treated the general like a figure out of *Great Men and Famous Women*.[57]

Exactly what Truman thought of MacArthur as a military man can be difficult to gauge since most of his negative comments have to do with showmanship. Along with aversion, one can observe elements of envy and awe. Truman would say that MacArthur was "a great strategist until he made the march into North Korea." We "leaned over backward in our respect for the man's military reputation," simply "one of the outstanding military figures of our time." Truman's private comment about "one of our greatest military commanders" almost matched letters that in late 1944 Southall Freeman wrote MacArthur, whom he then designated "the inheritor of the boldness and the strategy of 'Marse Robert' and 'Old Jack.'" MacArthur was touched, being another proud owner of Freeman's multi-volume biography, thanks to a Christmas present from the general's wife. "I am of Virginia," he replied, and had studied Lee and Jackson "all my professional life. . . . In some of my lonely vigils at night with momentous decisions pending . . . it seemed to me almost as though those great Chieftains of the Grey were there to comfort and sustain me." Freeman at the time had just completed his third volume of *Lee's Lieutenants*, a study of Civil War generalship that contemporary generals were toting in their haversacks, not to mention airmen filling time on bombing runs. MacArthur suggested that he now write the history of MacArthur in World War II: no one "has the divine gift of inspiration like yourself. It would be a contribution of military science beyond compare."[58]

No doubt Freeman was flattered, as he was in 1934, when MacArthur told him that *R. E. Lee* was a "masterpiece." Freeman, not above flattery himself, responded that "I had rather have your judgment of my book from the military point of view than that of any other person now alive." He said much the same thing in 1944 about MacArthur's conduct of war from New Guinea to Luzon, "a military classic of first rank" that "overcame inferiority of force" through speed and surprise, the operating procedure of Jackson and Lee. However, a suitable subject for the next great product in his literary career was not on Freeman's mind, for reasons other than his conviction that "the true history of a war cannot be written for at least eighty years." His own son was in the navy, yet to wage its worst battles in Japan's home waters. Freeman had decided to "launch a campaign in America for unification of the Pacific Command under your direction. . . . I am reasonably close to President Truman," he wrote MacArthur in June 1945. "I hope what I say will make a little impression, at least on him."[59]

Truman, according to Freeman, "does not trust his own judgment in matters concerning which he has no information. He seeks the best counsel and follows it." Lee's great biographer vowed "to cut loose with some violence on the subject [of military appointment] soon," but no evidence exists that he contacted the White House about MacArthur receiving sole command in the Pacific. One can only imagine what would have happened if he had said something to the president about the general resurrecting the soldiers who always set Truman's standard for excellence, even through the darkest days of the Korean War. (The Marine Corp conducted "one of the greatest fighting retreats that ever was. . . . There's only one man—no, two—that I've ever read about who could do as well, and I mean Stonewall Jackson and Robert E. Lee.") Even without Freeman's benediction of MacArthur, Truman would have a psychological disadvantage to his military commander in the Far East, whom he sardonically called "God's right hand man."[60]

Aside from Lee and Hannibal, Truman's heroes included Andrew Jackson and Woodrow Wilson, his prototypes of presidential leadership. He did not face irreconcilable problems balancing their actions with his own idea that a president's job was to help a general as much as, if not more than, generals worked for presidents. Jackson had conflicts about tactics with Winfield Scott during the Seminole War, but he got to the White House on his military reputation won at the Battle of New Orleans, War of 1812. Wilson, whom Truman called "one of the greatest of the great Presidents," could have presented a predicament if openly challenged by John Pershing, another Truman hero. The general certainly wanted to march on Berlin in 1918, but this dispute did not become public. Truman may have never known much about it because Pershing accepted Wilson's directive to stop at Sedan: later cited by George Marshall, Pershing's former aide, as model behavior in comparison to that of MacArthur. For Captain Harry Truman, Missouri National Guard, the war left a different legacy: that the country (not Pershing) crossed President Wilson by not accepting membership in the League of Nations. On 25 June 1950, after sending U.S. forces to stop the invasion of South Korea, Truman explained to an assistant secretary of state: "I did this for the United Nations. I believed in the League of Nations [Wilson's formula to ensure world peace]. . . . It failed because we weren't in it to back it up. Okay, now we started the United Nations . . . and in this first big test we just couldn't let it down."[61]

Truman tried to live up to Wilson's political legacy on behalf of international responsibility and to Jackson as a model of decisiveness. Senior army officers found him "a man of quick decision," especially compared to Franklin Roosevelt, from whom "you would never get your answer," said Lieutenant General John Hull, "if you didn't have a man like Harry Hopkins [his special assistant] to pin him down to the subject." Less than a month after Truman moved into the White House, he gave Hull, head of army war plans, an on-the-spot directive in May 1945 against negotiations with Germany for a unilateral armistice: "No, we can't do that." On this occasion, Truman lived up to the cultivated image of a take-charge guy perched behind a sign saying: "THE BUCK STOPS HERE." However, it must be noted that Hull simply wanted guidance. The War Department would gladly do as told provided it was told what to do. In this case, Truman "was ideal," Hull said, "from a purely military standpoint"[62]

The MacArthur episode was far different, one in which a legendary soldier had priorities more important to him than policy guidance from a president. Then, the sentiment Truman shared with much of the public came back to haunt him as to what role a head of state should play when war was raging. Douglas Southall Freeman was on Truman's side, although disenchanted with the "common" run of people now in the White House: Harry Vaughan being no Robert E. Lee. Neither was MacArthur, when it came to temperament, if one is to judge by what Freeman wired Truman the day he relieved the general: "You have applied courageously a basic constitutional principle asserted and maintained to the nation's benefit by discerning presidents in some of the most critical hours of American military history."[63]

The *Richmond News Leader*, Freeman's newspaper, was less complimentary but still with Truman. "There cannot be two commanders-in-chief," its editorials stated. "It is of the essence of military discipline that one must lead and the many must follow." Nonetheless, the paper conceded that it was not speaking for the masses: MacArthur, "a brilliant general [fired] by a less than brilliant President," certainly "fills our national hunger" for heroes, as did Lee, Jackson, Charles Lindbèrgh, and Joe DiMaggio. A New York taxi driver speaking to the *New York Times* was more pointed. "MacArthur was the general over there. Let him run the Far East. He knows more about it than anybody sitting in Washington." At another time, about another government, Harry Truman might have said much the same thing.[64]

Defense Policy on the Eve of the Korean War

1 **2** 3 4 5 6 7 8 9

In Washington it's never over till it's over—and it's never over.

PRESIDENT GEORGE W. BUSH, 2001

The roots of the Korean War conflict between Truman and MacArthur lay outside Korea, a minor issue in the United States before the North invaded the South in June 1950. The public, the president, and the political parties paid far more attention to the Chinese civil war, as did the commanding general military forces, Far East. International and domestic politics were joined at the hip in a circular, feedback fashion. Policy debates created partisan squabbles that inflamed policy debates about who was responsible for the communist victory on the mainland and what was to be done about Formosa, known as Taiwan to the Chinese. Whatever one called the island, it obsessed MacArthur as had the Philippines, once the geopolitical center of his world. By mid-1950, he convinced the Department of Defense that Formosa was vital to U.S. security. The State Department had other opinions, despite involving MacArthur in schemes to depose Chiang Kai-shek, the leader of the Chinese regime that had fled to Taiwan as "the last piece of clean land that had not been polluted by Communism." The diplomatic corps still dithered because they were more concerned with trying to turn the Marxist leadership in Beijing against the Soviet Union, a path recently taken by Tito's Yugoslavia. MacArthur, not one for equivocation, fell back in favor of Chiang, long-time favorite of Truman's most partisan Republican critics. These issues lived on in the Korean War, when Formosa exacerbated military, political, and personal tensions. If the Chinese residue were not present, Truman and MacArthur might have persisted despite rocky civil-military relations, as the general did with Franklin Roosevelt during World War II.[1]

U.S. Elections and China's Civil War

We don't want a Communist government in China, or anywhere else, if we can help it.

HARRY S. TRUMAN, NEWS CONFERENCE, 11 MARCH 1948[2]

Chiang Kai-shek's Nationalists are about "the rottenest government that ever existed."

HARRY S. TRUMAN, PRIVATE CONVERSATION, 30 DECEMBER 1949[3]

Nineteen forty-eight was Truman's banner year in both international affairs and domestic politics. Military, economic, and political assistance turned back communism in Turkey, Greece, and Italy; the U.S. airlift overcame the Soviet blockade of Berlin. None of this could have happened without Republican support for military spending and foreign aid. Normally, this was just fine with the president, who liked to draw party lines on domestic matters while disowning such behavior in foreign affairs. However, Truman was on the ballot, a decided underdog, and bucking the outcome of 1946, when Republicans won their first congressional election since 1930. They picked up fifty-five seats in the House, among them Richard Nixon, and thirteen in the Senate, including Joe McCarthy and William Jenner, who proved exceptions to Truman's rule on amiability: "You don't have to fall out with a man because you don't agree with him on politics."[4]

The Republican Party had yet to form a common stance on foreign policy, other than agreeing to an internal détente on the premise that unity ensured victory for its prospective nominee, perhaps Senator Arthur Vandenberg of Michigan or Senator Robert Taft of Ohio. The former, as chairman of the Committee on Foreign Relations, had become a leading advocate of bipartisan internationalism. Taft, an isolationist in respect to Europe, led the GOP on domestic matters, particularly reducing the grasp of the so-called socialistic state. He felt "foreign policy should be one of the main issues in the next election" but admitted, "I am not an expert on foreign relations." He would be less deferential after 1948, the year the Republican convention chose Tom Dewey of the Vandenberg persuasion, not Truman's main target during the campaign. The president lambasted "the do nothing 80th Congress" for obstructionism. Dean Acheson, to be his secretary of state, subsequently told him "you ought to be ashamed of yourself," because that session gave the administration virtually

Republican Congressional leaders on 26 July 1948, planning political strategy for their presumed victory in the November election. Sitting, left to right: Speaker of the House Joseph Martin and Senator Arthur Vandenberg, chairman of the Senate Foreign Relations Committee. Among those standing, second from left is Senator Kenneth Wherry, party whip, and furthest on the right Senator Robert Taft, chairman of the Senate Republican Policy Committee. *International News Service, courtesy of the Harry S. Truman Library.*

everything requested for international relations. "Well," replied the president, "it worked."[5]

Truman had trumpeted his global triumphs. "The whole world knows of the success," ran a typical stump speech; "the Communists will never forgive me." Neither would some Republicans, if only because he stole a stock issue they used when claiming New Deal Democrats dallied with communists. Truman used Jacksonian populism and guilt by association to concentrate his campaign on "hard-shelled isolationists" in the GOP who would look the other way while the communists "take over nation after nation in the world." It was clear in Truman's speeches, if nowhere else, that the "Communists want a Republican victory."[6]

Dewey, first famous as a Mafia prosecutor, was sorely tempted to hit "that bastard Truman," especially when called a "front man" for "powerful reactionary forces which are silently undermining our democratic institutions." However, as a clear frontrunner, he bit his barbed tongue because his opponent seemed to thrive as an underdog kicked by the favorite. "Don't get nasty," said Dewey's advisors; "keep cool, don't make any mistakes and you've got it won." They might have been right if the Chinese Nationalists/Kuomintang could vote absentee. Chiang Kai-shek, its leader, believed his days were numbered if Truman stayed in power. A few days before the election he addressed "the American people and their statesmen" in Dewey's flagship newspaper, the *New York Herald Tribune*. He touched the right rhetorical buttons, no doubt coached by his wife, Madame Chiang, a master at manipulating U.S. opinion. "History is repeating itself," Chiang said in alluding to appeasement in the 1930s. If the "democratic nations" turned their back on communist expansion, "the third world war would surely follow and mankind would once again be precipitated into a tragic disaster."[7]

The logic and language of thwarting aggression to prevent a wider war led Truman into Korea in mid-1950. Washington, however, had lots of experience in World War II with the Nationalist Republic failing to carry its share of defeating Japan so America could concentrate on Germany. The head of the U.S. military mission, Lieutenant General Joseph W. Stilwell, felt the only way to get a suitable effort out of the "grasping, bigoted, ungrateful little rattlesnake" leading the regime was to put all assistance to Chiang on a strict quid-pro-quo basis. This was too brusque for Franklin Roosevelt, who preferred charm and sympathy, at least initially. When that too failed to produce military performance, Roosevelt began vague talk (but produced no performance himself) about looking "for some other man or group of men."[8]

The Kuomintang (KMT) quandary thus fell to Harry Truman, who faced substantial problems cutting back support to what he called a bunch of "grafters and crooks." The new administration believed that if it "pulled out," the KMT would soon collapse, not what the White House wanted on its political record. Chiang also had a flock of friends in the Taft wing of the Republican Party on Capitol Hill, such as Joe Martin, speaker of the House, 1947 to 1949. He foreclosed potential presidential vetoes of assistance by tacking it to bills funding Europe and Korea, major interests of the administration. This ensured that the Nationalists obtained nearly $2 billion dollars between WWII and the war in Korea, 25 percent more money than lend-lease provided to help it against Japan. Truman still complained in 1947 that Chiang "will not fight it out," unlike the communists, who "are fanatical." George Marshall, envoy to China after World War II, agreed from firsthand experience: "Chiang won't listen to advice." As secretary of state in 1948, he testified to Congress that the United States could not affect the outcome of the ongoing conflict in China "under present conditions of disorder, of corruption, inefficiency, and impotence of the Central Government."[9]

Truman himself was trying to disengage as quietly and gracefully as he could. He felt no inclination to draw notice to his greatest failure to contain communism, especially when the American public, by a two-to-one majority, thought events in China a threat to world peace. The Dewey campaign, in the midst of this mess, had not mounted a sustained attack on what their candidate sporadically called the "grossly inadequate" assistance for the KMT. He not only believed in a bipartisan foreign policy, even when running for president. His advisors were working on governing the nation before they became the government. "We shall invite the [future] Minority Party," read Dewey's foreign policy plank, "to join under the next Republican Administration in stopping partisan politics at the water's edge." Those of the Taft persuasion would have attacked Democrats for anything tainted by communism, such as Roosevelt and Truman purportedly giving concessions to Joe Stalin at the World War II summit conferences, Yalta and Potsdam. The subsequent descent of Poland and China into communist hands had explosive content in American politics. However, the GOP would not make full use of this matter as long as these proponents of a partisan foreign policy remained the minority at the minority party's national convention.[10]

Dewey then lost to Truman, the day before the communist Chinese People's Liberation Army (PLA) occupied Mukden, central Manchuria's principal city. His campaign appeared "clean" and "dignified" to the public at large, including Douglas Southall Freeman, a rock-ribbed Virginian voting Republican for the first time in his life. Moral victories like that did not cushion the blow of a fourth straight loss of the presidency. The Taft wing, particularly bitter for bearing the brunt of Truman's attacks, felt justified to pounce on international issues now that Truman had done so to further his own political fortunes. James ("Scotty") Reston's *New York Times* column foresaw this development the week the Democrats held their convention: "Any attempt to claim party credit for the foreign policy record threatens the continuance of cooperation between the parties." He also might have predicted the Republican opportunity to reap revenge. Busts follow booms in international affairs as in Wall Street stocks and bonds.[11]

"I'm not worried about being elected," Truman said early in November, "but I am very worried about the coming four years. They are going to be very rough." There was one thing wrong with his prediction made shortly before opinion polls selected him the "most admired man in the world" for the first— and the last—time in his life. It was significantly understated. Within a year, communist leader Mao Tse-tung officially established in Beijing the People's Republic of China (PRC). The Soviets, meanwhile, detonated an atomic device. Dean Acheson created his own explosion just as the political debate over China was reaching a new intensity in January 1950. He was a proud, if not arrogant, man with no whiff of Truman populism. "If you truly had a democracy and did what the people wanted," Acheson believed "you'd go wrong every time." That maxim may have been on his mind at an encounter with reporters wanting to know "am I going to run away or say what I think." He defiantly responded: "I do not intend to turn my back on Alger Hiss" (brother of a protégé, former State

Department official, and U.S. delegate to Yalta revealed to be a spy). After that, Acheson later said, "all hell broke lose."[12]

Arthur Vandenberg admired George Marshall to the point of denying China was in imminent crisis as long as the latter was secretary of state. The senator was not consulted about Acheson, the replacement, whom he thought "soft at the core." Even in good health before 1948, Vandenberg barely had kept his party in agreement with the president: "God knows, I had a hard enough time." Now less robust and less deferential, he sided with the Taft-wing critics of the critics of Chiang Kai-shek. That GOP faction had its own Jacksonian rhetoric historically based in conflicts between Midwest small business and East Coast big bankers: "the wealthy crowd" on whom Taft blamed failure to get the presidential nomination in 1940, '44, and '48. He and his following turned on well-heeled individuals, often with Wall Street backgrounds, who staffed the highest rungs of the State and Defense Departments, such as Acheson, Averell Harriman, Paul Nitze, Robert Lovett, and John McCloy. It did not matter that several were nominal Republicans who originally came to Washington to conduct a nonpartisan defense policy at the behest of New York State Republicans Henry Stimson and James Forrestal. As far as Taft adherents were concerned, the "bipartisan bigwigs" were guilty of collaboration with Democratic presidents recruiting those who aped the White House line.[13]

Notwithstanding the *Chicago Tribune*, Acheson was not a "lackey for Wall Street Bankers, British lords, and Communist radicals from New York." He and his coterie were of the pragmatic opinion that "good and evil have existed in this world since Adam and Eve went out of the Garden of Eden." Hence, they were not averse to looking for Marxist allies in Belgrade or Beijing, provided they might turn against Moscow domination. This smacked of immorality to true believers in the cause of eradicating communism. That group flocked to Robert Taft, whose cloakroom dealings were more temperate than the public statements delighting his followers. "What gives you pause in politics," the senator once confessed, "is the number of nuts who write you with approval."[14]

Dwight Eisenhower would write that "when [Taft] starts making a public speech . . . he easily loses his temper and makes extravagant statements." In 1950, that talk targeted Dean Acheson, who seemed "visibly shook" to close colleagues by the pounding over "softness towards Communism." That fall, the secretary of state would shy away from conflict with Douglas MacArthur, at least over military policy in the war against North Korea. Truman, while also careful about the general, showed a thicker political hide. He replied in rage to accusations about "traitors in the high councils," although not one to take much umbrage at charges about creeping socialism. ("Look," he told offended members of his staff, "you fellows don't understand politics.") Such forbearance was a forlorn hope that partisanship could be confined to electioneering, the customary opinion in the majority party responsible for government. Now that much of the minority was mired in a partisan drought, Truman displayed his own partisan streak by condemning strident opponents as "the greatest asset that the Kremlin has . . . [their behavior being] just as bad in this cold war as it would be to shoot our soldiers in the back."[15]

Neither Truman nor his critics backing down, the American electorate would have the final decision in the congressional election of November 1950, a main focus of both sides. This was hardly an ideal environment to reconstruct a nonpartisan policy for international relations, particularly in respect to the situation in China. Three months after sworn into office in January 1949, Acheson told Britain's foreign minister: "The US henceforth will pursue a more realistic policy." That would have been in line with the observation of old China hands that Mao Tse-tung led "the most realistic, well-knit, and tough-minded group" in that country. One could hope that his band maintained its capacity to fight, at least against foreigners, now that the objective of the Truman administration was to prevent the largest country in Asia from turning into "an adjunct of Soviet power." Acheson, in need of a rationale for this reorientation, might look no further than Maoist propaganda maintaining that Chiang was just America's "colonial running dog." This oratory drove most Americans closer to the Kuomintang, even Acheson over the long run. In the short run, this sophisticate whom Truman called his "number-one brain man" used Chinese Communist Party (CCP) condemnation of the "U.S. imperialists" to leverage change in U.S. policy. Hostility would not abate as long as Washington protected the KMT redoubt. That would simply "provide Formosan fuel for the communist fire" by tending "to unite all Chinese regardless of political affiliations in a movement for the restoration of Chinese territory."[16]

Acheson's argument played to traditional opinion insofar as reiterating the U.S. commitment to Chinese territorial integrity pronounced in the "Open Door" policy of 1899 in response to Russian occupation of Manchuria. The czarists then in control of the Kremlin lost Manchuria in 1905 through defeat in the Russo-Japanese War, during which China favored Japan, no love lost for Russia, with whom it shared a boundary four thousand miles long. Moscow regained Manchuria in 1945, the objective of the last Soviet campaign of the Second World War. Taft Republicans blamed Democrats at Yalta for sacrificing the "Open Door" to a Russian sphere of influence, something also on Acheson's mind. He believed there was "no deep-seated antipathy towards Communism" in the Far East. Russian imperialism, another issue, would inevitably lead to rivalry with the PRC from Vladivostok to Afghanistan. On and off the record in January 1950, he and Truman compared Moscow's record of expansion versus "Open Door" opposition to Chinese fragmentation. Now that Chiang had failed to build a strong central government, Mao might consolidate the country and contain the Soviet Union behind another great wall of China.[17]

Acheson had not fathomed the depth of Mao's ideology, wherein the U.S. government was a "fascist clique of financial magnates and reactionary warlords" in addition to the "foreign masters" of the Kuomintang. Ideologies had not mattered to a practical man like Acheson, particularly in his diplomacy with Josip Broz Tito, "a staunch communist" engaged in his own "ideological war with the USSR." Moscow accused his Yugoslavia of "nationalist" deviations, what Stalin also thought of Mao. This dirty word in the Kremlin's lexicon meant preservation of independence won by one's own effort as opposed to installation by Soviet military forces. The U.S. embassy in Belgrade reported as of January 1949: "Tito has stood firm and has carried army, secret police, paramilitary, party, and mass organization with him with far fewer and less important defections than have occurred in many satellites enjoying full Moscow favor." Indeed, not simply defensive, he looked for disciples to spread his principles throughout the world. In Asia, to his reasoning, China seemed particularly apt to spearhead a Red reaction against "servitude to Russian imperialism."[18]

Stalin himself considered Mao a "second Tito" and his revolution "a fake," to quote Mao, who had a suspect record, if only for resisting outside edict about how to wage his civil war. In the immediate interest of the Soviet Union, Mao was supposed to stop fighting Chiang and hurl his forces at Japan, not what he had in mind. He preserved his resources during World War II for the internecine struggle against the KMT. Stalin, in frustration, could think him a Japanese agent, worse than what Stilwell said of Chiang. Mao, after all, had not been trained in Moscow, as were more malleable Chinese Bolsheviks, whom he thought "fools" for slavish adherence to teachings inappropriate to local Asian conditions. Still, while Mao founded "Maoism," testimony to an intellectual independence, he did not think himself a nationalist in the common meaning of the term, wherein one's own country is the more important matter. "We are not an independent communist party," he had told his adherents since 1935; "we are a branch of the Communist International. Our Chinese revolution is a part of the world revolution," if not the key element, because colonialism was "the weak lineage of the chain of international imperialism."[19]

Stalin, for his part, was unwilling to risk war in the Far East against the U.S. "lunatics" armed with atomic bombs. He told his chief lieutenants in late 1945 to remove "all our liaison officers and other people . . . from the operational zones of Mao Tse-tung's troops as soon as possible. The civil war in China is taking a serious turn, and I am worried that our enemies would later blame our people in these regions, who are not controlling anything, as the organizers of the civil war." Stalin subsequently increased his delivery of materiel assistance: thousands of artillery guns along with tanks and planes, as long as he could keep it relatively secret. He still lectured Mao at their first meeting (December 1949) that "the main point is not to rush and to avoid conflicts." The Korean War that began halfway through 1950 would not change Kremlin motivation all that much. Chinese envoys returned from Moscow in 1951 reporting Stalin's fear of a fight with the United States and apprehension that Beijing would emulate Belgrade, a rationale for his reluctance to engage America on China's behalf.[20]

Conflicts of interest beset Mao and Stalin, as well as common traits of personality, such as chronic suspicion and egotism approaching megalomania. This does not mean that Russia had no real reason to be wary, even if not hearing what Mao said in 1936: "We are certainly not fighting for an emancipated China in order to turn the country over to Moscow." In 1949, some U.S. experts already were predicting that Mao aspired to be the Lenin of the Far East, all the more dangerous for not bearing the "onus of Russian influence. . . . Image a dissident Bolshevism loose in Asia." Mao, for the time being, described himself as "Stalin's pupil," necessary to get Moscow to relinquish all holdings in Manchuria, finance Chinese reconstruction, and support the conquest of Taiwan. His emissaries made their case for assistance by telling the Soviets of a U.S. "plan of changing the CCP to echo the Tito clique." This was not a comfortable contingency for Stalin, who had eliminated debate inside the Kremlin and imperiously dictated orders to communist parties throughout the world. Dissidents such as Tito (or perhaps a Mao) were potential role models for rebellion. For such reasons, Stalin rejected in July 1949 China's membership in the Red internationale when he was orchestrating the trial and execution of the secretary general of the Bulgarian Communist Party and the Hungarian minister of internal affairs. One might recall his obsession with a meager band of Trotskyites and other sectarian Marxists said to be subversive elements in the 1930s. He had already taken the first steps toward a new purge of the party within the Soviet Union, although filled by now with handpicked underlings. This would culminate in the "Doctors' Plot" of the early 1950s, discussed in chapter 8 of this book.[21]

Sino-Soviet relations were in flux; so was U.S. policy toward China. The State Department had a "surprisingly unanimous" consensus, according to the senior foreign correspondent of the *New York Times*: "The Chinese situation is very fluid . . . we must wait and find out." Most people in the agency looked for a breather to debate whether Mao would follow Tito's fold once they realized that the Serbian strongman "is perhaps our most precious asset in the struggle to contain and weaken Russian expansion." Acheson, impatient with bureaucracy, was disposed to probe potential allies of convenience. To him, pause meant flexibility to adopt neutrality that was hardly neutral; suspension of American assistance was supposed to be a deathblow to Chiang's regime. The impact of its prospective demise on national security was still uncertain, considering the political situation within China. "Violent verbiage" against the West could always be a ploy to protect China from premature stories in the American press that Mao was on the cusp of emulating Tito. Belgrade thought his rhetoric had no real relevance, essentially the position of the U.S. counselor general in Shanghai: Mao "could not undertake at this stage any open or definite repudiation of Moscow" but would move in this direction "granted favorable circumstances and a reasonable attitude on the part of the democracies"—Washington take note; Moscow certainly did.[22]

The politburo studied Dean Acheson's "slanderous fabrications against the Soviet Union," saw they angled for rapprochement with Beijing, and preempted Washington by signing a Sino-Soviet alliance on 14 February 1950. Stalin, in the process, declared "to hell with Yalta," where he had recognized the Kuomintang in return for Manchurian bases, railways, and ports. He ceded these territorial concessions and adopted a more active stance in the ongoing civil war when he described the new pact as "a serious boost to Chinese Communists in their relations with the national bourgeoisie." The latter still had pockets on the mainland and were waging war from Taiwan, a topic to which Stalin turned a deaf ear as late as mid-1949. When Mao's emissaries then requested air force and navy support, he had replied that he dared not confront the United States lest he risk a global war before his country recovered from World War II. Now in 1950, from fear of Sino-American reconciliation, Stalin pledged to dispatch to China more than one thousand experts on air and naval combat, the military weak points of the PLA at war with the KMT, a conflict still under debate within the United States.[23]

Democracies, being disputatious bodies, rarely have a single point of view, especially before a national election. In 1950, when Congressman Richard Nixon was an aspiring candidate for U.S. senator from California, he said that Dean Acheson and his fellow "apologists for the Chinese communists [have] been taken in hook, line, and sinker." Twenty-five years later, after his own presidency exploited Sino-Soviet conflict, Nixon admitted to having used the immaculate moustache, clothes, and manners of the secretary of state "as a perfect foil for my attacks on the snobbish kind of foreign service personality." In the process, Acheson was guilty of "bare-faced appeasement" toward the PRC, a scathing indictment for those who had lived through Munich and thought it encouraged Hitler to begin World War II. Douglas MacArthur essentially agreed with Congressman Nixon, although the general would have to mince some words as long as he remained in uniform. Once relieved in 1951, he was completely free to speak his mind about the concept of limited war that Acheson and Truman supposedly hatched: a "new and yet more dangerous form of appeasement—appeasement on the battlefield."[24]

MacArthur and Mao, both Asia-firsters, avowed that events in the Far East held pinnacle significance in the mortal struggle between communism and the West. This put the leader of the CCP at odds with the leader of the Kremlin. It put the commander in chief, Far East, at odds with past and present U.S. army chiefs of staff George Marshall, Dwight Eisenhower, Omar Bradley, J. Lawton ("Joe") Collins, and, one might add, Matthew Bunker Ridgway, the deputy chief of staff for operations and administration who would replace MacArthur, then rotate to Europe before coming back to Washington to succeed Collins in 1953. MacArthur, once dismissed, said the "fools in Washington" who rebuffed his plans "lost most of the Asiatic mainland for the United States" with tragic results to be "visited on our children and our children's children." He rarely mentioned

Korea before the communist invasion nor argued with the Pentagon assessment of March 1949 that the military "has no strategic interest in maintaining troops and bases" on the peninsula. The Department of the Army, not inclined to throw around scarce assets to make a political point, began to reconsider this Northeast Asia deployment shortly after it began in mid-1945, when Truman was angry at Red Army occupations carried out in Eastern Europe. Essentially, he would keep the Soviets out of Seoul, because Yalta had not kept them out of Warsaw. "This," said Henry Stimson, "is the Polish question transplanted to the Far East."[25]

One might debate the beneficence behind a foreign commitment. Numerical inferiority in a forward position falls on its military face. The U.S. army felt no reason to "hold on tenaciously to what is essentially a weak position" in Korea, to be "liquidated . . . as soon as possible." MacArthur was also averse to a land war in Asia, as well as to the State Department, the agency most committed to retaining American forces on the peninsula. "It should be recognized," he wrote Washington in January 1949, "that in the event of any serious threat to the security of Korea, strategic and military considerations will force abandonment of any pretense of military support." As for "the coffee-drinking diplomats" who argued for retaining the troops, he told his staff that they could take over "the messy situation" and "stew in their own juice." MacArthur was thinking of a different battlefield in the Pacific area of operation, but not the one the Joint Chiefs of Staff (JCS) had in mind. They leaned toward Japan, to chairman Omar Bradley "about the only tangible thing left of the fruits of victory in the Pacific." MacArthur had his own opinion contrary to this sentiment of many Europe-firsters. He preferred Formosa, even to Great Britain. That would help make China a more important factor in the election of 1950 than in 1948.[26]

Washington, MacArthur, and Chiang Kai-shek

Chiang Kai-shek's downfall was his own doing.

HARRY TRUMAN, SEPTEMBER 1952[27]

Many Americans give [Sun Li-jen] the impression that he is our White Hope for China.

COLONEL LOUIS J. FORTIER, JUNE 1950[28]

America had begun the process of ending the occupation of Japan through a treaty that officially would conclude World War II. The Pentagon wanted any final agreement to include rights "to station as many troops as we want, where we want and for as long as we want." Douglas MacArthur, Supreme Commander Allied Powers, did not concur. He thought the whole occupation effort already was going downhill once Washington marginalized his authority to place social, moral, and political reform ahead of economic growth. He advised the neutralization of the island, dependent on Soviet concurrence. "Japan's role is to be the Switzerland of the Pacific." The administration, less enchanted with demilitarization, the memorial achievement of MacArthur's occupation, placed policy in the hands of John Foster Dulles, an establishment Republican of the Dewey-Vandenberg variety. He negotiated with Japanese officials, now bypassing SCAP headquarters, where MacArthur was in search of a new mission. The general would have moved toward redeploying military assets to Formosa, which he never would trade for any communist concession, such as ending the Korean War. Seventy was simply too young for a soldier to retire who had yet to fill his full destiny.[29]

MacArthur, making $18,761 a year in the army, already had signed a memorandum of understanding with Remington Rand Corporation guaranteeing $100,000 a year for service on its board of directors, not to mention housing at the Waldorf Astoria and speaking honorariums. This prospect, merely money, left him emotionally cold, as seen in the physical symptoms periodically displayed when his career was in limbo. His hands and legs trembled in 1949, although once he was able to write memos with what an assistant called "immaculate" script. He also seemed to lose his train of thought, unique for someone able to conduct what Eisenhower called "spell-binding" monologues on a wide variety of topics "far afield of military matters." A medical officer in Tokyo headquarters thought the general suffered from Parkinson's disease, a faulty diagnosis considering the symptoms would not persist. MacArthur was yearning for a new opportunity, namely the defense of Formosa, which seemed out of reach.[30]

In World War II, MacArthur's forte had been air and sea power, the biggest flaw in the PLA light infantry armed forces. If allowed to meet an amphibious invasion of Formosa, widely predicted for mid-1950, the general foresaw inflicting a "crushing defeat" able to rock the foundation of Mao's regime, still insecure because recently installed. MacArthur began this self-assumed undertaking in 1949 after the U.S. government closed down its military advisory mission to the Nationalists. Claire Chennault got assistance recruiting old American volunteers who had flown with him for Chiang and China prior to Pearl Harbor. Other veterans surreptitiously enrolled by the KMT's consulate in Tokyo were Imperial Japanese officers recently released from incarceration. Chinese communist newspapers accused MacArthur of freeing "fascists" armed with "American-made planes dropping American-made bombs" for the "traitor Chiang Kai-shek": they have "come again to massacre the Chinese people.... Obviously, therefore, Taiwan must be liberated."[31]

Washington could not do much about decaled U.S. equipment already in Chiang's hands. It asked CINCFE headquarters for a situation report about purported mercenaries and received a substantial understatement: a few "military adventurers . . . may have been smuggled into Formosa." Acheson, in frustration over what seemed a KMT ploy to implicate America, sputtered that "the communists would be criminally crazy if they did not put an end to [Chiang's military citadel] just as soon as possible." Moscow reacted with more resolution than the U.S. protests Taipei ignored. In February 1950, Soviets began to man air-defense batteries and radar units protecting coastal cites, particularly Shanghai, and then put their own pilots up in the sky.[32]

Between mid-March and mid-May, Russians gunned down five KMT aircraft, such as U.S. manufactured P-38s. This became something of a proxy war wherein the USSR, the USA, and PRC avoided direct confrontation. To Stalin, who kept his pilots back from the Taiwan Strait, that was a prudent form of military conflict, at least as long as America held the nuclear advantage. To MacArthur, it fell far short of reshaping the world through a decisive victory. Before history could pivot along his lines with a counterrevolution against Asian communism, three things would have to happen. First, Washington would have to decide to defend Formosa. Second, MacArthur would need to assume command, presumably as "military advisor to Chiang Kai-shek," of interest to the CINCFE since 1947. A lesser man might have recoiled at the recollection of what transpired in 1941, when another wish came true. Roosevelt adopted the total defense of the Philippines and returned MacArthur to active duty, wherein the general could beat back a Japanese invasion—or later go down saying "I shall return." In 1950, as a new decade began, nothing so monumental seemed in the offing without the occurrence of contingency number three. Mao would have to try to take Taiwan on MacArthur's watch. That July, after the CINCFE suddenly got responsibility to defend the island, he revealed his personal priorities to Matt Ridgway, a presumed protégé: "I pray nightly [the Chinese communists] will try."[33]

MacArthur and Dean Acheson obviously had disagreements as substantial as those dividing Stalin and Mao. The general still resented critical comments made in September 1945 about presuming to make national policy. He nonetheless managed to say to Foreign Service personnel a few nice things about the secretary of state, as when inviting him to visit Japan. MacArthur complained of neglect and isolation from the center of political power. However, when officials did visit, he found the meetings useless: "Not a damn one of them tells me exactly what is going on." Visitors might have gasped in disbelief. They remembered monologues where the general talked for hours while they tried, but failed, to get in a question or comment. Mike Mansfield, then a congressman from Montana and former professor of Asian history, would state: "I don't remember anything of what he said. He said too much to remember anything."[34]

George F. Kennan, the State Department's director for long-range planning, had a much different experience insofar as talking and remembering what was said in an open, wide-ranging, and surprisingly pleasant exchange of opinions. His own visit to MacArthur in March 1948 was scheduled to focus on change in economic plans partly due to events occurring in Mainland China. Japan would now be needed to maintain a balance of power in the Far East. Washington emphasized industrial expansion by curtailing antitrust action associated with demilitarization. MacArthur had been more New Dealish than the Truman administration, which was running for reelection on populist rhetoric attacking favoritism for large corporations. Whether the general recognized this political irony or not, he certainly sensed that his authority was eroding for Japan. He turned the encounter with Kennan into a broad exploration of military defense in Asia, an issue where he could exert substantial influence because the matter was in flux.[35]

Kennan and MacArthur came to agree on a broad policy that the government subsequently adopted as its grand strategy: that America should commit its assets in an offshore defense perimeter on islands east of continental Asia. The diplomat wanted to end participation in the Chinese civil war. The general, still clutching one of his cherished ideas, was reiterating the position he held with his father from the dawn of the twentieth century, but with a somewhat different cast of geopolitical entities. In mid-1936, MacArthur wrote the War Department that the Philippine and Alaskan island chains "will give the United States a position of such mastery in the Pacific as to give pause to any force of aggression," meaning Imperial Japan. This had not proved true in late 1941–early 1942, when Manila fell along with Malaya, Burma, the East Indies, and New Guinea. In 1948, one could hold that specific conditions were far more favorable now that America occupied Okinawa and Japan itself. Yet to be determined was the fate of Formosa, the former Japanese colonial possession from which Imperial forces had staged their attack on the Philippines, the most devastating event in MacArthur's life before the Korean War.[36]

Agreement on the perimeter defense policy relied on ambiguity, as often is the case on controversial issues in the U.S. government. Exactly what assets should be invested in exactly what places on the Pacific Rim? Would economic, military, and political assistance suffice, or would America deploy its armed forces beyond their base in Okinawa, presently the hub of the defense network? Specifically, did the perimeter concept foreclose sustained involvement on the continent of Asia? Yes, according to Kennan, Foreign Service officer. MacArthur and Dean Acheson thought otherwise, although otherwise in disagreement. The general would never turn his back on the Chinese mainland, to him a "disastrous" situation since 1944. The secretary of state remained a firm proponent of Korea, "where the line is clearly drawn between the Russians and ourselves." Formosa, about to become the most contentious problem, was not mentioned in Kennan's report of his conference with MacArthur. As of yet, the Nationalists had not fled wholesale to the island: no need to bring up an issue that could tear the frail consensus apart.[37]

All parties agreed that Formosa should not fall into the hands of a military threat. That certainly meant Stalin, who had in theater 4,150 military aircraft by MacArthur's account to Washington, November 1948: "It no longer appears realistic to consider the Far East as a static and secure flank in the military contest with communism." Was Mao also an imminent threat, or might he emulate Tito, said to have faced down the Soviet Union "with [a] consolidated Communist regime equipped with a consolidated power apparatus able and willing to go an independent way?" Acheson was not sure in his own mind, nor was the rest of the National Security Council (NSC), judging by its vacuous position paper about dangers to U.S. defenses from an unidentified "administration . . . susceptible of exploitation by Kremlin-directed communists." If and when this threat came from China, would America use Formosa as a base for projecting power back onto the mainland? One could not tell because of subtle differences in the concepts of perimeter defense. Kennan used words such as "corner-stone of Pacific security." MacArthur chose "spearhead." One may assume that neither usage was accidental. Both men were master craftsmen of the English language.[38]

MacArthur would have used Formosa as a cape luring Mao to make a fatal charge across the Taiwan Strait. By January 1949, according to the NSC, the island was being inundated with an "influx of refugee politicians and militarists from the mainland—many of them men whose gross incompetence has played into the hands of the communists in China." Acheson contemplated permanent neutralization under native Taiwanese or as a trustee of the United Nations, what he privately depicted as "taking over the island under the front of international action." He even pondered the esoteric point that Formosa technically belonged to Japan, at least until the forthcoming treaty officially ended World War II. By this reasoning its government fell to the SCAP (Japan), someone named Douglas MacArthur. One doubts this feature reassured the secretary of state, who remained ambivalent about Formosa at least as late as June 1950, when he advised that the issue of the island "required further study," the classic excuse for delay.[39]

MacArthur said of Chiang Kai-shek in mid-1949: "I believe in helping him as I would help anyone else who would fight Communism." The absence of positive comment about the regime ("not the best" but "on our side") testifies to MacArthur's ambivalence about the man whose presence on Formosa would play a major role in his relief. In 1951, shortly before dismissal, the general put renewed assistance to the island under the direction of a U.S. officer empowered to make sure the right items "got to the right places." This was no vote of confidence in the KMT command, which MacArthur supported on the basis of common enemies, including U.S. journalists. "Irresponsible propaganda aimed at my destruction" in articles critical of his doings in Japan seemed reminiscent of what the media said of Chiang. Their criticism started in America, then spread "over China with the ultimate yielding of the country and its people before the Communist advance."[40]

MacArthur held that MacArthur should have been the presidential envoy in 1946, rather than George Marshall, unable to handle "the practical features of Chinese life." He himself would have "made the military decision to meet [the communists] and it would have been easily handled," no wasting time with a futile ceasefire. Marshall, when appointed secretary of state in 1947, ignored proposals that MacArthur go to China. In 1948, when almost everyone expected a Republican sweep in the national election, the CINCFE welcomed GOP suggestions that he become Chiang's special advisor with unprecedented powers. These scenarios for an American viceroy would have saved China by making Chiang a figurehead along the lines of Hirohito, the head of state through whom MacArthur governed Japan. Although notions like this withered when Washington stayed in Democratic hands, a variant revived in Nanking when members of the U.S. embassy began feeling out dissident officers inside the Nationalist army to consider a coup. Dean Rusk, Paul Nitze, and George Kennan took up the initiative inside Washington. MacArthur, still looking for a mission to Formosa, met them more than halfway.[41]

After George Kennan returned to Washington from MacArthur's headquarters in March 1948, he started working on a project completed that June in NSC 10/2, the government charter creating a special subdivision in the CIA for clandestine operations, usually behind the Iron Curtain. He was still giving State Department guidance and oversight to the so-called Office of Special Projects when he received a "Dear Kennan" letter from MacArthur in June 1949. The general wrote from concern that Acheson was paying so much attention to Europe that "the oriental masses" might gather the impression that the United States was relaxing its commitment "to hold our Far Eastern position." In hopes for another conference with an influential thinker in officialdom, MacArthur invited the director of policy planning "to visit Japan again in the not too distant future. You may be sure of a hearty welcome." In return, he received a letter of introduction for Lieutenant Colonel Boris Pash, "related to a project of the greatest delicacy concerning which some of my associates and I have great interest."[42]

Pash, son of Russian émigré bishop of the Eastern Orthodox Church, had a long résumé that began in 1919 as a teenage volunteer doing signals duty on the flagship of the anti-Bolshevik Black Sea fleet. This was good preparation for what he did in World War II, aside from investigating communists in the Manhattan Project making the atomic bomb. He earned a reputation for bold action with a top-secret unit of scientists and assorted "cutthroats" who chased down German physicists and high-grade uranium before Stalin could gather these spoils for his own nuclear enterprise. After that, in the postwar era, Pash helped resettle defectors and collaborators in return for information about communist armed forces and the Red underground. Nineteen forty-eight brought assignment to the Central Intelligence Agency, where Pash headed "Program

Branch 7," a five-man cell with a charter entailing "assassinations, kidnapping, and such other functions as from time to time may be given it."[43]

No record is available of the MacArthur-Pash meeting, but one thing is clear: the general's criticism of the KMT leader subsequently escalated. In September, he told a congressional delegation visiting Tokyo: "Chiang is surrounded by corrupt officials including corrupt generals. The generalissimo is a highly intelligent individual but knows nothing of the art of war." In October, MacArthur received a request for "guidance" from the publisher of the *New York Times*, whose editorials were favorable to Chiang. He responded: "Formosa's defenders cannot be counted upon long to resist a determined enemy amphibious assault."[44]

Hyperbolic stories too often accepted as literal truth portray MacArthur chronically conducting activities unknown to Washington. He probably had more autonomy than any other officer in American history, but that did not mean he conducted unilateral enterprise—before or during the Korean War. He commenced operations at the behest of the national authorities, or at least with their acquiescence, although he might then drive the effort beyond boundaries that they had in mind. Take the case of replacing Chiang. The State Department hoped to reform the government of Formosa, creating a viable regime on the island as a fallback position if Mao failed to follow the Tito model and became subservient to Stalin. MacArthur wanted to gain command and control of anticommunist forces during what he thought would be the climactic campaign of the Chinese civil war. He would, in effect, recreate his role as field marshal of the Commonwealth of the Philippines, with better results expected this time. "The Communist tide can be turned with relatively little effort now," MacArthur briefed a congressional investigation on the Far East. The United States would just have to "make a ringing declaration that it will support any and everyone who is opposed to communism, place 500 fighter planes in the hands of some 'war horse' similar to General Chennault, and give sufficient surplus ships to the [Nationalist] Chinese Navy to blockade and destroy China's coastal cites."[45]

MacArthur and Washington were in general agreement about the generalissimo—for the time being—although both parties were underestimating Chiang. He had not proved very good at counterintelligence against first-class conspirators on the mainland, where his army was rent with communist agents conducting military debacles from within the KMT command. Still, Chiang was better at intrigue than was the United States government, hesitant if not inept in this field of endeavor where undermining governments can prove difficult. Even the KGB could never execute Stalin's orders to execute Tito, notwithstanding Kennan's rather envious depiction of "an apparatus of amazing flexibility and versatility, managed by people whose experience and skill in underground methods are presumably without parallel in history."[46]

The CIA discussed "the assassination of an [unnamed] Asian leader" in mid-1949. Pash, its presumed specialist, was out of the country. The issue went up the chain of the Agency, where the assistant to the director of special operations was recorded to have declared: "We don't engage in such activities." That testified to their secrecy within the most secretive surroundings. It also indicated that direct action was not Dean Acheson's primary plan. He proposed developing what he called "a spontaneous independence movement which could then lead to an agreement in the UN for a new deal for Formosa." Otherwise "an American-created irredentist issue [would exist in Beijing] just at the time we shall be seeking to exploit the genuinely Soviet-created irredentist issue in Manchuria and Sinkiang." This meant Acheson wanted his cake and wanted to eat it: to keep the communists out of Formosa but even more to coax Mao onto the Titoist track. Hence the secretary of state told the president that we must "carefully conceal our wish to separate the island from the mainland," essentially futile since Mao long suspected "this kind of U.S. plot" to replace Chiang with a more competent lackey to imperialist likings, perhaps disguised as a "pseudo-Taiwanese setup on Taiwan."[47]

With little to be gained from subtlety, Washington might have turned to Kennan's new proposal whereby the U.S. armed forces would "serve to take the eye of both the public and Congress off the record of the past." This was a strange proposal from someone known to despise domestic political influence on foreign affairs. Kennan, however, had come to doubt the capacity of a democracy to do the KGB specialty: use force "for the accomplishment of measures short of war." Hence in July 1949 he said that an invasion should take over Formosa with "sufficient resolution, speed, ruthlessness and self-assurance," like Theodore Roosevelt took Panama in 1902. The Pentagon, however, was not nearly so willing to send in troops, whether to defend or to overthrow Chiang Kai-shek. The State Department still had to hope for some new regime willing to accept "veiled but vigorous" guidance, in the words of Paul Nitze, Kennan's replacement as director of policy planning in 1950. Nonetheless, when it came to conducting a successful coup, best wishes from the United States were far less than required by Lieutenant General Sun Li-jen, on whom Americans such as Kennan had pinned their hopes as the leader of the "Western trained liberals" against the "reactionaries" within the KMT.[48]

By virtually all accounts of all Americans who had contact with the Kuomintang, Sun was "the most outstanding Chinese military leader." MacArthur would say that he knew very well this "able and gallant officer who graduated from our own VMI," no small matter to the Far East commander or his chief of staff, Ned Almond, a fellow graduate of the Virginia Military Institute. They cited Sun as evidence that the Nationalists could be "a formidable force" if provided sufficient support. This implied the KMT had a lot more Suns in the offing, hardly the case. A network of "informers, counterintelligence agents, and 'political commissars' engendered" what a senior U.S. advisor called "paralyzing fears, suspicions, timidity, and buckpassing throughout the whole structure of command." MacArthur for his part was mum about his own first meeting with Sun in March 1949, when Virginia connections probably entered KMT calculations. The Nationalist regime used Sun much the way the Kansas City machine had used Harry Truman, a hard-working, honest man who made the rest of the outfit look better than it was. Sun was supposed to acquire more technical assistance and equipment from the CINCFE. Behind closed doors he proved less loyal to Chiang than Truman was to Tom Pendergast. Sun discussed with MacArthur the "most urgent need" for anticommunists to adopt "a radical reform of our psychology and ways of doing things—in political as well as military fields."[49]

In 1955, after Washington signed a defense pact with Taiwan, Chiang dropped all pretense of abiding Sun and put him under house arrest for the next thirty years. This was the last in a decade-long series of punishments that already reduced him to a figurehead unable to shift a regiment or replace a colonel without approval from Chiang or his eldest son, schooled in commissar methods from a decade in Moscow military academies. They claimed this concentration of command was required to prevent traditional warlord behavior that afflicted Nationalist forces when leaders used their units as personal property. One might think Chiang a glorified warlord out to monopolize corruption or a patriot battling endemic Chinese problems. Either way, he did not obsess about a lack of U.S. support, no matter that certain politicians in Nanking and Washington blamed White House indifference to his plight. Chiang attributed communist success to its superiority in political discipline, organization, indoctrination, and mass mobilization. Consequently, he set out to remodel the KMT along the lines of the CCP, which he admired for what his own regime lacked: cohesive pursuit of a political cause.[50]

MacArthur and Sun Li-jen were following their own path of reform, as when they met secretly with leaders of Taiwan's independence movement out to remove their birthplace from the Chinese civil war. Secession from the mainland, while contemplated in Washington, was not the real objective of the CINCFE or the maverick Chinese Nationalist. "If we can hold together [a] sufficient fighting force at a suitable place," Sun wrote MacArthur in mid-1949, "it would be possible to recover our lost ground by a series of well-guided counter-attacks." MacArthur would propose much the same thing when recommending an invasion of south China to the Pentagon in 1951. As for now, before he and Sun could replace Mao, they believed they had to replace Chiang. Sources reported MacArthur conferring about the government he was to establish after KMT underlings urged the generalissimo to "take a trip abroad." This was far from assassination but yet too audacious for Livingston Merchant, the State Department's desk officer for Formosa. He opposed taking "the dangerous and risky effort to finance and promote a coup d'etat" that could embarrass America, "cause violent repercussions," and give "Communist propaganda [a helping hand] throughout Asia."[51]

Sun complained to MacArthur that "our efforts could hardly bear fruit without effective aid" and "I am afraid Washington is still undecided." It was certainly informed. Sun sent these letters through the Taipei consulate that forwarded copies to the State Department, all for naught. The consul general had concluded that Sun did not have the wherewithal for political leadership. Acheson and Merchant felt he lacked adequate administrative experience. One suspects they were searching for a pretext not to conduct a coup that might jeopardize their primary objective: wooing Mao away from Stalin by claiming to be the true ally of Chinese nationalism and territorial integrity.[52]

While Washington was fumbling over finding an obstacle to Russian expansion in Asia, Sun took the initiative in early June 1950. He proposed deposing Chiang in a hand-delivered letter to Dean Rusk, whom he knew in World War II, when the assistant secretary of state for Far East affairs was assistant chief of staff for plans and operations at Joe Stilwell's military headquarters. Rusk later claimed he was "startled" by the message, although he actually received prior reports of Sun's plans to "overthrow the Government and set up one responsive to the people's will." This seemed better to him than Mao deposing the entire Nationalist cause: "It will not leave a good taste if we allow our political problems to be solved by the extermination of our war allies." Rusk already had been moving in the direction of MacArthur insofar as feeling that Formosa was the best place in the Far East to take a stand against communist expansion. He now held that Sun should "be given firm assurances" of advice and support, although the CIA thought the scheme already had been compromised. Rusk took the subject up with Acheson, who said he would take it to Truman, to whom he already drew "one lesson to be learned from the China debacle. It is that if we are confronted with an inadequate vehicle [i.e., Chiang] it should be discarded or immobilized in favor of a more propitious one." Rusk, of a like mind, met secretly on June 23rd with a prestigious member of the Chinese community in exile, whom he hoped to enlist in the Sun Li-jen enterprise. Two days later the undertaking was overtaken by the onset of the Korean War. Its military and political exigencies would save the regime on Formosa through a convoluted process this book will address. The issue, crackling through the conflict, was a major factor in the dismissal of MacArthur.[53]

Formosa, the Far East Command, the State Department, and the Pentagon

Loss of the island is widely anticipated. . . . Formosa has no special military significance.

STATE DEPARTMENT, "SPECIAL GUIDANCE," 23 DECEMBER 1949[54]

The domination of Formosa by an unfriendly power would be a disaster of the utmost importance to the U.S.

DOUGLAS MACARTHUR, 14 JUNE 1950[55]

The fact that Dean Acheson reconsidered a coup testifies to mounting misgivings about the regime in Beijing, traced below. Mao had proved hostile to the United States, supposedly out to depose him. The U.S. military proved fearful of Formosa falling into hostile hands. Meanwhile Acheson was worried but not ready to renounce all hope for rapprochement. He still believed that China would eventually break with the Soviet Union, nor would he change his mind even after the PRC and America came to blows in November 1950. The operative question was always when the split would occur and how to advance its appearance. The United States would have to take "the long view, not of 6 or 12 months but of 6 to 12 years," Acheson told the Joint Chiefs of Staff in late December 1949. Would anyone—Acheson, MacArthur, Truman, the JCS, or the electorate—have this much patience or this much time to nurture some sort of Sino-American understanding?[56]

The White House and the State Department were not decisively committed to either contestant in the Chinese civil war. They had not provided enough support for the KMT to win, but more than enough to enrage the CCP. MacArthur, while disgusted that "the exigencies of the moment seem to be our guide," was also of two minds, at least shortly after failing to take command of Formosa in 1949. He entreated Senator H. Alexander Smith (Rep.-N.J.) to procure assistance for Chiang, "misunderstood" in Washington because of a "smear campaign." He also told a State Department officer recently stationed in Taipei that "there is no reason why we should need Formosa as a base. It would be of no earthly use to us against our only possible major enemy [elsewhere identified as Russia] and certainly they could not utilize it against us."[57]

That MacArthur comment at that time was not exceptional or unique. In March 1949 and February 1950, he discussed the offshore defense policy with no mention of Formosa other than to boast of constructing airfields on Okinawa able to launch 3,500 sorties a day. This would blanket any bases on Formosa, now of no significant military value—that is, until March 1950, when MacArthur switched his mind again. Thereafter, whether speaking to the president, the secretary of defense, the JCS, or the *New York Times*, he stated: "Formosa in the hands of the Communists can be compared to an unsinkable aircraft carrier and submarine tender located to accomplish Soviet offensive strategy." He also accepted Chiang Kai-shek once Washington showed little stomach for deposing him. "If he has horns and a tail so long as he is anti-Communist, we should help him," MacArthur told a member of the Foreign Service. "Rather than make things difficult, the State Department should assist him in his fight against the Communists—we can try to reform him later."[58]

The Joint Chiefs of Staff were also moving in the direction of defense of Formosa but not without their own equivocations on display in 1948. Enemy control of the island "could produce strategic consequences very seriously detrimental to our national security." However, the JCS did not propose a direct role for U.S. armed forces other than putting "minor numbers of fleet units at a suitable Formosan port." Next year, the army superseded the navy at the highest rungs of the Pentagon. General Omar Bradley replaced Admiral William Leahy as chairman of the JCS. Louis Johnson, formerly a colonel like Truman in the National Guard, replaced James Forrestal, an ex-naval aviator now exhausted in the position of secretary of defense. Meanwhile, according to Anglo-American intelligence estimates, the Soviets had 175 divisions fully equipped with armor, artillery, and aircraft in Europe. This was the prime concern of most army officers who had attained their high rank while fighting in that theater during World War II. Bradley, for one, already predicted war against the Russians over Berlin.[59]

Johnson, per Truman's guidance to balance the budget, set out to prune military spending against pressure from the services for greater allocations. This just heightened JCS attention to the "current disparity between our military strength and our many global obligations." Acheson could therefore cite Pentagon reluctance to defend Formosa, an opinion ebbing in the flow of events. The official foundation of the People's Republic of China in October 1949 nudged the military down the road toward intervention, if done economically. Bradley wrote Johnson that "a modest, well-directed, and closely-supervised program of military aid to the anti-communist government in Taiwan would be in the security interest of the United States." Joe Collins, the army's chief of staff, told Acheson that "by comparatively small expenditures Formosa might be placed in a position where it could hold out longer than otherwise, with a consequent significant effect on the ability of the Chinese Communists to consolidate their regime." Phrases such as "longer than otherwise" were not accidental. A study by the joint staff concluded: "Prompt military measures short of involvement of major United States military forces might gain time but presumably would not prevent Communist control of Taiwan."[60]

Acheson, like most good negotiators, made concessions as long as he could say they were theoretical. He was willing to nuzzle up to "the discredited, decayed KMT Government" provided it was necessary to "acquire an island essential to the defense of the United States." In response, he got Collins to give up a major point in late 1949 concerning geostrategic position: that Mao's acquisition of Formosa would not expose Okinawa to a much greater threat than it already faced from bases on the Chinese mainland. Within a week, the secretary of state told Senate Republican spokesmen on the Far East that the Okinawan linchpin of the offshore peninsula defense lay only 40 miles farther from China's coastline than it did from Taiwan, "a distance that has no significance in terms of airpower today." Alexander Smith and William Knowland did not correct the lapse in geography: the true distance is 120 miles. Like most laymen, they chose to cite an accommodating expert, in their case Douglas MacArthur, whose "opinion had not been taken into account."[61]

Civilians cited military authorities on behalf of positions they already took on their own accord. Acheson parried the reference to MacArthur by retorting it "was necessary in such matters to accept the considered judgment of the Joint Chiefs of Staff." Actually, political advocates and professional experts were all ambivalent: Acheson about a coup; MacArthur about Chiang; and the Pentagon about commitments to defend Formosa. Even Secretary Johnson, the foremost proponent of U.S. support to the island, had to write Truman: "It is not in our interest to become involved to the extent of placing the American flag. . . . The cost and the risk, in the opinion of the Joint Chiefs of Staff, would be excessive." Nonetheless, this founding partner of a major Washington law firm added a fateful proviso to the DOD position, phrased with double negatives that made no contribution to clarity: "There can be no categorical assurance that other future circumstances, extending to war itself, might not make overt military action eventually advisable from the over-all standpoint of national security."[62]

The president was the ultimate arbitrator between Acheson, Johnson, the JCS, and General MacArthur. If at all possible, Truman and the public at large would have wished to avoid affiliation with either side in the Chinese civil war. He did not recognize Beijing, a position favored by two-thirds of the people expressing their opinion in newspaper polls. He berated Taipei, as did 70 percent of the citizenry, now tired of aid to Chiang Kai-shek. "We have never been favorable to the Communists in China," Truman held in 1949. "We can't be in the position of making any deals with a Communist regime." On the other hand, he probed alternatives to conflict suggested by Acheson's grand strategy and Truman's own sense of practicality. The idea of reaching some sort of understanding with the likes of Mao did not seem unprecedented or completely farfetched to someone used to handling political strongmen, although primarily in a domestic American context.[63]

In 1945, Truman thought that he could "deal with Stalin," being "as near like Tom Pendergast [the boss of Kansas City] as any man I know." In the depth of the Cold War, he still thought of calling person-to-person the general secretary of the Communist Party, a plausible way to contain conflict provided "the old guy" was not to blame. "He had a politburo on his hands like the 80th

Congress," the president was wont to say. Foreign Minister Molotov "never gave Stalin all the facts unless he was forced to do it"—what "a perfect mutton head." That Truman could repeat such statements into the 1950s testifies to more than Stalin's genius for deception, an actor even greater than MacArthur. It reveals the president's enduring inclination to believe in the fraternity of politicos, that is, that sensible men could make sensible deals, be they Republicans, Democrats, or Marxist-Leninists.[64]

In the 1960s, Truman thought that if he had only been president in the late 1950s, he could have gotten Fidel Castro "on our side rather than Russia's." In 1949, he was inclined to think much the same thing about Mao Tse-tung, with whom he could agree on a "strong central government in China" able to prevent "probable Russian resumption of power in Manchuria." Acheson appealed to this slant that November, when he put forth his full case for attempting "to detach [the PRC] from subservience to Moscow." The president had qualms about appearing soft on communism but agreed with Acheson "in the broad sense," probably from his own recall of history. Truman's pro-Confederate parents deeply resented Yankee army occupation of the postwar South. Was that much different than Russian soldiers inhabiting the Orient? China itself "was fundamentally anti-foreign," and Truman would do all he could "to see that this anti-foreign sentiment is not turned in our direction." Irrespective of "military considerations" about Formosa, he therefore said "on political grounds he would decide with the State Department." On 5 January 1950, the president announced at his first news conference of the new year: "The United States Government will not pursue a course which will lead to involvement in the civil conflict in China. . . . [It] will not provide military aid or advice to [Nationalist] Chinese forces on Formosa."[65]

One might have thought that policy was finally settled. However, nine days after Truman delivered what diplomats called "an olive branch," Beijing police confounded Acheson's expectations by entering the U.S. consular compound to expel its personnel. Washington had thought China had every reason to maintain contact: food production was falling 25 percent, natural disasters afflicted some 40 million people, and the Soviet Union seemed too poor and crude to provide much help. Beijing would seek investment, trade, and technical assistance, according to State Department logic and the image some Chinese communists cultivated in the West. Mao was supposed to be a pragmatist straddling a "radical" faction that favored the Soviet Union and "liberals" led by Chou En-lai who thought the Kremlin "crazy" for "policies leading to war." This was seductive to U.S. officials searching for alternatives to Chiang Kai-shek, whether moderates within the communist party or reformers inside the KMT. Fifty years later Washington was still searching for reasonable leaders in Serbia, Iraq, and Iran, as well as the Taliban government of Afghanistan, that is, before 9/11/2001.[66]

Notwithstanding the logic in some circles of the West, Mao and his under-lings were convinced that reconciliatory rhetoric out of Washington was a "smokescreen" for imperialist schemes such as occupying Taiwan. U.S. diplo-mats, merchants, and clergy still on the mainland were thought to be part of "a large American espionage bloc" dedicated to utilizing "Japanese special service as well as Chinese and Mongols in a plot against the Chinese people, [their] revolutionary cause and world peace." Communists already had imprisoned the consul general at Mukden, serving a year on bread and water. Truman, out-raged, spoke of establishing a blockade and sending commandos to conduct a prison breakout. Acheson talked him out of this impulse, what one might expect from "the striped-pants set," to quote a CIA operative. Acheson in fact held that rapprochement "did not mean a policy of appeasement." He told Truman in November 1949 that "if the Communists took action detrimental to the United States it should be opposed with vigor." The secretary of state began to move along these lines in April 1950, about the time Washington imposed restrictions on six hundred items for sale to China. In May, he told Britain's foreign minister that while the administration did not expect Chiang to last very long, it had "reassessed more highly the strategic importance" of Formosa.[67]

All this indicated that Acheson was giving ground, with or without the challenge mounted within the Cabinet. In March 1949, he had felt impelled to say: "I trust that we may count on disciplined cooperation. . . . Members of the [National Security] Council will bear in mind the necessity of restraining evidence of zeal with regard to Formosa." Louis Johnson, the object of this homily, was brusque, competitive, and extremely ambitious. He tended to treat Acheson "like an office boy," according to a senator attending a joint briefing. Johnson had raised nearly $2 million for the 1948 election campaign, despite all odds against Truman. He then got his Pentagon posting but did not limit activities to what the president wanted: holding down military expenditures. Truman had to tell him not to meddle with policy for the Far East, which belonged to the State Department. Johnson did not take this as the final word but "had to be discreet about it," as least for now. "If war should break out," a long-time assistant told Chiang's ambassador, "it would be very different. Then the Secretary of Defense would take charge and have a great deal to say in relations with foreign nations."[68]

Johnson, chronically impatient, still went on the offensive by taking every opportunity to expose and refute any inconsistencies he could find in Acheson's stance. Foreign Service officers like George Kennan supported the offshore defense perimeter policy to avoid intervention on the mainland in the Chinese civil war. Johnson used it to undermine aversion to a pledge to defend Formosa, the last anticommunist stronghold in a country of utmost importance to the secretary of defense. However, he could not overcome the State Department position without more support within the Pentagon. The army, navy, and Joint

Strategic Survey Committee, as late as 10 June 1950, would not "recommend that U.S. forces be committed to hold Formosa" unless "preceded by partial mobilization and acceptance of possible commitment to global war," not the state of world affairs at the time of discussion.[69]

Omar Bradley did not think much of Johnson's grasp of military issues, his abrasive manners, nor his patent political ambition. People who really pushed for his appointment were Truman's military aides from the National Guard, associated with Johnson in the American Legion, where he was national commander in the early 1930s. However, Harry Vaughan and Louis Renfro were no prestigious blue-ribbon panel according to the JCS. Johnson therefore needed someone of greater standing if he were to dissolve the military's ambivalence about Formosa, for which he bore some direct responsibility. He, after all, was pruning the budget while trying to add this substantial mission. In mid-June 1950, with Bradley in tow, Johnson set out for Tokyo. Truman forbade a stopover visit to Taipei. He could hardly forbid consultations on Formosa with Douglas MacArthur, whose extraordinary powers of persuasion could provide crucial assistance, inside and outside the military establishment.[70]

MacArthur hardly needed much encouragement, even when Acheson and Truman were making their official announcements about the Far East in January. A "responsible source" in SCAP headquarters told the Associated Press that "a final decision on United States policy toward Formosa would emerge from a visit of the Joint Chiefs of Staff to Japan." In so many words, everything was tentative until MacArthur's own pronouncement, a position clarified in February when he told one diplomat: "It would be the Chiefs who would be educated, not the SCAP!" MacArthur by March had allayed his qualms about Chiang Kai-shek, which became evident when he arrested a leader of the Taiwanese independence movement working out of Japan. On June 15th, one week before the general met with Johnson and Bradley, the issue was permanently laid to rest upon receipt of a message to Charles Willoughby, MacArthur's deputy chief of staff for intelligence. This immigrant from Central Europe, fluent in several languages, had sponsored and counseled foreign officers attending the army staff college at Fort Leavenworth in the mid-1930s. One of them, Ho Shi-Bai, was now a senior officer at Chiang's headquarters. He passed to his former instructor a message to be passed onto MacArthur: "Generalissimo, aware of the danger of his position, is agreeable to accept American high command in every category and hopes to interest General MacArthur to accept this responsibility. . . . Soliciting his advice, guidance, and direction."[71]

Chiang had tried to lead a host of Americans down this garden path: Roosevelt, Hopkins, Stimson, Stilwell, and Marshall, not to mention a State Department officer at the Formosa desk in 1950. Those pleas for direction to put his own house in order seemed "an old story" to Washington. However, the situation was a little different because more desperate as of May 1950, when the Nationalists fled the communist invasion of Hainan island, the KMT's largest holding outside Taiwan. The U.S. consul in Taipei, busy planning to evacuate American dependents, forwarded reports that the generalissimo was shouting at visitors, throwing objects around his office, and cursing the United States for abandonment. Nonetheless, he had not played his last hand until June 16th, the day after MacArthur received his confidential message passed through Willoughby. Chiang sent a similar plea directly to Truman: "if the President would send someone to Taiwan who would not insult him, he would do anything the President asked," presumably including abdication. Ten days later, during the first days of the crisis in Korea, Truman mentioned how "the Generalissimo might step out if MacArthur were put in," incidentally the fulfillment of Mac-Arthur's dream. Acheson, however, dismissed this line of enterprise. Chiang would probably "resist and 'throw the ball game.'"[72]

MacArthur had a different opinion about what he could accomplish, as if Chiang would place real faith in a foreigner known to have been dabbling in plots to remove him from power. The generalissimo was far more interested in recruiting to his side an articulate advocate for his cause, reminiscent of what he did in World War II by playing Claire Chennault against Joe Stilwell. MacArthur was not prepared to accept a role confined to public relations but was ready for Johnson and Bradley on their arrival in Tokyo. Reports from the Pentagon had informed his headquarters that "the Joint Chiefs do not regard Formosa of prime strategic importance to the U.S. as a military base," although it might be "a valuable irritant against the Communist-held mainland, if the U.S. showed its determination to hold it." A statement from MacArthur was required to stiffen the opinion of the Department of Defense, which he did on the June 22nd with a memorandum given to the secretary of defense and the chairman of the Joint Chiefs. It "made the case," said Bradley, "for helping Formosa more eloquently than anything the JCS had produced."[73]

The military henceforth was a solid front on behalf of substantial assistance to the island, although the Pentagon had file cabinets full of reports about incompetence and corruption in the KMT. Still, no matter what it thought of its old Chinese ally, "U.S. military teaching rejects as a basis for action guesses as to what the enemy will do." Matt Ridgway used those words in June 1951 to distance himself from MacArthur, a self-declared expert on "Oriental psychology" who had said that China would not enter the Korean War. In 1950, MacArthur and the Pentagon were in closer harmony about the Taiwan Strait. DOD, per the Ridgway-stated rule of thumb, held that "the strategic value of these islands to the security of the U.S. should not be jeopardized by any wishful thinking that a *modus vivendi* between the U.S. and a Communist China can be effected." It did not share Acheson's faith that any ruler of China would never hand over any territory to any Russian, except for what the State Department called another "Spanish situation." The Soviet Union, leveraging its military supplies during the Spanish Civil War, treated the leaders of the Republican side "as colonists handle natives," to quote reports from Moscow's own operatives in the 1930s. In January 1950, Mao requested some two hundred fighters, eighty bombers, and specialty air and naval personnel to participate in the conquest of Taiwan. Anticipating this occurrence, State worried that U.S. support for the KMT would make Beijing more vulnerable to Kremlin penetration when Stalin could demand bases on the island in return for military support.[74]

NSC-68, the pivotal report on the Cold War, restated in April 1950 that "nationalism still remains the most potent emotional-political force. . . . If a satellite feels able to effect its independence of the Kremlin, as Tito was able to do, it is likely to break away." That language indicated China must make the overture. "We should be in no hurry," Truman already stated, "to recognize this regime." An impasse thus existed. Washington waited for Beijing to cut its ties to Moscow as Acheson stood on "the look-out for the development of a Chinese version of Titoism." Meanwhile Beijing awaited Washington cutting all ties to Taipei, not easy with mounting DOD concern about enemy penetration of the Pacific defense perimeter. That would risk "the current grand strategy" in the event of war with the Soviet Union: to "conduct a strategic offensive in the West and a strategic defense in the East." This at least avoided a land war in Asia, the worst-case scenario for generals such as Omar Bradley. Neither he nor any other member of the JCS yet advocated direct military protection of Formosa. Exactly what was needed to keep it out of communist hands and who would do the keeping was to be determined from a military survey of requirements. If and when the president approved, it would fall to the senior officer in the Far East, General Douglas MacArthur.[75]

Bradley showed no worry that he was beginning a process that could end up sucking scarce military assets ever deeper into a secondary theater. On June 24th, he returned to Washington weak with fever from his trip to the Far East. He pushed himself out of bed on the 25th to get unanimous JCS support for Secretary Johnson's prospective effort to reverse Acheson's Formosa policy at a meeting of the National Security Council to be held that night at Blair House, the White House then undergoing reconstruction. The general had just heard that the North Korean People's Army (KPA) had crossed the 38th parallel but did not think much of it, having recently been briefed by the head of the American military advisory mission in Seoul. Brigadier General William L. Roberts, flown to Tokyo, told of his fine performance training recruits of the armed forces of the Republic of [South] Korea, colloquially known to Americans as the ROKs. He was inclined to praise "my army" for physical fitness, tenacity, and toughness but also had sent less conspicuous reports that it was "dangerously reduced in firepower, mobility and logistical support." The chairman of the JCS, not one with time to comb these files, told the service chiefs that the ROKs would hold off the invasion "unless the Russians actively participate in the operation." If that should happen, "we may want to recommend even stronger action in the case of Formosa in order to offset the effect of the fall of South Korea on the rest of East Asia."[76]

From Bradley's perspective events on the peninsula enhanced the need for a survey team to gather information as to what was needed to prevent Formosa from "falling into unfriendly hands." John Foster Dulles already had informed Dean Acheson that the CINCFE "stands ready" to undertake this mission "personally." That news was hardly welcome to the secretary of state, officially opposed to the project since 26 January 1950, but still it was the first item on the NSC calendar at the historic meeting on June 25th. Bradley, at the prompting of Louis Johnson, began the conference by reading the entire memo MacArthur wrote on behalf of protecting Formosa as "the very center" of the "western strategic frontier." Truman, after breaking for dinner, turned to Acheson for an update on Korea and the response he started when Johnson was out of the country and Truman back home in Missouri. The secretary of defense, distressed at this digression from Formosa, began what he later called a "violent discussion" with Acheson. Truman, who had rushed back to Washington talking of smashing the aggressor, redirected the focus to Korea, where it largely stayed for the rest of the evening. Bradley suspected that the communist crossing of the 38th Parallel was just a "diversion to distract us from an imminent attack on Formosa," now clearly of strategic significance to the Pentagon. If this assessment proved wrong, the army and MacArthur could be falling into the land war in Asia no one at the meeting yet anticipated.[77]

The War against North Korea: From Commitment to the Pusan Perimeter

1 2 **3** 4 5 6 7 8 9

The Reds [were] using their now familiar tactics. The battalions were hit with a massive frontal attack by numerically superior forces. Then, after all American elements were engaged, large numbers of North Koreans moved around both flanks.

MEDICAL COMPANY CAPTAIN, KOREA, MID-JULY 1950[1]

One military theory proposes that war occurs when a rival seems too weak to prevent a contestant from working its will without much risk. Another holds that it happens when an adversary fears that if it doesn't act now, its opponent will amass enough power to win a future war at its convenience. Both concepts have validity for both sides in the case of Korea. Stalin thought the North Korean army should have little trouble overrunning the South but feared that a revitalized Japan, now allied with the United States, might reoccupy its old Korean springboard into continental Asia. The Truman administration thought the North Koreans were just a bunch of bandits, easy to defeat, but feared damage to its credibility if unwilling to commit its armed forces to this place in Asia where it had no plans to fight at all. Far better, from President Truman's perspective, to wage a limited conflict in Korea than an all-out war in Europe, where the West had yet to amass the strength to defend this primary prize. Washington might ensure the military standing to deter World War III, provided it was not defeated by the KPA, which proved far more formidable than first perceived. It therefore had to shift naval forces from patrol of the Taiwan Strait, a related commitment the White House also made late in June 1950 lest supporters of Chiang Kai-shek not rally behind a "police action" for Korea. Truman avoided use of the word "war" lest it lead toward escalation into direct confrontation with the Kremlin, thought to be probing U.S. resolve through its proxy in Pyongyang. Pawn or not, this opponent seemed on the brink of victory in August 1950, a blessing for Douglas MacArthur, who was looking for leverage to extract consent for the type of operation he long had wished to execute. He promised that a giant pincer movement would crush the enemy between a "hammer and an anvil." By seeming to snatch victory from the jaws of defeat, it covered the theater commander in the grandeur of military genius. That mystique would prove more dangerous to the U.S. Army than the actual landing at Inchon.[2]

The American Decision to Fight

You did everything you could to tell us you were not interested in Korea, but when the North Koreans went in, you put your troops there. We just can't trust you Americans.

ANDREI VYSHINSKY, SOVIET FOREIGN MINISTER[3]

U.S. defense policy regarding Korea had been clear and virtually unanimous before the onset of the war. Democrats, Republicans, Congress, and the Defense Department wrote off the southern half of the peninsula, as did General Mac-Arthur, who told the Joint Chiefs of Staff in January 1949 that it was "not within the capabilities of the United States to establish Korean security forces capable of meeting a full-scale invasion." The State Department was the only agency to have registered dissent. It maintained that South Korean exports, primarily food and fuels, were vital to Japanese prosperity and that the former Korean ward of American occupation had become "an ideological battleground upon which our entire success in Asia may depend." Still, as Dean Acheson would testify: "We cannot scatter our shots equally all over the world. We just haven't got enough shots to do that." The best he could do was delay departure until 1949 of a 7,000-man regimental combat team large enough to be a target but too small to be a shield. The U.S. ambassador would bluntly summarize the de facto plan: "Turn the problem over to the U.N. and get out of the way in case of trouble."[4]

South Korean intelligence agencies had been monitoring Soviet delivery of heavy weapons to its North Korean ally. They predicted an invasion was likely to occur in June 1950, a prediction not accepted by Americans because no such danger registered in their own electronic and photo reconnaissance. Charles

Willoughby, MacArthur's chief of intelligence, was paying far more attention to Formosa, as was Dean Rusk, the assistant secretary of state for Far East affairs. He testified on June 20th that "we have no indication that the people across the border have any intention of fighting a major war for . . . taking over Southern Korea." Five days later, Kim Il-sung, head of North Korea, sent 90,000 soldiers, 60 planes, and 154 Soviet-built battle tanks across the 38th parallel, what he had hoped to do since 1945.[5]

Kim was still a young man in his mid-thirties, although "Supreme Leader" of the North Korean Worker's Party thanks to installation by the Soviet army, where he had been a junior officer during World War II. He had something to accomplish in his own right, a reason more committed to expanding communism than his acknowledged leader, Joseph Stalin. The Kremlin, being pragmatic when facing formidable obstacles, had forbidden Kim to invade the south: an action considered "inexpedient, irrational, untimely and unwise." It focused on developing its own atomic bomb, along with rocketry, radar, jet planes, and air defense: testimony to Stalin's fear of U.S. strategic weaponry. The Soviets worried North Korea would provoke America but still shipped Kim heavy weapons, instructors, and advisors—some there to see that he did not cross the border, which he clearly wished to do. To get concurrence, Kim would tap Stalin's fear that U.S. departure from the peninsula was a prelude to an invasion of the North by the South without implicating Washington.[6]

Stalin's idea about an enemy hiding aggression behind withdrawal was the modus operandi he himself adopted when taking advisors out of North Korea's army in June 1950. Paranoid or not, he had provided enough assistance to create military imbalance on the peninsula. Hence Kim had a window of opportunity to unify the country under Marxist rule, even if Soviet generals felt KPA military staff could not work out the details by June 1950. Stalin still foresaw "a smooth and quick success" now that he believed America would not reenter Korea, no more than it returned to mainland China to save Chiang Kai-shek. This reckoning ran afoul of ironic fortune favoring the State Department's side in the debate about Korea with DOD. Its delaying action over when to withdraw the last military units inclined Syngman Rhee, the head of South Korea, not to prepare for self-defense, weakness being his best argument to keep the American army on the peninsula. It being too late for the ROKs to ready themselves after U.S. combat units finally left, Washington had to send its own troops back or see South Korea completely overrun.[7]

Why did the U.S. government choose intervention and thereby change its policy virtually overnight? It was not because the administration suddenly realized that national security was immediately at stake. One senior State Department official wrote another in August 1950: "Korea does not have the strategic importance of, say Formosa," an island the foreign service had planned to dump "as rapidly as events at home and abroad permit." Acheson, who had fought the Pentagon to keep military units in Korea, privately said in late July that anything on the peninsula would "be a mere sideshow" in any general or world war. He shed little light on the initial commitment at Senate hearings on MacArthur's dismissal in 1951. "Korea is of very great importance to the United States and the United Nations because it is there that the first great effort of collective security is being made to repel an armed attack." By then, it seemed America was fighting for Korea because America was fighting in Korea and did not want to be defeated.[8]

NSC-68, the major State Department policy statement about the Cold War, warned in April 1950 that U.S. commitments already exceeded capabilities. Washington in late June still dedicated scarce resources to Korea. Some specific reasons for this decision shed light on Truman's interactions with MacArthur. That fateful summer the president's mind had been on the congressional elections that fall. Any politician would be striving to please public opinion despite protests on June 25th that "we're not going to discuss politics." A lambasting for being "soft" on Chinese communism had certainly not shored up Truman's recent slippage in public approval: from 45 to 37 percent. He hoped to show that he was tough and successful, as he had in 1948. His initial commitment to Korea won 81 percent support, predictable because the American people invariably rally behind the president in an international crisis. Sticking with him through casualties and setbacks would be another story. From late June through November, Truman's concern to sustain his popularity would be manifest in his reluctance to confront MacArthur, a man ready to assure victory provided Washington did not interfere.[9]

Apart from the U.S. electorate stood the Western alliance: a cause of America's military commitment to Korea, a factor limiting its extent, and a feature in the future relief of MacArthur. The North American Treaty Organization (NATO) was more paper than substance in mid-1950. U.S. credibility was its greatest handicap, as State Department intelligence underscored on June 25th: "The capacity of a small Soviet satellite to engage in a military adventure challenging, as many Europeans will see it, the might and will of the US, can only lead to serious questioning of that might and will." Korea as "a symbol to the watching world" had consequence for Truman, whose favorite adage was that "the only new thing in the world is the history you don't know." He and much of the World War II generation—whether civilians such as Acheson or soldiers like MacArthur—viewed the invasion of South Korea through the lens of Munich and Manchuria, namely the belief that standing up to Germany and Japan in the 1930s would have backed down the aggressors and prevented a world war. The invasion of South Korea, according to Truman in late June, "is a clear indication of the pattern of aggression under a clear international Communist plan."[10]

Truman's line of reasoning was perfectly consistent with predictions he had made since late 1945: "Unless Russia is faced with an iron fist and strong language another war is in the making." The demise of Nationalist China

Right to left: Secretary of Defense Louis Johnson, President Truman, and Attorney General J. Howard McGrath on 27 June 1950, shortly after Truman announced the deployment of U.S. air and naval forces to South Korea. Johnson, already showing the strains of war, would be widely blamed for the poor initial performance of America's armed forces. Truman dismissed him on September 11th. *Courtesy of the Harry S. Truman Library.*

Secretary of State Dean Acheson and Assistant Secretary of State for Far East Affairs Dean Rusk leaving the White House on 27 June 1950. Neither man expected to fight a war in South Korea, but they helped make that commitment and vigorously maintained it when senior military officers proposed withdrawal after China entered the conflict in December.

precipitated more State Department thinking about a wave of Asian countries falling to communism and a "mounting militancy" in Soviet policy that
"borders on recklessness." In the subsequent case of Korea, Stalin was thought
to be using a proxy—also called a pawn or substitute—to test the will of the
noncommunist world. "If we are tough enough," Truman told his staff on June
26th, "there won't be a next step," meaning escalation of armed aggression.
Otherwise, "there is no telling what they'll do." The quick action Truman
subsequently took to defend South Korea helped dissolve doubts current in
mid-May, when European officials implored Acheson that America must be
ready to fight the day a conflict began. ("We can't afford to be liberated again.")
"Thank God," France's foreign minister subsequently said, "this will not be a
repetition of the past," that is, no appeasement and occupation while the United
States deliberated what it was willing to do.[11]

What Stalin actually would have done if America did nothing can never
be known. Charles Bohlen, State Department advisor to Presidents Roosevelt,
Truman, and Eisenhower, concludes that he "will always remain one of the
most enigmatic figures in history . . . his motives will never be known." Those
recently willing to venture a hypothesis cannot reach agreement despite unprecedented access to archival records released since 1990. Some support Truman's
proposition about a momentum building up behind communist expansionism,
specifically that Stalin used Korea to test "the prevailing mood" of weakness in
Washington. Others, such as Alexandre Mansourov, paint a different picture,
wherein Stalin looks a lot like Truman, trying to show determination lest the
enemy take advantage of the circumstances. "The South was determined to
launch an attack on the North sooner or later," the Soviet leader said to Kim in
April 1950, "and it was apparent to forestall this aggression."[12]

Stalin had his eye on border clashes for which Syngman Rhee bore substantial responsibility. U.S. advisors thought he used them to justify requests for
more military assistance, usually not approved. Rhee feared abandonment by
the Truman administration, which seemed to be abandoning China and cap-
ping military spending. He hoped closer relations with Japan would preserve
close relations with Washington, more attached to Tokyo than Seoul. Stalin,
embellishing the situation, deduced that Rhee would soon invite militarists
reclaiming power in Tokyo back into Korea, a "ready-made bridgehead on the
continent" from which Japan had often moved against Russia. Truman must
have been working his will through third parties, that is, according to Stalin—
more suspicious than ever, thought Kremlin insiders. That drove him to work
his own will through Kim and Mao Tse-tung, as he stated to the former two
months before the war. "The USSR was not ready to get involved in Korean
affairs directly, especially if Americans did venture to send troops." This was of
utmost importance to Stalin, perceived to "quiver" at the prospect of fighting the
United States. Its president and "his equally obstinate and aggressive Secretary

of State, that political half-wit Mr. Acheson" were purportedly looking for a reason to release their nuclear arsenal.[13]

Soviet production of intercontinental missiles was supposed to be "an effective straitjacket for that noisy shopkeeper Harry Truman." Western Europeans, while not nearly so crude or colloquial as Stalin, had similar concerns, particularly after the commitment to Korea gave some assurance that Washington had shed disengagement and demobilization. Ernest Bevin, Britain's foreign minster, would speak of the need to exert "sufficient control over the policy of the well-intentioned but inexperienced colossus on whose cooperation our safety depends." Those words had elements of jealousy and resentment from what was once a primary power, reduced to junior partnership. Britain now flexed its residual autonomy in the role of mediation as during the Berlin Blockade of 1948. Bevin, along with his Australian and French counterparts, told a U.S. official: "I know all of you Americans want a war, but I'm not going to let you have it."[14]

In mid-1950, NATO nations had related concerns about impetuosity: "The Far East is slated to become the bottomless pit into which America's might and wealth shall be poured." By mid-August, Acheson already found "a chill" overtaking "the peoples of Europe," anxious about the commitment to a secondary theater, meaning anyplace other than Europe itself. MacArthur made the problem worse, particularly when he threatened to attack China in 1951. Then Washington had to choose its Far East commander or NATO nations, often governed by left-of-center parties pressured to leave the alliance rather than fight the total war America might wage. No such inclination really existed in the White House, which got into the war on a presumption that the invaders were just a "bunch of bandits," to quote Truman on June 29th. Surely, a response to something on that order would not precipitate prolonged conflict. Omar Bradley, chairman of the Joint Chiefs of Staff, admitted: "No one believed that the North Koreans were as strong as they turned out to be."[15]

One is struck by the absence of institutional memory, although it is rarely the strong suit of those running most institutions. For years, the U.S. military had filed numerous reports about its inability to defend Korea, even when the proposal entailed no more than a UN task force conducting a police action, judged "militarily unsound" in June 1949. On 25 June 1950, the secretaries of the army and defense opposed "putting [in] ground forces," just a theoretical contingency under present misconceptions about combat capabilities. The air force and the navy had 639 high-performance planes in Japan and a fleet carrier in the Far East. They maintained they could "knock out" columns of KPA tanks. Joe Collins, army chief of staff, swayed his head in disbelief but kept relatively silent. No one yet advocated the type of land combat for which he bore responsibility. When Matt Ridgway, Collins's deputy, asked Bradley if he deliberately precluded ground troops, he got a one-word answer: "Yes."[16]

The high command hoped to conduct military operations on the peninsula much the way it planned to conduct the perimeter defense on islands off the coast of continental Asia, that is, with air and naval elements, its comparative advantage. Squadrons equipped and trained for air supremacy "dog fights," strategic bombing, or hitting large ships on the high seas now had to target enemy vehicles moving around the battlefield. In one engagement, they struck two in a formation of eighty. Ground forces consequently had to enter the breach. Still, as late as July 13th, Collins told MacArthur not to expect a substantial increase of soldiers. The CINCFE's reply: "Joe, you are going to have to change your mind," proved more accurate. "As each situation arose we extemporized," Collins wrote in retrospect, "until we were far more committed than we had expected to be."[17]

The United States would double the ground force contingent it already had doubled, eventually fielding eight divisions. The Department of the Army, never wanting to be in Korea, supported MacArthur as long as it believed his operations were the most rapid way to liquidate the commitment that prevented it from concentrating on Europe. The Joint Chiefs concurred with his dismissal when the CINCFE seemed to verge toward a major war with China on the mainland, making no sense to Bradley "from a global viewpoint." He told the U.S. Senate in 1951 that the former theater commander had been advocating "the wrong war, in the wrong place, against the wrong enemy," particularly true because MacArthur would "ignore the military facts and rush us headlong into a show-down before we are ready," a frank admission of national unpreparedness.[18]

In June 1950, Bradley, Collins, and Frank Pace, the secretary of the army, were not the only people at Blair House wary of falling into what Truman called "a general Asiatic war." No matter how bloody the battles in Korea became, the president maintained his bedrock belief that this was a limited operation, to be confined to the peninsula and waged to prevent a major confrontation between the major military powers: "Ours was an action, I said it before, designed to stop a war and not to spread it." This was not unlike Stalin's own planning, although neither he nor Truman grasped their parallel policies. In April, Stalin accepted the North Korean argument that the United States would not intervene in a place of inhospitable weather, mountainous terrain, and little strategic value, as least for Washington. On the eve of the invasion he still removed Soviet advisors from the KPA, where they had been planning the campaign, organizing logistics, and managing transportation units. Stalin, clearly tense to observers, worried that the capture of Soviet personnel could provide "a pretext" for American intervention, if not direct confrontation with the USSR. He did not conceive that Truman committed his own ground forces on the supposition that Russians were not present and were not likely to arrive, particularly once the Kremlin declared its adherence "to the principle of the impermissibility of interference by foreign powers."[19]

To the U.S. government, the conflict in Korea was essentially a proxy war to be waged against Kim Il-sung, a lesser opponent, in order to send a warning to Stalin, a far more powerful enemy. Not particularly new, this tactic was an extension of the Truman Doctrine inaugurated in March 1947, when the president announced action against "the seeds of totalitarian regimes." He had not mentioned the Soviet Union, although presumed to be directing the communist guerrillas in Greece. While not without risk, this commitment seemed far safer than Berlin, June 1948, when in the face of military misgivings, Truman put forces in exposed positions aside a Red Army region of strength.[20]

Americans, although engaged in proxy wars before and after the Berlin blockade, would not coin the term until mid-1955. Even then, Washington used it only to describe Soviet policy, as when utilizing North Korean stand-ins. Truman told the Joint Chiefs of Staff back on 26 June 1950 "to do everything we can for the Korean situation," but take note, "I don't want to go to war." Three days later, he solved his dilemma through a word game at a press conference. Truman emphatically insisted "we are not at war," then confirmed the term "police action" after a reporter chose those words to frame a question as to what was occurring in Korea. The president retained that unforeseen phrase for the rest of his presidency, if not his life. It would differentiate his own curbs upon MacArthur from the political interference that afflicted Hannibal, one of his heroes. "If we are at war, declared war with any nation," he later told Korean War veterans, "then the military are in control in the field and that's an Army of the United States. Where we are in action in conjunction with the United Nations to prevent aggression, that's a police action to prevent the whole world from being involved."[21]

The word "war" was already subject to redefinition, depending on whether one wished to arouse or restrain public opinion. In April 1950, to rally support for enhanced military spending, the State Department asserted that "the cold war is in fact a real war in which the survival of the free world is at stake." In June, Truman denied that the war in Korea was a war although facts on the battlefield soon called his terminology into question. "My God," a first lieutenant said to himself on July 1st, "maybe there was a real war going on." His undermanned and poorly armed regimental combat team, know as Task Force Smith, was supposed to stop North Korea by showing the flag and giving "moral support." This was not much different from a prewar plan to deter aggression by naval visits to South Korean ports of call. In fact, the first encounter killed or wounded 38 percent of the soldiers engaged. Americans were soon cracking gallows humor about the so-called police action. "Damn, these crooks over here got big guns."[22]

The president's phraseology could embitter those fighting for their lives in Korea. "Truman really slapped us in the face," some veterans said, when he did "not even dignify" the conflict "by calling [it] a war." The topic was also a stump speech theme in Republic Party oratory, October 1952, when "police action" in Korea raised heckles from crowds. The words still served a purpose for officialdom afraid of fighting a war while conducting one. "We can't ever have another war, unless it is total war, and that means the end of our civilization," Truman said in late 1945. "Limited," let alone "proxy," war had yet to enter the Cold War vocabulary, but the concept was still present in White House strategy. In April 1951, after finally relieving his theater commander, Truman said that he had restricted military action to Korea in order "to prevent a third world war. A number of events have made it evident that General MacArthur did not agree with that policy."[23]

Truman, while badly damaged politically by his conflict with MacArthur, survived because the Joint Chiefs of Staff supported his guiding principle of limiting operations in a secondary theater, as well as some of his terminology. Bradley told the Senate hearings on the dismissal of the theater commander that "I would hate very much to see us involved in a land war in Asia." Collins and George Marshall said much the same at much the same time: "In the event of war," the army chief of staff told the State Department, "we are going to have to carry the load out there." The secretary of defense told *U.S. News and World Report:* "Now we are in a very difficult period [for enhancing military preparedness] when there is no war." These three men obviously knew Americans were fighting and dying in Asia, a problem they dealt with every day. "We still considered Korea strategically unimportant in the context of a possible global war," Collins wrote in his memoir of the conflict called *War in Peacetime,* a telltale title.[24]

Washington, although drawn into Korea far more than it foresaw, would never commit all the resources MacArthur requested. This created another controversy, that about one's standard for success. Once China entered the war, Truman pinned achievement on prisoners refusing repatriation to communist regimes, as will be discussed in chapter 8. MacArthur never experienced any equivocation that out-and-out destruction of an opponent's armed forces remained the only score. Over his long career, he loved to replicate certain refrains despite differences in audience and occasion. In the letter to Congressman Joe Martin that triggered his dismissal in April 1951, he repeated what he wrote the Corps of Cadets for an Army-Navy football rally in 1949: "There is no substitute for victory."[25]

MacArthur, Chiang Kai-Shek, and the United Nations

I listened to an announcement that General MacArthur, one of the most unreconstructed nationalists this country has produced, was working for the United Nations. . . . I thanked the Good Lord that I had retired because I would never have been able to find my way around in an international police force.

UNIDENTIFIED GENERAL, JULY 1950[26]

In late June 1950, Douglas MacArthur was seventy years old, sinking into obscurity, and often inattentive to his office work. He would later be reported to have called the war in Korea "Mars's last gift to a warrior." Whether his words or those of an imaginative journalist, that phrase was not far from historical fact. North Korea's action was reminiscent of that of Japan in 1941, at least as far as MacArthur's career was concerned. In both cases, an enemy invasion rescued him from a backwater position of marginal authority over a waning occupation, the Philippines or Japan. However, in neither instance was he ready when the bell rang for the first round. Nine hours after the enemy attacked Pearl Harbor, MacArthur was locked away in his headquarters while his fleet of heavy bombers was destroyed on the ground. He did not respond to the invasion of South Korea with any more alacrity on June 25th, when his primary attention focused on Formosa. He initially believed that North Korea was only conducting a "reconnaissance-in-force," not substantially different from other border incidents over the last two years. Next day, MacArthur was "astonished" to receive directions to resist the invader: "I don't believe it; I can't understand it." John Foster Dulles, who favored a prompt military response, recorded him saying that anyone thinking of throwing American forces into the breach "ought to have his head examined." The CINCFE seemed so despondent and defeatist that Dulles advised Truman to bring him back to America. The president would send Frank Lowe, a trusted assistant, to inquire about MacArthur's state of health, but one doubts Truman would have done what Dulles suggested short of unanimous testimony from a blue-ribbon medical board. "The general is involved politically," he informed Dulles, as if this pillar of the Republican Party had no idea. He "could not recall MacArthur without causing a tremendous reaction in this country, where he has been built up to heroic stature."[27]

This confession to a man brought into the State Department to revive bipartisanship implicitly admitted that the defense of Korea relied on members of the political opposition. The GOP was more willing to support the general than a president who needed senior military officers to sustain his policy, particularly after Truman finally relieved MacArthur for reasons far from infirmity. Combat may cause neuropsychiatric damage in young men once the picture of health. For MacArthur, it was more like a fountain of youth two days after Washington responded to Pyongyang's attack, then said to be "the biggest surprise" in his life. He could travel by jeep for hours over rocks alleged to be roads without any indication of discomfort, something of a marvel to men as tough as Matt Ridgway. He seemed "buoyant" to one *Life* magazine photographer: "His eyes possessed that same luminous brilliance which I had sometimes seen in faces of fever patients." By then, the government probably wished its theater commander less vigor than he had.[28]

On June 29th, Washington sent MacArthur approval to bomb airstrips giving the invader more time over target than U.S. planes could muster out of Japan. The theater commander by then had already authorized an act foretelling his momentous clash with Truman over enemy sanctuaries: "Take out North Korean airfields immediately. No publicity. MacArthur approves." Dwight Eisenhower would have expected as much, judging by what he said that very day on a trip to the Pentagon from New York City, where he was president of Columbia University. He chewed out Collins, Ridgway, and the government in general for complacency, Korea still not having prime importance in their eyes. He recommended partial mobilization and consideration of nuclear weapons, a subject Eisenhower revisited in 1953 when president of the United States. He also lamented the forthcoming appointment of MacArthur to supreme UN military command, no place for "'an untouchable' whose action you cannot predict and who will himself decide what information he wants Washington to have and what he will withhold."[29]

Eisenhower's comment was of little consequence if kept inside the Department of the Army. It should have gone directly to the only person clearly senior to the five-star theater commander, meaning Harry Truman, the commander-in-chief. Eisenhower returned home without stopping at the White House, although then a welcomed visitor whenever he called. Still, if he had gone on this occasion, he would not have told the president anything not already known. The administration was soon admitting, through preferred newspaper columnists, that the government faced a problem containing its appointee. MacArthur "is a sovereign power in his own right, with stubborn confidence in his own judgment," wrote James Reston, whose *New York Times* columns frequently cited a "responsible official," also known as Dean Acheson. "Diplomacy and a vast concern for the opinions and sensitivities of others are the political qualities essential to this new assignment," Reston wrote on 9 July. "These are precisely the qualities General MacArthur has been accused of lacking in the past."[30]

MacArthur soon became an explosive issue within the NATO alliance, particularly concerning the Taiwan Strait, already a prickly problem for the Truman administration. The critical NSC meeting of June 25th that committed America to South Korea did not completely ignore Formosa, DOD's initial topic for discussion. General Bradley and Admiral Forrest Sherman, the chief of naval operations (CNO), said that America should move warships into the ninety-five nautical miles separating the island from the mainland. This could prevent attacks from the PRC on Chiang Kai-shek—or by Chiang on the PRC.

"We could not otherwise justify our action," Sherman then added. Two days later the administration adopted this policy of intervention under the rubric of "neutralization." The JCS would now have to live under the rules of engagement the admiral proposed and the Pentagon sent MacArthur on the 29th. It was essentially the same policy the general had advocated back in December 1949, when the administration was in the process of cutting its involvement in the Chinese civil war. MacArthur had countered that America should treat "as an act of war" an attack from the mainland on Formosa or from Formosa onto the mainland. This was not his ultimate objective, just the strongest position the situation permitted prior to Kim Il-sung's invasion of South Korea. Presumably, if and when Washington adopted "neutralization," MacArthur could argue for something still stronger, especially if circumstances proved the initial policy flawed, as occurred in mid-1950.[31]

In late June, the Seventh Fleet moved from its port in the Philippines north to the strait. Eight destroyers, one heavy cruiser, and a large aircraft carrier provided a lot more force than the "minor numbers of fleet units" the navy suggested in 1949. They could not remain on station because redeployed to Korean waters, where they were supposed to help the air force stop communist ground forces in their tracks. Four submarines remained to prevent a prospective invasion, not their forte in these circumstances. America built its subs to detect and kill steel-hulled vessels—the larger the target the better. They were relatively ineffective against the immediate threat: five thousand steamships, sampans, fishing boats, and other small craft whose wooden frames were too flimsy to detonate the triggers on torpedoes. They still had the collective capacity to lift the 200,000 soldiers gathering along the coastline for transport to Taiwan, according to U.S. intelligence agencies, then of the opinion that "the current [Nationalist] Chinese Navy, operating alone, would be practically impotent against . . . an all-out amphibious operation."[32]

Mao did not seem to understand his advantage in the Taiwan Strait on June 24th, the day before North Korea crossed the 38th parallel. The Chinese government then decided to demobilize its peasant-based army, not because Beijing was declaring peace or even a cease-fire. It had founded a naval academy and procured a Soviet mission staffed with five hundred advisors. The PRC envisioned a new Chinese force structure: marines, troop transports, landing craft, and naval fire platforms. It apparently dreamed of conducting the kind of amphibious invasion MacArthur would mount at Inchon in September 1950. By then, the threat America presented in Korea preempted the conquest of Taiwan. China went back toward light infantry maneuvering in closed terrain. Mao would throw this force armed with handheld weapons against the U.S. army on the supposition that stealth could offset heavy firepower, an idea he rejected in the Taiwan Strait. That winter, artillery, frostbite, and starvation devastated his soldiers by the tens of thousand. China would have stood in better stead if it had used its low-tech, guerrilla flotilla far to the south on the way to Taipei.[33]

The modernization Mao envisioned for his navy might have created what the military calls a "target rich environment" for a U.S. fleet sure to retain superior technology. It then could have delivered "the bloodiest victory in Far Eastern history," to use MacArthur's words of August 1950. The general was not one to compromise his military plans on behalf of the convoluted policy he was supposed to carry out in the Taiwan Strait, even if inconsistency was standard procedure for Washington during the Chinese civil war. Truman and George Marshall may have despised the "reactionary clique" that ran the KMT, but they still sent support in the 1940s. Now, Truman hid his de facto reentry into the conflict by claiming he was only preventing each side from attacking the other, a police action of sorts, one could have said.[34]

The U.S. course of action had some true aspects of neutrality, namely preventing Chiang Kai-shek from bombing the mainland, as he did before the Korean War. However, while saving some noncombatants in the People's Republic, it seemed to have saved the whole regime on Taiwan. Therefore Chiang quickly agreed to the terms of Washington's aide-memoire, June 27th: to discontinue "air and sea operations by forces under Your Excellency's command against the Chinese mainland or against shipping in Chinese waters or on the high seas." This proved a good example of unforeseen consequences. An invasion force is most at risk when bunched in a harbor, as opposed to disbursed when executing its maneuver plan. Mao's prospective operation was especially exposed for not having won supremacy over Chiang's best military asset, the air force that U.S. advisors trained and equipped in the 1940s. Truman, by preventing renewed bombing raids, gave Communist China its singular opportunity. Consequently Taiwan was in more danger than it had been before U.S. intercession, good reason why its Tokyo military mission notified MacArthur on July 16th of "serious Communist activity" building jet airfields opposite the island. The CINCFE promptly forwarded the message to Washington: "IN SELF-DEFENSE COUNTERMEASURES INCLUDING BOMBING MUST BE TAKEN IMMEDIATELY."[35]

One doubts MacArthur's prodigious memory ever forgot the most criticized military action in his career to date, not releasing B-17s to bomb Formosa while Japan was assembling eighty-four transports to invade the Philippines in 1941. Whatever the general's agenda in July 1950, his concurrence with the KMT request was not welcome news to Harry Truman, then personally reading message traffic from MacArthur. The president said that this "has very dangerous implications" and promptly instructed Acheson to confer with the Department of Defense. They were to "instruct General MacArthur that an attack by the Chinese Nationalist Government on the Mainland will be considered an unfriendly act," that is, by the government of the United States—no need to mention Beijing.[36]

Washington was telling MacArthur to defend Formosa under the guise of "neutralization." It was also imposing rules of engagement that undermined that mission, a point MacArthur made in passive voice since it was not judicious to attribute direct blame to Acheson or Truman. "The United States is placed in the position of neither assuming the defense of these islands nor permitting the Nationalist Government freedom to deploy its own military resources. . . . The enemy," he maintained to the Pentagon on July 29th, "is being given the distinct military advantage of being permitted to prepare for such a military operation in which our own forces, as well as the Chinese [Nationalists] are to be engaged." The crux of the matter was whether Mainland China should remain a sanctuary, an issue over which Truman relieved MacArthur in 1951. For all one knows the question might have exploded that July when American officers on the spot "had serious misgivings about our capability of defending Formosa in case of attack." The problem would dissipate when the PRC began sending troops north to Manchuria. Even MacArthur soon conceded that Formosa seemed secure, at least for the time being. He did not seem to grasp that safety in the strait occurred because the American army in Korea was falling into danger by the massive Chinese redeployment.[37]

The government was not oblivious to the difficulties it put in MacArthur's path: "The borderline between offensive and defensive operations in an area of military conflict is necessarily blurred." International politics still dictated military policy in the Taiwan Strait, where Truman could not claim, as he always did for Korea, that America was simply playing its part as a member state in a UN operation. Mere association with Chiang Kai-shek discredited the attempt to "give the United States a moral diplomatic position" by conceivably making Taiwan a trustee of the United Nations. NATO partners and other countries, such as India, took no solace that America shed isolationism when it came to KMT territory. To make the action taken toward Formosa as inoffensive as possible to the international community, Acheson maintained that it was merely an "interim policy" to freeze the "security situation" until it could "be clarified." More to the point, as he told Louis Johnson, then secretary of defense, "we should take considerable military risks rather than place ourselves in the role of an aggressor."[38]

Britain and the United States had agreed to form a common policy about China in 1949, when the NSC conceded that coercive measures would "tend to drive the regime into a position of complete subservience to the USSR, thus making impossible of attainment the primary objective," one of splitting the PRC from the Soviet Union. Anglo-American methods soon came into conflict as the United Kingdom moved toward official recognition of Beijing. "The British had not played very squarely with us on this matter," Truman told Acheson that October. Washington would apply pressure in the name of strength, as opposed to making concessions thought to be appeasement. Whitehall had not budged from its own position, if only to maintain some diplomatic balance. In July 1950, along with India, it proposed a conference to freeze the Korean War by ceding support for Taiwan and its seat in the United Nations. Beijing was interested, as one would expect, a communist victory in the Chinese civil war being its highest priority. Russia, however, was not receptive, also no surprise. The KPA, a more subservient satellite, seemed rolling toward its own victory in its own civil war. Taiwan, moreover, served a function in Kuomintang hands as something keeping Mao inside the Kremlin's political orbit. The Truman administration still took the onus of rejection off Stalin's hands. It tersely rebuffed the "British-India maneuver," although well aware of problems caused to its coalition "by reason of the Russian ability to play on the Korean situation, Formosa, and the Chinese Communists."[39]

Washington did not act out of close relations with Taipei. "They were hardly on speaking terms," Dulles still observed. However, once the United States took its initial stance in the strait between the East and South China Seas, Formosa (like Korea) became as much a symbol as a place. A principle was now at stake, not just Chiang's distasteful regime: if the communists could "extort concessions for desisting from unlawful conduct, the ability of the free world to prevent aggression would be totally lost." The emotional intensity of this diplomatic message disconcerted the government in London, although already feeling that Acheson had lost his way under "the vicious campaign against him in the USA. . . . He dare not put forward a constructive policy." Meanwhile, in August, the secretary of state shared his own fear with the president that support for seating China in the United Nations "would whip up opinion here against our Allies." No matter what Acheson did, Taft-wing Republicans still said he and his so-called fellow-appeasers would trade Formosa for peace in Korea at some "Far-Eastern Munich." France and Britain put less stock in the administration's conclusion that credibility, international relations, and deterrence hung in the balance, along with domestic support. Those factors that drove Truman to put troops into Korea politically were now attaching him to Taiwan despite the president's insistence that "it will not be necessary to keep the Seventh Fleet in the Formosa Strait if the Korea thing is settled."[40]

Europeans wanted to keep the war on the peninsula hermetically sealed from Mao and Chiang lest it rouse Beijing's wrath against potential hostages, particularly Hong Kong and Indochina. NATO nations, from their own perspective, were only asking the United States to maintain the position Truman stated on 5 January 1950: noninvolvement in the Chinese civil war. As of July, administration policy alienated many allies but compromised Taiwan's opportunity to preempt its enemy. It could also create an incident leading to a U.S. war with China, as Acheson warned the secretary of defense after communist fighters engaged a reconnaissance plane near its coastline. Why get oneself into this predicament? It was not simply because the government changed military policy to solve a clearly identified military defense problem. The JCS contended that Formosa should be part of the perimeter defense but usually based this major force commitment on conditions not existing at this particular time: national mobilization to enhance capabilities and exemption from conducting a land war in Asia.[41]

When a conclusive explanation cannot be found in terms of national security, one can turn to domestic politics, the first field a prospective president has to understand. Formosa and Korea have often intertwined in political debate, as in the House of Representatives on 19 January 1950, two weeks after Truman announced the end of aid for Chiang Kai-shek. In turn, the administration lost by one vote a $120 million appropriation for South Korea, defined by Republicans as a "Dunkirk without a flotilla, a dead-end street without an escape." In this setting the president could not expect Congress to accept the defense of Korea other than to offer the opposition a deal foreshadowed that January when Robert Taft declared that America "should take steps to see that the communists do not cross over into Formosa. I would use the Navy to keep them out." John Foster Dulles, the Republican consultant to the State Department, advocated much the same policy in a private memo to Dean Acheson in May. The fleet "would neutralize Formosa not permitting it either to be taken by the Communists or to be used as a base for military operations against the mainland."[42]

Truman already wrote favored Republicans that "the breakup of the bipartisan foreign policy at this time would mean but one thing—victory for Russia in Europe, and in all probability a definite approach to a shooting war." Along these lines, the administration and Congress agreed in May on an omnibus spending bill for Asia as a "general area," whereby South Korea, Formosa, and French Indochina all received assistance. Once the war began in late June, Truman offered the Republicans another trade, something of an omnibus/general area policy for military protection. Temporarily, he would defend Chiang on Formosa, a Republican cause. In turn, they would support Truman's military effort in Korea, questionable to the Senate Republican Policy Committee on 25 June 1950, when it favored sending equipment to embattled Koreans but not committing Americans to wage war. By the 28th, Truman's procedure seemed quite politically successful. David Lawrence, a prominent newspaper columnist not friendly to the administration, said: "Republicans and Democrats are again united on an unpartisan foreign policy." James Reston, having written that "there is in Washington a spirit of far greater cooperation than at any time in the last few years," added in July that when Truman neutralized the Taiwan Strait he was "neutralizing Senators . . . who had been condemning his 'hands-off Formosa' policy."[43]

Truman's policy that summer of 1950 got him through threats of congressional disruption. A military commitment requires greater consensus than necessary for domestic legislation. However, like most short-term solutions, "neutralization" could not solve a long-term problem, especially when the step was taken too late to dissolve the partisan bitterness flourishing over Formosa. The administration, by no means consistent, had moved beyond some GOP proposals for aid and advisors by deploying combat-capable units. However, Truman still held Chiang at arm's length. The navy patrolled the waters as best it could while also on duty for Korea, but Washington would not place forces on Kuomintang territory. It held that "neutralization" was separate from the "future political settlement of the status of the island." This meant the United States was protecting a region, not the Nationalist regime, as privately explained by Philip Jessup, ambassador at large and Acheson's close confidant. "Necessity has required a change in our Formosa policy but so far as I know we have made no deliberate decision to the effect that we wish to be closely re-associated with Chiang Kai-shek."[44]

Ironically, Washington still recognized the Kuomintang as the government of the mainland, where it no longer existed, but distanced itself from the KMT in Taiwan, which Chiang actually governed. This stance was a desperate attempt to keep together a broad coalition fundamentally at war with itself: the Taft bloc in Congress and NATO governments containing left-wing socialists. The Republican faction would turn on "neutralization" as U.S. protection for the PRC: what right did Truman have to tell Chiang he could not fight to regain his country? Meanwhile European radicals, inclined to believe the worst of U.S. capitalism, were not immune to neutralism augmented by a "peace campaign" against "American Warmongers." Britain was the irreplaceable base from which to stop Soviet expansion in Europe. Acheson already had cited London's objections to selling tanks and planes to the Kuomintang. In July, the Foreign Office was quick to point out that "armed conflict" with China, precipitated by Taiwan, "would promptly throw . . . the whole of Asia into the USSR camp." The same might be said of militants in the Labour Party who described the diplomatic corps as a privileged bastion of the establishment. Their left-wing version of Taft-wing rhetoric served a pointed purpose, that of taking over major ministries from the reigning moderates who now ran them, by exploiting grassroots hostility to the KMT, Douglas MacArthur, and America's Far East policy. This insurgency would not be quelled by State Department claims that its measures "have involved no political commitment to Chiang Kai-shek; nor is any such commitment contemplated."[45]

In 1951, MacArthur split the shotgun marriage between American conservatives and British socialists by threatening to attack China. He almost cracked this fractious coalition in 1950 by positions taken as theater commander with overall responsibility to assess military capabilities in his area of operations. He would testify to Congress that he "got a series of messages from the Joint Chiefs of Staff expressing the gravest concern about the situation" in the strait, perfectly understandable when Americans on the spot held that "the present regime [is] unable to defend Formosa." The JCS recommended "all-out aid" to the Nationalists. Truman responded by finally allowing CINCFE headquarters to dispatch a survey team. Two weeks before that decision on July 27th, MacArthur informed Joe Collins that he would go as soon as the battlefield stabilized in Korea. On the 30th, the Department of the Army deferentially suggested: "You may desire to send a senior officer," essentially "for the purpose of gathering information," although it conceded that "if you feel it necessary to proceed personally . . . the responsibility is yours."[46]

The State Department had an "understanding" that MacArthur would not go to Formosa "at this time," that is, for the indefinite future, which was just fine with the diplomatic corps. His presence would call into further question its policy of "neutralization," a word already lacking credibility in London, Paris, New Delhi, and Beijing. One might well assume that in late July the general was paying total attention to the North Korean army threatening to break through his Pusan defense perimeter, some fifty miles wide and ninety long at the southeast corner of the peninsula along the Naktong River. The last position like this MacArthur had occupied was in the Philippines, when engaged in a similar fight to the bitter end in 1942. Bataan had become a personal obsession, the nickname for MacArthur's staff ("the Bataan gang") and the name of his personal airplane. The general still rejected any taint of defeat that an analogue to Bataan might portend. Common soldiers in the field had a different point of view; to quote one corporal in a medical company: "We were convinced that by September the U.S. would be pushed out of Korea."[47]

On July 29th MacArthur told the American ambassador in Korea: "We [are] going to have a very difficult five or six weeks." He also conceded to Joe Collins the necessity of deploying reinforcements into the Pusan perimeter, although having hoped to keep troops in Japan for an envelopment far north of the Naktong. MacArthur said nothing of what he would do in two days: take his staff to Formosa for a fateful appointment with Chiang Kai-shek, what he wanted to do since the KMT fled the mainland in 1949. The fact that the general did it while the fate of Korea was in doubt suggests he still felt the Chinese civil war was the most important thing in Asia, if not the whole world. Immediately upon returning to Japan, the Far East theater commander issued a statement that shattered distinctions between defending Formosa and protecting Chiang, now called "my old comrade-in arms" whose "indomitable determination to resist Communist domination arouses my sincere admiration. His determination parallels the common interests and purpose of Americans that all people in the Pacific area [meaning the mainland] shall be free." One wonders what had happened to the MacArthur who said in 1949: "There appears to be constant bickering among senior [KMT] officials with little unity of purpose."[48]

The report the Far East command group soon sent the Department of Defense had some echoes of the older assessment: Chiang's "appointments and directives, in many cases are based on personal obligations and influences rather than on the capability or efficiency of the appointee." Nonetheless, the MacArthur entourage took heart: "Many times" the generalissimo "expressed his willingness and desire to conform to any suggestions that the CINCFE might have." Chiang broke similar vows to George Marshall in 1946. However, according to MacArthur, that man was not suited to the mission. ("Marshall's fine patrician Virginian nose does not tolerate the daily smells of Asia.") On August 11th, within two weeks of returning to Japan, MacArthur wired Washington that "reports indicate that without exception to date the Chinese have done everything within their power and capabilities to grant requests made by our officers." The general did not hide his presumption that if and when the PRC launched its prospective invasion, he would not remain a mere mentor. MacArthur hoped to "dictate Nationalist military actions," along with gaining the "freedom to strike military concentrations on the mainland."[49]

Washington had little independent information whether MacArthur made arrangements with Chiang to wage war on China. The CINCFE "made clear" that because "the talks were purely military in nature . . . what was said and done was his sole responsibility, and not that of the State Department." Acheson consequently had no representatives at the meeting. MacArthur had not informed the U.S. consulate in Taipei, contrary to both common procedure and what he later claimed. This caused substantial anxiety as well as substantial complications. "The fact that we are kept in ignorance," Philip Jessup complained, "makes it difficult for us to clear up any misunderstandings." The general, back in Tokyo, tried to make amends to the White House in a press conference held on August 3rd: "I have never known so high a degree of mutual support without the slightest friction or misunderstanding." Taipei, unlike Truman, took heart, according to America's ranking diplomat on station: "Authorities feel situation well cared for in hands of MacArthur who will straighten out US policy toward Formosa and Nationalist Government." Chiang already had issued an official statement in this general spirit, along with a picture of him and the CINCFE beaming at each other: "An agreement was reached between General MacArthur and myself on all the problems discussed in the series of conferences held in the last two days."[50]

Acheson wrote his representative in Tokyo headquarters about being "increasingly disturbed" that MacArthur was "taking foreign policy in[to] his own hands." Truman, visibly angry, already worried that the general was assuming too much autonomy, even in the military arena. He had ordered the secretary of defense, in the name of the president of the United States, to order the Far East Theater commander to make "full and complete reports on the situation every day." It is, he said in late June, "just as hard to get information out of MacArthur as it had been during the war," Korea still being a police action. The Pentagon handled the issue with more delicacy. "The President has asked you to be advised of his personal desire to be kept fully informed [of] your operations daily . . . personal from [four-star] General J. Lawton Collins to [five star] General of the Army Douglas MacArthur," 1 July 1950.[51]

Some conclusions reached that August regarding Formosa were unfounded, aside from the bogus tale that MacArthur sent no one in Washington any indication of his impending visit, including DOD. The consulate in Taipei wired the State Department that the CINCFE had made secret arrangements to station three fighter squadrons, an allegation repeated in Acheson's memoirs published in late 1969. In mid-1950, a concurrent story in the Associated Press held that the KMT bombed boats congregating on the Chinese coast and that

Chiang Kai-shek, Madame Chiang, and General Douglas MacArthur beaming at each other on 30 July 1950, during the general's trip to Formosa. In 1949, MacArthur had tried to replace Chiang through a coup, but he later became a very prominent supporter. *U.S. Army Signal Corps, courtesy of the MacArthur Memorial Library.*

MacArthur sanctioned this "offensive action." These accounts were incorrect but not illogical, with the Seventh Fleet sent off to the coastline of Korea. The general was just pursuing "authorization [for] familiarization flights" such as refueling. For the time being, he presented no plans for permanent basing "except in event [of an] actual attack on Formosa by Communists."[52]

Whatever MacArthur really did, his trip to Formosa carried "strong political implications," as the Pentagon advised the CINCFE: our "orders were to limit such operations as are practicable without committing any forces to the island of Formosa itself." Truman, always worried that he was being kept in the dark, was personally approving communications to the general, as well as reading the daily reports of the JCS Intelligence Group. This testified to his fear that he might lose all control, despite his contrary opinion that politicians should not manage military operations. On August 5th, he passed a message to MacArthur through a personal letter from the secretary of defense: "No other person than the President as Commander-in-Chief has the authority to order or authorize preventive action against concentrations on the mainland.... The most vital national interest requires that no action of ours precipitate general war or give excuse to others to do so."[53]

Truman obviously realized that Louis Johnson and the Joint Chiefs of Staff essentially agreed with MacArthur: Chiang should be allowed to bomb "amphibious concentrations" and mine "those mainland water areas from which an assault could be staged." To them, this position was a logical extension of the offshore defense policy using island-based weaponry "to prevent the assembly and launching of any amphibious forces from any mainland ports in east-central or northeast Asia." To be sure, those words written in July 1950 referred to U.S. assets on Okinawa, not the island of Formosa that had become the major issue of the moment, aside from the military units barely hanging on at the Pusan perimeter. There, MacArthur had issued fight-or-die instructions, not at all binding on the Pentagon. It had to consider the distinct possibility of conducting a forced evacuation to Japan whenever North Korea crossed the Naktong.[54]

In mid-1952, the chairman of the JCS told leading figures in the State Department: "We have said many times and still say that the loss of Formosa would be bad, but it would not be so bad as to justify U.S. forces there to hold it." In mid-1950, the military situation undermined this military preference. "A rash of intelligence reports" predicted China's invasion of Taiwan. That impelled the service chiefs to "suggest" to MacArthur "the desirability to sweep [the Seventh Fleet south from Korea] toward Formosa." Clearly overburdened, they needed help protecting two areas with one force. Their solution to what they called "this unfortunate position" meant erasing the present distinction between the island at risk and its government: vulnerability "can be corrected in part if the Chinese Nationalists can make timely efforts to defend Formosa." To the KMT this meant bombing the mainland: "Is it a sin to fight the Communists?"[55]

From the military perspective of MacArthur and the JCS strategic planning staff, "the present United States policy of withholding military aid from the Chinese forces on Formosa [should] be modified as a matter of urgency." It seemed common sense to grant Chiang Kai-shek arms, ammunition, training, and the freedom to launch a preemptive attack. Truman reflected some of this same feeling, judging by a private letter he sent on 6 July: "The present so-called Communist Chinese Government" is "nothing but a tool of Moscow just as the North Korean Government is." However, one should not confuse exasperation with national policy. Acheson told Louis Johnson on July 31st that any attack on Mainland China by any party was "unacceptable from a foreign policy point of view."[56]

Formosa and Inchon: A Crucial Connection

A failure at Inchon could very well so inspire the North Koreans that they would overrun the Pusan perimeter.

OMAR N. BRADLEY, CHAIRMAN OF JOINT CHIEFS OF STAFF[57]

Bradley is a farmer.

DOUGLAS MACARTHUR[58]

Back in late December 1949, when Louis Johnson broached substantial assistance for Formosa, President Truman rejected his proposal on grounds that political issues superseded "military considerations," common practice during peacetime. Since then, U.S. combat forces had entered Korea and begun patrol in the Taiwan Strait. The president was still not ready to make a wholesale change in the rules of engagement off the coast of China despite a military phalanx against "neutralization." No American politician would have liked to bring this opposition to light, no matter what the British Labour Party might have thought of Chiang Kai-shek. Truman, while angry that MacArthur endorsed the generalissimo, was disinclined to face the domestic explosion that would occur if he faced down his theater commander on the eve of an election, especially absent JCS support. On 4 August 1950, two days after MacArthur returned to Japan from his trip to Formosa, the general received direction to do what he had just done: "Initiate without delay a survey of the need and extent of military assistance required to enable the Chinese Nationalist forces to prevent the capture of Formosa by the Communists."[59]

W. Averell Harriman, senior White House assistant, kept up the effort to meet MacArthur more than halfway by telling a press conference that the CINCFE's trip to Chiang Kai-shek was known and approved "by the President, the Secretary of Defense, the Secretary of State, and me." Harriman, ambassador to the Soviet Union in World War II, had hoped to become secretary of state when George Marshall left the post after Truman's first term. The president gave the position to Dean Acheson. Harriman wound up with a consolation prize, that of national security advisor, although that exact title did not exist until 1953. The office, under the likes of Henry Kissinger, would later grow into a mini–State Department. Acheson would have never stood for such infringement but welcomed Harriman in July 1950: "I am spending half of my time overcoming obstacles that are thrown in my way by Louis [Johnson. I need] . . . someone to take these miseries off me." The president personally penned Harriman's job description, as much domestic politics as foreign affairs: "Dean's in trouble. I want you to help."[60]

Truman had trouble himself, particularly with MacArthur, a task for someone with experience as liaison between Roosevelt and Stalin, along with Acheson and Johnson—where Harriman quickly proved his loyalty. The secretary of defense, having long believed that war would provide the occasion to rid himself of Acheson, proposed a joint effort to depose the secretary of state, after which he would see that his coconspirator filled the vacancy. Harriman craved the job but bristled at the offer. "I could not be bought that easily," he told President Truman. Walter Lippmann, the newspaper oracle, would have felt vindicated. He wrote how "well-suited" Harriman was for the post he filled in the White House, about the last favorable thing Lippmann wrote about the administration during the Korean War. He made no comment about how fitting Harriman might be for a mission to MacArthur conceived to forestall the CINCFE from provoking war with the PRC. In the 1920s, when the general was superintendent of West Point, he had been a frequent guest at the Harriman estate on the Hudson River. Now his old host provided an opportunity to establish a back channel to the Oval Office, particularly important when on thin political ice around the Taiwan Strait. On August 4th, when informed that Harriman was on his way to Tokyo, MacArthur wired the president: "I am delighted. . . . I hold him in highest esteem." Next day, the general personally greeted his visitor on the airport tarmac, not his usual procedure: "Hello, Averell"; "Hello Doug."[61]

Truman's troubleshooter was not the only person on the chartered airplane dispatched to Japan. Matt Ridgway and Frank Lowe, two generals in the delegation, would also play significant roles in the conflict between Truman and MacArthur. Ridgway became a household word, about the only national figure whose stature would grow in the Korean War once he seemed to save the US/UN side from a crushing defeat in 1951. Major General Lowe, U.S. Army Reserves, remained in the shadows by mutual agreement with Harry Truman, who personally called this Maine utilities executive to active duty for the third time in his citizen-soldier career.

Lowe, like Truman, had been a reserve-commissioned battery commander during World War I. In World War II, he was working on ROTC programs when the War Department assigned him to the Truman Committee investigating favoritism, fraud, and waste in contracts and expenditures. The Pentagon had been holding information back to "a ridiculous extreme," to quote Harry Vaughan, Senator Truman's personal assistant. One presumes it thought Lowe would protect its interests against a bunch of civilians sticking their noses where they did not belong. Nothing could have been further from the truth or from Truman's initial suspicion that the new man on board would spy for his military bosses. Lowe had lots of accumulated resentment against the Department of the Army for perceived mistreatment of reservists, far worse in his opinion than the navy or the Marine Corps. He shared with Vaughan his peeves about snobby staff officers, West Pointers, and assorted athletes said to be dodging the draft

MacArthur on 6 August 1950, greeting W. Averell Harriman, special advisor to President Truman. This was one of several White House attempts to mend conflicts with the general. It led to the Inchon operation in mid-September. *U.S. Army Signal Corps, courtesy of the MacArthur Memorial Library.*

by playing football for the Academy. He would also write him glowing reports about a general "like you and me; he is basically a citizen-soldier, except that he has adopted the Regular Army as a career."[62]

Truman quickly developed great personal trust in and affection for Lowe, although the latter made no secret of his rock-ribbed Republicanism. He probed and passed to the committee highly restricted information in a discreet, low-profile manner, including the existence of the project producing the atomic bomb, of which Truman knew more than he professed. The senator, thanks to Lowe, could learn the most closely held military secrets while escaping accusations that a politician was impeding the war by grilling generals, the accusation history filed against the Congressional Committee on the Conduct of the (Civil) War. In 1945, after Truman entered the White House, he sent his special assistant to report on the Philippines, first stop MacArthur headquarters, where he immediately gravitated to Courtney Whitney, fellow reservist, old friend from the American Legion (where Lowe had been a vice commander), and confidant to the theater commander on personal, political, and legal matters. Lowe therefore became acquainted with MacArthur and promptly fell under his spell, probably for three related reasons. Number one, the general turned on his considerable charm, as he was apt to do when it served his purpose. Two, Lowe (like Truman) could adore, as well as despise, the professional officer corps, something that explains his acclaim for "the old Pershing school of leadership," about as far from citizen-soldier informality as one can possibly go. Three, MacArthur and his staff were hardly popular with the Department of the Army, as indicated by run-ins described in chapter 1. Lowe, feeling victimized by the Pentagon himself, gravitated to the enemy of his enemy, so to speak.[63]

Presumably, MacArthur did not rub salt in Lowe's GI resentments by discussing Academy athletic teams, as he did with a fellow West Pointer on a training maneuver one week before Japan attacked Luzon in 1941. ("He spent two minutes on the exercise and forty-three on Army football," one company commander recalled.) The general, instead, took the opportunity to patch up developing problems with the new president, who "never had a more loyal nor a more conscientious subordinate," if one is to believe what MacArthur then said. Lowe repeated those words in July 1950, when entreating Truman: "I would cheerfully give a leg to be ordered back to active duty under your command and sent to the Far East in the same status I undertook to serve as your subordinate in World War II."[64]

It was no easy matter to reactivate a reservist two months shy of sixty-six. Harry Vaughan had to get personal authorization from the secretary of the army by threatening to put the president himself on the telephone line. That type of behavior got Vaughan into trouble as an "influence peddler" meddling with regulatory committees. Financial profit was not at stake in this particular case. Lowe closed down business as a "gentleman farmer" on a beautiful manor and ran down to Washington in a hunting coat and pith helmet, two stars about to be emblazed. He was plied with inoculations and, at his insistence, given field binoculars and a .45-caliber pistol. Lowe apparently planned to stay in theater far longer than the orders originally cut for a four-day trip to Tokyo as a participant in the Harriman delegation. The advisor for national security returned. Lowe remained and took up "the pattern of our old Committee," namely "keeping my eyes and ears open and my mouth shut."[65]

The president wanted to receive unvarnished reports about rank-and-file concerns rather than rely on self-serving self-assessments from some general's staff about food, clothing, leadership, equipment, morale, and so on. "There are a great many things that I am in the dark about and can't talk about with anybody except someone who has been on the ground and understands the situation, if I am to get the truth." Given this mission, his agent got as close to the front lines as "Task Force Lowe" could get: one old reservist, his aide, a sergeant manning a .50-caliber machine gun, two drivers, one jeep, and a van loaded with food and coffee for worn-down frontline soldiers. Lowe thus became familiar with units like the marine reconnaissance company about to

Major General Frank Lowe, special representative of the president in Korea, awakening in a slit trench on 27 September 1950. When not sharing the conditions of front-line soldiers one-third his age, Lowe tried to cement good relations between Truman and MacArthur, the two men he most respected and admired. *Courtesy of the Harry S. Truman Library.*

trudge back across the Han River in the face of enemy fire. The division commander had to step in and refuse inclusion despite authorization Lowe flashed to go wherever and whenever he wished, signed President Harry S. Truman on White House stationary.[66]

In Tokyo, between stints on the battlefield, Lowe took up another task close to his heart, that of building a bridge between Truman and MacArthur. In that self-assumed responsibility, he transmitted pledges of mutual support and admiration between individuals who suspected but used one another. However, Lowe was only, so to speak, the chargé to MacArthur, being the second highest diplomat in an ongoing mission. Averell Harriman was the de facto ambassador to the Tokyo compound, often thought of as "a hostile and suspicious foreign government." He could do more than convey good wishes and iron out problems of communication. Harriman had the authority to get right down to business, per the president's marching orders to him on 3 August: tell MacArthur to "leave Chiang Kai-shek alone. I do not want to have him get me into a war with Mainland China." In return, "find out what he wants, and if it's at all possible to do it, I will give it to him," that is, as long as the general waged war only against North Korea.[67]

Truman had offered Republicans temporary protection for Formosa in return for support in Korea, bargaining more familiar to tariff legislation than grand concepts of national strategy in time of war. He now sent Harriman to offer MacArthur personal support for what he might want in Korea if he would not back up the KMT regime. The White House needed a deal because its policy regarding Formosa was terribly twisted, not what one would want to argue with MacArthur. Truman then was dealing with someone "not only highly intelligent," according to the secretary of the army, "but also highly sensitive to situations." The general "had the most uncanny talent for anticipating the real meaning of a question and providing a pertinent answer. I guess it's a quality of genius." Still, need one be an Einstein to answer an enquiry about "what do you want?"[68]

Dean Acheson had been outraged when MacArthur made no room for State Department personnel on the general's trip to Chiang Kai-shek. Foreign Service officers were equally in the dark when it came to the conference with Harriman taking place down the hall in the Dai-Ichi building, U.S. government/military headquarters Tokyo. "No details of his talks with MacArthur were made known, not even to SCAP officials," wrote the senior State Department representative in Japan. "In fact, the underlying purpose of Harriman's visit never was entirely clear to us, although we had a definite stake in it." Their concern nonetheless was minor compared to that of the CINCFE, who was probably quite ambivalent about the offer Harriman transmitted. For MacArthur, as for the Republican caucus in Congress, Formosa had always been a higher priority than Korea, a place he long expected to fall to invasion. On the other hand, a battle for Taipei was just a contingency, while what was happening on the peninsula was a war by anyone's definition, with the possible exception of Harry Truman.[69]

Until rather recently, Douglas MacArthur had held that public opinion foreclosed armed conflict between nation states, probably why he appeared "a crusading apostle for peace" in the words of the *Saturday Evening Post*. The conflict in Korea was an unexpected windfall, breaking out one month after MacArthur assured a *New York Times* correspondent that there would not be another war. It was not only a war but one on a peninsula jutting into the ocean, hence providing an exceptional occasion to conduct war the way he wished, far behind enemy front lines. MacArthur had tried to train regiments for double envelopments even when preparing to defend the beachheads at Luzon. Later, he executed this maneuver behind enemy strongholds, as when landing at Hollandia (New Guinea) in April 1944, an operation as close to perfection as real warfare can come. Charles Willoughby, his chief of intelligence and court historian, compared it to Hannibal's grand tactics at Cannae, a battle enshrined in military immortality. However, whatever attention his two-division maneuver deserved for style and skill, it was soon eclipsed by the allied invasion that Eisenhower orchestrated at Normandy.[70]

Douglas MacArthur, in personal manner, acted according to careful calculation, if one is to accept the U.S. ambassador to Korea: "I don't think MacArthur even blinked his eyes without considering whether it was to his advantage to have his eye blink or not." In military planning, the CINCFE gave more latitude to inspiration and emotion as opposed to the detached computation that marked other members of the military profession. His own forte, said senior officers and personal assistants, was imagination, determination, and "a vast store of information on history, on the Bible, on plays, on sports, on human behavior, on almost anything." He conceived daring ideas, usually with little initial support. "Most of his decisions," said his World War II aide, "were against the majority of his staff." Their job was to fill in the details that made specific plans from his broad concepts, such as a spectacular return to the Philippines in 1944 that might "eradicate the memory" of what MacArthur called "the stinging defeat of 1942." He conceived simultaneous landings (that is, a double envelopment) at Leyte and Luzon, four hundred miles apart. The JCS, however, was making its own decision for Leyte alone while MacArthur was beyond radio contact onboard a blacked-out ship. There was transport to put only five divisions ashore, whereas Luzon (the location of "200,000 Nips") needed four to six divisions by itself. Little would remain of MacArthur's initial vision for a large-scale double envelopment were it not for what former aides including Eisenhower recall: the general's fondness for "the idea of historical repetition" and his "phenomenal memory, without parallel in my knowledge."[71]

Korea, far from being the root of the Truman-MacArthur conflict, intervened to establish a momentary truce in a dispute embedded in Formosa and the Chinese civil war. The administration gave the general a new opportunity to conduct a climactic battle before a world audience that could ensure him a premier place in the annals of war. Hannibal and Napoleon had executed this kind of double envelopment but not MacArthur, except on a relatively small scale at backwater places in the coastal jungles in New Guinea. Now he could set the standard by conducting what he variously called "modern," "triphibious," or "three-dimensional" warfare: the synchronization of air, sea, and ground operations. But to get his long-awaited chance for a dream operation, he would have to give up something, at least in the short run.[72]

On August 1st, at the conclusion of the talks with Chiang Kai-shek, MacArthur declared that it was "my responsibility and firm purpose" to defend Formosa from the invasion force then doubling its size on the mainland, according to Nationalist intelligence. On the 6th, he still informed Averell Harriman that he did not think the PRC would try to conduct the operation "at the present time," a signal that the CINCFE was willing to put Formosa on the back burner. MacArthur had said much the same thing in 1941 about a prospective Japanese invasion of the Philippines, a miscalculation that did not seem to reduce his confidence in his own acumen, He proved correct in mid-1950, whether from insight, luck, or placation of the administration. The

Chinese communist authorities decided to postpone the invasion a few days after America's intervention in Korea. In late July, Beijing began to deploy forces to Manchuria, although most intelligence circles scarcely noticed, and there was certainly no consensus until late September, when the typhoon season creates impassable seas in the Taiwan Strait. Until then, message traffic from DOD reported "imminence of invasion of Formosa by Chinese Commies." MacArthur responded about the time the first communist military units began moving north: "Nothing that has been received here warrants an assumption of an early threat to Formosa . . . Request you make all such information available." One doubts either the CINCFE or the Pentagon forgot their respective predictions three months later when MacArthur forecast no Chinese intervention while on his way toward the Yalu River.[73]

Intelligence reports, negative assessments, doubts, and caution rarely upset MacArthur's preconceived plans. In August 1950, he told Harriman that there was no immediate need to bomb China because the threat had receded, exactly what the White House wanted to hear. He also made a remark about letting Chiang land on the mainland as an expedient way to "get rid of him." Later, that type of operation would be MacArthur's method proposed to crush Mao. Now, it slyly invoked his recent collaboration with Washington's attempt at an anti-Chiang coup. The general then proceeded to tell of his plans, incubating for a month, if not six years, for a "hammer and anvil" grand envelopment. A landing at Inchon, far behind enemy front lines, was to link up with a break-out from the Pusan perimeter, the position America was barely holding at the southern end of the Korean peninsula. The presentation "raised the hair on the back of my neck," said Harriman's military aide, Vernon Walters. Harriman himself was certainly impressed, hardly a surprise. Professional soldiers, such as Eisenhower and Matt Ridgway, testified to the infectious quality of MacArthur's confidence. One could hardly expect more resistance from a civilian told by a president, "Find out what he wants and if at all possible to do it, I will give it to him," a political deal with military content.[74]

On August 9th, Harriman returned to Washington and immediately went to the White House, where he told Truman, in so many words, that the theater commander agreed to his half of the bargain, that is, to "leave Chiang Kai-shek alone," and to agree "as a soldier [to] obey any orders that he received from the President." Harriman also told him about Inchon, what MacArthur wanted in return. Truman then told him "go and see Louis Johnson and General Bradley. I want them to act on it rapidly," meaning don't study it to death. Harriman stopped at home to shower and eat breakfast before arriving at the Pentagon two hours later. Truman already had phoned Bradley once and Johnson twice, leading them to question, "Averell, what have you been doing to the President?" When answered, "I was there [in Tokyo] entirely for political reasons," Johnson responded, "Well, the President has told me he wants this plan of MacArthur's supported."[75]

Truman had ample experience with Pentagon obstruction, whether to desegregation, armed service unification, or cutting of favored weapons such as a new class of aircraft carriers. Suspicion was warranted about the reception to Inchon in view of what the secretary of the army later said. The Joint Chiefs "uniformly thought it a bad idea," that is, once privy to the plan. On June 29th, when DOD was finding the commitment to Korea growing far beyond initial expectations, Joe Collins wrote MacArthur that the JCS would "welcome any suggestions" about "different measures for achieving basic objectives." On July 3rd, the CINCFE requested personnel trained to handle troop transports and landing craft, no reason then given. On the 7th, MacArthur explained that once the enemy "is fixed, it will be my purpose fully to exploit our air and sea control and, by amphibious maneuver, strike behind his mass of ground force." This had not been what the Pentagon had in mind. The chiefs heard more in a tele-conference with Tokyo headquarters in late July but did not take their chance to inoculate the White House by taking Inchon up with the president. Perhaps they feared that Truman, in the manner of Franklin Roosevelt, might get enthusiastic for an operation judged to have "very little chance of success."[76]

Omar Bradley called Inchon "the worst possible place ever selected for an amphibious landing." The architect of invasion planning at Omaha Beach knew a lot about the standard since "shaken to find that we had gone against [an enemy in June 1944] with so thin a margin of safety." The sea channel chosen for 1950 was narrow, was easy to mine, and led to a sixteen-foot wall, no inclined beach this time. Tides were of sufficient strength to carry land-ing craft only once a month; otherwise they would mire on soggy mud flats. In that case it seemed that the double envelopment most likely to take place was one conducted by the North Korean army. It might penetrate a depleted Pusan perimeter on multiple fronts, shades of Bataan with one big difference. The Japanese sank the potential relief expedition at Pearl Harbor. This time MacArthur would be the party who made sure the navy, stuck at Inchon, could not come to rescue his army.[77]

Bradley, Collins, and Forrest Sherman professed their "desire to help in every possible way." MacArthur spoke only in broad generalities on July 24th except to conclude a telecom conference with admonishments that "I cannot emphasize too strongly the necessity for complete secrecy with reference to this matter." That meant no one was to discuss the prospective invasion outside the present room, exclusively filled with officers of three- and four-star rank. There were certainly good reasons for silence. Inchon could succeed only if no substantial opposition met MacArthur at the invasion site. One still doubts whether operational security need be stressed to experienced military men such as Bradley, who felt MacArthur "always considered us a bunch of kids." The CINCFE's own homily did not prevent him from leaking his plans to the Tokyo press corps, which devised their own sardonic code name, "Operation Common Knowledge." Maggie Higgins of the *New York Herald Tribune*, one of eighty-six correspondents about to cover Inchon, telephoned her publisher, who telephoned the Pentagon to secure her passage on a "very important navy mission." DOD was appalled.[78]

These facts, conditions, and circumstances lead one to conclude that MacArthur swore the JCS to strict secrecy so they could not examine his Inchon proposal in meaningful depth. The service chiefs are CEOs of mammoth corporations at the beck and call of their boards of directors sitting in the U.S. Congress. They must rely on large staffs, now out of the loop, to assess the details, usually the weak suit in MacArthur's plans. This theater commander, being an artist pursuing an inspiration, could be called to account by technical experts good at facts and figures if he were not keeping these fine points within his loyal circle of support. MacArthur was also preparing the press, another one of his standard procedures at variance with proposals from the Joint Chiefs. They advocated censorship; not so the CINCFE, although known to control the press in Japan by expelling critics as security risks. Now he turned the tables on the JCS by citing its own White House–based instructions to avoid all appearance of unilateral action. Censorship, purportedly, could not be initiated save by the direction of the United Nations, which meant the media would be free to print whatever it got from Tokyo headquarters. MacArthur could thereby avoid the problems he faced in World War II, when the secretary of war stopped him from taking his case to the public, as he would do, one way or the other, if Washington dragged its heels on Inchon.[79]

Collins and Sherman went to Tokyo in late August, "to try to argue General MacArthur out of it," to quote Louis Johnson's description of the setting for the most important conference on the Inchon landing. The chief of naval operations, said to be "unquestionably opposed to the plan," encouraged dissent from the naval component in CINCFE headquarters. He met with Rear Admiral James Doyle, the resident expert on amphibious operations, who got much different guidance, in a "most dictatorial manner," from MacArthur's chief of staff. Major General Ned Almond directed "do not linger over details"; MacArthur is "just" interested in "the broad picture." Doyle shot back "he must be made aware" and next day had his say at the grand assemblage: "I have not been asked nor have I volunteered my opinion about this landing," testimony to MacArthur's indifference to technical expertise. It "will be extremely difficult and will take considerable destruction ashore . . . the best I can say is that Inchon is not impossible."[80]

MacArthur made one concession to the possibility of failure before his climactic conclusion: "We shall land at Inchon and I shall crush them." If necessary, he would pull out of the channel, as if one could throw the fleet into reverse. "General," Doyle politely pointed out, "we don't know how to do that. Once we start ashore we'll keep going," hardly something MacArthur did not know. The general had commanded more landings in the last war than any other solider—or sailor, or marine. With his encyclopedic knowledge and photographic memory, he had an impressive grasp of fleet issues, if one is to believe Arleigh Burke, deputy chief of staff for the CINCFE's naval forces. Mac-Arthur was resorting to every potential argument, including the bone he threw to doubters, as before landing on the Admiralty Islands in February 1944. Then, the general also talked of withdrawing his so-called reconnaissance-in-force if the enemy were nearly as strong as intelligence assessments suggested. Even this could seem a rare moment of humility to observers of MacArthur. "It was more than confidence which upheld him," thought Major General Oliver Prince (O. P.) Smith, the marine selected to command the assault division at Inchon. "It was [a] supreme and almost mystical faith that he could not fail."[81]

Quotes like this are common from fellow senior officers who said that MacArthur "believes in himself, his destiny, and in his place in history." This, however, may be a bit superficial when delving into an actor better than John Barrymore, according to the U.S. ambassador to Korea. Drama probably helped MacArthur handle his responsibilities, not simply while away his time as an inveterate watcher of movies, especially about cowboys, Indians, and the army on the western frontier. Theatrics had a role in situations such as Bataan, where "the commanding general enjoins upon all officers that demeanor of confidence, self-reliance and assurance which is the birthright of all cultured gentlemen and the special trademark of the Army officer." This would be particularly true for one fated to carry the destiny of the MacArthurs, although no guarantee of ultimate victory. The general admitted to Harriman in October 1950 that "though the [Inchon] action was now successful, he had taken a grave responsibility."[82]

Unlike MacArthur, Collins and Sherman felt no need to hide their apprehension about taking an awful gamble, at least at a closed conference of fellow flag officers presumed to be a frank exchange of opinion. MacArthur still held that nothing but the Inchon operation could sever the enemy's main supply route running through Seoul to the Pusan perimeter. For once he overlooked tactical airpower, the weapon on which he usually relied, as when he later told Truman at Wake Island: "Now that we have bases for our air force in Korea, if the Chinese tried to get down to Pyongyang, there would be the greatest slaughter." Collins, for his part, made his own reversal about whether the air force could turn back an offensive. A skeptic at Blair House on June 25th, he took a different stance now, although one failing to persuade the CINCFE. Once the weather cleared up over enemy lines of communication, "the logistics support of the North Korean forces will rapidly dry up," thanks to air supremacy. Then, according to the army chief of staff, MacArthur should launch a short envelopment at Kunsan astride enemy positions along the Naktong.[83]

The Kunsan alternative could provide immediate relief to the battered Eighth Army, the reason why favored by its commander, Lieutenant General Walton ("Johnnie") Walker. It was far less dangerous than a deep envelopment at Inchon that separated MacArthur's major military components by 180 miles, not to mention North Koreans holding a central position that could split, isolate, and defeat them in detail. MacArthur did not pay much attention to what worried the Pentagon: a month of combat over rugged terrain before U.S. forces might ever link up. Sherman would walk away mumbling: "I wish I could share that man's optimism." MacArthur's pessimism seemed confined to what would happen if he was not allowed to execute Inchon: "a war of indefinite duration, of gradual attrition and of doubtful result, as the enemy has potentialities of reinforcement and build-up which exceed those of our own availability," tactical airpower be damned.[84]

Because MacArthur would not budge from his position, Sherman and Collins might have stayed home and saved the treasury their airfare. The JCS had marginal authority, organizational bar charts to the contrary. Its executive agent in the case of MacArthur was the army chief of staff, who had been a captain teaching tactics at the infantry school when the CINCFE held the post Collins now had. The older man did not hold youth against officers he judged worthy of being protégés, such as Matt Ridgway and Ned Almond. In World War II, he still thought Collins "too young" for high command in SWPA, a potential career-stopper in 1943. Thanks to George Marshall, under whom Collins served at the infantry school, he shipped out of the Pacific for Europe, where Collins became Bradley's favorite corps commander. In 1949, when the latter became chairman of the Joint Chiefs, Collins was his candidate for successor as army chief of staff and hence the JCS representative to any theater commander responsible to the Department of the Army.[85]

Thirty years after the Korean War, Collins conceded that MacArthur was "a fine strategist up to a certain point." The problem was that he "lacked knowledge of the fighting side of the Army," one way of saying that the CINCFE fell in love with his abstract plans. However, before defeat in late 1950 revealed feet of clay, Collins had to judge MacArthur's judgment on the basis of his record in the theater Collins left behind. It "was sheer brilliance," he would say of MacArthur in World War II, "one of the most brilliant campaigns that I know of in military history." This state of mind was hardly conducive to a confrontation over Inchon, no matter that Collins was certainly no shirker at Guadalcanal, Normandy, or the Battle of the Bulge. The army has an informal way of preventing the predicament he faced, where the nominal authority calls a man "general" and he, in turn, is called "Joe." When an individual such as Collins becomes chief of staff in his early fifties, passed-over officers usually put in for retirement. This was especially likely for those not part of what MacArthur called the "Marshall clique" that ran the Department of the Army after World War II. His former ground component commanders, Walter Krueger and Robert Eichelberger, had already retired; not so the CINCFE—especially if a war with China over Formosa might be on the horizon.[86]

The Pentagon is always reluctant to overrule a theater commander placed in that position to be the expert on the spot. This is particularly true when that officer has the backing of the White House: "pretty slick," Truman said in retrospect. O. P. Smith, about to command the First Marine Division, had gone to Tokyo headquarters for discussions on Inchon. He found its staff "had absolute contempt for the Truman administration. Their idea was that the only man in the world who knew anything about the situation in the Far East was General MacArthur." The CINCFE himself said nothing so negative, at least at this time, when Averell Harriman provided a pinstriped back channel to the Oval Office, where a potential benefactor might reside. MacArthur, on the eve of the military operation of his life, still must have worried that neither personal etiquette nor a particular liaison could seal the final deal with Harry Truman. He had known what he needed to know about Franklin Roosevelt, whom he loathed but with whom he worked. He had not met and measured FDR's successor, having refused his invitation to address Congress right after World War II. Best keep Frank Lowe on the premises under these circumstances, even when MacArthur privately complained that he was "a pain in the neck."[87]

MacArthur trusted no one loyal to someone in the White House, although Lowe showed him every message he was about to send. However, if turned to MacArthur's side, Truman's man would enable him to supplement the Harriman connection a propos the military principle of redundancy: keep second volleys in reserve lest the first strike fails. On August 15th, he sent Lowe, the khaki-clad envoy, to give to the president a "first hand report of the situation here"; that is, reiterate why Inchon was essential. Truman was susceptible because always anxious to get frank "observations with regard to the High Command which cannot be put in writing." His agent felt the prospective landing "will reflect tremendous and everlasting credit to our country and to all concerned." Of particular concern to Lowe was saving GIs from winter warfare in Korea, horrendous to contemplate, even when drenched in summer heat: "Our battle-weary veterans *must* have relief and rest." They would not get it, and neither did Lowe, who refused to live like most presidential emissaries, whether giving his gloves to a Negro private when the weather was 27 degrees below or manning the final marine gangplank out of North Korea with his .45-caliber pistol cocked in late December 1950: "Go up boys, I'm an old man, and I'll protect your rear as long as I can."[88]

Back in August, most other people were not thinking of winter weather combat. MacArthur said the Inchon operation would end the war with total victory. The service chiefs, on the other hand, feared defeat. They "inclined to postponing Inchon," Omar Bradley would write, "until such time that we were certain Pusan could hold." Even that was a major concession to the CINCFE; the JCS did not want to conduct Inchon at all. "But Truman was now committed," Bradley explained, a fact that contradicts another fact: "Truman was relying on us to an extraordinary degree for military counsel." The general did not explain this paradox, not the responsibility of the chairman of the Joint Chiefs, who has quite a few other things to do. Historians, less gainfully employed, can trace the inconsistency to conflicts between professional soldiers and within Truman himself.[89]

The president long held that "crazy politicians" burdened "the great [military] Captains of History," such as Hannibal and Lee. He may now have estimated that MacArthur was attempting his own double envelopment per Cannae or the crossing of the Rhone River, where the "greatest general in all history" caught his opponents in a vise by slipping upstream, then doubling back. Inchon also must have looked like the strategic turning movements described in Douglas Southall Freeman's biography of Lee, to Truman "the best history of the Civil War that's ever been written." There was the great victory at Chancellorsville in 1863. There was also the engagement at Fraiser's Farm, where the opportunity "for a Cannae" slipped away because the Army of Northern Virginia was not prepared to execute a double envelopment in 1862. It was "the bitterest disappointment Lee ever sustained and one he could not conceal," Freeman wrote in volume 2. This time would Truman bear the blame rather than an exhausted corps commander? The president did not specifically mention any analogues for Inchon in his memoirs, even if he remembered all the history he read, as several people attest. He simply said that MacArthur had proposed "a bold plan worthy of a master strategist."[90]

The Decline and Fall of Louis Johnson

> *He is the most egomaniac I've ever come in contact with—*
> *and I've seen a lot.*

HARRY TRUMAN, 14 SEPTEMBER 1950[91]

Truman claimed that General Collins and Admiral Sherman "advised me that the Joint Chiefs had approved [MacArthur's] plans," hardly the whole story although serving a purpose. It enabled the president to maintain to his own conscience—and the nation at large—that politicians did not meddle in the conduct of war, at least when Harry Truman was in charge. This proposition, while not completely accurate, was coming true in the case of Louis Johnson, a politician now losing the power to obstruct an operation like Inchon, not really to his liking despite essential agreement with MacArthur on the Chinese civil war.[92]

The secretary of defense had been trying to expand American's defense perimeter to include Formosa, even when cutting defense spending. He also had been saying since 1949 that "we'll never have any more amphibious operations." In this instance, his force structure matched his policy insofar as having cut into "the whole damned navy," particularly its army, the United States Marines. The Corps lost 540 landing craft. Only 91 troop transports remained in the inventory. Forces would be carried to Korea in an international flotilla provided by France, Holland, Britain, and its commonwealth, not to mention "Japanese boats that smelled to high heaven of dead fish." America scrounged up 30 LSTs (tank landing ships) sold to commercial enterprise, along with foreign sailors to help man these vessels. "Everybody believed," said one marine, "that he was being ferried to Inchon by a Japanese [fisherman] who had been an admiral at Midway."[93]

The commandant had said that "my biggest worry is to keep the Marine Corps alive." This same concern infused some ranking members of the House Armed Services Committee. They tried to create a third Leatherneck division, not to Truman's liking in mid-August 1950, when he responded that "the Marine Corps is [merely] the Navy's police force and as long as I am president that is what it will remain." Frank Lowe, known to be the president's "personal spy," got a post-Inchon reaction at forward Marine headquarters from the "greatest fighting men I've ever seen." Senior officers played up to him, as had Mac-Arthur, seeing Lowe as an aficionado ready to make their case to a hostile figure in the Oval Office. Rank-and-file marines, being a less courtly lot, painted "Truman's Police" on their vehicles and "MP" on their tanks.[94]

Johnson for months was undergoing a less good-natured criticism. Hawkish elements in the press accused him of "not telling the truth about national defense." His own claim to "lick Russia with one hand behind our back" caught up with him during Korea, although it was unfair to make him shoulder all the blame. Johnson reflected Truman's priority to grow the economy by reducing the public debt, no matter that the president admitted to close confidants that the armed forces would be strapped if facing sustained conflict. (The atomic bomb was "all he had; that the Russians would have probably taken over Europe a long time ago if it were not for that.") The secretary of defense struck a suitable public pose, at least on behalf of government finance. "If Johnson were any less crude, direct and ruthless," one columnist wrote, "he probably could not have carried through what he has accomplished." Nonetheless, every collective disaster winds up in someone's lap, as it did once Kim Il-sung crossed the 38th parallel. In the U.S. presidential system, as opposed to parliamentary Britain, some subordinate resigns. The secretary of defense fit the bill, according to Drew Pearson, Washington reporter to whom Johnson leaked stories to taint political coverage: "It is true Truman had to have a scapegoat, but you can't make as many enemies as Johnson has made inside the services, inside the Congress, and the country generally without automatically nominating yourself as scapegoat."[95]

The president had wanted "the hardest, meanest so and so" to beat down the military budget, scheduled for a 10 percent reduction in the next fiscal year. Now he was concluding that Johnson, a blunt bureaucratic infighter, had "an inordinate egotistical desire to run the whole government." The secretary of defense abused the White House staff, fought turf battles with other agencies, and espoused a preventive war against the Soviet Union. (In the "name of law and order and for the establishment of peace," the United States should request a UN agreement to use the atomic bomb.) The perennial problem of policy toward China came into particular play. Johnson sneered about government disloyalty for criticizing Chiang Kai-shek and passed information to Robert Taft, with whom he allied to defend Formosa. Truman eventually would dismiss MacArthur for behavior much like this. He delved into Johnson's replacement but had not taken definitive action, partly because of his reluctance to fire anyone he appointed. Eleanor Roosevelt felt compelled to write her husband's successor about the groundswell against Johnson as the person "responsible for our poor showing" in Korea, where the army had fallen back to Pusan perimeter. Truman politely informed the matriarch of his party, best known for her family welfare work, that she was misinformed: "Adequate forces and supplies are now being built up." Fours days later, on August 26th, Johnson finally suffered an irreparable deathblow, largely thanks to fallout over Douglas MacArthur.[96]

On August 25th, the ambassador to the United Nations assured its general secretary that the United States would not use Formosa as a base from which to strike China. Next day, Acheson handed Harriman, for Truman's personal perusal, a late-breaking public statement out of CINCFE headquarters. The general, in lieu of a personal appearance, had sent the annual convention of the Veterans of Foreign Wars a message reiterating the memo on Formosa he gave Johnson and Bradley on the eve of Korea. By now, MacArthur's stance about the necessity to keep the island out of communist hands was virtually identical with that of the JCS, with one substantial difference. Their advice was confidential; his went for public broadcast. It argued the strategic position of the geographical entity with no explicit mention of the Nationalist government, much like Truman's own statement of June 27th that "the occupation of Taiwan by Communist forces would be a direct threat to the security of the Pacific area." Now that the White House seemed to have adopted the MacArthur doctrine, MacArthur could maintain that his VFW message "was most carefully prepared to fully support the President's policy decision" recorded in state papers that "the future historian will regard as the focal and turning point of this era's struggle for civilization": message "personal for President Truman," July 20th.[97]

This flattery notwithstanding, MacArthur felt Truman's stipulations against preemption stymied Taipei's self-defense. His communication to the VFW, going out to the public under "Formosa Must Be Defended," gave the general his opportunity "to clarify any fogginess in current American thinking generated by such misinformation being circulated in public discussions both at home and abroad." In other words, it applied pressure on Washington to change the rules of engagement in the strait while laced with protective compliments to Truman for lighting "into flame a lamp of hope throughout Asia." MacArthur had said virtually the same thing to another president in August 1941, after Roosevelt called the military forces of the Philippines into federal service: a proclamation that "had a momentous effect throughout the Far East. Locally, it changed a feeling of defeatism to the highest state of morale I have ever seen." FDR, genial on the outside but a cynic underneath, would claim MacArthur deceived him. Truman was certainly not won over, although his press secretary had praised MacArthur for praising the "great state papers" the president issued.[98]

It was not so much what MacArthur said in late August as what he failed to clarify, especially to the international community long on Truman's mind. The president issued an official statement on July 19th "in order that there may be no doubt in any quarter about our intentions regarding Formosa. The United States has no territorial ambitions whatever concerning that island." Acheson thanked India for passing these statements to China. He was far less thankful to MacArthur for raising indiscreet issues among neutrals and European allies, let alone Beijing. The general's statement seemed to portend plans to build air bases on Taiwan, anathema to Britain, already in possession of reports of conversations where MacArthur referred to the island "as a means of entry into China." The UK ambassador was quick to question whether U.S. policy on "Formosa was firmly based on the President's statements," not standard fare for diplomatic discourse, which is usually quite circumspect.[99]

The White House maintained that MacArthur's statements "would serve to confuse the United Nations and the world." A disinterested party could have filed a rejoinder that those bodies had been baffled since Truman's press conference on 5 January 1950. To a denial of any inclination "to establish military bases on Formosa," the president had added a proviso ("at this time") that Johnson inserted, to Acheson's dismay. In June, Truman pledged to prevent an invasion altogether but prohibited U.S. airfields on the island that this mission required. However, he was less attentive to these shortcomings than to the "tenor" of MacArthur's own message: "critical of the very policy he had so recently told Harriman he would support." The CINCFE seemed to be breaking their personal peace treaty, as Truman had been cautioned to suspect. "I did not feel that we came to a full agreement," Harriman had told him. MacArthur "will act accordingly but without full conviction."[100]

Full conviction was also absent when the general told the VFW that the president had "swept aside in one great monumental stroke all of the hypocrisy and the sophistry which has confused and deluded so many people distant from the actual scene." If anything, MacArthur was praising Truman for seeing the mortal sins of his past and pledging to turn over a new leaf. Actually, as of then, all policy changes were partial and temporary, to last no longer than the Korean emergency, as Truman repeatedly said. They also fell under "neutralization" of the Taiwan Strait, a carefully chosen phrase. Acheson had reminded Johnson that this depiction was necessary "to obtain international support for a step which had no United Nations sanction." MacArthur, in his own message, characterized neutrality in the Chinese civil war as "appeasement and defeatism in the Pacific," emotive words for the Munich generation. Harriman, adamant that the phrase be excised, checked it for the president's personal inspection.[101]

Truman, who seethed when accused of "appeasement," must have thought MacArthur disloyal to someone who had been loyal to him, the worst offense in Truman's code of political honor. Having backed the Inchon plan, he already told Frank Lowe to tell the general: "I have never had anything but the utmost confidence in his ability to do the Far Eastern job and I think I've shown that by action, as well as words." MacArthur probably thought this nothing but vacuous verbiage, such as he piled on the president. The JCS chain of command had yet to give final word of approval for the grand envelopment. The people clearly coming to the CINCFE's side were what Truman called the "Chiang Kai-shek Republicans" critical of the administration for disengaging from the Chinese civil war. Senator Joe McCarthy, who recently had charged that the State Department was rife with communists, called MacArthur's letter to the VFW "the most intelligent, clear-cut, irrefutable and valuable document which has been brought to the attention of the public for many months."[102]

No one need be surprised that Truman was enraged at MacArthur for handing "the Acheson-haters an argument behind which they could gather their forces for the attack." The president later claimed that he "gave serious thought" to relieving the general then and there, a statement that obscures as much as it reveals. Truman privately discussed dismissing MacArthur with Louis Johnson, no one else present. This one-man council of advisors virtually assured that he not relieve the CINCFE, considering the way the president made most decisions. "Even on the most important issue," Truman later said, "my reaction might be immediate. I'd tell the people around me what my decision was, and then, if they thought I was wrong, it was up to them to talk me out of it. I was talked out of a lot of things," notwithstanding his favored image as a take-charge guy. The prospective relief of MacArthur in August 1950 was no exception to the standard procedure. Secretary Johnson felt the CINCFE was "one of the greatest, if not the greatest, generals of our generation." He convinced Truman, as Truman later put it, that "we needed MacArthur to run the war."[103]

Truman was much less convinced that he needed Johnson to run the defense department, thought to be the secretary's secondary interest. "He began to run for President the day I appointed him," Truman wrote in retrospect. Johnson was not ready to take on MacArthur with anything resembling a reprimand, although not shy to battle the service chiefs over budgets and Dean Acheson about China policy. In this case ambition dictated prudence: MacArthur's "stature is so great." Hence Johnson stalled for time despite Truman's angry statement: "Send an order to MacArthur to withdraw this letter. That is an order from me. Do you understand?" The secretary of defense, proud if not impervious, still debated the issue with Acheson and confused Truman by saying "a long lot of stuff that I couldn't understand." Finally Truman "certainly set [someone] straight," even if he had to do it two times. He again directed Johnson to direct MacArthur that "the President of the United States directs that you withdraw your [VFW] message."[104]

The incident could not be kept out of the public domain, to the joy of Truman's critics. Joe Martin, House minority leader, already had entered the general's statement to the VFW into the *Congressional Record*. This helped precipitate Truman's own public statement: "In the field of foreign relations there can be but one voice in stating the position of the United States." His claim might be true regarding civil-military relations, at least when the president exercised his full prerogatives as commander in chief. It ignored the complexity of the Constitution and congressional control of appropriations, which had pushed Truman toward begrudging acceptance of Chiang Kai-shek in return for support of NATO and South Korea. However, lest the reluctant commitment to Formosa now get out of hand, the president exercised control where he could, over what public statements a military officer can make.[105]

MacArthur, self-important but quite sensitive, desperately wanted to avoid the humiliation of rescinding his message to the VFW. He wrote a personal note to the secretary of defense, as if the general were a lawyer making every conceivable argument for a desperate client, contradictions notwithstanding. He alleged that his statement was "calculated solely to support" Truman's declared policy. It was, on the other hand, "purely personal" from a citizen giving his opinion on an issue "freely discussed in all circles, governmental and private, both at home and abroad." Unfortunately for the plaintiff, the one-man judge and jury already had rendered its verdict. Nonetheless, Harry Truman, having vented his anger, was willing to soften his reprimand in a personal letter to MacArthur on August 29th. The president enclosed some UN statements of policy so that "you will understand why my action of the 26th in directing the withdrawal of your message to the Veterans of Foreign Wars was necessary." He concluded with praise for the person he admonished, reminiscent of passages to the VFW where MacArthur heaped applause on the president he also criticized. In the process, Truman signaled he would not renege on the original understanding about setting policy on Formosa but letting MacArthur run military operations. "General Collins and Admiral Sherman have given me a comprehensive report of their conversations with you and of their visit to the United Nations forces now fighting under your command in Korea. Their reports were most satisfactory and highly gratifying."[106]

MacArthur, in a "most earnest request to the President for reconsideration of the order," already had pointed out that the message to the VFW could not be retrieved from the hands of the press. In so many words, the damage had been done, but a full accounting of the injuries had yet to be compiled. Truman's alleged neutrality toward Formosa suffered in the eyes of NATO nations and the People's Republic of China, fearing or convinced that it was a fabrication. Harm was also done to MacArthur's ego, of no small consequence. Frank Lowe, his on-call channel to the Oval Office, passed on his claim that in some fifty years of military service he had never received "such abrupt messages" as those just received. Many commentators looking at MacArthur's behavior in 1951 conclude that the general virtually forced the White House to dismiss him. His provocative behavior could well have had some roots in resentment festering since the humiliation of late August 1950.[107]

Louis Johnson had predicted that the Formosa issue would cause Truman to get rid of Dean Acheson. The island and MacArthur mortally damaged Johnson's own standing despite the common wisdom of the White House staff that "nothing can be done before the election." On 11 September, four days before the U.S. landing at Inchon, the president asked Johnson for his resignation. "He wept and said he didn't think I'd make him do it," Truman noted, about "the toughest job I have ever had to do. . . . I feel as if I had just whipped my daughter."[108]

Averell Harriman, who once appeared to have smoothed Truman's problems with MacArthur, had given up on handling Johnson, one of his original responsibilities as senior advisor to the president. He heard of the dismissal of the secretary of defense when out for drinks with Stuart Alsop, a well-connected columnist. He thereupon danced and hugged Mrs. Alsop, whose husband was of the opinion that this type of "reaction was duplicated just about everywhere in Washington." The euphoria, however, proved premature. Johnson's replacement was George Catlett Marshall, on whom the White House felt it could rely to handle the remaining problems in Korea; "he's of the *great*," said Truman. Marshall took office in a honeymoon period evident in the tributes MacArthur issued from the deck of a battleship the day before Inchon. He said the president chose the right man for DOD and that Eisenhower had been a good army chief of staff. Bad days would follow, not to be resolved by Marshall's aura of authority. It actually furthered the forthcoming confrontation between Truman and MacArthur: politics, policies, and personalities had yet to be aligned.[109]

The War against North Korea: From Inchon to the Yalu River

1 2 3 4 5 6 7 8 9

I find it amazing that highly trained professionals with extensive combat experience could have approved and tried to execute the tactical plan of operations . . . in November 1950. It appears like a pure Map Exercise put on by amateurs, appealing in theory but largely ignoring the reality.

MATTHEW BUNKER RIDGWAY, GENERAL (RET.), 27 FEBRUARY 1985[1]

United Nations forces wore down the North Korea army at the Pusan perimeter before Douglas MacArthur conducted his Inchon landing in mid-September 1950. However, few Americans had grasped the critical condition of the KPA. Truman, always hesitant to be a politician interfering with military operations, now deferred to the general as a genius, particularly when they met at Wake Island three weeks before the congressional election. This was no time for a civilian to dispute a field commander whose prestige was sky-high, even when a "police action" near the border of the Soviet Union and China might escalate into war with a major power—just what the intervention in Korea was supposed to deter. Dean Acheson and George Marshall, on whose counsel Truman strongly relied, had reservations about the military situation. Still, they did not take their concern to the president, for personal as well as political reasons. They too were apt to avoid a confrontation with MacArthur, especially when they could still hope it might not be necessary. The administration could not really fathom what might motivate China to intercede in North Korea, thought to be a Moscow satellite and hence not vital to Beijing. Washington's commitment to Formosa, partly a byproduct of MacArthur's influence, had become a factor, along with Mao's plan to force the United States to disengage from the Taiwan Strait by crushing its army north of Pyongyang.

Inchon: Expectations and Execution

I am firmly convinced that early and strong effort behind [the enemy] front will sever his main lines of communication and enable us to deliver a decisive and crushing blow.

DOUGLAS MACARTHUR, 23 JULY 1950[2]

Matt Ridgway said MacArthur could "cause opposition to melt and doubters to doubt themselves." The CINCFE actually got his way by mixing persuasion with stealth. The Joint Chiefs of Staff did not send him their approval to conduct Inchon until August 29th—and then it was "conditional" upon his delivery of "timely information" about the disposition of the enemy. On September 7th they asked for a new "estimate as to feasibility," obviously not satisfied with what one officer subsequently called "some slap-dash answer telling them we would make it." MacArthur dispatched a major who gave a briefing on the 14th, D-Day (Inchon) minus 1, perfect execution of his guidance: Don't arrive "too soon." By then, criticism or concurrence was largely academic for what had become a fait accompli. "General MacArthur had a talent for creating good fortune," the secretary of the army would say.[3]

The fact that MacArthur could have his way by withholding information indicates that the burden of proof lay on the Joint Chiefs. He did not have to show them that Inchon was right as much as they had to convince him it was wrong. The Pentagon still demurred, and MacArthur wondered who "in Washington lost his nerve? Could it be the President?" No, it was not, despite what MacArthur, still angry a decade after his dismissal, wrote in his memoirs. On August 27th, with the battle at the Pusan perimeter reaching its climax, Frank Lowe wrote the White House confirming "the prediction I made in Washington [twelve days ago.] Tremendous air strikes have had fearful effect on the enemy, and our ground troops have followed up and are fighting their hearts out. Right now the initiative just may pass to us at any moment."[4]

Truman jotted down "thank Frank for me." Neither he nor his personal agent drew the logical conclusion that Inchon was not necessary now that US/UN forces were winning the war at the Naktong. Lowe had fallen under MacArthur's aura. The Department of Defense was also disarmed, especially the navy, although the chief of naval operations planted a new deputy chief of staff for the commander of the naval component in Far East military headquarters. "Send a personal radio dispatch to me directly at least once a day," Forrest Sherman told Arleigh Burke. "I want you particularly to study the plan for this upcoming Inchon assault. If you think it likely to fail, let me know and I can block the operation." MacArthur, meanwhile a step ahead, won Burke over much the same way he seduced naval officers serving under him in World War II. He gave them direct access, above or around gatekeepers on his staff, so that they (the experts) might tell him how to do whatever he wanted them to do. "I was the first Army man to give all my ground forces to the Navy to handle," MacArthur told one marine. "I trusted them to land me, cover and guard me," what Burke appreciated. He had his fill of land force commanders who "do not understand that they can obtain better naval support by telling the Navy what they need and letting an able Navy do it." By October 5th, when he wrote those words, Inchon was history. Burke would say of MacArthur, "this operation really shows the greatness of that man."[5]

MacArthur may have listened to the navy, but only when he wanted. He would not turn the landing force over to a man in its department such as Lieutenant General Lemuel Shepherd, commander of the Fleet Marine Force. Nor did he invite ranking marines to attend the key conference about Inchon on August 23rd, lest someone like O. P. Smith, commander of the First Marine Division, give his opinion "that there was a complete lack of understanding at GHQ concerning the manner in which amphibious forces were mounted out." MacArthur still used service rivalry, as when telling Shepherd that "for political reasons" the Department of the Army wanted to keep marines out of the war. This appeal to prestige was no small way to garner support for Inchon, judging by what Rear Admiral Burke would say: "Against a strong, virile aggressive opponent, our Army ground units were unable to advance while our Marine Corps against the same kind of opposition forced the enemy to take to his heels in full retreat."[6]

High hopes about Inchon also enticed the army, anxious to get out of Korea, quick and permanent. A deep envelopment cutting just logistics lines would force North Korea back beyond the 38th parallel but leave them able to recross when replenished. That might drag U.S. forces back to the peninsula in some future emergency, an end state not worth the operational gamble America ran at Inchon. MacArthur offered something of more value when he described the prospective operation to Generals Bradley, Collins, and Ridgway, or other officers of influence. It was to be a decisive battle in the Napoleonic sense of the term, that is, an action that so totally destroys the enemy armed forces that it ends the entire war. He would catch the North Koreans between "the anvil" of the X Corps, landing behind its lines at Inchon, and "the hammer" of the Eighth Army, sweeping up from its positions at the Pusan perimeter. "I shall crush them," and presumably without too much difficulty. His chief of staff, Ned Almond, got command of the X Corps despite inexperience with assault landings and his own concern that "I can't do two jobs at once." The CINCFE dismissed further discussion: "Oh, we'll all be back [in Tokyo] in two weeks."[7]

At least for MacArthur, the ultimate objective of the Inchon landing transcended the destruction of the North Korean army, seemingly on the verge of its own victory by busting through the Pusan perimeter. The operation was supposed to have a profound effect on the vital center of his geopolitics: "The prestige of the Western world hangs in the balance. Oriental millions are watching the outcome." A slow buildup in the Eighth Army followed by a cautious crossing of the Naktong River would simply not be commensurate with this rare opportunity for a spectacular victory that would provide "a strong magnet in the East." The JCS, with different priorities, felt Korea had become a burden to the defense of Europe. However, like other people stuck with something they did not really want, they seemed to have engaged in wishful thinking about the product at hand. On September 7th, the same day the Joint Chiefs asked MacArthur to reconsider his envelopment, Omar Bradley wrote Louis Johnson: "After the strength of the North Korean forces has been broken . . . south of 38 degrees, . . . operations on the ground should be conducted [only] by South Korean forces. . . . In this connection it is considered that all United States forces should be removed from Korea as early as practicable."[8]

Forrest Sherman gave a timeline to "practicable" when telling Arleigh Burke that his staff responsibilities in theater would last three to four months. Burke actually stayed in CINCFE naval headquarters sixteen months, before being reassigned to Washington halfway through the Korean War. This reveals a lot about Inchon, surely one of the best-conducted military operations of the twentieth century. It was tactically "miraculous" and "flawless," said some former skeptics, among them Joe Collins, who would now call it "the masterpiece of one man, General Douglas MacArthur." Prevailing fears to the contrary, the narrow channel to the harbor was not mined. Fire support was nearly perfect; the disembarkation was conducted virtually as drawn, only twenty-five fatalities. Unfortunately Inchon was also a failure, at least at a strategic level. It certainly did not end the war.[9]

Some 50,000 North Koreans escaped across their southern border, partly because personal agendas and prewar resentments affected execution of the plan. Tokyo headquarters, a place of luxury, had treated even Colonel John ("Mike") Michaelis, a decorated paratrooper, "like an absolute bum because I was in Eighth Army." He became a national hero for beating back penetrations around the Pusan perimeter, the most important campaign of the entire war. Lieutenant General Walton ("Johnnie") Walker, commander of the Eighth Army, still felt his force had something to prove. He was touchy, proud, and prone to public posturing, much like his mentor, George S. Patton. Complaints from MacArthur about a tardy transition to offensive operations north of the Naktong did little for his temperament. Walker felt he faced 90 percent of the enemy but had to ration ammunition because Ned Almond, his hated rival for recognition, got overwhelming support at Inchon to face down "a handful of green troops." Once the Eighth Army got across the river several days after Almond's landing, it captured some 9,000 prisoners. It might have gotten substantially more if Walker had not concentrated on linking up with the X Corps outside Seoul: shades of Patton's Third Army rescuing the 101st Airborne at the Battle of the Bulge in 1945.[10]

Almond, with whom Walker was constantly at odds, was exceptionally brave, self-centered, and blunt. One officer on his staff called him "the cruelest man I've ever run into." An aide named Alexander Haig said he was "the most reckless man I have ever known." Almond, obviously primed, had something to prove—or disprove in his case. He had compiled what *Time* magazine called a "spotty" record as a division commander in Italy during World War II. For this he blamed the War Department, MacArthur's own bugbear, for sending him so-called defectives, as he characterized African Americans from his native South. That helps explain his devotion to MacArthur, the "only [man] who has ever given me such a chance" at the major command in the major operation of a war. Almond thought him the greatest soldier of the twentieth century, although "hard to compare the present day with the time of Napoleon, Caesar, or Hannibal." Per the CINCFE 's wishes, Almond was supposed to occupy Seoul by September 25th, exactly three months after the conflict began. That was reminiscent of MacArthur's hope to grab a symbolic headline by liberating Manila on 26 January 1945, his sixty-fifth birthday. Then, there was to have been a triumphal celebration with the general reviewing his soldiers marching down the main boulevard. However, MacArthur could not quell rear-guard resistance from Japanese marines until March 3rd, by which time the city was largely in ruins. Meanwhile much of the Japanese army managed to flee into the mountains of Northern Luzon, where over 110,000 of the enemy held out for months, if not the rest of the war.[11]

The escape of a substantial body of Imperial Japanese soldiers foretold what would happen in Korea during the Inchon operation. General Walker, if allowed to plan the US/UN breakout, would have landed at Kunsan, a day away from the Eighth Army along the Naktong. His opinion, against Inchon, had little bearing on Almond or MacArthur, who were subject to emotional temptations over political-geographical objectives such as Seoul that diverted them from the enemy's army, the decisive point in most military plans. Walker would have bypassed the city, partly from memory of bogging down in Metz, an urban fortress that cost his World War II command over 2,500 casualties in late 1944. Six years later, field-grade officers in marine, navy, and X Corps staffs identified Seoul as just "an initial objective area"; blocking forces must occupy positions further east. MacArthur, sober-minded after China's intervention, wrote Matt Ridgway in 1951 that the occupation of the capital "would, of course, present certain diplomatic and psychological advantages . . . but its military usefulness is practically negligible."[12]

One finds no such counsel from MacArthur in 1950. He thought the North Koreans would "evaporate very shortly" from the city, unlike Lemuel Shepherd, who jotted in his journal: "It will take a week of fighting before Seoul is secure." Almond, getting reports of "enemy fleeing," ordered posthaste attack, preferably a double envelopment, the CINCFE's favored tactic. Marines still moved deliberately, to Almond's utter frustration. When they got to the capital on September 24th, they faced the bloody resistance the Marine Corps foresaw. Civilians, not the KPA, for whom they were mistaken, had abandoned the area. Artillery, tanks, and "strong defensive positions" lined the streets, where, according to one sergeant, "there were roadblocks at almost every city block." Next day, long marked to be the one of liberation, Almond dutifully issued a command communiqué: "The military defenses of Seoul were broken." Down in a reconnaissance unit a private responded, "It was news to us."[13]

Back on August 23rd, MacArthur told Collins and Sherman: "The seizure of Inchon and Seoul will cut the enemy's supply line and seal off the entire southern peninsula." The first half of the proposition was true, although North Korean logistics already was taking a terrible beating under U.S. air supremacy from Pyongyang to the Pusan perimeter. The latter half was fanciful because the reach of MacArthur's envelopment exceeded his grasp. The X Corps, a bit less than 70,000 men, could barely stretch to Seoul, let alone constitute an anvil 200 miles across Korea. It left a gap of 175 miles and four major mountain passes across the 38th parallel. One doubts this was a shock to MacArthur. He had sensed the inherent weak spot in the operation, judging by his original hope to land forces on both sides of the peninsula, Wonsan as well as Inchon. A major force deposited on the east coast might have produced the barrier of which MacArthur spoke. As it was, he barely had enough sealift for one landing, let alone two, reminiscent of 1944, when he lacked the capacity to land simultaneously at Leyte and Luzon. MacArthur, again having to make do with what he had, proceeded to undertake more than his force could accomplish. It could beat back and seriously damage the enemy army: exactly what he did. The final "destruction of the North Korean Armed Forces," MacArthur's official mission as of September 27th, would have to take place north of the inter-Korean border.[14]

Inchon: Reputation vs. Results

There's no stopping MacArthur now.

DEAN ACHESON TO AVERELL HARRIMAN, SHORTLY AFTER INCHON[15]

One can say that compromise between Truman and MacArthur marked the initial period of the Korean War, from the communist invasion to the Inchon operation. The general stopped making statements about Formosa; the president accepted his campaign plan for Korea. Now, in period number two—from the crossing of the 38th parallel to the Chinese offensive of late November—concession was predominant. The White House deferred to the theater commander who had been a hero after Bataan, despite defeat. After Inchon, his putative superiors treated him much in the manner of his Tokyo subordinates. "MacArthur took military chances that few commanders take and he got away with so many that his own staff and commanders regarded him as God," said a field-grade intelligence officer. "They really thought he could do no wrong."[16]

After subsequent events took a lot of the shine off the MacArthur mystique, the Pentagon, the White House, and the State Department would differ as to who should bare the blame for abdicating authority to the theater commander. Averell Harriman said that "General Bradley and the Chiefs of Staff were afraid of General MacArthur," a depiction not essentially challenged by Joe Collins, although he preferred "somewhat overawed." All this is no mystery considering the CINCFE's readiness to exploit victory—over North Korea or Washington. Carefully cultivated newspapers reported on September 16th: "Sources close to General MacArthur [codename for Courtney Whitney] said both Collins and Sherman opposed the landing at Inchon." The Pentagon press office made an immediate denial, essentially saying what Collins claimed as late as 1975: "We did question MacArthur about it, he defended his position, and ultimately the Joint Chiefs, after we had gotten his plans, gave approval." No, not exactly. The JCS had worried, dallied, and delayed. Thereafter, they were naturally reluctant to oppose their theater commander and be embarrassed again.[17]

Senior civilian officials were no different from their constitutional subordinates in the armed forces, excepting that they often made concessions to MacArthur earlier than did some military men. Truman made a deal over Inchon the first week of August. The State Department signed on by the 25th, when granting him authority to "make operational amphibious landings behind the North Korean lines, north of the 38th parallel" if he wished, just as long as he stayed "well clear of the Russian frontier." Cabinet secretaries, service chiefs, and White House staff would worry that a march toward the Yalu might precipitate Soviet or Chinese intervention. (Bradley told the British military chiefs on October 25th: "We all agree that if the Chinese Communists come into Korea, we get out.") Nervous though Washington was, it could take solace that MacArthur was a "larger than life military figure [who] had so often been right when everyone else had been wrong," as Matt Ridgway described the situation. Acheson called him the "sorcerer of Inchon," along the lines of what Frank Lowe said. He wrote Truman from onboard ship in Inchon harbor that MacArthur pulled "*this* white rabbit out of a hat. . . . I have witnessed a miracle, no less; which many considered impossible. I need not tell *you* of the doubts in many minds concerning the success of this mission."[18]

Washington officialdom, civil and military, might have retained critical judgment by a more careful examination of results. It accepted MacArthur's self-serving characterization of Inchon, expressed again in 1951 by Hanson Baldwin, the influential and well-connected military analyst of the *New York Times*: if it had not been for the grand envelopment at Inchon, "we would now still be holding the Pusan perimeter against a yet undefeated North Korean Army." This assessment is flawed but understandable. In early September 1950, on the eve of Inchon, the U.S. Army suffered the highest weekly casualty rates it sustained during the entire war, including the Chinese ambush in late November or the bloodletting battles of attrition subsequently fought at Heartbreak Ridge or Pork Chop Hill. This did not prove that it had been on the verge of stalemate or defeat. North Korea, in utter desperation, was depleting its last resources in a frantic gamble to win the war while it had anything left, reminiscent of the 77,000 casualties Germany inflicted at the Battle of the Bulge, now known to have been its death rattle on the Western Front.[19]

MacArthur won over common opinion, notwithstanding his failure to deliver the decisive battle he promised. The UN command could have accomplished what it did—throw a crippled enemy out of South Korea—by simply pushing out of the Pusan perimeter, no need for a deep envelopment at all. Even with the detachment of the X Corps, MacArthur had a two-to-one advantage in manpower and five-to-one in armor along the Naktong, not to mention domination from the sea and sky. Aircraft had rained ordnance on the opponent since mid-July, now truly effective. It "had all but stopped movement of enemy troops, armor, and truck convoys during daylight," according to the army's official history. Battleships held the far flanks, in particular the *Missouri*, Harry Truman's favorite means of travel abroad. Its 16" guns fired 2,000-pound shells twenty-eight miles, arriving faster than the speed of sound from beyond the range of sight. North Korean infantry, suddenly caught in a manmade earthquake, would succumb to uncontrollable panic, no small matter for what was the most severely disciplined army in the world.[20]

Only time, care, and captured communist documents could puncture the myth that Inchon saved the day. Joe Collins, in retrospect, would put the operation in true perspective, beginning with the truly decisive action, the defense along the Naktong River. By mid-August, he wrote in his memoir of Korea, "T-34 dominance of the battlefield was definitely at an end"; by mid-September, the North Korean "offensive was spent." Then came the Inchon counteroffensive. The X Corps did "all that actually could be expected of it but it simply could not extend its lines to cover all escape routes." However, in summary, Collins concurred that Inchon "remains a Twentieth Century Cannae," equal to Hannibal's own high-water mark. This hedging is no mystery, Collins having spent so much effort denying he ever opposed Inchon at all. The legendary status of the operation thereby withstood analysis even after analysis took place. One can imagine its reputation in October 1950 and that of its architect, who would maintain that the "principle of envelopment . . . has always proved the ideal method for success by inferior in number but faster moving forces." MacArthur certainly did not want to entertain the proposition that his force was actually larger but not swifter once the enemy got off the main roads and took to the mountain passes. He would dispute the actual force ratio figures when subsequently published by the army's office of military history. "These conclusions are completely unwarranted and based upon figures concocted by the author with little substantiation."[21]

MacArthur obviously had a vested interest in what he said in September 1950—and repeated until he died—that Inchon was "the only hope of wresting the initiative from the enemy." One presumes the Joint Chiefs of Staff did not care that it was "the happiest moment of my life." They still concurred with his immediate conclusion that the operation "completely changed the tide of the battle in South Korea," even if this further cast them in the shadow of their supposed subordinate, the CINCFE. Washington did not grasp that the whole military maneuver really was a pile-on tackle, to use football metaphors in the manner of MacArthur: the KPA ball carrier was already falling down at the Naktong River line of scrimmage. The White House was quick to make amends to the hero of the hour as when Harry Vaughan, through Frank Lowe, sent General MacArthur a communication that "we feel the unfortunate matter of the message to the VFW was due to an overzealous public relations staff member, which happens to the best of us." At the Wake Island conference that October, the administration thought it was in the presence of "a military genius," to quote the secretary of the army. That meant Inchon had accomplished its moral and mental objectives, but not on the particular audience MacArthur specified. A lightning strike from an unexpected direction that heaped contempt upon the enemy was supposed to have an enormous "effect on Oriental peoples." The problem for the subsequent war effort was that Washington was more intimidated than Beijing.[22]

A lot had happened since June 29th, when President Truman told the secretary of the army that MacArthur could have "all the authority he needs . . . to keep the North Koreans from killing the people we are trying to save," except for one ironclad limitation: "He is not to go north of the 38th parallel." On September 9th, an NSC report proposed that if the enemy rejected peace terms, the UN commander be "directed [to] continue operations north with major forces for the purpose of occupying North Korea." Policy drafts are one thing; serious preparations are another, especially when one could hope that Inchon would end the entire war. In October, American ground forces headed north with useless maps and without winter clothing. This would not present a major problem as long as the United Nations conducted the short-term cleanup then foreseen. Washington and CINCFE headquarters might have considered the retrospective wisdom of an enlisted man: "The mess and confusion of combat are things that don't readily lend themselves to planning."[23]

Pursuit toward the Yalu

One day [in late October] I Company fell out for some kind of ceremony and "passed in review." When we lined up together the platoons looked no larger than squads. We became quite emotional. We asked ourselves, "Is this all that's left?"

FIFTH CAVALRY REGIMENT PRIVATE FIRST CLASS VICTOR FOX, N.D.[24]

In late September, Douglas MacArthur told a prominent correspondent that "as a matter of fact, if you stay on here [in Korea], you will be wasting your valuable time." Joe Alsop, having covered the recapture of Seoul, agreed that the war was all but over. He returned to America to write columns espousing the "liberation" of the communist North, an idea already tempting Harry Truman. The president's political rhetoric had long had "grandiose" and "sweeping" passages, to the dismay of George Kennan, leading light of State Department policy planning. The Truman Doctrine of 1947 declared "that it must be the policy of the United States to support free people who are resisting subjugation by armed minorities or by outside pressures." In late August 1950, this morphed into presidential instructions for State and Defense to begin preparing plans to unify the whole peninsula, free of communism. With the enemy reeling in September, liberating a satellite could provide an attractive platform in the upcoming congressional election, much like saving Greece helped in 1948. The American public supported crossing the border by five to three, not to mention swing voters of Eastern European extraction still angry with Democrats about Yalta and Soviet occupation of their ancestral homeland. They could always hope that North Korea would set a precedent for Poland, somewhat the way Truman had sent the XXIV Corps to Seoul in 1945, after Warsaw fell behind the Iron Curtain.[25]

The Pentagon, while advising "caution and discretion," still favored pursuit. A mop-up operation ensuring total victory could free it from further duty on the peninsula. North Korea, if left to reconstitute, could strike at its convenience, not unlike the Soviets always eyeing Berlin. The State Department, while united in June for the commitment to Korea, was more equivocal despite potential fallout from Republican charges of plans to "subvert our military victory." Department hawks—in particular Dean Rusk, assistant secretary for the Far East—did not want aggression to escape serious penalty. Its doves, such as Kennan, feared operations north of the border could precipitate the war with Russia or China that Washington felt it was fighting to avoid.[26]

The result of this mixture of hope and fear was NSC guidance to MacArthur described as "a matter of policy," rather than specifying "in no circumstances," a phrase the government excised from an early draft. It told the general to destroy North Korea's armed forces and hold its territory, the Pentagon position since July 31st. Only South Korean troops were supposed to operate in the provinces along the Yalu, per Acheson's modification of the military proposal for the "pacification and occupation of all Korea." No one, however, drew a wall U.S. soldiers could never breach, aside from the border of the PRC or the USSR. American action, presumably restrained, would not provoke their intervention. If either communist power did enter the war, MacArthur was to stop in place and await instructions, as if military circumstances would not dictate decisions on the spot. When Acheson's personal assistant pointed out the ambiguity, the secretary of state replied: "For God's sake, how old are you? Are you willing to take on the Joint Chiefs?"[27]

Foreign service officers discussed their misgivings about this compromise in State Department corridors. The secretary of state, meanwhile hoping for the best, said, "[I]f we were lucky and neither the Russians nor the Chinese intervened in North Korea, General MacArthur could act consistently with our overall political plans." Rather than dwell on the danger, Acheson took the opportunity to turn his attention to his first love, matters having to do with Europe. George Marshall, the new secretary of defense, would handle Mac-Arthur. Unfortunately, his personal messages to the CINCFE, never known to Acheson, would add more confusion to Washington's equivocation: good intentions, bad results.[28]

In almost all other cases with all other people, George Marshall was emotionally aloof. He did not resort to charm, whether out of principle or from recognition that he lacked the knack MacArthur honed to a fine art. Marshall tersely forced dozens of officers he had known for decades to retire when he was army chief of staff in the Second World War. They were too old for the stress and the strain of battle: "I have been absolutely cold-blooded in this business." Younger men rising to the top were not treated with much more empathy; for instance, Eisenhower, told after Normandy: "You're not doing too badly, so far." MacArthur got exceptional treatment as to appropriate age for command and Marshall's command and control of a subordinate commander. Marshall visited only once although more conferences were needed because MacArthur's communiqués hardly kept him well informed. By contrast, Marshall's side of the transmission line took far more care and far more time. His chief of plans could send messages in Marshall's name anywhere excepting SWPA. The army chief of staff insisted on writing those himself to ensure they were "phrased in a very polite language." Marshall did much the same thing when secretary of state, 1947–1949. Rather than meet MacArthur, he sent George Kennan to Tokyo but only after a personal tutorial. He was to avoid what Marshall later called the "many prejudices and intense feelings" making MacArthur "supersensitive" to any slight: let him expound on "our world strategy," probably at great length, and maintain a posture of approval, particularly in public.[29]

Marshall, who retired at the end of Truman's first term, returned to government as secretary of defense on 21 September 1950, then far from prime physical health. His formal courtesy strayed into cajolery as he tried to build a bridge to MacArthur. On September 28th, the CINCFE sent the Pentagon a copy of the demand for surrender he proposed to send the enemy "in whatever part of Korea situated." Next day, Marshall sent a personal letter he came to regret: "We want you to feel unhampered tactically and strategically to proceed north of the 38th parallel." (Notice "we," a personal pronoun, rather than "the President of the United States" or "the Department of Defense.") Nothing indicated what MacArthur could not do: leeway and license to a man of ambition, courage, and willpower. On the 30th, MacArthur (not Marshall) clarified how far north "north of the 38th parallel" might be: "Unless and until the enemy capitulates, I regard all of Korea open for our military operations." On October 1st, the day MacArthur broadcast the demand for capitulation, he reiterated to DOD: "If the enemy fails to accept the terms of surrender set forth, our forces in due process of [the ensuing] campaign will seek out and destroy the enemy's armed forces in whatever part of Korea they may be located."[30]

This message traffic set a pattern lasting to December. The theater commander was far more clear to Washington about his plans than Washington was to him about its stipulations. Marshall acted as if praise could fill the vacuum in command, as when sending MacArthur a note simply signed "Marshall," no hint of higher rank, in "a personal tribute to the courageous campaign you directed in Korea." (Inchon was "the perfect strategical operation.") The CINCFE immediately reciprocated, "[T]hanks George." He praised his nominal superior for "the perfect unity of cooperation which has always existed in our mutual relationships and martial endeavors." All this reminds one of the way Franklin Roosevelt once tried to handle Chiang Kai-shek: long on compliments and positive mental attitude; short on blunt warnings about withdrawing support. Marshall had thought this futile when it came to the KMT. Paul Nitze and Acheson would admit the same thing in 1954 when discussing the right way to have dealt with the CINCFE. If the Department of Defense had sent the general an order to stop "and had cleared that with the president in advance so that there wasn't any problem about whether the president said something else at Wake [discussed below] or not, MacArthur would have obeyed it, because," they agreed, "he was the kind of fellow who would obey a specific, concrete order even though he'd do every darned thing he could to weave his own way underneath."[31]

In October 1950, before the benefit of hindsight, everyone in the government avoided preemptive language that would have created a confrontation with MacArthur, seemingly a senseless action after Inchon. Marshall in a message to the CINCFE agreed the operation "virtually terminated the struggle." Frank Lowe confirmed on the 8th in a letter to Truman: "The enemy has no air forces, no artillery worthy of its name, and troops with little or no skill in musketry. It's a strange war, if one chooses to dignify it as 'war.' To me, it has degenerated [into] bushwhacking." This feeling of triumph set the tone for

Truman's first (and last) face-to-face meeting with MacArthur, that taking place at Wake Island on the 15th. George Marshall would not attend, nor would Dean Acheson, who found "the whole idea" of traipsing off to see MacArthur "distasteful." It "did not seem wise" to treat him like "a foreign sovereign," although he "had many of the attributes." The absence of the senior cabinet officials responsible for national security may have primed an atmosphere of camaraderie between the president and the theater commander. It did little to enhance Washington's control of activities in Korea—apparently not the main purpose of the conference, as MacArthur quickly sensed.[32]

In August, MacArthur went to Formosa on his own initiative when the North Korean offensive was in high gear. In October, when he was conducting what he called "merely a mop-up operation," the general was enraged at "being summoned for political reasons," no matter that he already maintained "there are no organized army enemy units in the rest of North Korea." Marshall's short message on the 10th telling him of the meeting at Wake Island only said the president would discuss "the rehabilitation of Korea . . . as well as other matters." This cryptic description was not likely to dispel suspicion of a photo opportunity to pose with the hero of the hour, nor should it. No one on the National Security Council had proposed this conference with MacArthur, although the JCS felt the need to remind him of the possibility of Chinese intervention. The meeting was a product of political staff thinking about "good election-year stuff," particularly when partisan critics of the administration long had urged Truman to go get MacArthur's views on the Far East. The president balked at the suggestion out of pride of office and some reluctance to engage in politics while Americans were fighting in Korea. A special counsel soothed his conscience by reminding him that in 1944 (the midst of World War II), Franklin Roosevelt had trekked off to Hawaii to meet MacArthur on the eve of a national election, that one with Truman also on the ticket.[33]

Averell Harriman, once again the mediator, landed on the island before the rest of Truman's entourage. He proceeded to MacArthur's quarters, where he explained "the strong support the President had given him for the [Inchon] operation," meaning Truman had fulfilled his side of the bargain Harriman had engineered two months before. MacArthur, until then, may not have known or thought that Truman steered Inchon through a JCS minefield. He must have sensed a new opportunity for a new understanding to preclude interference with his plans to conclude the war with the total conquest of the enemy, certainly not farfetched. "The President wanted to be very sure that General MacArthur was being properly supported," said Secretary of the Army Frank Pace, the senior DOD official at Wake Island. "I think that he could see that if there were some problem that would arise, the allegation could arise, 'It happened because we hadn't done our job back in Washington.'"[34]

Americans tend to equate politicization of military operations with restraining, not supporting, a commander in the field. Take Harry Truman, a very

Truman, MacArthur, and MacArthur's military secretary, Courtney Whitney, conferring at Wake Island on 15 October 1950. To perpetuate the good feelings manifested at the meeting, Truman soon promoted Whitney to major general. *Courtesy of the MacArthur Memorial Library.*

typical American, describing Hannibal: "the greatest general in all history," defeated because his own government "would not support him." The president could have drawn a different lesson from the Second Punic War, one less accommodating to military initiative. Hannibal's obsession to conquer Rome created a reaction in which the enemy resolved, under mortal threat, "Carthage must be destroyed." MacArthur, also obsessed with total victory, could seem another Hannibal, especially after his own Cannae at Inchon. The danger in that parallel did not appear to Truman, although worried about war with Moscow or Beijing. The president was primed to cooperate with, not confront, the CINCFE, who was ready to reciprocate in a public pronouncement: "I don't know any field commander in the history of war who has had more complete and admirable support from the agencies in Washington."[35]

That compliment, while written by Harriman's staff, was virtually a copy of MacArthur's press release to mollify Washington after endorsing Chiang Kai-shek. Truman was not impressed in early August. Mid-October was another story. Acheson, who met with the president right after Wake Island, recorded that Truman "had been aware of the possibility of things going wrong and was therefore particularly glad that all of the pitfalls had been avoided." That was the typical reaction to meeting MacArthur, at least when on his good behavior. "Without any doubt his personality makes one of the most charming first impressions I have encountered," said the chief foreign correspondent for the *New York Times*. The White House delegation at Wake Island would have agreed. Dean Rusk thought the general "could not have been more agreeable," apparently mistaking good manners for compliance. So did Harry Truman, the man who really mattered. He found MacArthur "very deferential and seemed fully aware that he was talking with his Commander-in-Chief." The president concluded: "I liked him."[36]

With MacArthur out to turn his considerable charm on the president, one wonders how he could have failed to salute him on the tarmac, an incident mentioned whenever Wake Island comes up. One thing is clear, aside from the fact that every reporter covering the conference noticed the gaffe. It was not typical MacArthur behavior. When Frank Pace, barely in his thirties, visited Tokyo shortly before the general's dismissal in April 1951, he wondered if the CINCFE would seat him on his right, where the secretary of the army belongs as his constitutional superior. MacArthur did precisely what protocol required, although "when he was Chief of Staff of the U.S. Army, I was at Hill School in Pottstown, Pennsylvania." Why was formal etiquette at fault at Wake Island, whether greeting the president with a firm handshake, instead of a salute, or declining an invitation to stay for lunch from the president who came half-way round the world? Omar Bradley would call this "insulting . . . whether intended or not."[37]

MacArthur rejected an invitation that could have been imposed by the president's mere presence because the general was not so brazen to pick up and

Truman, in good spirits, meets his national security team on 18 October 1950, shortly after returning from Wake Island. Left to right: W. Averell Harriman, presidential advisor; George Marshall, secretary of defense; Dean Acheson, secretary of state; Philip Jessup, ambassador at large (partly obscured); John Snyder, secretary of the treasury; Frank Pace, secretary of the army; and General Omar Bradley, chairman of the Joint Chiefs of Staff. *Abbie Rowe, National Park Service, courtesy of the Harry S. Truman Library.*

leave before someone of superior rank. What he did is reminiscent of October 1945, when MacArthur said he could not come to Washington for honors the government planned to bestow. Then he cited "the extraordinary dangers" lurking in Japan. Now, virtually five years to the day, he said that he had to get back to running the war in Korea, although scarcely credible considering other comments that a "poorly trained, led, and equipped" opponent was "pursuing a forlorn hope." Contrast this with MacArthur's behavior in early August 1950, when there was a true military crisis around the Pusan perimeter. He and his staff took two days off to visit Chiang in Formosa, not his usual procedure for trips out of Japan. MacArthur always managed to return from Korea (and now Wake Island) the same day he arrived.[38]

Perhaps at Wake Island a flash of anger was seeping through MacArthur's persona of courtesy: Dr. Jekyll having another Mr. Hyde moment. One could also consider what Pace has said: "MacArthur never made an uncalculated or emotional move." If so, the general was probably sending the president a subtle message to the effect: you will have to deal with me much the way we came to an agreement on Inchon, a triumph that prevented your opponents from blaming defeat in Korea on you. I will endorse the administration right now, three weeks before an election against Republicans I actually favor. In return, I expect carte blanche on the peninsula, never mind the self-effacing salutation I will give you when you leave, quite properly before me. "Goodbye sir," the *New York Times* recorded. "It has been a real honor to talk with you."[39]

Truman had his own concerns at Wake Island, aside from the upcoming election and lunch with MacArthur. Now that the general's command was about to capture Pyongyang, the capital of North Korea, the president sought confirmation that neither Russia nor China would intervene. "I have been worried about that" were among his first words to MacArthur when out of earshot from reporters. Recent change in policy reflected this alarm. NSC guidelines had been that the United States would deliver "air and sea attacks in Communist China directly related to the enemy effort in Korea." Acheson, mixing threat with reassurance, told Beijing through Indian intermediaries that it "need not fear US military action unless it lends itself to indirect or direct aggression against neighboring countries." In early October, when U.S. armed forces were just about to cross the 38th parallel, China sent back a warning that it "did not intend to sit back with folded hands and let the Americans come up to [our] border." This did not stop Truman in his tracks but did cause new directives to MacArthur as of October 9th, two days after crossing into North Korea. The general would now have to "obtain authorization from Washington prior to taking any military action against Chinese territory." On the other hand, he received wider latitude against its ground forces, previously reason to stop and await DOD instruction. If "major Chinese Communist units [enter Korea] without prior announcement, you should continue the action as long as, in your judgment, action by forces now under your control offers a reasonable chance of success."[40]

For Truman, always wanting to avoid military conflict with China, this scenario might have led to reconsideration of further movement north. He could rest assured and therefore not impede MacArthur as long as he shared MacArthur's faith in MacArthur's infallibility. On July 1st, still skeptical, the president called the general a "supreme egotist who regarded himself something as a God." Now, after Inchon, MacArthur crossed the dichotomies by which Truman separated professional soldiers: he had gone from the bad into the good, if not the truly great, heretofore reserved for Hannibal and Lee. The president even asked MacArthur about "possible Chinese interference in Indochina"—a long way from his immediate responsibility in Northeast Asia. The CINCFE's staff had tracked the units and location of some 400,000 soldiers present in Manchuria by mid-October, quite an achievement in the face of directives precluding air reconnaissance over the mainland. They could not identify purpose or objective, political questions "beyond the purview of local collective intelligence," as Charles Willoughby, the G-2, professed several times, including the day before MacArthur met Truman on Wake Island.[41]

MacArthur had no such reservations, nor did Truman, who should have relied on CIA and State Department political intelligence assets for assessments of communist thinking. He asked the theater commander "what are the chances for Chinese or Soviet interference" and accepted his reply: "Very little." A wily politician such as Franklin Roosevelt would have known there was no authoritative answer to the question posed. He still would have posed it to shift blame to the theater command if something went wrong. Truman took this way out after China intervened in late November, but not from malice or forethought. He sincerely held that MacArthur "made his march into North Korea without the knowledge that he should have had of the Chinese coming in. That's what caused most of his trouble."[42]

MacArthur did not have a great record in geostrategic prognostication, judging by what he said in June 1939: people who think "Japan covets these islands [the Philippines] . . . fail fully to credit the logic of the Japanese mind." Truman, however, was not anxious to question an oracle who told him what he wanted to hear about China. "I have seldom seen him in better spirits," Omar Bradley would recall. "It was a relief to all of us that the Korean War would soon be over." The Pentagon had activated electronic intercepts focused on the mainland but still knew little about the theater other than what MacArthur had told it. One way or the other, 90 percent of the information flowing into DOD came from sources in the Far East Command, not to be blamed, according to MacArthur, when he apportioned blame in December. Then he placed failure to predict Chinese intervention at the feet of "political intelligence," that is, other agencies of the federal government. "Field intelligence," meaning theater command, "was so handicapped [with restrictions on air reconnaissance] that once the decision to commit was made, this new enemy could move forward . . . without fear of detection."[43]

Mid-October was another story, or should one say another play. MacArthur at Wake Island, with a great actor's instinct, knew what role to perform and words to say, regarding Formosa as well as Korea. "I supposed my letter to the Veterans of Foreign Wars had been right down the line of the president's policy. Had I not thought so," he told Harriman, "I would not have sent it." The clear implication of this statement was that MacArthur would not defy Truman—nor should he. Truman gave no indication he would resist MacArthur. The president told him Formosa was "a closed issue," thereby foreclosing an ideal opportunity to warn the general face to face that he must clear all policy statements. Despite Truman's pretense to be an "ass kicker," he was polite, pleasant, and accommodating, except when reporters back in Washington asked, "Are you now in complete agreement with General MacArthur on Formosa?" This question had merit regarding abdication of authority, probably why Truman snapped, "He is loyal to the President in his foreign policy . . . wish a lot of your papers were."[44]

MacArthur told Harriman at the end of the Wake Island meeting, "Newspaper accounts [of the president] do not do him justice." The whole conference had been steeped in optimism and mutual flattery. Truman announced, "There was no disagreement between General MacArthur and myself"—essentially true because there was no real discussion of the original order restricting military operations near the Yalu border. Nor did anyone thrash out what would be done if Mao and Stalin were not as passive as MacArthur presumed. Dean Rusk, the senior State Department official in the absence of Acheson, pointed out that Chinese intervention "might not be impossible," hardly strong words. Still, "that young whipper-snapper asking questions" (as MacArthur privately described Rusk) could not force an airing of fallback plans. Truman passed him a pointed message: "I want to get out of here before I get into trouble."[45]

No wonder an "effervescent" MacArthur was "at his sparkling best" on the plane ride back to Tokyo, to quote a fellow passenger. Trouble, nonetheless, was on the horizon. Truman's deference to the theater commander, so reported in Beijing, confirmed the hard-line proposition that the PRC had no choice but war because the MacArthur clique allied with Chiang Kai-shek personified U.S. policy. That was not correct but was not unforeseen a week before Wake Island. Philip Jessup warned Acheson that Moscow and Beijing were apt to misinterpret a Truman-MacArthur meeting as proof of American intent to maintain its foothold north of the 38th parallel, if not cross the Yalu River. The secretary's closest friend at the State Department had been a professor of international law, hardly formal training for Marxist dialectics. He still sensed enemy thinking, at least until direct exposure to MacArthur's personality: "very cordial and full of self-confidence, particularly his statements about the Chinese. He was," said Jessup, "absolutely sure what the situation was and would be."[46]

Washington would have been better off if more attentive to the fact that communist regimes underestimate the competition, contradictions, and confusion in U.S. policy decisions. In August 1949, Mao declared that there was "not any lack of desire on the part of the Truman-Marshall group, the ruling clique of American imperialism, to launch direct aggression upon China." The president, since then, according to the PRC, "sent General MacArthur to confer clandestinely with Chang Kai-shek on concrete measures for using Taiwan as a base to wage war." This was certainly news to the White House, replete with its own fears of what MacArthur and Chiang might have done behind closed doors. *Isvestia*, official news organ of the Soviet government, still had no doubt about Wake Island, where Truman and MacArthur planned to "expand American aggression." Meanwhile in Beijing, the press was calling the conference "the final phase" leading up to outright attack.[47]

Notwithstanding Sino-Soviet ideology, Wake Island did not entirely settle America's course of military action. State, Defense, MacArthur, and the White House exchanged message traffic for the next five weeks, but ambiguity still ruled the roost. This was acceptable as long as all parties believed enemy resistance was quickly winding down. Individuals then could return to pursuits to which they had been dedicated before war diverted their concentration. Truman refocused his attention on the fall election. Some generals returned to literary avocations. Omar Bradley edited his memoir of World War II, scheduled for publication in early 1951. Charles Willoughby did much the same thing with MacArthur's official World War II history of the Southwest Pacific Area of Operations, "dearer to his heart," said the U.S. ambassador in Seoul, "than keeping touch with what was going on in Korea."[48]

Willoughby had come to MacArthur's attention in 1935, when teaching military history at Fort Leavenworth. That subject was a major interest of this army chief of staff but a minor matter at the army's staff college, which scheduled the class right after lunch, in what was generally known as "the slumber hour." The instructor defied all odds by keeping his students awake. "That intrigued MacArthur," Willoughby later said. In 1938, when MacArthur was field marshal for the Philippines, Willoughby applied "for the privilege of serving under you directly." He sent a copy of the history text he created for the infantry school, Fort Benning, that happened to begin with a quote from MacArthur: "More than most professions, the military is forced to depend upon intelligent interpretation of the past for signposts charting the future. . . . [It illustrates] the basic and inviolable laws of the art of war." The recipient found the publication "fascinating" and replied that he read it "at one sitting," presumably including the lesson analyzing Japan's crossing of the Yalu River against Russia in 1904.[49]

Next year, 1939, Willoughby joined MacArthur's staff and published *Maneuver in War*, a book that made his reputation as an officer "with a flair for the drama of military history." It also revealed his contempt for Chinese military forces at war with Japan: "a tell-tale index of the efficacy of troops with adequate modern weapons over improvised organizations." This opinion was also on display in October 1950, when by Willoughby's own count some 400,000 soldiers were assembling in Manchuria, 244,000 being regulars constituting thirty-eight Chinese divisions. He was still astonished in early November when Beijing conducted a limited probe of US/UN positions. He initially held that captured prisoners were actually Koreans, what one might expect from this expert on Central European languages, cultures, and armies really hired to be the command's historian. Thereafter more cautious, Willoughby would report in mid-November 64,200 Chinese soldiers south of the Yalu plus "a continued build-up," virtually twice the estimate of MacArthur, essentially his own intelligence officer.[50]

Matt Ridgway, far from dismissing Willoughby as a buffoon, would say that the "intelligence he had of the Chinese order of battle . . . was very accurate." Still, the day before China attacked in late November, the Far East Command Intelligence Summary saw "indications" that "point to the possibility of a withdrawal of CCF [Chinese Communist Forces] to the Yalu River or cross the border into Manchuria." This was consistent with MacArthur's long-held opinion, that "relatively little effort will be required to turn the tide in China." That itself was not uncommon in military circles in the fall of 1950, when old China hands told Marine rookies about to face the enemy, "Just give them a carton of cigarettes and they'll surrender." The recent communist victory over the KMT did little to enhance the reputation of the successor regime. PLA superiority was thought to result from the poor quality of the competition, except among a handful of American observers such as Major General David Barr. The commander of the Seventh Infantry Division had led the last advisory mission on the Chinese mainland, where he reported that the communists used ideology to overcome "faulty Nationalist traits and characteristics. . . . Their [own] leaders are men of proven ability. . . . The morale and fighting spirit of the troops is very high." Barr, however, was known to be so polite he was "almost entirely lacking in force." No one ever said that of his immediate superior, Ned Almond, soon enjoining Barr's division to go "all the way to the Yalu. Don't let a bunch of Chinese laundrymen stop you."[51]

In May 1975, Averell Harriman said: "Willoughby's intelligence may have been wrong, but General MacArthur's knowledge of the Chinese was obsolete." In October 1950, elements of the Eighth Army began overrunning dumps of ammunition incompatible with North Korean arms supplied by the Soviet Union. ("When you asked the natives, they would say, 'It's for the Chinese.'") Nonetheless, on the 17th, two days after MacArthur returned to Japan from his meeting with Truman, the general moved the northern boundary for U.S. operations to the Songjin-Sonchon line, approximately forty miles south of the Yalu River. This was north of the limit the Joint Chiefs of Staff cited back on September 27th. If the Pentagon noticed, it could take heart that the CINCFE still specified that only South Koreans were to cross the new boundary, although this restriction did not last long. On October 24th, the latest line of restraint became the newest line of departure as MacArthur enjoined field commanders "to drive forward with all speed and with full utilization of all their force." He forwarded no copy to the Pentagon, for which he got a mild reminder that the Joint Chiefs "would like to be informed . . . as your action is a matter of some concern here." They only heard about his order from an undisclosed leak in the Far East theater. The JCS reminded the CINCFE of their original message that no one but South Koreans were to approach the border. MacArthur reminded them that, in their original words, that was "a matter of policy" and "this entire subject was covered in my conference at Wake Island." No one in the Pentagon could refute this claim without trekking to the Oval Office for information about the closed conversation, some forty minutes long, that the CINCFE privately had with the commander in chief. "I don't know what was discussed between the President and General MacArthur," Omar Bradley later admitted to the Senate.[52]

On October 26th, the day after the MacArthur-JCS exchange ended in favor of freedom for MacArthur to continue his pursuit, Truman entered the discussion, although through the national press corps, not the chain of command. A reporter asked the president "whether we plan to go directly to the border?" He replied: "The Korean divisions will occupy . . . the whole northern frontier of Korea." Question: "Not the American troops?" Answer: "No. That is my understanding." Truman had felt no need to read the message traffic to MacArthur since the departure of Louis Johnson from the Defense Department in mid-September. The president, no "crazy politician" if he could possibly help it, had turned the Washington end of the war over to "General Marshall," as he was always addressed, even when secretary of state. MacArthur, a five-star general still on active military duty, reentered the discussion on October 29th with a depiction of events at odds with what Truman stated at his news conference. "Dear Mr. President," the CINCFE wrote. "It is my current estimate that the next week or so should see us fairly well established in the border area, after which it shall be my purpose as I outlined during the Wake Island conference, to withdraw American troops as rapidly as possible. . . . The country's interests had been well served through [our] better mutual understanding and exchange of views."[53]

Fear, Ambition, Concession, Aggression: Washington, MacArthur, and Mao

The military activity of Chinese troops in Korea so far is not sufficiently extensive to indicate a plan for major operations.

SPECIAL ASSISTANT, STATE DEPARTMENT
INTELLIGENCE, 17 NOVEMBER 1950[54]

The debate as to whether U.S. troops would proceed all the way to the border did not conclude with the discourse between General MacArthur, President Truman, and the Joint Chiefs of Staff. One more party had yet to be heard. On November 1st, fifty miles south of the Yalu, elements of two Chinese divisions struck some 800 soldiers of the Eighth Cavalry Regiment, a surprise to both sides. Mao Tse-tung's target was the South Korea army: so-called puppet forces guarding America's flanks. When they suffered a crushing blow, MacArthur was supposed to stop his advance and give China time to prepare a fortified defense in depth. The CINCFE, hit rather advertently, fell back for the next five days and wired Washington: "men and material in large force . . . pouring across all bridges over the Yalu."[55]

MacArthur had been taking the initiative on his own authority since June 27th. On November 6th, he ordered the destruction of the Yalu bridge network, paying scant attention to existing directives against dropping bombs on China. The U.S. air force commander, who received the mission and knew the rules of engagement, wired the Joint Chiefs. They were certainly not indifferent to MacArthur's situation, no matter what he may have thought about the so-called Marshall clique. The JCS would remind the secretary of defense of NSC documents the president approved in September specifying that the U.S. command "should be authorized to take appropriate air and naval action outside Korea against Communist China." However, that was only policy in a broad sense. The JCS did not have the power to approve the operation in question. It ordered MacArthur to "postpone all bombing of targets within five miles of [the] Manchurian border." He immediately wired back to bring the matter "immediately to the attention of the President," quite understandable since Averell Harriman had alluded to Truman backing Inchon against all opposition.[56]

There was added reason for MacArthur to expect accommodation from the president on November 6th, next day being the congressional election, no time for a catfight with a theater commander. The CINCFE warned Washington that "the restrictions you are imposing" would create a military disaster. Unstated was the offer Harriman carried to Tokyo in August—that Truman would support the general in every way he could, the sort of thing Jefferson Davis told Robert E. Lee. True, the president had then been talking strictly about Korea while telling MacArthur he could not attack China to preempt its attack on Formosa. Now that UN forces were approaching the Yalu, the line between Korea and the PRC was difficult to draw. Truman still tried to draw it by granting MacArthur permission to bomb only the southern or Korean side of the bridges, rather impracticable for high-speed aircraft operating in the face of enemy fire. The planes cut only four of the twelve spans in question, but the central political fact as of November 7th was that Truman modified the rules of engagement in response to MacArthur's pressure and appeal. A so-called lesson learned probably misled the CINCFE in due course. He would later push for an all-out attack on China that Truman never would concede.[57]

Some people well acquainted with MacArthur mention his "mercurial temperament," a trait pronounced in November 1950 in regard to the Chinese communist army. On the 8th, in a personal message to George Marshall, he said that "the Chinese people have become militarized. . . . They now make first class soldiers" and are in the process of "developing competent staffs and commanders." His warning about their "dominant aggressive tendencies" was a far cry from his previous contempt for this "grossly overrated" army. It also was the sort of thing Marshall had heard before—in another war against another enemy after MacArthur redeployed to Australia in 1942. The latter then predicted that if not reinforced with men, ships, and planes posthaste, his whole area of operations would be subjected to onslaughts "similar to those which produced the disasters that have successively overwhelmed our forces in the Pacific since the beginning of the war."[58]

MacArthur did not exude optimism until 1943, when he found that forecasts of victory were a better way of getting what he wanted than predictions of catastrophe. In late November 1950, after China's full-scale intervention in Korea, the dismal message MacArthur sent Marshall on the November 8th reappeared—often word for word—in personal letters to close supporters as well as MacArthur's subsequent address to Congress after his relief in 1951. Suddenly, however, on November 9th that type of threat assessment vanished for three weeks, apparently overcome by MacArthur's ambition, his emotion, and his disdain for opponents unable to conduct "modern, three-dimensional warfare": air and sea as well as ground forces. U.S. and Chinese units broke contact. Military headquarters—in Washington and Tokyo—had to ask and answer how many Chinese troops were involved, where were they positioned, and what was their mission. The Pentagon wired MacArthur that "this new situation indicates your objective . . . 'the destruction of the North Korean Armed Forces' may have to be reexamined."[59]

This threat to MacArthur's great finale was about the worst communication he could receive, although a reasonable response to his own message that a "potential buildup of enemy strength [could reach] a point of threatening the safety of the command." Having made that remark on November 7th, let alone his comments about "first class" enemy soldiers, the CINCFE could not simply order a hasty charge to the border, at least in those exact words. He therefore advised mounting "a reconnaissance-in-force," a favorite term also used in February 1944, as if his high-risk landing in the Admiralty Islands was a probe of Japanese positions. In mid-November 1950, the phrase was a smokescreen to resume his drive in the manner of mid-October. Officially, MacArthur maintained that "only through such an offensive can an accurate measure of the enemy strength be taken." Actually, he had reverted to the conclusion that some "voluntary personnel" were filling holes in depleted North Korean ranks, nothing particularly new. Months before, MacArthur and military intelligence out of Taipei had reported Chinese communist elements within KPA units, none of them subsequently able to stop the Inchon operation or the capture of Pyongyang.[60]

The North Korean leadership might still escape to Russia or China, maintain a government in exile, and come back across the Yalu—an action to be expected from a regime of former guerrillas experienced with waging war from hideouts in Siberia. MacArthur advised the Pentagon to press forward "to complete victory which I believe can be achieved if our determination and indomitable will do not desert us." He recently had claimed that North Koreans, already beaten, were "only fighting to save face." Willoughby offered a similar hypothesis about the Chinese going through the motions so that they could claim some moral credit for trying to assist Kim Il-sung. One might have thought that the substantial damage the CCF inflicted would have caused headquarters to doubt its expertise on Asian motivation as well as Western military doctrine for conflicts with so-called backward people. MacArthur, however, was chronically reluctant to admit error. He was far more prone to hang on to his predilections with greater intensity.[61]

Standard operating procedure for military action in the age of colonial empire had held that the defense was to be avoided because it raised the prestige of one's military opponents. Those said to have "profound knowledge of the Oriental" took the offensive relentlessly and thereby "cowed whole provinces" of India for rule by the Crown. "Asiatics do not understand such vigor"; they lacked "steadiness in adversity," along with the discipline to practice security measures common to a civilized force, such as patrolling one's perimeter. Arthur MacArthur, "a master of his profession," had taught this essential doctrine at the advanced school for infantry officers and practiced these principles against guerrillas in the Philippines. His son, a Victorian surviving into modernity, toured British military posts with his father as far as the Khyber Pass in 1906. This experience "was without doubt the most important factor of preparation in my entire life."[62]

Passages of MacArthur's fateful message to the VFW drafted in his own hand display viewpoints reminiscent of the sayings by officials of the rajah, such as "never show a sign of hesitation" and "savages must be thoroughly brought to book and cowed or they will rise again." MacArthur himself criticized those who "did not grasp that it is the pattern of Oriental psychology to respect and follow aggressive, resolute, and dynamic leadership" versus one "characterized by timidity and vacillation." His nineteenth-century rhetoric may have seemed rather purple to mid-twentieth-century Americans, but related concepts existed in the State Department. Senior staff of the Office of Northeast Asian Affairs wrote in late August that "the significance in Asia of the unification of Korea under UN auspices would be incalculable. . . . Those who foresee only inevitable Soviet conquest would take hope." A payoff such as that justified the purported risk MacArthur soon ran at Inchon. In late November, with the army deep in North Korea, he again would resort to his favored double envelopment: "The United Nations massive compression envelopment in North Korea against the new Red armies operating there is now approaching its decisive effort [that would] close the vise."[63]

The phrase "new Red Armies" acknowledged something different had taken the field, but no one really knew their size, purpose, and location. This made the potential threat different from that at Inchon, where KPA positions had been identified. Some U.S. officers thought weather and the terrain, virtually by themselves, nullified MacArthur's scheme for converging the army commands east and west of the Taeback Mountains running down the middle of North Korea. The road net between Almond's X Corps and Walker's Eighth Army was a narrow gorge twisting through the high ground. "A platoon of Boy Scouts" could hold up progress, a battalion S-2 told the commander of the Seventh Marines. One might think the mission now reminiscent of Ahab pursuing

Moby Dick. Ned Almond's deputy chief of staff later said he sometimes felt "like I was in a nut house with the nuts in charge." MacArthur nonetheless repeated with assurance on November 25th that the "the giant UN pincer moved according to schedule today." To back off now with total victory at hand would seem to forfeit the aura of invincibility he supposedly won at Inchon. "Asiatics adore a winner and despise a loser," he was fond of saying.[64]

All this made sense provided MacArthur did not meet an opponent with far greater capabilities than the English met in India or his father faced in the Philippines. If he did, then the CINCFE might be grouped with George Armstrong Custer, as Truman did in 1945, when splitting graduates of West Point into the Lees, Pershings, Eisenhowers, and Bradleys as opposed to the "Custers, Pattons, and MacArthur." Custer and MacArthur had records with some outstanding achievements, the reason why they were the youngest generals in the U.S. Army of their respective eras. However, both careers came to a climax when they split their forces to conduct double envelopments versus primitive rowdies bent on escaping their grasp—hardly effective tactics when actually against a large force ready to counterattack.[65]

Signals intelligence focused on Manchuria picked up Chinese government message traffic about raising volunteers to serve in Korea. It was still difficult to acquire tactical information on its light infantry army infiltrating the peninsula while hiding from photo and electronic reconnaissance. Civilian refugees reported construction of enemy positions and "many, many" Chinese. The information was fragmentary, was not quantifiable, and evoked skepticism because not authenticated by Far East command capabilities. If one were searching for a rationale to terminate MacArthur's offensive that fall, he might recall much the same situation occurring that spring. South Koreans operating behind North Korean lines reported substantial activity, predicted imminent attack, but were discounted for lack of U.S. confirmation. Analogues, however, were hardly proof of what might happen in November. MacArthur did not ignore hard facts independently verified on the Korean countryside. Intelligence officers in field and Tokyo headquarters, as well as the last CIA analysis, testify to few facts to ignore, at least in the peninsula area of operations.[66]

MacArthur filled the vacuum with prejudice, intuition, and positive mental attitude—exactly what he did for the Inchon operation. He would have stood in better stead if adopting "worst casing," as did some marine and navy officers now that UN forces were moving north of the Pyongyang-Wonsan line. O. P. Smith passed on to James Doyle "a feeling" that the Chinese "would come into the war." Arleigh Burke and Forrest Sherman began hoarding ships delivering supplies in anticipation of an emergency evacuation, subsequently conducted from North Korea in late December 1950. The performance of the navy in removing the X Corps at Hungnam would be as brilliant as delivering it at Inchon. However, if this component of the Far East command had something more credible than a premonition that proved correct, it was a secret to the national intelligence agencies as well as Douglas MacArthur. Their estimates on November 9th and 24th concluded that the PRC lacked the modern weaponry to undertake a full-scale military action. Its loud propaganda line emphasizing "American impotence in a war with China" seemed geared to intimidation and coercive diplomacy.[67]

Mao once thought the U.S government out "to gain control of all China without fighting" by supplying "pawns" and "running dogs" like Chiang Kai-shek. This was far more than an annoyance but less than a mortal threat, as Washington would "make trouble, fail, make trouble again, [and] fail again till their doom." Mao's apprehension grew in June with the interposition of the Seventh Fleet in the Taiwan Strait, called "an open exposure by the United States of its true imperialist face." The administration never seemed to realize exactly how its change in policy toward Formosa escalated tension with the PRC. Dean Rusk, the State Department's foremost defender of the island, told Chiang's representative in late July that he could not concur with the proposition that "men like Mao Tse-tung would be willing to carry out the orders of the Kremlin rather than work for the welfare of the Chinese people." Presumably, this was not at stake in North Korea, thought to be Stalin's stooge. When the PRC sprang its deadly trap in late November, for which "there is no conceivable justification," Truman thought that "the only explanation is that these Chinese have been misled or forced to further [Stalin's] imperialist designs."[68]

It now seems surprising that Washington was surprised, but China's objectives were not clearly settled. It had maximum and minimum goals, as do most governments in most situations. The minimum, that of keeping a military launching pad out of America's hands, prevailed from the onset of the Korean War in late June until initial military contact with the U.S. army early in November. "If the U.S. imperialists win," Mao told his politburo during this period, "they may get so dizzy with success that they may threaten us." Consequently, he began a major redeployment of his army from staging bases opposite Taiwan to a strategic defense on behalf of North Korea. As if to issue a credible warning to the United States to halt and withdraw, he made no effort to hide his buildup in Manchuria. Indeed, bogus message transmits purposefully painted a larger force than he actually had, closer to 300,000 soldiers than the 450,000 Willoughby reported by October or the 1,000,000 subsequently estimated early in December.[69]

Whatever the United States did north of Pyongyang, Mao felt Washington was building Taiwan as a base from which to attack the mainland. If war was inevitable, the strait was not the best place to wage it. Korea was more advantageous, being adjacent to Soviet bases that could provide airpower, equipment, and logistics to sustain his infantry. The same strategic thinking during the civil war drove the communist side toward "maintaining a defensive posture in the South while waging the offense in the North." Stalin promised help in 1950 but long proved cautious from disinclination for direct confrontation with the

United States. In October he disclosed his air force would not participate. Stalin would later reverse that reversal insofar as providing air defense behind the front lines—but only on a temporarily basis: he told the Chinese that "China must have its own cadre in order to stand on its own feet." More bluntly he told his own politburo: "We are not ready to fight."[70]

Mao must have been disappointed but might have known better. Aggrieved Chinese concluded by the mid-1940s that Moscow was afraid of Washington. Stalin maintained a good Marxist justification behind China's back in late 1950: they were not true communists, only Tito-like revisionists, but still of use to him, particularly now. He egged them on with a ploy also used before the war when Mao seemed reluctant to back Kim Il-sung's plan of attack, a diversion from his own sacred task of Taiwan. Stalin held out support for the invasion of the island, what he had avoided in 1949 on grounds it would cause World War III. Mao came around but still hoped to cross the strait and take Taipei before Kim got to Seoul. His desire was still transparent to Stalin on October 1st, when entreating Mao that military defeat would force America "to abandon Taiwan." It would also keep "the Japanese reactionaries" from restoring their "militaristic potential" in collusion with the United States.[71]

Mao seemed "a strange kind of communist" to Stalin, never being pliant putty for Moscow's foreign policy. The Chinese leader feared his own "open clash" with America in late 1950: "Our whole plan for peaceful construction will be completely ruined" and "malcontents" among the bourgeoisie would exploit discontent. This was not good news for Korean communists, largely defeated according to Mao: they would have to "change the method of the struggle and rely on guerrilla war." Mao was willing to provide the regime a haven, relatively low-risk for Beijing, but not to directly take on the United States armed forces under present circumstances. China first must mass "four times as many troops" and three times U.S. "firepower," although itself then critically short in aviation, artillery, and armor. Mao told Stalin nothing else could "guarantee a complete and thorough destruction of one enemy army."[72]

The Kremlin presumed that Mao had fallen for the "tricks of the Anglo-American block calling for the Chinese to be patient in order to avoid a catastrophe." Stalin pointed to a pledge to provide assistance to Korea made at a time when Mao still maintained that the United States "would not start a third world war over such a small territory." Now cautious in the face of adverse force ratios that October, Mao admonished his field commander: "We should proceed on a practical basis and never try what is impossible." That was reminiscent of his watchword in the Chinese civil war: "Don't fight battles you may lose," a maxim for discretion that had paid big personal and political dividends. Mao became head of the Communist Party and therefore the entire state, whereas rash rivals suffered defeat in the field by taking the offensive without patent advantage. At present, he intended to remain on the defensive until "our troops are fully equipped and well trained, as well as having achieved overwhelming air and land superiority." Then, in early November, Beijing was forced to react when US/UN forces moved within fifty miles of its border. The result was an astonishing success at odds with Mao's old dictum that "there can be no victory in war without advance planning and preparations."[73]

British observers in Hong Kong, a listening post for China, soon noted a different tone in the Communist Party press: talk of "annihilating and repulsing unconsolidated American invading troops" replaced discussion of a "long-term war of attrition." This reflected Mao's rethinking of enemy capabilities. He had suddenly developed great contempt for the U.S. army, easily "dazed and completely demoralized," unfamiliar "with night fighting or hand to hand combat," and able to operate only in open terrain because dependent on "weapons too heavy to be mobilized in the mountains." The worst insult came on November 22nd, three days before Mao launched his all-out assault: "The American forces have lower combat effectiveness than some capable troops of Chiang Kai-shek." One might think this ridiculous overstatement were it not for comments from U.S. officers when in retreat from the Chinese. "We have a cream puff army and not an army of soldiers," read one *New York Times* quotation, dateline November 2nd. MacArthur, too angry to maintain any charm, exploded at Walton Walker, never one of his favorites. "This again reflects the embarrassment at the loose and unbridled comments emanating from your forces." Put on notice, the commander of the Eighth Army was averse to dragging his heels, as he would have done if left to stop at the narrow neck of North Korea, where Walker would have created a buffer between himself and the Chinese.[74]

Mao told Stalin "many comrades believe that here prudence must be displayed." Military officers still felt their force too primitive to inflict on MacArthur anything more than a temporary setback. Party members typically thought more profitable targets were on hand at home: enforce land reform and extend party edict over Tibet and KMT pockets still existing on the mainland. However, Mao and the "small inner clique" taking China into war had a different assessment. "We could," he now said, "eliminate all enemy units," testimony to ideology and the cult of his infallibility that had pervaded party ranks since World War II. Against MacArthur, he planned to use an old tactic previously fashioned against Chiang, one of luring the enemy deep into a devastating ambush.[75]

MacArthur, the JCS, the CIA, and the State Department counted on Mao continuing to recognize his weakness to wage modern war. The CINCFE, while claiming to be on the cutting edge of this military capability, was also relying on inspiration and intuition, rather than hard data and military science. MacArthur "could leap across space and arrive at a conclusion," say authorized biographers and trusted assistants. "He could then leisurely marshal his facts and justify his conclusion in reverse," hence having no need for a staff "except to do the details." Critics like Acheson say Far East headquarters was a "court" of "sycophants" worthy of a potentate. This blurred the most significant difference between MacArthur and Mao, aside from a preference for double envelopments as opposed to lure and destroy. The American had less power to dictate policy. In the final analysis, MacArthur had to sell his opinions to constitutional superiors such as Acheson; no such problem existed for Mao. With effective control of the secret police, the party, and the armed forces, he had "emerged," in the words of a major informant, "as the most powerful emperor in Chinese history."[76]

Mao felt he had a special opportunity in an ideal theater of operations now that the U.S. army was proceeding north of Pyongyang. His force could use its experience and competitive advantage—light infantry in mountainous terrain already identified in a Communist Party publication as "an ideal graveyard for the imperialist invaders." This would forge a "turning point in history" far greater than containing the most recent wave of imperialist expansion, which had been Mao's objective until first military contact with American units. Now he would not only "liberate the whole Korean peninsula." He would dismantle Washington's offshore chain of bases. The United States would have to give China a dominant position in the forthcoming peace treaty with Japan, thereby forestalling the plot against the people's republics in Asia to "rear up again a fascist power." Even more important, Mao could conclude the Chinese civil war. A week before he launched his all-out offensive, East European communists at the United Nations specified the conditions "volunteers" held for going back across the Yalu, stipulations Beijing reiterated on 28 November 1950 and 20 January 1951. "In order that peace and security in the Pacific and in Asia may be ensured," the United States was to remove the Seventh Fleet from the strait, stop all assistance to the Nationalist government, and hand over China's seat in the United Nations. The generalissimo's circle, having once fled to Taiwan, would flee further west toward Hawaii, along with America on its way out of Japan.[77]

For the war to end as Mao envisioned, Washington would have to allow MacArthur what he wanted, permission for all-out attack. The ambush in late October–early November blew much of the facile optimism out of the Truman administration, certainly not comforted by reports received from its consulate in Taipei that "the Chinese communists plan to throw the book at the United Nations forces in Korea." This would prove correct but was hardly conclusive when sent on November 6th. KMT intelligence, the prime source, was known to be prone to "wishful thinking" about a full-scale war between the USA and the PRC. One thing was clear although the immediate future was in doubt. Washington faced a difficult decision in the face of ambiguity. It could withdraw its forces some twenty miles, as its British allies soon proposed. This would leave the UN command at the narrow neck of North Korea, where it would be relatively safe from envelopment but still in possession of Pyongyang. It would also leave the UN commander short of his objective, which had become an obsession reminiscent of the Philippines in World War II. "To give up any portion of North Korea to the aggression of the Chinese Communists would be the greatest defeat of the free world in recent times."[78]

Omar Bradley held that "militarily the farther back the line the better off we would be." MacArthur, mounting a rebuttal, could appeal to the Pentagon's fear of "indefinite retention of our military forces" on the Korean peninsula. This concern was particularly compelling in November 1950, when Bradley told Joe Alsop that "a good many" people in the government expected war with Russia in Europe by next spring. "A great many more," apparently more optimistic, thought the confrontation more likely to occur in two years. In either scenario, without extensive preparation right now, the United States was likely to be thrown off the Continent. The JCS therefore had firm plans to begin deploying four divisions to Europe in the next few weeks, provided MacArthur wrapped up operations in Korea.[79]

A push to the Yalu could tempt the secretary of state as the way to prevent "major proportion of US forces committed indefinitely in Far East." At the same time Britain's ambassador found "Acheson and his associates very deeply troubled about the present situation [in Korea] and its possibilities." The man who called himself the "first minister" of the U.S. government would later say that in the face of this "grave crisis" he had responsibility to step forward and tell the theater commander, "Whoa, reverse your policy, order your troops back; the line [of furthest advance] is that of Pyongyang." Nonetheless, since Inchon, Acheson had not been willing to take on MacArthur, which was clear once again at an NSC conference on November 9th. "Defense believes, and we [at State] agree, that General MacArthur's directive should not be changed at present. . . . [He] is free to proceed with his operations in the hope that they might be successful."[80]

Acheson's pronouncement took place two days after the congressional election. Beyond Washington, where politics always affects policy, it might seem to be a brief period where the pressures of public opinion and partisan competition would temporarily abate. Colonel Chesty Puller, on his way toward the Chosen Reservoir in the First Marine Division, wrote his wife: "I hope and pray that now that the elections are over, President Truman will call out the National Guard. . . . Since the last war we have only had a big mouth and no stick." Britain, more fearful of Russia and China, thought it time to stop movement north. MacArthur felt this akin to the "historical precedent [England set] in the action at Munich." In fact, the foreign office sometimes seemed as frightened of the Anglophobia that it found among "Americans of all classes and types." Republican isolationists were apt to blame Britain for dragging the United States into two world wars. Democrats had their own resentments, fanned by occupations of Ireland and Palestine. The foreign minister already had warned his colleagues that their ally is "likely to be irrational . . . towards the United Kingdom where our policy diverges from that of the United States."[81]

MacArthur, not one to appreciate British circumspection, was always quick to blame its "very powerful" influence on U.S. policy. Actually, the foreign government with the greatest impact on Washington had no embassy in the city. When China hit American forces a few days before the election, it reminded voters that it went communist on the administration's watch. Democrats lost twenty-eight seats in the House and five in the Senate, among them that of Millard Tydings, running for his fourth term shortly after chairing an investigation denouncing Joe McCarthy for charging that the State Department "is thoroughly infested with Communists." The electorate seems to have repudiated Tydings's repudiation of "fraud." Truman privately reproached himself for failing to carry the public and for letting his supporters down. His wife never saw him more overcome with remorse, although certainly no stranger to defeat. In 1946, when his party lost twice as many seats as in 1950, Truman's press secretary wrote his sister: "Nobody here in the White House is downcast. . . . The consensus is that President Truman is now a free man and can write a fine record in the coming two years." Contrast that with the mood on election night 6 November 1950, when Truman went to bed drunk, the only time in his presidency. He not only attributed defeat to the "McCarthy-Jenner-Nixon poison" about being soft on communism, he spoke cryptically of "hero worship," suggesting that he might have thought he lost the election to images of Douglas MacArthur.[82]

Democratic candidates for office said the Korean War had been a political liability, right behind communists in the government. Truman, in low spirits, was not prepared to change on his own initiative the climate of cooperation forged at Inchon. A get-tough approach toward MacArthur could always find its way into the Oval Office were Dean Acheson to act on his dictum that cabinet responsibility meant presenting the president with "the real issues . . . extraneous matter stripped away." That precept, if practiced in late 1950, might have aroused Truman's own belief that the past had practical lessons for the present. He had thought MacArthur an egotist, what he also thought of Jeb Stuart, the glory-grabbing cavalry commander conducting unauthorized raids that led Robert E. Lee astray in 1863. Truman's hero, lacking scouting reports he needed deep in enemy territory, could not grasp the strength of the force he faced at Gettysburg, a battlefield Truman subsequently walked with Douglas Southall Freeman's *Lee* in hand. MacArthur might be thought to be falling into a comparable trap of his own making had Truman received straightforward counsel from his closest advisors. Acheson, while normally far from reticent, was not ready to face the president "with the gravest sort of problem," to which Acheson himself "could not offer any solution. So," he said in retrospect, "I did not go."[83]

That November, the secretary of state wrote his British counterpart: "Giving up the part of Korea we do not occupy would at this time undoubtedly be interpreted as a sign of weakness." One wonders whether Acheson was thinking of his own image as well as that of the United States. He was damaged goods in Washington, where common wisdom blamed him for the outcome of the election. One U.S. representative thought it more style than substance: "He ought to sound as though he had cow manure on his feet." If Acheson's own behavior was any indication, he thought the vote had more to do with policy. James Reston, a confidant, wrote nine days after the voting: "Consciously or unconsciously, he has certainly avoided any recommendation that could be interpreted as an appeasement of the Chinese Communists"[84]

Appeasement of the secretary of defense was another issue once George Marshall replaced Louis Johnson. If the latter had remained and supported MacArthur, Acheson would have been sorely tempted to dissent, if only out of spite. ("If Johnson would say, 'That's white,' Acheson would say, 'That's black,'" said one of Truman's military assistants.) Marshall was treated much differently, an object of Acheson's adoration for his character, commitment to duty, and sheer "presence" whenever entering a room. This man, as head of DOD, could hand MacArthur a blank check because Marshal had unlimited credit in the administration: no one second-guessed *his* decisions. Ironically, his position was strengthened by ill health, "a four-engine bomber going on one engine," as Acheson described him in 1948. Marshall came back to government office in September 1950 with one kidney and considerable discomfort, sometimes unable to put in a full day's work. In these circumstances, Acheson was particularly loath to raise issues that might cause Marshall more problems in sensitive areas, such as those having to do with the theater commander.[85]

At a White House meeting on November 21st, Marshall "expressed [his] satisfaction that Mr. Acheson had stated his belief that General MacArthur should push forward with the planned offensive." This was hardly the way to bring to the surface Marshall's own sense of unease. "It was clear" to the secretary of the army that the secretary of defense "had concerns about General MacArthur's inner drive, his egocentricity." Nonetheless, just as Acheson deferred to Marshall, Marshall deferred to the CINCFE, consistent with the American military tradition that one supports or relieves the officer in charge. "After all," said Bradley earlier that month, "MacArthur is the commander in the field." This simple statement carried weight with Acheson, another Civil War buff, although he thought in terms of U. S. Grant, not one of the president's particular favorites. Truman, when looking past the likes of Jeb Stuart, said the South lost because of "crazy politicians," despite Lee's battlefield brilliance. The North, according to Acheson, won because Lincoln acknowledged having "made a supreme mess in interfering with the strategy, tactics, and choice of commands of the Federal Armies in the East and determined to turn all of this over to General Grant."[86]

The historical record was not so simple, before or after Grant got supreme command. Lincoln had been no warlord, nor did he then slink completely off the scene. But whatever actually occurred in the Civil War was now less important than Inchon's inclining Acheson toward what he called "uneasy respect for the MacArthur mystique." One could not replace the general for incompetence or disobedience. He never violated direct orders, Acheson, Nitze, Marshall, and the entire JCS would admit. They rarely sent him anything except broad guidance, what one would expect because MacArthur seemed on a roll and no one had hard evidence that he was now mistaken, even if the U.S. army was "scattered from 'hell to breakfast,'" as Ridgway later described the military situation.[87]

Marshall already had noted that units were 20 percent under strength, widely dispersed, and bound down on broken terrain. On November 17th, a DOD deputy secretary for foreign military affairs pointed to the risk of a world war: Washington must act because MacArthur would never "recommend a change in military objectives from complete victory." The State Department did not concur with this call for an emergency meeting with the theater commander. The worst scenario it could conjure was a "probability" that the Kremlin and Beijing would join to hold "the northern fringe of Korea." However, no one showed that such a force was then in place. Marshall would not buck the tide on this basis, although not at all complacent. He remarked that the recent absence of contact with the enemy was reminiscent of "similar withdrawals . . . in the past . . . [that] preceded definite offensive action," such as he had observed when Truman's representative to China after World War II. He had warned Chiang not to chase Mao's army deep into Manchuria. The generalissimo disregarded his advice, extended his lines, and spread his soldiers thinly into isolated positions where they were subsequently crushed. Mao thus won his war for the mainland years before he anticipated. In late 1950, he was eager to put his military method back into operation, this time against MacArthur, Chiang's apparent ally.[88]

Marshall looked past his experience with China as well as that with MacArthur during the Second World War: "so influenced by his own desires that it is difficult to trust his judgment." The secretary of defense, despite these qualms, had written another "very personal and informal message" to the theater commander: "Everyone here, Defense, State, and the president, is intensely desirous of supporting you in the most effective manner within our means." Words like that had not mattered in late 1941–early 1942, when Washington had nothing to give MacArthur to defend the Philippines. Now, it gave him the opportunity to go out to "hit the jackpot," as MacArthur put it, and bring his army "home by Christmas." Mao Tse-tung had different plans, to put it mildly. He ignored overtures by Sweden and Britain to negotiate a buffer zone that would protect his border except as part of a comprehensive settlement by which Washington would stop all support for Chiang Kai-shek. Politically impossible for the Truman administration to accept, this position foreclosed the final chance for diplomacy.[89]

Mao would not have been disappointed that Washington lost its leverage to stop MacArthur south of the Yalu. If America would not hand over Taiwan, he would forcibly take it in the North Korean wastelands. Both Charles Willoughby and the CIA now "firmly" counted in Manchuria nearly 850,000 Chinese soldiers, regulars plus territorial reserves. Other commanders might have paused, dug in, or withdrawn. MacArthur drove forward with renewed intensity. He may have calculated that the swelling numbers in the potential communist order of battle gave him one last chance to make the Yalu "the bloodiest stream in all history" if China dared cross now. Plausibly, he could beat them to the river, excepting the 30,000 Chinese already plugging the ranks of a withering North Korean army. Any more than that "would have been detected by our Air Force and our Intelligence." MacArthur had hoped China would try to storm the Taiwan Strait on his watch, if not actually provoking their effort, which he planned to shatter with airpower and seapower in mid-1950. By late November, he was more bull than matador for Mao's military tactics, vintage 1938: "Lure the enemy into the deep and strike it when it is unprepared and isolated. . . . Concentrate before hand under cover along the route through which [he] is sure to pass, suddenly descend on him while he is moving, encircle and attack him before he knows what is happening, and conclude the fighting with all speed." A crisis for U.S. policy was in the offing. Personal and political conflicts, kept under reasonable control, would rupture the consensus in the American camp.[90]

The War against China: Winter 1950 to Spring 1951

1 2 3 4 **5** 6 7 8 9

I've worked for peace for five years and six months and it looks like World War III is here.

HARRY TRUMAN, 9 DECEMBER 1950[1]

The Chinese attack roused Truman's fury at MacArthur, who assured him no such thing would happen. However—for military, political, and personal reasons—the president would not relieve the theater commander. MacArthur thereby retained his position to affect events in Korea, including the appointment of Matt Ridgway to ground forces command. Presumed to be a protégé, he was supposed to help MacArthur execute another Inchon-like maneuver, now behind enemy lines into Mainland China. Formosa was to be the launch pad, certainly no sudden inspiration. MacArthur's standard method was to use new circumstances to conduct operations previously conceived. Dire reports about military conditions in late 1950–early 1951 could justify an attack on China first considered by the CINCFE in 1949. The Joint Chiefs of Staff had other priorities for shipping, particularly when considering withdrawing from Korea. Truman still wanted the army to hang on lest China's reputation grow as U.S. prestige crumbled. Ridgway prevented defeat but not the way MacArthur wanted. He proved able to preserve South Korea without having to invade, bomb, and blockade the PRC largely thanks to Stalin's failure to provide offensive airpower to his communist ally. With Mao too weak to win, Truman need do no more against the mainland than insert covert agents to conduct relatively minor acts of disruption. However, the result of this mutual restraint proved to be military stalemate. That impasse set the stage for the climactic confrontation between President Truman and General MacArthur.

Retreat from the Yalu; Decisions about China

The Chinese military forces are committed in North Korea in great and ever increasing strength. . . . This command has done everything humanly possible within its capabilities but is now faced with conditions beyond its control and its strength.

DOUGLAS MACARTHUR, 28 NOVEMBER 1950[2]

On November 25th, forty-five days after Wake Island, Truman wrote his first critical memorandum about his meeting with MacArthur, heretofore considered fruitful for having avoided civil-military conflict. The president, a former haberdasher said to be "immaculate" even in a trench, recorded that "General MacArthur was at the Airport with his shirt unbuttoned, wearing a greasy ham and eggs cap that evidently had been in use for twenty years." The wardrobe was bad, the advice even worse. The CINCFE "said the Chinese Commies would not attack, that we had won the war, and that we could send a Division to Europe from Korea in January 1951." Truman would be bitter for the rest of his life, apparently thinking the general a swindler or a fraud: "I considered him a great strategist until he made the march into North Korea without the knowledge that he should have had of the Chinese coming in."[3]

These comments only meant that high-placed people in Tokyo were no smarter than those in Washington. China's intervention "was really a great shocker," said the secretary of the army; "nobody had expected [it] at all." Nearly everybody subsequently tried to pass fault up or down the line. The Eighth Army staff held that the "strategic responsibility and collective capability for determining the intentions of [the Chinese] Government . . . were vested in the Central Intelligence Agency, the Department of the Army and the [Far East] Theater Command." Theater headquarters wanted no place on the liability list it centered on the White House. There, the president seemed more outraged at MacArthur than at Joe Stalin and Mao Tse-tung. "Like all egotists do, he wanted to place the blame as far from himself as possible."[4]

Truman notwithstanding, one could say the same of Truman insofar as blaming a collective U.S. failure completely on MacArthur. By so doing, he moved away from his old inclination to find fault with "the crazy politicians" rather than the generals. A president so clearly disillusioned with his senior military commander must have had strong illusions about that man's prowess before tarnished by defeat. Truman thought about relieving MacArthur but did not do it for more substantial grounds than his explanation: "I had no desire to hurt General MacArthur personally." There were also good reasons of national security, as Truman told the NSC on November 28th. "We could not cause the Commanding General in the field to lose face before the enemy." The president did his best to maintain his pretense of confidence, even to a writer given special access to the White House: "People who don't know military affairs expect everything to go well all the time. . . . The greatest of generals have had to take reverses [even] Robert E. Lee and Stonewall Jackson. . . . I'm not upset, like most people, about these reverses MacArthur is taking."[5]

Better Oval Office actors like a Roosevelt or Reagan could have pulled this off, but not so Harry Truman. He told the press that MacArthur "is continuing to do a good job" but told his staff, "MacArthur says he's stymied." So was Truman in relation to the general, partly for fear that Stalin would see his dismissal as proof of U.S. desperation. That might arouse the Soviet proclivity to exploit success by reinforcing Chinese infantry with submarines and airplanes out of Vladivostok and Port Arthur, its installations east and west of the Korean peninsula. America long hoped in vain that a strong, united China would deprive Russia of some of these facilities. If Stalin used them now, the United States would have three alternatives, according to the JCS on December 1st. One: watch the slaughter of the allied ground contingent, over 500,000 soldiers. Two: try to conduct a Dunkirk-like emergency evacuation to Japan. Three: immediately decimate the bases in question, which meant dropping atomic bombs.[6]

The nuclear option might be necessary but was hardly welcome, as seen in Truman's press conference remarks on November 30th about "a terrible weapon [which] should not be used on innocent men, women and children who have nothing whatever to do with this military aggression. That happens when it is used," as he, of course, did in World War II. Since then, Truman periodically made rueful remarks like this when unable to avoid the whole unpleasant topic. Eisenhower had found him "pretending to defend Europe without mentioning the atomic bomb," to this general "one of the silliest damn things." In the case of Korea, Truman had to walk a nerve-wracking line between that weapon, policy, politics, and military personnel. ("What a hell of a two weeks I've had," he told Dean Acheson.) The president still announced that the bomb was under active consideration: "It's a matter that the military people will have to decide. . . . The military commander in the field will have charge of the use of the weapons, as he always had."[7]

This was vintage Truman commentary as to politicians keeping their hands off military operations, no matter that law and his own directives required his own release of the atomic bomb. Truman's statement may have salved his soul concerning a Hannibal or Lee. It upset his NATO allies more than anything yet said or done about Chiang Kai-shek, MacArthur, and Taiwan. In Britain, public opinion and parliamentary factions of all stripes pushed Prime Minister Clement Attlee to rush to Washington for "intimate discussions" with the president of the United States. He arrived on December 3rd, when high-level consultations were going on inside the government, where the Department of Defense had long requested "a comprehensive statement of national policy" in regard to nuclear weapons. Truman had hemmed and hawed through the Berlin crisis ("no time to be juggling an atomic bomb around") until he finally told the military he would do what was "necessary." Now, when the Joint Chiefs asked about use of the bomb in the Korean War, he answered he would face that decision "when it comes."[8]

The grim scenario of nuclear warfare did not seem far-fetched to the Pentagon, never happy to be in Korea at all. The JCS advised immediate evacuation. Truman saw things a little differently despite daily intelligence reports through December 7th about "heavy vehicular traffic moving south across the [Yalu] border." Time would show that the threat was overstated. Mao ordered his force south without effective means of supply. No one in Washington knew this in late 1950, when Truman ignored "all my military advisors" and thereby risked becoming one of those crazy politicians who lost their army. He threw in some verbal provisos about not intending "to take over military command of the situation in Korea—I leave that to the generals." Even so, "they told me there was no chance to hold the line. But I still wanted them to try." On December 11th, Truman informed the NSC that he simply refused to "surrender to these murderous Chinese Communists. We will have to be pushed out and that will take them a long time."[9]

These inconsistent statements about the president's proper role during war must have helped Truman navigate contradictory convictions, some dreadful tasks, and the input of Dean Acheson, his preeminent advisor. The president habitually tried to protect him from accusations of interference in military affairs: "Acheson has attended strictly to his business as Secretary of State." This was correct for most of November insofar as acceding to MacArthur proceeding north of the Pyongyang-Wonsan line. Ashamed now of that compliance, Acheson was particularly assertive, once getting over his initial panic on November 28th, when he expected the Soviet Union to exploit the situation by renewing aggressive action in Europe. "We don't want to beat China in Korea—we can't," Acheson then told the NSC. "We don't want to beat China any place—we can't. . . . Our great objective" must be "to terminate the fighting, to turn over some area to the Republic of Korea, and get out." Such defeatism was out of character, as was his acquiescence to military men. Acheson's geopolitical thinking, as reported by James Reston, premised that "the dangers of intervention are less than the dangers of non-intervention, since the latter policy was tried before without noticeable success," meaning Munich. He therefore resumed his habit of taking military risks to make a diplomatic point, whether in Korea or Southeast Asia, to which he forged a commitment in early 1950 despite reports from area experts that "the chances of saving Indochina were slim." He had said something similar about Korea to Joe Collins on June 26th: "It was important for us to do something even if the effort were not successful." On December 1st, he insisted that America stay and fight irrespective of the immediate outcome, although Collins was of the opinion that the peninsula was "not worth a nickel" while the Russians held bases on both flanks.[10]

MacArthur, at a news conference the next day, weighed in with his own statement about the "new war with a new opponent and a new army." The Chinese and North Koreans, according to his briefing, had 600,000 well-armed men in theater. "It is a modern ground force in every sense of the term," virtually the same assessment MacArthur made in his personal message to George Marshall on November 8th. Then, by the 10th, he discarded that opinion when looking to renew his pursuit to the Yalu. Now he brought it out of proverbial storage to explain his retreat. Within one month the assessment proved erroneous as some 400,000 ill-equipped light infantry reached their military culminating point. Acheson could not know these limitations when putting forth his appraisal that "there is a danger of our becoming the greatest appeasers of all time if we abandon the Koreans and they are slaughtered. If there is a Dunkirk and we are forced out, it is a disaster but not a disgrace," apropos Winston Churchill after Tobruk in mid-1942.[11]

Acheson in early December sounded something like MacArthur in mid-November, when the latter claimed that the prestige of the United States was irrevocably committed in Korea. The secretary of state only wanted to go out fighting, not conquer the entire peninsula as the general once insisted. However, he could not browbeat the same concessions from the Department of Defense that frequently treated MacArthur (to quote Matt Ridgway) with an "almost suspicious awe." According to Omar Bradley, chairman of the JCS, "neither Acheson or [Dean] Rusk fully appreciated the complexities and risks of a military evacuation under heavy enemy fires." The greatest fear was—and would remain—full commitment of the Soviet Far East air forces, some five thousand planes able to "establish air superiority in this area immediately," Ridgway would say. Hoyt Vandenberg, air force chief of staff, expressed his "great worry" that "our ground forces, unaccustomed to hostile air attack, might well be unable to become acclimated before a disaster could occur."[12]

Bradley maintained that under these immediate conditions it would be wise to abandon Korea but still "repay the Chinese Communists for their deeds." He put his own spin on credibility, a factor also present in mid-1947 when the army staff pointed to the benefit of leaving the peninsula on its own accord rather than be forced out in battle, a true blow to "the prestige of the United States." Now that the latter scenario seemed in the offing late in 1950, Bradley asked: "Would anyone believe [in deterrence] if we don't react to the Chinese attack?" The JCS advocated "a complete blockade and a concentrated air effort over the major cities of China," although its chairman subsequently said, "We would probably not use the A-bomb."[13]

DOD held to its essential global strategy, one minimizing ground warfare in Asia because the Soviets were the major enemy, Europe the primary prize, and the Korean peninsula a bad place to put one's infantry. Marshall and Bradley, facing forced evacuation, "reserved the right to take action against China" with air and naval power. MacArthur—perhaps confused about exactly who proposed exactly what, when, where, and why—later told the U.S. Senate that the service chiefs supported his plans. That claim had credibility at least through December 5th, when MacArthur told Joe Collins that in lieu of the prompt and substantial reinforcement Collins deemed impossible "the command should be evacuated [as soon] as possible."[14]

For the next six weeks the Far East commander confronted Washington with a terrible dilemma: attack China or vacate Korea. Not everyone in his headquarters was nearly this pessimistic, provided field forces could consolidate. Major General Edwin ("Pinky") Wright, assistant chief of staff for plans and operations, came back from an inspection trip on December 6th, from which he concluded that "we have the capability to delay and punish the enemy enormously, retain our status in Korea and be better prepared to meet the eventual political decisions." Collins, on a concurrent visit to tactical headquarters, found conditions better on the peninsula than in the mind of MacArthur. Walton Walker conveyed confidence that Eighth Army could withdraw intact, something Collins repeated when he returned to Washington and promptly informed the White House on December 8th: "Our troops were not in a critical condition today."[15]

The army chief of staff had a receptive audience within presidential circles, if only for telling them what they longed to hear. One still wonders what Collins might have reported if briefed by the captains rather than the colonels. For at least one company commander "things have become a damned mess. Everyone is running." Enlisted men prayed the high command felt the way they did: get out of Korea as rapidly as they could. True, Collins conveyed a breath of optimism, but only relative to the predictions of imminent destruction. The army's representative on the JCS did not tell the NSC that US/UN forces could hold their positions at the narrow neck of North Korea, at Pyongyang, the 38th Parallel, or even Seoul. Like Walker, he foresaw passing through eight defensive lines all the way down to Pusan.[16]

George Marshall, neither buoyant nor defeatist, felt "there seems to be some improvement in the Korean situation . . . for a time we can hold a line . . . unless exposed to heavy Communist air attacks." MacArthur meanwhile had bounced from alpha to omega. He first thought Walker could hold Pyongyang. By December 4th, he was skeptical about even holding Pusan, unless "material reinforcement in a reasonable time can be provided." He blamed Truman;

Truman blamed MacArthur. Other Americans blamed the South Koreans. Collins emphasized their "inability to maintain the integrity of their assigned sectors." Frank Lowe, Truman's eyes and ears in theater, said the ROKs had "little value." Best concentrate on rearming the Japanese, "the only people who have whipped the Russians and the Chinese," plus "they are militant in their adoration of General MacArthur," probably not what Truman wanted to hear.[17]

Whether the latest scapegoat or not, South Koreans were hardly the only people scared. One GI retreating south gave a graphic depiction of being caught in a double envelopment such as MacArthur loved to conduct: "We're like the meat in a sandwich and the Chinks are the bread." Even those spared the ordeal of running a gauntlet back toward Pyongyang or Hungnam had "the ominous feeling that the Chinese, whenever it suited them, were going to come down and bust our asses." MacArthur said much the same thing, although in more polished language and in a strategic context: a "new and dominant power in Asia" was about to sweep through Tibet and Indochina, let alone Korea. Granted, the CINCFE was a temperamental man prone to overstate success or failure. Still, his depiction of the PRC as an "excessively imperialistic [nation] with a lust for expansion" was not far different from that of intelligence agencies tracking Chinese soldiers and equipment heading south and southwest to Tonkin and Tibet, not just north against MacArthur.[18]

On December 23rd, in the midst of the debate over what the U.S. army should do, Walton Walker died in a traffic accident. MacArthur, who preferred Ned Almond and the X Corps, had been known to admonish Walker with "grave disfavor," particularly for a slow start across the Naktong River in mid-September. All was forgiven now that he was dead; MacArthur even told Walker's son, about to escort the casket home, that the defense of the Pusan perimeter was the best campaign an American had conducted since Stonewall Jackson in the Shenandoah Valley. The CINCFE, while not about to admit that Walker's fight at the Naktong made Inchon unnecessary, nominated him for the Medal of Honor, later downgraded by DOD. The Pentagon was more receptive to MacArthur's immediate recommendation for Walker's replacement, Matthew Bunker Ridgway, whom MacArthur considered "a protégé of mine for over thirty years."[19]

MacArthur did not adhere to strict traditions of seniority, whether as a captain in the War Department in direct contact with the army chief of staff or as superintendent of West Point shortly after World War I. There, he gave special access to junior officers judged to have exceptional promise, not to Omar Bradley and Joe Collins, "lowly" instructors of math and chemistry who saw little of the "legendary general." (He "maintained an aloof position"; "the gulf between us was vast indeed.") On the other hand Ridgway, while assigned to teach French and Spanish, received special appointment as faculty director of athletics, the jewel in MacArthur's educational crown. No subject was more important than participation in sports: "Nothing brings out the qualities of

Lieutenant General Matthew B. Ridgway, commander of the U.S. Eighth Army, greeting MacArthur in Korea on 20 February 1951. Their close and supportive relationship was beginning to fray as Ridgway's stature grew while MacArthur's declined. *U.S. Army Signal Corps, courtesy of the MacArthur Memorial Library.*

leadership, mental and muscular co-ordination, aggressiveness, and courage more quickly than this type of competition." That meant Captain Ridgway had "no boss" other than Brigadier General MacArthur, "the same status as the head of a Department at West Point," ordinarily reserved for full colonels. "I had a great deal of contact with him," Ridgway would recall, to be resumed in Korea. The day Walker died MacArthur extolled the new commander of the Eight Army: "To me personally, [your appointment] will mark the resumption of a comradeship which I cherished through long years of military service."[20]

One star West Point athlete under their personal tutelage had been Earl ("Red") Blaik, who returned to the Academy to coach a football dynasty that garnered two national championships and twenty-eight straight victories until upset by Navy in the midst of the Chinese offensive. ("Its terrible, devastating to morale army-wide," one officer blurted to a dumbfounded soldier fearing more bad news about casualties on December 2nd: "The score was 14 to 2. We lost the game.") Periodically, MacArthur sent Blaik plays to run. He received, in return, notes of appreciation like that of January 1945: "In the midst of the sweeps, hidden ball plays, and traps that your command has so brilliantly executed in the Pacific, your congratulatory cable to the West Point team sent the spirit of the Corps of Cadets to an all time high." In late 1950, to use this kind of football lexicon, MacArthur had developed a special play to reverse the recent drive by the Chinese team and take back the big game in Asia. For this the CINCFE wanted Ridgway in field command.[21]

MacArthur had not forgotten that when Ridgway was still deputy army chief of staff for plans and administration, he had been about the only officer in the Pentagon unequivocally in favor of the Inchon operation. Five weeks before the landing, Ridgway did not hesitate to call it the way to "decisive success," meaning the destruction of "hostile main forces in South Korea by early winter." MacArthur's presumed protégé did not have the authority at that particular time to convince his superiors, Bradley and Collins. The CINCFE therefore cultivated Averell Harriman and Frank Lowe, Truman's liaison team. In December, MacArthur must have felt Ridgway would have more weight as a field commander, not readily second-guessed according to American military practice. That could be significant when MacArthur presented the Joint Chiefs of Staff with a proposal for a grand envelopment reminiscent of Inchon, which Ridgway had praised as testament "to the incomparable brilliance of your unsurpassed leadership and judgment."[22]

MacArthur had been gathering experts in amphibious warfare at his head-quarters since mid-May 1950, although DOD then scoffed at assault from the sea. The CINCFE had not identified specific scenarios, certainly not involving Korea, of little importance to him five weeks before the war began. Now in December, his latest operation was for a far greater prize than the peninsula. News reports out of Tokyo (not Taipei) said on the 28th that Chiang Kai-shek was preparing his own forces to invade the PRC. MacArthur's staff probably planted this story in preparation for his petition to Washington on the 30th to "release existing restrictions" and thereby allow "for diversionary action (*possibly leading to counter-invasion*) against vulnerable areas of the Chinese mainland" (italics mine). The general kept the details of his plan on close hold, as was his habit. Talk about a diversion was almost certainly a smokescreen. MacArthur had in mind a major commitment of the navy, the air force, logistics, and, although not yet stated, the Eighty-second Airborne Division to capture airfields on the coastline. Chiang's army of 500,000 men, operating as the heavy assault force on the beaches, would be the final element in this application of "triphibious" warfare, MacArthur's favorite military concept.[23]

Truman would write that he could not "make myself believe that Mac-Arthur, seasoned soldier that he was, did not realize that the 'introduction of Chinese Nationalist forces into South China' would be an act of war." One doubts MacArthur could believe that the issue was in doubt at all. Number one, the word spooked him less than Truman, who did not use "war" even in the context of Pyongyang, a less dangerous opponent than Beijing. Two, MacArthur now had a chance to fulfill a long-standing ambition, that of inflicting a mortal blow on the Chinese communist cause. The opportunity was just a contingency in mid-1950, when he hoped to crush a prospective invasion of Formosa. U.S. operations in Korea then foreclosed the possibility by drawing Chinese forces north into Manchuria. Before December, the idea that he could take the initiative was politically impossible. Washington and Beijing were not in direct combat. Once Mao's armed forces crossed the Yalu, MacArthur plainly believed the United States and PRC were now at war. This being the case, "nothing we can do would further aggravate the situation as far as China is concerned."[24]

The People's Republic was deep in combat but fatally out of position, according to MacArthur's latest analysis. Far East headquarters reported 1,350,000 soldiers situated from Manchuria to Pyongyang. "It is quite clear," the CINCFE told the JCS, "that the entire military resource of the Chinese Nation, with logistic support from the Soviet Union, is committed to a maximum effort against the United Nations Command." This evoked events of last September, when North Korea committed the bulk of its army to the battle around the Pusan perimeter. Another insertion at lightly held positions behind enemy lines could be in the works. MacArthur would land across the Taiwan Strait on an indented coastline pocked with good harbors, more than could be said for the Inchon area of operations. He would not only save Korea for a second time. He would "inflict such a destructive blow upon Red China's capacity to wage aggressive war that it would remove her as a further threat to peace in Asia for generations to come."[25]

Matt Ridgway lacked MacArthur's encyclopedic recall of historical events, such as Britain's amphibious invasion of China in the Opium War. He still was a daring paratrooper who had dropped behind German lines, now reason to appreciate MacArthur's explication that China was "wide open in the South." Actually, that briefing that the CINCFE gave Ridgway on December 23rd was not completely accurate as of mid-November, when Mao sent instructions that all efforts in southeast China "should be based on the premise of a U.S.-K.M.T. landing attack." Ridgway, knowing nothing of this, informed Joe Collins, his West Point classmate, of MacArthur's latest scheme of maneuver: "It would be negligent were I not to state my full concurrence at once." He thereby placed himself beyond the Pentagon's consensus opinion at this moment of apparent crisis. The JCS could favor bombing and blockading the mainland, but never the invasion that was MacArthur's ultimate plan. Ridgway, too, proved less amenable, at least when it came to MacArthur's political mantra: "There is no substitute for victory." He later admitted that "no rally cry could have been better calculated to stir the blood of Americans." However, in Ridgway's mind an attack on the PRC was to be a true diversion, not a way to become decisively engaged in a decisive battle of a decisive war.[26]

Ridgway later wrote that "the military concept had always been all-out war, where everything is used in order to achieve victory." In October 1950, he had to manage army departments growing larger every day but still took the effort to try to uncover new ideas about "the manner of waging war," particularly the nexus between combat power and political objectives. In a message to Collins, Ridgway proposed that the destructive capacity of contemporary weaponry pointed "to the necessity of a break with the orthodox past. . . . The more fruitful the military results" of a force-on-force confrontation for control of Europe "the more barren will be the economic, political, and spiritual results." Ridgway, in response to Soviet aggression, might not target its industrial heartland in the manner of the U.S. Air Force. He proposed striking "back with hard blows around the periphery," akin to MacArthur's arguments against policy anchored on forward defense in Germany. Ridgway could not say how to strike, nor could President Truman, whose failure to cope with the era's military problems then seemed to this particular officer tantamount to "criminal neglect." Ridgway proposed a comprehensive reassessment of grand strategy by three to five "individuals of the highest possible caliber," Dwight Eisenhower being his candidate for committee chair.[27]

Two months later, when Ridgway went to Korea, he was prone to keep an open mind in an uncharted situation, a principle learned under George Marshall in field exercises at the infantry school advanced course, 1930. MacArthur's opinion to the contrary, Ridgway was not his private protégé, despite mutual admiration. He would dedicate his own Korean War memoir to Marshall, "whose character and achievements in peace and war have not been surpassed" by any other American soldier save George Washington. Ridgway, while searching for fresh answers in the field, still reflected Marshall's geopolitical priorities, what one might expect from a man who had fought World War II in the northwest European theater of operations along with Eisenhower, Bradley, and Collins. MacArthur believed that the fate of mankind turned on the outcome of the conflict between Communist China and the United States. Ridgway felt that Chinese soldiers, "a shade of the beast," were just "human canaille that the Soviets [were using to] destroy our men while conserving their own."[28]

Ridgway favored evacuation from Korea when still assigned to the Pentagon on 3 December 1950. Suddenly made field commander, he arrived in theater on the 26th. He peremptorily declared, "There will be no more discussion of retreat. We're going back"—at least according to legend and some dated recollections. An individual hero holding off the enemy is a captivating story, be it Lee at Spotsylvania, Jackson at Bull Run, MacArthur at Inchon, or Ridgway south of Seoul. However, a sudden rebound was not the whole truth and nothing but the truth, which had several sides and contradictions. Ridgway told the President of South Korea, "I aim to stay," a relatively upbeat message but not as unequivocal as "I shall return"—in this case to the 38th parallel. US/UN forces continued south for three more weeks while the command of the First Cavalry Division placed bets on returning to Japan. As late as January 16th, Ridgway told Joe Collins only of his confidence that he could remain in Korea for another two to three months, barring some unforeseen event. Collins wired Bradley on the 17th: "On the whole 8th Army is now in position and prepared to punish severely any mass attack." No one mentioned staying, but Ridgway "does not want to [leave] before army is back to old [Pusan] beachhead." This meant the new field commander was sanguine in the sense of saying that his retreat was no rout. Ridgway drew no firm line where he would stop, nor that he would stop short of extraction, the subject of messages he sent MacArthur on 6 January.[29]

Ridgway then exuded far less confidence about executing his plan for "withdrawing to a bridgehead line only under pressure and inflicting maximum punishment." The "operation [being] dependent upon the conduct of ROK Army on East flank," he asked MacArthur for a decision "made without delay" to allow embarkation and its protection by chemical agents, also known as poison gas. Ridgway was apparently thinking along these lines six days before being called to Korea, judging by his December 16th entry in the journal he kept at the Pentagon. It notes committee work on "clandestine introduction [of] wea[pons] of mass destruction." All this could be contingency planning, what the military calls "worst-casing," but nothing appears conditional or contingent in Ridgway's language to MacArthur. He seemed profoundly aware of his military vulnerability: "One [enemy] A-bomb could take out 4/5s of our [total ammunition] reserves." Ridgway would not feel confident that he could still save his troops, let alone South Korea, until personally assured by naval commanders in theater, which happened subsequent to his message to MacArthur.[30]

Ridgway did not want to run from the enemy, nor did he want to risk destruction of his army. He seems to have navigated contradictory impulses by sending Washington and Tokyo different types of messages. He was upbeat to the Department of the Army in early January 1951: "The power is here everything is going fine. We shall be in for some difficult days but I am completely confident of the ability of the Eighth Army to accomplish every mission assigned." At the same time, he was bleak to MacArthur, who took his warnings literally for personal and political reasons. The CINCFE trusted the messenger: "You have my complete confidence." In addition he trusted the message, no mystery. It resembled, if not resurrected, his own opinion, as of 1949, that Korea was "indefensible." It also could be construed to fit his present predilection to take the war to China. The theater commander, otherwise, might have reacted in the manner of the deputy chairman of the JCS in mid-April, shortly after Ridgway replaced MacArthur and requested authority to conduct an evacuation. Vice Admiral Vernon Davis thought Ridgway was "just trying to get himself lined up to meet any emergency," hardly what MacArthur said in early January. Then the fact that retreat always looks like defeat gave MacArthur another chance to argue his case to Washington. On the 8th, he wired about the serious situation, "the solution of which is dependent largely upon the highest policy determination not yet received here." This wordage was courteous because cryptic. Two days later, having received a response indicating no change in policy or size of troop commitment, MacArthur sent a message to the Department of the Army too clear to be polite: "Under the extraordinary limitations and conditions imposed upon the command in Korea, its position is untenable, but it can hold for any length of time up to its complete destruction if overriding political considerations so dictate."[31]

Joe Collins would say that MacArthur "always gave me the impression of addressing not just his immediate listeners but a larger audience unseen." Dean Acheson thought much the same thing about the CINCFE's message to Washington on January 10th: a "posterity paper" written for the public record, not the government chain of command. As such, it resembled the general's message to the Pentagon in early November, during the first (brief) Chinese intervention: "I cannot overemphasize the disastrous effect, both physical and psychological" of restrictions on bombing the bridges spanning the Yalu. "I trust that the matter be immediately brought to the attention of the President." In both instances, early November and early January, MacArthur was telling the administration that if it ignored his warning, the blood of American soldiers would be on its hands. In late 1950, Truman had modified the rules of engagement to allow an attack on the southern section of the spans. In late 1953, a student of government from Harvard University named Henry Kissinger asked Acheson for his reaction in 1951. "You mean before or after I peed in my pants?" replied the former secretary of state.[32]

Hostile newspapers later printed MacArthur's message of January 10th, no doubt given copies by the White House defense team after the general's relief on April 11th. They contrasted his so-called panic with statements from Ridgway "that the situation was under control," thus condemning him by comparison with a personification of steady professionalism at the front. Various pundits, in the process, have accused MacArthur of "trying to reverse policy by using the threat to the Eighth Army's engulfment as a lever to force Washington to adopt his program." They did not see the grim message traffic Ridgway had been sending theater headquarters, nor did Dean Acheson, who simply thought MacArthur deceitful and dishonest for trying to "involve us in [a] wider war." That accusation about his calculations has validity but is also incomplete for ignoring other aspects of MacArthur's personality. This manipulative but complex man had an artistic temperament more subject to mood and imagination than senior officers basing their own assessments on numerical data concerning force ratios in the field. Thus MacArthur could bounce between extremes, whether claiming victories while facing impending failure in Luzon, late 1941, or predicting disaster on the eve of success in Korea, early 1951.[33]

Even then, inconsistencies abound, as when MacArthur visited the X Corps in retreat from the enemy on December 11th. The situation would precipitate gloom-filled messages to Washington that were not at all evident to the corps G-3 seeing MacArthur for the first time. The general spoke in a "very low voice" as if his sentences were "coming right out of a fixed lecture. . . . What impressed me," said Colonel Frank Mildren, "was how calm he was about the whole business." Were it not for a personal letter, one could think MacArthur was simply doing what Ridgway did—exuding confidence to subordinates but not to certain superiors, lest complacency delay prompt response to his requests. In reply to a birthday greeting from a long-retired West Point classmate for whom there was no earthly reason to put on any act, MacArthur wrote on January 16th: "China hurled its entire military might at our relatively small force. . . . Just what is in store I do not know. . . . If you hear of my last roundup at the end of a rope from an Oriental telegraph pole, don't be surprised or shocked."[34]

This message was more figurative than factual, although indicating MacArthur's morale. No general writing from Far East headquarters on the east side of the Tsushima Strait was likely to be lynched, short of a total collapse of the offshore perimeter defense ensured by the U.S. navy. Politically, MacArthur's calculation was never worse, if words of woe were just a ploy to change government policy toward China. Far better to exhibit a bit of the confidence on display before Inchon, as Frank Lowe did while "most earnestly" entreating the president to adopt the CINCFE's scheme of maneuver. "ALL SECURE SAFE AND GOOD HEALTH ABSOLUTE MINIMUM CASUALTIES," he wired the White House on the way out of North Korea the day before Christmas. "[DISREGARD] REPORTS OF DIRE PREDICTIONS AT HOME OF DISASTER HERE." On January 6th, he "privately" wrote "the Boss in Washington," meaning not shown to theater command. "I hope that we will go to the Pusan sector, wire in a tight perimeter defense where our battalions will have *not more* than 900 yards of front, 'secure' (as they say in the Navy) our two airfields there, and clobber these monkeys until it really hurts. We have sufficient forces for that purpose, including reserve and without counting on the ROKs," on whom Lowe had given up. "Our Navy and Air can then have a chance at the Chinese elsewhere," which happened to be MacArthur's ultimate objective, provided one included the invasion of the mainland.[35]

It was not foolish for MacArthur to hope Washington would enhance its commitment rather than accept defeat. The Pentagon, however, was caught in its own contradictions between objectives, resources, and responsibilities. That January, the JCS sounded like MacArthur in memos to the secretary of defense: "Support establishment in China of a government friendly to the US . . . remove now the restrictions on operations of Chinese Nationalist Forces and give such logistic support as will contribute to effective operations against the Communists." At the same time, its committee on strategic plans reported that "we must not lose sight of the fact that the USSR is our principal enemy. With this in mind our concept for a strategic defense in the Far East is to reduce the forces of Communist China to impotence . . . with the minimum practicable commitment of U.S. resources," that is, use "limited military operations and political, economic, and psychological pressures." These propositions, while all well and good, were incompatible at their core. A marginal commitment against a significant opponent cannot secure meaningful victory. The Joint Chiefs certainly filed no request for a full share of a Normandy-type onslaught against the PRC, particularly when the Eighth Army was swamping it with requests for fire support along its present line of retreat.[36]

The Defense Department had an opportunity to present its case when directed by the NSC to prepare "a detailed study of the military effectiveness of the possible use of Chinese forces on Formosa against the mainland of China." In March, it would conclude that "even with U.S. air and naval support the ultimate success . . . is questionable." This synopsis, while not encouraging, was actually better than its opinion back in December: amphibious operations by the Kuomintang "are not considered feasible due to logistical problems and the danger of annihilation." Senior KMT officers would confide, "They are not ready to assault the mainland unless they have very substantial outside assistance." Their U.S. counterparts knew this meant "US service forces based on Okinawa, Guam, Japan, etc., to supply all types of equipment—ammunition, POL [petroleum, oil, and lubricants], medical supplies, transportation equipment, etc., etc." One might then ask whose strength would be diverted from Korea by an invasion of China: the USA's or the PRC's? Chiang Kai-shek told American reporters about ending all "Chinese Communist aggression" with a devastating offensive to be conducted "after necessary and adequate equipment and supplies are available." This meant he was ready to receive a limitless transfer of materiel but otherwise not willing to do much more than advise his American advisors to blockade China and bomb Manchuria. His wife added bombing Moscow, presumably for good measure.[37]

Joe Collins, when inspecting Formosa in late November 1951, found its armed forces "not prepared for modern combat," exactly what he anticipated. DOD long felt the KMT "incapable" of "withstanding a prolonged and determined all-out assault by Chinese Communist forces," let alone take a beachhead out of their hands. Chiang's "medieval infantry force"—ignorant of "teamwork" between armor, artillery, air force, and navy—was hardly likely to survive a landing and conduct a follow-on breakout. Then Mao in a mere coup de main might occupy Taiwan, now considered "essential" by the JCS for "the conduct of air and naval operations in the strategic defense of our offshore island chain." MacArthur's argument of 1950 that Formosa was too important to risk had come back to haunt him in 1951. France and Britain, meanwhile fearing a "sudden and overwhelming" sweep of China across Asia, were insisting that the U.S. navy stand ready to evacuate thousands of soldiers and even more citizens from Hong Kong and Haiphong down to Singapore. This was "in part [a] quid pro quo arrangement" for basing rights in Europe, as the Department of the Army explained to MacArthur, once again a casualty of adverse global priorities.[38]

Washington had to concede what NATO feared: "The danger of Communist Chinese attack would be increased by the adoption of a strong stand against the regime." MacArthur, in the meantime, was thinking of his own attack. He would have assembled enough transport to sealift 100,000 KMT soldiers into the region around Shanghai. "The objective," he wrote on February 7th, "was the domination of South China behind the protective line along the Yangtze River." This plan for a territorial division of the mainland was not unprecedented, being Chiang's last hope in 1949. It also once appealed to some U.S. officials, lest communism roll "onwards from Manchuria, China, and Korea toward Indo-China, Malaya, and India." Now, when that danger seemed at hand, the plan risked assets necessary for the evacuation of Southeast Asia, let alone Korea. One need consider Acheson's insistence on maintaining credibility by fighting to the last instance and MacArthur's assessment that his command could not hold. This seemed to foretell another desperate battle at the Pusan perimeter reminiscent of August 1950, when the navy was overburdened to patrol Korea and protect Formosa at the same time. The Pacific command, always short on sealift, barely had on-hand capacity to beach two regiments. The Defense Department hardly wanted to commit that asset to an invasion of China when it could be tasked to evacuate its own army and the citizens of its allies.[39]

Formosa would still have a function in the Korean War, although different from the role MacArthur conceived. Washington was adopting the general's concept of the offshore defense perimeter as a base for power projection, meaning a sword, not just a shield. The size of the weapon to be wielded was still in dispute in May 1951, when Truman approved NSC 48/4 authorizing plans to use Chinese Nationalist forces "offensively" against the PRC. Nothing specific was mentioned aside from "appropriate military action in the event UN forces are forced to evacuate Korea." What would be done to relieve the military pressure on the peninsula if the command held but fell into strategic stalemate? MacArthur would have launched what he called "triphibious warfare." The administration was content with relative pinpricks via covert operations with guerrilla contacts, hardly a rapier, let alone a battleaxe.[40]

Publicity about these secret doings would have undercut persistent Republican Party attacks on "neutralization": Truman had "no right to prohibit Chiang from aiding guerrillas on the mainland." Plausible deniability still served a purpose within the international community. It kept the operation out of discussion unless Mao Tse-tung raised the issue or struck bases on Taiwan. The effort was not worth his while as long as the Truman administration did not change its own rules of engagement for conventional forces: no major action except in response to a communist invasion. Chiang himself was no substantial threat despite claims that at least a million guerrillas awaited him in China. Hanson Baldwin wrote that the KMT had little contact with dissidents there at all. Some six hundred CIA operatives based in Formosa tried to step into the vacuum by providing the support and direction the Nationalist government did not supply. Forrest Sherman, chief of naval operations, identified the national objective: "establishment in China of a government friendly to the United

States." However, when it came to specifying action, he just listed "give logistic support NOW to effective guerrilla activities."[41]

"Effective" might be difficult to measure, but covert activity had some things in its favor, particularly on the cost side of the government ledger. Guerrilla operations were relatively cheap in manpower, equipment, and national prestige, of no small interest to Sherman and the rest of the Pentagon. They were mindful "to avoid a general war" at least "until we have achieved the requisite degree of military and industrial mobilization." The downside of their prudence lay in limited payoff. Clandestine action only had a "nuisance value," although individuals inserted behind enemy lines certainly ran enormous risks. "Large-scale defections" would not happen, according to the JCS, "until it is believed that the Nationalists have a good chance of remaining ashore and expanding their bridgehead." MacArthur, a proponent of decisive battle, was not very interested in something short of changing the enemy regime. By his analysis that would not occur "until a major force has gained a lodgment. . . . United States identification with guerrilla warfare should be a prelude to larger operations which have a substantial prospect of overthrowing Communist authority in China."[42]

MacArthur hoped to topple the Beijing government, widely thought unstable. CIA analysts in October 1950 had thought it would never intervene because too beset with dissent: "The regime's very existence would be endangered." Mao assessed the situation differently, dissidence being a reason to wage war. He planned to use external conflict to suppress the internal opposition that his foreign enemy tried to support. This became a familiar procedure of his statecraft in the late 1950s and the mid-1960s, as well as during the Korean War. The specter of U.S. aggression would justify the economic displacement of the Great Leap Forward into industrialization; it mobilized the population behind the Cultural Revolution, Mao's greatest attempt to suppress all critics. Back in 1951, American assistance to insurgents was particularly useful because of the compromises Mao had to make in the Chinese civil war, where his propaganda downplayed revolution in order to present his cause in bourgeois terminology of modernity, efficiency, and honest government. Many who happened to oppose entry into Korea also opposed the rapid communization of society. Mao, impatient with caution on both counts, could seize upon the war as a time to go after "enemy agents, backbone members of reactionary parties and groups, or heads of reactionary secret societies." They purportedly were stirring in the south when he sent his army north to hold off MacArthur. Once he was winning initial victories, Mao was riding a wave of national prestige. He used it to deploy over 100,000 soldiers and policemen in a "purification" campaign that eliminated up to two million "political bandits" and "individualists." If not killed or imprisoned, many fled into Vietnam, where they had to fight through the Viet Minh communists to wind up in Hanoi, a French sanctuary, at least for the time being.[43]

Mao, once stronger at home, might be more forceful abroad. As for now, he and Truman could work along the lines Stalin used at the onset of the war. Moscow removed Soviet military advisors from the North Korean army for fear their capture could provoke a direct altercation with the United States. Beijing and Washington tempered their own confrontation that might lead to a world war in the nuclear age. Officially, Red Chinese soldiers were merely "volunteers," as were "former" U.S. army officers "seconded to a civilian status" when working for Western Enterprises Incorporated, the CIA front engaged in guerrilla support operations. Two of them, Richard Stilwell and Bill DePuy, eventually became four-star generals. None were supposed to go on the mainland because exposure would embarrass stated U.S. policy. Some, dressed in Chinese military uniforms, still went, if only to retrieve the common soldiers they considered the best and the bravest people the Nationalists had. (They "suffered hardships with extraordinary good nature," unlike scornful KMT officers.) Thirteen Americans were captured and held without publicity until late 1954. Mao did not want to call more attention to U.S. aid for the resistance, probably worried that news of outside support could embolden the opposition. Well-informed Americans might have thought him more apprehensive than the situation warranted. *New York Times* reports out of Hong Kong in mid-1951 concluded: "The main preoccupation of most [anticommunist] groups is simple self-preservation." A CIA operative would later be quoted as saying, "If I ever find a[n indigenous] guerrilla, I'm going to stuff him and put him in the Smithsonian."[44]

Crisis in Korea; Return to Seoul

It looks like the beginning of the end. The Chinese are kicking hell out of us. There are just too many of them in Korea for us to fight. If the big wheels in Washington continue fighting it will be the biggest mistake they ever made.

JAMES CARDINAL, PRIVATE FIRST CLASS, FIFTH CAVALRY,
8 JANUARY 1951[45]

We don't frighten now like we did in November and December and there's no talk of them pushing us out of Korea. Their losses . . . have been almost beyond belief. Their dead are piled up in front of our positions by the thousands.

JAMES CARDINAL, CORPORAL, FIFTH CAVALRY, 30 APRIL 1951[46]

In December 1950, the Pentagon tried to force a basic reassessment of defense policy in the face of global responsibilities. It realized MacArthur was getting mixed messages because a dialectic process pervaded Washington: the military's request for a clear statement of political objectives elicited a State Department inquiry as to military capabilities—and vice versa. This produced a synthesis hardly helpful to a theater commander: do the best you can with what you got. On the 26th, the day after Matt Ridgway arrived in the Far East, Omar Bradley asked George Marshall to revisit the issue through a memorandum to the president along the following lines: "It is highly important to be able to select the time and place for evacuation rather than withdraw from Korea under conditions approximating a military rout. Therefore the decision should not be based on political grounds; rather it should be based on our best military judgment . . . made now for the evacuation of United States forces whenever it becomes apparent that the Chinese Communists are massing their troops in the vicinity of the Kum River."[47]

The Defense Department informed MacArthur on December 30th to expect orders "to commence withdrawal to Japan" when the enemy reached the Kum, about halfway between Seoul and the sea. This was not what the CINCFE had in mind if evacuation did not trigger a change in policy that took the war directly to China. MacArthur apparently feared that a terminal exit was in the offing and replied there was no need to make that decision prior to a breach of a new defensive position under preparation thirty-five miles outside Pusan. As things turned out, the enemy would never get to the banks of the river, let alone the so-called Davidson line. Few might have ventured that calculation on January 12th, when the JCS wired the CINCFE after consultation at the White House: "Based upon all the factors . . . particularly those presented in your recent messages, we are forced to the conclusion that it is infeasible under existing conditions, including sustained major effort by Communist China, to hold for a protracted period a position in Korea."[48]

It might seem that as of mid-January the military was finally in control of military strategy, although it still had to accommodate State Department concerns insofar as the JCS informed MacArthur to make the best fight he could for the sake of "United States prestige worldwide." Dean Acheson, Harvard Law 1918, held that MacArthur's message was "not wholly clear in some respects." Joe Collins, West Point 1917, clarified that "the question was not on a decision to evacuate or not to evacuate but of the timing of the issue of orders to begin the evacuation." The secretary of state still said the CINCFE could use more information about "the political basis of American foreign policy." The next day MacArthur received a personal letter from the president of the United States, no longer talking about liberating North Korea or even regaining Seoul. The military mission as of January 13th was "to deflate the dangerously exaggerated political and military prestige of Communist China." Hold, Truman said, "an important portion of Korea," provided this was "practicable" with "the limited forces" on hand. This reiterated what MacArthur already had heard from the Pentagon on the 9th: that despite Chinese intervention "there is little possibility of policy change or other external eventuality justifying strengthening of our effort in Korea."[49]

In postwar memoirs claiming that they were coiling for counterattack, MacArthur and Courtney Whitney spoke highly of Truman's communication, particularly for its clarity. For once, they overlooked an opportunity to criticize Washington. Truman told MacArthur that the telegram "is not to be taken in any sense as a directive." Hence, if one is to give the president high marks, it must be in comparison to muddled messages along the lines of save your army, save Japan, save Korea, all the above. Truman's telegram looks like something Franklin Roosevelt might have sent MacArthur in the Philippines, provided Roosevelt were not even more opaque. Truman said the main enemy lay elsewhere, now Russia as opposed to Germany. "We must act with great prudence" in the CINCFE's particular "area of hostilities," second to Europe once again. His mission was primarily symbolic—that of providing "a rally point around which the spirits and energies of the free world can be mobilized to meet the world-wide threat which the Soviet Union now poses." MacArthur was to fight another losing battle in order to preserve national prestige, although one doubts the White House could have turned Pusan into a rally as strong as "Remember Bataan."[50]

The CINCFE entreated Washington for a direct command, either evacuate or stand and die in place. Truman and MacArthur, contrary to their cultivated reputations, were really both saying the buck stops at the other guy's desk. The general, in response to the president's message, did not give his traditional war cry: "There is no substitute for victory." He opted for his characteristic phrase in periods of pessimism, although now using a collective pronoun. "I can but do my best," he said during grim times in Manila. "We shall do our best," he now said, ten years later. MacArthur had lost the assurance on display when holding ground at Pusan and then moving past Inchon and Pyongyang to points north on the way toward the Yalu. Washington, meanwhile reducing its own objectives, simply wanted to make China pay a toll for its conquests but inflict that punishment within the confines of Korea. That was hardly a green light for what MacArthur wanted, a decisive victory culminating in the crumbling of the communist regime. Nonetheless, anybody in attendance at the Blair House meeting back on June 25th could attest to a truism not heard when tactical airpower was supposed to stop the enemy in its tracks: one can never know where a military effort ends once it is begun, whether against North Korea in 1950 or the People's Republic of China in 1951.[51]

In the final analysis, facts on the ground would be more important than Truman's hope to avoid a wider war, MacArthur's aspiration to overthrow the PRC, the Joint Chiefs' inclination to limit its commitments, or Acheson's desire to preserve credibility. On January 17th, the Strategic Plans Committee of the JCS filed its carefully measured conclusion that "the most optimistic estimate of our military capability is to hold selected beachheads in South Korea." The same day, Matt Ridgway finally turned around to make a tentative probe of enemy positions, where some 174,000 Chinese soldiers were supposedly on his heels. "*If* you can go up there and stay twenty-four hours," he told the commander of the Twenty-seventh Infantry, "I'll send up the division behind you. *If* it stays there twenty-four hours, I'll send up the corps." (Italics mine.)[52]

The Eighth Army had withdrawn the last 130 miles for "no apparent reason," recalled a British brigadier, "other than some ominous red arrows marked on the operational maps, showing that the whole of the U.N. forces were about to be encircled." Ridgway tested these notions with what Joe Collins described as "reconnaissances-in-force," an accurate depiction of these movements to contact, no smokescreen for deep attack in the manner of MacArthur. Ridgway himself no longer talked about breaking with military orthodoxy, as he had in the Pentagon last fall. The campaign he just began would be quite conventional: "a coordinated, phased advance for the purpose of developing the enemy situation in their front." The field commander, in his own words to the CINCFE, was "inflicting maximum losses with minimum sustained, and prepared to exploit . . . up to the Han [River]," provided the ability to support the operation "logistically was clear beyond any reasonable doubt." Whether overly cautious or not, this proved more successful than Ridgway initially presumed, as revealed in his modest claims at a press conference held before heading north: "The Eighth Army can take care of itself." Notice, he did not promise success, aside from avoiding a shattering defeat. He did not know the true size or condition of the enemy forces he faced, discovered only after he sprang his attack. On January 19th, Collins could finally write George Marshall that the Chinese "were showing little disposition to fight." They had "little or no transport and practically no artillery because of our constant air action."[53]

Neither the JCS, the field commander, or the CINCFE had been quick to grasp what the Chinese army recently had acknowledged to allies and itself: that it was a spent force needing months of replenishment before conducting another major offensive, to be mounted in late April 1951. The Chinese could execute a successful ambush provided they had total surprise and fought at night on closed terrain. Once America broke contact and reconstituted defensive positions, the attack stalled for lack of heavy weapons, close air support, transportation, medicine, gloves, boots, and food: the weak points of a light-infantry army used to local supply from sympathetic peasants, such as they had found when fighting the KMT in North China.[54]

Early in November 1950, Mao had been quite aware of these military limitations. However, by the end of the month, he was instructing his senior officers: "Do not request a winter break." This was more than broad political guidance from a head of state, such as Truman gave MacArthur. Mao was his own commander of military operations, a Chinese Napoleon as well as a Lenin. In December, he filled much of his materiel deficit with equipment, clothing, and "many luxury items" abandoned by Americans giving up ground. Messages purportedly culled by communist espionage could also buttress hopes for a decisive victory. In the Chinese civil war, Mao frequently knew enemy plans through agents operating inside the KMT. During the conflict in Korea, he got his information about Western intentions from Soviet intelligence. Kim Philby, future recipient of the Orders of Lenin and the Red Banner, was the Washington-based liaison officer between U.K. and U.S. secret services, a position from which he allegedly reported that Joe Collins told President Truman and Prime Minister Attlee on December 8th that "the situations of the United Nations' and America's forces in Korea has become hopeless."[55]

Mao passed on to his field commanders that the enemy "cannot organize a protracted defense because the American forces have suffered very heavy casualties, great losses of equipment, and an extreme deterioration in morale." He might have suspected this was not what Collins said, since the testimony came to his Kremlin attaché thanks to the good offices of Joseph Stalin, who was desperate to keep Mao on the offensive. "I have no doubt," Stalin wrote him on December 1st, "that in a war against a modern and well-armed army, the Chinese army will acquire a rich experience in modern warfare . . . in the same manner as the Soviet army did in the struggle against the superbly-armed German army." One might have thought that one would have shuddered at emulating World War II on the Eastern front. Mao, however, did not waver from using the Korean War to extract the heavy weapons he long sought from the Soviet Union. It, he told Stalin, "has clearly shown . . . the extreme necessity for improvement of the equipment of our troops." "We badly need anti-aircraft guns, artillery ammunition and anti-tank grenades." By mid-1952, when the Chinese had suffered some 500,000 casualties, Stalin was still cheering on his ally: "Americans don't know how to fight," their infantry is "weak," and "people are weeping in the USA" although fighting only "little Korea."[56]

Stalin would not have much compunction at lying about what his spies were really reporting in December 1950. Deception was a way to get and keep Mao committed to a full-scale offensive before realizing how far his political ambition exceeded the capabilities of his force structure. Peng Dehuai, the titular commander of Chinese forces in the field, was better acquainted with specific deficiencies, as one might expect. In October 1950, he opposed military entry into Korea without guarantees of Soviet close air support. In early December, when Peng warned of substantial deficits in food, ammunition, and air cover, he advised against trying to chase America even south of Pyongyang, a far cry from the viewpoint held by Mao, his old comrade in arms. They had run-ins in the 1930s and 1940s, when Peng dared doubt Mao's military acumen. At the end of the civil war on the mainland, the chairman drove him into an offensive costing 15,000 casualties before Peng saved his force with a tactical retreat in 1949. In early January 1951, he advised another withdrawal from contact—of little interest to Mao, whose accession to supreme authority left little room for anything but acquiescence to the wisdom of the leader of the Chinese Communist Party. "Move away when one could not win" once was Mao's watchword in a protracted military conflict. Now he held forth that war was a "contest of human power and morale," wherein weapons were important but "not the decisive factor." Mao was approaching the point where he would eventually say that "the relationship between politics and numbers is like that between officers and soldiers: Politics is the commander."[57]

Peng, never one to believe in the cult of Mao, muttered to his staff in the midst of the offensive that "the Schoolmaster is getting drunk with success." Mao, although a student of Chinese classics, was violating their ancient writings that "military matters are not determined by the ruler's commands; they all proceed from the commanding general." Whereas Truman, a less egotistical man, delegated too much to MacArthur, Mao assigned too little to Peng, told to push the enemy into the sea. This proved impossible against the U.S. army, soon on its way back beyond the Han to Seoul, then points further north. It was "far different," Ridgway later wrote, "from the reckless and uncoordinated plunge toward the Yalu." One lieutenant colonel summed it up: "Barreling down the road was off." It was "simply the old tactical story of making sure of one position before attacking the next."[58]

The Chinese had no effective counter, including falling back. Its vintage lure, exhaust, and ambush strategy presumed a cooperative enemy performing its prescribed role, such as Chiang usually played except when heeding outside advice. In the 1930s, he listened to German General Staff officers, to whom he also sent his adopted son for extensive schooling in Berlin. (His eldest attended the Red Army academy in Moscow.) The German contingent convinced him to move slowly, consolidate his rear, and fortify positions with some three thousand blockhouses. That hemmed the communists into a dwindling base until Germany recalled its military mission and Japan diverted the KMT, a deus ex machina for Mao, who rose to the fore in the CCP after rivals wasted soldiers in fruitless assaults on these firebase forts. He reconstituted the People's Liberation Army and resumed the civil war in 1945, when Chiang played less heed to foreign advisors such as George Catlett Marshall.[59]

MacArthur, also averse to listening to Marshall, had scattered his own army in November 1950 across the landscape of North Korea, where it left numerous gaps for the enemy to exploit. The First Marine Division, in much better condition, had executed its own blockhouse strategy, although not so named by its commanding general, O. P. Smith. Like other marines, he was uncomfortable putting his regiments "out on a limb" by operating far inland beyond the reach of the navy. Unlike army generals, he had some institutional independence from Ned Almond, whose "supercilious manner" rubbed Smith the wrong way. In November, when ordered north of the Pyongyang-Wonsan line, he built airfields and supply depots in his wake, testimony to his lack of "confidence in the tactical judgment of the Corps [command.]" This proved of crucial importance in December, when the division conducted a retrograde movement that inflicted some 37,500 casualties on the Chinese. Truman, who called it "one of the greatest fighting retreats that ever was," bestowed the only

Presidential Unit Citation won by a division during the Korean War. He even thought the operation worthy of Lee and Jackson—no higher praise possible other than throwing in Hannibal. Truman would never repeat what he said about marines in mid-1950, that the "Navy's police force" had "a propaganda machine almost equal to Stalin's."[60]

In mid-January 1951, when Matt Ridgway headed back north, he too denied the enemy the opportunity it needed, as Peng later informed Mao. "The enemy forces are so clearly knit together that there exists no gap. Tactically, they advance and retreat so steadily and entrench themselves at every step. We could not make a breach unless we penetrate into [the] depth and bear a fierce fight." Ridgway did not eradicate the Chinese army nor drive it completely out of Korea, objectives he could not achieve without running prohibitive risks in what was still a secondary theater for the Washington authorities. However, he and his command certainly discredited Mao's dreams of conquest, Truman's objective for MacArthur back in January. Ironically, by so doing, Ridgway upheld the original MacArthur-Willoughby thesis that a primitive force, even of substantial size, will not defeat a modern army possessing air and naval supremacy, firepower, and mechanical mobility.[61]

MacArthur and his staff had managed to place their command in truly exceptional circumstances where their truisms about military superiority were not true. The enemy was not the "splendidly trained and equipped" force they initially reported in late November. "It was," Willoughby came to say, simply "the right kind of war for the illiterate Chinese coolie under the opiate of the Red gospel, reinforced with modern Russian tommy [sic] guns." Mao bet against materiel indices and won—in the short run. In the long run, quantitative calculation is more apt to be correct than intuition, inspiration, and excessive self-confidence, the attributes that also misled MacArthur on the way to the Yalu in late 1950. The American general blamed defeat on politicians in Washington and London. Peng would eventually bear the burden for Mao's own shortcomings. In 1959, the general was purported to be the head of a "Right [wing] opportunist anti-Party clique," certainly a way to discredit his objectives. Peng wanted to professionalize the army, a lesson many Chinese officers took from Korea. Mao would make it an instrument of radical ideology. All soldiers were to be trained and equipped with his "Little Red Book," Chairman Mao's thoughts being "the supreme commander, the soul and guarantor of all work." Veterans were purged or promoted on the basis of slavish loyalty to the head of state, reminiscent of Chiang Kai-shek at his worst. Peng, being one of the losers, was arrested, was beaten to force a confession of plotting for the Soviet Union, died in a prison hospital, and was buried in obscurity under a false name. Chiang's Kuomintang emerged the big winner, thanks to disruption in the PLA. The Chinese Red Army could not return to serious preparation for the unfinished business with Taiwan until after Mao's death in 1976.[62]

Peng deserved far better treatment for mitigating a military disaster when dragging his heels against demands for headlong pursuit in Korea, not unlike O. P. Smith back in November. The Chinese field commander had grasped the essential facts before confusion, fog, and fear dissipated on the American side in late January 1951. Even in the darkest days, the condition of the U.S. army was not as bad as depicted by reports from Mao, MacArthur, and various newspapers. Stories portrayed Eighth Army troops throwing down their weapons and running for their lives. Some individuals had panicked, as did some units, mostly from the Second Infantry Division. These instances of "bugging out" made for sensational copy that put its stamp on events, however inaccurate across the entire front. The army, as a whole, withdrew south at the same rate of speed it went north in October. Otherwise, it could not have conducted the scorched-earth policy of destroying everything that could feed, clothe, or shelter an enemy already low on essential supplies. The military never quite appreciated its own military accomplishments because its data-gathering system was primitive and slow. It did not collect and publicize war diaries from units such as the IX Corps, which reported "an orderly withdrawal to selected defensive positions" through "a long series of delaying actions."[63]

The American army essentially needed a transfusion of confidence. In wartime, this can be a huge task, one for which MacArthur was no longer suited, having been reduced to something like a military manic-depressive, bouncing from "hysterical optimism to deepest pessimism" in the words of Omar Bradley's aide. The commander of the Eighth Army became a legend for stepping into the void, although initially called "wrong-way Ridgway" for heading north at all. Whether his accomplishment was somewhat inflated might never be resolved. "A retreating, despondent, defeated army was turned around by the power of the personality of its commander," said Harold K. Johnson, battalion commander, Distinguished Service Cross recipient, and future army chief of staff. James Polk, another lieutenant colonel on his way to full general, thought differently: no one at three- or four-star rank "is going to change morale in an outfit very fast. His impact isn't that great." As for Joe Collins, he could come down on either side of the issue, depending on what passage one may choose to cite. On December 4th, when visiting Korea three weeks before Ridgway took command, he found "no signs of panic" at tactical headquarters and left "reassured that the Eighth Army could take care of itself," what Ridgway would also say on January 10th. Collins still called him "the man who turned things around, there is no question about it. The Eighth Army was a badly defeated army, its morale was zero, practically."[64]

One gets the impression from these contrary statements that the Ridgway saga, like many other legends, rings both true and false. The general "played the army like a piano," according to one admiring marine who passed on the story of the field commander kneeling in the snow to tie the shoes of a soldier lugging a heavy radio. James Van Fleet, Ridgway's successor at Eighth Army, was less impressed with someone he thought a showboat for displays such as hanging grenades from his shoulder strap. Few, however, questioned that military mettle bounced back on Ridgway's watch, even if it never had hit rock bottom and the real catalyst was not his force of personality. "There is nothing so essential to the morale of an army as success in the field," wrote a lieutenant out of the Twenty-seventh Infantry; it "had the effect of a bolt of lighting." Ridgway, in this context, flipped the right switch. He maximized America's materiel strength and exploited China's corresponding weakness. He selected battles hard for him to lose while Mao made demands impossible to attain. Miracle or not, one U.S. officer said of Ridgway, "He put offensive spirit into us."[65]

Ridgway and MacArthur: The Parting of the Ways

MacArthur "demanded complete loyalty; if he didn't get it he would have nothing to do with you."

BRIGADIER GENERAL BONNER FELLERS,
FORMER MILITARY SECRETARY TO DOUGLAS MACARTHUR[66]

Once Matt Ridgway restored military normalcy by wiping away Mao's moment of overacheivement, the only thing MacArthur could do was take credit for his subordinate's accomplishments. On January 20th, at army headquarters (Taegu), he told the assembled press, with Ridgway present: "There has been a lot of loose talk about the Chinese driving us into the sea . . . a lot of nonsense. . . . This command intends to maintain a military position in Korea just as long as Washington decides we should." In MacArthur's memoirs and books by his staff, this speech preceded Ridgway's attack, rather than occurring three days later. The CINCFE would not suffer such embarrassment again. From now until dismissal in April, MacArthur went to field headquarters on the eve of an offensive, where he would announce the imminent operation. "Our security people had a heart attack," one Eighth Army officer wrote his wife, "but no one could stop the Supreme Commander. . . . It's shocking."[67]

The absence of adequate censorship had long been a source of aggravation to people who could not manipulate the media with the aplomb of General MacArthur. Frank Lowe wrote Truman in December that "the enemy has but to read the local papers to know about all he needs to know of our troop disposition and strength." The CINCFE's press conferences made the problem worse than ever, said James Quirk, Philadelphia newspaper editor called up from the reserves to handle public affairs at Ridgway headquarters. MacArthur, without due notice to Eighth Army, returned to Korea on February 20th, where he announced to the press: "I have just ordered a resumption of the initiative" across a fifty-mile front. "The story ran everywhere," moaned Lieutenant

Colonel Quirk. "Chinese intelligence could shut down their staff since all their work was [now] done for them."[68]

Twenty years later, Ridgway said that MacArthur "had no part in any way of suggesting or even influencing [my] operational plan, none whatever," regardless of what he claimed "right in front of my face." During the war, Ridgway could have felt misled and betrayed. MacArthur told him on 25 December 1950: "The Eighth Army is yours, Matt. Do with it what you like," implicitly a promise to stay out of Korea; "Now," said Ridgway, "the full responsibilities were mine." The CINCFE acted accordingly, as long as US/UN forces continued to retreat. The new situation allowed the restoration of his reputation through proximity with victory on the eve of attack. "Our father who art in Tokyo," according to Quirk, has "nothing to sustain him but his supreme ego."[69]

Quirk probably slipped his assessment into the *Washington Post* and the *New York Herald Tribune*, where stories about MacArthur's spite and jealousy surfaced in the days surrounding his relief. Ridgway, for his part, made no comment while MacArthur held theater command, although usually not prone to be mum. Ridgway later wrote with pride about risking his job by denouncing "ill-conceived tactical schemes" that would have "resulted in useless slaughter," for example, a projected airdrop into Vietnam, 1954. In 1955, his objections to a president's military budget prematurely terminated his tour as army chief of staff. However, back in 1951, Ridgway was far more compliant in asking approval, even for plans already cleared by CINCFE message traffic that backtracked on handing over the ground war in Korea. Ridgway would say that a "conversation alone with General MacArthur gave me a completely satisfactory and unambiguous understanding of his ideas . . . and of the authority accorded me for the future conduct of operations by the Eighth Army." The precise time and place of these meetings was another story to be addressed with delicacy: "Look forward with deepest pride and pleasure to your visits," Ridgway wrote on March 5th, two days before he launched an offensive across the Han River just south of Seoul. The enemy "knows, as does all the world, of your fearless personal gallantry" and "tactical acumen. . . . [Therefore] it may well follow that the pattern of your many visits will clearly point to him the conclusion that some major tactical action is pending. . . . If this reasoning seems valid to you, would not your visit on D plus one or even later annul the value of his deductions?"[70]

The Pentagon, if asked, could have told the commander of the Eighth Army about the futility of packaging in flattery sober-minded messages to MacArthur. Back on December 9th, when Ridgway was still in the Pentagon, the Department of the Army wrote the CINCFE that "the JCS desire that you confine communiqués, with due regard to security, to completed phases of military operations." None of this had worked very well before or after the Chinese offensive reached its culminating point. Different priorities lay on MacArthur's end of the communication line. The specter of utter defeat that he had raised was thoroughly discredited by the end of January. Thereafter, the only way to reverse the policy of limited war was to raise the prospect of protracted stalemate, starting months before Ridgway reached his own culminating point a little north of the 38th parallel in June 1951.[71]

In mid-February, as UN forces moved north toward the Han, MacArthur sounded a note of triumph to the assembled press, although a far cry from promising the decisive victory he had proclaimed before the Chinese counteroffensive last November. "The enemy," he said on February 13th, "has suffered a tactical reverse of measurable proportion. His losses have been among the bloodiest of modern times." However, MacArthur cautioned, "we must not fall into the error of evaluating such tactical successes as decisively leading to the enemy's defeat." One presumes the general went public because Washington had not paid particular heed to his secret message sent on the 11th: "Unless authority is given to strike bases in Manchuria, our ground forces as presently constituted cannot with safety attempt major operations in North Korea." He would not even guarantee the preservation of the status quo, Washington's basic objective. The enemy, with its major installations left intact, always "retains the potential to employ a force which will enable him to resume the offensive and force [another] retrograde movement upon us."[72]

Six weeks later the front lines were at or near the prewar boundary between North and South Korea. For the Truman administration this presented an ideal opportunity for a peace settlement: each side could retain its territorial integrity, having held it on the battlefield and hardened its lines. For MacArthur, this situation simply meant protraction, his whipping boy since September 1950, when arguing for Inchon on grounds that a deep envelopment was the only alternative to a "war of indefinite duration, of gradual attrition, and of doubtful results." He predicted the same outcome in March 1951 if Washington rejected his plans to take the war beyond the peninsula. "Red Chinese aggression in Asia could not be stopped by killing Chinese, no matter how many in Korea, so long as her power to make war remained inviolate." In impromptu press conferences for the media, MacArthur called Ridgway's step-by-step movement an "accordion war," elaborated in prepared remarks about the "heavy cost in Allied blood," the "unprecedented military advantage of sanctuary protection" in China, and the need to answer these "abnormal military inhibitions" at a level "far beyond the scope of the authority vested in me."[73]

No longer ebullient, MacArthur often seemed "tired and depressed" to those who had seen him last fall. What is more, his body had "the shakes," his recurrent symptom of emotional distress. "He did not manifest his usual confidence and flamboyance," said one lieutenant colonel, of the opinion that "he was a beaten man." This was not exactly true since the theater commander had some cards left to play. Frank Lowe, his back-channel to the White House, wrote the president on February 28th that "General MacArthur is on the verge of pulling twin white rabbits out of a black silk hat," a reference to a new plan—or should one say an old one—for a spectacular military operation. He had thought of conducting landings behind enemy positions on both sides of the Korean peninsula in July 1950, a plan subsequently scratched for lack of men and landing craft. MacArthur now dusted off this design for a double amphibious envelopment, to be supplemented with airborne and KMT troops. Courtney Whitney called it "Inchon all over again, except on a far larger scale."[74]

One may question these predictions of dramatic success. Peng, having studied MacArthur's proclivity for seaborne envelopments, was deposing reserves at coastal areas on both sides of the peninsula. MacArthur knew nothing of this or never seemed to care. He would assert that his enemy was sitting there "naked, without ammunition, without sufficient anything. . . . He could have walked around 'em and trapped the whole damn Chinese army." On occasion, the general maintained that he simply could not understand why Washington turned his proposal down. More often he had an all-purpose explanation, namely personal resentments by prejudiced parties associated with George Marshall, including Matt Ridgway since 1951. By then MacArthur felt himself subjected to a "carefully outlined campaign of propaganda" to discredit his generalship. This would climax with the proposition from columnists well connected to the administration that "General Ridgway, rather than MacArthur, has actually been in full command of the United Nations forces in Korea."[75]

This claim that MacArthur had lost his military significance, while somewhat overstated, reflected an essential fact. Washington had marginalized the general, as it had in Manila and Tokyo, until the onset of wars against Japan and North Korea breathed new opportunities in 1941 and 1950. Nothing similar was likely to reoccur in 1951 as long as Truman refused to attack China or conduct "triphibious" warfare that would give the theater commander responsibility transcending the tactical battlefront Ridgway largely controlled. MacArthur, as of now, had little more to do than go to Korea and make vacuous statements such as he did on his last trip, April 3rd: "Our strategy [meaning *my* strategy] remains unchanged. . . . It is based on maneuver and not positional warfare." A press conference performance like this could not relieve frustrations that brought to the surface his worst qualities. At some level of consciousness, he might have felt that Ridgway had played him for a fool back in early January, when secret requests for release of poison gas preceded the CINCFE's final message of disaster to the Pentagon. MacArthur was certainly not beyond conspiracy theories about enemies plotting against him, including people once thought personal protégés. This combustible mix of emotions could stir feelings similar to his reaction to the success of "that traitor Eisenhower," who had joined the War Department cabal against his old responsibility to protect the Philippines. For this Eisenhower purportedly got a major World War II command and fame to rival that of his former boss. MacArthur thought Ridgway now was doing much the same thing.[76]

If anything, MacArthur was rather slow to take offense at someone coming out of the Marshall-Eisenhower-Bradley-Collins directorate in Washington. As of February 4th, he praised Ridgway for his "performance of the last two weeks in concept and in execution. [It was] splendid and worthy of the highest traditions of a great captain. . . . Before long I hope to drop in on you for a personal chat." When MacArthur got there on the 20th, he said: "I am entirely satisfied with the situation at the front." On his next visit, March 7th, he still told his field commander: "Matt, you do what you think is right every time, and never anything just because you think I want it done. If you do that and make mistakes, I will back you 100 percent." A series of public statements then poisoned their association, starting with what MacArthur read to reporters that same day: "Assuming no diminution of the enemy's flow of ground forces and material to the Korean battle area, a continuation of the existing limitations upon our freedom of counter offensive action . . . cannot fail in time to reach a point of theoretical military stalemate."[77]

Washington initially paid MacArthur's statement little heed, although George Marshall later said it called into question the sacrifices made. The CINCFE had a more immediate impact on the common soldier in Korea, who tersely characterized his message as "why die for a tie." James Quirk, glumly by MacArthur's side when he delivered his prepared remarks, quickly responded to their "adverse effect on the morale of the troops." Within a day, he advised Ridgway's aide to offset the damage with a press release "to give purpose and direction to the soldier who is called upon to do the fighting." On March 11th, the general held his own news conference, quite different in tone from that of MacArthur: "It would be a tremendous victory for the United Nations if the war ended with our forces in control up to the 38th Parallel." Granted, Ridgway admitted to reporters, "you might call it a draw from one angle. We didn't defeat China. [However] we didn't set out to conquer China. We set out to stop [the expansion of] communism."[78]

Ridgway's statement, although treading on political policy, was essentially a "that-a-boy" to soldiers engaged with a fierce enemy on rugged terrain. They had just conducted a dangerous crossing of the Han River, where resistance would not subside until March 13th. One doubts MacArthur could conceive the psychological harm he himself had done; it was far easier for him to think his subordinate was in league to disparage a real war cry like "There is no substitute for victory." Ridgway's comments "pleased" UN officials, a group that long seemed eager to trade Formosa to Mao for peace in Korea. They certainly had influence in Washington, as the Pentagon had informed the CINCFE back in November 1950: "Our position of leadership in the Far East is being most seriously compromised in the United Nations. The utmost care will be necessary to avoid the disruption of the essential allied line-up in that organization." Conceivably, this could be reflected in Ridgway's recent pronouncement that MacArthur misconstrued.[79]

MacArthur reading a prepared statement on military stalemate in Korea, 7 March 1951. Standing glum-faced on his immediate right is Lieutenant Colonel James Quirk, Ridgway's public affairs officer. On the far right is Major General Doyle Hickey, MacArthur's acting chief of staff. *U.S. Army Signal Corps, courtesy of the MacArthur Memorial Library.*

The commander of the Eighth Army was no coconspirator with the international community, judging by a message he sent MacArthur shortly after his force turned north in mid-January. "The command, I am convinced, will do far more [than just punish the enemy]. Knowledge of this conviction, I am convinced, particularly if it likewise is your conviction, might accordingly alter our national policy and decisions vis-à-vis member states of the United Nations." Subsequent progress revealed diversity and discord not present when the immediate objective was to avoid defeat. By mid-March, when all talk of forced evacuation from Korea was a thing of the past, the UN, Washington, MacArthur, and Ridgway would have to forge some consensus or admit irreconcilable differences, classic grounds for separation. On the other hand, if the various parties were just aggrieved by some failure to communicate, a conscientious intermediary might still salvage something, Averell Harriman and Frank Lowe at the ready.[80]

There were potential areas of greater agreement if MacArthur had been attentive to changes in Washington. The State Department already had told its NATO allies that any concession on Formosa would only "whet [Beijing's] appetite for further conquest" and "consolidate its internal political position," the classic accusation against appeasement. However, no matter who said what about that island, Ridgway was no clone of MacArthur, particularly concerning substitutes for total victory. The "demand for the destruction of all opposing forces," he wrote last October, "must be reversed if civilization is to avoid self-destruction." Still, when now pressed about Korea, Ridgway had to admit that peace was not yet at hand under present military conditions. MacArthur held that this situation pointed to the need to strike China, no benign nation forced into self-protection by Western imperialism. Ridgway agreed: "There is nothing temporary about communist determination to destroy us completely." Nonetheless, to him, the appropriate response was military preparedness, limited war, and political containment, that is, the evolving strategy of the Truman administration. Moreover, as reporters in Korea noted, Ridgway was always sensitive to the sensitivities of allied commanders and their governments. This meant that while fighting his own war, he did everything he could to prevent disruption of the NATO alliance Dwight Eisenhower was bringing forth halfway around the world.[81]

Policy, pride, and pique may help explain an incident never covered in the press. In late March, MacArthur sent Ridgway a personal reprimand when a single battalion fell into a firefight after theater headquarters ordered a corps-wide advance to stop. This harsh (although unofficial) response to an inadvertent mishap was a far cry from previous statements: "Form your own opinion and use your own judgment." It was indicative of a permanent change in MacArthur's attitude toward his erstwhile protégé, later manifest when calling him part of "the Marshall clique" that "monopolized the power and who bore the onus of the misfortunes which had occurred" in the Far East. Ridgway, supposedly, had been in full agreement with plans to win the war but then, at Washington's so-called behest, did "a complete flip flop in 24 hours." MacArthur, the "outsider," would tell a reporter in 1954 that Ridgway was the worst of all field commanders reporting to him in two wars.[82]

MacArthur, however bitter toward the man he would call "a chameleon," was not wrong to feel that Ridgway's repute severely damaged his own standing. If one believed that the personal strength of a field commander turned the war around, then it was logical to think a badly flawed superior created the mess that had to be fixed. Whether this scenario was simplistic or not, Ridgway entered the pantheon of America's great commanders on par with, if not topping, his old patron. Back in March 1951, when his reputation was still growing, he had known the CINCFE in far better circumstances. Consequently, he first thought GHQ staff hatched up the rebuke out of personal jealousy: "MacArthur would never write a letter like that." Ridgway would not learn that he had done it over staff objections until a week or two after becoming CINCFE. Prior to that revelation, he promptly went to see MacArthur after appointed to replace him. The general said "that my performance had been brilliant" and was told, in turn, "that he knew that for more than thirty years he had my personal devotion and he could count on that remaining completely unchanged." MacArthur, said Ridgway, "seemed touched."[83]

One might judge MacArthur's state of agitation on the eve of his dismissal by his behavior toward a fellow soldier of long acquaintance who really wished him well. The press poured salt on the wound by lionizing Ridgway, what Mac-Arthur seemed to consider a cabal. "In my twenty campaigns," he wrote in 1957, "I have never known portions of the newspaper coverage to be so inaccurate, so slanted and so harmfully prejudicial." His personal staff was well aware that "sensitivity to criticism . . . is his Achilles' heel." Courtney Whitney continued to battle reporters in Japan judged unfriendly to the theater commander. Sid Huff, long-time member of the MacArthur inner circle, hid critical press copy published outside the reach of headquarters. All this effort went for naught, thanks to the general's stateside following. At his behest they clipped and sent articles about him on a daily basis via air express. As one journalist put it: "He knew everything we said."[84]

China and the Balkans:
The Korean War in a Global Context

Surprise invasion South Korea by North Korea in strength may indicate riskier Soviet policy. . . . If successful Soviets may venture similar attacks in Yugoslavia.

PENTAGON TO MACARTHUR, 27 JUNE 1950[85]

The Truman administration in early 1950 tired to withdraw from the Chinese civil war largely because Europe seemed more important to United States security. Combat in Korea against Chinese troops did not change the essential principle restated in the Department of Defense on December 4th: do not "fall into the Russian trap of engaging our strength in a depleting war with China." This decision was strictly military, Washington now having little faith in a political rapprochement with Beijing. "We had hoped that Titoism would develop in Communist China," the undersecretary of the army wrote Frank Pace. "Unfortunately, the evidence is all of a contrary sort." The government still raised the topic in psychological warfare, an enterprise gaining considerable steam. It took a stab at Stalin's paranoia by spreading disinformation that Mao always was a Titoist at heart.[86]

Dean Acheson, once receptive to Chinese independence, now relied on forceful means to drive a "wedge" between Moscow and Beijing. Grand strategy was to mete out pain and suffering on China inside Korea, force it to rely on Russia, then reap the inevitable windfall from disillusion after the USSR failed the PRC. In August 1951, the civil affairs and education section of Eighth Army headquarters drew up a public statement for the foreign press: "Letting China take a hideous pounding from the United Nations does Sino-Soviet relations no good at all. It may mean China eventually goes the way of Yugoslavia's Communist Marshall Tito if her regime holds up, which is doubtful." Dean Rusk already had said much the same thing in private consultation with Canada's foreign minister: by inflicting "hugely disproportionate Chinese losses," US/UN operations could cause a substantial change in Beijing. The "pro-Moscow elements of the Communist Party are now on top," proven by China's intervention. Defeat could redistribute the allocation of power, putting the "nationalist element" in command.[87]

Rusk made no reference to MacArthur, a self-professed expert on "Oriental psychology." Titoism, whether dead or alive on the mainland, diminished the chance of ever executing the general's plan to make war on Beijing. Washington remained quite wary of a Soviet plot "to involve the United States [deeper] in a struggle with China so as to create a situation in which Russia could have the highest degree of freedom in making a move against Yugoslavia." The Balkans had become a geographic buffer keeping the Red Army away from Greece and

Italy. This was far more important to the State Department than keeping Mao out of Korea or Formosa, let alone bringing Chiang Kai-shek's forces back to the mainland. Yugoslavia was also practical, at least to the Pentagon. It had over a million men at arms, the single largest force in Europe not in Stalin's camp. Joe Collins, on a secret tour of inspection, said they were "tough and traditionally have made fine soldiers." Their weakness lay in equipment, particularly aircraft and armor, alarmingly reminiscent of ROK incapacity for self-defense at the onset of the Korean War.[88]

The Pentagon had warned MacArthur back on 27 June 1950 that the "sudden invasion" of South Korea might indicate Stalin was willing to move against Yugoslavia. Kim Il-sung's initial progress reinforced fears that a Soviet proxy such as Romania, Hungary, or Bulgaria would launch its own blitzkrieg on Belgrade. However, with relatively little assistance, the Serbs were likely to be quite effective, because "able and aggressive," to quote Collins. Omar Bradley went further when things were at their worst in late November 1950: military assistance for Yugoslavia would help "get them to act as a threat" to the Soviet Union itself. Grand strategy thus had gone a long way from 1944, when the U.S. army zealously opposed a commitment to the Balkans lest it risk Kremlin "resentment" during World War II. Six to seven years later, in the Korean conflict, one could not be sure how Stalin might react. The same thing often could be said of the Truman administration. It had not anticipated the invasion of the south or its own commitment to prevent that conquest. Washington now seemed to be searching for a dividend from its investment, that is, strategic validation for getting stuck in this secondary theater. It proposed that by prohibiting the Kremlin from "securing [its] eastern flank," the war effort in Korea had prevented the Soviet Union from "concentrating its offensive power in other areas, particularly in Europe."[89]

MacArthur would hold that "the Truman-Acheson-Marshall-Bradley-general staff group concentrated its resources at the center to the neglect of the vital ends." Wise or foolish, Washington seemed to operate on the premise that by limiting its investment, it limited its liabilities. To divert Stalin, yet not be diverted itself, it would ration the size of the U.S. force to what it already committed to Korea as of late 1950, about a quarter of a million Americans. It also limited military operations to the peninsula. One Pentagon paper proposed a rationale judiciously not publicized because too cold-blooded to pass muster with the American public: "A [U.S.] victory in Korea could make Soviet imperialism turn elsewhere for fields to conquer," such as Europe or the Mid-East. Those regions were clearly more important to Washington than was a relatively barren stretch of continental Asia jutting into the Sea of Japan. The supreme military commander in this secondary theater felt undercut by such government priorities and by a field commander's conduct of the war. He would take his personal frustrations over policy into the political area and thereby precipitate an irreconcilable clash with the president of the United States.[90]

Truman Fires
MacArthur

1 2 3 4 5 **6** 7 8 9

Only God or the Government of the United States can keep me from the fulfillment of my mission.

DOUGLAS MACARTHUR, N.D.[1]

Relations between Truman and MacArthur went through three stages during the Korean War. In stage one—from intervention through Inchon in mid-1950— implicit bargaining and compromise was common. Stage two—the late fall— was one of CINCFE ascendancy over Truman, an "inveterate idealist about generals" according to an assistant, who said the president would "passively await the outcome of MacArthur's plans for victory." Stage three began with China's intervention in late November and gathered momentum as Matt Ridgway discredited MacArthur's call to attack the mainland. Verbal obstruction then became the theater commander's mode of interaction with the administration. He openly criticized its policy of limiting the war to Korea; it issued restrictions on these pronouncements that barely restricted the pronouncements at all. After that, Truman did his best to ignore these comments while Ridgway handled combat operations. This civil-military stalemate during a stalemated war lasted until April, when MacArthur embedded his objections to government policy in a new forum, a personal letter to one of Truman's most partisan critics in Congress. The issue then no longer seemed whether a politician should manage a professional soldier, the perception that had staid Truman's hand. The soldier now became a politician, or so it struck the president, who still needed other military men to support his relief of MacArthur. The Joint Chiefs of Staff had to concur lest the public think Truman was the person who politicized the war. The final irony was that relieving the theater commander was about the last thing a shrewd politician would do. Better to have kept him as a figurehead in Japan than have him return to America, where he could rally his supporters.[2]

Moving toward the Threshold

The President was reluctant to relieve General MacArthur . . . he leaned over backwards to see whether he couldn't work things out.

PAUL NITZE, NOVEMBER 1986[3]

Douglas MacArthur, unlike his government, never doubted what to do about Chinese bases beyond the Yalu River. On 1 December 1950, a weekly magazine asked him if restrictions against attacks on these targets were "a handicap to effective military operations?" "An enormous handicap," he replied, "without precedent in military history," and then sent the transcript of the interview to the United Press for nationwide distribution. One can understand his sense of outrage. A sanctuary of this size and importance was certainly uncommon, not excepting restrictions imposed on Chiang Kai-shek's air force when Washington "neutralized" the Taiwan Strait. Then, in late June, the Kuomintang was not engaged in daily combat with the PRC. MacArthur and the JCS would still have precluded a potential invasion of Taiwan by allowing a preemptive bombing of the mainland. Few military men anticipated that America would do any less if its own army confronted a major Chinese force.[4]

The CIA had assumed that the threat of retaliation would keep the PRC out of the war. MacArthur concurred when discounting China's commitment to Korea in the fall of 1950. His confidence encouraged the government to postpone hard decisions about policy until Chinese presence was uncontestable. The NSC met on December 2nd, the day the press published MacArthur's aforementioned complaint. The administration focused on his statements, not just the communist offensive. Acheson insisted "that it was essential to get some kind of censorship in the Far Eastern Command immediately." George Marshall, maintaining his role as mediator between the CINCFE and the State Department, said "that this would be a rather difficult thing to do." Truman, torn again, tried to take control but remain conciliatory, that is, blend his belief in presidential leadership along the lines of Andrew Jackson with his personal and political desire to avoid conflict with MacArthur.[5]

The result of this ambivalence was a transmission from the White House commonly known as "the gag order," although that is rather hyperbolic considering its content. That designation was more appropriate to the kind of directive Dwight Eisenhower issued George Patton following remarks in 1944 about the "evident destiny of the British and Americans and, of course, the Russians to rule the world." Winston Churchill, on Truman's side in 1951, felt the U.S. army brouhaha was a "tempest in a teapot." Hitler was not one to be shocked into escalation. Eisenhower, still taking a general's "hide off" in a manner Truman only fantasized, told Patton to say nothing in public without prior submission for direct approval: "Officially and definitely, if you are again guilty of any indiscretion in speech or action . . . I will relieve you instantly."[6]

Truman was hardly this forceful on 6 December 1950. Washington's instructions to MacArthur went out "in the light of the present critical international situation," thereby implying a temporary measure lasting no longer than the emergency. Clear all "public" statements on foreign policy with the State Department, military policy with the Department of Defense. Submit them in advance to the "White House for information"; the word "approval" was not present at all. Two days later the Pentagon sent a clarifying message that clarified equivocations and escape clauses: "Intent of instructions not to prohibit speeches by military on suitable occasions. Necessity of imparting sound and authoritative information to the public is as important as it always has been. . . . Dept of Army is prepared to assist with advice and clearances when you are in doubt"—this to a man who rarely seemed to entertain much doubt at all.[7]

All the major military commands got a copy of the "gag order," as did all members of the cabinet and the federal directors for selective service, central intelligence, national resources, price stabilization, and economic cooperation. This was hardly a round-up of the usual suspects, the draftsman of the message eventually confirmed: it "would bring torrents of criticism" if sent only to Mac-Arthur, "especially from his Republican supporters in Congress." The general himself could not be mollified by any pretense he was just part of a crowd. "This has been by far the most open drive from Washington against me with but little effort to conceal the individuals responsible." MacArthur steered clear of open defiance, at least while his army was in retreat. The criticism befalling his command seemed proof that the government was searching for an excuse to justify his dismissal. "I have made no effort," he wrote a confidant on December 20th, "to clarify any further questions raised concerning the Korean campaign."[8]

Back on December 8th, MacArthur submitted for approval a press release attributing surprise to failures in "political intelligence," meaning other federal agencies. The Department of the Army replied that statements issued in the field should make no comments "relative to political or domestic matters," but then undercut the authority just asserted: "Compliance with the foregoing will obviate any need for referring your communiqués to Washington." MacArthur conformed without comment and removed the statement on hand, far from his resistance to withdrawing his August message about Formosa to the Veterans of Foreign Wars. He subsequently grasped the opportunity to issue more pronouncements on debatable grounds that they dealt with military matters, not political affairs, when he blamed outside factors for China's success. "Field intelligence was handicapped by the severest limitations," he told the press the day after Christmas. "Aerial reconnaissance beyond the border . . . was forbidden."[9]

MacArthur, obviously testing the waters, made this scarcely hidden accusation of political interference in passive voice, no subject named. Truman bit his lip, although the ultimate target for responsibility. Opponents had denounced him for silencing the general in the VFW incident, remarkable considering how public that whole incident had been. In response to the gag order, the press was asking embarrassing questions as to whether Washington had "stripped General MacArthur of authority to speak freely on the Korean War," even "issue decisions on current ground or military operations." Truman dodged the topic of political intrusion, always a very sensitive subject for him: "It is not true. If you will call up the Defense Department, they will confirm what I am telling you." Acheson would later defend his boss with an argument worthy of a senior partner, Covington & Burling law firm, Washington bar. No "authority had been taken away from General MacArthur to issue communiqués on the real situation of the military operations in Korea," no mention made of military policy toward mainland China. The day the president finally relieved the general, Courtney Whitney, personal lawyer in residence on MacArthur's staff, cited White House statements that it never curbed the prerogative to communicate. Truman's proclivity to compromise with his theater commander thereby undercut accusations of disobedience.[10]

Whatever eventually happened, Truman initially thought he mitigated his problem with MacArthur by striking a reasonable balance between command and conciliation. The president had not told the general to withdraw his statement about responsibility for failure, perhaps because MacArthur did not directly blame the White House. Nor did Truman say "cease and desist"; only forward statements on policy matters for concurrence. Since hoping for the best he could cite Wake Island, a cause for hope that MacArthur "would respect the authority of the President," at least in the president's memory of the event. The theater commander, who apologized for "any embarrassment" he had caused concerning Chiang Kai-shek, supposedly promised to clear what he said. The first incident was true, but the so-called pledge was a product of the president's imagination regardless of how polite MacArthur may have been in circumstances not likely to reappear. Truman had held out a significant reward for good behavior, much as Franklin Roosevelt did in World War II when discussing a return to the Philippines and the prospective invasion of Japan. In the fall of 1950, Truman talked of support for another total victory, because against the lowly North Koreans. Now that he would not attack Communist China, the president had little to promise in return for compliance. MacArthur was therefore likely to dance along the sideline of defiance until he finally stepped out into what Truman would call "rank insubordination."[11]

MacArthur made public comments about the "unification of Korea" in mid-February. He still grumbled "this old soldier cannot obtain approval on any statement more significant than a [company status] morning report." A critical confrontation with the president was in the works despite Frank Lowe's mediation mission. "I note the wolves are howling back home," he wrote Harry Vaughan two days after Ridgway took ground command. "If the wolves prevail and we lose General MacArthur, then it would be a bad day for all of us and a dim day for all of our chances out here." Lowe, who was reluctant to speak ill of any soldier other than Department of the Army staff, gave the field commander his due in late February. "I cannot undertake to describe the 'lift' that General Ridgway has given to the troops out here," he wrote the president; "it is remarkable, to put it mildly." However, because Lowe would not have built the monument to the new hero on the grave of MacArthur's reputation, he resented press reports that JCS directives going straight to Korea were making the CINCFE a nonentity. "MacArthur's strategy and Ridgway's tactics are paying off in a big way. It is tough going and a hard life, but we are doing all right."[12]

Truman agreed that MacArthur and Ridgway were "really making a fighting team," perhaps to salve the CINCFE's ego or console Lowe, another subject of concern. "Your reports [about supplies, conditions, and morale] are very valuable to me and I don't want them to stop by your being too brave at the front." The president paid less attention to his friend's volatile opinions on national defense. Lowe, when falling back with the troops in December, called for "a show-down with the Russians once and for all." Two months later, he praised Truman's effort "to prevent a world wide holocaust [that] will make World War I and II look like a skirmish." By then, the president must have felt Lowe's judgment was wearing thin. "Being on the ground you absorb certain views points but when it became my responsibility to lay out the whole picture, it has a different look." Lowe, reduced to sending bitter commentaries about "newspaper embryonic Napoleons," began to rant about "hear[ing] too damn much about the Eighth Army and the Commanding General." On April 5th, Truman ordered his "eyes and ears" home on grounds "you have used up your share of good luck." So had MacArthur, as things would soon turn out.[13]

Lowe had been faithful as a monk to his vows of anonymity, at least until after MacArthur's dismissal. The president's personal agent then briefly sought the limelight to right what he felt was a terrible wrong previously mentioned in an "eyes only" message to Truman about "certain Pentagon channels" in March 1951: they "resent my presence and resent it militantly," just as they resented Harry Vaughan, MacArthur, and the Marine Corps. Lowe repeated the same themes to the press in January 1952: "that damned Pentagon crowd" prevented his reports from reaching the Oval Office, where they would have plugged the rupture in relations with MacArthur that led to the "disgraceful stalemate" in Korea. One can always debate the wisdom of Lowe's grand strategy: "Throw everything at 'em and get it over with." There was no substance to his charge about interference with his message traffic, according to a confidential White House enquiry into the accusations.[14]

Lowe was brave, noble, and naïve: the Don Quixote of the Korean War. Sabotage was not the factor that severed Truman and MacArthur, unless it was the damage caused by Courtney Whitney—Lowe's friend and MacArthur's military secretary, speechwriter, confidant, and attorney. Virtually no one in the Far East command, aside from Lowe and MacArthur, had much to say for this "slimey son of a bitch." He "was a good lawyer," the others admitted, being "smart, ruthless, and incisive" or, if one preferred, "crafty and deceitful," not to mention "pompous, arrogant, mean, rude [and] shrewd." This apparently fit the conditions for a counselor to MacArthur on topics like his divorce in the 1920s from a high-society wife bored to death in the Philippines. Otherwise, the general's staff dismissed Whitney as a "politician," which was not completely fair. He put in ten years of military service before taking up the bar; the staff put in time on political activities when MacArthur made prospective runs for the presidency. There obviously was a lot of personal jealousy in play.[15]

George Kennan, when visiting Tokyo headquarters in 1948, thought of the "internal intrigue" prevalent in "the latter days of the court of Catherine II." Whitney won the competition for special place aside the throne. Losers who had served MacArthur longer, such as Charles Willoughby, could not understand Whitney's "considerable influence" other than his "Jewish credentials, training, and background." Others less disposed to anti-Semitic paranoia emphasized that Whitney was a "civilian," actually a citizen-soldier, as were MacArthur's personal aides in both world wars. The general could not "let down his hair" with a professional soldier, let alone a fellow West Pointer, said Edwin ("Pinky") Wright, assistant chief of staff for plans and operations. Such men retained residual ambitions—even Willoughby, not the complete sycophant outsiders often depict. Whitney, however, was "almost a servant," according to Wright. He was "a fellow to whom he could tell his troubles" because "willing to commit himself totally."[16]

MacArthur said that he and Whitney got along so well because their "minds just meet." This may explain what another staff officer observed: the "pervasive, insidious power Whitney seemed to have, not over, but with the general." Frank Lowe, while acting from the best intent, played a part in preserving this situation in which a Mr. Hyde figure, like Whitney (nicknamed "Rasputin" by one associate), swamped the Dr. Jekyll aspects of MacArthur's personality. In January 1950, when Lowe was still comfortably retired in Maine, he did his best to prolong Whitney's military carrier by entreating the president that the man had been "stymied" as a brigadier general because he was "a reserve officer" although "he is one of our very best. . . . Knowing the War Department as I do, General MacArthur's request [for Whitney's promotion will not] be granted except at your hand and by your act." Truman responded in late October, during the era of good feelings following the conference at Wake Island. Once he saw to Whitney's upgrade to major general, the advisor could stay on active duty by the CINCFE's side round the clock. This would prove detrimental to relations with the White House, aside from one act on which all parties agreed. Whitney would draw up the citation presenting Frank Lowe with a Distinguished Service Cross, the country's second-highest combat decoration. Awarded on April 10th, the day before the president dismissed the theater commander, it was about the last general order MacArthur ever issued.[17]

Other than respect for Frank Lowe's bravery, Far East Military Headquarters and the administration agreed on very little, including the meaning of the gag order issued back on December 6th. Whitney supplied a legal veneer to noncompliance when he advised MacArthur that the directive applied "solely to formal public statements and not to communiqués, correspondence, or personal conversations," also known as briefings to the press. One might debate who was at fault: the counselor not serving his client's best interests or the client requesting the advice he received? Either way, Whitney could certainly poke holes in any potential suggestion that MacArthur be court-martialed for insubordination, despite Truman's retrospective claim "that's what ought to have happened to him." The general did not violate a clear order directed "to the subordinate personally," as specified in the sixty-fourth Article of War. That might keep him out of court, but it would not assure retention unless Washington continued to lean over to avoid a confrontation.[18]

Concessions from the White House along these lines would have to be based on the premise that the form of a MacArthur message was more important than its content. Did he make a "formal public statement" on policy as opposed to what the CINCFE called a "routine communiqué," what he purported to do on March 24th? Ridgway's field command had reestablished the territorial integrity of South Korea by throwing the invader back across its border. The Truman administration, feeling an opportunity for peace was at hand, drafted a proposal for an armistice as a point of discussion toward "a common point of view" within the UN coalition. Acheson told reporters that consultations were taking place with other nations participating in the war, as well as with General MacArthur, who had already been informed that a pending action could produce a ceasefire: "State has asked JCS what authority you should have to permit sufficient freedom of action for next few weeks to provide security for UN forces." It was less judicious to have told him the political rationale behind the peace feeler: "Strong UN feeling persists that further diplomatic effort should be made before any advance with major forces north of 38th parallel."[19]

Neither the United Nations nor military compromise was popular in MacArthur's headquarters, particularly after the General Assembly, led by an India-Egypt-neutralist bloc, sweetened the peace-talk proposal to Beijing by considering the status of Taiwan and China's seat in the UN. These ideas, widely discussed since July 1950, always made the Truman administration nervous that its own China policy would alienate the international community. It consented to the distasteful resolution but still hoped the PRC would not exploit the opportunity to sever the alliance, particularly before a true cease-fire. MacArthur, not content with ceding the initiative, broadcast his own communiqué on March 24th that preempted any prospective message out of Washington.[20]

The general may have taken an action that incidentally helped the administration escape embarrassing discussions about Formosa. Truman and Acheson were still not grateful. The president had planned to suggest that "a prompt settlement of the Korean problem would greatly reduce international tension in the Far East and would open the way for the consideration of other problems in the area." This was diplomatic code for Formosa, not really on his trading bloc. Truman was more forthright in a passage conveying would happen if inducement failed. "Until satisfactory arrangements for ending the fighting have been reached, United Nations military action must be continued," no hint made of directly attacking the mainland. MacArthur, by contrast, explicitly withheld the carrot in question: "There should be no insuperable difficulty in arranging decisions on the Korean problem if the issues are resolved on their own merits, without being burdened by extraneous matters such as Formosa or China's seat in the United Nations." He also waved a larger stick, his customary doings, as when warning North Korea the previous October that "the early and total defeat and complete destruction of your armed forces and war-making potential is now inevitable." This time he gave notice to the PRC that the UN command could "depart from its tolerant effort to contain the war to the area of Korea. . . . An expansion of our military operations to its coastal areas and interior bases would doom Red China to the risk of imminent military collapse."[21]

A close reading of MacArthur's message revealed his personal frustration: "Red China" did not really risk "collapse" as long as Washington remained "tolerant." The general could still get some satisfaction from bragging about what he thought he had the raw capacity to do. That refurbished the military motif in his mind before China ever ambushed U.S. forces, judging by what he now said. "Of even greater significance than our tactical success has been the clear revelation that this new enemy, of such exaggerated and vaunted military power, lacks the industrial capacity to provide adequately many critical items essential to the conduct of modern war." This certainly got the attention of China, not one to draw distinctions between different personalities in the so-called imperialist camp. MacArthur seemed to be "new evidence" that the United States was preparing for "direct aggression against our homeland." Beijing certainly would not negotiate under an ultimatum widely dispersed to its own soldiers in MacArthur-command leaflets that depicted the Chinese army as defeated on the battlefield. That would have cost the regime the prestige acquired when throwing the enemy out of North Korea, its primary achievement during the war. Mao had not gained Taiwan, one major objective, but had consolidated the mainland under Communist Party control. Its new status as a world power helped the politburo mobilize its population to crush the remnants of the opposition, particularly in South China.[22]

No counterrevolution was in the offing, but the Far East command had still done what Truman asked MacArthur to do back on January 13th. It deflated China's prestige by stopping its expansion. It had not done damage commensurate with MacArthur's communiqué, aptly called by critics "an ultimatum of terms of surrender." Truman could only put his own proposal away and reply "no comment" to questions about the general's proclamation. Otherwise, the president would have drawn more attention to the disarray in America's chain of command, a topic of serious discussion abroad. There, MacArthur was said "to be wearing his self-tailored mantle of pro-consul." George Marshall later testified that it became "more difficult for us to work to a more harmonious and intimate accord" with Britain, France, and the United Nations. Leaders of opinion in London and Paris felt MacArthur personified Caesarism or Bonapartism, the threat a military strongman can pose to republican government. In April, the president of the United States agreed that the presidency was at stake. However, in late March, while the U.K. embassy was protesting MacArthur to the U.S. government, the administration was remarkably subdued. Robert Lovett, the deputy secretary of defense, warned Acheson that "if the president challenged" the general's pronouncement, the White House "would be in the position at once of being on the side of sin."[23]

Truman's rhetoric, in comparison, was uninspiring because constrained by fear of stroking a fervor for total war. His low-keyed delivery was even worse, especially when reading scripts prepared to prevent off-the-cuff comments, such as those scaring Britain about use of the atomic bomb. MacArthur's message, on the other hand, was a cry for decisive victory in the tradition of a Lincoln, Roosevelt, or Churchill. No one in Washington insisted that he withdraw his statement in the manner of his old pronouncement to the VFW. Dean Acheson had learned something since shoving his foot down his own throat over Alger Hiss. He told Lovett that George Marshall had best stick to "no comment," rather than speak of an officer entering areas of policy. Otherwise, "it would appear that the argument was between General MacArthur and the Department of State or the president and was not a matter of concern to the Department of Defense."[24]

Acheson knew that he needed the Pentagon to take on and take down the Far East military commander. In the meantime, unnamed elements in the State Department issued what the press called "an implied rebuke" by saying "the political issues which General MacArthur has stated are beyond his responsibility as a field commander." The agency later went on to state that "so far as they could determine General MacArthur's statement was not cleared in Washington before he issued it in Tokyo." Truman, along these lines, directed the Department of Defense to tell the CINCFE to "direct that your attention be called to the order as transmitted 6 December 1950," that is, make no announcements on policy without government concurrence. "P.S.: Honest this time," was the essence of this modest message, according to a Herblock political cartoon for the *Washington Post*, where the MacArthur figure says "File it with the others" while motioning over his shoulder to a wastepaper basket.[25]

The Advent of the Critical Event

The most obvious fact about the dismissal of General MacArthur is that he virtually forced his own removal.

NEW YORK HERALD TRIBUNE, EDITORIAL, 12 APRIL 1951[26]

Dean Acheson found Truman angry and perplexed but "perfectly calm" after MacArthur issued his communiqué to the PRC on March 24th. He also seemed composed on April 5th, at least when newspapers published a report that the general told a British military analyst that "it was not the soldier who had encroached on the realm of the politician but the politician on that of the soldier." The theater commander had been making such comments off and on since December. His language, however, was growing particularly pointed about obstruction of victory. Even so, there is no record of reaction in the Oval Office. The president's attention was on another news story breaking that day about another politician.[27]

Joe Martin, the Republican minority leader in the House of Representatives, had just disclosed a letter from MacArthur written in response to a request that he give the government his views on military policy, nothing particularly new. Truman's critics had been passing resolutions since March 1949 "requesting" the general testify to Congress about conditions in the Far East. MacArthur responded to Martin on 20 March 1951, the day he received word from the Pentagon about the president's prospective proposal for negotiations but four days before he received gag order number two. The CINCFE praised a speech the congressman delivered on February 12th in which Martin declared that "our great ally, the established government of the Republic of China," should be released to establish "a second front on China's mainland." Hence the issue of Formosa raised its head once more. It sparked conflict between Truman and MacArthur before Kim Il-sung sent his army across the 38th parallel. It caused Truman to ponder relieving MacArthur for his VFW letter, then highly praised by Congressman Martin in mid-1950. Now, the spring of 1951, the Chinese civil war set the stage for the act directly leading to the general's dismissal from command in a conflict ostensibly waged about Korea.[28]

Martin clearly preferred full utilization of KMT armed forces, some 800,000 strong, but "a series of commando raids" was a viable option for him, as it was for Joe McCarthy and Robert Taft. The senator from Wisconsin implored

Congress to issue "a mandate to our foreign policy planners" that General MacArthur be given "complete freedom" to arm and use Nationalist forces for guerrilla warfare. Taft, while not so directive, could not fathom neutralization, "utterly indefensible and perfectly idiotic." None of them mentioned—perhaps did not know—that the administration was already in the process of using Taipei against China in covert form. Martin proposed cleaning out the State Department because, "as now constituted," it "is never going to permit a single soldier from Formosa to participate" in any action against the mainland. Otherwise, Dean Acheson and company "would have to admit that we should have supported Chiang Kai-shek all along." The White House could not tout its actual activity lest it alienate Britain and concede MacArthur's point about where to be waging the war. One of the covert agents conducting the ongoing action wrote, "Having listened to the critics of the Truman administration hammer ceaselessly on the theme that Truman had abandoned Chiang Kai-shek, it was a major revelation to me to learn that this was far from the truth."[29]

In America, one rarely has to worry about compromising secret operations, most of which wind up in the newspapers. Reports surfaced in May that "a United States program of aid and organization for anti-Communist guerrillas on the mainland of China has been considerably increased in recent months." If in print earlier, the story still would not have affected Joe Martin very much. Domestic politics, not military strategy, was his bottom line. The speech—in origin, nature, and purpose—was a manifesto from a man hoping to regain the position of speaker of the house won in the 1946 election, lost in 1948, and nearly won back in 1950. Election 1952 was to be his day of "deliverance," one in which America answered the question "what are we in Korea for, to win or to lose? If we are not in Korea to win, then the Truman administration should be indicted for the murder of thousands of American boys," an opinion not far from that of MacArthur. "The only way," Martin continued, "to achieve the leadership we so desperately need is by a landslide Republican victory."[30]

Martin, later wanting to rebut responsibility for the relief of MacArthur, claimed that "fresh Democratic attacks" forced him to contact the general: "The Republicans were entitled to the truth if we were effectively to defend our side of the argument." One wonders to what he was referring. The *New York Times* and the *Congressional Record* contained nothing about his speech in the two months between its delivery and MacArthur's dismissal. It consequently seems that the congressman was more concerned that it got no attention, scarcely the heated criticism allegedly generated. If so, he enlisted MacArthur to give the statement the significance it finally got when the general responded, "As you point out, we must win. There is no substitute for victory."[31]

MacArthur thought nothing was wrong with Martin's exposition, particularly to deploy Chiang's armed forces: "In the past" America "never failed" to "meet force with maximum counter-force." The issue, nonetheless, was not so much military policy as linking it to a political party, customarily outside the mainstream of the officer corps, nonpartisan by tradition. The scathing rhetoric of Martin's speech did not curb MacArthur's praise: "You have certainly lost none of your old time punch." The general might have known that close association with the man in question might not help his cause. Herbert Hoover soon advised MacArthur to keep his distance from Martin in order to present himself as a soldier above and beyond the political fray. He subsequently claimed that the congressman put a personal letter into the public record "for some unexplained reason and without consulting me." This was scarcely credible. MacArthur had not marked his letter "confidential," nor did he show resentment at its release. When a crowd met the general at the airport in Washington for his "farewell address," he went directly to the House minority leader for a special greeting: "How do you do, Mr. Speaker?"[32]

Anyone half as astute as MacArthur would have realized the partisan benefits Martin derived when citing "advice from our Far Eastern Command." The person to be quoted had already gone through something like this in 1944, when a Roosevelt-hating congressman sent the general his complaint that "left-wingers and New Dealers" were establishing a "monarchy . . . which will destroy the rights of the common people." MacArthur responded: "I do unreservedly agree with the complete wisdom and statesmanship of your comments." Then caught in a political tempest by its publication, he claimed that he had "merely" written some "amiable acknowledgments to a member of our highest law-making body." The constitutional authority of the legislature had not been the issue. Nor would it be in 1951, although MacArthur ended the year on a speaking tour lamenting the "despotic power" of the chief executive. For the time being, the only thing that really mattered was what the president would do: whether Harry Truman would essentially ignore the letter to a hostile congressman as Franklin Roosevelt did.[33]

MacArthur's "consuming desire for favorable publicity is going to give him a hard bump some day," Dwight Eisenhower recorded in his diary on 15 November 1939. On 6 April 1951, Harry Truman recorded in his own journal that the MacArthur-Martin incident "looks like the last straw." This language, while equivocal because not stating this "*is* the last straw," suggested that there was a clear, linear progression of events over a substantial period of time finally culminating in the CINCFE's dismissal. In fact, despite Truman's post facto claims, he had no plans to relieve the general for sabotaging his foreign policy on March 24th. The theater commander had still not done what only he could do, force his removal by a man long willing to endure almost anything he did. Then on April 5th, Roger Tubby, deputy press secretary, rushed into the Oval Office with a ticker-tape copy of MacArthur's letter of endorsement implanted in Joe Martin's political attack. "It is high time," the Republican leader said, "that the administration and the Pentagon came clean with the Congress and with the American people."[34]

Truman, a military history buff, had been engrossed in reading Omar Bradley's memoir of World War II serialized in *Life* magazine. Not wanting to be disturbed, he quickly passed over the wire service release and calmly told Tubby, "The newspaper boys are putting him up to this." The gag order of the previous December was supposed to handle such problems: MacArthur was "to refrain from direct communications on military or foreign policy with newspapers, magazines, or other publicity media in the United States." He routinely ignored the directive when defending his damaged reputation by laying defeat at the door of the White House. Truman had still not penalized him for his comments, perhaps because the president could always blame his own critics in the "sabotage press." They already "made the world believe that the American people are not behind our foreign policy. I don't think," he had said on November 28th, that "the Communists would ever have dared to this thing in Korea if it hadn't been for that belief."[35]

Truman was disinclined to think any such thing of almost any soldier, including Douglas MacArthur. The general's recent ultimatum to China had still not shown the president how far he would go. Acheson noted Truman's "disbelief" in what MacArthur did even after the general did it. Truman wrote: "I do not believe that he purposefully decided to challenge civilian control of the military." This reveals his ongoing reluctance to face up to the state of affairs. Who knows what might have happened if Roger Tubby had not persisted despite admittedly holding a junior position that did not warrant involvement in high matters of government policy? He insisted that MacArthur "is not only insubordinate, he's insolent and he ought to be fired." Truman only then carefully read the press copy, where he apparently found some new factor. He looked up and said: "By God, Roger. I think you are right."[36]

Newspapers had played no role in this statement from MacArthur, despite Truman's initial reaction to Tubby. Any provocation lay in the lap of the congressman from Massachusetts, although this source was subsequently slighted in most White House claims. In mid-May, Truman denied MacArthur's letter to Joe Martin was the cause of his relief: "I have been carefully studying the situation over, and reviewing the facts for the past year." This was not inaccurate in the narrow sense that the idea of relieving MacArthur probably crossed his mind. It then was discarded until the Martin incident emphasized by partisan Republicans who held that the president was not presidential: he fired MacArthur out of "political pique" when an opponent tweaked his nose with a statement from the soldier. Truman wished to discredit this accusation for political as well as personal reasons. He always tried to maintain that he had a bipartisan foreign policy in the best interests of the nation at large. He frequently employed Republicans of the Arthur Vandenberg variety to respond to criticism launched from the Taft wing—before, during, and after the bitterly fought 1950 election. By drawing subsequent attention to MacArthur's diktat to China in March 1951, Truman could maintain this pose rather than share something he called "regrettable and shameful," namely ever making war "a football in a partisan political campaign."[37]

The White House perpetuated a mantra that echoed over time that the proclamation to China caused MacArthur's relief. This had surface credibility because the incident had international impact. "That worried us more than the Joe Martin letter," Truman told the White House counsel in late April. However, his statement that the general's behavior in March "was inexcusable" ignores the fact that he excused it, unlike the exchange between Martin and MacArthur that Truman deemphasized only in retrospect. The president apparently felt he had to present a case of greater substance to the public, the government, and his own conscience. In 1952, his staff told the *National Cyclopedia of American Biography* that the action against MacArthur "was taken following an unauthorized ultimatum containing unauthorized terms." In 1955, Omar Bradley told two research assistants working on Truman's memoirs that the message to China "was the straw that broke the camel's back . . . that was when the President finally gave up." Truman put forth this proposition without equivocation in the book published the following year: MacArthur's communiqué "left me no choice." End of story were it not for backtracking in unprepared remarks, such as a TV interview in 1960, where he said MacArthur "was in private contact with the Republican minority."[38]

In the immediate aftermath of MacArthur's March message to China, Truman had not mentioned dismissal to Acheson or Marshall, or in his own diary, where he habitually entered momentous events. "Everybody thinks I don't have courage enough to do it. We'll let 'em think so, then we'll announce it" followed the Martin episode in April. Then Truman finally did what friendly newspapers were already beseeching him to do: "grasp the nettle in the manner of Lincoln and Polk" and thereby provide the "really forceful, frank and energetic leadership" that would "demonstrate once and for all he is master in his own house." Far better to claim after the fact that "my mind was made up before April 5." Otherwise, the president would have to confess to dereliction of a duty long overdue by his own admission: "I should have relieved General MacArthur" for his message to the VFW and for letting "all the world know that he would have won [the war] except for the fact that we would not let him have his way."[39]

Truman noted in his diary on April 5th: "The situation with regard to the Far Eastern General has become a political one." Why now, not before? Truman certainly felt that certain soldiers leaned in a particular political direction, for example Eisenhower, whom he thought a "Democratic general" on the basis of a speech Ike made at age eighteen when briefly under the influence of a hometown party leader. MacArthur's political identity was a lot more clear, particularly in the White House, where staff members regarded him as a Republican "playing the Republican line in Far Eastern and Asian policy."

They put the cart before the horse. The GOP was playing the MacArthur line as an opportunity to pose as the political alternative that would not politically interfere with the conduct of the war. However, MacArthur had not yet endorsed Republicans, at least directly. This was an important distinction to Harry Truman, as one columnist might have mentioned when tracing the president's thinking to his training in an urban political machine: there the real constitution was a "relationship of unquestioning political loyalty, given and returned, between 'the boss' and his subordinates." The general had been less than loyal to Truman's policies on East Asia long before writing to Martin, "As you point out, we must win." That comment was no different from what he told numerous visitors to his Tokyo headquarters, as the national press soon remarked. What was different now, and therefore a determinant factor, was the venue of the CINCFE's opinion. "MacArthur shoots another political bomb," Truman entered in his diary on April 6th, "through Joe Martin, leader of the Republican minority in the House."[40]

One might hold that Martin did not do anything Truman had not done, that is, use MacArthur's stature in an upcoming election on his own political behalf. The president, in October 1950, had gone to Wake Island, where he posed with the general and got his praise as commander-in-chief three weeks before the nation went to the polls. Truman would not see events that way, hardly surprising since he had qualms about a president stumping for his party when the country was at war. However, as of now only his opinion mattered, at least about MacArthur's tenure in command. The political opposition could react, and so would the American people, but the Oval Office had the initiative on this particular issue. A memo of record Truman wrote about Wake Island seemed of particular relevance: MacArthur had said "that he was not in politics . . . that the politicians had made a 'chump' of him in 1948 and that it would not happen again." On April 6th, the day after the Martin incident, Truman sent this document to key assistants. Two days later he consulted his history books on how Presidents Polk and Lincoln, respectively, handled Generals Winfield Scott and George McClellan.[41]

Truman always "found the teachings of history to be valuable in my approach to current problems." Korea echoed Munich. Taft-wing Republicans embodied "all the Know-Nothing business that led to the line of weak Presidents we had up until the Civil War." The "crowd" he faced in 1950 degraded the presidency in front of the enemy, who "keep a close eye on our dissensions." Essentially, he repeated that December, vis-à-vis China, what he had said in August about war with North Korea: that "the antics of McCarthy, Taft, and Wherry have as much as any other one thing to do with bringing on the communist attack." This point of view was very relevant on 11 April 1951, when Truman turned his thoughts toward generals along with certain members of Congress. The day he announced the discharge of the theater commander he told his White House staff that MacArthur, like McClellan in 1862, "worked with the minority to undercut the Administration when there was a war on," no mention of police action this particular time.[42]

Analogues to Munich and McClellan helped Truman make difficult decisions, but similes lack the complexity of actual events. McClellan was not the brazen schemer depicted in a six-page booklet the White House distributed to help its case against MacArthur. Despite attacks from Republican ideologues, McClellan did not issue a political endorsement before being relieved from command in 1862. Truman, a border-state Democrat, would normally be an enemy of McClellan's enemy, the Committee on the Conduct of the [Civil] War. It called the general "an imbecile if not a traitor" for what might now be dubbed appeasement: in this case restoring to the Union the seceding states with their prerogatives intact. Joe Martin and Robert Taft could have fit into the committee mold for unrelenting war provided one substituted "Communist China" for "chattel slavery."[43]

Truman was not interested in a line of reasoning that tied him to McClellan as fellow proponents of limited war. Any such pairing would have made his difficult decision about MacArthur more difficult to make. The president, instead, maintained a perception of his own behavior that added fuel to his fire of indignation. He always tried to avoid identification with the nefarious crowd of "crazy politicians" who brought down the likes of Hannibal and Lee. Now that MacArthur had joined the ranks of Taft and Martin by blending with McClellan, the president could think that the military man politicized the war. The professional soldier was then fair game for a professional politician who had not been disloyal to him. Note Truman's reply when later asked why he did not stop MacArthur from proceeding north of Pyongyang: "You pick your man; you've got to back him up. . . . That was my decision—no matter what hindsight shows."[44]

The president, according to the president, supported someone who now aligned with the opposition—moreover, not the loyal opposition, such as Vandenberg. Truman said of a hostile newspaper columnist clearly outside the chain of command: those who "contribute to the breakup of the foreign policy of the United States help bring on World War III." He would not think much differently about MacArthur, especially when searching for scapegoats for what went wrong in Korea by blaming the general's supporters in Congress for having weakened his presidency. Down in the depth of Truman's gut, he felt that MacArthur was collaborating with the de facto collaborators of the communist enemy. Still, for all Truman's outrage, the final decision for dismissal was still not inevitable on April 5th. He ended his episode with Roger Tubby by declaring, "I can take just so much. I'm talking to Marshall about this."[45]

Truman's remark was testimony to his habitual reliance on his tight coterie of trusted advisors, even when dealing with "this stuff [that] makes me boil." He would admit that a primary function was to talk him out of his initial impulse, which his close counselors often did. On occasion he might interrupt opposition, as he did in January 1950 at the sole White House meeting exclusively held on building the hydrogen bomb. Then Truman's mind already was firmly made up—not exactly true when it came to his Far East commander, to be handled with utmost circumspection. "I never knew whether he liked or disliked MacArthur. That's not the way he was," said Admiral Robert Dennison, military officer who acquired a host of White House staff responsibilities. The president would not act precipitously or on his own when it came to this general. He called three meetings in the next four days with his inner circle: Acheson, Harriman, and Marshall, now joined by Omar Bradley since the Joint Chiefs had a major role to play. None of them yet knew about a decision to fire the CINCFE, no particular mystery. Truman had not made the definitive determination, regardless of what he said in his diary, a way by which he discharged steam: "I've come to the conclusion that our Big General in the Far East must be recalled."[46]

On April 6th, the first meeting of Truman's high council, Averell Harriman was the only person with no doubt about dismissing MacArthur "forthwith," other than to say it should have been done in 1949. He had spent more time and effort than anyone else trying to accommodate the general, who privately thought him a "pacifier" with many social graces but "not enough iron in his veins." Other people noticed other aspects of this presidential advisor, particularly a smoldering temper for which he would be nicknamed "the crocodile." (Harriman looked quiescent, wrote Joseph Alsop, until "the great interests of the United States are attacked. Whereupon the great jaws open and another fool finds that he is figuratively missing a leg.") That spring Harriman felt that MacArthur's "indiscretions" defied all "rational explanation," aside from ingratitude. "Truman stood squarely back of him when he made his blunders in Northern Korea."[47]

Dean Acheson was not as ready for the confrontation, already being burdened with Alger Hiss, Formosa, and accusations of plotting to replace MacArthur. He did his best to conceal the distressing effect of this criticism beneath the cropped mustache on his stiff upper lip. He nonetheless knew he would be the prime target for the likely rebuttal on behalf of the general that would pit decorated warriors against striped-pants diplomats who dared tell them how to wage war. As late as 1968, Acheson mentioned the "great trouble" he expected for taking on MacArthur, notwithstanding that his antagonist was then four years dead and Acheson was facing some favorable juries, such as the Pulitzer Prize award committee passing judgment on his memoirs. He faced much longer odds in 1951. Consequently, at the first Oval Office meeting on the dismissal of MacArthur, Acheson advised the president that they must reexamine all the facts very carefully.[48]

Usually Acheson did not hesitate to argue with the Pentagon about commitments and policy, aside from October–November 1950, when MacArthur marched toward the Yalu River. At present, the secretary of state was acutely aware that military men had become the arbitrators of domestic politics. Robert Lovett wrote him on March 24th that the Joint Chiefs thought "the consequences of relieving MacArthur are startling. It would have its effect at once in the field and it would probably prejudice the success of the Japanese peace treaty negotiation." This clearly was cause for caution to anyone wanting to avoid any dispute that appeared to set soldiers against civilians, particularly now that the administration already suffered two-to-one disapproval in public opinion polls. If Truman and company were to survive, they would need the unequivocal support of the JCS: "a completely united front," as Acheson would put it, "no cracks whatsoever."[49]

The Military's Role in Policy and Politics

How can it have happened that we have sunk to the point where two [political] parties are rallying around opposing generals?

WALTER LIPPMANN, 21 MAY 1951[50]

A narrow focus may be convenient but not illuminating. One cannot understand the clash of policies over Korea without understanding disagreements about Formosa. Nor can one understand the relief of MacArthur—or its consequences—without understanding political functions played by senior military officers. JCS support for a decision it did not really recommend was essential if the White House was to weather the public outcry over a five-star general. Dean Acheson chose his bodyguard advisedly, judging by opinions ranging from Walter Lippmann to the *Saturday Evening Post*. They expressed "doubt whether military leaders at any previous time in American history have figured so largely in nonmilitary affairs." This meant more than the proclivity to place officers in posts heretofore filled by civilians, from ambassadorships to the Soviet Union, Panama, and Paraguay to the directorship of the Department of Veterans' Affairs. The administration also pushed the military into a political function, that of rounding up public support for its policies. The officer corps had a reputation for a "sound conservatism" comforting to the body politic during a period of substantial change in global obligations, interests, allies, and enemies.[51]

Lippmann, in favor of a governing elite such as Acheson presumably embodied, emphasized the particular condition of the incumbent administration, mired in "mediocrity, inexperience and political vulnerability." Truman was certainly aware that his own self-defense against vituperative attacks suffered from a look of partisan pleading. He therefore found "a devoted patriot," Fleet Admiral Chester Nimitz, to ward off charges that subversives pervaded the government. The chair of the President's Commission on Internal Security and Individual Rights may have been, in Truman's words, "our greatest naval strategist." Did this qualify the World War II commander of the Central Pacific theater to "seek the wisest balance that can be struck between security and freedom"? Whether or not the admiral could fulfill this charter of the so-called Nimitz Commission, Lippmann might attest that he carried more weight than Senator Millard Tydings, Truman's erstwhile defender on Capitol Hill. There, General Omar Bradley would soon shape the debate about General Douglas MacArthur. General Dwight Eisenhower already dominated discussion about the North Atlantic Treaty Organization.[52]

Most Republicans felt their victory in the November 1950 election confirmed the utility of partisanship in foreign policy. "Over and over I pointed out," said senator-elect Richard Nixon, "that had it not been for the fall of China, the Korean War would not have happened." This confrontational mood had not dissipated by 24 March 1951, the day MacArthur issued China his ultimatum. Dean Rusk told the British Foreign Office: "The state of Congress has never been more deplorable and difficult." Europe was an issue, as well as the Far East, when Truman threw down the gauntlet to send NATO four more divisions. The administration felt the invasion of South Korea proved only armies at the borders could prevent aggression such as occurred after it withdrew the XIV Corps, originally deployed in 1945. The Robert Taft bloc favored national defense via long-range bombers rather than "policing" what it called "the 20,000 mile Soviet perimeter." Weaponry, however, was not its only focus; the president's manner and the Constitution were at the forefront.[53]

Truman had entered the White House with hopes for restoring relations on Capitol Hill frayed under Franklin Roosevelt. By the Korean War, he was telling Rusk that his favorite president was James K. Polk because "he had the courage to tell Congress to go to hell on foreign policy matters." In July 1950, he claimed to an assistant, "I just did what was in my power. . . . [The commitment to Korea] was none of Congress's business." That contention was quite vulnerable politically in January 1951. Public approval for Truman's decision hit 35 percent. He still held that "under the President's constitutional powers as Commander in Chief of the Armed Forces" he "has authority to send troops anywhere in the world." Truman did not dodge the ensuing hailstorm with begrudging statements that he would "appreciate" support for a troop deployment to Europe, "but I will do whatever is necessary to meet the situation."[54]

What proved necessary was Dwight Eisenhower, called back to Washington after being called back to uniform in December 1950 as supreme allied commander, Europe. Only 31 percent of the public favored Truman's stance on NATO, even less popular than Korea. Eisenhower was still able to appeal to Congress and to the American people in a nationwide radio address identifying European apprehension of U.S. hesitation as the greatest obstacle he faced. This got the attention of the upper chamber in a "sense of the Senate" resolution in favor of his appointment, a meaningless motion that had meaningful content in a stipulation that withdrew the cap on deployment of divisions that the Senate had just passed. The convoluted details of the legislation were less important than who did—and who did not—carry the day. Dean Acheson had lost substantial credibility over what he said in 1949 regarding the United States making a substantial troop commitment to NATO: "clear and absolute, no." Taft thought his judgment "probably as bad as anyone I have ever seen in [this] position." It was good enough to absent himself from this so-called great debate on military policy taking place days before Martin read MacArthur's fateful message.[55]

The Democratic leadership on the Senate floor rallied support by saying that any troop ban "would be a direct slap at General Eisenhower and the great work he is doing in Europe." This did not pass by newspaper columnists, both for and against White House policy: "President Truman has lost all national authority"; "in effect the Senate [had been] voting disapproval of Mr. Truman's past record" in foreign affairs. Such cries of gloom and doom, overstated or not, were important within Washington, where supremacy resides where it is perceived, often by the national press. Even James Reston, despite his access to Acheson, paid him little heed in the New York Times on 8 April 1951: "Today, prominent soldiers are supplying much of the balance, statesmanship and confidence so sorely needed by the Administration."[56]

Acheson, a self-interested observer of this domestic balance of power, was disinclined to take on MacArthur without Pentagon unanimity, still to be obtained. George Marshall's staff, far from enamored with the CINCFE, long had disliked his secrecy and condescension, what they described as the "idiot treatment." Bradley agreed that MacArthur's message traffic "might well be called lectures to the 'youngsters.'" The JCS would abide this behavior as long as they thought him irreplaceable, although now because of politics, not brilliance in battle. "MacArthur had been 'kicked upstairs' to chairman of the board," Bradley later put it. "Insofar as military operations were concerned, [he was] mainly a prima donna figurehead who had to be tolerated."[57]

Bradley had yet to agree that this period of permissiveness was over, although later saying that MacArthur was notorious for disobedience. In 1951, when scuttlebutt would not suffice, the Pentagon held "there is little evidence that General MacArthur ever acted in opposition to an order of the Joint Chiefs." At most, when pressed by the Senate, Joe Collins said that the theater commander had violated "the spirit" of the gag order. Bradley, when pressed in 1955, said "military people should be left alone in the field when they are fighting a battle. If General MacArthur is talking about that I don't think you can criticize him." That sentiment caused hesitation in 1951—also the product of plain self-interest for someone otherwise showing a readiness to relieve fellow generals from military command. In World War II Bradley sacked seven flag officers, not to mention George Patton, lucky to have escaped his wrath for slapping two privates. ("I would have relieved him instantly" if having the authority in 1943.) Now, when directly consulted about MacArthur, whose misbehavior had far more significance, Bradley worried about receiving a "savage mauling [from] the right wing primitives." He had witnessed the abuse heaped on Acheson and Marshall. On the eve of retirement after forty years in uniform, Bradley "did not relish going out on a sour note," a prospect that left him "bitter and sad."[58]

George Marshall, more used to this kind of abuse for allegedly losing China, had absorbed the insults of extremists with remarkable composure, confident that overstatement would undermine their credibility. Nonetheless, when it came to a prospective fight over MacArthur, the preference of the secretary of defense was that of Bradley, his old subordinate in the tactics department at the infantry school, Fort Benning. Marshall long requested substantial enhancement in defense appropriations not forthcoming before Kim Il-sung invaded South Korea. The initial KPA onslaught drove up demand for military spending, but only 35 percent of the public still favored an increase, on Marshall's mind since October 1950, when others were ecstatic at Wake Island. He saw the downside of announcements that "the war will be over by Thanksgiving." This would signify to Congress and the sovereign citizenry that the country could win a war despite ill preparedness. The secretary of the army, recalling the desperate defense at the Pusan perimeter, asked, "Would you say I was naïve if I said that the American people had learned their lesson?" Marshall replied, "No, Pace, I wouldn't say you were naïve, I'd say you were incredibly naïve."[59]

The tactical disaster on the way to the Yalu saved the day for defense appropriations, at least in the short run. Congress voted an emergency $16.8 billion dollar supplement for the military budget in December 1950, more than doubling the sum originally given for the fiscal year. However, four months later, Marshall said he "never dreamed" of what next happened: another "180 degree turnabout in public and congressional sentiment." Complacency resurfaced once Matt Ridgway stabilized the battlefield, the downside of doing what Washington wanted him to do. Consequently Korea was not a headline story by the first week of April 1951, when public attention concentrated on a different form of police action, the first televised hearing on organized crime.[60]

The Sopranos, 1950s style, featuring Frank Costello, Tony Accardo, and the other "Godfathers" of the era, made a hot political prospect of Estes Kefauver, a Democratic version of Tom Dewey. This first-term senator from Tennessee was suddenly rising to the top of his party for investigating gangsters protected by machine politicians, including those from Kansas City, uncomfortably close to Truman's political roots. The president, already appearing too weak to run for reelection, thereby fell even further. Decorated veterans home from the war also lost their political balance. First Lieutenant Alexander Haig, aide-de-camp to Ned Almond, was "struck by the atmosphere of business as usual." Captain Margaret Blake, combat nurse and first female in the war to win a Bronze Star, told the United Press: "New clothes, new cars, vacations and parties are 'firsts' in the minds of too many people." Lew Millett, platoon leader traveling to the White House to have the president bestow his Medal of Honor, got the distinct impression from talking to townspeople that many of them "didn't care anything about what was happening over there" in Korea.[61]

George Marshall feared the impact of this apathy on U.S. army capabilities finally nearing a capacity to form new units without stripping old ones of their best personnel. On March 28th, he held his first formal news conference since assuming the position of secretary of defense. He avoided all discussion of MacArthur's ultimatum to China while registering a plea for "an enduring program of national security." It had no discernible impact; public support for enhanced spending plunged once again. Two weeks later, on the day before the president relieved MacArthur, Congress ruled on universal military training, "vitally important" to Marshall. A voice vote sufficed to reject his measure for an "established system" to overcome the condition faced at the outset of Korea: "a state of bankruptcy as to available trained reserves." This entire issue shaped his opinion on how to deal with MacArthur: bring him back for consultation and another appeal for cooperation. Dismissal would be self-defeating if the CINCFE's congressional coterie dealt preparedness a mortal blow. They could revenge their hero with no fear of electoral retribution or qualms about subverting a policy they rejected, one of avoiding escalation in Asia and saving resources for a force build-up in Europe.[62]

One might have thought a concern like this would have inhibited Dean Acheson, an architect of NSC-68. The Korean War set in motion this massive defense-spending plan, just a study paper before mid-1950, when he held that "the advantages of power lie in the hands of the Soviet Union." The secretary of state was convinced that "the United States Government was in the greatest danger in its history," but he hesitated less at disrupting a potential period for rearmament, as also had been true in mid-1941. Marshall, then army chief of staff, aimed "to do all in our power" to delay battle with Japan from concern for "our state of unpreparedness and because of our involvement in other parts of the world." Acheson, as assistant secretary of state for commerce and foreign trade, led the fight to embargo petroleum on the assumption that this sanction would deter the threat. The subsequent attack on Pearl Harbor might have caused a lesser man to doubt his judgment when in charge of the department ten years later and facing fallout over the general who eventually accepted the surrender of Japan. Acheson, however, felt guilty for not taking a stand to reign in MacArthur in late 1950. On April 7th, he joined Harriman in favor of dismissal when Truman held his second meeting on the topic.[63]

The civilian caucus in Truman's gang of four had reported. It was still up to the two-man military squad—generals of the army Bradley and Marshall. "I cannot understand why MacArthur behaved this way," Bradley said some two or three times. He and Marshall had hoped to draft a "personal and confidential letter" to MacArthur "telling him how much his actions were embarrassing the government." One wonders if their last hope was hopeless. Marshall already had tried something like this in the fall of 1950, although in a different context and without hint of penalty, when he wrote MacArthur personal letters that just encouraged the recipient to do what he wanted. This may have been why Acheson was no longer deferential to Marshall's deference to MacArthur. More appeals would be counterproductive, according to the reasoning of the secretary of state. They would enable the CINCFE's supporters to organize opposition to his prospective relief. MacArthur "had to be stripped of his power and authority so that he returned [to America] as a private citizen. . . . Though we'd have a difficult enough time with that battle," Acheson maintained, "it would still be an argument about the past and not an argument about the future."[64]

That type of argument from the president's "number-one brain man" may have given Truman the encouragement he needed. The Joint Chiefs of Staff had other concerns on April 8th, when they held their own major meeting about the dismissal of MacArthur. The JCS believed there were "military reasons" in the present situation to get a new theater commander. Soviet airpower was growing in theater, along with fears of its sudden deployment in an attack likely to kick off the communist offensive expected later that month. Washington would still not delegate authority to react, for suspicion MacArthur might preempt and thereby precipitate a global war. This apprehension notwithstanding, the JCS would still not "recommend" dismissal for reasons suggested in Bradley's confidential memorandum for record: "Military considerations were only a small part of the question involved."[65]

One would like Bradley to have filed a full explication as to whether he was referring to constitutional factors, domestic politics, or some other issue beyond the JCS charter. Whatever the answer, the question was not pursued in mid-May, when the general told the Senate hearing on MacArthur's dismissal that the Joint Chiefs "unanimously agreed that from a purely military point of view they thought he should be relieved." In point of technical fact, the JCS had merely "concurred," a word with a particular definition within military organizations. It did not mean advocated, but rather accepted without objection, if "that should be the President's decision." Granted the distinction could be subtle, particularly in the midst of a tension-ridden moment. Truman faced a historic decision, looked for support, and eventually got it from Marshall and Bradley, who dropped debate about alternatives to dismissal. Loyal military men understand when it is time to execute their commander's plan, like it completely or not. Truman, glad for unity, could now state, if not overstate, "It is the unanimous opinion of all that MacArthur be relieved."[66]

Taft-wing Republicans, disputing Truman's claims, would make their own dubious allegation that "there was no serious disagreement between General MacArthur and the Joint Chiefs of Staff as to military strategy in Korea." Such accord did not exist, nor did JCS initiative aside from a "spontaneous reaction" by Admiral Forrest Sherman, who suggested that Marshall go to Tokyo and try to reconcile MacArthur to governmental policy. Bradley thought

Sherman "urbane, intellectual, diplomatic, and smart as a whip" but passed over his proposal. Still, the JCS did not "recommend" that MacArthur "must be relieved"—contrary to claims in DOD's press office, its department of legal/legislative affairs, and stories planted in the columns of some prominent newspapermen.[67]

Joe Collins, although "exasperated" with MacArthur, characterized the Joint Chiefs as a "sad and sober" group. In early April, they were not saying much more than that a president has a right to have the theater commander a president wants to have. If Truman were to get through the storm his decision would create, he would need more than their "concurrence" should hostile senators reveal the passivity of that elusive phrase. The JCS would need to testify that administration strategy was about to force the enemy to conclude the conflict, even if the fighting was confined to the peninsula. Hanson Baldwin wrote on April 13th: "General MacArthur's sudden replacement is certain to dramatize the need for some definite answers to pressing questions," particularly "how can the Korean war be ended?" The public certainly had no idea, according to informal surveys of opinion. Drew Pearson, a reporter savvy in the ways of Washington, thought the Joint Chiefs equally mum. "It looks as if Harry Truman is going to have to fight his battle almost alone. None of the military men on whom he has leaned so heavily in the past appears ready to face MacArthur."[68]

The Axe Finally Falls

Truman succeeded in making a popular hero out of MacArthur— something the general was never able to do for himself.

LETTER TO DWIGHT EISENHOWER, 18 APRIL 1951[69]

Truman stood convinced that MacArthur was purposely provoking his own dismissal. The president did not venture what might be the motivation but recognized the danger to his presidency of releasing the general from military service. MacArthur could no longer be contained to making remarks to reporters or sending telegrams to Capitol Hill. Republican critics of the president had been calling for Congress to subpoena his appearance because he "has been muzzled by the Truman Administration." Democrats, in rebuttal as late as April 8th, cited the "impracticality" of the proposal on grounds of his "critical responsibilities at a fighting front," the sort of thing MacArthur would have loved to read in newspaper coverage from Korea. Three days later he was relieved and thereby acquired a nationwide audience. Taft-wing conservatives anticipated "the biggest windfall that has ever come to the Republican Party." They talked of staging "a 'Pearl Harbor' inquiry" into the whole affair, particularly whether the "Truman-Acheson-Marshall triumvirate" was conducting wholesale appeasement of China, "a super-Munich" according to Joe Martin. No one need wonder who would be the star witness.[70]

A more cunning occupant of the Oval Office, less outraged by what he felt was personal disloyalty, would have kept in mind what Eisenhower mentioned upon hearing of MacArthur's relief: "When you put on a uniform, there are certain inhibitions you accept." One consequently might have looked for a position to keep a troublesome critic busy outside the United States, as the Truman administration did in 1949 when the chief of naval operations aligned with Congress to preserve the latest line of aircraft carriers. Admiral William Denfeld chose retirement rather than accept command of the Atlantic fleet, but the MacArthur family, thin-skinned or not, had a different history. In 1905, Arthur went off to the Orient at the behest of the despised William Howard Taft. Thirty years later, Douglas left for the Philippines, although Franklin Roosevelt reduced his rank before he even got on ship. Harry Truman would not need to make a meticulous search through the federal employment service to preoccupy a former CINCFE in some relatively minor fashion. The administration had largely made MacArthur's other job, that of Supreme Commander Allied Powers (Japan), a ceremonial post whose "former responsibilities" were in State Department hands, as the general himself told Matt Ridgway the day after his relief.[71]

MacArthur would have been left with the pomp and circumstance of office, in which he played the lead in *The King and I*, according to Canada's foreign minister visiting Tokyo in 1950. One doubts that diplomat knew how accurate this simile might be in light of the inspection tour the MacArthurs had conducted through the Far East forty-five years before. They had a delightful state dinner with the "progressive monarch" of Siam on whom the aforementioned play was based. (MacArthur's mother, a dominant figure in his life, was particularly charmed: "Your Majesty, you're a darling.") His well-run fiefdom in Southeast Asia seems to have been a model for what MacArthur hoped to do from his office in the Dai Ichi Building across the street from the Imperial Palace of Japan. In late October 1950, he told a confidant, "I'd like to finish my work here—that is unless Washington recalls me."[72]

In 1951, the important factor was not that MacArthur was the venerated ruler receiving from ordinary Japanese half a million letters for help and advice. What counted was that he well might have kept the show open in Tokyo whatever Truman did about supreme military command in the Far East. The day after the general's ultimatum to China, he turned to one of his standard methods for digging in against his government. He told his State Department advisor that as an allied official technically responsible to a coalition commission, he could not be dismissed from Japan by Washington on its own accord. "There's nothing they can do to me. There has to be an international agreement."[73]

MacArthur, to ensure his tenure, was desperately searching for something resembling the Soviet veto at the United Nations. Washington could have met him halfway with claims about the general's irreplaceable relations with the Japanese people and the multilateral nature of his appointment as an allied occupation commander. This would seem to require his retention in Japan until the final signing of the treaty between that nation and the coalition powers that would officially end World War II. The White House might then find enough red tape and bureaucratic roadblocks to prevent ratification until convenient to dismiss MacArthur. The Pentagon, fearing Russian reaction to Japanese independence, certainly wanted to delay the treaty until peace in Korea freed military assets for enhanced protection of Japan. John Foster Dulles, head negotiator, filed no brief to relieve the general. He saw a great deal of MacArthur, whom he described as "a high strung person" of the opinion that "the only way to make his thinking an element in policy making was through indirect channels," namely Congress and the press. The general's aide, Sid Huff, foresaw benefits from a recall to Washington: it would enable his boss to "clarify some of the hazy thinking there."[74]

The American ambassador to South Korea said, "MacArthur is one of the biggest brains I've ever come in contact with, but he had gotten to the age where he was no longer in touch with the situation." If the general's keen receptivity to nuance had gone into decline, the president needed to foreclose all ambiguity by issuing detailed directives with crystal clarity. The so-called gag order, not really a direct order at all, hardly met this standard. Truman was not comfortable sending soldiers preemptive commands, for political reasons as well as personal discomfort over meddling with the military at time of war. Neither would he revisit bargaining on a quid-pro-quo basis, to which he came close in mid-1950 when Harriman brokered Inchon for Formosa. Something like this in mid-1951 would demean the constitutional office held by Harry Truman, who called himself "the man who runs the greatest republic" ever created.[75]

In late August 1950, Louis Johnson ostensibly convinced Truman not to fire MacArthur when the issues were Formosa, China, Chiang Kai-shek, and Mao Tse-tung. George Marshall, a man of much higher standing, could not convince the president to try other options after the MacArthur-Martin incident. Apparently, personal disloyalty, partisan politics, and the McClellan precedent had to be added to long-standing disagreements over foreign policy and military strategy. Then Truman approximated his ideal of a take-charge/ take-no-prisoners chief executive officer along the lines of his hero, Andrew Jackson. If he had been that firm, resolute, and clear to MacArthur from 1950, not to mention 1945, there might have been no need for drastic action in 1951. This now was water over the dam, except for a matter of personal pride, no small issue in itself. Truman refused advice to say in his speech announcing the general's dismissal that he was acting with "the consent" of his military and civilian advisors. He told his staff, "I am taking this decision on my own responsibility as president of the United States. I want nobody to think I am sharing it with anybody else."[76]

The passage of time and testimony by Truman loyalists helped solidify this image, whereby "feisty old" Harry S. Truman eventually became an American icon reminiscent of "Old Hickory." Averell Harriman said at a memorial conference twenty-five years after the fact that Truman dealt with MacArthur simply "as the president of the United States would deal with a subordinate who was not carrying out of the president's orders. . . . General Marshall was cautious in dealing with him; General Bradley was also cautious. . . . Truman was the one man who had the courage to step up and deal with it." That was basically true by April 1951, although Harriman also stepped up. MacArthur had to admit that Truman was "a man of raw courage and guts . . . the little bastard honestly believes he is a patriot." Yet gracious or gruff, this overlooks the preceding years of Truman's dealings with MacArthur, hardly presidential by the president's own standards.[77]

Exactly what MacArthur thought he was doing was and remains a point of debate. Walter Lippmann, unable to decide between plausible proposals, wrote that "General MacArthur chose to force the president to relieve him—or he thought from what he had seen during the past year that the president would give in and would take his orders from Tokyo." This type of explanation is part and parcel of the opinion that "MacArthur never made an uncalculated move," to quote Frank Pace, the secretary of the army. It made no concession to the proposition that raw emotion also had a role in early April, when the acting chief of staff at theater headquarters thought MacArthur "about ready to explode." People acquainted with the situation agree that the general could not tolerate the standing policy. To this common observation about his disposition, they attribute different causes—patriotism, politics, or personal pique. The head of public health and welfare in occupied Japan recalled MacArthur's fury at the administration: "I do not believe that the American people will permit their sons to be killed if they know that they are being killed senselessly under such a [no win] directive."[78]

Did MacArthur fully understand that he would be fired? Sometimes yes, sometimes no, often maybe. He could think he had a great destiny, testimony to feelings of invulnerability while imprudently facing sniper fire in two world wars and Korea. He also felt the presence of a hazardous enemy in Washington conspirators out to get him. Hence eyewitnesses describe contradictory incidents, as if *Rashomon* along with *The King and I* was playing center stage at Far East headquarters, starting with the colloquy of the man in the lead role. MacArthur maintained in memoirs and conversations that he was utterly astonished. "Up to the moment of my recall, I had been receiving laudatory commendations from the President," a man he considered clearly subject to "violent temper and paroxysms of ungovernable rage." Truman dismissed him "ignominiously. . . . He had never been told why."[79]

This profession of surprise was more than a MacArthuresque pose set forth in retrospect, if one accepts press accounts and State Department testimony.

William Sebald, political advisor at the embassy, said the general was "shocked." John Foster Dulles wired Acheson that MacArthur and his staff had all expressed doubt he would ever be relieved. The UPI correspondent in Tokyo was dispatching stories that they felt his stance was more popular than ever, probably why Charles Willoughby soon wrote MacArthur about "this incredible news." There is also, however, reliable evidence that the theater commander made a better threat analysis than his assistant chief of staff for intelligence. On April 9th, two days before Truman's axe fell, MacArthur told Ned Almond, "I may be relieved." "Pinky" Wright remembered less equivocation. "MacArthur felt for some time that he was going to be relieved. . . . There was no question in his mind." Still, he thought he would be brought back to Washington for a conference then eased out through another assignment, something like George Marshall apparently had in mind. "It was the method that surprised him," Wright said.[80]

MacArthur felt himself the victim of a willful insult, although not true. His relief was executed by government snafu. The administration planned to contact Frank Pace, then in Korea, who was supposed to inform MacArthur in a personal visit to Japan. In the meantime, word of an "important resignation in Tokyo" got to reporters for the *Chicago Tribune,* part of the McCormick-Patterson newspaper syndicate. The chain's East Coast outlet, the *New York Daily News,* soon called the White House for a comment on a story that the paper was about to run saying no presidential action was pending on the CINCFE. For months, if not years, the president had felt these particular publications were "traitorous" for undermining his presidency. He also thought them in league with Douglas MacArthur. Their call, according to this kind of assessment, seemed a plot to lull the administration while the general announced that he could no longer abide its policies. This was no small matter to Truman, anxious to reassert supremacy in foreign affairs. That might be forfeited if MacArthur quit, as opposed to being relieved. "I wasn't," said Truman, "going to let the SOB resign on me."[81]

MacArthur planned no such thing, wondrous to the White House that could not understand that he still might want to hang on in Japan. It accelerated the pace of its own plan, now to notify the CINCFE in a photo finish. The secretary of the army was supposed to get the message and rush it to Tokyo just before announcement of the general's replacement, rescheduled for tomorrow afternoon. Pace never got word due to a power breakdown in a transmitter at Pusan. Far East headquarters heard of the dismissal over commercial radio. MacArthur, being a great actor, showed no emotion when so informed while hosting a luncheon for a delegation from the United States Senate. He finished his meal and politely took his leave, but remained bitter for the rest of his life at being fired "after fifty-two years of service in the Army." He would take no comfort at faring better than some other generals who crossed his path: Peng Dehuai, Sun Li-jen, and Lee Sang-cho, the head of political intelligence, North

Korean army. They faced long-term imprisonment by their own heads of state: Mao Tse-tung, Chiang Kai-shek, and Kim Il-sung.[82]

Douglas MacArthur appears to have been a conflicted man subject to a host of contradictions before Truman made the final move. He could fret about dismissal, as in his belief about plots to depose him. He could still think he could prevent it, whether because of his historical destiny or his personal charm. In March 1941, he flattered Franklin Roosevelt rather shamelessly to return to active duty. He did much the same thing to keep his post with Truman in April 1951. On the 10th, Courtney Whitney, MacArthur's gray eminence, wrote a "Dear Harry/Faithfully Courtney" letter to his fellow reservist, Harry Vaughan:

> I hope you people back there are not too much disturbed by the efforts of what the General terms the "scuttlebutts" to make it appear that there is a developing schism between the President and himself. The General is in the President's corner one hundred percent, just as he has always been. It was the President's message to him on 13 January which was the turning point in the Korean campaign. For it showed in no uncertain double-talk that the President wanted him to hold. He went to Korea and instructed that the word "evacuation" be deleted from the Eighth Army dictionary, ordering that the Army reassume the initiative, and since has periodically moved to insure that the President's wishes as he interprets them are carried out. You may be sure of one thing, and that is that come hell and high water our forces will hold a position in Korea until the President clearly indicates a change in objective.[83]

Whitney was spreading flattery awfully thick. Truman actually said on January 13th that his communication was "not to be taken in any sense as a directive." As for Whitney to Vaughan, the message did not receive the accustomed "Dear Courtney" reply. Truman fired MacArthur the next day. The theater commander, when not thinking this the deed of a sick and afflicted man, felt it was part of a Washington scheme to dismantle America's position in Asia. However, the immediate question was what he would do now, not why Truman had done what he did. Joe Martin called to urge rushing back to America, not then on MacArthur's mind. He and his wife, "bewildered by all this," had been talking of taking a "leisurely tour" of Europe after living in the Far East for the last twenty years. However, because the general professed to being "out of touch with events," he wanted to speak to Herbert Hoover, his mentor in political economy and the only recent president he did not hate. Hoover, who had been trying to contact MacArthur, thought it disgraceful not to retain him for the peace settlement with Japan, a place where the general was "a real genius." He now described a deluge of favorable mail and strongly advised returning at once, if only to head off the attack enemies were about to launch. MacArthur, getting off the phone, told his wife that they were promptly going back by airplane.[84]

This particular incident tends to discredit the Frank Pace hypothesis that MacArthur was "promoting his own dismissal" so that he could return to America "under dramatic circumstances" and get the Republican nomination. ("He had no doubt he could beat Harry Truman.") Nonetheless, the idea was not so foreign that the general would not pounce on the emerging prospect, his standard procedure in military or political operations. North Korea's push toward Pusan in July 1950 gave him the opening to launch a grand envelopment long on his mind. Being fired by Truman for wanting to win a war was certainly a new opportunity to run for president. MacArthur was still too properly polite to leave before graciously welcoming his successor on April 12th. Matt Ridgway, apparently expecting the depression and dismay common to officers recently relieved, said MacArthur's "indomitable spirit seemed undiminished." He spoke of plans to move to New York and take advantage of the many offers to "raise hell."[85]

Republican legislators with whom MacArthur spoke ran over initial Democratic resistance to his addressing a joint session of Congress, an honor offered to the five-star commanders at the end of World War II. Truman filed no objection lest he appear petty. He therefore gave MacArthur a golden opportunity to make the opening statement for the plaintiff in what was to become a public litigation against the administration. One marvels at the general's aplomb, as did riflemen who saw him at the frontlines in tactical situations he understood much better than American public opinion. MacArthur certainly had no good record in political prognostication since 1936, when he forecast the defeat of Franklin Roosevelt because "I do not believe one can buy or corrupt a majority of American votes." In 1951, he told one confidant: "If I could just get the facts to the American people, I am sure they would make the right decision." Truman also counted on the proposition that "the good people of this great Republic do not like a below the belt approach." He told his staff that April, "I can show just how the so-and-so double-crossed us. . . . [MacArthur] is going to be regarded as a worse double-crosser than McClellan." The protagonists, having made their respective predictions, would soon present their case to the sovereign citizenry of the United States of America. Their dispute over policy, spurred on by personalities, had definitely fallen into a political venue.[86]

Public Verdict and Consequences: Military and Political, Home and Abroad

1 2 3 4 5 6 **7** 8 9

Who was responsible for the stalemate in Korea and the failure of the United States to win?

EDWARD POND, COMMON CITIZEN, 19 FEBRUARY 1958

Their government took the decisions involved. . . . Had the American people harbored an overwhelming desire for different decisions these would have been taken.

MATTHEW B. RIDGWAY, GENERAL (RET.), 25 FEBRUARY 1958[1]

The public's initial response to the dismissal of Douglas MacArthur was largely one of outrage at the presumption of Harry Truman, a politician not held in high esteem. A few adept senators on the president's side, particularly Richard Russell, defused the fury by demonstrating that the general did not speak for the entire military profession, particularly for Omar Bradley, chairman of the Joint Chiefs of Staff. Congressional hearings forced the administration and MacArthur to explain comprehensively their respective policies. A wealth of material disclosed the global context of the Korean War. That provided a field day for newspaper columnists and Soviet intelligence able to monitor JCS confessions about not being ready for a showdown with the USSR. "The military facts," once openly revealed, undermined the primary reason for the war, to deter Joseph Stalin with a demonstration of American strength. Understandably, the administration was upset with what it had to do to discredit MacArthur. The general public also was upset with this inside view of U.S. strategy. Laymen want experts to agree, not to dispute momentous issues, especially the likelihood of war with Russia should America attack China. Britain, completely against this option, became another international factor in the internal U.S. debate. Its government purged its radical, anti-American faction lest MacArthurites blame the general's dismissal on a nefarious foreign influence. Truman, meanwhile, turned again to Bradley for necessary credibility. The so-called GI general, free of political blemish, had the personality to carry forth the policy of maintaining NATO.[2]

The People Upbraid the President: The Senate Holds a Hearing

The great point to face the [Senate] investigators already has emerged. . . . It involves the degree of agreement between the Joint Chiefs and General MacArthur as to how, purely as a military matter, the Korean campaign should have been conducted.

NEW YORK TIMES, 21 APRIL 1951[3]

On April 26th, a reporter asked President Truman to comment on a statement from Courtney Whitney that "General MacArthur did not have the faintest idea why he has been relieved." Truman responded, "Everybody else knows why!" This repartee caused considerable laughter at the press conference, but neither remark was correct. The general had a ready explanation, thanks to "a friend of mine" supposedly close to the White House physician who was said to have diagnosed Truman as having "malignant hypertension characterized by bewilderment and confusion of thought." Matt Ridgway, to whom MacArthur told this story, was hardly convinced that these tendencies were symptomatic of the president as opposed to the former CINCFE. MacArthur was "so monumentally egotistical," his replacement said in retrospect, "that he could conceive of no possible reason why Truman would relieve him except there was something wrong mentally." To Ridgway, this was "really amazing," but not so to a substantial body of the American public. In mid-1951, a lot of people felt the president had departed from his senses.[4]

Truman had not prepared the nation for MacArthur's dismissal for a number of reasons—some noble, some not. When the CINCFE had interfered with foreign policy, Truman usually declared, "There is no disagreement between General MacArthur and myself"; he "is taking orders." Elsewhere, his typical comment in a public forum was "I have no comment." Before the 1950 congressional election, Truman wanted to bask in the general's popularity: glory (not guilt) by association. After China ambushed MacArthur in late November, the president said, "He is continuing to do a good job." Otherwise, Washington might have encouraged further enemy offenses by confirming the precarious condition in Korea. The situation stabilized by late January, but Truman still withheld open criticism. He did not want to admit that his theater commander was often acting beyond his effective control.[5]

Even government insiders who knew of the tension between the president and the general were shocked when Truman relieved MacArthur. "I can't believe it, Mr. Secretary," Ridgway told Frank Pace, when the latter got the message from the White House. "I can't either," said the secretary of the army, "so I'll repeat it. You're now the Supreme Commander." Officialdom, unaware of MacArthur's impending relief, could not leak the story and thus prepare the public, standard practice in Washington. Reporters did write a host of articles finding fault with MacArthur, based on government sources trying to reduce the aura under which the general disparaged policy. None of the writers gave any indication that he would be discharged, almost certainly because Truman had not made the decision himself. Hence, on March 30th, the national security correspondent of the *New York Times* said no change was in the offing, at least "until a peace treaty with Japan is signed or the Korean War is settled." As late as April 10th, the most influential newspaper in the United States ran a front-page story citing "usually reliable sources" discounting all "suggestions that Mr. Truman might be sufficiently angry to order the General's removal from his military command."[6]

In retrospect, one sees that Truman had a breaking point, although previously disparaged as a supplicant who did "not dare act against [MacArthur] either for political or military reasons." Now the president suddenly became someone who "can be absolutely ruthless without regard to consequences." Politically, the worst problem with this transformation was that when Truman discharged the general, to widespread astonishment, he could seem "small and petty," if not "emotionally unstable." This belief was not confined to Taft-wing Republicans, who would place White House praise of MacArthur into their critical report of the president's action. A letter from a constituent to a U.S. senator from the solid Democratic South expressed this same point of view with no tint of partisan slant: MacArthur "has served his country wonderfully well. Even a common laborer is protected from dismissal without prior notice. Too bad that such protection might not have been given to one of our finest officers."[7]

In times of crisis, the public tends to look for leaders with an air of superiority, such as Franklin Roosevelt after Pearl Harbor. In May 1951, a White House administrative assistant rued that "in a clash of personalities, MacArthur seems to outrank Truman." The president had never quite transcended his political origins in the Kansas City machine, a past that opponents periodically revived. One had reason to expect comments on "pip-squeak politicians" and "ex-Pendergast ward-heelers" in correspondence to MacArthur from citizens "sick of politics, sick of Truman." More surprising, the general also garnered a certain populist advantage despite the concern of Herbert Hoover and others who advised against his employment at Remington Rand: it would serve "the objective of [those] who want to smear [you by] making the average man believe General MacArthur is 'falling in line for the capitalists.'" Typical letters to him still read, "the so called 'little people'"—and "the 'average Guy'"—"are all behind you," the sort of thing that enabled Truman to beat Tom Dewey in 1948.[8]

Granted, citizens are more likely to write those they support than those they oppose. Many of the same pro-MacArthur themes occurred in letters to Truman, addressed as "a cheap, tinhorn politician" and "the little necktie salesman." He could not find much sympathy for the underdog against "the man of the ages" even inside his own political party. A plurality dismissed his dismissal of MacArthur, 42 to 39 percent. Manual workers would reject Truman 46 to 35, although for the first time he won approval of the rich, famous, and accomplished listed in *Who's Who*. They favored the removal of MacArthur 51 to 46 percent, whereas the general public disapproved 66 to 25. Congressional mailbags confirmed the polling data with language more colorful than the Gallup questionnaire. Messages labeled Truman "the smallest man that ever occupied the seat of the Presidency": "WHEN AN EX-NATIONAL GUARD CAPTAIN FIRES A FIVE-STAR GENERAL IMPEACHMENT OF NATIONAL GUARD CAPTAIN IS IN ORDER." One constituent asked Richard Russell, a Senate baron about to play a critical role in the controversy, "Who was the president that told George Washington what to do at Valley Forge?"[9]

In mail to all parties—Truman, MacArthur, and Capitol Hill—Dean Acheson was a figure of particular opprobrium: to be "discharged and deported." In anticipation of this firestorm, Acheson and Paul Nitze asked Truman to batten down the proverbial hatches by dumping his "Missouri gang" of wheeler-dealers brought into the White House from personal affection. Most notorious was Harry Vaughan, whom Acheson long treated as persona non grata: "I don't want to hear anything he thinks about anything." Truman, however, was faithful to those he thought faithful to him, whether individuals or nation-states. He did not like the authoritarian nature of the Rhee regime in South Korea but told the JCS, "We cannot desert our friends when the going gets rough." Closer to home, he thought much the same about some hangers-on who helped businessmen skirt regulatory committees in return for campaign contributions, mink coats, and household goods. Truman would no more fire Vaughan than replace his secretary of state, although the Democratic leadership on Capitol Hill was tramping to the White House to plead not to face another election "carrying Acheson on our backs."[10]

The president's position gave his opponents an opportunity to wrap up in one target the most unpopular elements of his administration: the courthouse cronies with the foreign policy elites. The Senate minority report about MacArthur's dismissal spoofed the Acheson-led criticism of Chiang Kai-shek: "It ill behooves the Government of the United States to level charges of corruption against any friendly nation. 'People who live in glass houses should not throw stones.'" It was, agreed one Texan, "a classic example of the pot calling the kettle black."[11]

The favorable mail the president received focused on the constitutional principle of civilian supremacy, not on Harry Truman versus Douglas MacArthur, man-to-man. In the White House mailroom, home territory, Truman lost two to one on character issues of honor, integrity, and the like. This was nothing new; opponents long had criticized him for demeaning the dignity of the highest office in the land. Now, as if defensive about this charge, the president adopted a self-defeating plan that the MacArthur controversy would die down provided he said "nothing to keep the fire going." He was therefore loath to criticize the general, least of all on the night he announced the dismissal. Truman rejected a draft for his nationwide radio address on April 11th that began with "I relieved General of the Army Douglas MacArthur. . . . I want to tell you why. . . . Time and time again, in violation of direct orders, he made official pronouncements on foreign policy." Instead, per Acheson's advice, Truman made it a discourse on reasons to limit the war to Korea. Three-fourths of the way through the presentation there were two short paragraphs: "A number of events [none identified] have made it evident that General MacArthur did not agree with that policy. I have therefore considered it essential to relieve . . . one of our greatest military commanders." The speech, said Omar Bradley, was "a complete flop."[12]

In May 1952, Truman gave West Point a speech about the presidency that he probably wished he had given MacArthur at Wake Island and the entire American people the day he relieved the general. He told the corps of cadets that the person called to fill "the most important office in the world must do everything he can to cause all the people, at home and abroad, to respect that office for what it is." However, in April 1951, he forfeited the opportunity to set the terms of debate before MacArthur's whirlwind return to the United States. Truman remained closed-mouth on the topic for the rest of the year—in particular when the Senate was holding hearings on the general's dismissal from May through July. His response to MacArthur's continuous flow of criticism was "I can't comment on that now" or "I have no opinion to express." The president may have backed away because of political discretion, personal feelings, or

Truman showing emotional strain when making his radio announcement of the dismissal of MacArthur, 11 April 1951. *Courtesy of the Harry S. Truman Library.*

public civility. He was proud to claim he never bawled anyone out in front of anyone else. Robert E. Lee, a role model, "never scolded anybody at all." Truman periodically discharged his anger by writing critics hostile letters that his White House staff managed to suppress. He withheld a four-barrel response to MacArthur until a month before he left the White House, when he finally said in December 1952, "He didn't [have] the courtesy . . . of reporting to the President when he came back [to America]. . . . Any decent man would have done it."[13]

Meanwhile, through 1951, disapproval of the dismissal of MacArthur hovered around 60 percent despite Truman's prediction that public opinion would soon move toward his side. The president would float trial balloons through third parties about his willingness to "sacrifice" his health and run for reelection in the cause of world peace. The administration, unable to sustain a political rebound, spent its efforts merely trying to contain the damage with the assistance of third parties who help presidents remain presidential. Operatives inspired surrogates to attack MacArthur, sometimes with rather shabby stories in regard to a career "adroitly managed by his mother." More important, the general "did not think the North Koreans would overrun the South Koreans." Actually, MacArthur made no such statement, although it must have seemed quite credible in light of transcripts of the Wake Island conference also being leaked, at Truman's direct order in this particular case. The Far East commander had certainly said that China would stay out of Korea. With these types of forecasts printed in the papers, what was one to think of his latest assurance that the Soviet Union would not enter the war if America bombed Manchuria as he advised?[14]

Headline coverage of a U.S. Senate committee specially created to investigate policy in the Far East soon eclipsed other reportage about the dismissal of MacArthur. By congressional consensus, it was led by Richard Russell, the courtly Georgia gentleman who chaired Armed Services, rather than Tom Connally, the crusty chair of Foreign Affairs clearly on Truman's side. Russell's Senate mailbag was full of suspicions that the investigation would be a "whitewash" job for the White House, reminiscent of charges against the Tydings Committee, another special Senate inquiry into how the administration was coping with the threat of communism. Its chair, Millard Tydings, rebuked Joe McCarthy's charge of subversion in the State Department as a "conscious hoax." This, in turn, was widely thought to have cost Tydings his election to a fourth term. That occurrence aggrieved Truman in November 1950. Now it rebounded to his benefit. The gavel Tydings held at Armed Services fell into hands that could really help the president, if so inclined. A body commonly called the Russell Committee would conduct the enquiry into Truman and MacArthur.[15]

Russell stood by some abiding beliefs, not all of them favoring Truman, whom he thought prone to civil rights legislation that would "do away with the states by creating a massive totalitarian centralized government." As to the military issues immediately at hand, the senator never favored limited war: before, during, or after Korea. He had held that America should punish Germany and Japan until they begged for unconditional surrender. This was not unlike the position he would take on the war in Vietnam, a geopolitical "rat hole" that had to be won, although in his opinion foolishly begun. In 1951, the conflict in Northeast Asia was also not to Russell's liking. He had sided with Republicans for more aid to Chiang Kai-shek, one alternative to Russell's "nightmares" about falling into a land war with China. He would have pulled out of Korea, then bombed the mainland into submission: far more like General MacArthur than like President Truman.[16]

Partisan identity and personal ambition still swung the senator subtly to the president's side. Russell was a steadfast Democrat, as shown in 1948 after running second to Truman at the national convention: 263 to 947. He refused to join the latter-day secessionists who formed the Dixiecrats, partly because he hoped to win the nomination in 1952. That way he could return the political "house of my fathers" to its states' rights tradition and the South to the leadership it lost during the Civil War. To win acceptability from a broader spectrum of Democrats, Russell softened his position against organized labor and civil rights. One can imagine his incentive not to side with MacArthur if he ever hoped to carry the national convention.[17]

Russell, if moving toward the center, might diverge from his home-state constituency. His staff worried about another round of the "very dangerous" demagoguery "used to destroy [the] Tydings Committee." That fear was widespread in Washington, especially among liberal Democrats. They despised MacArthur but foresaw an awful backlash if the public felt cheated of what Russell promised all parties: hearings "without the color of prejudice or partisanship." As if diving for a foxhole, they fell in behind the senator from Georgia, whose parliamentary maneuvers had won the designation "greatest southern general since Robert E. Lee." That designation was not frivolous, at least to Russell, who considered Douglas Southall Freeman's biography of that particular soldier "my most prized possession," something Truman also could have said. However, there is no indication Russell ever mistook MacArthur for Marse Robert, "a subject who has held my life-long admiration and interest." The senator voraciously studied what he always called the "War between the States" but showed no dismay about what dogged the president, going down in history as a critic of military commanders in the manner of the Joint Congressional Committee on the Conduct of the War.[18]

Alongside Russell in the probe of Korea was a freshman senator from Texas "he came to love as though he were a son," said another member of the committee. Lyndon Johnson sought appointment to Armed Services in 1949 as a part of his plan to climb the slope of power by cultivating Russell, whom *The New York Times* described as "incomparably the most influential man on the inner life of the Senate." Behind him and Russell sat George Reedy within whispering distance of each man's ear, an excellent position from which the chief member of the committee staff could probe and expose every weakness MacArthur might reveal. This was a labor of love for the only non-Texan and the most liberal person in Johnson's office, now on loan to the senator from Georgia. Reedy would not describe him with military analogues common to his colleagues from the South. They portrayed a "master of tactics and strategy," not so this son of the Irish working class, who won a scholarship to the University of Chicago. Reedy said Russell combined "the political craftiness of a nineteenth-century Tammany leader with the culture and breath of an Oxford don."[19]

Reedy, who loathed MacArthur, would have liked to ask him, "Do you know of any other 'old soljur' who has just 'faded away' into a $100,000 dollar a year job? Was your toupee made in the U.S. or Japan? When did you stop beating your wife?" But being no babe in the political woods, he realized the danger of opening up "a slashing attack" upon a national hero "greeted with an evangelical fervor." Since the general seemed "invulnerable," at least for the time being, best leave all criticism to "some source outside the committee—and preferably outside the administration." Russell, Johnson, and other Democrats should hold much of their case in reserve until "the political climate changes." For now, direct criticisms of MacArthur "should be avoided like the plague. Communists are certain to turn up the next day carrying them on banners."[20]

By mid-May, Reedy and Russell would hand the task of challenging Mac-Arthur over to Omar Bradley and the Joint Chiefs of Staff. In the meantime, Lyndon Johnson needed no reminders about the ins and outs of political survival. He would profess his own "inadequacy" when respectfully asking Mac-Arthur for his opinion: "We have a Nation to save and not an election to win." He was less deferential outside the public glare, then pouncing on Reedy's observation that "none of our military leaders made any estimate of the requirements for manpower and equipment which adoption of MacArthur's proposals would entail." Johnson surreptitiously told the JCS to prepare answers about "Soviet strengths" and American deficits in the Far East: "It would be quite a convincing story against the MacArthur strategy."[21]

Nine years before the hearing, virtually to the day, the young politician met the old soldier in 1942. Congressman Johnson, in uniform as a lieutenant commander, United States Navy Reserve, booked an inspection trip to the South Pacific, first major stop MacArthur headquarters. The general, unimpressed, said, "God only knows what you're doing here," the sort of thing he probably mumbled while awaiting Harry Truman at Wake Island. He reconsidered after Johnson showed why he was known for his knack of getting what he wanted: he said he was going back to Washington, where he sat on the Naval Affairs Committee, "which had something to do with military appropriations." MacArthur, thereupon switching into mode of gracious host, assigned a one-star escort, and promptly approved a request to go on a bombing run, where his guest claimed he could "see personally for the President just what conditions are like."

When Johnson returned, MacArthur pinned on a Silver Star for valor, the only reward granted that day to anyone in his airplane crew. LBJ soon was calling MacArthur "the number one hero of World War II."[22]

MacArthur was always ready to court Congress, especially when he felt he had an enemy in the White House, mid-1942 or mid-1951. The general may have thought that he had won (perhaps bought) a friend for perpetuity. If so, he was wrong, although Johnson wore to the hearings—and all other public events for the rest of his life—the combat ribbon the general gave him for coming under fire. (One wag called it "the least deserved but most often displayed Silver Star in American military history.") To MacArthur, Johnson now said, "I have always had great admiration and respect for you as a man, as a military leader, and as one who lives up to his responsibilities." This might have tricked the people back home sending mail in favor of the general, "a hundred to one easily" according to the senator's brother. MacArthur, no fool for such flattery, must have been suspicious of Johnson's probe of issues MacArthur tried to dodge. Asked about universal military training, hardly popular with the public, the general claimed he had not given the matter "the slightest thought."[23]

Johnson was walking his own political tightrope. He already had described Korea on the public record as a "futile, indecisive, little war." This was not much different from the words of MacArthur—or, for that matter, Richard Russell, when later discussing Johnson's conduct of the war in Vietnam. In 1951, long before LBJ got to the White House, they had distanced themselves from Truman, "about as popular as measles in Texas." Under this guise of neutrality, they could give the president more help than senators listed on the White House side. "I certainly have no reason to undertake to defend the Truman Administration," Russell replied to an impassioned MacArthur supporter, such as those writing him that the general was a "scapegoat for the parlor pinks." Meanwhile MacArthur, in a Dr. Jekyll phase of avoiding the low road himself, won the praise of the national press for showing no trace of "bitterness and the disparagement of personalities." He thereby set the proper "tone" per advice from Herbert Hoover, the Democrat's favorite whipping boy for having caused the Great Depression. The former president, not unlike the Truman administration, was looking for a popular military figure to buttress his own political position. Hoover thought MacArthur one of the few people able to lead the nation back in his direction, provided he received proper advice. Publicly, he called the general "the reincarnation of St. Paul," although privately regretting his "arrogance" and "Napoleonic bent." He counseled: play your strengths, that of "a soldier by profession" and "a partisan of no group"; your goal should be "prolonged peace" while still understanding that "victory" must be the military objective.[24]

MacArthur made these points right off the bat in his farewell address to Congress on April 19th: "I do not stand here as advocate for any partisan cause." Reporters thought his presentation "a masterpiece of restrained emotion," only equaled (not surpassed) by Winston Churchill. "There is little doubt," said

Hanson Baldwin in the *New York Times*, "that as of today [MacArthur] is perhaps the most popular man in the nation; one able to sway and influence thousands by his persuasive charm and his photogenic television personality." Of all the things MacArthur said in the greatest speech he ever made, one proved especially important. Audience applause hit its high-decibel mark in response to his stating that his view about how to conduct the war was shared by "practically every military leader concerned with the Korean campaign, including our own Joint Chiefs of Staff." The Pentagon's press office issued an immediate rebuttal: the dismissal of the general "was based upon the unanimous recommendations of the President's principal civilian and military advisers, including the Joint Chiefs." This staked out the issue that would dominate the subsequent Senate hearings, although neither side was telling the whole truth and nothing but the truth, so help them God.[25]

The JCS had tentatively agreed with the CINCFE, particularly in early December 1950. MacArthur and Whitney, having saved and filed every message, made that case to those already on their side. Taft-wing Republicans in Congress and conservative newspaper barons were traipsing to MacArthur's latest headquarters (set up at the Waldorf-Astoria) giddy at the chance to hang out Democratic scalps. They did not comprehend that the JCS concurrence so helpful to their cause was situation-specific to the worst days of China's winter offensive. The Pentagon had not foreclosed an attack on the PRC if a crisis reemerged but had withdrawn support for MacArthur's policy once Ridgway's operations held out hope for success without substantial escalation. MacArthur refused to acknowledge this state of affairs, as displayed in comments on his first day of Senate testimony. "I am not aware of having had any differences with the Joint Chiefs of Staff on military questions at all." Their opinions had "coincided almost identically. . . . I don't know a single exception."[26]

The secretary of the army said that MacArthur "was not only highly intelligent but also highly sensitive to situations. If you do not couple sensitivity with intelligence, you miss the man." One grants the general validity of this depiction. There also was a contrary tendency of misperception based on chronic suspicion. MacArthur long felt that enemies in the War Department had it out for him, as when cutting his superintendent tour at West Point short of the typical four-year term. However, he now felt the JCS was on his side. What explains his failure to grasp the gap between his position and that of the Pentagon, something clever senators like Russell and Johnson were bound to uncover? It might have been advancing age, erratic neurology, or faith in his destiny. A moment of silence in early December also could have played a part.[27]

Ten days after China sprang its trap, MacArthur told Joe Collins of his plans for evacuation in lieu of reinforcement. The army chief of staff later described his reaction, or rather his lack of direct response: "While I did not presume to argue the point with General MacArthur, I did not feel that, even with the limitations likely to be placed upon the United Nations Command, the

Chinese could force its withdrawal from Korea." Collins had reason to hold his tongue, having questioned MacArthur about conducting Inchon and ending up with egg heaped on his face. The CINCFE, in all probability, thought silence meant agreement, common practice in the army. This points to a recurrent problem in the case of MacArthur, as the Russell hearings made clear. Even newspapers favorable to Truman commented, "The timidity of the Pentagon authorities in communicating with General MacArthur—sometimes confusing him, sometimes leaving him quite uninformed—has been exposed before the Senate committee."[28]

MacArthur might also have expected the officer corps to support him as one of their own, particularly in front of politicians, an outside body to the profession of arms. He could have thought he set a precedent in the early 1900s when first appearing before a congressional committee as a cadet summoned to testify about hazing at West Point. Some upperclassmen had reduced Mac-Arthur to convulsions by forcing deep knee bends above a sharp sword. Still, no matter how brutal they had been to him, he was careful to bear witness in a manner that protected all participants not yet expelled from the Academy. Even then, MacArthur did not quite live up to the standard set forth in his memoirs, where he maintained he divulged no names at all. ("Come what may I would be no tattletale.") He apparently expected much the same from fellow military men such as Marshall, Bradley, and Forrest Sherman, who actually had done about all they could to head off his dismissal. That effort having failed, what would they say when called before the Senate? Bradley, peppered at a forum on NATO in mid-April, ducked the issue of the hour by saying "the question of General MacArthur's relief is primarily a political one" and military "advice should be confidential." Then, the strongest statement of JCS support for the president came from the director of public information at the Department of Defense, a civilian appointee without much credibility to the Washington press corps.[29]

Drew Pearson noted how "the brass hats" lined up to greet MacArthur at the airport: "The military boys were siding with their fellow military men from Tokyo." The columnist did not know that the White House helped choreograph the reception to discredit the presumption that DOD had something personal against MacArthur. One could expect the general to take his own welcome at face value, especially when his destiny was at stake. George Marshall still set the record on the side of the civilian leadership, from which he sought advice about his Senate testimony. "From the beginning of the Korean conflict," he said in his opening statement on May 7th, "down to the present moment there has been no disagreement between the President, the Secretary of Defense, and the Joint Chiefs of Staff."[30]

Marshal kept his comments as polite as possible, MacArthur being "a brother Army officer, for whom I have tremendous respect as to his military capabilities and military performances." He would not discuss MacArthur's worst error, the double-pronged pursuit to the Yalu, lest he criticize to civilians a fellow general's generalship. Marshall liked to maintain that combat operations had little to do with his own role in the CINCFE's relief. He focused on policy, as did the JCS, specifically that MacArthur espoused objectives at odds with the commander in chief. Richard Russell and George Reedy, connoisseurs of congressional testimony, thought this useful—but certainly no knockout. The secretary of defense did not display the same confidence MacArthur had about possessing a plan to win the war. Nor did Marshall—"patient, deliberate, businesslike"—have anywhere near the same public appeal and "dramatic flair."[31]

When MacArthur testified, senators deserted the floor to flood the hearing room. When Marshall took the stand, even members of the committee strolled in and out, barely half of them ever present at one time. For this situation, Truman bears some blame, having sent Marshall on a mission impossible to China: to patch up a civil war between irreconcilable enemies. The fallout from the inevitable failure had tarnished his reputation, particularly in conservative newspapers of the McCormick, Hearst, Scripps-Howard, and Gannett chains. In September 1950, when about to become secretary of defense, Marshall cautioned Truman that he might not be able to provide much political assistance. Reedy, understanding what Truman needed, felt Omar Bradley would be "the administration's best bet." He "has the type of personality which inspires genuine affection among the people with whom he comes in contact."[32]

Dwight Eisenhower in mid-1943 urged Ernie Pyle to "go and discover Bradley," never mind that America's favorite World War II correspondent usually wrote about the common soldier. Pyle soon put in print: "I don't believe I have never known a person to be so universally loved and respected." Such gushing veneration for "a great general" and a great human being "in every sense of the word" is always subject to dispute, even when coming from someone treated as the kid next door writing to the folks back home. As of late, military historians tend to think Bradley a rather mundane field commander, not what Richard Russell called him: "one of our ablest fighting generals." S. L. A. Marshall, head of U.S. army field historians in the European theater, was particularly critical of the "image played up in Ernie Pyle. . . . The idea that [Bradley] was idolized by the average soldier is just rot." True or false, one thing is still clear. A few columns from someone syndicated in three hundred dailies and ten thousand weeklies carried more weight with the public than the collective works of the American Historical Association. "As a political proposition," said the State Department's legal counsel, "you take the view of General Bradley as against General MacArthur."[33]

Richard Russell cited Ernie Pyle when introducing Omar Bradley as the "GI general." Actually, the new star witness had some trepidation about participation in the MacArthur controversy. He now was paying the price for his image as a homespun hero, simply too appealing for Truman's side not to exploit. The big question was how forceful the general would be, always an issue when a soldier faces the Senate. American history is replete with instances where a congressional committee has intimidated military men, no matter how many battle decorations they may have had. In this particular instance, however, the White House had not left much to chance. "At the direction of the President," Bradley and the service chiefs met with Marshall, Acheson, Averell Harriman, and Paul Nitze on April 24th "to discuss and agree on objectives and procedures" for the forthcoming Senate hearing. "The fate of the Truman administration," said the secretary of the air force, "was now in the hands of the military."[34]

Bradley's opening statement on 15 May 1951 hit its mark: the Joint Chiefs "have recommended our present strategy in and for Korea," no ifs, ands, or buts. This confirmation of Marshall's prior testimony was a lifeboat to the White House, even if the public still preferred MacArthur's military methods two to one. Polling data was not the issue when the former CINCFE claimed complete support by his fellow experts in the JCS. Anyone glancing at the headlines understood that testimony proved that they disagreed with MacArthur, crystal clear because Bradley personally added to his opening statement personal pronouns such as "our" and "myself." He subsequently told a hostile senator in no uncertain terms, "If we are following the wrong tactics [in Korea] . . . then all of our top military people that are here and who are responsible for world-wide strategy and who have knowledge of our capability are all wrong, and you are right."[35]

George Reedy put Bradley's stinging statement at the top of his testimony "highlights." Pro-administration senators sent the general fan mail: "You did beautifully today." He had performed the essential task of discrediting MacArthur's best gambit, that of making the issue one of soldiers versus politicians. However, by day four, the Reedy-led assessment team on the committee staff felt Bradley's presentation had grown repetitious and lost a lot of its "punch." Russell was therefore ready to move to a new witness, as were the Republican members, 66 percent from the Robert Taft wing. There was, however, fundamental disagreement as to who the next witness should be, heretofore not typical of the Russell/Taft consortium. They had run the Senate, to quote Lyndon Johnson, "with a wink and a nod." A few Republicans proposed a formal alliance between the South and Midwest blocs. Russell preferred an ad hoc coalition of convenience, now in abeyance when it came to Truman and MacArthur.[36]

Ten days before the hearings began, the GOP demanded extended testimony by the JCS and full exploration of its content. Once having witnessed Bradley's power and intent, they tried to go straight to Dean Acheson. Democrats blocked this maneuver by a straight party vote, although the committee did not learn much new after Bradley and Marshall staked out the Pentagon position. The Russell-Johnson-Reedy triumvirate stacked the witness lineup with flag officers, preventing quick comparison shopping, such as Robert Taft invoked on April 27th: "The choice which this country has is between Acheson and MacArthur. That is the only issue"—or at least the one he wanted. Russell's parliamentary counter was contrived but hardly without precedent. MacArthur stacked his own deck at a military conference on 23 August 1950, when he did not invite marines of two- and three-star rank to discuss their doubts about a landing at Inchon.[37]

In mid-1951, the public would lose interest before Acheson made his committee appearance. It was "just politics" to three-fourths of those polled that June. Bradley, in retrospect, did not disagree. "I was asked one type of questions by Republicans and an entirely different type by the Democrats," whereas to Bradley the real military issue "was not either black or white." Nonetheless, when caught in the crossfire of this Washington firefight, the chairman of the JCS certainly sided against those who "were trying to embarrass the President; they were not particularly interested in the truth." Walter Lippmann was equally disturbed, although with the role military officers had come to play. The hearing was "merely a culminating point of this most un-American and most unrepublican evolution of our affairs. . . . No civilian is regarded as having any authority or can get a respectful hearing, unless he has a general to speak for him." This was a lament over abdication, no accusation of a coup. It also was an elitist cry for government by the best and brightest, along with a note of jealousy from a source used to speaking to and for those holding highest office—from Woodrow Wilson to Charles de Gaulle. Still, it was relatively easy for a national oracle to stand for purity when not required to face the electorate. Acheson always thought Lippmann never understood the practical problems of real government.[38]

Particular Republican senators had been as peeved as Lippmann but less philosophical about it, at least by the third day of Bradley's testimony. Alexander Wiley of Wisconsin insisted on his "rights as a Senator to interrogate" when trying to override a Russell ruling that Bradley need not testify about "details" of "private conversations" with the president. One might question Russell's depiction of consultations about MacArthur and Korea that Truman directed the general not to discuss. Wiley's challenge to Russell's reign still went down 18 to 8 at the hands of a coalition containing the crucial swing blocs on Capitol Hill, moderate Republicans and the Southern Democrats whom reporters dubbed "Dick Russell's Dixieland Band." Had the vote gone the other way the chairman of the Joint Chiefs might have faced contempt of Congress charges if withholding that he actually "thought the military considerations were only a small part of the whole [MacArthur] problem." This quote out of a confidential Bradley memorandum was certainly not the path Russell wished to pursue. The JCS general should be questioned, according to George Reedy, exclusively about decisions "based on purely military considerations."[39]

Joe McCarthy, the junior senator from Wisconsin, sprang forth to support Wiley by calling Truman's directive to Bradley more "gagging" of the armed forces, as if reminiscent of orders the president tried to impose on MacArthur. Disgruntled charges of "cover-up" and "iron curtain" rulings were effective against Millard Tydings in 1950. They fell on their face against Richard Russell, a model of "firmness, fairness, and dignity almost unmatched in recent Congressional history," to quote *Life* magazine, usually on MacArthur's side. Praise like this crossed a spectrum spanning from Rev. John Cochran of Groton School to a Mrs. Beatrice Horan, who blasted Harry Truman for "his stupidity and his loyalty to Dean Acheson," a Groton graduate himself. The committee chair certainly had parliamentary talent, judging by letters from those thinking his hearings "a far cry from the white-wash tactics employed by Tydings in regard to the valid charges raised by Senator McCarthy." Russell also had the advantage of defending an Ernie Pyle icon loath to violate his orders. Bradley was far more popular than Tydings's clientele, namely Acheson's State Department diplomatic corps. In short, Wiley and McCarthy launched their political attack at the wrong time and the wrong place, and against the wrong enemy, to paraphrase what Bradley said about attacking China. Reedy had good reason to gloat, having predicted five days ago: "Attacks upon Bradley are likely to boomerang."[40]

Joe Collins and his service counterparts in the navy and the air force subsequently added nearly five hundred pages to the official record. They were forthcoming about their own conclusions during the MacArthur discharge process, essentially the position Bradley posted. They concurred with the White House; they did not propose the general's relief, even if they thought it correct "from a purely military point of view." One could not expect civilians, unfamiliar with military procedures and terminology, to hang on every word and fathom the difference between "concur" and "recommend." However, all in all, the JCS was less equivocal in front of Congress that May than when Bradley polled them in April on behalf of the president. This helped create one of the most widespread misconceptions about the Korean War, ranking with the notion that MacArthur at Inchon snatched victory from the jaws of defeat. Even O. P. Smith, commander of the First Marine Division, said the JCS "recommended MacArthur's relief."[41]

By early June, *Time* magazine was reporting "that Republicans [have] just about abandoned their hope that the hearings would find the Joint Chiefs siding with MacArthur against the President." The general would not hold an open grudge, at least when it came to Democratic politicians, perhaps because he never placed much faith in them at all. He graciously exchanged pleasantries when bumping into Averell Harriman in the late 1950s, about the time he told a mutual acquaintance he would be glad to meet with Harry Truman: "I certainly bear him no ill will for exercising the authority he had and doing what he felt was his duty." MacArthur would also be courteous to Lyndon Johnson, perhaps the biggest winner at the hearings. He had handled difficult issues under the watchful gaze of Richard Russell, who was looking for "a can-do young man," especially after his own run for the presidency failed. His protégé, thanks to his sponsorship, soon became head of the Senate Democratic caucus, a big step forward in 1953. In 1964, after LBJ reached his political finish line, he paid a presidential visit to MacArthur at Walter Reed Army Hospital, where the terminally ill patient also received a telegram from a White House predecessor issued in the spirit of Wake Island: "You are putting up a valiant fight to overcome this difficulty and I hope that you succeed, Harry S. Truman." The general, too, showed no sign of rancor, at least when it came to the sitting president whose photo he observed in a morning newspaper. "I see," MacArthur said of Johnson, "he is wearing the Silver Star I awarded him in World War II."[42]

MacArthur had shown no such grace and forbearance when discussing the military men he described to the Russell Committee as "personal friends of mine." That phrase had been a temporary attempt to forge solidarity with officers in Washington despite long mistrust. Thereafter, his hostility reached new depths in conversation with intimates, such as West Point's football coach. The service chiefs were merely "press agents, pretty boys, speech-makers, and front men." Joe Collins was a man of little ability, completely unqualified to be army chief of staff. Bradley was not much better, especially when led around by Marshall, long jealous of MacArthur's rapid rise to general while he remained a little-known field-grade officer. This "errand boy of the State Department" got his revenge by obtaining "unanimous [JCS] agreement that MacArthur must go."[43]

One could call this conviction about opposition to "MacArthur's advancement under any conditions" a textbook case of psychological projection. He thought Marshall had it out for him because he had it out for Marshall, whose career stagnated in backwater appointments when MacArthur was chief of staff. One thing is certain. MacArthur professed that he would die regretting the Defense Department's interference in Korea. Dean Acheson felt quite differently about the Pentagon, at least when it came to the Russell Committee, which he faced after seventeen days of protective testimony from Marshall, Bradley, Collins, and company. Acheson in less critical situations resented wasting time with legislators he thought ignorant about the issues and primarily concerned with public posturing. He had been known to respond to cross-examination with "that is a pretty stupid question, Senator." Lyndon Johnson would later drive Dean Rusk, his own secretary of state, into uncontrollable laughter by lampooning Acheson looking "around the room [of a Senate committee] as if he were sniffing out a skunk."[44]

Senators, for their own part, did not enjoy Acheson's company, especially when "decapitated," said one observer, "by a single whistling sentence." Taft-wing Republicans, in particular, were not inclined to heed the plea of one Democrat: "Let up so that he can resign with honor." The hearing had become a battle for supremacy, now primarily staked out on policy over the defense of Formosa, the issue where Acheson had been most at odds with the Joint Chiefs of Staff. The secretary of state prepared for the confrontation by combing prior testimony and agency records with staff from policy planning and public relations. After several long nights he put on the public record 400,000 words in forty hours over eight days of testimony, a bravura presentation "by common consent."[45]

Newspaper columnists wrote that Acheson gave an epic demonstration of "the skill of his mental processes" and "almost matchless abilities" for "lucid" articulation worthy of a ranking near MacArthur himself. None of this changed the widespread assessment that he was a political casualty of war, except for specifying that the obligatory resignation would probably occur when armistice talks on Korea begin, presumably in a month or two. This fate was a standard fact of life in Washington for anyone so unpopular, along with the kind of perfunctory letter Truman wrote Acheson, whom he barely knew, when Acheson resigned as assistant secretary of state in August 1945: "You have my best wishes for your success and happiness." Few people saw the heartfelt note Truman wrote two years later: "As Marse Robert said when Stonewall lost his arm at Chancellorsville, 'General Jackson has lost his left arm, I have lost my right'— that's the way I feel when you leave State."[46]

Truman said of Acheson on 13 September 1951, "As long as I am President of the United States, he is going to be Secretary of State." He had used the same "as long as I am President" about Louis Johnson right before dismissing him in 1950. This time Truman really meant it: "You can quote it as I have said it again and again." Other people were also in the secretary's corner, for example Omar Bradley: "one of the best colleagues in a fight I have ever known." Then, there was Richard Russell, although thought to be "impartial," even in the White House scouting report on the membership of his committee. The chairman, in preserving his judicious reputation for neutrality, could place some protection in front of Bradley but not interfere with the grilling Acheson had to endure, the longest span of testimony anyone could remember. Russell won public praise for a "fine job" from Robert Taft as well as Acheson, at least in retrospect. The senator could not swing the whole committee behind the administration, nor could anybody else. He could subtly waste MacArthur's prime time in the limelight. "This is the sort of political management at which 'leaders' in the Senate become past masters," Acheson subsequently wrote. "If it does not heal old wounds, it does not inflict new ones. It records that the virulent period of a political virus has passed."[47]

United States Foreign Policy and the Fate of Formosa

The United States "no longer felt, as it had in January 1950, that there was any real possibility of inducing Chinese Titoism in the foreseeable future."

DEAN ACHESON TO WINSTON CHURCHILL, JANUARY 1952[48]

The ordeal Acheson underwent from Alger Hiss through Douglas MacArthur took ten years off his life, according to his widow. The secretary of state, who maintained he "enlisted for the duration," no longer looked to one reporter "altogether like a British viceroy of India" while conducting his business "almost with a swagger." By 1952, Acheson "seemed visibly afraid of what senators from Nebraska and Wisconsin might say." Often this was not about Korea, Joe Collins noted in some bewilderment. "More time was spent in attacking and defending the Administration's policies in the Far East than in enquiring into the circumstances surrounding the recall of General MacArthur."[49]

A topic under particular discussion was a memo Acheson circulated in December 1949, where he denied that the prospective fall of Formosa "would seriously damage the interest of either the United States or other countries opposing communism." Now that war with China made such indifference unacceptable, Acheson called his old position resistance to defeatism: "If a captain in command of a company finds that companies on either side of him are falling back and taking punishment, what he says to his men is 'Don't give it a thought. It doesn't matter at all. You are doing fine. Dig in. Hold it. Its all right.'" Columnists wrote that that Acheson "prepared with a trial lawyer's skill." On this occasion, poetic license was the faculty on display. The secretary of state was portraying himself in the Matt Ridgway role of rallying the troops in January 1951, a device to blend with the only person to emerge from the struggle in Korea with his national standing substantially enhanced.[50]

Ridgway, when first sent to Korea, continued to withdraw south lest he fight on dangerous ground. Acheson's policy toward Formosa was also in retreat for the sake of survival, in this case behind a JCS line of defense. When they were wary to defend the island in January 1950, he was happy to cite them because they agreed with him. It was "necessary in such matters," he then told supporters of MacArthur, "to accept the considered judgment of the Joint Chiefs." Pentagon opinion now seemed closer to the Republican bloc, something Acheson took into account by holding, "We are going to use all our means to prevent it [Formosa] from falling into unfriendly hands." On occasion, he even crossed the barrier separating protection of the island from endorsement of the regime. Senator Wiley asked in mid-1951, "Is there any question in the minds of our Government as to the personal integrity of Chiang?" Secretary Acheson: "No sir; I don't know of any." That kind of statement gave MacArthur an ironic victory. The general soon claimed to have been dismissed for advocating the position the secretary of state swore under oath "to have been and to be the invincible and longstanding policy of the United States."[51]

Acheson, although contemptuous of public opinion, was following the body politic that had moved a long way on Formosa policy due to his own stance on Korea. In January 1950, by a four-to-one majority, respondents preferred the "hands-off"/no-support position regarding the island that Acheson then articulated. These numbers changed very fast after he helped commit troops to fight North Koreans four months before they made contact with Chinese communists. In July, when "neutralization" was supposed to be in practice, military aid for Chiang had a 13 percent plurality. In the winter, Mao's offensive in Korea virtually rang down the debate with a solid five-to-three majority for sending "war materials" to the KMT. Roy Howard, newspaper magnate, still wrote MacArthur on December 5th, "Now the tide has turned. . . . It is almost inconceivable that the administration should agree to an abandonment of Chiang Kai-shek and Formosa. On the basis of Washington's performance to date, however, and so long as Acheson is in the State Department saddle, I would make no bet."[52]

The day before Howard wrote this letter, Acheson, Truman, and Marshall met with Clement Attlee, head of government in Great Britain. The prime minister still believed that Mao could be another Tito and opposed intervention in Taiwan. The president, while a gracious host by nature, was now more in line with Howard, whose "snotty little sheet in Washington" (the *Daily News*) was in his opinion "among the worst" newspapers in the United States. Truman held that the Beijing regime was "Russian and nothing else." Marshall chimed in that they "regarded the Russians as co-religionists," not what he said in 1946. Marshall then held that relations between the Kremlin and Chinese communists were "extremely obscure." Dean Acheson said much the same thing, at least until Beijing's recent offensive. The secretary of state, as an erstwhile proponent of the British position on China, got special coverage from Howard's local outlet. The *Daily News* would print a story in which a company commander facing the Chinese says, "I'm not going to shoot too many of those guys Dean Acheson loves so much. I might be court-martialed."[53]

The secretary of state once told the Joint Chiefs of Staff that when it came to Formosa "political considerations," meaning international relations, had to outweigh their concerns. He was not about to persevere against the new military security consensus in Washington and the latest Gallup Polls. Eighty-one percent of those surveyed believed China entered the war on orders from Moscow and Acheson should be replaced, three to two. He brought politics back into the picture, this time as public opinion, by warning Britain what would happen if Washington gave in to foreign feelings disfavoring Formosa: "The attitude of the American people" was likely to change toward one of passively "adjusting ourselves to power and aggression everywhere."[54]

This was not the first (or the last) time Acheson raised the issue of American isolationism, a specter haunting London since the end of World War II. Whitehall thought him so busy compromising with Republicans that there was little hope for settlement with Beijing. This proposition overlooked an essential fact. The secretary of state was deferring less to Robert Taft than to the JCS, who endorsed substantial aide to the KMT before China ever launched its offensive. The Pentagon was not on a crusade as was MacArthur. It primarily acted out of practicality when unable to ensure "neutralization" of the Taiwan Strait while fighting nip and tuck in Korea. The president had been wary lest he upset his allies and precipitate war with the PRC. Stark facts then overtook policy and undermined the State Department's old preference against that of DOD. "If in taking a chance on the long future of China, we affect the security of the United States at once, this is a bad bargain," Acheson now told Attlee. "Instead of our making an effort to prove that we are their friends, we ask them to prove that they are ours. Formosa is too dangerous a thing for them to have to play with."[55]

This discussion took place five months before MacArthur's relief. The Senate hearings on that action solidified this policy by putting it on the public record where it was difficult to hedge, let alone retract. The *New York Times* noted that the administration "made it plainer than ever before that it would do all it could do to see that Formosa, during the war or after, shall not fall into Communist hands." All this was a way station on a path to a change still not completed by mid-1951, when Washington deployed a military "assistance" (not "advisory") group to Taipei. This distinction meant that U.S. personnel would distribute materiel, not just supervise its use—what advisors did for the Greek army in its civil war against communism. Chiang's supporters had reservations about these restrictions, last placed on the military mission to Nationalist China in 1948, when Taft-wingers failed to pass "Greek-Turkish provisos" on behalf of the KMT. They now had some powerful proponents on their side, such as the army chief of staff. Joe Collins argued for an advisory group, no provisos or fine print: "The only ground forces available for operations in defense of the island are those of the Chinese Nationalists"; take them or forget Formosa, so to speak.[56]

For various reasons, foreign and domestic, the interregnum on military assistance to Chiang Kai-shek was a thing of the past. MacArthur gave himself the credit, particularly on a nationwide speaking tour in mid-1951, when he asserted that he had been fired for his message to China on March 24th. He said it prevented the administration from executing a scheme to trade Formosa for peace in Korea. That was overstated but not out of character, as one syndicated columnist wrote of MacArthur: if the general "cannot be a savior, he will at least be a martyr." His real impact on policy about Formosa was more indirect. By bringing Mao Tse-tung into the military conflict in Korea, MacArthur forced Acheson to defer to the Joint Chiefs as experts on military policy who defended the dismissal of MacArthur. The U.S. government never waged war on China the way the general wanted, but he won the conflict over protecting Formosa where it was decisively waged, Washington, D.C.[57]

The White House must have felt that the exigencies of war and politics left it with a geopolitical lemon. Acheson, within the confines of the National Security Council, continued to oppose JCS plans to develop the full potential of Formosa, although the senior military thought it one of the few reliable places left them in the Far East now that independence was impending for Japan. The U.S. chargé in Taipei, another great supporter of the Nationalist cause, would brief the president in September 1952 about governmental progress and regime cooperation. Truman, retaining his good manners, attentively listened to "an interesting story." Two days later, he returned to ranting that "Chiang Kai-shek's downfall was his own doing. His field generals surrendered the equipment we gave him to the Commies and used his own arms and ammunition to overthrow him. Only an American Army of 2,000,000 men could have saved him and that would have been World War III."[58]

Such opinions were more common in Washington than was that of the chargé. "The regime is rotten and beyond redemption," wrote the State Department's desk officer. This finding was about to change, much to the surprise of the Foreign Service, some military advisors, and the CIA, of the opinion that the Kuomintang "exists only because of U.S. support." The ruling circles on the island cleaned up key agencies, such as that regulating foreign exchange, a cesspool in the 1940s. Taipei would not be democratic until the 1980s, when the Taiwanese took over Taiwan. Few outsiders thought the government could ever be effective, dictatorial or not. "It was quite a remarkable feat," said one old China hand; "I don't think those of us who had been associated with the KMT in China had any confidence that they could turn things around like they actually did."[59]

Washington did not deserve major credit for this turnabout in Taipei. Public declarations of unwavering support robbed Americans of the leverage reformers hoped to use by making aid strictly contingent on change within the Kuomintang. Utter desperation and new circumstances proved to be the remedy not existing as long as the regime remained in Nanking. Taiwan was literally its last stop short of individual exile in a foreign land, not attractive to Chiang Kai-shek, more interested in power than the luxuries tempting many of his compatriots. MacArthur blamed Washington for losing China; the administration blamed Chiang: too dumb, said Acheson, not to stand "in front of a locomotive." In fact, the generalissimo understood that a political culture of greed and sloth primarily was at fault. Mao, being master of a mass totalitarian party, could wipe out cliques, robber barons, and warlords festering on the mainland, along with any other challenge to his authority. Chiang, trying to hold on to his own factious organization, could do no such thing. He could, however, govern a relatively small island where feudalism and family favoritism had not taken hold, thanks to rule by Japanese technocrats finally exiled in 1945. "General," he told MacArthur in August 1950, "if I could have created on the China mainland a land reform act as you did in Japan, I would never have had to leave. I could never control my landlords to the extent where we could take a part of the land."[60]

The worst economic, military, and political elements in the Kuomintang never immigrated to Taiwan, which seemed foredoomed to fall to a communist invasion, especially once Acheson and Truman said in January 1950 that the United States was "not going to get involved militarily in any way." Hong Kong, Singapore, Hawaii, and New York seemed a far safer destination for the likes of Chen Li-fu, retiring to New Jersey after fighting off reform within the KMT. Emigration thus substituted for suppression of the many miscreants Chiang had to abide. Now he could use economic reformers to develop political resilience on Taiwan. The "breakaway province" could therefore play a major role in the subsequent containment of Communist China, not unforeseen by DOD in its bureaucratic battles with the State Department over policy before the Korean War began.[61]

In 1949, the army chief of staff said that China might not expand toward Southeast Asia "so long as they had Formosa to contend with or subdue." By the 1990s, the place had become the anchor of MacArthur's old perimeter defense. Training, planning, and equipment in the People's Liberation Army refocused on Taiwan scenarios, to the relief of other neighbors spared the threat of PRC hegemony. Had time proved MacArthur a brilliant prophet or a crank who made a lucky guess? Either way, the island in question never did become the fulcrum for the general's ultimate objective, that of overthrowing the mainland regime. The flash point of contemporary conflict in the strait is Taipei's flirtation with national secession, something abhorrent to MacArthur, Mao Tse-tung, or Chiang Kai-shek. They all adhered to Taiwan being part of China while disputing who governed China, once and for all.[62]

Dean Acheson would not have cared. He was always less concerned about what "devil" runs China as long as "he is an independent devil . . . [not] a stooge of Moscow." By 1952, the secretary of state had given up much hope for a Chinese Tito. Ironically, by then, the Korean War was actually accelerating the pace of schism within the communist camp. Through 1950, Mao and the CCP deferred to the Soviet Union as the "the great leader of working people throughout the world," notwithstanding resentment at the Kremlin's penchant for taking positions out of narrow national self-interest. Within two years, Mao began to think that China had saved radical revolution from imperialism by directly taking on the United States, which Stalin feared to do. By 1957, despite receiving more economic assistance than ever occurred during Korea, Mao said in contempt of his Moscow benefactors that they "know who is powerful and who is weak."[63]

The Precarious Prevention of Military Escalation

It is necessary that the Chinese rely only on their own aviation at the front.

JOSEPH STALIN, 13 JUNE 1951[64]

Most of the pilots were Russian. . . . We weren't prepared to do something about it. We had our hands full.

PAUL NITZE, CA. NOVEMBER 1986[65]

In 1951, the future roles of China and Taiwan were not clear. Taft-wing Republicans focused on aid to Formosa here and now, a stance popular with the public. Senate critics of MacArthur tried to change the topic by shifting the questions onto global grounds, particularly whether the general risked world war before the country was ready to wage it. This line of argument fell to Brien McMahon, known as "one of the sharpest, smoothest apples" on Capitol Hill, no small statement covering a field that included Lyndon Johnson. The Democrat from Connecticut forced MacArthur to admit that he "had no more information [about the nuclear arsenal] than the average officer," nor did he know the locus of international communism, was it Moscow or Beijing. "I don't pretend to be an authority on these things. The Chiefs of Staff or others here are the ones to answer that query."[66]

About Korea, MacArthur spoke with "considerable force and eloquence," wrote James Reston, "a personal triumph." His reluctance to address the world-wide balance of power exposed his weak suit, or so McMahon thought. ("Now I've got him," he whispered to an assistant, "I've really got him.") Questioned about Europe, the general responded, "I have been away in the Far East for 14 years and I don't pose as—not only an expert, but having anything more than the ordinary run-of-the-hopper knowledge of the special conditions that exist there." He was rarely so reluctant to voice an opinion on prospective threats or anything else. He was probably dodging an issue that could alienate isolationists, a significant component of his general support. If MacArthur were really ignorant about what Washington had in mind, he could go over other testimony before the Russell Committee, "the first time in all human experience," wrote Walter Lippmann, "that a people has conducted a council of war in the presence of its actual and possible enemies."[67]

Richard Russell knew he was walking a fine line. He had received numerous letters from people "shocked to hear you want to hold hearings behind closed doors." He replied that he was interested in protecting "the lives of men fighting in Korea more than pleasing the people with television shows," a reference to the Republican Party preference for something like the Kefauver hearings on organized crime. That broadcast uncovered local politicians consorting with gamblers in Democratic strongholds such as St. Louis, where a Truman appointee to the party's national finance committee was attorney for subpoenaed racketeers. This just raised more public suspicion about more government cover-ups. Hence the vice-president said "the Administration" could not be "in the position of trying to cut off the [MacArthur] hearings."[68]

Washington had other reasons for embarrassment than association with shady characters. Robert Lovett, deputy secretary of defense, grumbled that the MacArthur hearings were "contributing to the knowledge of the enemy in a shocking manner." This helped conduct the administration down a circular path. It entered the Korean War to avert World War III by demonstrating strength to Stalin. Now, it was publicly discussing ill-preparedness so it could discredit MacArthur on grounds he would precipitate war with the Kremlin before properly equipped. By so doing, the government had to worry that it would undermine the credibility deterring wider conflict. Omar Bradley testified that it is "very harmful to our security and to our country to have to pass on to Russia all of our intentions, all of our thoughts, all of our capabilities. . . . Since it is demanded by the people and is inherent in our form of government, here it is." Corporal William Manning, meanwhile recovering from wounds in Korea, wondered why Bradley and Marshall "insist on saying over and over that we are not prepared to wage World War III but that we may be ready in the future. Why," he asked Russell, "is it necessary to forewarn the Russians?"[69]

The Kremlin had to digest JCS statements about the "the shoestring" size of the U.S. air force and fears about "a show-down before we are ready." It also had to deal with disinformation from Washington intelligence agencies working off suspicions that Stalin had agents within the British embassy. The CIA appears to have fed Moscow figures that doubled true capacity to rain nuclear weapons on the Soviet Union. This could be a major factor in limiting Russian participation in Korea, unless the Russell Committee showed that Washington warmongers were afraid to conduct war. Stalin probably thought the hearings were the real charade because spies need not even wade though newspapers, as Corporal Manning did. Nor did they have to read all 3,651 pages of official transcripts released by the government. A cartoon in the *New Yorker* would suffice, wherein a Soviet general questioned, "But why delay, comrades? The testimony brought out by their own Senate committee proves that this is *exactly* the time for us to attack."[70]

MacArthur tried to use arguments about vulnerability to refute the administration's repudiation of his strategy: "At the lowest point of our disarmament it plunged us into war" but now "pled weakness before our fellow citizens." Senator Charles Tobey by mid-June 1951 was reluctant to make any point at all. This New Hampshire Republican cited the wholesale distribution of sensitive information as good reason to "ring down the curtain. . . . We have got the whole country by the ears putting out bulletins. Mr. Stalin subscribes to it every day." Presumably, the all-knowing leader of the working peoples of the world was less confused than the average American. The contradictions and inconsistencies of MacArthur and the administration cause one to wonder if what they believed dictated policies or policies dictated what they believed. In support of limited war, Marshall and the JCS held that Korea was relatively unimportant in comparison to Europe, the major target of Soviet expansion. At the same time, they warned that an attack on China would precipitate war with the Soviets in the Far East, where they have "sufficient forces and supplies to carry on operations for some period of time." World War III would be the "immediate" result according to Truman's side, although they didn't explain why Russia would fight an Armageddon in Asia, not its prime objective at all.[71]

MacArthur was equally inconsistent about Soviet policy, capabilities, and ambition. His letter to Joe Martin argued to augment his theater as the place where "the Communist conspirators have elected to make their play for global conquest." A month before dismissal, the general told Washington that "the Soviets have stationed offensive forces of great magnitude in Siberia": 4,500 aircraft, according to his military intelligence, four times that of the United States. "The lack of balance existing between Far East Command air forces and those of the potential enemy indicates that additional power will be needed on D-Day," when the Soviet Union presumably attacked the base of U.S. power in Japan. However, having made his case for reinforcement, MacArthur had to mitigate his greatest vulnerability: the fear that he would precipitate World War III. He therefore ridiculed ideas that an attack on China would bring in Russia, as he did in testimony about the decrepit state of the Trans-Siberian Railroad. It was not "within the capacity of the Soviet Union to mass any great additional increment of force to launch any predatory attack from the Asiatic continent. I believe that the dispositions of the Soviet forces [in the Pacific region] are largely defensive"—no mention of 4,500 aircraft now.[72]

The administration was forming its new opinion "that the top command of the Chinese Communists was thoroughly indoctrinated in Soviet theory and practice and completely loyal to Moscow." MacArthur maintained that Beijing "for its own purposes is [just temporarily] allied with the Soviet Russia," the same thing one would have heard from Dean Acheson before the Korean War. The implication of this position was that Stalin had no reason for war in East Asia, whether thinking of Marxist solidarity or military capability, at least when it came to railroad lines. Such logic might have led one to maintain the policy giving China a sanctuary status. In a global conflict against communism fought in the name of containment, why commit more resources where the Soviets were not likely to be belligerent? The failure of the administration to make this particular case was probably no oversight. The White House had a vested interest in a substantial Soviet threat posed in the Far East, lest it lose its best argument against striking China, that of provoking Russian retaliation. MacArthur, unlike the Pentagon, was taking a position similar to testimony of

JCS intelligence in mid-1949: "If the Soviets would like to move by means of armed aggression, Korea would be at the bottom of their priority list."[73]

The *New York Times* did not think much of MacArthur's theory that China was an autonomous entity vis-à-vis the Soviet Union. This proposition ran "a risk too large to be taken at this stage" according to this paper, which often spoke of "the North Korean puppets of the Chinese puppets of the Kremlin." That commentary matched its editorials favorable to the KMT, at least no tool of Joe Stalin. Right or wrong, the paper was more consistent than major figures who were reversing what they previously had said in this controversy. The administration once maintained that China and Russia were inherent adversaries, particularly along their common border. Washington sent ground troops to Korea in mid-1950 on the premise that it could wage a proxy war because Moscow would make no troop commitment on behalf of someone in this region of the world. Things looked far different to Dean Acheson by mid-1951. "China is the Soviet Union's largest and most important satellite," he told the Senate. Since it is "difficult to see how the Soviet Union could ignore a direct attack upon the Chinese mainland," that option would be a "catastrophic solution" for America's problem in Korea.[74]

Much the same caution was the main lesson the Joint Chiefs of Staff drew from the war. The deputy director for politico-military affairs wrote the chief of the joint staff that the government should not make decisions regarding China "on an ad hoc basis as was the case in Korea. As you recall we entered that fracas by steps without a thorough study of the possible consequences." The circumspect deliberation for which he spoke in December 1950 could not create a consensus with MacArthur, who clearly doubted to reporters that the Soviet Union "would launch itself into such a conflict in defense of the Chinese." He may well have been right, seeing how Stalin tried to get Mao into the war so that Russia could avoid a major combat role. MacArthur still showed a rare touch of humility when asked by William Fulbright [Dem-Ark.] if Mao had "close personal relations with Moscow." He replied, "How would I know, Senator?" Acheson was not nearly this modest before or after combat commenced with China. The previous January, he had cited Russian retention of bases in Manchuria as an issue pushing Beijing out of the Soviet orbit. In mid-1951, he said that MacArthur would provoke Stalin by bombing territory actually ceded back to Chinese sovereignty in February 1950. Acheson was unable to cite any precise provisions of this Sino-Soviet defense treaty, which merely specified "repetition of aggression by Japan." He could only raise the specter of some secret clause and resort to vague phrases such as "opportunity" and "leverage." Taft-wing Republicans, not impressed, asked whether Russia ever kept any treaties at all, another reference to Yalta, never far from their mind.[75]

The Truman administration was thus under considerable pressure to cite evidence on behalf of prudence concerning China. It would still not mention the Soviet commitment to air defense of its ally along the Yalu River Valley, potentially public exhibit number one. MacArthur testified that "no one would have been more opposed to doing any bombing in Siberia than I would." Acheson could have answered that the general's plan to bomb Manchuria would have killed a lot of Russians. Stalin sent, in total, 72,000 pilots, mechanics, technicians, and gun crew operators to cover the area north of Pyongyang into the depths of Manchuria. This was his quid-pro-quo to keep China keeping America in a "drawn out war." That, he told Mao, "shakes up the Truman regime" and "harms the military prestige of the Anglo-American troops."[76]

The Kremlin still tried to keep its air defense contribution covert, not unlike CIA operations out of Formosa. This made the Soviet air force play a different role than it took in 1970, open battles over the Suez Canal to garner gratitude from the Arab world. In 1951, when the proxy of a superpower was not the opponent, Stalin lived in fear of U.S. atomic weaponry. Khrushchev found him "trembling inside." Chinese infantry consequently got no close air support from Soviet planes in theater, lest they fly over areas where they might fall into American hands. Fellow pilots strafed those ditching in the high seas rather than risk their capture by U.S. patrols in the area to rescue their own crews. Washington still had proof of Soviet presence through electronic intercepts. Red Army airmen in the midst of deadly dogfights did not transmit in local dialect learned from rush training in elementary Chinese. Had the United States desired, it could have played the tapes of guttural Russian, if not put some of these crewmen on display by "sucking a few MIGs," to quote one U.S. general, "into combat over our lines."[77]

Acheson only told the Senate that if MacArthur had his way, Stalin "could turn over to the Chinese large numbers of planes with 'volunteer' crews for retaliatory action." He said nothing to them about Soviet air defense activity, let alone notify the citizenry at large. The administration feared stirring up "tremendous pressure" to escalate the conflict into "a war with Russia," not needed as long as the Red Air Force stayed on the strategic defensive. "We had only fighters and AAA," a senior Soviet officer recalled, and therefore were "unable to overcome the Americans." Its force still managed to gun down 569 planes, virtually unknown to the American public. However, Stalin never did what Mao wished and what Washington feared: commit major assets to offensive operations, even if Russians would not pilot the weaponry. "The air force belongs to the state," he told Chou En-lai. "Chinese volunteers should not use a state-owned air force," excepting in defense, a limited mission Russia turned over to China as soon as it could.[78]

MacArthur had his own notions about long-range bombers, at least those in the anticommunist inventory. In mid-1950, he objected to restrictions on KMT deployments off the coastline of South China, where at issue was the prospective invasion of Formosa. In mid-1951, he railed against communist sanctuaries in Manchuria, with even less impact on national policy. The Department of Defense was not on his side this time, as it had been twelve months ago.

Marshall and the JCS gave secret testimony that "we are fighting under rather favorable rules for ourselves," a tacit recognition of Stalin's concessions. "We had no ground troops in Korea," said a Soviet general. "We understood that might result in a big war." The same concern stirred Washington, then getting assessments that the Soviets had fifty atomic warheads and enough long-range aircraft to penetrate North America, a capacity not actually acquired until after war.[79]

Mao implored Stalin for "well prepared bomber units" attacking barracks, warehouses, and other targets in US/UN rear areas. In Stalin's own concept of operations, Chinese and North Korean infantry had a virtual monopoly on taking the fight deep to the enemy. He admonished Mao not to rely on localized lure-and-ambush operations, the sort of "bit by bit" strategy Peng Dehuai called "reasonable leadership." The USA, said Stalin, is not the Kuomintang: prepare for "a serious strike against the Anglo-American troops." Meanwhile, no Soviet submarines and bombers entered the fray. Not one vessel from any UN country would be attacked in waters surrounding the peninsula; none of its planes were challenged outside MIG Alley. The United States paid no penalty for inattention to its own air defense, although Pusan and other major ports, choked with ordnance, could by JCS admission have been "blown right out of sight."[80]

Looking for Light at the End of the Tunnel

Technical arguments about "civilian control" won't mean a thing to the people at large. We cannot afford to slack off in our constant emphasis and reiteration that MacArthur stood for war and the President stands for peace. This and this alone will sink in with the general public.

GEORGE ELSEY, WHITE HOUSE COUNSEL, 29 MAY 1951[81]

China was making full use of its limited capabilities. The Soviet Union, when it came to troop commitment, barely reached the threshold of limited war. Because the Kremlin and the White House both avoided escalation, each risked falling into stalemate. Politically, Stalin had less to lose. There was no MacArthur in his armed forces or vocal opposition in the nation at large. Truman, on the other hand, would have to show light at the end of the proverbial tunnel or be discredited in comparison to MacArthur's claim that his own proposal provided "the best chance possible of ending this war in the quickest time and with the least cost in blood." George Reedy knew the general struck political gold: "All the people want to know is whether we are going to get out of the place." He memoed Russell that the public would reject a plan "only because they think a better plan is available." Regrettably, it seemed the administration had "nothing to offer except a perpetual war in Korea."[82]

MacArthur told Congress in his farewell address that the objective of war must be "victory—not prolonged indecision." As of April 27th a pro-MacArthur columnist had no qualms saying that "the idea of a stalemate which shall keep American troops engaged indefinitely seems to be the policy of the Administration." Within weeks of that criticism, the White House received a windfall from the bloody battlefields north of Seoul, where the communists had launched their spring offensive, the most severe test of administration policy to beat China's army without attacking China. A million and a quarter enemy soldiers, over twice the size attacking the previous November, set out to drive the length of the peninsula. They advanced some thirty miles to the outskirts of the capital, where the US/UN/ROK opposition held and inflicted enormous casualties, over 100,000 killed, wounded, or captured. "The Chinese lying near us pulled back," said a reconnaissance company PFC. "How odd, I thought, in the past they would have entered the attack. . . . When my patrol returned to the CP, I saw plenty of Chinese prisoners. It seemed they were dispirited and discouraged."[83]

Nobody seemed to realize the problems that repatriating prisoners would eventually create for resolving the war. The Pentagon witness list faced the Russell Committee about the time the communist spring offensive clearly fell apart. This gave a great opportunity for southern Democrats subtly on Truman's side to prompt Marshall, Bradley, and Collins to discredit MacArthur while discussing conditions in Korea with ostensible objectivity. Lyndon Johnson: "You are in disagreement with General MacArthur on that specific question [of stalemate]?" General Collins: "Yes sir: I am." The JCS had come to place its faith in what MacArthur once conceded: "Even under our existing conditions of restraint it should be clearly evident to the Communist foes . . . that they cannot hope to impose their will in Korea by military force." The Washington command told the Senate that by "inflicting maximum casualties," our side had "beaten up" the enemy "pretty badly." If the war continued in this manner, "the trained fabric of the Chinese Communist forces will be pretty well torn to pieces." Presumably this would change the opponent's "attitude" so that "some kind of arrangement can be reached and a settlement made."[84]

Statements about "some kind of arrangement" were vague but certainly more upbeat than marching orders from the president back in January: no "surrender to these murderous Chinese Communists. We will have to be pushed out." However, suppositions about an opponent's unwillingness to bear more pain underlay the prediction that punishment would produce a suitable settlement. More predictable—and just as important—was the impatience of the American people, the subject of George Marshall's old dictum that "a democracy cannot fight a Seven Years' War." A protracted conflict to protect the status quo "is not in our temperament," he reiterated in 1951. It would not be a major problem provided peace was truly at hand. Senator McMahon, outspoken advocate of administration policy at the Russell hearings, stated the case in a televised debate with Robert Taft on May 20th. "We are inflicting the maximum amount of damage and casualties to the enemy with the least loss to ourselves. That can only result in victory for our side without the risk of bringing on a global or third world war."[85]

George Reedy would have liked "a clear simple statement that the United States can win the Korean War" issued by someone with wider authority than the junior senator from Connecticut. Marshall testified that "it is exceedingly hard to decide what may be said . . . because it really amounts to disclosing a war plan." Letters to Russell thought him evasive: "He doesn't talk straight from the shoulder like MacArthur," wrote one citizen. The secretary of defense and the chairman of the Joint Chiefs appeared hopeful but were always more guarded than politicians wished. They would not definitely guarantee "we are going to get decisive results under what we are doing," that is, "inflicting severe casualties on the enemy and proving to them they are not invincible." Marshall and Bradley had already seen quite a few predictions belied by events and conceded that if prospects worsened in Korea, they might have to implement MacArthur's ideas by taking the war outside the peninsula. This contingency still seemed hypothetical, Reedy concluded. It was "reasonable and logical" for the military to mention this fallback position, even if they felt a cease-fire was in the offing.[86]

When the communist offensive failed in May, UN forces pushed back across the 38th parallel. Republicans became more wary of association with MacArthur, now vulnerable to damage from an acceptable peace. In June, Marshall made an unannounced trip to Korea on the heels of his Senate testimony, an arduous task for an old man in poor health. One has difficulty accepting "I came to Korea to congratulate our Army leaders on their achievements." He inspected troops and the replacement system, what one might expect from the secretary of defense. More important, under hellish wind squalls, he flew over the front lines where a prospective armistice would be drawn. It was the first time Marshall saw Korean battlefields—and the last battlefield he ever saw. He returned with high praise for UN forces having conducted a "military classic." They "counterattacked immediately, disrupted the Communists' morale, and certainly hurt the Communist prestige. I don't think they'll ever forget it." As for domestic U.S. morale, he issued an implicit reprimand. "Whenever we start something and don't finish it the same afternoon in our country that's a stalemate."[87]

In private, Marshall was glum, if one is to believe Ridgway's public affairs officer, the only witness to an exchange between the secretary and the new CINCFE. It occurred as enemy resistance was stiffening once again. Marshall is said to have admitted that neither he nor anyone else in Washington understood how bad the situation was. When back in the States, he was going to tell the president to warn China about getting "a taste of the atom" unless willing to negotiate. No record exists that the government threatened to use such weapons, an issue that will reappear when chapter 8 examines how a settlement occurred in mid-1953. One can determine that on 14 June 1951 Marshall did send Ridgway a message of such sensitivity that a copy cannot be found, other than a record of its placement in a sealed envelope, such as he used during World War II for documents of the utmost secrecy pertaining to code breaking and the production of the atomic bomb.[88]

Coincidence or not, the Soviet representative to the United Nations said on June 23rd that his government favored talks for a cease-fire. In response to this announcement, western journalists and communist diplomats predicted a quick conclusion, probably within a month. Ridgway, certainly no sentimentalist, "thought peace might be just around the next corner." Mao Tse-tung mentioned two weeks. Dean Acheson, relatively skeptical, said the odds on a settlement "was at least fifty-fifty, perhaps a little better." Truman's public approval ratings reflected this state of euphoria by shooting up 10 percent. Asked if the prospective armistice justified his relief of MacArthur, the president told reporters "yes." Now all he needed to get out of the woods were honorable terms quickly signed and sealed. Few people suspected how distant that would prove to be, probably why Marshall could retire with good conscience on September 1st.[89]

Anglophobia, NATO, and Omar Bradley

Britain's "argument seemed to be that more could be accomplished in Asia by appeasement than by moral resolution."

DOUGLAS MACARTHUR, 1964[90]

MacArthur held that the Soviet Union would not let China drag it into war with the United States. NATO nations feared the general would drag them into war with China. The day of his relief a *New York Times* correspondent wrote that "the left-wing of the Labor [*sic*] party and a good part of the English press have been clamoring for MacArthur's scalp for some time." Having finally got it, they could be blamed for what they wished, as Dean Rusk forewarned his majesty's ambassador on March 24th: if the president were "explicitly to disown Mac-Arthur . . . foreign policy might be jeopardized including troops for Europe." The subsequent dismissal was far less popular in the United States than in the United Kingdom: 66 percent disapproved at home, 19 percent abroad. Senator Kenneth Wherry, the Republican Party whip, charged the president of the United States with succumbing to pressure from "the Socialist Government of Great Britain." This had been a staple theme of villainy in Taft-wing oratory since Labour came to power in 1945. Critics of Democratic domestic policy long accused it of following London's lead down the path of "slavery to government and crippling debt." Now, according to Wherry on national radio, Britain had the raw "audacity to insist that Formosa be turned over to Red China," nothing but a bunch of "Moscow-directed bandits."[91]

Wherry was not the only one in Washington applying pressure on Whitehall, which had excused its reluctance to condemn China as repugnance for "MacArthuritis." Acheson wrote his London embassy that the U.S. government was ready to "'cash-in' on the removal of MacArthur from [the] scene. . . . It is important" that the British "do not regard the MacArthur action as appeasement toward their point of view or as appeasement toward Chi. Commies." The White House, in so many words, expected its ally to do what it itself was doing in regard to Formosa, that is, move down what Britain called "the MacArthur road" by accepting a lesser version of his Far East policies. [92]

A major obstacle to this accommodation was Aneurin ("Nye") Bevan, the minister of labor and leader of resistance to U.S. pressure for doubling the defense budge, already 7.2 percent of gross domestic product. Inflation, commodity shortfalls, and substandard housing were hot-button issues when everyday life in London still meant coldwater flats and one pound of rationed hamburger per week. This could have geostrategic significance, as Acheson noted in August 1950: "undue strain on the economy" might open "the back door to Communist inroads through political means." That contingency seemed apparent in December when a parliamentary uprising from left-wing backbenchers helped drive Clement Attlee to Washington for his summit conference on Korea, MacArthur, nuclear weapons, and China. The president rejected concessions to Beijing as "political dynamite in the United States," then set up a private meeting with the prime minister. "Bevan and his group" took center stage along with their American equivalents, what Truman called "the problem of the men composing the Senate opposition who seemed violently determined to disrupt the nation's foreign policy." "We talked," the president said, "as only two men could talk who have spent a lifetime in politics."[93]

Bevan was out to leverage what one London reporter called "a rebellion of free Europe against the kind of leadership America was giving the West on the Korean issue." Specifically, he used dread of Douglas MacArthur to attack the moderates who led his party, allegedly complicit with the Far East Command. They should give him a key ministry, such as Foreign Affairs, said to be guilty of trading "socialist principles" for a lock-down alliance with "capitalist America." The dismissal of the CINCFE robbed the far left of "the antics of an insolent military politician" who had become a two-edged sword in the fight between Labour Party factions. The Attlee group used MacArthur against the Bevanites just as the Bevanites used him against them. Participation in Korea enhanced Whitehall's influence in Washington, if one were to believe the prime minister, the Foreign Office, and stories claiming that they removed the atomic bomb from MacArthur's hand at the December meeting with Truman. Now they said, with gentlemanly modesty, that they could not take "the whole credit" for the dismissal of the general, a joyous event in Britain. Bevan, with no place to go, resigned his own ministry on April 21st with a public attack on former colleagues "dragged behind the wheels of American diplomacy." They, in turn, attacked him as the type of egotist who dreamed "he was General MacArthur."[94]

Whitehall and the White House preserved the Western alliance by ridding themselves of divisive figures who thrived off each other. The United States, according to the Bevanites, was an imperialist state: witness how a Douglas MacArthur–Joe McCarthy–war profiteer consortium dictated policy that did "more damage to Western Europe than Stalin can ever do." MacArthur's following countered that Britains lacked "the will to fight for their own freedom": note Bevan's oratory, Hong Kong trade pouring into China, and resistance to enhanced commitment to Korea. In late 1950–early 1951, when Taft-wing Republicans opposed further U.S. deployments to NATO, they stressed that America "has put up 90% of the forces and suffered 90% casualties of the forces furnished by United Nations members." Adherents to the alliance—from the secretary of state to the *Washington Post*—had a grim rebuttal during the communist spring offensive, when the Gloucester battalion of the British Commonwealth Division suffered 90 percent casualties of their own while holding off the Sixty-third Chinese Army at a place to be memorialized as Gloucester Hill. Acheson, reviled in letters to the Senate for being "strongly pro-British," called this "one of the great stories in military history" at the Russell Committee hearing. "I think our troops recognize that these are comrades that they are very glad to have."[95]

A gritty infantry battle in Truman's hour of need was not the only answer to charges of "appeasement" from opposition elements in America. Mainline British papers and politicians fully realized that "the next few weeks will be very tricky with the U.S.A. going haywire over MacArthur." Whitehall would have to lean toward Washington's new guiding principle, what could be called a "closed door" policy of no contact with China. The week of the general's dismissal London agreed to embargo trade of strategic materials such as rubber, no doubt a counter to the charge laid down by Senator Wherry about conducting "a thriving business with the Communists." Britain also moderated its policy on Chiang Kai-shek insofar as its foreign minister announced it would not discuss the future of Formosa until after the end of the Korean War. "It would certainly be idle to expect that American policy will suddenly soften," newspaper editorials held.[96]

Whitehall was careful because it was no sacred cow in American politics. Taft-wing Republicans had no compunction about trying to bait George Marshall that the administration dismissed MacArthur because of "severe pressure by the Allies." The secretary of defense said that this was a State Department issue: "I can only give you second-hand." However, he confirmed that by keeping MacArthur in command "we were jeopardizing our entire relationship on a collective security basis," a theme to be sustained by the Joint Chiefs of Staff. Their prestige was largely intact, unlike Britain's, Marshall's, or Dean Acheson's. They certainly stood in favor of the effort for NATO epitomized in the president's January 1951 State of the Union address, which Truman called "the most important declaration I'd ever been called upon to make." In it, the Western alliance trumped the Korean War in priority of placement and number of pages in the text, where "the heart of our common defense effort" was said to be "the North Atlantic community."[97]

On this and other issues related to MacArthur the administration fostered a role for the military. It pushed them into the political function of gathering support for politicians who lacked the prestige to carry policies on their own accord. That modus operandi was not about "to fade away," no matter what MacArthur said about "old soldiers." In 1949, the White House used Omar Bradley to prevent a backlash resulting from merely signing the NATO treaty: "Without western Europe, the New World would stand alone," read the general's press release; "we must count on western Europe if we are to endure." Bradley resumed this topic in May 1951 at the Senate hearing on the military situation in the Far East. MacArthur, with his attention on the fight in Korea, testified that "we have plenty of allies but" they have contributed "only token forces" in the war at hand. The chairman of the Joint Chiefs, in rebuttal, implied that Korea was still a minor conflict: "I would hate very much to see us involved in a land war in Asia." He was more compelling when he held that it was "up to us to gain strength through cooperative efforts with other nations."[98]

Truth be known, Bradley had a streak of Anglophobia almost worthy of MacArthur or Wherry. He had seethed under British derision of the American army during World War II, even telling Patton he was far too compliant in mid-1943. However, Bradley could separate personal feelings from public policy better than MacArthur, who could not do it at all. This enabled him to be something of a dream witness for Russell Committee staff formulating a series of questions that would underscore the "value of our allies in Europe." Without these partners, according to Bradley's testimony, the Soviet Union would gain control of "the entire Eurasian land mass" and thereby "build the military power to rule the world."[99]

In so many words, the chairman of the JCS was telling the public that MacArthur could cost them NATO and thereby give them Soviet hegemony on a global scale. His message resembled that of the president, excepting one factor: Bradley had more credibility than Truman. The general had become a majordomo of the administration despite his military posting, professional training, and disinclination even to vote while still in uniform. To him and the officers of his generation the whole MacArthur incident was terribly upsetting. A wellconnected journalist wrote of a veil falling from the eyes of an officer corps who "recognized for the first time how deeply the military had got mired in domestic and world politics." In some form or degree, politicization of military policy was inevitable as long as politicians took conflicting positions on national defense like they do on taxes, public works, and tariffs. Somewhere a demarcation lay between policy and politics, but it was badly blurred by mid-1951. It was not likely to diminish, nor was confusion about respective roles in civil-military relations. Two five-star generals, MacArthur and Eisenhower, were about to square off for the Republican nomination to replace President Truman.[100]

Ending the War without Truman or MacArthur

1 2 3 4 5 6 7 **8** 9

There [is] no easy way out of the Korean war. . . . The only program I could offer is far from a satisfactory solution.

GENERAL DWIGHT D. EISENHOWER, JUNE 1952[1]

Harry Truman could retain political viability despite dismissing Douglas Mac-Arthur as long as he could hold out credible hope that he was about to end the war. That claim lost plausibility once the president insisted that prisoners of war get to choose their place of repatriation, a symbolic victory despite deadlock on the battlefield. Several thousand communist soldiers indicated they would go to Taiwan, something Beijing would not abide because denied recognition as the one and only government of China. The fighting therefore continued, a fatal blow to an administration not resorting to military escalation to break the impasse. Stalemate, politically, can be worse than defeat because it keeps the conflict current when the nation holds its next election. The party in office, unlike the opposition, cannot say it's time for a change. Therefore the most important political contest in 1952 was for the Republican presidential nomination, which MacArthur lost to Dwight Eisenhower on personality as much as policy. Now Eisenhower would have to end the war on acceptable terms, what eluded Truman. The new president made motions toward executing a MacArthur-like strategy of attacking China. Joseph Stalin's death then auspiciously broke the diplomatic logjam. This rang down the curtain on the Korean War, except for debates about what actually caused the enemy concession on POWs and how to contain communist expansion in the Far East. Eisenhower chose to emphasize the impact of threats to use atomic weapons, a handy claim when cutting Truman's military spending. Matt Ridgway, now army chief of staff, protested these reductions in the name of preventing a return to the state of unpreparedness afflicting ground forces in June 1950. Conflict in Vietnam was already on the horizon, but Eisenhower dismissed the hero of Korea with more alacrity than Truman handled MacArthur.

Peace Talks and Prisoners of War

Establish the principle that the treatment of POWs, after their transfer to places of internment, shall be directed toward their exploitation, training, and use for psychological warfare purposes.

NSC-81/1, 9 SEPTEMBER 1950[2]

Boundary lines between the antagonists were troublesome but not grounds to delay the armistice until July 1953. The prospective point of cease-fire reflected military facts and emplacements, not policy decisions by heads of state. As of June 1951, it did not lie precisely at the 38th parallel, which separated North and South Korea when the war began. Syngman Rhee, the leader of the South, fervently wanted to regain Kaesong, the ancient capital of his nation situated two miles below the parallel west of Seoul. It was still in enemy hands as the United Nations dug its own defensive positions on the east side of the peninsula twenty-five miles north of the prewar borderline. Talk could not resolve the issue, so the line of contact dictated the terms both sides accepted by November 1951: retention of occupied territory per the ancient Latin principle of *uti possidetis:* "if you are in possession."[3]

Other issues were also compromised because neither side had the power or the will to dictate terms. Nor were they willing to assume the international opprobrium of rejecting a reasonable solution to a war the world community wanted to conclude. Mutual agreement was reached about rotating and replacing army units during armistice negotiations as well as building jet airfields. Even the status of Taiwan, a major problem in Sino-American relations, temporarily went into eclipse, although present from the onset of the war. A week after Kim Il-sung crossed the 38th Parallel in June 1950, Chou En-lai told the Soviet ambassador about the "negative" impact of the operation on Chinese plans to liberate the island in question. In August, he protested to the United Nations "direct armed aggression on the territory of China," meaning the dispatch of the U.S. Seventh Fleet to the Taiwan Strait. That November, Mao thought he could force this disengagement by decisively beating America north of Pyongyang. Frostbite and firepower decimated his gloveless infantry wearing tennis shoes better suited for storming the Kuomintang redoubt. Mao thereby lost his best opportunity to conquer "the renegade province."[4]

In June 1951, Mao told Kim that "the question [of Taiwan] should be raised in order to bargain" but "if America firmly insists that [it] be resolved separately, then we will make a corresponding concession." Three months later, the communist side still tried to slip the status of the island into the agenda for negotiations under the rubric of "other questions related to peace." The United States responded by adding the word "Korean," so it now read "other Korean questions related to peace." China countered by throwing in "etc.," meaning just about anything anybody could infer. Direct discussion of the province was to be postponed for a future conference, eventually held in Geneva, 1954. It settled nothing of substance aside from the French evacuation of Vietnam that helped set the stage for America's next land war in Asia.[5]

In the meantime Mao told Stalin that the conflict in Korea demonstrated "the extreme necessity for improvement of the equipment of our troops." Armament for sixty divisions "is the minimal requirement in Korea this year." Stalin must have realized that Mao was using the war to acquire the vast volume of military equipment for which he long had appealed, including naval capability. Stalin already professed no "objections from our side," completely understandable from a Russia point of view. The war was diverting and dividing NATO, of far less importance to the PRC. Stalin thus reverted to his ultimate inducement to Chou En-lai in 1952: "The Chinese comrades must know that if America does not lose this war, then China will never recapture Taiwan."[6]

Mao certainly knew the price of the war he was conducting: nearly 46 percent of government expenditures and, in total, 2,300,000 soldiers. He had come to realize that he lacked the capacity to drive the enemy clear out of Korea, let alone out of Taiwan. The issue of the island remerged in an indirect fashion via disagreement on repatriation of prisoners of war. Technically, this was not an armistice issue about military security during a cease-fire, but it would still drive Truman out of the White House by blocking agreement to end the conflict. The specific point of controversy was his insistence on allowing captured soldiers to refuse return to the nation-state they had served. The demilitarized zone on the Korean peninsula ensured each side much the same expanse of territory that it had before the war began. There was, however, an enormous disparity in possession of POWs. The communists had 11,559 prisoners, 34 percent American. The United Nations held over 130,000, 38 percent Chinese. Two-thirds of them, some 14,000 men, decided to go to Taiwan. By so doing, they brought the island back into the political forefront of the Korean War.[7]

In March 1950, Paul Nitze and Robert Lovett talked of capitalizing on "the desires of the Poles, etc. for liberation"; "there are plenty of partisans and dissidents on the enemy's borders and within who are willing to fight." This type of thinking led toward recruiting refugees from communist states. The U.S. Army's Bureau of Psychological Warfare added voluntary (versus mandatory) prisoner repatriation to this mix in 1951. Few professional soldiers sought a posting to that particular detachment, lacking ladders of promotion to senior troop command. Eisenhower stuck Brigadier General Robert McClure in the director billet back in World War II because he thought him "the only career officer at the time who had the slightest notion of what psychological warfare was all about. . . . Most [others] were ready to dismiss it as just another 'crackpot' conception." McClure, whether oddball in a backwater or visionary on the cutting edge, felt psychological operations (PSYOPS, for short) "must become a part of every future war plan."[8]

McClure had direct experience with Stalin's method of stemming surrender in the Red Army when the prospect of Nazi captivity did not suffice. The Kremlin inflicted grim reprisals on those surviving incarceration to be shipped home at the end of World War II. Dean Acheson, Averell Harriman, and some others in the State Department had qualms about participation in this coercive process, as did Henry Stimson, secretary of war, who held "the time-honored rule of asylum should apply." The army, however, wanted to recover 23,500 U.S. POWs held in camps that Soviet forces overran. At Yalta, that hot-button issue in postwar politics, the general staff wrote provisions stipulating transfer of Americans and Russians back to their respective armies "without delay." By mid-1946, when all GIs were out of communist-held territory, U.S. units had repatriated over two million Eastern Europeans, frequently rather forcefully. Omar Bradley recalled moving Russians and Poles into the Soviet zone: "This was the first time that I realized these fellows didn't want to go home. We had a deuce of a time."[9]

The Soviet Union had patently blackmailed the U.S. military. Had people been able to refuse to live under its regime, communism would have sustained a damaged image in the opening rounds of the Cold War. By 1947, a propaganda contest along these lines had replaced the wartime coalition. This had profound consequences on domestic, foreign, and military fronts. To the distress of Richard Russell, the United States could no longer afford racial segregation. Central Intelligence reported, "The bulk of Moscow's criticism appears to be focused on U.S. discrimination against Negroes." George Marshall, meanwhile denying his complicity with forced repatriation, made much of individuals trying to flee Stalinist captivity. This would become a major motif in the Korean War and a counter to communists calling American bombing a "link in the same chain" that oppressed "colored people in the U.S."[10]

In mid-January 1951, Bradley as chairman of the Joint Chiefs of Staff sent a message to Marshall with wordage lifted from position papers passing around Washington for the past six months: America had to develop "measures of economic, clandestine, subversive, and psychological character to foment and support unrest and revolution in selected strategic satellite countries and Russian political divisions." Robert McClure could have hardly had a more supportive setting that July when pointing out to his superiors that "inducements to surrender will be meaningless if it results [after repatriation] in the prisoner's death or slavery." Bradley soon wrote Lovett, now secretary of defense, that "in the light of the ideological struggle throughout the world for the minds of men, it would be of great value to establish . . . the principle of United Nations asylum from terrorism." The general may have been carried away by his recent role as public spokesman for the administration, all the while professing "no intention of entering the foreign policy field." His rhetorical flourish did not last very long. By October, Bradley, the JCS, and Lovett reverted to the position the armed forces held at Yalta, that anything less than total exchange of captives meant "bargaining with the welfare of our own [men as] prisoners."[11]

The Pentagon really wanted all its soldiers out of Korea, POWs or not. The borders were settled, but not the war, if the enemy refused to allow 70,000 soldiers in UN captivity to do what they apparently wanted, to go to Seoul or Taipei, not Pyongyang or Beijing. Two-thirds of the Chinese were former Kuomintang joining the communist ranks when their officers defected with units intact in the late 1940s. Switching to the winning side was standard procedure for Chinese warlords as well as docile soldiers deferring to superiors. However, their new regime took ideology far more seriously than preceding governments had done. So-called radishes (red on the outside but white underneath) underwent a rush course in "revolutionary heroism" two weeks to three months long. Then, after pep talks about easy victory, they were pushed to the front as an opportunity to make amends for oppressing the people when serving Chiang Kai-shek. Taiwan had attractions to those not seeking martyrdom for Mao or reeking from humiliation, criticism, and forced confession during communist rehabilitation. "I wanted," said one prisoner, "to crawl into the nearest hole."[12]

McClure had a truly captive audience for his own PSYOPS program in Civil Information and Education mandatory for all POWs. That gave Taiwan-recruited teachers a great opportunity to proselytize former defectors to defect back to their original side. This would spare them prospects for more incarceration awaiting them in the PRC, where they were likely to be thought agents planted by Taipei intelligence. True communists were supposed to go out like commissars from the Political Department, last seen blowing out their brains lest they fall into imperialist hands. These "beet" revolutionaries (red all the way through) were the real problem Ridgway faced in Korea when they enforced unit cohesion through party propaganda and the pistols they packed. The new CINCFE simply doubted PSYOPS was worth much blood and treasure against "hard bitten, thoroughly indoctrinated Communist troops." He paid lip service to the program when suggesting enemy troops end their "futile war" by revolt against their leadership. He also tried to discourage defections getting in the way of armistice negotiations. Prisoners were to hear of the fate likely to await their families if they failed to return home, much what Soviet officers said in 1945.[13]

Initially, the POW issue was a side effect of the Korean War, particularly for U.S. combat units, always skeptical of psychological operations. ("The West Point colonels," said one former practitioner, "could not find even a cup of coffee for us.") However, tails can eventually wag dogs; effects can become a cause. Otherwise, voluntary repatriation would not have raised ferocious opposition in Beijing and Pyongyang. The Soviet Union was the major enemy, but McClure was not oblivious to the impact of the policy upon the Chinese civil war. He had written Collins that defections would strengthen Formosa vis-à-vis the mainland by transferring soldiers from the PRC into the KMT. For him, repatriation was a pragmatic matter of force-ratios in the field. For Asians engaged in armed struggles for supremacy, it had symbolic repercussions "for the entire revolutionary camp." Letting Chinese or Koreans choose Chiang Kai-shek or Syngman Rhee belied communist claims that they constituted their countries' only governments.[14]

The United States prevented so-called Communist China from representation in the United Nations, international recognition of national sovereignty. Mao had planned to get the UN seat, along with Taiwan, by crushing imperialist obstruction on the battlefield. By mid-1951, he acknowledged that he could do no more than take on one battalion at a time, certainly not annihilate "an entire U.S. army once and for all," as he had hoped to do in late 1950. Reputable sources confirmed a desire for settlement in the PRC, expending in Korea materiel and manpower needed to impose a communist revolution across its own territory. Nonetheless, two weeks after a U.S. negotiator officially presented his government's position about repatriation on 2 January 1952, his Chinese counterpart replied on behalf of Beijing, "If anyone dares to hand over any of [our] personnel captured by the other side to the deadly enemy [on Taiwan], the Chinese people will never tolerate it and will fight to the end."[15]

The United States ambassador already had warned opinion makers visiting Moscow that any "solution to the Korean crisis [must] permit China and the Soviet Union to save 'face' which is so important in the Orient." If anything, this understated Beijing's motivation: looking for a major claim on international military standing. The PRC packed photographers snapping pictures for worldwide distribution at the site of cease-fire negotiations, where the UN delegation, depicted as supplicants, was to fly white flags on their jeeps when crossing into communist-controlled territory "politically more favorable to us." Truman, also interested in preserving prestige, would not step back from voluntary repatriation. "To return these prisoners of war in our hands by force would result in misery and bloodshed to the eternal dishonor of the United States and of the United Nations. We can not buy an armistice," he loudly declared in May 1952, "by turning over human beings for slaughter or slavery."[16]

Compassion was not the only reason voluntary repatriation was important to Truman, even after most professional soldiers came to write it off. George Marshall shed light in conversation with Frank Pace, although not speaking about POWs per se. "The American people will never understand this war," the secretary of defense said. "War is to be won or lost; it is not to be temporized. Since we've always won, this is a convenient philosophy"—at least until the nuclear age. The Virginia gentleman was pointing to familiar beliefs in the American heartland, Truman's permanent place of residence. There probably was no president more representative of the common people than this midwestern farm boy, bankrupted small businessman, and temporary occupant of government housing who jotted down in his diary, "I hope I'm still the country man from Missouri." One suspects that he, like most of his fellow citizens and his own speechwriters, had trouble faulting MacArthur's most riveting sentence: "There is no substitute for victory."[17]

One State Department official with access to the White House in mid-1951 found speechwriters stymied because they felt they "cannot compete emotionally with such solutions as are offered by General MacArthur." Voluntary repatriation filled the void since also about winning, at least politically. Joe Martin and Robert Taft had criticized the administration for "default in the field of psychological warfare"—"unimaginative, and without appeal to the oppressed peoples of the world." In fact, the project had been under discussion since 1947, the same year the president enunciated the Truman Doctrine stipulating the obligation to keep "hope alive" among those living under "totalitarian regimes." Lots of people were looking for a relatively safe and inexpensive way to set back the Kremlin, aside from conservative Republicans espousing total victory and balanced federal budgets. In April 1951, Truman created by secret directive the Psychological Strategy Board (PSB), an interagency body responsible for coordinating PSYOPS activity across State, Defense, and the CIA. Expectations exceeded capabilities, not unusual for new institutions, even when becoming the largest component in the National Security Council. By mid-1952, a senior member of the PSB staff, 130 strong, professed dismay at the "rising tide of public pressures for a spectacular political offensive based partly on unrealistic conceptions of what political warfare can achieve."[18]

There were not many options aside from PSYOPS for someone such as Harry Truman, caught between military stalemate and his inclination to exclaim, "The only way to meet communism is to eliminate it." The day the president relieved MacArthur he used vague phraseology such as "successful conclusion" of the conflict. Matt Ridgway, being the hero of the hour, could get away with a clear statement that "it would be a tremendous victory for the United Nations if the war ended with our forces in control up to the thirty-eight parallel." He accomplished that objective in command of the Eighth Army but confided in September that he would need six or seven more divisions to conquer the enemy. Truman did not have the manpower. Nor did he have the moral authority to end the Korean War without some kind of conquest. He found it in something far less tangible than liberating North Korea, his objective in the fall of 1950 when first tempted to go beyond the restoration of the prewar state of affairs.[19]

Truman had redefined war by calling Korea a "police action." Now he redefined victory as voluntary repatriation of POWs, nothing near bringing down communism, of which he daydreamed three weeks after the United States told the enemy of its policy not to return soldiers without consent. It was time for an "ultimatum with a ten day expiration limit," Truman vented in his diary. We would then blockade China and destroy "every military base in Manchuria"—but why stop there when one might be truly decisive? Russia must withdraw from Eastern Europe and stop all aid "to thugs . . . and stop now. We of the free world have suffered enough." This fantasy about "the final chance for the Soviet Government to decide whether it desires to survive" was certainly more combative than any real message MacArthur ever sent Mao. "All out war" would be waged in Moscow, Leningrad, Vlaldivostok, Beijing, Port Arthur, and "every manufacturing plant in China and the Soviet Union." Truman then got over his emotional spasm for unconditional surrender, except for a distorted memory when he said in 1960 that MacArthur "wanted to bomb China and Eastern Europe and everything else."[20]

By mid-1951, U.S. forces in Korea were conducting low-risk operations: "offensive action" carried out only "to regain key terrain lost to enemy assault." Ridgway later wrote the JCS that his command "could not, repeat not, inflict a decisive military defeat." An attempt would run "a serious risk of a successful enemy counter-offensive." Victory still had emotional appeal in the American political arena, judging by the Republican Party's own offensive in June 1951, after Acheson expressed a willingness to consider a truce along the 1950 border. Taft told a partisan rally, "The whole policy of punishing aggression has become a joke." The next month, upon the termination of the Russell hearings on national policy in the Far East, the Taft-wing caucus filed their minority report holding "that cessation of hostilities, based upon restoration of the status quo at the thirty-eight parallel will be a victory for aggression." Letters to the White House were consistent with this partisan condemnation of "Munichlike respites which are only surrenders in disguise." They assailed the principle of containment, as opposed to victory, although the public refused to sustain the objective it claimed to support. Only 10 percent of those polled said that they backed all-out war; 60 percent favored reaching some "agreement with Communist China on Korea." Compared to World War II, "the apathy has been shocking," wrote a syndicated newspaper columnist.[21]

Voluntary repatriation was a bridge between America's call for total victory and its reluctance to fight total war. It was also a Western face-saving issue for those pursuing a propaganda triumph even when contravening customary practice and international law. Ten months before North Korea crossed the 38th parallel, the secretary of state signed Article 118 of the Geneva Convention Relative to the Treatment of Prisoners of War. The document, created to regulate conflict between nation-states, did not foresee civil wars. It therefore restated the principle and practice of blanket return to the country of origin: "as soon as the war ends, prisoners must be released and repatriated without any delay," what the U.S. army did to Russians at the end of World War II. The

Senate did not ratify this treaty until 1955, but its provisions were still present in August 1951 when the State and Defense departments took up POWs. Acheson advised strict adherence to the treaty; the JCS favored voluntary repatriation. Within six months, they switched their respective stances.[22]

Repatriation policy became the latest interagency dispute over Korea, a place that never had much strategic value for most U.S. military officers. Joe Stalin professed his own opinion to Chou En-lai in August 1952: "Americans want to decide the POW question on their own in defiance of all international laws," suddenly sacrosanct to Marxist-Leninists. Beijing signed the Geneva Convention in July and cited it repeatedly. This gave a first-rate attorney like Acheson a juridical escape if deeming to point out that the Geneva accord said nothing about repatriation against one's will. However, the secretary of state and his department decided to adopt the very "principle of no forcible repatriation." A concession on the issue would "seriously jeopardize the psychological warfare position of the United States in its opposition to Communist tyranny." Conversely, acceptance of this stipulation by the communist side would "leave no shadow of a doubt in anyone's mind that our will has been imposed upon the enemy."[23]

Destruction of a political system is the goal of total war. Korea, being far more limited, was the type of conflict in which prisoners could become major objectives. In the 1700s, they were booty to be sold or exchanged, usually at fixed rates according to military rank. In the 1950s, where ideology trumped bookkeeping, captives were to be converted rather than ransomed. PSYOPS became prominent, even in statements of officers more familiar with troop ratios, supply depots, and dominant terrain. MacArthur claimed his ultimatum to China was "largely prepared as part of psychological warfare." Marshall said that the major payoff for defeating the enemy's spring offensive had been disrupting "Communist morale." Thousands of enemy soldiers were now making motions toward refusing repatriation to regimes that claimed their loyalty. This, said the chief of naval operations, would have an "extremely adverse affect on worldwide Commie prestige."[24]

European allies saw far less benefit for NATO, already subject to dissension over America's position on Formosa. Walter Lippmann spoke on behalf of his contacts in the chancelleries of Europe: "The best and most reliable friends we have on earth feel only sorrow and dismay at the terrible disunion which our passion for Chiang is bringing into the grand alliance of free nations." Repatriation policy added fuel to this fire, no matter what party ruled Whitehall. None had expressed any qualms about returning any Russian in 1945: willing or unwilling, soldiers and civilians. Anthony Eden did not reconsider the issue after resuming the post of foreign minister when the Conservatives took power from Labour in October 1951. Acheson "could not have been more rigid and difficult," he thought. "It almost seems as if [the] United States Government were afraid of agreement."[25]

Words like these would have pleased Mao Tse-tung, concerned that accepting Acheson's terms would "inevitably make the enemy even more ambitious and undermine our prestige." He had his own wedge policy, different from that of the United States and the United Kingdom. They had hoped to sever China from the Soviet Union; Mao talked of splitting the Anglo-American coalition, as when he addressed the party faithful in September 1950: U.S. "disharmony with [its] allies" would eventually assure China's "triumph over" the United States. Parts of this prediction seemed close to coming true by November 1952. Canada and Britain tried to resolve the diplomatic impasse on POWs through a face-saving gesture that would "give us the words and the other side the decision," as Acheson described conditions to Truman. In most other cases, under most circumstances, the secretary of state represented foreign opinion to other government agencies, such as DOD, angry at London for appeasing China over Formosa. "We can bring U.S. power into play," Acheson responded, "only with the cooperation of the British." Now, over some Chinese prisoners, he threatened those whom he had called "the only real ally on whom we can rely."[26]

Others in Washington officialdom cautioned "not to break up our alliances" in pursuit of psychological warfare. Acheson still revisited what he brought up to Canada in July 1950, when he said that "if the United States had to do all the fighting in Korea, there was a real danger that public opinion . . . would favor writing its allies off." He now warned Western diplomats that if his government got no support "on this essential matter" of voluntary repatriation, there "would be no NATO, no Anglo-American friendship." People in the Foreign Office privately described him in words once reserved for the likes of MacArthur: Acheson was becoming an "American tough guy shooting his way out of an awkward position and scattering his friends on every side." No matter, he told Truman about telling them that "you are going ahead with General Grant to 'fight it out on this line if it takes all summer.'" One presumes the president would have been happier with a comparison to Robert E. Lee, although willing to credit Grant with "bulldog persistence" such as NATO did not welcome when it came to POWs.[27]

Military Stalemate and the 1952 Election:
Truman, MacArthur, and Eisenhower

The nation has been put through one emotional binge after another for twenty years. It's time for peace and quiet.

DWIGHT EISENHOWER, CA. OCTOBER 1952[28]

"Anybody is a damn fool if he actually seeks to be President," Eisenhower said in May 1951. He was later heard to say that "the country has not been in such grave peril since the darkest days of the Civil War." His diary as of late October recorded a readiness to take the plunge "in response to a clear call of duty," but he still told reporters that his fondest wish was to keep the armed forces out of politics. The general would solve his dilemma in June 1952 by putting in for retirement, a way to avoid "embarrassing the government or the Army" and to abide regulations against political activity. Douglas MacArthur would not follow suit although he was also in the hunt for delegates to the Republican National Convention. He did not interrupt his lifelong appointment to five-star rank, again suggesting Truman might have kept him under some institutional wraps if willing to provide another assignment or keep him in Japan with a nominal command.[29]

While Eisenhower and MacArthur mulled over their options from mid-1951 to mid-1952, combat in Korea hardened into trench warfare along the lines of World War I, except that communist positions had almost twice the depth the Germans dug on the Western front. The U.S. command, unwilling to try to penetrate twenty miles of mines and strong points, began a massive bombing campaign against North Korean cities, towns, installations, factories, and nearly everything else worth destroying between the front lines and the Yalu River. Pyongyang was ready to concede after twenty-four months of unremitting warfare, despite Stalin's offer to supply ten divisions of antiaircraft artillery. He and Chou En-lai recognized that "a certain group of leading Korean figures is in a state of panic," a substantial change in allies once thoroughly committed to "national liberation." Still, the damage done to Kim Il-sung could not be decisive because the communist rulers who kept the war going resided in Moscow and Beijing. "We are somewhat in the position," said a U.S. air plans officer, "of trying to starve a beggar by raiding his pantry when we know he gets his meals from his rich relative up the street."[30]

In mid-May 1951, Stewart Alsop wrote in his syndicated newspaper column that Omar Bradley "clearly intimated [to the Russell Committee] that another indecisive winter campaign wholly confined to Korea is almost inconceivable." Next year the U.S. Army was privately agreeing with MacArthur's prophecy of endless war: "It appears that within current capabilities and existing policies, there are no military courses of action that will ensure a satisfactory conclusion to the Korean struggle." The American people would not disagree if informed of this top-secret memo from the deputy army chief of staff for plans. Seventy percent already said they could not see a way to end the conflict, a subject of frustration and ambivalence. At times, 53 percent felt we should "stop fooling around and do whatever is necessary to knock the Communists out of Korea once and for all." Other times, this fell to three in ten. One way or the other, only 23 percent approved of Harry Truman, the lowest rating for a sitting president in the history of the Gallup Poll. He could not hope to win the upcoming election under conditions described in another Alsop column, August 1952: "We cannot resume the offensive in Korea because our national strength is not sufficient. We cannot build national strength without going on a full-war basis. We cannot expect the enemy to sign a truce unless punishment makes it worth his while to do so. And we cannot sign a truce and surrender ourselves."[31]

Even during the heady days following the defeat of the Chinese spring offensive, public opinion tended to favor MacArthur's policy. The subsequent stalemate hardened the conviction of his adherents, always more committed to their position than those who supported the Truman administration. (Seventy-one percent of those favoring MacArthur did so "very strongly" in June 1951, as opposed to 61 percent of those backing Marshall and Bradley.) Dean Acheson himself could tacitly concede that the situation in Korea confirmed the former CINCFE, although certainly not directly praising the general by name. In January 1952, the secretary of state told Eden and Winston Churchill that the United States would bomb and blockade the mainland if China launched another major offensive or violated an eventual cease-fire. By then, the American public admired MacArthur more than any other man in the world. However, he would still not reap the ultimate political reward. Only 36 percent of those polled thought he would make a good president. Far more people wanted Truman's replacement to be Eisenhower, beating MacArthur 57 to 21 percent in the nation at large.[32]

Eisenhower obviously was an expert on military issues. As for political matters, he had a strong personal opinion on the constitutional issue of the hour: "When the day comes that American soldiers can in war successfully defy the entire civil government then the American system will have come to an end." Nonetheless, in public, he stayed low in the foxhole provided to the Supreme Commander North Atlantic Treaty Organization, responsible to twelve different nations. His professions of prohibitions against involvement "in an American debate" could have been sincere or a lame excuse to put off the likes of Averell Harriman, soliciting public support for President Truman. Either way, Eisenhower wrote a confidant, "So far as all the MacArthur-Korean-administration-partisan politics affair is concerned, I have kept my mouth closed in every language of which I have ever heard." People on both ends of the issue and the majority flipping back and forth could think him on their side, whatever side they were on. Democrats polled the week Truman fired MacArthur wanted to run Eisenhower in 1952. He beat Truman 43 to 18 percent, better numbers than he got from a preference survey of Republicans in March 1952, where Taft beat Eisenhower 34 to 33, with MacArthur in third place at 14 percent.[33]

Eisenhower, while still reluctant to have to campaign for the White House, did not think much of the alternative candidates, starting with the incumbent. Truman, while "a fine man" on a personal basis, was caught "in the middle of a stormy lake, [and] knows nothing of swimming. A lot of drowning people are forced to look to him as a lifeguard. If [only] his wisdom could equal his good intent." The Republicans did not look much better, despite Eisenhower's prefer- ence for the party's pro-business positions compared to "minorities work[ing] their hands into our pockets and their seats to the places of the mighty." Dewey, for whom he had voted in 1948, had been labeled a perennial loser. Taft was the odds-on favorite, with MacArthur a dark horse ready to take over if the frontrun- ner faltered. Either option appalled Eisenhower. He first came into meaningful contact with the senator from Ohio in early 1951, after Truman brought the NATO commander back to Washington to defeat the Taft-led policy of legisla- tive limitations on troop deployments to Europe. Taft would make no pledge to approve six more divisions. Eisenhower would not discard his strongest piece of leverage by pledging not to run for president, what he was prepared to offer up. Their fruitless meeting, according to the general's brother, turned this professional soldier toward a political career.[34]

"Nothing," said Eisenhower in 1948, "especially qualifies for the most important office in the world a man whose adult years have been spent in the country's military forces." Informed members of the press interpreted this profession of disqualification as a collateral shot against MacArthur, whose prospective candidacy seemed more troubling than ever in 1952. MacArthur and America's European allies had barely tolerated each other for years. Over his insistence on attacking China, they were locked in a political conflict particu- larly portentous for Eisenhower. He had spent the last decade of his life building the grand alliance, often in the face of egotistical generals wrapped up in their personal ambitions. He swallowed snide remarks in World War II from the likes of George Patton and Bernard Montgomery: "If I can keep the team together, anything's worth it." Now he thought NATO "the last remaining chance for the survival of Western civilization." Fear of its disintegration shaped his assessment of a prospective MacArthur presidency, personal aversion aside. "My God," he already had said, "anything would be better than that!"[35]

Before primaries came to dominate the nomination process, political con- ventions still mattered. To stop Eisenhower by deadlocking the convention in 1952, MacArthur and Taft joined forces, although they had been rivals for the nomination Dewey won in 1948. Then, the general dismissed the senator as "very shopworn" and "provincial." Taft certainly was not receptive to expansive global missions, long having warned about the "real danger of becoming an imperialistic nation." He still confided in mid-1951, "We cannot possibly win the next election unless we point out the utter failure and incapacity of the present Administration to conduct foreign policy and cite the loss of China and the Korean War as typical examples." As for MacArthur, who personified these issues, Taft simply declared that a Taft administration "would make maximum use of his unique abilities and knowledge."[36]

An evasion this blatant could not escape the likes of George Reedy, preparing questions for Senate Democrats during the hearings on MacArthur's dismissal. He advised them to focus their attack on the general's supporters, "vulnerable because they have taken contradictory positions," in favor of him and in favor of Taft. Ask "how many *additional men* would be needed to garrison America's fronts under MacArthur's policy and how many *additional men* would be needed to fight his war in Asia." Taft himself, prone to rely on seapower and airpower, was assailing "the fallacies of our land generals," said to hold that wars must be won with bayonets. This was a stab at Eisenhower as well as George Marshall, an old infantryman of the opinion that "war may, and probably will, start in the air, or maybe on the sea, but it's going very soon to be [conducted] in the mud." It was also a crack at Omar Bradley and the Joint Chiefs of Staff, "absolutely under the control of the administration." True or not, this accusation was another way to reach out to MacArthur, a war hero now ready to accuse the Pentagon of becoming a "praetorian guard owing sole allegiance to the political master of the hour." Taft certainly knew MacArthur "has a fine sense of the dramatic," of no small importance to someone quite aware that "I don't know how to do any of the eloquence business which makes for applause." To Stewart Alsop, "it was perfectly obvious that Senator Robert A. Taft has bet his political shirt on General Douglas MacArthur."[37]

Republicans of the Dewey-Vandenberg variety tended to gloat at what they considered a shotgun marriage between an adventurous unilateralist and the leading isolationist. "Taft is very badly discredited by the MacArthur show," one Dewey-backer wrote his leader. He "has forfeited his reputation for intellectual honesty." This conclusion was not completely fair to someone who genuinely shared the general's staunch commitment to Formosa, of less consequence than the Atlantic to members of the Northeast governing elite. Henry Stimson, a charter member, had sparred with MacArthur over global priorities during World War II, no way to allay Taft-wing opinion that Stimson was a "renegade" Republican for serving in a Roosevelt administration. In turn, GOP internationalists blocked Taft's bid for the presidential nomination in 1940, '44, and '48. In late 1951, as a faction in search of a candidate, they were rallying to recruit Dwight Eisenhower.[38]

The publisher of the *New York Times* warned Eisenhower that if he did not declare his candidacy relatively soon the nomination would fall to Taft. He got no definitive reply because Eisenhower still wanted to win by acclamation, that is, get the political prize without becoming "just another political seeker." Dewey pressed another button in April 1952 by adding the MacArthur factor.

He suggested that the former CINCFE could sweep the Republican convention in a wave of emotional fervor, not unprecedented in the party's recent history with political outsiders and international crisis. In 1940, a Wendell "Willkie blitzkrieg" swept a deadlocked field of officeholders, including Robert Taft, shortly after the Nazis marched into Paris. MacArthur supporters subsequently talked of "pulling a Willkie" of their own. Taft, bland even when brilliant, could not compete in this venue tailor-made for MacArthur unless Eisenhower grabbed the call for a photogenic general. That role first had crossed his mind in 1948, according to close associates, who thought him willing to accept a bid if MacArthur seemed the answer to a Dewey-Taft deadlock. One can rarely prove simple causation of a historical event, but a time sequence seems pretty clear. Shortly after Dewey's message to NATO headquarters, Eisenhower put in for retirement.[39]

Committed members of the Taft wing, as proud partisans in foreign policy, thought Eisenhower an unprincipled collaborator with Truman's "Military–Internationalist–New Deal group." The general was equally negative about the convergence of MacArthur and the senator with whom Eisenhower locked horns in the fight for troop enhancement to Europe. "Now, as always," he said of MacArthur, he "was an opportunist seeking to ride the crest of the wave." This was a bit one-sided, but not incorrect. His old boss was certainly one to take advantage of new circumstances. However, MacArthur's thinking also had ideological factors entangled with deep personal suspicions. He would speak about the "threat of turning us into a military state," out to suppress critics with "the moral courage to question its omniscience." In Britain, such remarks were the staple of the far left. In America, they stood with Taft's right-wing ideas against a prospective Eisenhower presidency. According to one columnist in mid-1951, the "inner circle of the MacArthurites" indicated that their leader would warn the GOP that no "military man should aspire to a political office; that the civilian must be paramount in the field of politics." In March 1952, the former CINCFE declared, "It would be a tragic development indeed if this generation was forced to look to the rigidity of military dominance and disciple to redeem it from the tragic failure of a civilian administration."[40]

Taft also criticized military men going into government, although not taking it too seriously behind closed doors. ("Oh, I suppose that's as good a reason as any" to oppose Marshall.) It certainly did not prevent the Taft wing from going into the convention with talk of running MacArthur as vice president. He then might be "deputy commander in chief" with responsibility for "the formulation of all foreign policy bearing upon national security," something "worthy of the general's stature" according to the general's own aides. That prospect resembled their forlorn attempt to land the nomination in 1944 on grounds that "the shortest way to victory would be to place an experienced military man in the White House." This did not take the nomination from Tom Dewey in the midst of World War II. It was not more likely to stop Eisenhower during a so-called police action, although the gambit mirrored the GOP position in the Russell hearings that MacArthur was "in complete accord with the traditional American way of fighting a war."[41]

Eisenhower, unlike his rivals, offered no "clean-cut answer to bringing the Korean War to a successful conclusion." That June, he rejected the escalation option of attacking China on grounds similar to Truman's. It would "start another war far more difficult to stop then the one we are in now." It would also tie us to a spot of secondary importance, Japan being "the real outpost of our civilization" in the Far East. Such sobriety about defeating the enemy may have been disconcerting to those searching for military victory. Politicians still saw redeeming value in Eisenhower's candidacy, even when they "personally" preferred Taft. The general beat any prospective Democratic nominee by double-digit margins in opinion polls taken on the eve of the national convention. Taft barely edged Truman, the weakest standard-bearer the opposition had. His last hope to stop the odds-on favorite was to use MacArthur to rout the convention with the magnetism Taft admittedly lacked.[42]

The senator, in control of party machinery, recruited the former Far East commander to deliver the keynote address. The Eisenhower campaign protested, thinking a groundswell for MacArthur was the primary threat. His speech would certainly violate army regulations since he had not applied for retirement. Truman, when asked about this breach of military code, said, "I have no comment. The Army is handling that." When entreated, "But, sir, you are Commander in Chief, are you not," he replied, "Yes, I am Commander in Chief, but I am not exercising that authority in this case." The president might have said the same thing after Wake Island, when MacArthur was advancing toward the Yalu River. Once again Truman was trying to avoid a confrontation with the general, partly out of political calculation. This entailed aid and comfort to Taft, whom he called "my favorite candidate" for the Republican nomination, probably for the reason, commonly stated, that "Taft can't win."[43]

Truman, according to a White House correspondent, felt the GOP "would rue the day it hitched its chariot to [MacArthur's] white charger," No such thing happened in mid-1952 when the general addressed the Republican National Convention, although greeted with thunderous applause. In the past, his hands trembled at times of transition, nor was he really comfortable before strange crowds. Now MacArthur moved up and down on his toes, gesticulated with his right hand, and recited without vigor shopworn words heard with better delivery last year. People dozed off or left the hall while he launched his final salvos: the party must choose a candidate "true to its great traditions"; it must stand against those "permitting Soviet forces to plant the red flag of Communism on the ramparts of Berlin, Vienna, and Prague." In so many words, to hell with the crossover vote locked up by his rival, culpable of compliance with Stalin in World War II. Delegates, although not hard of hearing, gathered back to give 845 votes to Eisenhower. Taft received 280, a California favorite son got 77, and

MacArthur 4—one of them from Joe Martin, to whom he wrote his fateful letter about "no substitute for victory" in March 1951.[44]

Diehard adherents of Taft and MacArthur refused to switch their vote and make Eisenhower's nomination unanimous, the typical gesture on behalf of party unity. This did not auger well for the GOP. Rarely has a convention so bitterly contested been followed with electoral victory. Furthermore, Eisenhower had never run for public office. He was therefore bound to make even more gaffes than normally sprinkle a political campaign. However, Eisenhower did have one overwhelming advantage, aside from the goodwill a national hero gets. The election would be a referendum on Harry Truman, reason why the Democratic candidate would soon conclude, "The President wants to win this campaign more than I do."[45]

Success by a handpicked successor would enable Truman to punish detractors thought to have spread disunity, weakened his presidency, and therefore encouraged China to enter the war. He toyed with the idea of running Omar Bradley, who had joined his military pantheon alongside Hannibal, Lee, and Marshall. ("Bradley's march to Berlin is one of the greatest maneuvers of the world.") Truman, however, admitted somewhat contritely that he failed to groom him politically. Bradley, for his part, professed to recoil from the spectacle of an "Ike versus Brad" contest, something that might have breached the final barrier between domestic politics and the profession of arms. One still suspects some temptation to best his former boss, like Eisenhower beating MacArthur for the Republican nomination. Old scores were still around from the Battle of the Bulge, when Eisenhower handed Bernard Montgomery control of U.S. First Army, the largest single component in Bradley's XII Army Group. "I trust you do not think I am angry," Bradley had informed allied headquarters. "I am goddamn well incensed"—not the sort of thing one would have read in Ernie Pyle.[46]

Other men were eager to run for the White House, two of whom Truman would have loved to support were it not for glaring weak points he saw on their resume. Averell Harriman, his close advisor, was "the ablest of them all" but also a "Wall Street banker and a railroad tycoon," just the type Truman made a career denouncing on the campaign trail. Richard Russell, then basking in acclaim for his stewardship of the Senate hearing on MacArthur, was making a concerted effort to secure the nomination as restoration of the South. He "has all the qualifications as to ability and brains," Truman lamented; "too bad he has to be born in Georgia." Estes Kefauver, from border-state Tennessee, was also riding national exposure in a congressional hearing, in his case quite successfully. Russell carried more weight within the Senate but not among voters in Democratic preference polls, where Kefauver beat him 41 to 8 percent. The latter went on to sweep the primaries on a pledge to break up "the unholy alliance between the criminal elements and some men in politics," the subject of his televised investigation of the Mafia.[47]

Adlai Stevenson, the governor of Illinois, did not thirst for the nomination, since he felt Eisenhower was a "cinch" to win. Truman entreated him to run and threw all the White House influence his way lest the convention turn to "Senator Cowfever," as he called his gadfly within Democratic party ranks. The president did not know much about Stevenson other than a reputation for clean government and strong support for the United Nations, where he had served in the delegation founding the institution in 1945. Stevenson might appeal to moderates of both parties, not excluding Eisenhower, who later told his son, "I would have stayed in uniform if I had known the Democrats were going to nominate Stevenson." At the convention in late July 1952, Truman pledged to the party faithful, "I am going to take my coat off and do everything I can to help [our candidate] win"—everything, that is, except stay home.[48]

Truman had been loath to go out and campaign in 1950, feeling a president should avoid politics when the country was at war. He never totally upheld that standard, but broke it completely in 1952 when going out on another whistle-stop tour reminiscent of 1948. Reporters noted how "fit and pleased he was with the rigorous job of 'giving em hell.'" This was a catharsis from his daily grind of "soothing sensitivities" in Washington. It also was an opportunity to simplify feelings about the officer corps he could deify or damn. "Military training and military life does not qualify a man to be President," Truman now declared. Generals are likely to be "used as a tool," in this case by "the reactionary old guard." Eisenhower might have shaken his head, having seen Truman in circumstances where he noted the president's "adulation for people in high military positions." He saw "greatness in me clear beyond any reasonable limitations," well at least as long as Eisenhower was a potential Democratic candidate. When that hope proved futile, Truman unleashed the negative side of his feelings about the high command. Eisenhower emerged as someone who "could ruin our prosperity, wreck our whole policy, and endanger the peace of the world." Such charges that the GOP was running "a stooge of Wall Street" had hurt Dewey in the last election, when the country was at peace. They would now have to work against a five-star replacement running when a war was raging in Korea. Dewey, in late October 1952, asked the public to ponder, "Who is Stalin most afraid of, Adlai Stevenson or Dwight Eisenhower?"[49]

Stevenson was "frantic to distance himself" from the administration, according to a close advisor. He still took no step back from the war in Korea, to him "a major turning point in history." The candidate said that "America has been called to greatness," like England against Nazi Germany. He entreated the public to accept "a costly struggle likely to take a long time." Unfortunately, this clarion call to duty fell flat from a former civilian assistant to the undersecretary of the navy running against the former Supreme Commander Allied Forces Europe, World War II. His opponent, as a leading figure in the crusade against Hitler, was not inclined to speak of the momentous importance of armed conflict on a neck of land in the Far East. "If there must be a war there," Eisenhower said repeatedly, "let it be Asians against Asians"; "our boys do not belong on the front lines." Stevenson called this proposition "scuttle and run," a phrase the State Department also used in 1947 when objecting to army proposals for pulling out of the peninsula. "It is not a war that just concerns Koreans," Stevenson maintained with no hesitation. "It is our war too."[50]

The Democratic position may have validity at an academic seminar on geopolitical strategy. The general public thought the war was a mistake by nearly two to one; over 75 percent approved the "Koreanization" Eisenhower proposed. Domestic matters fell in favor of the Democrats by 10 points, 43 to 33, but offended some voters such as the lady telling one reporter, "the Democrats seemed to be saying prosperity is more important than the life of my boy." The war was the most important issue to 52 percent of those polled; seven out of eight eligible voters said Eisenhower "could handle Korea best." This was a strong indictment of the competition since half the public doubted this general could actually end this war. That notion was not at odds with Eisenhower's own opinion. The candidate privately confided to an old friend that a "decent armistice" was about the best he could get, providing he could provide it at all.[51]

Barely 3 percent of the public thought the Democratic Party able to handle the Korean War, but the Republicans still began to lose their big lead in October, thanks to residual memories of its last occupant in the White House. Herbert Hoover, symbol of the Great Depression and mentor to MacArthur, preferred the Far East general or the senator from Ohio. This did not free the Eisenhower campaign from fear the Democrats would pull off another miracle finish as in 1948. It consequently changed its cautious strategy, appropriate for a frontrunner, to come up with a headline-grabbing speech exploiting Eisenhower's personal strength: "[I shall] forgo the diversions of politics and concentrate on the job of ending the Korean War. . . . That job requires a personal trip. . . . I shall go to Korea." Omar Bradley thought this "pure show biz." A plurality still thought the trip would help end the war: 48 to 38 percent. The statement said nothing about policy but nailed down Eisenhower's election—at a substantial risk to his presidency. His pledge meant the war would no longer be Truman's war, Acheson's war, or the war of Douglas MacArthur. Eisenhower beat Stevenson by 6,500,000 votes in November. In January, Korea—"the first, the urgent and the unshakable purpose of [my] new administration"—was wrapped around Eisenhower's neck by his appeal to the populace.[52]

The election ruffled more than a few political feathers among winners and losers alike, for example MacArthur, who disparaged Eisenhower as "a mere clerk, nothing more." Publicly, he had said Eisenhower's outstanding quality was his pleasant personality and ability to get along with people, the same reeking condescension that incited Eisenhower's anger toward critics of his generalship. He could have used MacArthur to build bridges with orthodox Republicans, the reason the candidate held some well-publicized meetings with

Taft. However, he never sought the advice of MacArthur, invoked his name, or had him speak on his behalf. Truman did this for Stevenson, whether Stevenson liked it or not. Then the sitting president said of Eisenhower, "This fellow don't know any more about politics than a pig knows about Sunday." That was of little damage when politicians were held in ill repute; neither was it just election year stuff as Truman later maintained. Such remarks expressed a lot of personal resentment that Eisenhower had gone over to the opposition. As late as 1959, Truman denied to the man he once admired the accolades he bestowed on Hannibal, Lee, Marshall, and Bradley: Eisenhower was a great military leader provided "he had someone to tell him what to do."[53]

The new president, whether used to election-year theatrics or not, held that Truman's "barnstorming . . . shocked my sense of [what was] fitting and appropriate" for any occupant of the White House. One thing was certain, aside from the fact that in the final round between Truman and MacArthur, America chose Eisenhower. When the people's choice became commander in chief responsible for ending the Korean War, he felt no responsibility to seek the counsel of the former president or the former CINCFE. Eisenhower wanted to build bipartisan support for his foreign policy, as every president does. He still maintained with "a cold, hard look" that he would not appear on the same platform with Truman "no matter what was at stake."[54]

In retrospect, there was nothing strange about the country electing a soldier or about it being Eisenhower, not MacArthur. Truman preached that while "our generals" are "great men in their line [of work]," they are not fit or prepared "for the responsibilities of civil government." As a student of U.S. history, he might have known about public frustration with politicians in times of crisis and disunity. Then, when America is sick of officeholders, it tends to elect military men to the White House, especially if part of a particular breed. Zachary Taylor, Ulysses Grant, and Eisenhower were known for informality in dress and manner along the lines of citizen-soldiers. They stood in stark contrast to generals not selected: Winfield Scott ("Old Fuss and Feathers"), George McClellan ("the Young Napoleon"), or Douglas MacArthur, apparently too daunting to carry a national nickname.[55]

Truman observed that "the hero of the Mexican War was Zachary Taylor because he was an ordinary, everyday fellow like everybody else." This same was also said of Eisenhower, especially in comparison with MacArthur. The latter "was not a common man, nor ever intended to be. And he sure wasn't going to represent himself that way," said one acquaintance of both men. "Ike on the other hand did it the other way and pretended to be a lot of things he was not." In short, MacArthur may have been the great actor many people thought him to be but could not play the role of a plain, likable guy: no one but Averell Harriman readily called him "Doug." By contrast, GIs felt no qualms waving "Hi, Ike" to a grinning five-star general waving back while passing through in his chauffeured jeep. The poor kid from Kansas had joined the elite but could seem to be the fellow down the block: "I got where I did by knowing how to hide my ego and hide my intelligence," Eisenhower said.[56]

Personality was important to provide a sense of comfort in trying times. Policy—or its absence—was another factor when generals ran for the presidency. Scott and McClellan had clearly defined positions on the divisive issues of their day: the powers of the federal government or the Emancipation Proclamation. Taylor and Grant, less distinct than the losers, promised to "cement the bonds of our Union" or ran on a platform promising to "bring order and peace out of the present confusion." MacArthur would have escalated the scope and intensity of the Korean War despite the trepidation pervading the nuclear age. Compare "There is no substitute for victory" to Eisenhower's slogan about putting "America [on the] straight road down the middle." The latter made political sense for someone whose personal appeal transcended partisan and ideological divisions: Democrats as well as Republicans, moderates and conservatives. Few people knew for what Eisenhower stood in 1952, other than "it looks like he's pretty much for mother, home, and heaven," as a disgruntled Taft loyalist said. Fifty years later, just as few know what he would have done to end the war, save for the fortuitous death of the Soviet head of state.[57]

Eisenhower in the White House; an Armistice in Korea

If a national decision were made to expand the effort in Korea, it would be necessary to conduct military operations outside Korea to achieve success.

GENERAL OMAR BRADLEY, 20 MAY 1953[58]

When Dwight Eisenhower was army chief of staff, he concluded that the Pentagon had to remove its contingent from Korea. In mid-1950, when Truman took a stand on terrain Eisenhower called "an awkward place to fight," the general recorded in his diary, "I have no business talking about the basic political decision." He was less reticent about the limited scope of the military commitment, scarcely different from Douglas MacArthur, for whom he wrote speeches in the 1930s. "An appeal to force cannot, by its nature, be a partial one," he harangued Joe Collins and Matt Ridgway on June 30th. "Do everything necessarily to finish the Korean incident." If we do not "take a firm stand" now, "we'll have a dozen Koreas soon."[59]

In 1953, after Eisenhower became president of the United States, political decisions became his primary line of work, particularly about what he had called "the Korean mess." After sustaining 155,000 casualties, America could not simply withdraw from the peninsula, as it began to do in 1949. In theory, one could commit overwhelming military force as Eisenhower suggested back in 1950. This might be popular with the MacArthur-Taft wing of his party, which had attacked Truman for being "afraid to win." It would be very unpopular with Eisenhower's foreign constituents in NATO, who already feared that an "anti-Communist hysteria" had taken over Washington. Republican senators such as those on the Russell Committee had been blaming stalemate, MacArthur's relief, and failure in foreign policy on the Truman-Acheson tendency "to conciliate certain of our associates rather than to advance the security of the United States." Concessions to that position on Asia might push European allies toward neutrality in what they considered a right-wing crusade.[60]

MacArthur, still hoping to affect policy, tried to assure Eisenhower that his presidency held "the power to make the greatest impression on civilization made since the Crucifixion of Christ." Eisenhower, not inclined to such hyperbole or MacArthur's cause, navigated between polar positions: that of destroying China or giving up Korea. His most important constituency, the broad body of America, was sick of stalemate and Asia alike. Majority opinion in newspaper polls wanted "to knock the Communists out of Korea once and for all," if only to get out of Korea, also once and for all. The administration found itself "in a position of trying to reconcile the irreconcilable," to quote the undersecretary of state. The new president took something—never everything—from the left, the right, and the center. He would allow the communists to keep what territory they now occupied, by and large the prewar status quo. Symbolic issues of political victory were another story, despite Eisenhower's mixed record on POW policy before and after 1953.[61]

In 1945, Eisenhower accommodated forty Red Army officers assigned to mass repatriation of Soviet soldiers at the end of Word War II. He was not about to risk postwar cooperation with Moscow for the sake of some foreigners who might not want to go home, particularly when he calculated that Stalin's successor would be Field Marshall Georgi Zhukov, his own friend and fellow soldier. Zhukov, in fact, was falling under a communist cloud for "Bonapartism," what Europeans would say of MacArthur. His real crime was resisting party dictation in the armed forces, the sort of thing that finished off Peng Dehuai and Sun Li-jen. Zhukov fared better when recalled from exile to the Odessa military district and later brought to the Geneva summit conference of 1955 as a goodwill gesture from the politburo to the president of the United States. There, he and Eisenhower had what Zhukov called "a heart to heart talk" that gave each man a private opportunity to make a personal appeal. The Russian gave "his word as a soldier" that the Kremlin was not planning aggression; hence America need not continue German rearmament. Eisenhower put forth his own big step toward détente when asking Zhukov to "exercise his good offices" to win release of twelve U.S. pilots downed over North Korea in January 1953. This was covered in the Korean armistice agreement provided China had been, in the president's words, "a civilized nation ready to work with us in good faith."[62]

The fact that Eisenhower had not been ready to resume war in Korea to release imprisoned Americans casts doubt on any inclination to have sustained casualties so he could give Chinese prisoners the right to choose their country of repatriation. This had been Truman's quest for something to label "victory." Eisenhower certainly felt no personal obligation to the predecessor who had accused him of being "owned by the big money boys." However, the national honor had been committed along with that of Eisenhower when he ran on a platform criticizing Truman for failure to comprehend the "full import of a psychological effort put forth on a national scale." The implied promise to beat communism without waging World War III targeted swing voters of Eastern European extraction angry at Washington for purported passivity while Stalin imposed his rule on helpless satellites. Taft-wingers had been making that staple accusation against Democrats since 1946—and against Eisenhower in the fight for the Republican nomination. The candidate himself criticized "political decisions" made at Yalta, Teheran, and Potsdam, none of his responsibility as a soldier. PSYOPS was another story, by definition part of military operations. It had been an Eisenhower pet project since 1944, when he assigned Robert McClure to run the Psychological Warfare Division. That man was still on the job in 1953 when Eisenhower moved into the White House, to the joy of the PSYOPS community, which expected him to elevate the status of their art and agencies. It would ill serve the new president to begin his tenure by losing the first round in what he called "a struggle of ideas," even if Truman chose the time and place of battle through repatriation policy.[63]

In regard to conventional warfare, a more expensive form of conflict, America would simply not abide further military stalemate. The president therefore began to prepare military options against China, some old contingency plans for a different political purpose. MacArthur aspired to dismantle the regime in Beijing; Truman considered direct operations against China, but only to save UN forces from destruction when battles were going badly in December 1950. Eisenhower, different from both men, would attack the PRC to end the war on Truman's terms far short of unconditional surrender. The Department of Defense did not disagree at this stage of the war. In mid-1951, before Truman made voluntary repatriation a major political objective, the Pentagon could reasonably maintain that it could secure a suitable peace without fighting beyond the peninsula, least of all with nuclear weapons, still in short supply and dedicated to European contingencies. However, JCS chairman Omar Bradley would put down a nonpublicized proviso that "inconclusive operations in Korea over an indefinite period of time with attendant attrition of manpower and material may become unacceptable."[64]

The forebodings of late 1951 came true eighteen months later. In the interval, America had mobilized military resources, whose scarcity had been one reason the Pentagon waged only limited war. The nuclear stockpile was up from 298 to 1,161 bombs. Bradley, once a spokesman for the Truman position, now agreed with the new commander in chief that they had to take "more positive action" because "small attacks on small hills would not end the war." It seemed necessary "to use the atomic bomb" and "to expand the war outside of Korea" because there were "no good strategic targets within the confines" of the peninsula. Joe Collins, the JCS member most reluctant to have entered Korea, was the sole remaining holdout (easily outvoted) for the old thesis that US/UN forces had a distinct advantage in a war with mutual sanctuaries: China, Pusan, and Japan.[65]

The contingency plans under construction in the Pentagon provided virtually no role for Chiang Kai-shek's forces on Formosa, simply "eyewash" according to Bradley. Eisenhower still hoped the KMT could apply some pressure on Beijing to accept his stipulations: *uti possidetis* and voluntary repatriation. In his first State of the Union Address, February 1953, the new president announced the discontinuation of the Seventh Fleet as a peacekeeping force in the Taiwan Strait: it had become "a defensive arm of Communist China," which could then "with greater impunity kill our soldiers and those of our United Nations allies in Korea." This tilt toward MacArthur was primarily verbal, since the Truman administration never disclaimed "neutralization," even when abetting raids and sabotage out of bases in Formosa. NATO governments professed "shock" at the new pronouncement. They "were entirely unprepared for it," said *Newsweek*'s London bureau chief.[66]

Eisenhower sent his secretary of state, John Foster Dulles, on a fence-mending mission that secretly assured his European allies that the United States had no plans to "unleash" Chiang. Much like Acheson, Dulles thought him "bitter, arrogant, and difficult. . . . He has a vested interest in World War III." Talk about utilizing his military capabilities was psychological operations and rhetorical bones thrown to the right wing. Real war plans compatible with those of Mac-Arthur did not appeal to Eisenhower unless circumstances pushed him toward escalation when caught in a dreadful bind. The president's true preference emerged in reaction to Major General William Chase, a self-identified "Mac-Arthur man" who had led the First Cavalry Division into Manila back in 1945. Six years later, shortly before dismissal, the CINCFE selected Chase to head the military mission to Taipei. MacArthur's protégé was frank, informative, and utterly inappropriate when *Newsweek* interviewed him two days after Eisenhower's State of the Union address. Chase said that the KMT was improving daily but not ready to "play in the big leagues," that is, on mainland territory. A remedy was still available: "it all depends on how quickly the new Administration sends more hardware and how many more military advisers."[67]

Eisenhower wanted statements loud enough to get Mao's attention but soft enough not to sever the NATO alliance. Neither should they lead Stalin to think that "we had immediate and warlike intentions," to quote the director of the NSC. Chase, on the other hand, was too clear for compatibility with the contradictions enwrapping U.S. policy, reason for the president to steam about comments from those in uniform. "I don't like it a damn bit. If it doesn't stop I know what to do about it." That very day, February 5th, Chase got a real gag order. "No, repeat no, further interviews be given," Bradley wired Taipei, a far cry from the ambiguous message Truman sent MacArthur in December 1950.[68]

Back then, MacArthur's strategy against China had three elements: invasion, blockade, and bombing. Invasion, the major component of his plan, was essential if the policy was to replace the regime, not merely end the war. Because Eisenhower had no faith in a landing, particularly by Chiang's KMT, he would have to put more weight into bombing, even with atomic weapons, not part of MacArthur's plan while in command despite what Truman later claimed. In a December 1960 television interview, the former president accused the general of advocating extensive use of nuclear arms. MacArthur promptly replied this was "fantastic. . . . We did not need the atom bomb any more than we did in the war against Japan," provided Washington was ready to win. He forced a backhanded concession from Truman: "I have no documentary proof," he said before pointing out what MacArthur overlooked, that the atomic bomb ended World War II. Truman rarely brought up this unpleasant subject, except when necessity prevailed, whether warning communist governments at a press conference in December 1950 or putting down MacArthur ten years later.[69]

Washington had contacted MacArthur (not vice versa) on 21 December 1950 when the Defense Department requested a list of "atomic targets which should be destroyed to retard Soviet advances in the event of general war." What actually happened regarding such weapons in 1953 lacks equivalent clarity. Anyone studying the end of the Korean War should be skeptical of assertions conveniently suited to support someone's postwar agenda, whether Chairman Mao or President Eisenhower. The latter, when back from his trip to Korea, declared, "We face an enemy whom we cannot hope to impress by words, however eloquent, but only by deeds—executed under circumstances of our own choosing." These words notwithstanding, Eisenhower could not go straight to deeds, at least when it came to atomic bombs. He had to give some sort of warning about using something that once struck him as "horrible and destructive," lest he affront his own sensibilities as well as the conscience of the world.[70]

The administration later claimed that it "discreetly" dropped "the word" through a third party about using the atomic bomb. The actual threat was even more ambiguous. "The United States would probably make a stronger rather than a lesser military exertion," Dulles told India's prime minister on 21 May 1953. Discretion got the better of blunt speaking, as it often does in nuclear policy. Mark Clark, who had replaced Matt Ridgway as CINCFE, thought Washington was talking about hitting sanctuaries with conventional explosives, although he might have hoped for clarity from his old army buddy now in residence at the White House. Eisenhower knew from firsthand experience in and after World War II how badly generals want unambiguous statements about policy. He still proved no more willing than Truman to be pinned down as to when, where, and why he would use atomic weapons, although he himself complained in 1948, "I can't understand what the war plan is."[71]

Europe was a factor in what the United States might really do to stop the Korean War, begun in mid-1950 partly to solidify Washington's credibility in NATO. Since then, Britain, its Commonwealth, and France had a contributory role in MacArthur's dismissal, as George Marshall admitted in mid-1951, "He set up a very serious reaction among our allies, which threatened our collective action . . . and our position in the world." Eisenhower, that October, said much the same thing about Korea itself, a commitment that prohibited "building up defensive strength elsewhere," meaning his NATO command. Its members, while also aggravated, set limits on the way he could now end the conflict. "If we decided upon a major, new type of offensive," Eisenhower stated in his presidential memoirs, "the present policies would have to be changed and the new ones agreed to by our allies. . . . An American decision to use [the atomic bomb] would have created strong disrupting feelings."[72]

Eisenhower obviously was well aware of fissure issues in alliance politics. German rearmament and more defense spending already sparked dissension in Western Europe. War against China and POW policy had the potential to crack the Atlantic pact. On May 28th 1953, when the press asked the president about NATO support for American terms, he made misleading statements that "on the basic factor that there shall be no forced repatriation of prisoners, I have seen no wavering anywhere." Two days later, when getting down to business about what to do in the Korean War, his sensitivity to allied sensibilities was quite evident. A high-level White House meeting discussed atomic artillery, not an atomic bombing of the Chinese mainland. "The President," according to official notes, "emphasized that the weapons would be used tactically and that he saw no reason why our allies should disagree on the employment against enemy troops."[73]

The Western alliance that held together by hook, crook, and compromise staid Eisenhower's hand. NATO nations, although junior partners and not heavily committed in Korea, helped induce the United States not to take the war to China. An opposite influence occurred in the Sino-Soviet Pact, where the major power suffered the least casualties but still spurred its ally to fight. Stalin did begin to provide the trucks, artillery, and ordnance China desperately needed when he fed it false intelligence about American weakness in late 1950. "The Korean War should not be ended in a hurry," he would explain, "because a prolonged war will allow Chinese troops to learn about modern warfare." This particular education cost his ally some $2.7 billion dollars, approximately one-third for purchasing Soviet equipment, some of which was lend-lease stock left over from World War II. This meant secondhand American goods for American cash accumulated in the Chinese banking system thanks to years of assistance to Chiang Kai-shek. Other currency was not appreciated, Stalin explained to Chou En-lai in 1952. "British pound sterling have limited circulation."[74]

United States policy had foreseen this kind of situation in hope of splitting the Sino-Soviet camp. The Kremlin failed to fulfill Chinese pleas for proletariat generosity, redolent of the Spanish Civil War in the late 1930s. Then, to obtain equipment and advisors, the Republic had to liquidate all 510 tons of gold it shipped to Moscow for safekeeping. Beijing, not under direct siege, was not this desperate in 1952. Stalin must have sensed that resistance to him could be brewing, especially after Chou hinted to India that he might accept a settlement short of total repatriation. The Soviets called this "ludicrous" on the floor of the United Nations. Its foreign ministry tried to transfer peace talks to the Security Council, where the USSR could exercise its veto. One way or the other, it held its side together, as demonstrated on 7 February 1953. Mao reiterated his vow to carry on the fight as long as "U.S. imperialism persists in holding Chinese and Korean prisoners of war."[75]

Stalin had not been one to risk in Asia war against America, as Chinese communists periodically complained since 1945. He had long told Kremlin comrades that Truman was a warmonger out to drop atomic bombs. If Washington, out of frustration, now turned to escalation, Stalin would face a distressing dilemma: being humiliated for deserting Beijing or becoming ground zero for the Strategic Air Command. The conflict in Korea was apparently worth the danger because it helped him finish some important business inside his regime. *Pravda*, on 13 January 1953, revealed the so-called Doctor's Plot involving Jewish physicians hoping to "become rich, bourgeois, and so on." They purportedly were scheming with traitors in government circles and the "well-known agency of the American intelligence" to kill off the "leaders of the cadres of the USSR." Secret trials in Moscow and Leningrad already had condemned to death thirteen of these "terrorists" and six communist party turncoats, just the tip of the iceberg. Voroshilov, Molotov, Mikoyan, and other long-serving members of the inner circle were denounced for cowardice and capitulation in the "difficult struggle with the capitalist camp [that] lay ahead."[76]

Even a totalitarian state has difficulty calling its population to "conduct an uncompromising, relentless struggle with complacency." The war in Korea could enhance the credibility of charges likely to be filed against anyone in any position to replace Stalin. The supreme leader, having recently revitalized his propaganda agencies, was now about "to educate" the peoples of the Soviet Union to America's fiendish plan to restore Chiang Kai-shek, sweep its own troops across the Sino-Soviet border, and destroy the Kremlin with nuclear weapons sneaked into the U.S. embassy. Production and dissemination of this scenario assumed more of Stalin's attention than any battle on the Korean peninsula. He could take ten days to reply to Mao about heavy weaponry but send questions for his secret police to grill suspects on his watch list. The confessions he subsequently reviewed set the stage for party articles and convention speeches he edited despite declining health. They were to have culminated in a repetition of the Great Terror of the 1930s, save a few name substitutes. The

United States replaced Nazi Germany; Zionists supplanted Trotskyites. Korea provided the background once supplied by the Spanish Civil War, a prior subject of intense pageantry regarding foreign fascists and internal saboteurs.[77]

Stalin's death on March 5th saved untold numbers of Soviet Jews and quite a few government officials. It also widened the fault lines inside the communist bloc. Dean Acheson foresaw this development back in January 1950, but events belied his prediction that Russia would be the recalcitrant party. The Kremlin became preoccupied with succession and stability, no matter what Truman and Eisenhower once believed about the politburo pushing Stalin into the Cold War. The members of that body hoped to ensure personal and institutional survival by making less demands on a body politic trained to genuflect to Stalin's cult of infallibility. This meant production of consumer goods from textiles to foodstuffs for a population living barely above subsistence nutrition, while the military sectors of the economy grew 50 percent per annum through the Korean War. Talk consequently had to turn toward resolving international conflicts with "peaceful means."[78]

Nikita Khrushchev recalled that "we believed that America would invade the Soviet Union." One wonders if China also expected what Eisenhower later claimed: the "full-scale war or an atomic attack" that he purportedly threatened. Beijing, upon Stalin's death, found Moscow rejecting its latest requests for the heavy weapons essential to its military effort and Mao's ambition to become a world power. On 19 March, shortly after the Kremlin decided upon "concluding the war in Korea as soon as possible," it sent messages to Mao and Kim Il-sung that "the time has come to solve the entire issue." Within two weeks, Chou En-lai issued a proposal for repatriation that brought the warring parties back to Panmunjom a month before John Foster Dulles dropped his vague statement about taking a "stronger" military action that "might well extend the area of conflict." Thirty-seven percent of China's imprisoned soldiers subsequently ended up in Taiwan, where most of these 14,000 men reentered the Nationalist armed forces from whence they came in 1949. America thereby got the substance of voluntary repatriation—that is the "decision," to quote Acheson, now retired from government because "the country got tired of us." That was akin to the end of a love affair, as he told James Reston. "I sit here [in my law office] getting more money for more people who don't need it or deserve it. After State, I hate it."[79]

Beijing got the "words" or style, insofar as Washington did not demand that "voluntary" appear in the armistice document specifying that "each side shall release all those remaining prisoners of war, who are not directly repatriated, from its military control and from its custody and hand them over to the Neutral Repatriation Commission for disposition." Those wanting asylum would revert to civilian status and be released to go where they wished. The Eisenhower administration, wary of something like MacArthur's ultimatum in March 1951, did not insist on inflicting more humiliation than China was willing to accept.

Truman, remaining bitter, would say that his successor "surrender[ed] to the Kremlin in 1953," not unlike MacArthur when implying that Eisenhower and Truman gave Stalin central Europe in 1945. China was even less impartial about the final settlement. It would congratulate itself upon a "glorious victory" over an "enemy with superior technology." Repatriation suddenly became one of several "minor issues," this one all about "kidnapping" and "secret agents" of Chiang Kai-shek.[80]

China's last combat operation in the war, like its propaganda turnabout, was an attempt to save face. On July 13th, it launched its largest offensive since spring 1951 and drove "the enemy to come to terms," if one accepts the claims: "VICTORY AT THE NEGOTIATIONS: Punishment for Syngman Rhee." The ten thousand casualties he suffered were supposed to be retribution for releasing POWs into the population instead of transferring custody to UN personnel. Rhee actually let loose only Koreans; Chinese remained in their compounds as the armistice specified. More to the point, whatever Rhee wished, he would have to comply with Washington. The PRC attack on the "puppet troops" of South Korea, rather than the U.S. army, resembled America bombing Pyong-yang, not what really mattered: Moscow and Beijing. Mao's offensive camou-flaged political retreat under claims that if the imperialists "had not accepted the truce, their whole battle line would have been broken through and Seoul would have fallen." The premier of the People's Republic, like the president of the United States, would cite the end of the war in Korea as proof for his post-war agenda. Eisenhower claimed concessions won from the communist side proved the efficacy of nuclear weaponry vis-à-vis ground forces, too expensive for his fiscal policy. Mao used his own claim of victory to secure China's global significance as the true model for "oppressed nations" of the colonized world, an assertion that challenged the Soviet Union as well as the United States.[81]

Beijing and Washington both claimed to have forced the other to sign the armistice that occurred eleven days after the Chinese offensive. Neither party actually accomplished the clear-cut victory MacArthur and Mao craved. America had been thrown back to its starting line by China, recently considered a ramshackle state. China declared success for the "CCP's leadership and the heroic Chinese people" but could not recover all its imprisoned soldiers, a right every sovereign nation heretofore exercised. Nor did it recoup its last rebellious province, let alone emerge the reigning power in the Far East. Mao died in 1976, deeply disappointed that he never "liberated" Taiwan. Harry Truman, dying in 1972, had come to refer to Formosa as "the free Chinese." Notwith-standing his opinion of Chiang Kai-shek and the KMT as a den of thieves, Truman long had ceased to see any difference between Stalin and Mao, head of a "cutthroat organization [that] will never be recognized by us."[82]

Voluntary repatriation, Truman's triumph, was also subject to a harsh evalu-ation, judging by what Washington did after the Korean War. The policy had cost 125,000 dead and wounded—what UN forces suffered during stalemated peace talks. The United States gave no such choice to enemy subsequently captured in Vietnam, Iraq, Grenada, or anywhere else. They were all sent home like Russians in 1945. Nor did symbolic success in 1953 comfort Mark Clark, the conflict's last CINCFE. "I gained," he soon wrote, "the unenviable distinction of being the first United States Army commander in history to sign an armistice without victory."[83]

Eisenhower and Ridgway; Korea to Vietnam

The United States by example, persuasion, pressure, inducements, assistance, and agreements has established itself as the leader of the Western resistance. . . . [This] may involve action by U.S. military forces in many different types of climate and terrain, such as the mountains of Greece and Korea or the jungles of Indochina.

ARMY CHIEF OF STAFF MATTHEW B. RIDGWAY
TO SECRETARY OF DEFENSE, 27 JUNE 1955[84]

There were no gracious winners or losers at the cease-fire signing in Korea on 27 July 1953, unlike ceremonies concluding some other military conflicts, for example at Appomattox. James Reston, a witness of the final meeting at Panmunjom, thought both sides appeared as if they were "signing a declaration of war instead of a truce." No subsequent treaty would be signed for Korea, or for Asia in general. Hence, as one magazine recapped in 1995, the "war that wasn't a war ended in a peace that wasn't a peace." Decisive victories tend to produce prolonged periods of stability, such as Europe after Waterloo and World War II. The loser knew it had lost, accepted the verdict of war, and did not attempt to upset the geopolitical status quo. This was not true of the Far East post-Panmunjom, as Syngman Rhee forewarned Matt Ridgway in mid-1951: "A settlement which settles nothing is really no settlement at all."[85]

In these circumstances, old contestants prepared for a new conflict in Asia founded on mutual fear that their failure to win had emboldened their opponent. A secret State Department study concluded in mid-1953 that the United States "lost prestige in Asia vis-à-vis the Chinese communists as a result of the Korean war." Mao in mid-1958 told a Communist Party conference that U.S. leaders "looked down upon us [because] we have not yet completely shown and proven our strength." Dwight Eisenhower, the man immediately on Mao's mind, had distinct opinions about how to wage the next war and where authority for its conduct must reside. Back in 1949, he had counseled Harry Truman to "put [dissenters] on sharp notice" that "every Presidential decision is a command that must compel complete and loyal support." This was his own watchword when occupant of the Oval Office from 1953 to 1961. He exercised control of the officer corps with far more alacrity than the man he once advised. Aside from the case of Major General William Chase on Formosa, discussed above, one might consider the experience of Matt Ridgway, wrestling with contemporary strategy since October 1950, when he proposed that Eisenhower, then a university president, head a blue-ribbon panel on defense policy. "It behooves nations particularly those of the Western World, to examine the means used in war—lest destruction become so great that in the application of military power they will have defeated their purpose."[86]

Ridgway and Korea to the contrary, Eisenhower still held that "there are really no limits that can be set to the use of force." He rejected theories of limited war and flexible response buzzing through his own administration. Dulles worried that if America resorted to massive retaliation with nuclear weapons, such as he once publicly proposed, "we will, in the eyes of the world, be cast as a ruthless military power, as was Germany." Not pressing the issue, he served a second term, unlike Ridgway, army chief of staff from 1953 to 1955. Communication between the new president and the new member of the Joint Chiefs soon resembled that of Robert Taft and Omar Bradley in 1951–1952, when the senator favored airpower at the expense of infantry. He never made it to the White House, but that did not spare Ridgway from a budget beating that cost the army one-third of its soldiers and 40 percent of its appropriations. George Marshall's fear of a reduction in ground forces came true in the Eisenhower administration.[87]

When Eisenhower was Taft's rival for the Republican nomination, the general blasted those "who preach that we need do nothing except maintain a destructive retaliatory force for use in the event the Russian army should march." Since then, they had become "right good friends" and political allies. The senator stood by the president against members of the Taft wing opposing confirmation of an appointee guilty of accompanying Roosevelt to Yalta. Eisenhower took up Taft's cause of tax and debt reduction, a way of responding to the senator's warning against "taking us down the road Truman traveled." In this situation, Ridgway began writing memoranda about "highly placed, very influential people in our Government playing with the idea that because of tremendous atomic and nuclear capability . . . we can scrap our conventional weapons. . . . That will lead us to disaster" because "history is too replete with the records of people who could not be conquered, except by people who moved in on the ground."[88]

Eisenhower found Ridgway's words passé. "He's talking theory. I'm talking common sense," said the new devotee of strategic airpower. The army chief of staff still held to the lessons he learned about compliance with cutbacks during Louis Johnson's reign at DOD. "I thought," Ridgway said, "of the brave men who died in those early days in Korea, when the skeleton regiments fought and fell back until they finally stood with their backs to the sea." His case, dismissed by the White House, wound up in Congress, where the opposition party egged on an officer who thought the executive branch more concerned with "political expediency" and fear of "fiscal bankruptcy" than with national defense. Ridgway did not readily take to a MacArthur-like role. "It isn't up to me or to any other officer in uniform to oppose a decision by the constituted authorities of our Government." Still, when prodded by political opponents of the president, he admitted to thinking he "was being called upon to destroy, rather than to build" army capabilities. He recommended elimination of the cuts in personnel, the sort of thing that drove Eisenhower to complain that officers "tend to kowtow to the Congress and to make speeches inconsistent with the decisions of their superiors," namely him.[89]

Political pressures pushed Ridgway into premature retirement. Eisenhower grumbled that he should be fired. The whole episode, while reminiscent of Truman and MacArthur, was of less importance to the country, not yet mired in combat. However, because the Korean armistice had not settled supremacy in Asia, the stage was set for another proxy war described by Dean Rusk when secretary of state in January 1966: "Although Hanoi is the prime actor in this situation . . . it is the policy of Peking that has greatly stimulated Hanoi." This area of operations was a topic of discussion at Wake Island in October 1950, when Rusk was the senior State Department official at the conference held a few days after 20,000 communist-led Vietnamese overran 3,000 French Legionnaires blocking supply from insurgency base areas in China. The setback puzzled both MacArthur and Truman, who soon foresaw the potential for a string of defeats. The president warned the prime minister of Britain six weeks later, "After Korea, it would be Indochina, then Hong Kong, then Malaya."[90]

MacArthur, equating personal dismissal with national defeat, in mid-1952 told a diplomat that "our failure no doubt is a prelude to the loss of all the Asiatic mainland." The next occupant of the White House, Dwight Eisenhower, had little stomach for consultation with the former CINCFE. They did have a three-hour meeting in 1954, where according to the crestfallen visitor, the president did all the talking, presumably revenge for all the "monologues" he had to endure when a member of MacArthur's military staff. Eisenhower certainly struck the vulnerable spot of a sensitive man "never consulted by my government about the Far East, an area which I know and understand better than any living American." Things changed after a new president, John F. Kennedy, gave the old general a new chance to regain his influence, which he also gave Dean Acheson, the old secretary of state. "DA looks better and younger than I have seen him in years," wrote his personal secretary in April 1961. However, he soon felt treated like "a pampered and tolerated ghost" after failing to recapture control of national security policy. Acheson might have done better if he had emulated MacArthur, who charmed JFK much the way he charmed Truman at their Wake Island meeting. Nonetheless, the general now had a much different message than he ever gave Truman concerning China. He advised Kennedy and later Lyndon Johnson to stay out of Vietnam: "There is no end to Asiatic manpower."[91]

Harry Truman had not been so chary when he dismissed MacArthur in 1951: "Our resolute stand in Korea is helping the forces of freedom now fighting in Indochina and other countries in that part of the world. It has already slowed down the timetable of conquest." In a retirement hastened by the removal of MacArthur, he would not talk about the war in Vietnam, other than to write in a posthumous publication that Eisenhower initiated the misconceived commitment. Truman had good reason to forget certain unpleasant facts about inauspicious military theaters and intangible political objectives such as national credibility. This had led him to initiate the American military mission to Vietnam in April 1950, two months before making his combat commitment to Korea. In late June, when explaining his action on the peninsula, Truman also told leading members of Congress that it was "equally necessary for us to draw the line in Indochina, the Philippines, and Formosa." Both Korea and Vietnam proved far most costly than originally conceived. However, the former did uphold containment and exacerbated fissures in the Sino-Soviet camp.[92]

The U.S. military, already strapped in Korea and Europe, opposed a force deployment for Indochina lest it become "involved in fighting on the mainland of Asia." Dean Acheson emphasized a different issue in May 1952, when he told Britain's foreign secretary that "we are lost if we lose Southeast Asia without a fight." The communists, according to intelligence agencies, already controlled three-fourths of the population of Vietnam and two-thirds of the territory. Credibility, thought Acheson, could be preserved in defeat—but not in concession. This time, however, he would not have used ground troops to make his political point as he did in June 1950. He and his State Department, as well as the Pentagon, held that if China intervened to help the local communists in Southeast Asia, Washington must be willing to blockade and bomb the PRC, even if this entailed "danger of war with the Soviet Union."[93]

Korea left an ironic legacy of contradictory lessons for the war in Vietnam. MacArthur, on the one hand, would oppose the basic commitment. The Truman administration, on the other, had tacitly conceded the general's view for an attack on the mainland. Lyndon Johnson took neither option when he had to make his own decisions in 1965. He declared, "I am not going to be the President who saw Southeast Asia go the way China went." He also adopted the old Truman-Acheson strategy, whether Acheson had second thoughts or not. The Johnson administration sought "to create conditions for a favorable outcome by demonstrating to the VC/DRV [communists] that the odds are against their winning" but to do it "without causing the war to expand into one with China or the Soviet Union." Some senior military officers were doubtful that attrition worked in Korea and felt the White House was too concerned with Beijing, not likely to enter the fight if U.S. forces extended the war. Johnson had a riveting retort, per Wake Island: "That's what MacArthur thought."[94]

Truman and MacArthur: Summary, Conclusion, and Postscript

1 2 3 4 5 6 7 8 **9**

Writers who claim to recap 267 pages of text in a 7-page conclusion are admitting to have wasted 260. The attempt must still be made to prevent details from eclipsing the most essential points. The conflict between President Harry S. Truman and General Douglas MacArthur had three major components: policies, politics, and personalities, including a hunger for honor and renown. The same thing might be said of most every dispute between public figures in U.S. history, but this only outlines the topic that needs to be fleshed out if one is to get beyond a skeleton table of events.

The conflict over policy had much to do with definitions of war and victory. Truman chained himself to the phrase "police action," adopted on 29 June 1950 to avoid all the ramifications of war. He always maintained that the purpose of intervention in Korea was to prevent or preempt a direct confrontation with the Soviet Union that would lead to World War III. Disputes with MacArthur could be contained as long as operations focused only on North Korea, assumed to be a pawn of the Kremlin but not a critical interest. This was an opportunity for the president to defeat a proxy for which Stalin presumably would not wage war. Truman could then establish his military credibility by showing his willingness to fight while not having to fight the major threat.

China's intervention in late 1950 shattered the modus vivendi between the president and the general, although they were now united on a subject heretofore dividing them. MacArthur had been a firm opponent of any movement to abandon the anticommunist side in the Chinese civil war, even after its leader, Chiang Kai-shek, fled to the island province of Formosa in 1949. The administration, on the other hand, was less antagonistic to the new regime in Beijing, expected to turn against the Soviet Union as a natural opponent of its national interests along their common border. Once China entered the war in Korea, Washington saw it as a Russian puppet in the manner of Pyongyang. The administration still had an important difference with MacArthur insofar as now believing that Moscow would not stand by and witness China under U.S. assault. MacArthur's proposal to win the war in Korea by attacking the PRC would bring about a third world war, or so the White House feared. Hence the general, chained to his own phrase that "there is no substitute for victory," would precipitate precisely what Truman went into Korea to preclude.

Truman's memoirs talked of MacArthur's "view that the Korean action had become a war with Communist China," although it acknowledged that Beijing launched an "open, powerful, offensive attack." The general emphasized that fact every time he asked, "How could Red China have been more at war against us?" He held that because he was facing "the entire Chinese nation," the PRC relinquished all claim to escape direct reprisal. This assertion, logical or not, was lost on Washington. The government feared MacArthur, at best, would win a Pyrrhic victory. Asia generally, Korea specifically, was of secondary importance to it vis-à-vis Europe, whereas the Far East theater commander long thought "the lands touching the Pacific with their billions of inhabitants will determine the course of history for the next ten thousand years."[1]

Actually, Korea held no special interest for MacArthur until Truman made the military commitment in mid-1950. China and its province of Formosa were his political and military objectives. Now, the general would have expanded the conflict on the peninsula into war on the mainland through amphibious landings launched from Formosa far behind Chinese forces concentrated to conduct their campaign in Korea. Truman had approved a similar concept of envelopment on a smaller scale behind North Korean army lines at Inchon in mid-September 1950. The general then argued that the alternative was military stalemate, not at all convincing in retrospect. Better battlefield damage assessment would have held that Inchon was not necessary since the North Koreans were already ground down from attrition around the Pusan perimeter. On the superficial observation that the enemy collapsed after the Inchon operation occurred, the landing was thought to have caused the collapse. By MacArthur's reasoning, the tried and true method of his masterpiece should be used against China irrespective of conflict with Truman's concern about precipitating World War III.

Inchon had been part of an implicit deal Truman struck with MacArthur through Averell Harriman, an old acquaintance and current White House senior advisor. Truman would approve the type of operation MacArthur had wanted to conduct since 1944, when planning the liberation of the Philippines in World War II. The general, in turn, would stop his agitation on behalf of Chiang's regime in Formosa, at least in mid-1950. The invasion plan for 1951, something of a super-Inchon, would be conducted under conditions lashing the United States to the Kuomintang. MacArthur held there was no alternative but an unending string of frontal battles against communist armies with reservoirs of manpower impossible to drain. This specter of indefinite stalemate, if not outright defeat, was the strongest military argument he could muster in support of items long on his political agenda, particularly his desire to reverse the results of the Chinese civil war. Presenting it as a way to save South Korea, MacArthur would return Chiang's army to the mainland from which it had fled after defeat eighteen months before.

MacArthur's plan, in MacArthur's mind, would have solidified his claim for military immorality worthy of a Hannibal or Robert E. Lee—Harry Truman's own heroes. Their legends heretofore made the president reluctant to impose restrictions on MacArthur, lest history condemn the president as one of those "crazy politicians" who caused a military genius to lose a war. The Joint Chiefs of Staff now gave him military reasons against MacArthur's strategy. Chiang's army could be destroyed if it ever tried to conduct an amphibious invasion, a very difficult operation far beyond its capabilities. The Chiefs felt this should not be risked for two substantial reasons. The U.S. navy had to remain on the waters around Korea as long as ground forces might need evacuation from Chinese human-wave attacks. Formosa itself might be forfeited for lack of Nationalist forces no longer dug in on their own beachheads. This would be a substantial blow to U.S. security, or so the Pentagon believed after MacArthur convinced it of the need to keep the island out of communist hands.

Notwithstanding an attempt in late 1950 to liberate North Korea, Truman's abiding objective was to contain communism as opposed to bringing down Chinese or Soviet regimes. The administration hoped to obtain this objective by inflicting punishment on the enemy soldiers without taking combat beyond the confines of the peninsula. This seemed perfectly feasible after General Matthew Ridgway threw back Chinese offensives. However, in late 1951, the president introduced a new political factor that undercut the progress his military policy was making on the battlefield. His stipulation that prisoners of war get to choose the government to which they would repatriate was certainly short of MacArthur's demand for a decisive victory that could collapse Beijing. It would still be a symbolic, psychological, and propaganda defeat for the communist side, as shown when Mao Tse-tung would not make peace under provisions allowing his soldiers to go to Chiang-ruled territory.

Mao had given up all hope of driving the United States completely out of Korea, let alone from the offshore islands of Japan and Taiwan. Worse, however, would be acceptance of voluntary repatriation: an implicit admission that Mao's hated rival, Chiang, had an ongoing claim to be head of state. This contentious issue thereby culminated the incremental reentry of the United States into the Chinese civil war, something Truman disavowed in January 1950 when declaring that the "government will not pursue a course which will lead to involvement in the conflict." By late June, he and Dean Acheson announced the so-called neutralization of the strait between Formosa and the mainland. That policy froze the geopolitical state of affairs by stopping Mao from overrunning Chiang's island redoubt. In mid-1951, through clandestine operations, the Central Intelligence Agency advised and supplied anticommunist guerrillas inside China to divert forces that could have been committed to Korea. The prisoner-of-war issue was not at all covert, becoming an official demand at the armistice conference held between belligerents.[2]

Truman had moved toward MacArthur's position about participation in the Chinese civil war but not about taking major operations directly to the mainland. The general could criticize but not change policy on his authority as theater commander. The president stomached his sniping comments for political and personal reasons. The American public does not like civilians meddling in military business. Neither did Truman, even when he did it. His period of begrudging forbearance ended in April 1951, when MacArthur linked his policies to domestic politics, particularly the president's opponents in the Robert Taft–Joe Martin wing of the Republican Party. In Truman's mind, MacArthur thereby lost his aura as a soldier by collaborating with the partisan opposition. Indeed, the president was more outraged at the general, because he was a general, than at the critics who touted MacArthur's support. "You don't have to fall out with a man," Truman felt, "because you don't agree with him on politics"—provided the man in question was a fellow politician.[3]

In America, policy is made through politics. If one cannot abide a position and cannot convince the government to change, the alternative to acquiescence is making it an issue in an election campaign. MacArthur, still unwilling to give up his military post, could not take the logical step of retirement before dipping into partisan affairs. Indeed, lest he be removed for clearly naming Truman the culprit, MacArthur usually filed his objections in passive voice: he "was handicapped" and "was forbidden." However, once MacArthur explicitly endorsed Joe Martin's speeches on Formosa and an invasion of the Chinese mainland, the president could no longer pretend that the general was not defiant. He then relieved him from command, exactly what the Taft wing wanted since MacArthur seemed more popular than Truman. A more cunning incumbent would have found a way to keep the soldier in uniform rather than do something so out of favor. Personal feelings overcame political calculations that heretofore had staid the president's hand, even when MacArthur obviously disagreed with presidential policy.

Truman and MacArthur had more in common as to personality than they did about politics and policy. Both were quite courteous in most circumstances, although MacArthur was less genuinely friendly because fundamentally suspicious and inclined to introversion. His family raised him to believe he had a public destiny, that of soldier, sage, and Caesar. To fulfill the role he could switch on considerable charm: Wake Island, October 1950, provides a case in point. The sole time MacArthur ever met Truman mutual manners and self-calculation kept differences over policy and politics in check. The general feared the president might stop his plunge deep into North Korea, a spectacular coda to his career. The president, on the eve of a congressional election, wanted a photo opportunity with the hero who pulled off Inchon. They consequently avoided a frank exchange of opinions that might have clarified concerns and thereby controlled their clash when China entered the conflict six weeks later. That event created a crisis for Truman and MacArthur—and the world at large. The president thought it could set off World War III. The general, falling from his pinnacle of glory, looked like a fumbler, if not a fool.

In this period of distress, emotions erupted that civility normally contained. Truman and MacArthur uttered bitter comments about personal enemies politically associated with the man he recently had met at Wake. The general long had felt that White House attention being poured on other theaters reflected more than an honest difference of opinion about global priorities. He said after driven from the Philippines in 1942, "There are some people in Washington who would rather see MacArthur lose a battle than America win a war." In December 1950, after driven out of North Korea, he made comparable comments about "Europhiles" who controlled the government, sowing seeds for disaster by "their blind and stupid effort to undermine public confidence in me." At much the same time, Truman said much the same thing about his own critics in Congress and the press, not coincidentally favorable to MacArthur: "They would rather see the country go down than for the Administration to succeed."[4]

History is not an experimental science. Individual elements cannot be added or subtracted to determine with precision their relative importance. The best that this particular historian can do after observing Truman and MacArthur some fifty years after the fact is to state my assessment that their conflict was not the product of policies, politics, or personalities. In the final analysis, it was a combination of all three factors, wherein the whole was greater than the sum of its parts. Personal dynamics added intensity to their disagreement, which was not susceptible to mediation by Averell Harriman or anyone else. Still, this civil-military fissure might not have become a compound fracture if both protagonists had not felt the nation would sustain them. Millions of people lined the streets to cheer the general's homecoming. The president has become an American folk-icon. Neither fact changes the outcome of the Truman-MacArthur conflict. Both were exiled from their position of power, a cold war case of mutually assured public destruction. The electorate turned to Dwight Eisenhower, about whom Truman and MacArthur held a common point of view on personal, political, and policy grounds. They each thought him an old adherent who had become a traitor in patent pursuit of private ambition.

The story of generals, presidents, policies, and politics did not end in 1952. Traces of MacArthur will probably pop up as long as field commanders are at odds with Washington. Take the recent case of Wesley K. Clark, Supreme

Commander NATO during the conflict with Serbia. In 1963, he witnessed MacArthur's memorable speech on "duty, honor, country" to the West Point corps of cadets. He became a director of the Douglas MacArthur Memorial Foundation thirty-six years later, after being prematurely retired from the army by the secretary of defense and Joint Chiefs of Staff. In 1951, their predecessors thought Yugoslavia more important than Korea, to MacArthur's consternation. In 1998, when more concerned about Korea, they rejected what Clark called his "candid" and "straightforward" assessment that ground forces were necessary to carry out his mission in the Balkans. True, he proposed nothing on the scale of invading China. The chairman of the JCS, on behalf of the secretary of defense, still imposed a gag order such as George Marshall and Omar Bradley never gave MacArthur: "Get your f-----g face off the TV. No more briefings, period. That's it."[5]

President Bill Clinton, implying some sort of police action, had gone on record saying, "I do not intend to put our troops in Kosovo to fight a war." Clark, a "loyal, courageous, dutiful warrior" by his own account, still prepared to bring in reinforcements, concealed this plan from DOD, and exploited fear of national failure to try to get his way. This could evoke memories of MacArthur. Associates who conceded Clark's brilliance often thought him too political, egotistical, and ambitious: his "need to win, right down to the core of his fiber" made him "highly manipulative." One might add resentful, also reminiscent of MacArthur, whose aplomb he could not match when first informed of his relief, in Clark's case two months short of the minimum two-year theater command tour. ("Wes," said a witness, "looked like he was hit by a car.") In 2004, he ran for president in large part to redeem his honor and renown, purportedly besmeared by certain Pentagon enemies.[6]

Alexander Haig was a link on a chain between Clark, his former aide-de-camp at NATO, and Douglas MacArthur, whom Haig served in 1950 as aide-de-camp to his chief of staff, Far East military headquarters. When secretary of state in the early 1980s, he fell at odds with the White House by insisting that communism in Central America could not be stemmed by operations confined to Nicaragua, something of a pawn like North Korea. The agitation must be stopped "at its source," that is Cuba, to him the communist China of the Western Hemisphere. Haig "stood virtually alone," as he described Ronald Reagan political operatives concerned that escalation would upset the electorate. The administration would not rally behind his counsel to "turn that fucking island into a parking lot." Others might favor some "limp-wristed, traditional, cookie-pushing bullshit," but Haig apparently could take heart from MacArthur, "a figure like Pompey or Wellington out of the pages of history." The CINCFE, according to Haig's recall of events in Tokyo, "announced his daring plan to the Joint Chiefs of Staff to mount an amphibious assault at Inchon against their unanimous advice and that of President Truman." Take it, "gentlemen," or "you will have a new Supreme Commander."[7]

In mid-1982, Haig gave a similar ultimatum to Reagan, for whom he had intellectual contempt. To his amazement, the president took him literally and announced his letter of resignation before Haig wrote anything of the kind. In 1988, he ran for the Republican nomination but fell to Reagan's vice president, George H. W. Bush. Sixteen years later, Wes Clark criticized Bush's son for policies ironically suggestive of MacArthur, but now about the Middle East. He said President George W. Bush was paying too little heed to opinion held in Europe and too much attention to exiled rivals of the enemy regime, in this instance Ahmad Chalabi against Saddam Hussein as opposed to Chiang against Mao Tse-tung.[8]

Clark's candidacy had some significant advantages at the beginning of an election year when a retired general, in the manner of Eisenhower, might promise some way out of a growing quagmire. Clark, however, ran a self-defeating campaign reminiscent of MacArthur's, at least in style. The latter lashed out at the Truman White House when embittered because stuck on the defensive and purportedly not allowed to win. Clark accused the Bush II White House of scheming to get the country into war, not completely fanciful in retrospect. However, at the time, one commentator remarked that his "resort to conspiracy theories about government plots sounds like Al Haig." The press, which noted the "bruising attacks" on Bush, thought Clark "strident and combative." That was not the image this candidate needed in his new line of work. The electorate assumes military men can always be aggressive. From them, they look for balance in political affairs: what Eisenhower demonstrated in 1952. Clark fell in the primaries to a former lieutenant in the U.S. Naval Reserve who subsequently lost the election to someone who never served in combat but still attained what eluded Clark, shot four times in Vietnam. Bush opened up a double-digit lead (52 to 41 percent) over John Kerry as "better qualified to be commander-in-chief." Whatever war had in store after 2004, he could for the time being project a winning aura of confidence, mission, and determination reminiscent of MacArthur taking offensive action north of the 38th parallel before China's intervention. "The way to secure Iraq and bring our troops home is not to wilt or waver or send mixed signals to the enemy."[9]

Notes

Introduction

1. David M. Pletcher, *The Diplomacy of Annexation: Texas, Oregon, and the Mexican War* (Columbia: University of Missouri Press, 1973), 456n44; Stephen W. Sears, *George B. McClellan: The Young Napoleon* (New York: Ticknor and Fields, 1988), 227–28; Donald Smythe, *Pershing: General of the Armies* (Bloomington: Indiana University Press, 1986), 220–22. In February 1966, Johnson said to Westmoreland "I hope you don't pull a MacArthur on me." Westmoreland subsequently wrote in his memoirs that "I had no intention of crossing him in any way"; see William C. Westmoreland, *A Soldier Reports* (New York: Dell Paperbacks, 1980), 207; Bernard W. Rogers (Mark Clark's executive officer in June 1953) to LTC Scott Stephenson, 3 May 2000, copy in possession of this writer. General Wesley Clark's campaign is treated in the postscript of this book.

2. Since this is a book about U.S. government policy and frequently quotes government documents, I chose to spell Chinese proper nouns as did officialdom during the period under discussion. Not until January 1979 did the U.S. government adopt the pinyin alphabet that changed Mao Tse-tung into Mao Zedong, Chiang Kai-shek into Jiang Jieshi, Chou En-lai into Zhou Enlai, and the Kuomintang into the Guomindang. However, when the original source I quote uses the pinyin spelling, I will copy it as so used.

Truman and MacArthur, before Korea

1. LTC Gerald Wilkinson to British Foreign Office, quoted in Christopher Thorne, *Allies of a Kind: The United States, Britain and the War against Japan, 1941–1945* (New York: Oxford University Press, 1978), 370n39.

2. WWII Australian General Thomas Blamey, quoted in D. M. Horner, "Blamey and MacArthur: The Problem of Coalition Warfare," in William M. Leary, ed., *We Shall Return! MacArthur's Commanders and the Defeat of Japan 1942–1945* (Lexington: University of Kentucky Press, 1988), 58.

3. Quote on physical condition from Lieutenant Colonel (LTC) James Quirk, 20 Feb. 1951, in Rory Quirk, *Wars and Peace: The Memoir of an American Family* (Novato, Calif.: Presidio Press, 1999), 169. The intermittent speculation about MacArthur's physical condition had to be tentative. He rejected annual medical examinations, army regulations notwithstanding; see Roger Olaf Egeberg, M.D., *The General: MacArthur and the Man He Called 'Doc'* (New York: Hippocrene Books, 1983), 38, 93, 212. Egeberg mentions MacArthur's "usually very mild intention tremor." Colonel Norman Scott, M.D., was able to examine MacArthur thoroughly as his attending physician in 1964. The doctor says "unequivocally, he did *NOT* have Parkinson's Disease," see Scott to Pearlman, 13 Dec. 2000, in possession of the author.

4. Paul Rogers, *The Good Years: MacArthur and Sutherland* (New York: Praeger, 1990), xvi, 240–41, and Major General (MG) Edwin K. Wright, "Oral History," 28 August, 1971, 43, Douglas MacArthur Memorial Foundation Library [hereafter MMFL]; quote on MacArthur as an actor from William Allen White in Carol Morris Petillo, *Douglas MacArthur: The Philippine Years* (Bloomington: Indiana University Press, 1981), 122; Mrs. MacArthur cited in *Understanding and Remembering: 50th Anniversary of the Korean War International Symposium* (General Douglas MacArthur Memorial Foundation, 2003), 143; West Point Chaplain James David Ford quoting MacArthur in PBS videofilm, *West Point: The First 200 Years.*

5. Entry, 17 June 1945, in John W. Huston, *American Airpower Comes of Age: General Henry H. "Hap" Arnold's World War II Diaries* (Maxwell Air Force Base: Air University Press, 2002), 2:335; Brigadier General (BG) Charles J. West, "Oral History," 14 July 1977, 86, MMFL; Egeberg, *The General*, 93, 169.

6. For Pinky, see MacArthur aide T. J. Davis, cited in Charles Burton Marshall, "The Very Image of a General," *Washington Post Book World*, 11 Oct. 1970, 21; Kenneth Ray Young, *The General's General: The Life and Times of Arthur MacArthur* (Boulder, Colo.: Westview, 1994), 130, 164; MacArthur, 18 Nov. 1951, in Doulgas MacArthur, *General MacArthur: Speeches and Reports, 1908–1964*, ed. Edward T. Imparato (Paducah: Turner Publishing, 2000), 196, and 8 Sept. 1942, quoted in Petillo, *MacArthur: Philippine Years*, 251–52.

7. Young, *General's General*, 17–19, 74–79, 288, 294, 298; John Hersey, *Men on Bataan*, (New York: Knopf, 1942), 45; classmate quoted in Geoffrey Perret, *Old Soldiers Never Die: The Life of Douglas MacArthur* (Holbrook, Mass.: Adams Media, 1986), 42; MacArthur, ca. 1918, quoted in Stanley Karnow, *In Our Image: America's Empire in the Philippines* (New York: Ballantine, 1990), 260.

8. Young, *General's General*, 308–10, 320–21; Roosevelt quoted and issue discussed in D. Clayton James, *The Years of MacArthur* (Boston: Houghton Mifflin, 1970–85), 1:40–44.

9. James, *Years of MacArthur*, 1:92; Douglas MacArthur, *Reminiscences* (New York: McGraw-Hill, 1964), 36, 89; MacArthur quoted in Hersey, *Men on Bataan*, 48; final quote in Young, *General's General*, 344;

10. MacArthur quoted by newspaper reporter, 22 Nov. 1944, in James Forrestal, *The Forrestal Diaries*, ed. Walter Millis (New York: Viking, 1951), 18; Young, *General's General*, 142–44.

11. Arthur MacArthur in Young, *General's General*, 302–303, and Petillo, *MacArthur: Philippine Years*, 55–56, also see 171–74 for FDR; MacArthur, April 1936, in *A Soldier Speaks: Public Papers and Speeches of General of the Army Douglas MacArthur*, ed. Vorin Whan (New York: Praeger, 1965), 80; Dwight D. Eisenhower, *At Ease: Stories I Tell to Friends* (Garden City, N.Y.: Doubleday, 1967), 223.

12. MacArthur quoted, Aug. 1937 and June 1939, and described in Frazier Hunt, *The Untold Story of Douglas MacArthur* (New York: Signet Books, 1964 [orig. 1954]), 39, 172–76, and Perret, *Old Soldiers*, 196; Richard Bruce Meixsel, "Manuel L. Quezon, Douglas MacArthur and the Significance of the Military Mission to the Philippine Commonwealth," *Pacific Historical Review* 70 (May 2001): esp. 257–58, 271.

13. MacArthur, Jan. 1945, described in Egeberg, *The General*, 116; Eisenhower, 1932 through 1938, in *Eisenhower: The Prewar Diaries and Selected Papers, 1905–1941*, ed. Daniel D. Holt and James W. Leyerzapf (Baltimore: Johns Hopkins Press, 1998), 230, 304, 311, 363, 368, 395, 454; MacArthur and later Eisenhower quoted and situations described in Stephen E. Ambrose, *Eisenhower* (New York: Simon and Schuster, 1983–84), 1:91–92, 111.

14. Eisenhower, "Oral History," 28 Aug. 1967, 3, MMFL; MacArthur quoted in Theodore H. White, *In Search Of History: A Personal Adventure* (New York: Harper and Row, 1978), 109; T. J. Davis cited in Marshall, "Very Image of a General," 21; MacArthur, n.d., quoted by Roger Egeberg, interviewed by Al Hemingway, "The Real MacArthur," Sept. 2000, www. thehistorynet.com/WorldWarII/articles/2000.

15. Hunt, *Untold Story of MacArthur*, 186; MacArthur to Early, 21 March 1941, Early Papers, Franklin Roosevelt Presidential Library, Hyde Park, New York.

16. MacArthur, 14 July 1939, quoted in Perret, *Old Soldiers*, 220; unnamed American soldier quoted in White, *In Search Of History*, 108; Eisenhower quoted in *New York Herald Tribune* [hereafter NYHT], 1 April 1951, 2; Eisenhower's comments on himself and MacArthur, from 1936 to 1939, in Eisenhower, *Diaries and Papers*, 311, 381, 410–11, 423–24; 439; opposite comment on MacArthur from MG Wright, "Oral History," 43. Uriah Heep, a character in Charles Dickens's novel, *David Copperfield*, personified base flattery.

17. MacArthur on Sutherland, 25 Oct. 1938, in Hunt, *Untold Story of MacArthur*, 178; Rogers, *Good Years*, 39–40; Eisenhower, *Diaries and Papers*, 384, also see 455; West, "Oral History," 51; for Eisenhower to aide, see David Eisenhower, *Eisenhower at War 1943–1945* (New York: Vintage Books, 1987), 199; for MacArthur's comments and Eisenhower's resentment, see Robert Murphy, *Diplomat among Warriors*, (New York: Pyramid Books, 1965), 379, and Carlo D'Este, *Eisenhower: A Soldier's Life* (New York: Henry Holt, 2002), 227, 233, 294–95, 751n44.

18. Edward Miller, *War Plan Orange: U.S. Strategy to Defeat Japan* (Annapolis: Naval Institute Press, 1991), esp. chapters 8, 19, and 20.

19. MacArthur, 1940–41, quoted and described in Brian McAllister Linn, *Guardians of Empire: The U.S. Army and the Pacific, 1902–1940* (Chapel Hill: University of North Carolina Press, 1997), 232, 234–38, and James, *Years of MacArthur*, 1:591, 596.

20. MacArthur to Adjutant General, "Sub: Operations Plan R-5," 1 Oct. 1941, RG 2, Box 1, MMFL; Marshall to MacArthur, 18 Oct 1941, "Sub: U.S. Army Forces in the Far East, War Plans Division Correspondence, 1940–1942," WPD 4175–18, RG 165, National Archives and Records Administration [hereafter NA], College Park, Maryland; MacArthur described and quoted in Louis Morton, *The Fall of the Philippines* (Washington: Office of the Chief of Military History, 1953), 67.

21. Morton, *Fall of Philippines*, 84–88, 104–11, 125, 141, 161.

22. Eisenhower, *Crusade in Europe* (Garden City: Doubleday, 1948), 21–22; BG Leonard Gerow to Marshall, 3 Jan. 1942, quoted in James, *Years of MacArthur*, 2:51; "Memorandum of Conversation between MacArthur and Robert Murphy," 30 April 1952, Dean Acheson Papers, Box 63, Harry S. Truman Presidential Library [hereafter TPL], Independence, Missouri; Stimson Diary, 21 Jan. 1919, 20 March 1935, and 5 April 1942, microfilm available from Yale University Library.

23. Henry Stimson and McGeorge Bundy, *On Active Service in Peace and War* (New York: Harper and Brothers, 1948), 397, 404; Stimson also quoted in George Catlett Marshall, *George C. Marshall Interviews and Reminiscences for Forrest C. Pogue: Transcripts and Notes, 1956–1958* (Lexington: George C. Marshall Research Foundation, 1986), 2:238; Marshall to MacArthur, 22 Dec. 1941 in Dwight David Eisenhower, *The Papers of Dwight David Eisenhower*, ed. Alfred Chandler (Baltimore: Johns Hopkins Press, 1970–), 1:17; John Gunther on FDR in Joseph Persico, *Roosevelt's Secret War: FDR and World War II Espionage* (New York: Random House, 2001), 96–97; Roosevelt, 9 Feb. 1942, quoted in Petillo, *MacArthur: Philippine Years*, 207.

24. MacArthur quoted in Clark Lee and Richard Henschel, *Douglas MacArthur* (New York: Henry Holt, 1952), 184; messages from Washington and MacArthur in Richard

Connaughton, *MacArthur and Defeat in the Philippines* (Woodstock: Overlook Press, 2001), 154–55, 220, 237; Marshall to MacArthur, 13 Jan. 1942, in *Papers of Eisenhower*, 1:54–55.

25. Roosevelt, 8 April 1942, quoted in Jonathan Wainwright, *General Wainwright's Story* (New York: Bantam, 1986), 98.

26. *Washington Post* [hereafter WP] 27 Jan. 1942, quoted in Connaughton, *MacArthur and Defeat*, 257; Dwight David Eisenhower, *The Eisenhower Diaries*, ed. Robert H. Ferrell (New York: Penguin Books, 1981), 49, 54; for Roosevelt, see Michael Schaller, *Douglas MacArthur: The Far Eastern General* (New York: Oxford University Press, 1989), 64–65; Petillo, *MacArthur: Philippine Years*, 113–14.

27. MacArthur quoted in Connaughton, *MacArthur and Defeat*, 259, 295–96, and Hunt, *Untold Story of MacArthur*, 254, 278; Marshall, 21 Nov. 1956, in *Interviews and Reminiscences*, 345.

28. Reporter, 22 Nov. 1944, cited in Forrestal, *Diaries*, 18; MacArthur, ca. Oct. 1943, in Perret, *Old Soldiers*, 356; Roosevelt quoted in Rogers, *Good Years*, 255; MacArthur and Marshall quoted and issues described in Marshall, *Interviews and Reminiscences*, 2:380, 394–95, and *The Papers of George Catlett Marshall*, ed. Larry Bland (Baltimore: Johns Hopkins University Press, 1982–), 3:297.

29. Stimson Diary, 29 Oct. 1942; Edward V. Rickenbacker, *Rickenbacker* (Englewood Cliffs, N.J.: Prentice-Hall, 1967), 296, 332.

30. Bonner Fellers, "Diary of Office of Military Secretary," 17 June, 16 July, 29 July, 29 August, 1945, RG 44a, Box 5, MMFL; Huston, *Arnold's War Diaries*, 2:334–35.

31. Truman Diary, 17 June 1945 in Harry S. Truman, *Off the Record: The Private Papers of Harry S. Truman*, ed. Robert H. Ferrell (New York: Penguin Books, 1982), 47.

32. MacArthur on FDR in Fellers, "Diary of Office of Military Secretary," 9 July 1945, RG 44a, Box 5, MMFL; MacArthur quoted in Paul H. Nitze, *From Hiroshima to Glasnost: At the Center of Decision, a Memoir* (New York: Grove Weidenfeld, 1989), 39; Marshall and MacArthur, 19 and 21 Oct. 1945, in Truman, *Memoirs by Harry S. Truman* (New York: Doubleday, 1955–56), 1:521; MacArthur quoted in Notes of Clovis Byers, 20 Oct. 1945, Byers Papers, Box 36, MMFL.

33. Faubion Bowers (MacArthur's former military secretary), "The Late General MacArthur, Warts and All," reprinted in William M. Leary, ed., *MacArthur and the American Century: A Reader* (Lincoln: University of Nebraska Press, 2001), 254. (The statement about Truman as a Jew was certainly extreme but apparently not unique. In 1947, and in a fit of jealousy, MacArthur made reference to Eisenhower's "Jewish blood"; eyewitness quoted in Michael Schaller, *The American Occupation of Japan: The Origins of the Cold War in Asia* [New York: Oxford University Press, 1985], 117). For quotation on "persecution complex," see Robert E. Sherwood, *Roosevelt and Hopkins: An Intimate History* (New York: Harper and Brothers, 1948), 878; Bowers, "Oral History," 18 July 1971, 22; MMFL; Dean Acheson, *Present at the Creation: My Years in the State Department* (New York: Norton, 1969), 126. MacArthur, ca. August 1945, quoted on preparedness in Philip F. La Follette, "With MacArthur in the Pacific: A Memoir," *Wisconsin Magazine of History* 60 (Autumn 1980): 106, and in Egeberg, *The General*, 193.

34. MacArthur on Truman quoted in Notes of Clovis Byers, 20 Oct. 1945, Byers Papers, Box 36, MMFL; Truman quoted by Jack Sverdrup in ibid. and in Bonner Feller's "Diary of Office of Military Secretary," 29 Aug. 1945, RG 44a, Box 5, MMFL; Ickes quoted and incidents discussed in Schaller, *American Occupation of Japan*, 21.

35. Drew Pearson, *Drew Pearson Diaries: 1949–1959*, ed. Tyler Abell (New York: Holt, Reinhart, and Winston, 1974), 27, 254; Eben A. Ayers, *Truman in the White House: The*

Diary of Eben A. Ayers, ed. Robert H. Ferrell (Columbia: University of Missouri Press, 1991), 81; McCloy described and quoted in D'Este, *Eisenhower: Soldier's Life,* 288, 517.

36. Bonner Fellers, "Diary of Office of Military Secretary," 23 Oct. 1945, RG 44a, Box 5, MMFL; McCloy at meeting with secretary of state and secretary of war, 6 Nov. 1945, quoted in Herbert Feis, *The China Tangle: American Effort in China from Pearl Harbor to the Marshall Mission* (New York: Antheneum, 1965), 389–92, and diary notes quoted in Kai Bird, *The Chairman: John J. McCloy, The Making of the American Establishment* (New York: Simon and Schuster, 1992), 266–67; McCloy to MacArthur, 9 Nov. 1945, RG 5, Box 2, MMFL; Russell Brines, *MacArthur's Japan* (Philadelphia: J. B. Lippincott, 1948), 62.

37. Stalin, 24 Oct. 1945, quoted in Feis, *China Tangle,* 393; Rusk quoted in Thomas J. Schoenbaum, *Waging Peace and War: Dean Rusk in the Truman, Kennedy, and Johnson Years* (New York: Simon and Schuster, 1988),120; Truman to Stalin 17 Aug. and Stalin to Truman, 22 Aug. 1945, *Foreign Relations of the United States* [hereafter *FRUS*] 6:670, 687–88.

38. Vladislav Zubok and Constantine Pleshakov, *Inside the Kremlin's Cold War* (Cambridge, Mass.: Harvard University Press, 1996), 62, 67; Ickes quoted in 1945, Truman, ca. Oct. 1947, quoted by Sec. of the Army Kenneth Royal, and conflicts over occupation policy described in Michael Schaller, "MacArthur's Japan: The View from Washington," in Leary, ed., *MacArthur and American Century,* 293, 299–302.

39. Truman quoted and described in James David Barber, *The Presidential Character: Predicting Performance in the White House* (Englewood Cliffs, N.J.: Prentice-Hall, 1977), 262–63; Robert J. Donovan, *The Presidency of Harry S. Truman* (New York: Norton, 1977–82), 1:180–82; Eisenhower to MacArthur, 28 May 1846, Reel 331, Correspondence, MMFL; Jean Edward Smith, *Lucius D. Clay: An American Life* (New York: Henry Holt, 1990), 525.

40. Brines, *MacArthur's Japan,* 64–65; James, *Years of MacArthur,* 3:18–19, 694.

41. Dennison, "Oral History," September–November 1971, 108, TPL.

42. Truman described and quoted in David McCullough, *Truman* (New York: Touchstone, 1992), 141, 969; Truman, *Memoirs,* 2:492; Truman, n.d., quoted in William Hillman, *Mr. President: Personal Diaries, Private Letters, Papers, and Revealing Interviews of Harry S. Truman* (New York: Farrar, Straus and Young, 1952), 11; quote about "nicest man" in Donovan, *Presidency of Truman,* 2:25, last two quotes from Margaret Truman, ed., *Where the Buck Stops: The Personal and Private Writings of Harry S. Truman* (New York: Warner, 1989), 2, and Barber, *Presidential Character,* 249; for best description of the personality conflicts within Truman, see Alonzo L. Hamby, *Man of the People: A Life of Harry S. Truman* (New York: Oxford University Press, 1998), esp. 15, 45, 165, 305, 309, 484, 586.

43. Truman Diary, May 1931, 14 May 1934, and ca. mid-1952, President's Secretary's File [hereafter PSF], Box 334, TPL; letter of 14 Dec. 1918 in Harry S. Truman, *Dear Bess: The Letters of Harry to Bess Truman, 1910–1959,* ed. Robert H. Ferrell (New York: Norton, 1983), 286; quote per "gods," n.d., in Truman, ed., *Where Buck Stops,* 8.

44. Alfred Steinberg, *The Man From Missouri: The Life and Times of Harry S. Truman* (New York: G. P. Putnam's Sons, 1962), 134; Truman Diary, ca. mid-1952; PSF 334; Otto Baker to Truman, 17 Sept. and Truman to Baker, 24 Sept. 1949, PSF, Box 298, all in TPL; Truman's date is confirmed by the official history of the 129 Field Artillery, published in 1920; Diary, 11 Nov. 1954, and "Outline of Preliminary Volumes," ca. 1 July 1953: both in PSF, Box 334, TPL; Truman, 28 Nov. 1952, in Harry S. Truman, *Strictly Personal and Confidential: The Letters Harry Truman Never Mailed,* ed. Monte M. Poen (Boston: Little Brown, 1982), 55.

45. Robert H. Ferrell, *Harry S. Truman: A Life* (Columbia: University of Missouri Press, 1994), 70; LTC Peek to Col. Broadhurst, 16 March 1936, and Truman to MG Heintzelman, 15 Feb. 1935, military record files, TPL; Truman quoted in *Kansas City Star*, 11 March 1935, 4; unnamed general quoted on Lowe in Robert Debs Heinl, *Victory at High Tide: The Inchon-Seoul Campaign* (Philadelphia: J. B. Lippincott, 1968), 134.

46. Truman on Vaughan in Diary Entry, "Executive Assets," ca. late 1952, PSF, Box 334, TPL; "Friendship Racket," *Life Magazine*, 27 (1 Aug. 1949), 19; Ayers, *Diary*, 11, 21, 42, 146, 149, 175, 245–46, 322; Willoughby to Vaughan, 14 Feb. 1949, and Vaughan to Willoughby, 13 July 1949, White House Office File, Box 686, TPL.

47. Truman Diary, 17 June 1945, in Truman, *Off the Record*, 47; Truman Diary, May 14 1934, PSF, Box 334, TPL; BG Louis H. Renfro, "Oral History," 12 and 15 March 1971, 135, TPL.

48. Letter, 29 July 1945, in Truman, *Dear Bess*, 522; Truman Diary, 14 May 1934, PSF, Box 334, TPL.

49. Walter White, "Hannibal," in Charles F. Home, ed., *Great Men and Famous Women* (New York: Selmar Hess, 1894), 1:17–18; [Jacob Abbott], *Makers of History: Vol. 9: Hannibal* (New York: Harper and Brother, 1906), 228 and passim; Hillman, *Mr. President*, 102.

50. Douglas Southall Freeman, *R. E. Lee: A Biography* (New York: Scribner's, 1934–35), 2:310; for comments on Grant, see Merle Miller, *Plain Speaking: An Oral Biography of Harry. S. Truman* (New York: G. P. Putnam's Sons, 1974), 326, and Truman Diary, 14 May 1934, PSF, Box 334, TPL; McCullough, *Truman*, 43.

51. Ayers, *Diary*, 179; Truman, *Dear Bess*, 395–97; on Lee's revisionists, see Harry Truman, *Mr. Citizen* (NY: Bernard Geis, 1960), 235. The rest of this paragraph is based on Michael A. Palmer, *Lee Moves North: Robert E. Lee on the Offensive* (New York: John Wiley, 1998) and Steven E. Woodworth, *Davis and Lee at War* (Lawrence: University Press of Kansas, 1995); Freeman, *Lee*, 4:94; Emory Thomas, *Robert E. Lee: A Biography* (New York: Norton, 1995), 13.

52. Truman, 25 Sept. 1947, in Forrestal, *Diaries*, 319; McCullough, *Truman*, 126, 130; Robert H. Ferrell, *Collapse at Meuse-Argonne: The Failure of the Missouri-Kansas Division* (Columbia: University of Missouri Press, 2004), 90–92, 106–107; Dennis Giangreco, "The Soldier from Independence: Harry S. Truman and the Great War," *Journal of the Royal Artillery* 130 (Autumn, 2003): 56–59.

53. Giangreco, "Soldier from Independence," 58–59, Truman, 19 Dec. 1918, in Truman, *Dear Bess*, 287; Forrestal quoted in Keith D. McFarland and David L. Roll, *Louis Johnson and the Arming of America: The Roosevelt and Truman Years* (Bloomington: Indiana University Press, 2005), 191.

54. Hillman, *Mr. President*, 91; Truman to Bill, 31 Oct. 1959, in Truman, *Strictly Personal and Confidential*, 152; last quote, n.d., in Steinberg, *Man From Missouri*, 184.

55. Truman to A. E. Augustine, 23 Aug. 1951, OF Dismissal File, Box 1401, TPL; News Conferences, 26 April and 24 May 1951, *Public Papers of the Presidents of the United States: Harry S. Truman, 1945–1953* [hereafter PPOPT] (U.S. Government Printing Office, 1961–66), 244, 299, Eisenhower, *Crusade in Europe*, 160; John W. Spanier, *The Truman-MacArthur Controversy and the Korean War* (New York: Norton, 1965), 10; William Leahy, *I Was There* (New York: McGraw Hill, 1950), 96–97.

56. Eisenhower, *At Ease*, 213; Truman, *Off the Record*, 265, 404; Truman, *Memoirs*, 2:443.

57. Averell Harriman, "Oral History," 20 June 1977, MMFL; Nitze, *From Hiroshima to Glasnost*, 39, and Nitze, "Interview given for BBC Documentary, 'Korea'," ca. Nov. 1986, Nitze Papers, Box 130, Library of Congress.

58. Truman in 1959 quoted in Ralph Weber, ed., *Talking with Harry: Candid Conversations with President Harry S. Truman* (Wilmington: Scholarly Resources, 2001), 194, and Truman, *Memoirs*, 2:348, 443–44; Truman to Mrs. W. Coleman Branton, 19 April 1951, OF 584 Dismissal File, Box 1401, TPL; Freeman to MacArthur, 29 December 1944, in Personal Correspondence, Microfilm Reel 331, MMFL; Freeman and MacArthur quoted and flyers described in David E. Johnson, *Douglas Southall Freeman* (Gretna, La.: Pelican, 2002), 271–72, 287.

59. Johnson, *Freeman*, 169, 272; MacArthur to Freeman, 12 Jan. 1945; Freeman to MacArthur, 8 and 15 June 1945 with unpublished magazine article attached: all in Personal Correspondence, Microfilm Reel 331, MMFL; Freeman on history in Burke Davis, *Marine! The Life of Chesty Puller* (New York: Bantam, 1964), 321; Freeman Diary, 14 Aug. 1945, Freeman Papers, Box 1, Library of Congress.

60. Johnson, *Freeman*, 284–85, 292; Freeman to Col. Frank McCarthy, 7 June 1945, Freeman Papers, Box 62; Truman quoted in John Hersey, "Profiles: Mr. President," *New Yorker*, 5 May 1951, 39; Truman, *Off the Record*, 196, 199.

61. Truman, *Off the Record*, 388, 404; Marshall, 9 May 1951, in Senate Committees on Armed Services and Foreign Relations, *Hearings to Conduct an Inquiry into the Military Situation in the Far East and the Facts Surrounding the Relief of General of the Army Douglas MacArthur from His Assignments in That Area* [hereafter *MacArthur Hearings*], 82d Congress, 1st Session, 1951, 381; Truman, 25 June 1950, quoted in Donovan, *Truman Presidency*, 2:199.

62. John E. Hull, "Oral History," April 1973, 4:19–20, United States Military History Institute [hereafter USMHI], Army War College, Carlisle Barracks, Pennsylvania.

63. Johnson, *Freeman*, 271, 335.

64. *Richmond News Leader* editorials, see 11 April, 10, 12 April, 14, 20 April 1951, 10; taxi driver quoted in "Public Here Splits on MacArthur Case," *New York Times* [hereafter *NYT*], 12 April 1951, 12.

Defense Policy on the Eve of the Korean War

1. Chiang, 26 Oct. 1946, quoted in Odd Arne Westad, *Decisive Encounters: The Chinese Civil War, 1946–1950* (Stanford: Stanford University Press, 2003), 58–59. The Chinese, whether communist or anticommunist, used the word "Taiwan," as did most of the rest of the world. Americans, in the 1950s, still referred to the island as "Formosa," its name when held as a colony of Japan from 1895 to 1945. I will use "Taiwan" or "Formosa" depending on whether Chinese or Americans are referring to this territory.

2. *PPOPT*, 180.

3. Truman to Congress Walter Judd quoted in Gordon Chang, *Friends and Enemies: The United States, China, and the Soviet Union, 1948–1972* (Stanford, Calif.: Stanford University Press, 1990), 62.

4. George M. Elsey, "Oral History," 17 July 1971, 97, TPL; Truman in Weber, *Talking with Harry*, 247.

5. Arthur H. Vandenberg, Jr., *The Private Papers of Senator Vandenberg* (Boston: Houghton, Mifflin, 1952), 76, 82, 318–19; Taft quoted in James T. Patterson, *Mr. Republican: A Biography of Robert A. Taft* (Boston: Houghton Mifflin, 1972), 157, 372, 384; Truman quoted in Acheson, "Oral History," 30 June 1971, 11–13, TPL.

6. Campaign speeches, September and October 1948, *PPOPT*, 474, 765–66, 845, 859–60, 884–86, 925–30.

7. Issues discussed and quotes in Richard Norton Smith, *Thomas E. Dewey and His Times* (New York: Simon and Schuster, 1982), 515–16, 535–37, 546; Chiang interview, 31

October 1948, printed in U.S. Department of State, *United States Relations with China, with Special References to the Period 1944–1949* (Washington, 1949) [hereafter *China White Paper*], 686–89.

8. Joseph Stilwell, *The Stilwell Papers*, ed. Theodore White (New York: William Sloane, 1948), 207, 252; Barbara W. Tuchman, *Stilwell and the American Experience in China, 1911–1945* (New York: Macmillan, 1970), 239.

9. Truman, 19 Nov. 1945, in Ayers, *Diary*, 96; William Albert Hasenfus, "Managing Partner: Joseph W. Martin, Jr., Republican Leaders of the United States House of Representatives, 1939–1959" (Ph.D. diss., Boston College, 1986), 176, 208, 216; Truman and Marshall at Cabinet Meetings, 26 March 1947 and 26 Nov. 1948, respectively, Mathew Connelly Papers, Box 1, TPL; Marshall testimony, 20 Feb. 1948, quoted in Schaller, *American Occupation of Japan*, 73.

10. Poll taken from 11/26 to 12/1/48 in George H. Gallup, *The Gallup Poll, Public Opinion, 1935–1971* (New York: Random House, 1972), 1:773; Smith, *Dewey*, 470–71, 523; Athan G. Theoharis, *The Yalta Myths: An Issue in U.S. Politics, 1945–1955* (Columbia: University of Missouri Press, 1970), 55, 63–64.

11. Johnson, *Freeman*, 323, 334; Reston, "Foreign Policy Plank Puts U.S. Policy into Campaign," *NYT*, 14 July 1948, 4.

12. Truman quoted in Dennison, "Oral History," 56, 86; *Gallup Poll*, 1:774; Acheson on democracy quoted in Michael Hunt, *Ideology and U.S. Foreign Policy* (New Haven, 1987), 180; Acheson Statement, 17 Feb. 1955, Post-Presidential Papers, Box 641, and 10 Oct. 1954, in *Princeton University Seminar Meeting of Truman Administration Officials* [hereafter *Princeton University Seminar*], reel 3, track 1: both in TPL.

13. Vandenberg quoted in Walter Isaacson and Evan Thomas, *The Wise Men: Six Friends and the World They Made* (New York: Touchstone, 1988), 467, and Pearson, *Pearson Diaries*, 159; Patterson, *Mr. Republican*, 229, 236, 256, 330, quote on 286; Stimson depicted and final quote from Sen. Kenneth Wherry (Rep. Neb.) in H. Bradford Westerfield, *Foreign Policy and Party Politics: Pearl Harbor to Korea* (New Haven: Yale University Press, 1955), 130–34, 372. Truman could lambaste "Wall Street" and still hire individual Wall Streeters because the antithesis of the proverbial humanitarian who loves mankind but not people.

14. *Tribune*, 1950, quoted in Eric F. Goldman, *The Crucial Decade—and After, America, 1945–1960* (New York: Vintage Books, 1960), 127–28; Acheson quoted in James Chace, *Acheson: The Secretary of State Who Created the American World* (New York: Simon and Schuster, 1998), 226; Taft in Patterson, *Mr. Republican*, 329.

15. Eisenhower, *Diaries* (ed. Ferrell), 1 July 1953, 242; Acheson described by Dean Rusk in Schoenbaum, *Waging Peace and War*, 198–200; Truman on domestic politics quoted in Dean Rusk, *As I Saw It: Dean Rusk as told to Richard Rusk*, ed. Daniel S. Papp (New York: Norton, 1990), 161; News Conference, 30 March 1950, PPOPT, 234–35.

16. Acheson and Walton Butterworth, then Assistant Secretary of State for Far East Affairs, quoted and discussed in Warren Cohen, "Acheson, His Advisers, and China, 1949–1950," in Dorothy Borg and Waldo Heinrichs, ed., *Uncertain Years: Chinese-American Relations, 1947–1950* (New York: Columbia University Press, 1980), 15, 24, 37, 40; John Patton Davies, *Dragon by the Tail: American, British, Japanese, and Russian Encounters* (New York: Norton, 1972), 393, 404; quote from foreign service officer Ray Ludden on 403; Acheson to President, 14 Jan. 1949; State Department, "To Determine Action Which Should Be Taken With Reference to U.S. Naval Forces. . . . ," 14 Dec. 1948, both in FRUS, 1949, 9:266 and 8:341, respectively; Truman on Acheson quoted in Ronald McGlothlen, *Controlling the waves: Dean Acheson and U.S. foreign policy in Asia* (New York: Norton, 1993), 19.

17. "Meeting on North Atlantic Union and Other Matters," 14 Aug. 1950, Acheson Papers, Box 67, TPL; News Conference, 5 Jan. 1950, *PPOPT*, 11.

18. Mao quoted on White Paper in Ross Terrill, *Mao: A Biography* (New York: Touchstone, 1993), 212–13, and Chang, *Friends and Enemies*, 37; Acheson, *Present at Creation*, pp, 332, 405; Ambassador to Yugoslavia to Sec. of State, 31 Jan. 1949, *FRUS*, 5:857; Adam Ulam, *Titoism and the Cominform* (Cambridge, Harvard University Press, 1952), esp. 220–22; C. L. Sulzberger, "Yugoslav Theorists Expect Form of Titoism in China," *NYT*, 3 March 1950, 10.

19. Philip Short, *Mao: A Life* (New York: Henry Holt, 2000), 137–30, 355, quotes on pp., 422, 425; Jung Chang and Jon Halliday, *Mao: The Unknown Story* (New York: Knopf, 2005), 187, 2371; final quotes from Mao in Michael Sheng, *Battling Western Imperialism: Mao, Stalin, and the United States* (Princeton, N.J.: Princeton University Press, 1997), 37, 195.

20. Stalin, 10 Nov. 1945, quoted in Westad, *Decisive Encounters*, 31; Stalin discussed in Dieter Heinzig, *The Soviet Union and Communist China 1945–1950: The Arduous Road to the Alliance* (London: M. E. Sharpe, 2004), 84–90, 127.

21. Mao quoted in Henizig, *Soviet Union and Communist China*, 8, 148; assessments by foreign service officers in *FRUS*, 1949, 9:346, 348, and by Congressman Walter Judd, ca. July 1949, in Chang, *Friends and Enemies*, 252; Sheng, *Battling Western Imperialism*, 56, 104–105, 148; Jonathan Brent and Vladimr Naumov, *Stalin's Last Crime: The Plot against Jewish Doctors, 1948–1953* (New York: Harper Collins, 2003), 30, 74–80, 339.

22. C. L. Sulzberger, *A Long Row Of Candles: Memories and Diaries, 1934–1954* (New York: Macmillan, 1969), 434; State Dep't Policy Planning Staff, 30 June 1948 and 10 Feb. 1949, quoted in Robert Blum, "Surprised by Tito: The Anatomy of an Intelligence Failure," *Diplomatic History* 12 (Winter 1988), 56, and Lorraine M. Lees, "The American Decision to Assist Tito, 1948–1949," *Diplomatic History* 2 (Fall 1978), 415; Counselors General Clubb and Cabot, *FRUS*, 1949, 9:196, 395.

23. Memorandum by Molotov, 17 January 1950, in *Cold War International History Project Bulletin* [hereafter *CWIHPB*], 8–9 (Winter 1996–97), 233; Stalin, 22 Jan. 1950, quoted and issue discussed in quoted in Alexandre Y. Mansourov, "Communist War Coalition Formation and the Origins of the Korean War" (Ph.D. diss., Columbia University, 1997), 242, 249, 269; Heinzig, *Soviet Union and Communist China*, 146, 155, 166, 209, 303–304; Shen Zhihua, "Sino-Soviet Relations and the Origins of the Korean War: Stalin's Strategic Goals in the Far East," *Journal of Cold War Studies* 2 (Spring 2000): 53, 57–59.

24. *RN: The Memoirs of Richard Nixon* (New York: Grosset and Dunlap, 1978), 110–11, 111, 413, 418; MacArthur, 3 May 1951, *MacArthur Hearings*, 39.

25. "Memorandum of conversation between MacArthur and Robert Murphy," 30 April 1952, Acheson Papers, Box 63, TPL and MacArthur, 20 Jan. 1954, quoted in *NYT*, 9 April 1964, 16; Records of JCS, 7 March 1949, quoted in Harry R. Borowski, *A Hollow Threat: Strategic Air Power and Containment Before Korea* (Westport: Greenwood, 1982), 197; *Stimson Diary*, 16 July 1945.

26. Howard Petersen, assistant to Secretary of Army Robert Patterson, 1 March 1947, in William Stueck Jr., *Rethinking the Korean War* (Princeton, N.J.: Princeton University Press, 2002), 49; JCS to secretary of defense, 25 Sept. 1947, in James F. Schnabel and Robert J. Watson, *The History of the Joint Chiefs of Staff: The Korean War* (Wilmington, Dela.: Michael Glasner, 1979), 1:13–14; MacArthur, ca. Jan. 1949, in J. Lawton Collins, *War in Peacetime: The History and Lessons of Korea* (Boston: Houghton Mifflin, 1969), 28, and Schaller, *MacArthur: Far Eastern General*, 162–63; Bradley in *NYT*, 7 Feb. 1950, 1.

27. Truman, *Off the Record*, 271.

28. "Memorandum for Colonel Bayer: Paragraphs of Colonel Fortier's report mentioned in General Bradley's message," 26 June 1950, Joint Chiefs of Staff, Geographical File [hereafter JCS, GF] 1948–50, RG 218, Box 23, NA.

29. Dulles quoted and issue discussed in Herbert Bix, *Hirohito and the Making of Modern Japan* (New York: HarperCollins, 2000), 639–42; MacArthur quoted in *NYT*, 2 March 1949, 22. In December 1952, 20 months after his relief, MacArthur suggested to president-elect Eisenhower a Korean peace settlement that included the neutralization of Japan, not Formosa; MacArthur, *Reminiscences*, 411.

30. "Memorandum Relating To Understanding . . . MacArthur and Remington Rand," 3 Oct. 1949, Courtney Whitney Papers, Box 5, MMFL; for MacArthur physical symptoms, see James, *Years of MacArthur*, 3:360, and Lee and Henschel, *Douglas MacArthur*, 193; aide Faubion Bowers, "The Late General MacArthur, Warts and All," 245; Eisenhower, "Oral History," 3, and *At Ease*, 214.

31. Schaller, *Far Eastern General*, 167, 170; Bix, *Hirohito and Making Modern Japan*, 595, 634, 649; Chinese editorial quoted and KMT described in June Grasso, *Truman's Two-China Policy, 1948–1950* (Armonk, N.Y.: M. E. Sharp, 1987), 116–17.

32. Nanking embassy to Secretary of State, 17 Aug. 1949; Consulate Shanghai to Sec. of State, 20 Sept. 1949 and 13 Feb. 1950; and CINCFE to DA, 2 March 1950, RG 8, Boxes 12 and 23, and RG 9, "China folder," MMFL; Acheson, 29 March 1950, quoted in Chace, *Acheson*, 224; Xiamong Zhang, *Red Wings over the Yalu* (College Station, Texas A and M Press, 2002), 79–80.

33. Schaller, *American Occupation of Japan*, 71; MacArthur, ca. 7 August 1950, quoted in Matthew B. Ridgway, *The Korean War* (New York: Doubleday, 1967), 37–38.

34. For continued resentment, see Arthur Krock, "Critics of Wake Island on Shaky Ground," *NYT*, 15 Oct. 1950, 4:3; "Oral Histories" of William Sebald [ranking State Dep't official in Japan], 30 July 1971, 6; LTG. Edward T. Almond, 4 Aug. 1971, 36; and Mike Mansfield, 16 Aug. 1977, 1: all in MMFL.

35. George F. Kennan, *Memoirs, 1925–1950* (New York: Bantam, 1969), 405–406; Schaller, *Far Eastern General*, 155.

36. MacArthur to Gen. Hugh Drum, 25 July 1936, quoted in Connaughton, *MacArthur and Defeat in Philippines*, 65–66.

37. MacArthur, 22 Nov. 1944, in Forrestal, *Diaries*, 17; Acheson on Korea, 13 March 1947, quoted in McGlothlen, *Controlling the waves*, 54; Kennan, "Memorandum of Conversation with MacArthur," 5 March 1948, *FRUS*, 6:700–703.

38. MacArthur, 9 Nov. 1948, in Borowski, *Hollow Threat*, 202; for description of Tito, see U.S. Ambassador to Yugoslavia to Sec. of State, 21 Jan. 1949, *FRUS*, 5:857; NSC, "Strategic Importance of Formosa," 1 Dec. 1948, *FRUS, 1949*, 9:201.

39. NSC, draft, "The Position of the United States with Respect to Formosa," 19 Jan. 1949, JCS, GF 1948–50, Box 22, NA; first Acheson quote, 4 March 1949, in David Finkelstein, *Washington's Taiwan Dilemma, 1949–1950: From Abandonment to Salvation* (Fairfax, Va.: George Mason University Press, 1993), 125–26; second quote in "Korean Situation," 26 June 1950, *FRUS*, 7:180.

40. MacArthur, 5 Aug. 1949, quoted in John Lewis Gaddis, "The Rise and Fall of the 'Defense Perimeter' Concept, 1946–1951," in Borg and Heinrichs, *Uncertain Years*, 75; second quote from MacArthur in mid-1947 cited in Douglas Macdonald, *Adventures in Chaos: American Intervention for Reform in the Third World* (Cambridge: Harvard University Press, 1992), 105; for "right places," see MacArthur's chief of staff, LTG Ned Almond, "Oral History," 28 March 1975, 63, 66, USMHI; MacArthur to Roy Howard, 14 Jan. and 1 Feb. 1949, RG 5, Box 28, MMFL.

41. MacArthur, ca. Aug. 1950, quoted in Joseph C. Goulden, *Korea: The Untold Story of the War* (New York: McGraw-Hill, 1982), 188; "Memorandum of Conversation between MacArthur and Robert Murphy," 30 April 1952, Acheson Papers, Box 63, TPL; "Minutes of Meeting of Secretaries of State, War, and Navy," 12 Feb. 1947, *FRUS*, 7:796–97; McGlothlen, *Controlling the waves*, 96–118.

42. Wilson D. Miscamble, *George F. Kennan and the Making of American Foreign Policy, 1947–1950* (Princeton: Princeton University Press, 1992), 106–11; MacArthur to Kennan, 16 June 1949, and Kennan to MacArthur, 27 July 1949, RG 5, Box 3, MMFL.

43. Leslie R. Groves, *Now It Can Be Told* (New York: Harper and Row, 1962), 192–93, 243; Boris T. Pash, *The Alsos Mission* (New York: Award House, 1969), 200, 225, 239; Pash activities described in Christopher Simpson, *Blowback: America's Recruitment of Nazis and Its Effects on the Cold War* (New York: Collier Books, 1990), 108, 152–53; for Pash in CIA, see *Final Report of the Select Committee to Study Government Operations with respect to Intelligence Activities* (Washington: U.S. Gov't. Printing Office, 1976), 4:128–32.

44. Comment to congressional delegation in Finkelstein, *Taiwan Dilemma*, 224; Sulzberger to MacArthur, 19 Oct. 1949, and MacArthur to Sulzberger, 28 Oct. 1949: both in RG 5, Box 3, MMFL.

45. McGlothen, *Controlling the Waves*, 118–20; Report of Congressman Charles B. Deane, ca. Oct. 1949, PSF, Foreign Affairs, Far East, Box 177, TPL.

46. Chang and Halliday, *Mao: Unknown Story*, 303, 308–309; Kennan quoted in Peter Grose, *Operation Rollback: America's Secret War Behind the Iron Curtain* (Boston: Houghton Mifflin, 2000), 89.

47. *Select Committee to Study Operations of Intelligence*, 4:132; Acheson quoted in Finkelstein, *Taiwan Dilemma*, 117, 124; Mao quoted and described in Sheng, *Battling Western Imperialism*, 81, 163–64; communist publication quoted in U.S. Military Attaché (Taiwan), Nanking, to DA, 3 Sept. 1949, RG 9, "China," MMFL.

48. Kennan quoted in Isaacson and Thomas, *Wise Men*, 437, and Finkelstein, *Taiwan Dilemma*, 178–79; Nitze quoted in Robert Accinelli, *Crisis and Commitment: United States Policy toward Taiwan, 1950–1955* (Chapel Hill: University of North Carolina Press, 1996), 20; for Kennan and Sun, see Bruce Cumings, *The Origins of the Korean War* (Princeton: Princeton University Press, 1981–90), 2:532–34, 872n90.

49. Albert Wedemeyer, *Wedemeyer Reports!* (New York: Henry Holt, 1958), 325; *MacArthur Hearings*, 56–57, 183; MG William Chase, 20 Aug. 1951, cited in Robert Barnett to John Allison, 11 Feb. 1952, State Dep't Central Files, RG 59, Box 2882, NA; Chen Cheng to MacArthur, 11 Feb. 1949; Sun to MacArthur, 5 March 1949: both in RG 5, Official Correspondence; U.S. Military Attaché (Taiwan), MMFL.

50. Hanson Baldwin, "Appraisal of Formosa," *NYT*, 2 April 1951, 4; "Discussion of Budget Policy and Military Program with President Chiang Kai-shek," 19 Sept. 1952, *FRUS: 1952–1954*, 14:106–108; Lloyd Eastman, "Who Lost China? Chiang Kai-shek Testifies," *China Quarterly* 88 (Dec. 1981): 661–64; Bruce Dickson, "The Lessons of Defeat: The Reorganization of the Kuomintang on Taiwan, 1950–52," *China Quarterly* 133 (March 1993): 61, 73, 75, 83.

51. MacArthur and Sun discussed and Livingston Merchant quoted, 4 and 24 May 1949, in Finkelstein, *Taiwan Dilemma*, 137, 142, 149, 155, 173, 227; Sun to MacArthur, 18 May 1949, RG 5, Office of Military Secretary, Correspondence, Sun Lie-jen File, MMFL.

52. Sun to MacArthur, 5 March and 18 May 1949, as cited above; Robert Strong (counsel, Taipei) cited in Accinelli, *Crisis and Commitment*, 21.

53. Schoenbaum, *Waging War and Peace*, 209; Leonard A. Kusnitz, *Public Opinion and Foreign Policy: America's China Policy, 1949–1979* (Westport, Conn.: Greenwood Press, 1984), 33 and 41n83; McGlothen, *Controlling the Waves*, 120–22.

54. Document reprinted in *MacArthur Hearings*, 1667–69.

55. "Memorandum on Formosa," 14 June 1950, *FRUS*, 7:165.

56. Acheson quoted in Finkelstein, *Taiwan Dilemma*, 281.

57. MacArthur, 18 May 1950, quoted in Sulzberger, *Long Row Of Candles*, 562; MacArthur to Smith, 26 Sept. 1949, and MacArthur to Kenneth Krentz, ca. 15 March 1949, both in Finkelstein, *Taiwan Dilemma*, 218, 239.

58. MacArthur in *NYT*, 2 March 1949, 22; Sulzberger, *Long Row of Candles*, 687–88; MacArthur, "Memorandum on Formosa," 14 June 1950, *FRUS*, 7:162; MacArthur quoted in William J. Sebald and Russell Brinan, *With MacArthur In Japan: A Personal History of the Occupation* (New York: Norton, 1965), 122.

59. Leahy to Forrestal, 24 November 1948, *FRUS*, 9:262; Phillip A. Karber and Jerald A. Combs, "The United States, NATO, and the Soviet Threat to Western Europe: Military Estimates and Policy Options, 1945–1963," *Diplomatic History* 22 (Summer 1998): 408–20, Bradley's prediction in Borowski, *Hollow Threat*, 125.

60. Admiral Louis Denfeld, "Memorandum for Secretary of Defense, Sub: The Strategic Importance of Formosa," 10 Feb. 1949, JCS, GF, 1948–50, Box 22, NA; Finkelstein, *Taiwan Dilemma*, 221, 246, 269; Bradley to Secretary of Defense Johnson, 23 Dec. 1949, *FRUS*, 9:461; Joint Strategic Staff Committee, "Possible United States Military Action Toward Taiwan Not Involving Major Military Moves," ca. Dec. 1949, JCS, GF, 1948–50, Box 22, NA.

61. "Memorandum of Conversation by Secretary of State," 29 December 1949; *FRUS*, 9:466–67; NSC, "The Position of the United States with Respect to Asia," 30 Dec. 1949, *FRUS*, 7:1219; Acheson, "Memo of Conversation on Formosa Problem with Senators Knowland and Smith," 5 Jan. 1950, *FRUS*, 6:260–61.

62. Acheson, "Memo of Conversation with Knowland and Smith," cited above; Louis Johnson to Truman, 15 Dec. 1949, copy in RG 6, Box 8, MMFL; "Draft: Memorandum for Secretary of Defense," 2 April 1949, JCS, GF, 1948–50, RG 218, Box 22, NA.

63. Opinion polls cited in Robert Beisner, *Dean Acheson: A Life in the Cold War* (New York: Oxford University Press, 2006), 191, 202; Truman quoted in Robert Blum, *Drawing The Line: The Origin of the American Containment Policy in East Asia* (New York: Norton, 1982), 28, 99.

64. Truman quoted in Truman, *Off the Record*, 53, 58, in 1949 by Jonathan Daniels cited in Daniel Yergin, *Shattered Peace: The Origins of the Cold War and the National Security State* (Boston: Houghton Mifflin, 1978), 119, on 18 Oct. 1947 in Ayers, *Diary*, 293, and Truman Diary, 2 June 1954, PSF, Box 298, TPL. This last document has a line drawn top to bottom through all three pages, as if Truman did not want to be held to what he had just written.

65. Truman, ed., *Where Buck Stops*, 65, 193; Truman concurring in "Memorandum of Conversation, by General Marshall," 11 Dec. 1945, *FRUS*, 7:768; Truman to Byrnes, 5 Jan. 1946, in Truman, *Off the Record*, 80; Truman and Acheson quoted in 1949 in Finkelstein, *Taiwan Dilemma*, 237; Truman, *Memoirs*, 2:328; Truman, 27 March 1950, quoted in *Private Papers of Senator Vandenberg*, 560; Louis Johnson, paraphrasing Truman on 20 Dec. 1949, in *MacArthur Hearings*, 2578; News Conference, 5 Jan. 1950, PPOPT, 11.

66. Vice counsel in Beijing quoted in Grasso, *Truman's Two-China Policy*, 113; Chou quoted in Clubb to Sec. State, 1 June 1949, *FRUS*, 8:358–60, and Heinzig, *Soviet Union and Communist China*, 249; for American diplomats on "moderate" Taliban in

the 1990s, see Steve Coll, *Ghost Wars: Secret History of the CIA, Afghanistan, and bin Laden, from the Soviet Invasion to September 10, 2001* (New York: Penguin Press, 2004), 328, 343, 565.

67. Mao paraphrased by Molotov in *CWIHPB*, 8–9 (Winter 1996–97), 233; Communist Party newspaper quoted in Chen Jian, "The Ward Case and the Emergence of Sino-American Confrontation, 1948–1950," *The Australian Journal of Chinese Affairs* 30 (July 1993): 162; Grasso, *Truman's Two-China Policy*, 99,109; for CIA operative, see John K. Singlaub, *Hazardous Duty: An American Soldier in the Twentieth Century* (New York: Summit Books, 1991), 148, 155. Acheson discussed and quoted, 16 Nov. 1949, to Truman in Finkelstein, *Taiwan Dilemma*, 101, 237, "Minutes of bipartite ministerial talks," 7 May 1950, quoted in William M. Leary and William Stueck, "The Chennault Plan To Save China: U.S. Containment in Asia and the Origins of the CIA's Aerial Empire," *Diplomatic History* 8 (Fall 1984): 362.

68. Acheson at 35th Meeting of NSC, 3 March 1949, JCS, GF, 1948–50, RG 218 Box 22, NA; McFarland and Roll, *Johnson and Arming of America*, 14–22, 138; Senator Henry Cabot Lodge II quoted in Robert W. Merry, *Taking On The World: Joseph and Stewart Alsop-Guardians of the American Century* (New York: Viking, 1996), 182; Assistant Secretary of Defense Paul Griffith to Wellington Koo, 3 June 1950, in Kusnitz, *Public Opinion and Foreign Policy*, 33, and Cumings, *Origins of Korean War*, 2:540.

69. McFarland and Roll, *Johnson and Arming of America*, 252–53; Rear Admiral A. C. Davis, director of Joint Staff, "Memorandum for Gen. Bradley: Denial of Formosa to Chinese Communists," 10 June 1950, JCS, GF, 1948–50, RG 218, Box 23, NA.

70. Omar N. Bradley and Clay Blair, *A General's Life* (New York: Simon and Schuster, 1983), 502; Renfrow, "Oral History," 80–81; Truman's action described in Kusnitz, *Public Opinion and Foreign Policy*, 42n87.

71. Associated Press story quoted in Finkelstein, *Taiwan Dilemma*, 265; MacArthur in Lester B. Pearson, *Mike: The Memoirs of Lester Pearson* (New York: Quadrangle, 1972–75), 2:147; Cumings, *Origins of Korean War*, 2:525; Willoughby to CINC, "Inquiry by Maj. Gen. Ho Shi-Bai," 15 June, 1950, RG 6, Box 1, MMFL.

72. Finkelstein, *Taiwan Dilemma*, 21, 33, 240, 304–306, 314, quote on 214; Chiang quoted by private envoy in Accinelli, *Crisis and Commitment*, 26; "Korean Situation," 26 June 1950 *FRUS*, 7:180.

73. Memorandum from General Akin to Colonel Bunker, 30 December 1949, RG 9, Box 121, MMFL; Bradley and Blair, *General's Life*, 530.

74. Ridgway Diary, 15 June 1951, Matthew Ridgway Papers, Box 20, USMHI; Office of the Chief of Naval Operations, "Report Containing Proposals For U.S. Assumption of Control over Taiwan," 3 Jan. 1950, JCS, GF, 1948–50, RG 218, Box 22, NA; Consul General at Shanghai to Sec. of State, 5 Jan. 1950, *FRUS*, 6:266; NKVD report cited in Stanley G. Payne, *The Spanish Civil War, the Soviet Union, and Communism* (New Haven: Yale University Press, 2004), 208.

75. "Report to the President Pursuant to President's Directive of 31 Jan. 1950," 7 April 1950 [hereafter NSC 68], *FRUS*, 1:247; Truman, 3 Oct. 1947, quoted in Miscamble, *Kennan and Foreign Policy*, 238; Acheson at meeting with British foreign office, 12 Sept. 1949, quoted in Lloyd C, Gardner, "Korean Borderlands," in William Stueck, Jr., ed., *The Korean War in World History* (Lexington: University of Kentucky Press, 2004), 132; NSC 48/1, 23 Dec. 1949, quoted in Shu Guang Zhang, *Deterrence and Strategic Culture: Chinese-American Confrontations, 1949–1958* (Ithaca: Cornell University Press, 1992), 38.

76. JCS Chairman Bradley, "Memorandum for General Vandenberg, General Collins, Admiral Sherman, and Admiral Davis," 25 June 1950, and attached memo to

President, n.d., JCS, GF, 1948–50, RG 218, Box 23; for Roberts, see Sebald, *With Mac-Arthur*, 182–83, and Allan R. Millett, *The War for Korea, 1945–1950: A House Burning* (Lawrence: University Press of Kansas, 2006); 212, 250–52; Roberts cited in Ambassador to Korea to Sec. of State, 29 May 1950, *FRUS*, 7:93. "White House" and "the Oval Office" refers to the presidency, not 1600 Pennsylvania Avenue, to which Truman returned in March 1952.

77. Bradley interview, 6 Feb. 1962, Merle Miller Papers, Box 3, TPL; Sebald to Acheson from Dulles, 22 June 1950, *FRUS*, 6:366; MacArthur, "Memorandum on Formosa," 14 June 1950, JCS, GF, 1948–50, Box 23; interview with Acheson, n.d., Miller Papers, Box 3, TPL; Johnson, 14 June 1951, *MacArthur Hearings*, 2580; Truman's comments quoted in Ferrell, *Truman: A Life*, 322; Bradley and Blair, *General's Life*, 532–34.

The War against North Korea

1. Captain Frank Thompson, Jr. in Donald Knox, *The Korean War: An Oral History* (New York: Harcourt, Brace, Jovanovich, 1983–88), 1:42.

2. For examples of the respective theories, see Stephen Van Evera, *Causes of War: Power and Roots of Conflict* (Ithaca: Cornell University Press, 1999) and Dale C. Copeland, *The Origins of Major War* (Ithaca: Cornell University Press, 2000).

3. Quotation, n.d., cited by Dean Rusk in Schoenbaum, *Waging Peace and War*, 208.

4. MacArthur, 19 Jan. 1949, quoted in James, *Years of MacArthur*, 3:401; issue discussed and Acheson, 1948, quoted in McGlothlen, *Controlling the Waves*, 50, 54–55, 62–66, 77; Acheson, 1 My 1950, quoted in Gaddis, "Defense Perimeter' Concept," 68; Ambassador John J. Muccio, "Oral History," 18 Feb. 1971, 14, TPL.

5. Millett, *War for Korea*, 214, 245; Rusk testifying to House Committee on Foreign Affairs as quoted in Donovan, *Presidency of Truman*, 2:182.

6. Charles Armstrong, *The North Korean Revolution, 1945–1950* (Ithaca: Cornell University Press, 2003), esp. 4, 54, 167–68, 213, 222; Mansourov, "Communist War Coalition," 43–45, 71, 159–61, 165, 183.

7. Mansourov, "Communist War Coalition," 290, 297–98, 358, 387; Stalin, Dec. 1949, quoted in Chen Jian, "In the Name of Revolution," in Stueck, ed., *Korean War in World History*, 100–101; "Russian Documents on the Korean War, 1950–53," *CWIHPB*, Issue 14/15, Winter 2003–Spring 2003, 373; Muccio, "Oral History," 22.

8. Ambassador at Large Philip Jessup to Deputy Undersecretary of State H. Freeman Matthews, 17 Aug. 1950, *FRUS*, 7:595; Livingston Merchant (Formosa desk officer) to Dean Rusk, 16 Feb. 1950, in Finkelstein, *Taiwan Dilemma*, 295; Acheson, 29 July 1950, cited in Pearson, *Mike*, 2:152; Acheson, 1 June 1951, *MacArthur Hearings*, 1818.

9. Truman quoted in Glenn D. Paige, *The Korean Decision: June 24–30, 1950* (New York: Free Press, 1968), 141; for polling data on the initial commitment to Korea, see William A. Scott and Stephen B. Withey, *The United States and the United Nations: The Public View, 1945–1955* (New York: Manhattan Publishing, 1958), 78. One senior national security official in the Clinton administration said of domestic politics, "It's the ever present but never acknowledged player"; Nancy Soderberg interviewed on National Public Radio, *Morning Edition*, 23 Jan. 2003.

10. State Department, "Intelligence Estimate," 25 June 1950, in *FRUS*, 1:336; Truman, *Memoirs*, 2:321, 326, 333, 463; Truman in 1951 quoted in Hillman, *Mr. President*, 81; last quote from "Points Requiring Presidential Decision," 25 June 1950, George M. Elsey Papers, Box 71, TPL.

11. Truman in Dec. 1945 quoted in Chace, *Acheson*, 152; Nitze, 8 Feb. 1950, in *FRUS*, 1:145–46; Truman quoted in Donovan, *Presidency of Truman* 2:199, 204–205; French saying quoted in D. W. Brogan, "For Bevan," *NYT Book Review*, 4 May 1952, 29; Robert Schuman, 25 June 1950, quoted in Charles E. Bohlen, *Witness to History, 1929–1969* (New York: Norton, 1973), 291–92.

12. Bohlen, *Witness to History*, 339; Kathryn Weathersby, "The Soviet Role in the Korean War: The State of Historical Knowledge," in Stueck, ed., *Korean War in World History* 70, 82; A. V. Torkunov and E. P. Ufimtsev cited in Shen Zhihua, "Sino-Soviet Relations and the Origins of the Korean War: Stalin's Strategic Goals in the Far East," *Journal of Cold War Studies* 2 (Spring 2000), 53, 57–59; Mansourov, "Communist War Coalition Formation," 104, 187, 189, 206, 221–22, 326, 365; Stalin in conversation with Kim quoted in Odd Arne Westad, *The Global Cold War: Third World Interventions and the Making of Our Times* (New York: Cambridge University Press, 2005), 66.

13. Millett, *War for Korea*, 192, 206, 210, 215–16; first quote on Korea from Stalin to Mao, 7 Oct. 1950, in *CWIHPB*, Winter 1995–96, 116; report on conference with Kim, March 30–April 25, 1950, reprinted in Kathryn Weathersby, "'Should We Fear This?': Stalin and the Danger of War with America" (Woodrow Wilson International Center, Cold War History Project, Working Paper No. 39, July 2002), 10; Stalin described and quoted in Jerrold Schecter, ed., *Khrushchev Remembers: Glasnost Tapes* (Boston: Little, Brown, 1990), 100–101, and Strobe Talbott, ed., *Khrushchev Remembers* (Boston: Little Brown, 1970–74), 1:299, 361, 2:356.

14. Stalin quoted, ca. 1947, in David Holloway, *Stalin and the Bomb: The Soviet Union and Atomic Energy, 1939–1956* (New Haven: Yale University Press, 1994), 247; British policy explained and Bevin, 12 Jan. 1951, quoted in Robin Edmonds, *Setting The Mould: The United States and Britain, 1945–1950* (New York: Norton, 1986), 194, 203, 229; for Berlin Blockade and other quote, see Bohlen, *Witness to History*, 278–82.

15. French military intelligence assessment quoted in Cummings, *Origins of Korean War*, 2:650; "Meeting on North Atlantic Union and Other Matters," 14 Aug. 1950, Acheson Papers, Box 67, TPL; Truman news conference, 29 June 1950, *PPOPT*, 502; Bradley, 15 May 1951, testifying at *MacArthur Hearings*, 732.

16. Dialogue between Truman and Air Force chief of staff in "Korean Situation," 25 June 1950, *FRUS*, 7:158–62; Acheson, 11 Oct. 1954, describing Collins at *Princeton University Seminar*, reel 2, track 7, 7, TPL; Washington-CINCFE Teleconferences, 25–26 June 1950, RG 16a, Box 5, MMFL; Matthew B. Ridgway, *Soldier: The Memoirs of Matthew B. Ridgway* (New York: Harper and Brothers, 1956), 192.

17. MacArthur quoted in Stanley Weintraub, *MacArthur's War: Korea and the Undoing of an American Hero* (New York: Free Press, 2000), 109; Collins, *War in Peacetime*, 393.

18. Bradley, 15 and 16 May 1951, *MacArthur Hearings*, 732, 948.

19. Truman Diary, 30 June 1950, in Truman, *Off the Record*, 185; Truman at Q and A, Ft. Leavenworth, 15 Dec. 1961, Merle Miller Papers, Box 6, TPL; Mansourov, "Communist War Coalition," 203, 301, 332; Stalin used the phrase "pretext to intervene" when describing to Mao Tse-tung why he would not directly participate in an invasion of Taiwan, see record of their conversation, 16 Dec. 1949, in Odd Arne Westad, ed., *Brothers in Arms: The Rise and Fall of the Sino-Soviet Alliance, 1945–1963* (Washington: Woodrow Wilson Center Press, 1998), 316; Paige, *Korean Decision*, 169–70, 259.

20. Richard F. Haynes, *The Awesome Power: Harry S. Truman as Commander in Chief* (Baton Rouge: Louisiana State University, 1973), 137, 140–45.

21. For first known uses of "proxy war," see *NYT*, 9 Jan. 1955, 8, and 18 Nov. 1956, 12; "Memorandum of Conversation," 26 June 1950, *FRUS*, 7:178–83; News Conference, 29

June 1950, *PPOPT*, 503–504; Truman, Q. and A. at Leavenworth, 15 Dec. 1961, Merle Miller Papers, Box 6, TPL.

22. NSC 68, *FRUS*, 1950, 1:259; Lt. Philip Day quoted in Knox, *Korean War: Oral History*, 1:16; MG John Church quoted and casualties cited in Roy E. Appleman, *South To The Naktong, North To The Yalu* (Washington: U.S. Army Center of Military History, 1992), 61, 75; unidentified soldiers, July 1950, quoted in T. R. Fehrenbach, *This Kind of War: A Study in Unpreparedness* (New York: Macmillan, 1964), 123.

23. Corporal Frank Bifulk and Colonel Richard Stephens quoted, respectively, in Knox, *Korean War: Oral History*, 1:669, and Fehrenbach, *This Kind of War*, 149; Louis Harris, *Is There a Republican Majority: Political Trends, 1952–1956* (New York: Harper and Brothers, 1954), 26; "Remarks at Pemiscot County Fair," 7 Oct. 1945, and "Radio Report to the American People on Korea," 11 April 1951, in *PPOPT*, 1945, 381, and 1951, 226. The term "limited war" was coined in 1907 by Julian Corbett, an English military historian and theorist, see Corbett, *England in the Seven Years War* (London: Longmans, Green, 1907), 1:28–29. However, in the aftermath of the world wars, it was common to believe that "modern war is total," as Winston Churchill said to a joint session of the U.S. Congress, May 1943.

24. Bradley, 15 May 1951, *MacArthur Hearings*, 753; for Collins, 18 April 1951, see *FRUS*, 7:361; "'Prepare for 10 Years of Tension:' Interview with George C. Marshall," *U.S. News and World Report* 30 (April 13, 1951): 27; Collins, *War In Peacetime*, 205.

25. Bernard K. Duffy and Ronald H. Carpenter, *Douglas MacArthur: Warrior and Wordsmith* (Westport: Greenwood, 1997), 112, 119, 123; MacArthur to Lt. Wm. Knapp, 6 Sept. 1949, RG 5, Box 3, MMFL.

26. General quoted in DeMaree Bess, "Are Generals in Politics a Menace?," *Saturday Evening Post* 224 (April 26, 1952): 29.

27. Quotes from MacArthur in Richard Rovere and Arthur Schlesinger, Jr., *The General and the President: The Future of American Foreign Policy* (New York: Farrar, Straus and Young, 1951), 104; Goulden, *Korea*, 53, William Stueck, Jr., *The Korean War: An International History* (Princeton: Princeton University Press, 1995), 44; and by MG Earle Partridge, temporary Cdr. of Fifth Air Force, in Phillip S. Meilinger, *Hoyt S. Vandenberg: The Life of a General* (Bloomington: Indiana University Press, 1989), 163; Dulles quoted in Townsend Hoopes, *The Devil and John Foster Dulles: The Diplomacy of the Eisenhower Era* (Boston: Atlantic-Brown, 1973), 99–100; Truman, 1 July 1950, paraphrased in Ayers, *Diary*, 360.

28. MacArthur, 20 Jan. 1954, cited in *NYT*, 9 April 1964, 16; David Douglas Duncan quoted in Goulden, *Korea*, 90. In March 1951, Ridgway, and Major General Oliver Prince (O. P.) Smith, commander of the First Marine Division, took a five-hour trip to the front in Korea "bouncing around" in a jeep. At the end of the trip, according to Smith, "Ridgway bawled me out . . . 'Why in the hell didn't you suggest that we stop?' I replied, 'You're the senior. I figured it was up to you.'" MacArthur "got out of his jeep and marched over to his plane. Then everyone else just disappeared to the johns," O. P. Smith, "Oral History," 24 Aug. 1971, 15–16, MMFL.

29. James F. Schnabel, *Policy And Direction: The First Year* (Washington: Office of the Chief of Military History, 1972), 66, 74–78; Eisenhower described and paraphrased in Ridgway Diary, 28 June 1950, Ridgway Papers, Box 16.

30. Reston in *NYT*, 9 July 1950, E:3; also see 1 Jan. 1950, 4:3; James Reston, *Deadline: A Memoir* (New York: Random House, 1991), chapter 17.

31. "Korean Situation," 25 1950; JCS to CINCFE, 29 June 1950: both in *FRUS*, 7:158–59, 240; Under Sec. of Army Tracy S. Voorhees, "Memorandum for Secretary of

Defense, General MacArthur's views about Formosa," 14 Dec. 1949, copy in RG 6, Box 8, MMFL.

32. JCS to Secretary of Defense, 10 Feb. 1949, *FRUS*, 9:268; James A. Field, Jr., *History of United States Naval Operations: Korea* (Washington: U.S. Govt. Printing Office, 1962), 47, 60, 67, 128, 343–44; Memorandum, "Chief of Naval Operations for JCS on Defense of Formosa," 27 July 1950, JCS, GF, 1948–50, RG 218, Box 23, NA; GHQ Liaison Group Taipei to CINCFE, Groups-2, 9 Aug. 1950, RG 9, Box 40, MMFL; "Survey of Military Assistance Required by Chinese Nationalist Forces," 11 Sept. 1950, JCS, GF, 1948–50, RG 218, Box 24, NA.

33. John Gittings, *The Role of the Chinese Army* (New York: Oxford University Press, 1967), 26–28, 79; He Di, "The Last Campaign To Unify China," *Chinese Historians* 5 (Spring 1992): 2–5.

34. MacArthur in conversation with Averell Harriman, 6 and 8 August 1950, *FRUS*, 6:429; Marshall, 30 June 1947, quoted in Arnold A. Offner, *Another Such Victory: President Truman and the Cold War, 1945–1953* (Stanford: Stanford University Press, 2002), 326.

35. Secretary of State to Embassy, China, 27 June 1950, *FRUS*, 7:188; CINCFE to Department of the Army [hereafter DA] 16 July 1950, Radiograms, RG 9, Box 45, MMFL.

36. CINCFE to JCS and State Department, 16 July 1950, and Truman to Acheson, 18 July 1950: both in State Department, Selected Records Relating to the Korean War [hereafter Selected Records Korea], Box 6, TPL.

37. CINCFE to DA, 29 July 1950, RG 9, Radiograms, Box 45, MMFL; MacArthur in conversation with Averell Harriman, 6 and 8 August 1950, *FRUS*, 6:429.

38. First quote from "September Foreign Ministers Meeting: Formosa," 28 August 1950, State Department, Selected Records, Korea, Box 6; "Points Requiring Presidential Decision," 25 June 1950, Elsey Papers Box 71: both in TPL; Acheson to Secretary of Defense, July 1950, and Dean Rusk (for Sec of State) to Embassy, China, 14 August 1950, *FRUS*, 6:404, 435–36.

39. NSC 41: "United States Policy Regarding Trade with China," 28 Feb. 1949, quoted in Finkelstein, *Taiwan Dilemma*, 101; Truman to Acheson, 17 Oct. 1949, Acheson to Truman, 3 August 1950, quoted and China discussed in Grasso, *Truman's Two China Policy*, 97, 157, 159; Acheson, *Present at Creation*, 418–19.

40. Dulles quoted in Kusnitz, *Public Opinion and Foreign Policy*, 45; British Foreign Secretary to Secretary of State, 15 July 1950, and "Minutes of Meeting with Representatives of France, the U.K., and USA in Paris on Aug. 3, 1950," both in *FRUS*, 6:403–404, 408; for reaction in London and quote from foreign office minister of state, 14 May 1950, see Alan Bullock, *Ernest Bevin: Foreign Secretary, 1945–1951* (London: Heinemann, 1983), 768, 794; Acheson to Truman, 3 Aug. 1950, quoted in Grasso, *Truman's Two-China Policy*, 160; Ronald J. Caridi, *The Korean War and American Politics: The Republican Party as a Case Study* (Philadelphia: University of Pennsylvania Press, 1968), 104–105, 171, 193; Press Conference, 31 Aug. 1950, *PPOPT*, 607.

41. Acheson to Johnson, 31 July 1950, *FRUS*, 6:408.

42. See debate by Congressman Donald Jackson (Rep.-Calif.) and others in *Congressional Record*, 81st Cong., 2nd Session, esp. 644, 649, 652; Taft quoted in Finkelstein, *Taiwan Dilemma*, 264, 308–309; Dulles to Acheson, 18 May 1950, *FRUS*, 1:315.

43. Truman, 27 March 1950, in Vandenberg, *Private Papers of Vandenberg*, 558–59; Blum, *Drawing the Line*, 200–201; Paige, *Korean Decision*, 154; Lawrence, *NYHT*, 28 June 1950, 6; Reston, *NYT*, 28 June 1950, 1, and 28 July 1950, 8.

44. Westerfield, *Foreign Policy and Party Politics*, 369n64, 386, 396; "Statement by President of the Situation in Korea," 27 June 1950, and "Special Message to Congress Reporting on the Situation in Korea," 19 July 1950, *PPOPT*, 492, 532; Jessup, "Memorandum for Mr. Matthews," 2 Aug. 1950, State Dep't Central Files, RG 59, Box 2882, NA.

45. Caridi, *Korean War and American Politics*, 11, 60, 169; Bullock, *Bevin*, 685, 766, 773; Cumings, *Origins of Korean War*, 2:530; U.S. Ambassador (United Kingdom) to Acheson, 14 July 1950, *FRUS*, 6:382; State Dep't draft, "September Foreign Ministers Meeting," 28 August 1950, RG 6, Box 8, MMFL.

46. MacArthur, 4 May 1951, at *MacArthur Hearings*, 123; MG Burns and Captain Grem, "Defense of Formosa," 24 July 1950, State Department, Selected Records Korea, Box 6, TPL; "Report of Joint Strategic Survey Committee to JCS on General Policy of the United States Concerning Formosa," 21 July 1950, RG 6, Box 8, MMFL; Truman, *Memoirs*, 2:349; Collins, *War in Peacetime*, 271; DA to CINCFE, 30 July 1950, RG 9, Box 45, MMFL.

47. Dean Rusk to MG J. H. Burns, 7 July 1950, JCS, GF, 1948–50, RG 218, Box 23, NA; Acheson, "Meeting with the President," 3 August 1950, in State Department, Selected Records Korea, Box 6, TPL; corporal quoted in Knox, *Korean War, Oral History*, 1:81.

48. MacArthur, 29 July 1950, paraphrased in Muccio, "Oral History," 68; Strong to Acheson, 3 August 1950, *FRUS*, 6:411; Ned Almond, "Oral History," 28 March 1975, 65, USMHI; MacArthur's press statement reproduced in Courtney Whitney, *MacArthur: His Rendezvous With History* (New York: Knopf, 1956), 373; MacArthur to Arthur Hays Sulzberger, 28 Oct. 1949, RG 5, Box 5, MMFL.

49. CINCFE to DA, 7 and 11 Aug. 1950, RG 6, Box 8, MMFL; MacArthur on Marshall, n.d., quoted in Goulden, *Korea*, 188; DA to CINCFE, 29 July and CINCFE to DA, 31 July 1950, JCS, GF, 1948–50, RG 218, Box 23, NA.

50. CINCFE to DA, 31 July 1950, JCS, GF, 1948–50, Box 23; Sebald (State Department's Political Advisor to MacArthur), "Oral History," 6; Jessup, "Memorandum for Mr. Matthews," 2 Aug. 1950, State Dep't Central Files, RG 59, Box 2882; NA; MacArthur quoted in Sebald to Acheson, 3 August 1950, *FRUS*; 7:415; Chargé to Secretary of State, 3 Aug. 1950, *FRUS*, 6:411; Chiang quoted and picture published in *NYT*, 3 Aug. 1950, 6.

51. Acheson, 1 Aug. 1950, quoted in Cumings, *Origins of Korean War*, 2:712; Truman at White House conferences, 28 and 29 June 1950, in Dennis Merrill, ed., *Documentary History of Truman Presidency* (Washington: University Publications of America, 1997), 18:107, 127; Collins to MacArthur, 1 July 1950, RG 6, Box 9, MMFL.

52. Strong to Acheson, 4 August 1950, and Johnson to Acheson, 29 July 1950: both in *FRUS*, 6:401, 416–17; Acheson, *Present at Creation*, 422; CINCFE to DA, 7 Aug. 1950, RG 6, Box 8, MMFL.

53. DA to CINCFE, 14 July 1950, RG 6, Box 8; MacArthur to DA. 4 Aug. 1950, RG 9, Box 45: both in MMFL; Bradley and Blair, *General's Life*, 542; Johnson to MacArthur, 5 Aug. 1950, RG 16a, Box 5, MMFL.

54. JCS to MacArthur, 25 July 1950; Rear Adm. A. C. Davis, Dir. of Joint Staff, Memorandum for Secretary of Defense, "Defense of Formosa," 28 July 1950: both in JCS, GF, 1948–50, RG 218, Box 45, NA.

55. Omar Bradley statement, 9 April 1952, *FRUS*, 1952–54, 14:39; Joint Intelligence Committee, "Estimate of Taiwan Situation," 31 July 1950, JCS, GF, 1948–50, RG 218, Box 23, NA; Nationalist Chinese newspaper quoted in DA to CINCFE, 1 July 1950, RG 6, Box 8, MMFL.

56. Far East Command Survey of Formosa to CINCFE (Groups-2), 6 Sept. 1950, RG 9, Box 41; MMFL; Truman, 6 July 1950, quoted in David McLean, "American

Nationalism, the China Myth, and the Truman Doctrine: The Question of Accommodation with Peking, 1949–50," *Diplomatic History* 10 (Winter 1986), 40; Acheson to Johnson, 31 July 1950, *FRUS*, 6:402.

57. Bradley and Blair, *General's Life*, 547.

58. MacArthur, ca. 20 June 1950, quoted in Heinl, *Victory At High Tide*, 10.

59. Johnson paraphrasing Truman in *MacArthur Hearings*, 2578; DA to CINCFE, 4 Aug. 1950, RG 6, Box 80, MMFL.

60. Walter Waggoner, "Harriman Denies Shift," *NYT*, 9 Aug. 1950, 10; Rudy Abramson, *Spanning The Century: The Life of W. Averell Harriman, 1891–1986* (New York: William Morrow, 1992), 438–45; interview with Acheson, 18 Feb. 1955, Post-Presidential Papers, Box 641, TPL. Harriman officially became "mutual security administrator," a title that understates his place and influence in the Truman administration.

61. Harriman quoted in Goulden, *Korea*, 159; Lippmann quoted and MacArthur mentioned in Abramson, *Spanning the Century*, 445, 451; Harriman, "Oral History," 2, 7, MMFL; CINCFE to Secretary of Defense, 5 Aug. 1950, *FRUS*, 6:423–24; MacArthur to Truman, 4 Aug. 1950, RG 16a, Box 5, MMFL; *NYT*, 7 Aug. 1950, 1.

62. Lowe to Truman, 7 and 8 Feb. 1951, Lowe to Harry Vaughan, 26 March and 27 August 1951, and 25 Jan. 1952: all in PSF, Box 245, TPL; Vaughan, "Oral History," 14 and 16 July 1963, 61–63, TPL; "Truman's Top Korean Expert Defends 'Mac'," *Boston Herald*, 14 Jan. 1952, 1.

63. Truman to Lowe, 1 Nov. 1950, 1 and 29 Dec. 1950 and 5 Jan. 1951; Lowe to Harry Vaughan, 2 Dec. 1950; Lowe, "Presidential Mission to the Philippines, 15 May 1945–1 June 1945"; Lowe to Truman, 7 Feb. 1951: all in PSF, Box 245, TPL.

64. Capt. Thomas Trapnell quoted in Lewis Sorley, *Honorable Warrior: General Harold K. Johnson and the Ethics of Command* (Lawrence: University Press of Kansas, 1998), 36; Lowe to Truman, 12 and 23 July 1950 and 5 and 25 Sept. 1950: all in PSF, Box 245, TPL.

65. Renfrow, "Oral History," 147–50; Lowe to Truman, 12 and 23 July 1950, PSF, Box 245, TPL.

66. Truman to Lowe, 11 Dec. 1950, PSF, Box 245, TPL; Heinl, *Victory at High Tide*, 134, 193; Clifton La Bree, *The Gentle Warrior: General Oliver Prince Smith, USMC* (Kent: Kent State University Press, 2001), 120, 151, 200.

67. Quote on compound from Kennan, *Memoirs*, 403; Truman quoted in Harriman, "Oral History," 8, MMFL; Harriman, mid-May 1975, in Francis Heller, ed., *The Korean War: A 25 Year Perspective* (Lawrence: Regents Press of Kansas, 1977), 25; "Extracts of Memorandum of Conversation by Harriman," 20 August 1950, *FRUS*, 7:543, is not as detailed as Harriman's memory of events but it is a contemporary document that substantiates his recall of the same event whether speaking in 1954, 1975, or 1977.

68. Secretary of the Army Frank Pace, "Oral History," Jan.-June 1972, 73, TPL and Pace, "Oral History," 12 June 1977, 14, 19, MMFL.

69. Sebald, *With MacArthur in Korea*, 124.

70. Martin Sommers, "The Reconversion of Douglas MacArthur," *Saturday Evening Post* (25 May 1946): 212; MacArthur, 10 May 1950, cited in C. L. Sulzberger, *Seven Continents and Forty Years: A Concentration of Memoirs* (New York: Quadrangle, 1977), 105; Sorley, *Honorable Warrior*, 36; Major General Charles A. Willoughby and John Chamberlain, *MacArthur, 1941–1951* (New York: McGraw-Hill, 1954), 184, 191, 193.

71. Muccio, "Oral History," 73, 79, TPL; O. P. Smith, "Oral History," 29; quotes from Roger Egeberg, "Oral History," 30 June 1971, 13, 26–27, and Eisenhower, "Oral History," 7: all in MMFL; Perret, *Old Soldiers Never Die*, 411–14; General George Kenney Diary, 17 Sept. 1944, MMFL; Egeberg, *The General*, 113, and Eisenhower, *At Ease*, 214.

72. For double envelopment at Lae, see *Reports of General MacArthur: Vol. 2, Part 1: Japanese Operations in the Southwest Pacific Area* (Washington: U.S. Gov. Printing Office. 1966), 216; MacArthur, *Reminiscences*, 178.

73. MacArthur quoted and Nationalists cited in *NYT*, 3 Aug. 1950, 6; "Extracts of Memorandum of Conversations by Harriman and MacArthur, August 6 and 8, 1950," *FRUS*, 6:429; Michael M. Sheng, "Beijing's Decision to Enter the Korean War," *Korea and World Affairs* XIX (Summer 1995): 298; Gen. Burns and Captain Grem, "Defense of Formosa," 24 July 1950, State Department, Selected Records Korea, Box 6, TPL; JCS to CINCFE 25 July and CINCFE to JCS, 26 July 1950, RG 6, Box 8, MMFL.

74. Edward J. Drea, *MacArthur's Ultra: Codebreaking and the War against Japan, 1942–1945* (Lawrence: University Press of Kansas, 1992), esp. 59, 71, 223, 230; "Extracts of Memorandum of Conversations by Harriman and MacArthur, August 6 and 8, 1950," *FRUS*, 6:429; Vernon Walters, *Silent Missions* (Garden City: Doubleday, 1978), 190–201; Walter's comment about "hair on end" is in PBS videofilm, *The American Experience: Douglas MacArthur*, Part 2; Ridgway, *Korean War*, 143; Truman quoted in Harriman, "Oral History," 8, MMFL.

75. Harriman's memorandum reprinted in Truman, *Memoirs*, 2:349–53, quotation on 352–53; Truman and Bradley quoted in Harriman, "Oral History," 8–9, MMFL; Abramson, *Spanning The Century*, 453–54; Johnson quoted by Harriman, 4 Feb. 1954, *Princeton University Seminar*, reel 5, track 2, 7.

76. Frank Pace, "Oral History," 81, TPL; Collins to MacArthur, 29 June 1950; MacArthur to DA, 3 July and 7 July 1950: all in RG 9, Box 11, MMFL; Pace, "Oral History," 27–28 April, 1975, 15, USMHI.

77. Bradley and Blair, *General's Life*, 544; Omar Bradley, *A Soldier's Story* (New York: Henry Holt, 1951), 272. The best book yet written on this subject states that "Bradley, more than any other American commander, was responsible for the near defeat and heavy losses at Omaha Beach," see Adrian R. Lewis, *Omaha Beach: A Flawed Victory* (Chapel Hill: University of North Carolina Press, 2001), 157.

78. Collins to MacArthur, 22 July 1950 and CUNCFE to JCS, 23 July 1950, JCS, GF, 1948–50, RG 218, Box 22, NA; Telecon Conference, Washington and CINCFE, 24 July 1950, RG 9, Telecons, 17–34, MMFL; Bradley interview, 30 March 1955, Post-Presidential Papers, Box 641, TPL; Merry, *Taking On World*, 199; Heinl, *Victory at High Tide*, 70, 79; JCS to CINCFE, 12 Sept. 1950, RG 16a, Box 5, MMFL.

79. Collins. *War in Peacetime*, 35; Howard Schonberger, *Aftermath of War: Americans and the Remaking of Japan, 1945–1952* (Kent, Ohio: Kent State University Press, 1989), 69–70.

80. Johnson at *MacArthur Hearings*, 2618; Sherman described by LTG Lemuel Shepherd; Doyle and Almond quoted: all in Heinl, *Victory at High Tide*, 40, 43, and Duffy and Carpenter, *Warrior and Wordsmith*, 86–87, 92.

81. Doyle and MacArthur quoted in Heinl, *Victory at High Tide*, 38–40; E. B. Potter, *Admiral Arleigh Burke* (New York: Random House, 1990), 339; Edward Drea, "Military Intelligence and MacArthur," in Leary, ed., *MacArthur and American Century*, 19; Smith quoted in James, *Years of MacArthur*, 3:467.

82. Gen. George Kenny, MacArthur WWII air component commander, quoted in James, *Years of MacArthur*, 2:666; Muccio, "Oral History," 93, TPL; MacArthur quoted in Paul Rogers, *The Bitter Years: MacArthur and Sutherland* (New York: Praeger, 1991), 287; MacArthur cited in Harriman, "Oral History," 10 Jan. 1980, 10, TPL.

83. Collins, *War in Peacetime*, 81–83; statements at Wake Island Conference, 15 Oct. 1950, *FRUS*, 7:953; Clay Blair, *The Forgotten War: America in Korea, 1950–1953* (New

York: Times Books, 1987), 224; army chief of staff to CINCFE, 4 Aug. 1950, RG 5, Box 3, and CINCFE to DA, 8 Sept. 1950, RG 16a, Box 5: both in MMFL.

84. For Walker, see John Toland, *In Mortal Combat: Korea, 1950–1953* (New York: William Morrow, 1991), 207, 339; Sherman quoted in Schnabel and Watson, *History of JCS, Korean War*, 1:213; MacArthur quoted in Appleman, *South to Naktong, North to Yalu*, 495.

85. J. Lawton Collins, *Lightning Joe: An Autobiography* (Baton Rouge: Louisiana State University, 1979), 63, 70–72, 176; Bradley and Blair, *General's Life*, 471–72, 505. Since the Goldwater-Nichols Act of 1986, theater commanders directly report to and receive orders from the National Command Authority, meaning the president of the United States and the secretary of defense. Previously, the Joint Chiefs of Staff was the directing authority. It dealt with theater commanders through its member of the same service. Because MacArthur was an army general, Collins was the JCS executive agent.

86. Collins quoted in spring 1983, *CSI Report, No. 5, Conversations with General J. Lawton Collins* (Combat Studies Institute, U.S. Army Command and General Staff College, n.d.), 11; testimony of Collins at *MacArthur Hearings*, 1301; "Memorandum of conversation between MacArthur and Robert Murphy," 30 April 1952, Acheson Papers, Box 63, TPL. Other examples of young chiefs of staffs causing large retirements of the "gray beards" occurred when Harold K. Johnson became chief in 1963 and Edward ("Shy") Meyer in 1979.

87. Truman, ca. Jan. 1962, quoted in Robert Alan Aurthur, "Harry Truman Chuckles Dryly," *Esquire* 76 (Sept. 1971), 259; Smith, "Oral History," 13 and 23; MacArthur quoted in Heinl, *Victory at High Tide*, 134.

88. MacArthur to Truman, 12 Aug. 1950, Lowe Papers, Box 1, MMFL; Truman to Lowe 2 Feb. 1951, Lowe to Truman, 8 Aug., 22 Oct., and 15 Dec. 1950; Lowe described in Tommy Reed to Mary Lou [Lowe], 17 Jan. 1951, all in PSF, Box 245, and in Renfrow, "Oral History," 150–51: all in TPL.

89. Bradley and Blair, *General's Life*, 545, 547.

90. Truman Diary, 14 May 1934, PSF, Box 334, TPL; Truman quoted in Hillman, *Mr. President*, 102; for Hannibal's operation as described in a book on Truman's bookshelf, see [Abbott], *Makers of Modern History, Hannibal*, 76–77; Truman in 1959 quoted in Weber, ed., *Talking with Harry*, 95; Freeman, *Lee*: 2:199; for Truman's memory about history see, Dennison, "Oral History," 48, 94, and Chace, *Acheson*, 155; Truman, *Memoirs*, 2:348.

91. Truman, *Off the Record*, 193.

92. Truman, *Memoirs*, 2:358; McFarland and Roll, *Johnson and Arming of America*, 420n65.

93. Johnson in 1949 quoted in George W. Baer, *One Hundred Years of Sea Power: The U.S. Navy, 1890–1990* (Stanford: Stanford University Press, 1994), p; for force structure statistics and quote from anonymous marine per Midway, see Heinl, *Victory at High Tide*, 7, 48, and Duffy and Carpenter, *Warrior and Wordsmith*, 83–85; Sgt. Robert Dews quoted in Knox, *Korea War, Oral History*, 1:50.

94. Commandant Clifton Gates and Truman quoted in Franklin Mitchell, "An Act of Presidential Indiscretion: Harry S. Truman, Congressman McDonough and the Marine Corps Incident of 1950," *Presidential Studies Quarterly* 11 (Feb. 1981): 566–67; Lowe quoted and incidents described in Davis, *Marine*, 242, and Jon T. Hoffman, *Chesty: The Story of Lieutenant General Lewis B. Puller* (New York: Random House, 2001), 357, 368–69.

95. Joe and Stuart Alsop column, 13 Feb. 1950, and Johnson quoted in Merry, *Taking on World*, 181, 190; Ayers, *Diary*, 326; Truman, Feb. 1949, paraphrased by David Lilienthal

as quoted in Borowski, *Hollow Threat*, 156; Columnist Marquis Childs quoted in James Bell, "Defense Secretary Louis Johnson," *The American Mercury* 70 (June 1950), 653; Pearson, *Pearson Diaries*, 62, 131, 233.

96. Truman quoted in McFarland and Roll, *Johnson and Arming of America*, 171, and in Marshall, *Interviews and Reminiscences*, 4:421; for Truman's comments on his staff and Johnson, see Dennison, "Oral History," 47; for Johnson on preventive war, 6 July 1950, see Anthony Cave Brown, *Treason in the Blood: H. St. John Philby, Kim Philby, and the Spy Case of the Century* (Boston: Houghton Mifflin, 1994), 414; E. Roosevelt to Truman and Truman to Roosevelt, 9 August and 22 August 1950, Official File, 471-B, White House Central Files, TPL.

97. Acheson, *Present at the Creation*, 549–50; Collins, 25 May 1951, *MacArthur Hearings*, 1217; for entire letter to VFW, see *FRUS*, 1950, 6:451–53; MacArthur's comments in Whitney, *MacArthur*, 379–81; MacArthur to DA, "personal for President Truman," 20 July 1950, RG 16a, Box 5, MMFL.

98. MacArthur to Roy Howard and to Hugh Baillie, both 21 Aug. 1950, RG 5, Boxes 28 and 57, MMFL; MacArthur, "Formosa Must Be Defended," *U.S. News and World Report* 32 (1 Sept. 1950): 34–35; MacArthur, 30 Aug. 1941, quoted in Marshall to FDR, 9 Sept. 1941, *Papers of Marshall*, 2:604; Charley Ross cited in DA to CINCFE, 21 July 1950, RG 9, Korean War File, MMFL.

99. "Special Message to Congress . .," 19 July 1950, *PPOPT*, 531; Acheson to Embassy in India, 3 Aug. 1950, and Secretary of State to Under Secretary. 27 Aug. 1950, *FRUS*, 7:526; 6:453; MacArthur, 3 June 1950, in conversation with British Admiral Patrick quoted in Cumings, *Origins of Korean War* 2:542 and 874n110; UK ambassador quoted in Secretary of State to Embassy in UK, 13 Aug. 1950, *FRUS*, 7:419.

100. Truman's position described in Collins, *War in Peacetime*, 275; Truman's statement and Harriman's memorandum reprinted in Truman, *Memoirs*, 2:351–52, 355.

101. MacArthur to VFW, 20 Aug. 1950, *FRUS*, 6:452–53; Acheson to Johnson, 31 July 1950, ibid., 6:402, 452–53; George Elsey, "Memorandum For File," 26 Aug. 1950, in Merrill, ed., *Documentary History of Truman Presidency*, 20:418–26; Ayers, *Diary*, 368.

102. Truman, *Memoirs*, 2:457; McCullough, *Truman*, 172, 423, 447; Truman to Lowe, 11 Aug. 1950, PSF, Box 245, TPL; Truman, Diary, 21 June 1951, in Truman, *Off the Record*, 213; McCarthy to MacArthur, 29 Aug. 1950, RG 10, Folder 55, MMFL.

103. Truman, *Memoirs*, 2:355, 430; Johnson, 14 June 1951, describing MacArthur at *MacArthur Hearings*, 2587, 2590, 2617; Truman, January 1962, in Aurthur, "Truman Chuckles Dryly," 260.

104. Truman Diary notation, ca. 1 Jan. 1953, PSF, Box 334, TPL; Johnson, 14 June 1951, at *MacArthur Hearings*, 2603; Acheson, "Memorandum for Record of Events," 26 Aug. 1950, Merrill, ed., *Documentary History of Truman Presidency*, 20:21–26; Acheson to Truman, 25 July 1955, in Dean Acheson, *Among Friends: Personal Letters of Dean Acheson*, ed. David S. McLellan and David C. Acheson (New York: Dodd, Mead and Comp., 1980), 101–102; Acheson, 10 Oct. 1954, quoting Truman on Johnson at *Princeton University Seminar*, reel 4, track 2, 12.

105. James Warner, "White House Explains Order," *NYHT*, 29 Aug. 1950, 1, 4.

106. MacArthur (Personal) for Johnson, 27 Aug. 1950, RG 5, Military Correspondence, MMFL; Truman to MacArthur, 29 August 1950, printed in *MacArthur Hearings*, 3480.

107. MacArthur (Personal) for Johnson, 27 Aug. 1950, RG 5, Military Correspondence; Lowe to Truman, 11 Sept. 1950, Lowe Papers, Box 1B: both in MMFL.

108. Ayers, *Diary*, 369; Truman Diary, 14 Sept 1950, in Truman, *Off the Record*, 193; Truman quoted in Goulden, *Korea*, 163.

109. Merry, *Taking on the World*, 201; Truman to Bess Truman, 7 Sept. 1950, in Truman, *Off the Record*, 189; Heinl, *Victory at High Tide*, 87.

The War against North Korea

1. Ridgway to Morris MacGregor, Ridgway MSS, Box 53, USMHI.

2. Quotation in Heinl, *Victory at High Tide*, 24.

3. Ridgway, *Korean War*, 143; JCS messages, 28 August to 7 Sept. 1950, in Schnabel and Watson, *History of JCS, Korean War*, 1:211–13; quote from Gen. [then LTC] James H. Polk, "Oral History," 9 Dec. 1971, 26, USMHI; Heinl, *Victory at High Tide*, 19; James, *Years of MacArthur*, 3:474–75; Frank Pace, "Oral History," 15, MMFL.

4. MacArthur, *Reminiscences*, 351–52; Lowe to Vaughan, 27 Aug. 1950, PSF, Box 245, TPL.

5. Truman notation on Lowe to Vaughan, 27 Aug. 1950, cited above; Sherman and Burke quoted in Potter, *Burke*, 336–37, 340; MacArthur quoted right after Inchon in Davis, *Marine*, 241; Burke, 5 Oct. 1950, in "Burke Speaks Out on Korea," *Proceedings of the United States Naval Institute* 126 (May 2000): 71.

6. Issue discussed and Smith and MacArthur quoted in Heinl, *Victory at High Tide*, 3, 40, 44–45, 74, 259–61; "Burke Speaks Out on Korea," 69.

7. [Then] Major Vernon A. Walters, Harriman's aide and translator, "Memorandum of Conversation with General MacArthur," 6 August 1950, in Averell Harriman Papers, Box 306, Library of Congress; also see MacArthur to JCS, 8 Sept. 1950, in Appleman, *South To Naktong, North To Yalu*, 495; MacArthur quoted in Almond, "Oral History," 17, MMFL.

8. "Extracts of Memorandum of Conversation by Harriman," 20 Aug. 1950, FRUS, 7:543; MacArthur at 23 Aug. 1950 Tokyo conference on Inchon in *Reminiscences*, 350; Bradley to Johnson, 7 Sept. 1950, FRUS, 7:540.

9. Potter, *Burke*, 337; comments of MG Oliver Smith, commander of the (Inchon assault) 1st Marine Division and Rear Adm. James H. Doyle, naval task force commander: both quoted in David Chisholm, "Negotiated Joint Command Relationships," *Naval War College Review* 53 (Spring 2000): 93–94; Collins, *War in Peacetime*, 115.

10. General John H. Michaelis, "Oral History," 1 June 1977, 32, 35, MMFL; Wilson A. Heefner, *Patton's Bulldog: The Life and Service of General Walton H. Walker* (Shippensburg, Pa.: White Maine, 2001), 323; Toland, *In Mortal Combat*, 130, Walker quoted on 205; Heinl, *Victory at High Tide*, 147–48.

11. Almond described in General Frank T. Mildren, "Oral History," 24 May 1977, 7–8, MMFL and in Alexander Haig, *Inner Circles: How America Changed the World, A Memoir* (New York: Warner Books, 1992), 44; "Sic 'Em, Ned," *Time Magazine*, 51 (23 Oct. 1950): 29; Almond quoted in Margaret Almond to MacArthur, 12 April 1951, RG 10, Box 28, MMFL; for Almond's 90 day objective, see Heinl, *Victory at High Tide*, 157, 210–11; Connaughton, *Battle For Manila*, 83, 83, 179–87, 203.

12. Eugene Lynch, Walker's personal military pilot, cited in Dean Nowowiejski, "Comrades in Arms: The Influence of George S. Patton on Walton H. Walker's Pusan Perimeter Defense," unpublished paper, 2001, 12–13, USMHI; undated map in file operations order, JCS, GF, 1948–50, Box 43, NA; MacArthur to Ridgway, 4 Feb. 1951, RG 16a, Box 5, MMFL.

13. MacArthur, Shepherd, and Almond, quoted in *Victory at High Tide*, 199–200, 239; La Bree, *Smith*, 126, 129; final quotes in Knox, *Korean War: Oral History*, 1:293, 299.

14. MacArthur, *Reminiscences*, 350; Schnabel, *Policy and Direction*, 187n27; Schnabel and Watson, *History of JCS, Korean War*, 1:230.

15. Quoted in Isaacson and Thomas, *The Wise Men*, 532.

16. Polk, "Oral History," 25.

17. Harriman, "Oral History," 11–12, MMFL; Collins, *War in Peacetime*, 141, 158; newspapers quoted in JCS to MacArthur, 16 Sept. 1950, Merrill, ed., *Documentary History of Truman Presidency*, 18:475–76; Collins, mid-May 1975 in Heller, ed., *Korean War: 25 Year Perspective*, 25.

18. "Memorandum of Conversation by Special Asst. to Ambassador at Large Jessup," 25 Aug. 1950, *FRUS*, 7:646–48; Bradley, 23 Oct. 1950, quoted in Schnabel and Watson, *History of JCS. Korean War*, 1:263; Ridgway, *Korean War*, p, 61; Acheson, *Present at the Creation*, 447, 467; Lowe to Vaughan, 15 Sept. 1950, and to Truman, 16 Sept. 1950, PSF, Box 245, TPL.

19. Baldwin, "MacArthur—II," *NYT*, 29 March 1951, 3.

20. Appleman, *South to the Naktong, North to the Yalu*, 256, 392, 546–47; Field, *History of US Naval Operations: Korea*, 212; for testimony from postwar defectors about the effects of naval gunfire, see South Korean film documentary, *Korean War*, reel 2, *Tempest*.

21. Collins, *War in Peacetime*, 105, 113, 141, 155; MacArthur, late 1952, quoted in Hunt, *Untold Story of MacArthur*, 268; MacArthur to Major General Richard Stephens, 15 Nov. 1957, RG 10, Box 142, MMFL.

22. JCS to MacArthur and MacArthur to DA, both 8 Sept. 1950, RG 16a, Box 5, MMFL; Vaughan to Lowe 30 September 1950, PSF, Box 245, TPL; Frank Pace. "Oral History," 98, TPL; "Extracts of Memorandum of Conversation by Harriman," 20 Aug. 1950, *FRUS*, 7:543.

23. Truman at White House Conference, 29 June 1950, Merrill, ed., *Documentary History of Truman Presidency*, 18:123; Report by NSC to President, 9 Sept. 1950, *FRUS*, 7:719; PFC Victor Fox quoted in Knox, *Korean War, Oral History*, 1:324.

24. Knox, *Korean War: Oral History*, 1:421.

25. MacArthur quoted in Merry, *Taking On World*, 201; Kennan, *Memoirs*, 332; Truman, *Memoirs*, 2:106; James I. Matray, "Ensuring Korea's Freedom: The Decision to Cross the 38th Parallel," *Journal of American History* 66 (Sept. 1979): 325–27; American Institute of Public Opinion Survey, 13 Oct. 1950, cited in *Public Opinion Quarterly* 15 (Spring 1951): 170.

26. Department of Defense (DOD), "Draft Memorandum," 31 July 1950, *FRUS*, 7:509; Rep. Hugh Scott (Rep.-Pa.) quoted in *NYHT*, 22 Sept. 1950, 4; Rusk, *As I Saw It*, 23, 51–52; Kennan, *Memoirs*, 515–16.

27. JCS to MacArthur, 27 Sept. 1950, in Schnabel and Watson, *History of JCS, Korean War*, 1:230; "Draft Report by NSC on Courses of Action with Respect to Korea," 1 Sept. 1950, and DOD Draft Memorandum, "U.S. Courses of Action in Korea," 31 July 1950, *FRUS*, 7:687–88, 502–10; conversation between Acheson and Lucius Battle, ca. 27 Sept. 1950, in Isaacson and Thomas, *The Wise Men*, 532–33.

28. Louis J. Halle, *The Cold War as History* (New York: Harper and Row, 1967), 220; Acheson, 21 Sept. 1950, *FRUS*, 7:746.

29. Marshall, *Interviews and Reminiscences*, 2:13, 92–95, statement to Eisenhower on 338; Marshall to Theo. Roosevelt, Jr., 22 Dec. 1941, *Papers of Marshall*, 3:28; Marshall paraphrased and described in John Hull, "Oral History," 2:35–36, 3:21,33, 47–48; Kennan, *Memoirs*, 402; *Marshall Interviews and Reminiscences*, 222, 345, 573. Like Forrest Pogue, Marshall's biographer, I put no credence in the apocryphal story that Marshall told MacArthur that his military staff was a "court," despite Dean Acheson's claim that Marshall personally told him of this incident, *Present at the Creation*, 424.

30. For regret, see John Sutherland, "The Story General Marshall Told Me," *U.S. News and World Report* 47 (Nov. 2, 1959): 54; JCS to MacArthur, 27 Sept., Marshall to MacArthur, 29 Sept., and MacArthur to JCS for Secretary of Defense, 30 Sept. 1950: all in Schnabel and Watson, *History of JCS, Korean War,* 1:230, 242–43; MacArthur to DA, 28 Sept. and 1 Oct. 1950, RG 16, Box 5, MMFL.

31. Marshall to MacArthur and MacArthur to Marshall, both 1 Oct. 1950, RG 5, Box 37, MMFL; Nitze in *Princeton University Seminar,* 13 Feb. 1954, Reel 4 Track 1, page 8, Acheson assented to this statement.

32. Lowe to Truman, 8 Oct. 1950, PSF, Box 253, TPL; Acheson, *Present at Creation,* 456.

33. MacArthur quoted in Muccio, "Oral History," 79–80, 88, and 92; Marshall to MacArthur, 10 Oct. 1950, RG 16a, Box 5, MMFL; for the domestic political background, see John Edward Wiltz, "Truman and MacArthur: The Wake Island Meeting," *Military Affairs* 42 (Dec. 1978): 169–76; Charles Murphy quoted and Wake Island described in Donovan, *Truman Presidency,* 2:265, 284.

34. Harriman, "Oral History, 10, TPL; Harriman, "Oral History," 14, MMFL; Pace, "Oral History," 99, TPL.

35. Truman (1952) in Hillman, *Mr. President,* 102; Wake Island described and MacArthur quoted in Harriman, "Oral History," 14, MMFL.

36. Acheson, "Meeting with President," 9 and 19 Oct. 1950, Merrill, ed., *Documentary History of Truman Presidency,* 18:530, 598; Sulzberger, *Long Row of Candles,* 501; Dean Rusk, "Oral History," ca. 1986, 5, Rusk Papers, University of Georgia; Truman describing MacArthur in unpublished drafts of Truman's *Memoirs,* Box 22, TPL.

37. Donovan, *Truman Presidency,* 2:284; Pace, "Oral History," 106, TPL; Bradley and Blair, *A General's Life,* 576.

38. MacArthur, 21 Oct. 1945, in Truman, *Memoirs,* 1:521; MacArthur, 15 Oct. 1950, at Wake Island in *FRUS,* 7:949.

39. Pace, "Oral History," 11, MMFL; MacArthur quoted in *NYT,* 16 Oct. 1950, 5.

40. Truman quoted in Donovan, *Truman Presidency,* 2:285; NSC, 1 July 1950, quoted and issue discussed in Shu Guang Zhang, *Deterrence and Strategic Culture,* 85–88; Secretary of State to Embassy, India, 1 Sept. 1950, *FRUS,* 6:478–80; Indian Ambassador to China paraphrasing Chinese general on 25 September 1950 in Goulden, *Korea,* 281; JCS to MacArthur, 9 Oct. 1950, reprinted in Truman, *Memoirs,* 2:362.

41. Truman, 1 July 1950, in Ayers, *Diary,* 360; intelligence estimates in Schnabel, *Policy and Direction,* 179, 199; Willoughby's statements on 12, 14, 20, and 24 Oct. 1950 about limitations of theater intelligence assets in Goulden, *Korea,* 280, 284, and Patrick C. Roe, *The Dragon Strikes: China and the Korean War, June-December 1950* (Novato: Presidio, 2000), 116–17, 119.

42. "Substance of Statements Made at Wake Island Conference on 15 Oct. 1950," *FRUS,* 7:953; Weber, ed., *Talking with Harry,* 194.

43. Connaughton, *MacArthur and Defeat in Philippines,* 87, 142; Bradley and Blair, *General's Story,* 577; Collins, *War in Peacetime,* 173; MacArthur, 8 and 24 Dec. 1950, quoted in Schnabel, *Policy and Direction,* 285, and *NYT,* 25 Dec. 1950, 4.

44. Rusk, "Formosa," 14 Oct. 1950, State Department, Selected Records Korea, Box 7, TPL; News Conference, 19 October 1950, PPOPT, 679.

45. Harriman, "Oral History," 20 June 1977, 20, MMFL; News Conference, 19 October 1950, PPOPT, 679; Bradley interview, 30 March 1955, Post-Presidential Papers, Box 641, TPL; MacArthur describing Rusk, according to a state department officer, in *Princeton University Seminar,* 13 Oct. 1954, reel 5, track 2, 3, TPL; Rusk, "Oral History," 4.

46. John Muccio quoted in Wiltz, "Truman and MacArthur," 173; "Memorandum of Conversation [with Chinese informant], Prepared in Dep't of State," 2 Feb. 1951, *FRUS*, 7:1558; Jessup to Acheson, 9 Oct. 1950, *FRUS*, 7:916; Philip Jessup, "Oral History," 14 July 1977, 7, MMFL.

47. Mao quoted in Zhang, *Deterrence and Strategic Culture*, 21; speech by Wu Hsiu-Chan, special representative of PRC, at UN Security Council, 28 Nov. 1950, in *Important Documents Concerning the Question of Taiwan* (Peking, Foreign Languages Press, 1956), 36–37; *Isvestia* quoted in NYT, 16 Oct, 1950, 5; China newspapers described in Netherlands to Secretary of State, 17 Oct. 1950, *FRUS*, 7:974.

48. Bradley, *Soldier's Story*, ix and Bradley and Blair, *General's Life*, 583–84; Willoughby, "Oral History," 10 July 1971, 2, MMFL; Muccio, "Oral History," 89–90.

49. Willoughby, "Oral History," 3; Willoughby to MacArthur, 10 June 1938, and MacArthur to Willoughby, July 20, 1938, RG 1, Box 2, MMFL; *Outline of the Military History Course* (Infantry School, n.d.), 1, 12.

50. Willoughby described in Hanson Baldwin, "MacArthur-1," *NYT*, 28 March 1950, 4; Willoughby, *Maneuver In War* (Harrisburg: Military Service Publishing Co., 1939), 196, 205; Memorandum for Secretary Lovett, "Brief of MacArthur's Groups-2 Estimate, Korean Situation," 13 November 1951, and Memorandum for Record, "Chinese Communist Intervention in Korea," 10 November 1951: both in RG 330, Box 180, NA. In August 1995, LTG (Ret.) Philip Davidson told me that in 1950–51, as a newly minted lieutenant colonel, he privately briefed MacArthur about the enemy order of battle with no superior intelligence office present. When he left the room, Willoughby grabbed him and demanded to know, "What did he say?"

51. Ridgway quoted in Heefner, *Patton's Bulldog*, 276; intelligence summary quoted in Roy Appleman, *Disaster in Korea: The Chinese Confront MacArthur* (College Station, Texas A and M University Press, 1989), 41 MacArthur, 5 Sept. 1949, quoted in Finkelstein, *Taiwan Dilemma*, 224; unidentified Marine Corps senior officer quoted and issue discussed in Roe, *Dragon Strikes*, 53, 197; report by Barr, early 1949, in *China White Paper*, 338; Barr described by LTG Albert Wedemeyer, 1 March 1948, in Forrestal, *Diaries*, 383; Almond to LTC Don C. Faith, 28 Nov. 1950, quoted in Russell A Gugeler, ed., *Combat Actions in Korea* (Washington: Combat Forces Press, 1954), 69.

52. Harriman in Heller, ed., *Korean War: 25 Year Perspective*, 33; Michaelis, "Oral History," 13; CINCUNC [United Nations Command] to CG Eighth Army et. al., 24 Oct., JCS to CINCFE, 24 Oct., and CINCFE to JCS, 25 Oct. 1950: all in Schnabel and Watson, *History of JCS, Korean War*, 1:274–76; Collins, *War in Peacetime*, 177; Bradley at *MacArthur Hearings*, 928.

53. News Conference, 26 Oct. 1950, PPOPT, 691; MacArthur to Truman, 30 Oct. 1950, Merrill, ed., *Documentary History of Truman Presidency*, 20:52.

54. "Estimate of the Most Probable Course of Soviet-Chinese Action With Regard to Korea," 17 Nov. 1950, *FRUS*, 7:1188.

55. Appleman, *South to Naktong, North to Yalu*, chapters 13 and 14; "Mao's Dispatch of Chinese Forces to Korea, July–October 1950" and "Mao's Telegrams During the Korean War, October–December 1950," in *Chinese Historians* 5 (Spring and Summer 1992), 1:73–74, 2:67; MacArthur to Dept. of Army, 6 Nov. 1950 in Schnabel and Watson, *History of JCS, Korean War*, 1:293.

56. Schnabel and Watson, *History of JCS, Korean War*, 1:290–93; "Memorandum of conversation between MacArthur and Robert Murphy," 30 April 1952, Acheson Papers, Box 63, TPL; Bradley to Marshall, 9 November 1950; NSC Report to the President, 9 Sept.1950; and JCS to CINCFE, 6 Nov. 1950: all in *FRUS*, 7:718, 1057, 1120.

57. Messages in Truman, *Memoirs*, 2:375–76.

58. Frederick Shedden (secretary for War Cabinet of Australia) describing MacArthur in mid-Jan. 1943, as quoted in David Horner, "MacArthur: An Australian Perspective," in Leary, ed., *MacArthur and American Century*, 116; MacArthur to Marshall, 8 Nov. 1950, RG 16a, Box 5, MMFL; MacArthur, 5 Sept. 1949, quoted in Finkelstein, *Taiwan Dilemma*, 224; MacArthur to Marshall, 30 Aug. 1942, quoted in Marshall, *Interviews and Reminiscences*, 2:386.

59. MacArthur to Roy Howard, 20 Dec. 1950, RG 5, Box 28, MMFL; MacArthur, *Reminiscences*, 166; DA to MacArthur, 9 Nov. 1950, RG 9, Box 45, MMFL.

60. MacArthur to DA, 7 and 9 November 1950, *FRUS*, 7:1076–77, 1107–10; Egeberg, *The General*, 37; Joint Intelligence Committee, "Estimate of Situation in Korea," 13 July 1950, JCS, GF, 1948–50, RG 218, Box 39, NA; FEC Survey Group Formosa to CINCFE, 6 and 8 Sept. 1950, RG 9, Box 41, MMFL.

61. MacArthur to DA, 9 November 1950, and "Substance of Statements made at Wake Island," 15 Oct. 1950, *FRUS*, 7:949, 1107–10; Roe, *Dragon Strikes*, 175.

62. For quotes from 19th Century English imperialists, see V. G. Kiernan, *Colonial Empires and Armies: 1815–1960* (Great Britain: Sutton, 1998), 144, 157–59, 192; Arthur MacArthur described by a superior officer in James, *Years of MacArthur*, 1:26–27; MacArthur, *Reminiscences*, 31.

63. Kiernan, *Colonial Empires and Armies*, 160; handwritten draft of VFW message in RG 16a, Box 5, MMFL; draft by John Allison and John Emerson of Office of Northeast Asian Affairs, 21 Aug. 1950, *FRUS*, 7:620; MacArthur's communiqués, 24 and 25 November, printed Heefner, *Patton's Bulldog*, 282, 284.

64. Pat Roe, the S-2, letter to this author, 27 Dec. 2002; LTC William McCaffrey quoted in Heefner *Patton's Bulldog*, 247; MacArthur quoted in Whitney, *MacArthur*, 509.

65. Truman Diary, 17 June 1945, in Truman, *Off the Record*, 47.

66. James Bamford, *Body of Secrets: Anatomy of the Ultra-Secret National Security Agency from the Cold War through the Dawn of a New Century* (New York: Doubleday, 2001), 28–29; Roe, *Dragon Strikes*, 135, 163, 196, 258, 265; Millett, *War for Korea*, 245; author's personal interviews with (then) Captain Joe Pizzi, (in charge of enemy order-of-battle for Eighth Army in Korea), 26 Feb. 1996, and (then) LTC Phillip Davidson (in charge of enemy order-of-battle at military headquarters, Far East Command), 23 August 1995; CIA, "National Intelligence Estimate," 24 Nov. 1950, *FRUS*, 7:1221.

67. La Bree, *Smith*, 145, 156; Potter, *Burke*, 336, 339, 345; Burke in Knox, *Korean War: Oral History*, 1:613; National Intelligence Estimates, 9 and 24 Nov. 1950, *FRUS*, 7:1101–1104, 1220–21.

68. Sheng, "Beijing's Decision to Enter Korean War," 298–304, and Sheng, *Battling Western Imperialism*, 154, 191; for longer quote from Mao and further discussion of the issue, see Zhang, *Deterrence and Strategic Culture*, 15, 21–25; Mao, 28 June 1950, quoted in Tang Tsou, *America's Failure in China, 1941–50* (Chicago: University of Chicago Press, 1963), 561; Rusk to Wellington Koo, 25 July 1950, quoted in Kusnitz, *Public Opinion and Foreign Policy*, 46; "Special Message to Congress," 1 Dec. 1950, *PPOPT*, 730.

69. Mao quoted in Shu Guang Zhang, *Mao's Military Romanticism: China and the Korean War, 1950–1953* (Lawrence: University Press of Kansas, 1995), 63; Roe, *Dragon Strikes*, ix and Roe, "The Ghost Armies of Manchuria," in *Understanding and Remembering*, 89.

70. Sheng, "Beijing's Decision to Enter Korean War," 298–304; Mansourov, "Communist War Coalitions," 341; Stalin quoted and issues discussed in *CWIHPB*, Issues 6–7, Winter 1995–96, esp. 10–11, 60–61, 100.

71. Heinzig, *Soviet Union and Communist China*, 93–94; 208–12, 391; Zhihua, "Sino-Soviet Relations and Origins of Korean War," 65–67; Stalin and Mao, 1 and 6 Oct, in *CWIHPB*, Winter 1995–96, 116, and Winter–Summer 2003–2004, 376–77.

72. Stalin quoted and issue discussed in Heinzig, *Soviet Union and Communist China*, 34–38, 138; message(s) sent to Kremlin, 2 Oct. and 2 Nov. printed Evgeniy Bajanov and Natalia Bajanova, *The Korean Conflict, 1950–1953: The Most Mysterious War of the 20th Century—Based on Secret Soviet Archives* (Institute for Contemporary International Problems, Russian Foreign Ministry, 1998), 81, 98–99, and Sergi N. Goncharov, John W. Lewis, and Xue Litai, *Uncertain Partners: Stalin, Mao, and the Korean War* (Stanford: Stanford University Press, 1993), 177–78.

73. Soviet Ambassador to Stalin, 3 Oct. 1950, in Bajanov and Bajanova, *The Korean Conflict*, 100; Stalin described and Mao quoted in Evgeniy Bajanov, "Assessing the Politics of the Korean War," *CWIHPB*, Winter 1995/1996, 88–89; Mao to Peng Dehuai, 23 Oct. 1950, in "Mao's Dispatch of Troops," 1:80; Short, *Mao*, 290, 321, 324, 343, quote on 360. Mao to Zhou En-lai, 14 Oct. 1950, in "Mao's Dispatch of Chinese Troops," 1:73; "On Protracted War," May 1938, *Selected Military Writings of Mao Tse-tung* (Peking: Foreign Language Press, 1972), 242.

74. Consul General at Hong Kong to Sec. of State, 9 Nov. 1950, *FRUS*, 7:1128; Chinese assessments of U.S. infantry quoted in Appleman, *South To The Naktong, North To The Yalu*, 720, and Roe, *Dragon Strikes*, 230–31; Military Commission to 19th Army Corps, 22 Nov. 1950, in "Mao's Telegrams During Korean War," 2:74; Heefner, *Patton's Bulldog*, 245, 283–84; MacArthur to Walker, 5 Nov. 1950, quoted in U.S. Army, *History of the Far East Command*, 37, provided to author by Patrick Roe.

75. Mao, 3 Oct. 1950, quoted in Bajanov and Bajanova, *The Korean Conflict*, 98, "Mao's Telegrams During Korean War," 72, 74; for splits within CCP, see Zhai, "China and Korean War," 59; unidentified informant on "clique" quoted in "Memorandum of Conversation," 6, 7, 12, and 13 Jan. 1951, *FRUS*, 7:1483; Short, *Mao*, 221–22, 255, 390–95.

76. MacArthur described in Hunt, *Untold Story of MacArthur*, 35–36, 85, and Fellers, "Oral History," 14; Acheson, *Present at Creation*, 424; informant in "Memorandum of Conversation," Jan. 1951, *FRUS, 1950*, 7:1483.

77. *World Culture*, 31 Oct. 1950, quoted in Allen S. Whiting, *China Crosses the Yalu: The Decision to Enter the Korean War* (Stanford: Stanford University Press, 1968), 134; Zhou En-lai, ca. 1 Oct. 1950, quoted in Chen Xiaolu, "China's Policy towards the United States, 1945–1955," in Harry Harding and Yuang Ming, ed., *Sino-American Relations, 1945–1955* (Wilmington: Scholarly Books, 1989), 190; transmission from Eastern European cited in *FRUS, 1950*, 7:1197n11; speech by Wu Hsiu-Chaun, 28 Nov. 1950, *Important Documents Concerning Taiwan*, esp. 68–69.

78. For concerns of Truman Administration, see *Princeton University Seminar*, esp. reel 4, tracks 1 and 5; message from consulate to state department, 6 Nov. 1950, reprinted in Karl Lott Rankin, *China Assignment* (Seattle: University of Washington Press, 1964), 65; MacArthur to JCS, 9 Nov. 1950, *FRUS* 7:1108–1109.

79. Bradley at Minutes of 71st Meeting of NSC, 9 Nov. 1950, University Publications of America, microfilm, reel 1; Bradley in conversation with Alsop as quoted in Merry, *Taking On World*, 202; secretary of state to political advisor, Tokyo embassy, 20 Nov. 1950, JCS, GF, 1948–50, RG 218, Box 42.

80. Acheson in Minutes of 71st Meeting of NSC, 9 Nov. 1950, University Publications of America, microfilm, reel 1; Amb. Oliver Franks quoted and issued discussed in Peter N. Farrar, "Britain's Proposal for a Buffer Zone South of the Yalu in November 1950:

Was it a Neglected Opportunity to End the Fighting in Korea?," *Journal of Contemporary History* 18 (Fall 1983): 332–35; Acheson on "first minister" in Paige, *The Korean Decision,* 26; Acheson, 13 Feb. 1954, at Princeton University Seminar, reel 5, track 2. 9.

81. Quotation in Davis, *Marine,* 272; British intelligence officer quoted and issue discussed in Brown, *Treason in the Blood,* 388, 392; MacArthur to JCS, 9 Nov. 1950, *FRUS,* 7, 1108–1109; foreign minister, Ernest Bevin, 30 Aug. 1950, quoted in Stueck, *Rethinking Korean War,* 99.

82. MacArthur, *Reminiscences,* 341; Robert Griffith, *The Politics of Fear: Joseph R. McCarthy and the Senate* (Lexington: University Press of Kentucky, 1970), 100, 126–27, 130–31; Margaret Truman, *Bess Truman,* (New York: Macmillan, 1986), 363–64; Charlie Ross, 13 Nov. 1946, quoted in Hamby, *Man of the People,* 418; Donovan, *Truman Presidency,* 2:298; Truman at Cabinet Meeting, 7 November 1950, Connelly Papers, Box 1, TPL.

83. "'Why I Won' — 'Why I Lost,'" *U.S. News and World Report,* 29 (17 Nov. 1950): 26–33; Dean Acheson, "The Responsibility for Decision in Foreign Policy," *The Yale Review* 44 (Sept. 1954): 12; for Truman on Stuart, see Miler, *Plain Speaking,* 351; Acheson, 13 Feb. 1954, at Princeton University Seminar, reel 5, track 2., 9.

84. Acheson to Ernest Bevin, 16 Nov. 1950, State Department, Selected Records Relating to the Korean War, Box 3, TPL; 'Why I Won' — 'Why I Lost', 27–30; "Conversation with Congressman Clinton D. McKinnon," 5 Dec. 1950, George Elsey Papers, Box 92, TPL; Reston, "U.S. Politics Is a Handicap In U.N. Moves on Red China," *NYT,* 16 Nov. 1950, 6.

85. Renfrow, "Oral History," 131, 135; TPL; Acheson quoted in Chace, *Acheson,* 47, and Isaacson and Thomas, *The Wise Men,* 449.

86. Marshall quoted in "Memorandum of Conversation: Situation in Korea," 21 November 1950, in Merrill, ed., *Documentary History of Truman Presidency,* 19:46; Pace, "Oral History," 117, TPL; Bradley in Minutes of 71st Meeting of NSC, 9 Nov. 1950; University Publications of America, microfilm, reel 1; Acheson quoted in Chace, *Acheson,* 303.

87. Geoffrey Perret, *Lincoln's War: The Untold Story of America's Greatest President as Command in Chief* (New York: Random House, 2004), 316, 326, 340, 394; Acheson, *Present at the Creation,* 467; Ridgeway, "Oral History," 77. At the Senate hearings on MacArthur's dismissal in 1951 no member of the JCS claimed that MacArthur ever violated a military order.

88. Marshall at 9 Nov. 1950 meeting of NSC, University Publications of America, microfilm, reel 1; Maj. General James Burns, 17 Nov., and Marshall, 20 Nov., in Doris M. Condit, *The History of the Office of the Secretary of Defense: The Test of War* (Washington: Office of the Secretary of Defense, 1988), 81–82; John Davies, "The Problem," 17 Nov. 1950, *FRUS,* 7:1180; Short, *Mao,* 409–10.

89. Marshall cited in Secretary of War Henry Stimson Diary, 27 Dec. 1944, reel 9, 127; Marshall to MacArthur, 7 Nov. 1950, in Schnabel and Watson, *History of JCS, Korean War,* 1:296–97 for MacArthur, 21 Nov. 1950, on "jackpot," see Appleman, *South To The Naktong, North To The Yalu,* 736; Farrar, "Britain's Proposal for Buffer Zone," 339–46.

90. For intelligence estimates see Appleman, *South To The Naktong, North To The Yalu,* 762, and Sebald, *With MacArthur In Japan,* 203; Ambassador John J. Muccio, "Memo of Conversation with MacArthur," 17 Nov. 1950, *FRUS* 7:1175; Mao, *On Protracted War* (1938) as quoted in Mansourov, "Communist War Coalition," 55, and Whiting, *China Crosses the Yalu,* 134.

The War against China

1. Diary, 9 Dec. 1950, in Truman, *Off the Record*, 294.

2. CINCFE to JCS in *FRUS*, 7:1237–38.

3. Truman's described in Vaughan, "Oral History," 6; "Wake Island," 25, Nov. 1950, Merrill, ed., *Documentary History of Truman Presidency*, 20:57; Truman in Weber, ed., *Talking with Harry*, 194.

4. Pace "Oral History," 102, TPL; LTC James Tarkenton, Eighth Army assistant chief of staff for operations, quoted in Heefner, *Patton's Bulldog*, 276; Truman to Arthur Schlesinger, Jr., 5 Nov. 1951, in Merrill, ed., *Documentary History of Truman Presidency*, 20:400.

5. Truman, *Memoirs*, 2:384; Truman quoted at NSC Meeting, 28 Nov. 1950, *FRUS*, 7:1245; Hersey, "Profiles: Mr. President," *New Yorker*, 7 April 1951, 1.

6. News Conference, 30 Nov. 1950, *PPOPT*, 726–27; Hersey, "Profiles: Mr. President," 14 April 1951, p, 52; NSC Meeting, 28 Nov. 1950, and DOD-State Meeting, 1 Dec. 1950, *FRUS*, 7:1242–43, 1278.

7. News Conference, 30 Nov. 1950, *PPOPT*, 727; for comments between 1945 and '49, see Ferrell, *Truman: A Life*, 344; Eisenhower quoted in William B. Pickett, *Eisenhower Decides To Run: Presidential Politics and Cold War Strategy* (Chicago: Ivan Dee, 2000), 182; Hersey, "Profiles: Mr. President," 5 May 1951, p, 52.

8. Chargé in UK to Secretary of State, 3 Dec. 1950, *FRUS*, 3:1698; Borowski, *Hollow Threat*, 102–103, 113–17, 121–26, quotes on 129–30; Truman also quoted in Gregg Herken, *The Winning Weapon: The Atomic Bomb in the Cold War, 1945–1950* (New York: Knopf, 1980), 260; Truman at DOD-State Meeting, 1 Dec. 1950, *FRUS*, 7:1248.

9. "Daily Korean Summaries, Nov-Dec. 1950," in PSF, Intelligence File, TPL; Truman, *Memoirs*, 2:399, 402; Truman at 74th Meeting of the NSC, 11 Dec. 1950, PSF, Box 210, TPL.

10. News Conference, 30 Nov. 1950, *PPOPT*, 728; Acheson at NSC Meeting, 28 Nov. 1950, in Merrill, ed., *Documentary History of Truman Presidency*, 19:71, and Beisner, *Dean Acheson*, 411–12; Reston, "U.S. Must Wage Long Fight for Peace, Acheson Holds," *NYT*, 3 Sept. 1946, 4; Charles Reed, chief of State Dep't Division of Southeast Asia, 17 May 1949, quoted and Acheson described in Blum, *Drawing the Line*, 109, 204; Acheson to Collins on 26 June 1950, and Collins at DOD-State Meeting, 1 Dec. 1950: both in *FRUS*, 7:182, 1278.

11. MacArthur quoted in *Washington Post* [hereafter WP], 3 Dec. 1950, 6; Xu Yan, "The Chinese Forces and Their Casualties in the Korean War: Facts and Statistics," *Chinese Historians* 6 (Fall, 1993): 50; Acheson at DOD-State Meeting, 3 Dec. 1950, *FRUS*, 7:1324. At Tobruk (in Libya) some 33,000 British Empire soldiers surrendered to an Axis force half that size. Churchill reacted, "Defeat is one thing, disgrace is another."

12. Ridgway, *Korean War*, 61; Bradley and Blair, *General's Life*, 614; CINCFE [Ridgway] to DA. 12 May 1951, JCS, GF, 1951–53, RG 218, Box 14, NA; Vandenberg to General Stratemeyer, 28 Nov. 1950, RG 9, Box 121, MMFL.

13. "Meeting at the Pentagon," 3 December 1950, and "Memorandum of Conversation of the Executive Secretariat," 3 Dec. 1950: *FRUS*, 7:1330, 1335; for Sept. 1947 army study, see William M. Stueck, Jr., *Road to Confrontation: American Policy Towards China and Korea, 1947–1950*, (Chapel Hill: University of North Carolina Press, 1981), 86; Bradley and Blair, *General's Life*, 613–14.

14. Statements of Marshall and Bradley in Minutes of NSC Meeting, 11 Dec. 1950, PSF, Box 210, TPL; MacArthur at *MacArthur Hearings*, 13–14, 38, 48; DOH [Doyle

Hickey, MacArthur's acting chief of staff], "Memorandum for General Collins," 4 December 1950, RG 46a, Box 5, MMFL.

15. Wright quoted in Roe, *Dragon Strikes*, 385; Collins at White House on 8 December 1950 in *FRUS*. 7:1470.

16. Capt. Norman Allen [5th Cavalry Regiment] to mother, ca. 5 Dec. 1950, in Knox, *Korean War: Oral History*, 1:654; Appleman, *Disaster in Korea*, 441–42, 447–49; Collins, "Memorandum for the JCS: Report on Visit to FECOM and Korea, December 4–7, 1950," 8 Dec. 1950, JCS, GF, 1948–50, RG 218, Box 43, NA; DOH, "Memorandum for General Collins," 4 December 1950, RG 46a, Box 5, MMFL.

17. Marshall at Cabinet Meetings, 5 and 8 Dec. 1950, in Connelly Papers, Box 1. TPL.; DOH, "Memorandum for General Collins," 4 Dec. 1950, and Collins "Memorandum for JCS," 8 Dec. 1950: both in RG 46a, Box 5, MMFL; Lowe to Truman, 1, 3, and 19 Dec. 1950 and 20 and 21 Jan. 1951, PSF, Box 245, TPL.

18. Enlisted men quoted in Russell Spurr, *Enter the Dragon: China's Undeclared War against the U.S. in Korea, 1950–1951* (New York: Henry Holt, 1988), 193, and Knox, *Korean War: Oral History*, 1:654; MacArthur to Roy Howard, 20 Dec. 1950, RG 5, Box 28, MMFL; Report of Joint Plans Committee to JCS, "Possible U.S. Action in Event of Open Hostilities Between United States and China," 8 Dec. 1950, and Report of Joint Policy Committee to JCS, "Strategic Importance of Formosa," 28 Dec. 1950, JCS, GF, 1948–50, RG 218, Boxes 14 and 23, respectively, NA.

19. MacArthur to Walker, 5 Nov. 1950, quoted in Roe, *Dragon Strikes*, 231; CINCFE to DA, 27 Dec. 1950, and DA to CINCFE, 6 Jan. 1951: both in RG 16a, Box 5, MMFL; Sam Walker cited in Nowowiejski, "Comrades In Arms," 24; MacArthur to Roy Howard, 12 Feb. 1951, RG 5, Box 28, MMFL.

20. Hunt, *Untold Story of MacArthur*, 51; Bradley and Blair, *General's Life*, 51; Collins, *War in Peacetime*, 5; Ridgway, "Oral History," 77–78, MacArthur, *Reminiscences*, 81; MacArthur to Ridgway, 23 Dec. 1950, RG 16a, Box 5, MMFL.

21. Earl Blaik, *The Red Blaik Story* (New Rochelle: Arlington House, 1974), 521–22; quote from unnamed officer in Paul F. Braim, *The Will to Win: Life of General James A. Van Fleet* (Annapolis: Naval Institute Press, 2001), 391n16; Blaik to MacArthur, 1 Jan. 1945, general correspondence, reel 330, MMFL.

22. "Memorandum of Conversation, by Lieutenant General Mathew B. Ridgway," 8 Aug. 1950, *FRUS*, 7:541; Ridgway to MacArthur, 27 Sept. 1950, Ridgway Papers, Box 16.

23. Heefner, *Patton's Bulldog*, 154; Heinl, *Victory at High Tide*, 9; press reports discussed in news conference, 28 Dec. 1950, PPOPT, 761; CINCFE to JCS, 30 Dec. 1950, *FRUS*, 7:1631.

24. Truman, *Memoirs*, 2:415; Lindsay Parrott, "M'Arthur Reports," *NYT*, 28 Dec. 1950, 1.

25. CINCFE to JCS, 30 Dec. 1950, *FRUS*, 7:1631; MacArthur quoted in Goulden, *Korea*, 431.

26. Ridgway, *Korean War*, 11, 82, 144–45; Mao, 11 Nov. 1950, quoted in Qiang Zhai, *The Dragon, the Lion, and the Eagle: Chinese/British/American Relations, 1949–1958* (Kent, Ohio; Kent State University Press, 1994), 97; Roy E. Appleman, *Ridgway Duels For Korea* (College Station: Texas A and M University Press, 1990), 36, 588. Ridgway, "Oral History," 16–17.

27. Ridgway, "Oral History," 16–17, Ridgway to Chief of Staff, "Concept of War," 12 Oct. 1950, Ridgway Papers, Box 16; for Ridgway on Truman and Eisenhower, see Jonathan M. Soffer, *General Matthew Bunker Ridgway: From Progressivism to Reaganism, 1895–1993* (Westport: Praeger, 1998), 114.

28. Ridgway, *Soldier*, 41–42; Ridgway, *Korean War*, flyleaf; Ridgway to MacArthur, 9 Jan. 1951, RG 16a, Box 5, MMFL.

29. Diary, 3 Dec 1950, Ridgway Papers, Box 20; Ridgway in *NYT*, 28 Dec. 1950, 3; Sorley, *Honorable Warrior*, 106; Collins to Bradley, 17 Jan. 1951, RG 16a, Box 5, MMFL and Collins to Bradley, 17 Jan. 1951, JCS, GF, 1951–53, RG 218, Box 14, NA.

30. Ridgway to MacArthur, 6 January, 1951, RG 16a, Box 5, MMFL; Ridgway Diary, 16 Dec. 1950, Ridgway Papers, Box 20; concerns described in Ridgway, "Oral History," 67.

31. Ridgway to army chief and vice chief of staff, 3 and 11 Jan. 1951, in Collins, *War In Peacetime*, 251–52; MacArthur to Ridgway, 25 Dec. 1950, in Ridgway, *Soldier*, 201; Davis quoted and military situation described in "Discussions at a Department of State-JCS Meeting," 18 April 1951, *FRUS*, 7:357–60; CINCFE to DA, 8 Jan. 1951, JCS, GF, 1951–53, Box 15, NA; CINCFE and DA message traffic, 8 to 10 Jan. 1951, Schnabel and Watson, *History of JCS, Korean War*, 1:406–11.

32. Collins, *War in Peacetime*, 81; Acheson, *Present at Creation*, 515; CINCFE to JCS, 6 Nov. 1950, *FRUS*, 7:1058; Henry Kissinger, *White House Years*, (Boston: Little, Brown, 1979), 942.

33. "Who Was Right?," WP, editorial, 23 May 1951, 15; Marquis Childs, "Story of Joint Chiefs' Directive" and "JCS Version of Korean War," WP, 16 May 1951, 13 and 29 May 1951, 10; the quoted accusation from a critic of MacArthur is David Rees, *Korea: The Limited War* (Baltimore: Penguin Books, 1970), 181–82; quote from Acheson in Acheson, *Among Friends*, 285.

34. Mildren, "Oral History," 6; MacArthur to Charles Patterson, 16 Jan. 1951, RG 5, Personal Correspondence, MMFL.

35. Lowe to Truman, 24 Dec. 1950, copy in "Lowe File," Robert Dennison Papers; Lowe to Truman 1 and 6 Jan. 1951, PSF, Box 245: both in TPL.

36. DA to CINCFE, 22 Jan. 1951; Minutes of 80th Meeting of NSC Council, 17 Jan. 1951; "Courses of Action Relative to Communist China and Korea-Chinese Nationalists," 29 Jan. 1951: all in JCS, GF, 1951–53, RG 218, Box 14, NA; Field, *U.S. Naval Operations: Korea*, 308.

37. "Courses of Action Relative to Communist China and Korea—Anti-Communist Chinese," 14 March 1951, *FRUS*, 7:1604. JCS Decision on Joint Strategic Plans Committee, "Possible U.S. Actions in Event of War with Communist China," 27 Dec. 1950, and Chief of Naval Operations to JCS, "Chinese National Intentions," 22 Aug. 1952, in JCS, GF, 1951–53, RG 218, Boxes 14 and 16, respectively; Robert Barnett, "Memorandum of Conversation with General William Chase," 30 Aug. 1951, State Dep't. Central Files, RG 59, Box 2882: all in NA; "Chiang Offers Men For China Invasion," *NYT*, 17 May 1951, 5.

38. Collins, "Memorandum of the Joint Chiefs of Staff; Subject: Visits to Yugoslavia and other MDAP Countries," 13 Nov. 1951, Eisenhower Pre-Presidential Papers, Box 25, Dwight D. Eisenhower Presidential Library [hereafter EPL], Abilene, Kansas; JCS Decision on Joint Strategic Plans Committee, "Courses of Action Relative to Communist China and Korea-Chinese Nationalists," 29 Jan. 1951, and Bradley to Sec. Def., "Strategic Importance of Formosa," 2 Jan. 1951: both in JCS, GF, 1951–53, RG 218, Boxes 14 and 17, respectively; NA; DA to CINCFE, 16 Jan., 23 Jan., 26 Jan., and 20 March 1951, RG 9, Box 45, MMFL.

39. John Hickman, "Negotiating paper for Truman-Pleven Talks, January 29–30 [1951]," JCS, GF, 1951–53, RG 218, Box 14, NA; CINCFE to JCS, 7 Feb. 1951, RG 6, Box 9, MMFL; memo to Sec. of Navy and Army, ca. Sept. 1946, quoted in Douglas J. McDonald, "Truman Administration and Global Responsibilities," in Robert Jervis and

Jack Snyder, ed., Dominos and Bandwagons (New York: Oxford University Press, 1991), 118; Memorandum of CNO for JCS, "LST Requirements of CINCFE," 18 Sept. 1951, JCS, GF, 1951–53, RG 218, Box 15, NA; Marshall, Bradley, and Collins, at MacArthur Hearings, 333, 946, 1189.

40. Gaddis, "Defense Perimeter Concept," 114; Frank Holober, Raiders of the China Coast: CIA Covert Operations during the Korean War (Annapolis: Naval Institute Press, 1999), passim.

41. Tom Dewy, 10 May 1951, quoted in Caridi, Korean War and American Politics, 169; Baldwin, "Guerrillas Worry Mao," NYT, 29 Dec. 1950, 3; Memorandum by Chief of Naval Operations for JCS, "Courses of Action Relative to Communist China and Korea," 3 Jan. 1951, JCS, GF, 1951–53, RG 218, Box 14 NA.

42. DA to CINCFE, 22 Jan. 1951, JCS, GF, 1951–53, Box 14; Sherman, 16 January 1951, quoted in Peter Lowe, "An Ally and a Recalcitrant General: Great Britain, Douglas MacArthur and the Korean War, 1950–1," English Historical Review 105 (July 1990): 642; Memorandum by Chief of Naval Operations for JCS, "Courses of Action Relative to Communist China and Korea," 3 Jan. 1951, JCS, GF, 1951–53, Box 14; NA; CINCFE to JCS, 23 Feb. 1951, RG 6, Box 9, MMFL.

43. CIA, "Chinese Intervention in Korea," 12 Oct. 1950, FRUS, 7:934; Chen Jian, Mao's China and the Cold War (Chapel Hill: University of North Carolina Press, 2001), esp. 60, 203–204, 209–10, 236, 239, 279; Westad, Decisive Encounters, 79, 107, 210, 230, 324–25; Mao and other PRC officials quoted in Stueck, Korean War: International History, 100; He Di, "Last Campaign to Unify China," 8–11; and Short, Mao, 434–38; Henry Lieberman, "Anti-Mao Fighters In Southwest Quit," NYT, 15 June 1951, 3.

44. Goncharov, et., al., Uncertain Partners, 142–53; Holober, Raiders of Chinese Coast, esp. 11–19, 28–36; quote from Tillman Durdin, "Open Resistance in China Weakens," NYT, 3 Aug. 1951, 2; quotes in Nancy Bernkopf Tucker, ed., China Confidential: American Diplomats and Sino-American Relations, 1945–1996 (New York: Columbia University Press, 2001), 118, 152.

45. Knox, Korean War: Oral History, 2:14.

46. Ibid., 2:191.

47. Collins, War in Peacetime, 248; Bradley, "Memorandum for the Secretary of Defense," 27 Dec. 1950, JCS, GF, 1948–50, RG 218, Box 14, NA.

48. Collins, War in Peacetime, 247–48; JCS to CINCFE, 12 Jan. 1951, RG 16, Box 5, MMFL.

49. Schnabel and Watson, History of JCS, Korean War, 1:414–17; Meeting in Cabinet Room, 12 Jan. 1951, FRUS, 7:69; Truman to MacArthur, 13 Jan. 1951, in Truman, Memoirs, 2:435–36; JCS to CINCFE (Personal for MacArthur), 9 Jan. 1951, JCS, GF, 1951–53, RG 218, Box 14, NA.

50. MacArthur, Reminiscences, 382; Whitney, MacArthur, 427, 436–39; Truman to MacArthur, 13 Jan. 1951, in Truman, Memoirs, 2:435–36.

51. Meilinger, Vandenberg, 177–78; MacArthur to Truman, 14 Jan. 1951, JCS, GF, 1951–53, RG 218, Box 14, NA.

52. Joint Strategic Plans Committee, "Responsibilities for Supply in FECOM Post-Hostilities in Korea," 17 Jan. 1951, JCS, GF, 1951–53, RG 218, Box 41, NA; Ridgway quoted in John Michaelis (then commander of the 27th Regiment), "Oral History," 14.

53. Brig. Gen. Basil Coad, commander of 27th Commonwealth Brigade, n.d., quoted in Appleman, Disaster in Korea, 449; Collins, War In Peacetime, 253, 257; Ridgway to MacArthur, 3 Feb. and 22 March, 1951, RG 16a, Box 5, MMFL; Collins to Sec. of Defense, 19 Jan. 1951, JCS, GF, 1951–53, RG 218, Box 14, NA.

54. Shen Zhihua, "Sino-North Korean Conflict and its Resolution during the Korean War," *CWIHPB*, Winter 2003–Spring 2004, 15–16; Zhang, *Mao's Military Romanticism*, esp. 125–30, 167–68; Roe, *Dragon Strikes*, 420, 436–37.

55. "Mao's Telegrams During Korean War," 2:72, 76; Westad, *Decisive Encounters*, 142, 203, 224, 237, 253, 301; "luxury items" is from American reports cited in Appleman, *Disaster in Korea*, 430; Yuri Modin, with Jean-Charles Deniau and Aguieszka Ziarek, *My Five Cambridge Friends: Burgess, MacLean, Philby, Blunt and Carincross: By Their KGB Controller* (NY: Farrar, Straus, and Giroux, 1994), 137.

56. "Mao's Telegrams During Korean War," 2:81; Cave Brown, *Treason in the Blood*, 426; Stalin, 1 Dec. 1950; Mao to Stalin, 21 June and 5 Oct. 1951, all in Bajanov and Bajanova, Korean Conflict, 109, 136, 145; Stalin to Zhou Enlai, 20 Aug. 1952, in *CWIHPB*, Winter 1995–96, 13.

57. Zhang, *Red Wings over the Yalu.*, 68–69, 74–75, 97; Chang and Halliday, *Mao: Untold Story*, 151, 263, Westad, *Decisive Encounters*, 254; final quotes in Short, *Mao*, 364, 480.

58. Peng quoted in Spurr, *Enter the Dragon*, 252; writings quoted in John A. Lynn, *Battle: A History of Combat and Culture* (n.p.: Westview, 2003), 55; Ridgway, *Korean War*, 105; LTC Malcolm quoted in Appleman, *Ridgway Duels For Korea*, 180.

59. Short, *Mao*, 237–39, 246, 260, 263, 313; Davies, *Dragon by Tail*, 157–59, 194; Fenby, *Chiang Kai-Shek*, 257, 262, 280, 301.

60. La Bree, *Smith*, 106, 107, 128, 149, 151; Hersey, "Profiles: Mr. President," 5 May 1951, 39. Truman in Mitchell, "An Act of Presidential Indiscretion," 567–68.

61. Peng, 26 April 1951, quoted in Zhang, *Mao's Military Romanticism*, 149.

62. CINCFE to JCS, 3 Dec. 1950, *FRUS*, 7:1321; Charles A. Willoughby and John Chamberlain, *MacArthur, 1941–1951* (New York: McGraw-Hill, 1954), 350; Jian, *Mao's China and the Cold War*, 79, 81, 172.

63. Appleman, *Disaster in Korea.* 448–50; S. L. A. Marshall, *Infantry Operations and Weapons Usage in Korea, Winter of 1950–51* (Operations Research Office, Johns Hopkins University, n.d.), 116–19; Kelly C. Jordan, "Three Armies in Korea: The Combat Effectiveness of the United States Eight Army in Korea, July 1950–June 1952" (Ph.D. diss., Ohio State University, 1999), 207–209.

64. Bradley's aide, 5 June 1951, quoted in Sulzberger, *Long Row of Candles*, 639; Appleman, *Disaster in Korea*, 448; Johnson, "Oral History," 7 Feb. 1972, 43, USMHI, Polk, "Oral History," 37–38; Collins, *Lightning Joe*, 373; Collins in May 1975 quoted in Heller, ed., *Korean War: 25 Year Perspective*, 34.

65. Major (Ret.) Patrick Roe to author, 11 Jan. 2003; Braim, *Will to Win*, 309; Addison Terry, *The Battle for Pusan: A Korean War Memoir* (Navato, Ca.: Presidio Press, 2000), 57, Lt. Perry's comment is not specifically about January 1951 but about the effects of another battle; Lt. Col. Norwood G. Read quoted in Appleman, *Ridgway Duels For Korea*, 141.

66. Fellers, "Oral History," 11.

67. MacArthur quoted in James, *Years of MacArthur*, 3:558; MacArthur, *Reminiscences*, 383; Whitney, *MacArthur*, p, 459; LTC James Quirk to wife, 24 Feb. 1951, Quirk Papers, TPL.

68. Lowe to Truman, 1 Dec. 1950, PSF Box 245; Quirk to wife, 24 Feb. 1951, Quirk Papers: both, TPL.

69. Ridgway, "Oral History," 79; MacArthur quoted in Ridgway, *Soldier*, 201; also see Collins, *War in Peacetime*, 239; Quirk, 20 and 21 Feb. 1951, in Quirk, *Wars and Peace*, 169, and Quirk to wife, 24 Feb. 1951, Quirk Papers, TPL.

70. Report of *New York Herald Tribune* war correspondent Christopher Rand summarized in "Now It Comes Out," WP, 12 April 1951, 20; Ridgway, *Soldier*, 29; Ridgway to MacArthur, 5 March 1951, RG 16a, Box 5, MMFL.

71. DA to CINCFE, 9 Dec. 1950, RG 9, Box 9, MMFL.

72. MacArthur press conferences on 13 and 20 Feb. 1951 in MacArthur, *Soldier Speaks*, 234–37; CINCFE to DA, 11 Feb. 1951, RG 61a, Box 5, MMFL.

73. MacArthur's remarks, 6 to 20 March 1951, quoted in Whitney, *MacArthur*, 462, in James, *Years of MacArthur*, 3:582–83, and in news summary, 8 March 1951, Dennison Papers, TPL.

74. MacArthur described in Goulden, *Korea*, 453, and in Quirk, *Wars and Peace*, 169; Lowe to Truman, 28 Feb. 1951, PSF, Box 245, TPL; Schnabel, *Policy and Direction: First Year*, 187n27; Whitney, *MacArthur*, 461.

75. Spurr, *Enter the Dragon*, 68; Appleman, *Ridgway Duels For Korea*, p, 347; MacArthur paraphrased by associate, Arnold A. Saltzman, "Oral History," 17 May 1996, 6–7, MMFL; for MacArthur's feelings about Marshall and Washington, see Blaik, *Red Blaik Story*, 506, MacArthur to Roy Howard, 20 Dec. 1950, RG 5, Box 28, MMFL and Whitney, *MacArthur*, 454; quote from columnist Stewart Alsop, "Korea Is Still the Key," NYHT, 15 April 1951, 2:5; for Alsop's connections with the administration, see Merry, *Taking on the World*, 184–85.

76. MacArthur quoted in *NYHT*, 4 April 1951, 1.

77. MacArthur to Ridgway 4 Feb. 1951, RG 16a, Box 5, MMFL; MacArthur, *Reminiscences*, 384; MacArthur, 7 March 1951, quoted in Appleman, *Ridgway Duels For Korea*, 343, and James, *Years of MacArthur*, 3:582.

78. Marshall at *MacArthur Hearings*, 429; soldiers quoted in Goulden, *Korea*, 453; Quirk to Merrill, 1 Feb. 1950, and to LTC Walter Winton, 8 March 1951, Quirk Papers, TPL; "Ridgway Sees Parallel as Goal," *NYT*, 13 March 1951, 1 and 3.

79. "UN Dropping Idea of Unifying Korea By Military Force," *NYT*, 14 March 1951, 1; DA to CINCFE, 30 Nov. 1950, RG 9, Box 45, MMFL.

80. Ridgway to MacArthur, 16 Jan. 1951, RG 16a, Box 5, MMFL;

81. John Hickman, "Negotiating paper for Truman-Pleven Talks, January 29–30 [1951]," n.d. JCS, GF, 1951–53, RG 218, Box 14, NA; Ridgway to Chief of Staff, "Concept of War," 12 Oct. 1950, Ridgway Papers, Box 16; "Ridgway Can See No End to War Unless There Is Political Accord"; Christopher Rand, "Ridgway Hero to UN Army"; Mark Duffield, "Successor: Ridgway": all in NYHT, 9 April 1951, 1 and 6, 12 April 1951, 2, and 15 April 1951, 2:1, respectively.

82. For the Ridgway reprimand, see Wright, "Oral History," 33–38; MacArthur cited and quoted in "Memorandum of conversation between MacArthur and Robert Murphy, 30 April 1952," Acheson Papers, Box 63, TPL and on 20 Jan. 1954, in NYT, 9 April 1964, 16; in Ridgway, *Soldier*, 201; and in Ridgway, *Korean War*, 158–59.

83. Wright, "Oral History," 38; Ridgway, "Memorandum For Diary," 12 April 1951, Ridgway Papers, Box 20. MacArthur was "as courteous as ever," according to Ridgway, another indication of his exceptional ability to carry out a required role.

84. MacArthur to MG Richard Stephens, 15 Nov. 1957, RG 10, Box 142, MMFL; quote from Col. Sid Huff, *My Fifteen Years with General MacArthur* (New York: Paperback Library, 1964 [orig. 1951], 134; *Life Magazine* photographer Carl Mydans, "Oral History," n.d., 9, MMFL.

85. DA to CINCFE, 27 June 1950, RG 6, Box 9, MMFL.

86. Secretaries of Army, Navy, and Air Force, "Memorandum for Secretary of

Defense," 4 Dec. 1950, and Undersecretary of the Army Karl R. Bendestein, "Memorandum for Secretary of the Army," 5 Dec. 1950: both in Averell Harriman Papers, Box 305, Library of Congress; Gregory Mitrovich, *Undermining the Kremlin: America's Strategy to Subvert the Soviet Bloc, 1947–1956* (Ithaca: Cornell University Press, 2000), 74, 184.

87. Chang, *Friends and Enemies*, 52–53, 63, 92–95, 142; "Ridgway Sees Wedge Driven Between Chinese and Soviet," *NYT* 4 Aug. 1951, 1 and 2; Rusk, ca. 15 Feb. 1951, cited and quoted in Pearson, Mike, 2:176–79.

88. "Memorandum of Conversation: Charles Marshall, State Dep't Planning Staff and BG Frank Roberts, Harriman's Staff," 30 Jan. 1951, and "Memorandum on Discussions of State and JCS Meeting," 30 Jan. 1951: both in *FRUS*, 7:1534, 1537; Collins, "Memorandum of the Joint Chiefs of Staff; Subject: Visits to Yugoslavia and other MDAP Countries," 13 Nov. 1951, Eisenhower Pre-Presidential Papers, Box 25, EPL.

89. DA to CINCFE, 27 June 1950, RG 6, Box 9, MMFL; Hanson Baldwin, "Tito's Yugoslavia the Sensitive Point in an East Europe Standing to Arms," *NYT*, 26 March 1951, 14; Collins, "Memorandum of the Joint Chiefs of Staff; Subject: Visits to Yugoslavia and other MDAP Countries," 13 Nov. 1951, Eisenhower Pre-Presidential Papers, Box 25, EPL; Bradley, 29 Nov. 1950, quoted in Henry W. Brands, "Redefining the Cold War: American Policy toward Yugoslavia, 1948–60," *Diplomatic History* 11 (Winter 1987), 44; JCS document, May 1944, quoted and issue discussed in Mark A. Stoler, *Allies and Adversaries, The Joint Chiefs of Staff, The Grand Alliance and U.S. Strategy in World War II* (Chapel Hill: University of North Carolina Press, 2000, 173; Report to NSC, "United States Objectives, Policies and Courses of Action in Asia," 17 May 1951, *FRUS*, 6:34.

90. MacArthur, "Mr. Truman Yielded to Councils of Fear," *U.S. News and World Report* 40 (17 Feb. 1956): 49–50; "Joint Chiefs of Staff Report for Senate Committees on Korean Operations: Forcing Russia To A Decision," ca. 18 April 1951, Joint Chiefs of Staff, Chairman's File, [hereafter JCS, CF], RG 218, Box 8, NA.

Truman Fires MacArthur

1. Quotation, n.d., in John Gunther, *The Riddle of MacArthur, Japan, Korea, and the Far East* (New York: Harper's 1951), 13.

2. Richard E. Neustadt, (former member of Truman's White House staff), *Presidential Power: The Politics of Leadership* (New York: Signet Book, 1964), 138–39.

3. Nitze, "Interview given for BBC Documentary, 'Korea'," ca. Nov. 1986, Nitze Papers, Box 130, Library of Congress.

4. *NYT*, 2 Dec. 1950, 1 and 4; James, *Years of MacArthur*, 3:540.

5. Roe, "Ghost Armies of Manchuria," in *Understanding and Remembering*, 87; Dep't of State, "Memorandum of Conversation," 3 Dec. 1950, in Merrill, ed., *Documentary History of Truman Presidency*, 19:149.

6. D'Este, *Eisenhower: Soldier's Life*, 507–509; Eisenhower to Marshall, 15 April 1945, *Eisenhower Papers*, 5:2617.

7. JCS to major commands, 6 Dec. 1950, in Merrill, ed., *Documentary History of Truman Presidency*, 20:58; DA to CINCFE, 8 Dec. 1950, RG 9, Box 9, MMFL.

8. George M. Elsey, "Truman's Six Immaterial Legacies," in Robert Watson, Michael J. Devine, and Robert J. Wolz, ed., *The National Security Legacy of Harry S. Truman* (Kirksville, Mo: Truman State University Press, 2005), 1:55; MacArthur to Roy Howard, 20 Dec. 1950, RG 5, Box 28, MMFL.

9. Schnabel, *Policy and Direction*, 285; DA to CINCFE, 9 Dec. 1950, RG 9, Box 9, MMFL; MacArthur's communiqué in *NYT*, 26 December 1950, 4.

10. News Conference, 11 Jan 1951, *PPOPT*, 18; Acheson, 4 June 1951, *MacArthur Hearings*, 1864; "Text of Statement," *NYT*, April 12, 1951, 9.

11. Truman, "Wake Island" memorandum for record, 25 Nov. 1950, and "The Mac-Arthur Story," ca. 1953 transcript of early draft of Truman's *Memoirs*, both in Merrill, ed., *Documentary History of Truman Presidency*, 20:57, 419; Truman, *Memoirs*, 2:443. As for the facts of Wake Island, Marshall testified to Congress that MacArthur "had received no specific instructions or any instructions so far as I know on that subject [of clearing policy statements with Washington] until this message of December 6," see *MacArthur Hearings*, 342; for "rank insubordination," see Truman, Diary, 6 April 1951, in Truman, *Off the Record*, 210.

12. MacArthur quoted in *NYT*, 14 Feb. 1951, 3, and in Weintraub, *MacArthur's War*, 318; Lowe to Vaughan, 27 Dec. 1950; Lowe to Truman, 4 and 28 Feb. 1951, PSF, Box 245, TPL.

13. Truman to Lowe, 28 Dec. 1950, 2 Feb., and 10 March 1951; Lowe to Truman, 27 and 29 Dec. 1950, 3 and 25 Feb. 1951; Vaughan to Lowe, 17 Dec. 1950, 16 and 20 March 1951: all in PSF, Box 245, TPL.

14. Lowe to Truman, 29 March 1951; Robert Dennison to Truman, 30 Jan. 1952: both in PSF, Box 245, TPL; *Boston Herald*, Jan. 14 1952, 1–2.

15. Whitney described in Egeberg, "Oral History," 16; Willoughby, "Oral History," 8–9; West, "Oral History," 25; and Almond, "Oral History," 24–25, all in MMFL; for Willoughby's own political activities, see Vandenberg, Jr., ed., *Private Papers of Senator Vandenberg*, 78–81, 84.

16. Kennan quoted in Schaller, *American Occupation of Japan*, 125; Willoughby, "Oral History," 9; Wright, "Oral History," 61–63.

17. MacArthur quoted in James, *Years of MacArthur*, 3:378; West, "Oral History," 66–67; Lowe to Truman, 9 Jan. 1950; Vaughan to Whitney, 27 March 1951: both in PSF, Box 245, TPL; Whitney to Harry Vaughan, with note by Truman, 10 April 1951, Lowe File, Whitney Papers, MMFL.

18. Whitney, 12 April 1951, reprinted in *MacArthur Hearings*, 3552; DA to CINCFE, 9 Dec. 1950, RG 9, Box 9, MMFL.

19. MacArthur, *Reminiscences*, 387; Acheson quoted in *NYHT*, 22 March 1951, 14; JCS to CINCFE, 20 March 1951, State Department, Selected Records Korea, Box 10, TPL.

20. Sebald, *With MacArthur in Japan*, 201; Stueck, *Korean War: International History*, 152–54, 170–73; Cabinet Meeting, 1 April 1951, Connelly Papers, Box 1, TPL.

21. Truman's draft proposal in *Memoirs*, 2:439–40; MacArthur statement of 24 March 1951 in *MacArthur Hearings*, 3541–42.

22. MacArthur statement of 24 March 1951 cited above; "Red China Rejects M'Arthur's Offer," *NYT*, 29 March, 1951, 3; Jian, *Mao's China and Cold War*, 60.

23. MacArthur's statement characterized by Sen. Wayne Morris (Rep.-Oregon), 1 June 1951, in *MacArthur Hearings*, 1790; News Conference, 29 March 1951, *PPOPT*, 203; *London Daily Herald* (organ of the Labour Party gov't) quoted in *NYHT*, 27 March 1951, 7; Marshall, 8 May 1951, *MacArthur Hearings*, 349; Howard K. Smith, "Thou Art Soldier Only," *Nation* 172 (21 April 1951): 363, and Genet, "Letter from Paris," *New Yorker* 27 (5 May 1951): 59; Joseph Newman, "British Aim Is to Silence MacArthur," *NYHT*, 8 April 1951, 1; Memo, "Acheson-Lovett phone conversation," 24 March 1951, Acheson Papers, Box 66, TPL.

24. "Memorandum of call to Lovett," 27 March 1951, Acheson Papers, Box 77.

25. Statements in *NYHT*, 25 March 1951, 1, and 28 March 1951, 4; JCS to CINCFE, 24 March 1951, State Department, Selected Records Korea, Box 10, TPL; Herblock cartoon reprinted in *NYT*, 1 April 1951, 4:3.

26. "The Removal of MacArthur," *NYHT*, 30.

27. Acheson, *Present at Creation*, 519; *London Daily Telegraph* story republished in *NYT*, 5 April 1951, 2.

28. *Congressional Record*, 82nd Cong., 1st Sess., 3380; Martin speech republished in ibid., A813–15.

29. McCarthy quoted in "Troop Curb Moves Gains in Senate," *NYT*, 29 March 1951, 6; Taft in James Minifie, "World Debate On MacArthur Grows Intense," *NYHT*, 8 April 1951, 4; agent Joseph Burkholder Smith quoted in William M. Leary, *Perilous Missions: Civil Air Transport and CIA Covert Operations in Asia* (University, Ala.: University of Alabama Press, 1984), 133.

30. Newspaper quotation from Hanson W. Baldwin, "M'Arthur's Strategy," *NYT*, 13 May 1951, 4:4; Martin's speech in *Congressional Record*, 82nd, 1st Sess., A813–15.

31. Joseph W. Martin, Jr. as told to Robert J. Donovan, *My First Fifty Years in Politics* (New York: McGraw-Hill, 1960), 199, 203, 207. On 19 March 1951, Hugh Scott (Rep.-Penn.) raised the issue of KMT commitment to the mainland on the House floor, but the only response came from three other Republicans, all of whom agreed with his position, indistinguishable from Martin and MacArthur, see *Congressional Record*, 82nd, 1st Sess., 2619–23.

32. MacArthur to Martin, 20 March 1951, and subsequent discussion of the letter in MacArthur, *Reminiscences*, 386–89; notes of Bonner Fellers, esp. "Memorandum For Honorable Herbert Hoover," 7 May 1964, and "telephoned," 13 April 1951: both in Fellers Papers, MMFL; Martin, *My First Fifty Years in Politics*, 208–209.

33. Hunt, *Untold Story of MacArthur*, 126, 154–55, 290–93, and James, *Years of MacArthur*, 3:434–45; MacArthur, *Speeches and Reports*, 176.

34. Diary, Eisenhower, *Diaries and Papers*, 453; Truman Diary, 6 April 1951 in Truman, *Off the Record*, 210; Martin's speech in *Congressional Record*, 82nd, 1st Sess. A814.

35. Roger Tubby, "Oral History," 10 February 1970, p, 129, TPL and statement by Tubby in Francis Heller, ed., *The Truman White House, The Administration of the Presidency, 1945 to 1953* (Lawrence: Regents Press of Kansas, 1980), 147–48; Truman, 11 Sept. 1945, 1 Sept. 1949, and 28 Nov. 1950, in Ayers, *Diary* 76, 327, 383.

36. Acheson, *Present at Creation*, 519; Truman, *Memoirs*, 2:445; Tubby, "Oral History," 39–40. One would like to find some April 1951 documentation of this recollection in February 1970. However, the Tubby manuscript collection deposited in the Yale University library is closed until 2150.

37. News Conference, 17 May 1951, *PPOPT*, 289; for Republican charges, see "Precedent for Acheson," *NYT*, 20 May 1951, 4:1; News Conference, 21 Sept. 1950, *PPOPT*, 643; Clayton Knowles, "Dulles Will Reply to Hoover," *NYT*, 28 Dec. 1950, 1; Truman, comment at Ft. Leavenworth, 15 Dec. 1961, Merle Miller Papers, Box 6, TPL.

38. Truman, 28 April 1951, to Elsey and Eben Ayers in "MacArthur" notes of Elsey, Eben Ayers Papers, Box 7; Joseph Short to E. J. Williams, 25 July 1952, PSF, Box 298; Bradley interviewed by Hillman and Heller, 30 Mach 1955, Post-Presidential Papers, Box 641: all in TPL; Truman, *Memoirs*, 2:442; "M'Arthur Denies Truman Charge," *NYT*, 23 Dec. 1960, 1.

39. Truman quoted in Donovan, *Truman Presidency*, 2:355; "Bring MacArthur Home," *WP* editorial, 11 April 1951, 10; "Fog Over Korea," *NYHT* editorial, 7 April 1951, 8; and "The MacArthur Problem," *WP* editorial, 10 April 1951, 14; Truman, *Memoirs*, 2:384.

40. Truman Diary, 5 and 6 April 1951, PSF, Box 33, TPL; Steven Neal, *Harry and Ike: The Partnership that Remade the Postwar World* (New York: Scribner, 2001), 110, 221, 235; Ayers, *Diary*, 369; Stewart Alsop, "Truman and MacArthur," *WP*, 12 April 1951, 20.

41. "'Wake Island' memorandum received from President's personal secretary," 6 April 1951; Elsey, "Notes for April 8, 1951": both in MacArthur notes of Elsey, Eben Ayers Papers, Box 7, TPL.

42. Truman, *Memoirs*, 1:168; Truman in John Hersey, "Profiles: Mr. President," 14 April 1951, 42, 54; Truman, 5 Aug. 1950, quoted in Hamby, *Man of the People*, 500; Truman at staff meeting, 11 April 1951, Eben Ayers Papers, Box 7, TPL.

43. "Lincoln and General McClellan," six page mimeographed booklet, copy in Senator Paul H. Douglas Papers, Box 243, Chicago Historical Society; Bruce Tap, *Over Lincoln's Shoulder: The Committee on the Conduct of the War* (Lawrence: University Press of Kansas, 1998), esp. 102, 106, 115, 124–25, 133.

44. Truman quoted, ca. 1960, in Neustadt, *Presidential Power*, 124–25.

45. Truman's unsent letters to Arthur Krock in Truman, *Strictly Personal and Confidential*, 27–28, 57–58; Truman quoted in Tubby, "Oral History," 40.

46. Truman quoted in Tubby, "Oral History," 40; Aurthur, "Truman Chuckles Dryly," 260; for decision on H-bomb, see Borowski, *Hollow Threat*, 193–94; Dennison, "Oral History," 153; Diary, 6 April 1951, in Truman, *Off the Record*, 210–11.

47. "Truman memo to Ayers and Elsey," 28 April 1951, in "MacArthur" notes of Elsey, Ayers Papers, Box 7, and Truman, *Memoirs*, 2:447; MacArthur describing Harriman on 14 Sept. 1950 in Heinl, *Victory at High Tide*, 87; nickname described and Alsop quoted in Abramson, *Spanning the Century*, 603; Harriman to Eisenhower, 9 April 1951, Pre-Presidential Papers, Box 55, EPL.

48. Acheson, *Among Friends*, 268, 288; "Truman memo to Ayers and Elsey," 28 April 1951, in "MacArthur" notes of Elsey, Ayers Papers, Box 7.

49. Memorandum, "Acheson-Lovett phone conversation," 24 March 1951, Acheson Papers, Box 66, TPL; public opinion survey taken 4 to 9 Feb. 1951, *Gallup Poll*, 2:970; Acheson, 14 Feb. 1954, *Princeton University Seminar*, reel 7, track 1, 4.

50. Lippmann, "The Constitutional Crisis," *WP*, 21 May 1951, 7.

51. Bess, "Are Generals in Politics a Menace?," esp. 29 and 136; Morris Janowitz, *The Professional Soldier: A Social and Political Portrait* (New York: Free Press, 1960), 379 and 393n7.

52. Lippmann, "Taft and Bradley," *WP*, 30 April 1951, 11; Ayers, *Diary*, 350–51; Truman, *Memoirs*, 2:283–85.

53. Political issue discussed and Nixon quoted in Caridi, *Korean War and American Politics*, 98, 100–101, 107, 138; Rusk quoted and discussed Laura Belmonte, "Anglo-American Relations and the Dismissal of MacArthur," *Diplomatic History* 19 (Fall 1995): 656–59.

54. Ayers, *Diary*, 77–78; Truman, n.d., quoted by Rusk in Schoenbaum, *Waging Peace and War*, 194; Truman, 14 July 1950, quoted in George M. Elsey, *An Unplanned Life: A Memoir* (Columbia: University of Missouri Press, 2005), 195; poll data in Heller, ed., *Korean War*, 170; News Conferences, 11 and 18 Jan. 1951, PPOPT, 19, 21;

55. Poll in *WP*, 4 April 1951, 5; Eisenhower, *At Ease*, 367–69; Acheson quoted in Chace, *Acheson*, 205; Taft quoted on Acheson in Patterson, *Mr. Republican*, 480.

56. Sen. Ernest McFarland (Dem.-Az.) quoted in *NYHT*, 4 April 1951, 8; Stewart Alsop, "Spring Fever" and Mark Sullivan, "The Verdict on Truman": both in *NYHT*, 6 April 1951, 25, and 8 April 1951, 2:7, respectively; Reston, "U.S. Message to Europeans Is 'The Yanks Are Coming'," and "Our Foreign Policy Unchanged By Great Debate," *NYT*, 5 April, 12 and 8 April 1951, 4:3.

57. Staff quoted in Condit, *Test of War*, 77; Bradley to Assistant Sec. of Def. Marx Leva, 16 April 1951, JCS, GF, 1951–53, RG 218, Box 4, NA; and Bradley interview, 4 May

1971, in Schnabel and Watson, *History of JCS, Korean War*, 1:345–46; Bradley and Blair, *General's Life*, 623.

58. Bradley interview, 20 March 1955, Post-Presidential Papers, Box 641, TPL; Collins at *MacArthur Hearings*, 1209; Daniel Bolger, "Zero Defects: Command Climate in First U.S. Army, 1944–1945," *Military Review*, 71 (May 1991): 65; Bolger does not count Major General Terry Allen, whom Bradley relieved in Sicily; Bradley quoted in D'Este, *Eisenhower: Soldier's Life*, 441, 780; Bradley and Blair, *General's Life*, 633–34, 638; Bradley described on the day MacArthur was fired by Roger Tubby, "Oral History," 134. I have cited and will cite again recollections of White House counsel George Elsey. However, Bradley's own documents gainsay the passage in Elsey's memoir that Bradley "urged Truman to fire MacArthur forthwith," Elsey, *Unplanned Life*, 204.

59. Frank Pace, "Oral History," 17, USMHI; polls graphed in Bruce M. Russett, "The Revolt of the Masses: Public Opinion on Military Expenditures," in John Lovell and Philip S. Kronenberg, ed., *New Civil-Military Relations: The Agonies of Adjustment to Post-Vietnam Realities* (New Brunswick, N.J.: Transaction Books, 1974), 61–63; Frank Pace, "Oral History," 115–16, TPL.

60. "Tension Graver Than In November, Marshall's Belief," *NYT*, 28 March 1951, 1 and 20; James Reston, "Government, Too, Unready for the Long Pull," *NYT*, 25 March 1951, 4:3.

61. "Quizzing Kefauver," *U.S. News and World Report* 30 (April 20, 1950): 26; William Howard Moore, *The Kefauver Committee and the Politics of Crime: 1950–1952* (Columbia: University of Missouri Press, 1974), esp. 17–21, 146–47, 204–205; Haig, *Inner Circles*, 68; "U.S. Shocks a Nurse From Korea," *NYHT*, 8 April 1951, 2:3; Millett in questions and answers with Truman, Ft. Leavenworth, 16 Dec. 1961, Merle Miller Papers, Box 6, TPL.

62. "Marshall Pleas Fails," *NYHT*, 11 April 1951, 1, and "'Prepare For 10 Year's of Tension': Interview with Marshall," 24, 28, 31; Truman, *Memoirs*, 2:477. Despite Marshall's fears, defense expenditures still grew nearly thirty percent, thanks to Joe Stalin and military stalemate in Korea.

63. "Meeting on North Atlantic Union and Other Matters," 14 Aug. 1950, Acheson Papers, Box 67, TPL; Marshall and Harold Stark, 25 July 1941, quoted in Marshall, *Interviews and Reminiscences*, 2:183; Waldo Heinrichs, *Threshold of War: Franklin D Roosevelt and American Entry into World War II* (New York: Oxford University Press, 1988), 174, 177–78.

64. Bradley quoted in Roger Tubby, "Oral History," 208; Bradley, "Memorandum for Record," 24 April 1951, Bradley Papers, Box "Papers Declassified in June 1981," United States Military Academy; Acheson, *Princeton University Seminar*, 2 Feb. and 14 March 1954, reel 3, track 1, 5, and reel 7, track 2, 3.

65. Bradley, "Memorandum for Record," 24 April 1951, Bradley Papers, U.S. Military Academy.

66. Bradley, 15 May 1951, in *MacArthur Hearings*, 747; Truman Diary, 7 April 1951, PSF Box 333, TPL.

67. *MacArthur Hearings*, 3602; Bradley and Blair, *A General's Life*, 513, 632–35; Testimony of CNO Forrest Sherman, 30 May, and General Collins, 25 May 1951, *MacArthur Hearings*, 1308, 1576–77; E. M. Shafer [office of assistant secretary, legal and legislative affairs], memo to Theodore Tannenwald, Jr. [counsel to Averell Harriman], 24 August 1951, Tannenwald Papers, Box 4, TPL; for newspaper columns, see Stewart Alsop, "Truman and MacArthur," *WP*, 13 April 1951, 21.

68. Collins to Eisenhower, 26 March 1951, Pre-Presidential Papers, Box 25, EPL; Collins, *War in Peacetime*, 283; Baldwin, "U.S. Lacks Aim in Korea," *NYT*, 13 April 1951, 7; "Report for the Nation: The Reactions to General MacArthur's Week," *NYT*, 22 April 1951, E:5; Pearson, *Pearson Diaries*, 156.

69. Cliff Roberts to Eisenhower quoted in William Pickett, *Eisenhower Decides to Run: Presidential Politics and the Cold War* (Chicago: Ivan Dee, 2000), 111.

70. Roger Tubby, "Oral History," 208; Arthur Krock, "The Applecart and Its Badly Teetering Load," *NYT* 17 April 1951, 28; Sen. Styles Bridges [ranking Republican on the Senate Armed Services Committee] quoted in *NYHT*, 4 April 1951, and *WP*, 18 April 1951, 1; Senate Dem. Majority leader Ernest Ferguson quoted in *NYHT*, 9 April 1951, 10; Martin quoted in ibid., 15 April 1951, 2:1.

71. Eisenhower quoted in *NYHT*, 12 April 1951, 2; Ferrell, *Truman: A Life*, 340–41; Ridgway, "Memorandum for Diary," 12 April 1951, Ridgway Papers, Box 20.

72. Pearson, *Mike*, 2:145–46, and John English, *The World Years: The Life of Lester Pearson, 1949–1972* (New York: Knopf, 1992), 41; MacArthur, *Reminiscences*, 32; Petillo, *MacArthur: Philippine Years*, 92, 97; MacArthur, 9 Oct. 1950, quoted in "Marguerite Higgins Recalls a Prophetic Talk," *NYHT*, 12 April 1951, 3.

73. Sodei Rinjiro, *Dear General MacArthur: Letters from the Japanese During the American Occupation* (Lanham: Rowman and Littlefield, 2001), passim; MacArthur quoted in Sebald, "Oral History," 13; also see Sebald, *With MacArthur in Japan*, 222–24.

74. Melvyn Leffler, *A Preponderance of Power: National Security, the Truman Administration, and the Cold War* (Stanford: Stanford University Press, 1992), 427; "Memorandum by the Consultant to the Secretary (Dulles)," April 12, 1951, *FRUS*, 6:972–74; Huff quoted and issue discussed in Sebald, *With MacArthur in Japan*, 222–30.

75. John Muccio, "Oral History," 72; Truman, ed., *Where Buck Stops*, 4.

76. Truman quoted by Tannenwald in Heller, ed., *Truman White House*, 156–57.

77. Harriman, May 1975, in Heller, ed., *Korean War*, 235; MacArthur, 20 Jan. 1954, quoted in *NYT*, 9 April 1964, 16.

78. Lippmann, "The President and the General," *WP*, 12 April 1951, 11; Pace, "Oral History," 11, MMFL; Major General Doyle Hickey quoted in Hull, "Oral History," 4:33; Marquis Childs, "JCS Version Of Korean War," *WP*, 29 May 1951, 10 BG Crawford Sams, "Oral History," 25 Aug. 1971, 24, MMFL.

79. MacArthur, *Reminiscences*, 393; "Memorandum of conversation between MacArthur and Robert Murphy," 30 April 1952, Acheson Papers, Box 63. *Rashomon* is an acclaimed Japanese movie about a murder committed in feudal Japan. It is told from the accounts of five different participants, no two of whom agree about essential events.

80. Sebald, *With MacArthur in Japan*, 223–24; "Memorandum by the Consultant to the Secretary (Dulles)," April 12, 1951, *FRUS*, 6:972–74; columnist Russell Brines cited in *WP*, 12 April 1951, 11; Willoughby to MacArthur, n.d., Reel 335; Almond, "Oral History," 19; Wright, "Oral History," 54–55: all in MMFL.

81. Omar Bradley, "Memorandum for Record," 11 April 1951, Bradley Papers, U.S. Military Academy; Truman Diary, 14 Sept. 1950, in Truman, *Off the Record*, 192; Truman, 11 April 1951, quoted in Elsey, *Unplanned Life: A Memoir*, 205.

82. Memoranda, n.d., Bradley Papers; U.S. Military Academy; James, *Years of MacArthur*, 3:600; MacArthur quoted in Matthew Ridgway, "Memorandum For Diary," 12 April 1951, Ridgway Papers, Box 20.

83. Whitney to Vaughan, 10 April 1951, PSF, Box 245, TPL.

84. MacArthur, *Reminiscences*, 385, 388; Martin, *First Fifty Years in Politics*, 208–209; for MacArthur on Hoover, see Bowers, "Warts and All," 242; Memo. "Conference with Herbert Hoover," 14 April 1951, H. Alexander Smith Papers, Box 106, Mudd Library, Princeton University; notes of Bonner Fellers, esp. "Memorandum For Honorable Herbert Hoover," 7 May 1964, and "telephoned," 13 April 1951: both in Fellers Papers, MMFL.

85. Pace, "Oral History," 15, USMHI and "Oral History," 108, TPL; Ridgway, "Memorandum For Diary," 12 April 1951, Ridgway Papers, Box 20.

86. Hasenfus, "Managing Partner: Martin," 275; Cabinet Meetings, 13 and 16 April 1951, Connelly Papers, Box 1, TPL; MacArthur to Col. John G. O'Laughlin, 15 Sept. 1936, RG 1, Box 2, MMFL; Sams, "Oral History," 25; Truman Diary, 7 March 1951, in Truman, *Off the Record*, 210; Truman quoted in Donovan, *Truman Presidency*, 2:355.

Public Verdict and Consequences

1. Pond to Ridgway, 19 Feb., and Ridgway to Pond, 25 Feb. 1958, Box 21, Ridgway Papers.

2. Bradley on "military facts" at *MacArthur Hearings*, 732.

3. William S. White, "Democrats Await Changed Reaction," *NYT*, 21 April 1951, 7.

4. News Conference, 26 April 1951, *PPOPT*, 241; MacArthur, "Mr. Truman Yielded To Counsels Of Fear," 52; MacArthur quoted in Ridgway, "Memorandum For Diary," 12 April 1951, Ridgway Papers, Box 20, and Ridgway, "Oral History," 81.

5. News Conferences, 19 Oct. and 30 Nov. 1950, 11 Jan. and 8 Feb. 1951, in *PPOPT*, *1950*, 679, 726, and *1951*, 21, 147.

6. Pace, "Oral History," 106, TPL; Hanson Baldwin, "MacArthur—III," *NYT*, 30 March 1951, 3; W. H. Lawrence, "Republicans Move to Back M'Arthur," *NYT*, 10 April 1951, 1.

7. Lawrence, "Republicans Move," cited above; idem, "Truman—Portrait Of a Stubborn Man," *NYT Magazine*, 22 April 1951, 8 and 64; letters to Senator Richard Russell from Robert Moore, 1 May 1951, Mrs. George Wesley, 9 May 1951, and Miles Pinckey, 14 April 1951, Boxes 2 and 4, Richard Russell Papers, University of Georgia; report by the 8 Taft Republicans, ca. August 1951, in *MacArthur Hearings*, 3580.

8. David Lloyd to Truman speech writers, 30 July 1951, quoted in Edgar B. Robinson, et. al., *Powers of the President in Foreign Affairs, 1945–1965* (San Francisco, Commonwealth Club of California, 1966), 71; McCullough, *Truman*, esp. 214, 285, 320, 521; notes of Bonner Fellers, esp. "Memorandum For Honorable Herbert Hoover," 7 May 1964, Fellers Papers; quote from letter from LTG (ret.) Ennis Whitehead to Larry Bunker, 17 April 1951, MacArthur Correspondence, Reel 335: also see letters to MacArthur from Robert D. Ireland, Robert Taylor, Robert Salisbury, B. D. Cornell, and W. Harry R. Meeker, all on 10 or 11 April 1951, in MacArthur Correspondence, Reels 748 and 761: all in MMFL.

9. Letters to Truman quoted Mene Arthur Harris, "The MacArthur Dismissal—A Study In Political Mail" (Ph.D. diss., University of Iowa, 1966), 114, 124, 130, 143. Although people tend to praise those to whom they write, the White House survey of its own mail found 55 percent in favor of MacArthur, "Memorandum for the President," 8 May 1951, Merrill, ed., *Documentary History of Truman Presidency*, 20:227–28. On the issue of MacArthur's populist appeal, Truman's dismissal of the general won approval from 41 percent of those who graduated from college but only 23 percent of those with a grade school education, see *Gallup Poll*, 2:981, 983, 1020; Gallup Poll in *WP*, 20 May 1951, 5B;

American Federation of Labor members in *NYT*, 3 June 1951, 31; for correspondence to Congress, see telegrams reprinted in Rovere and Schlesinger, *General and the President*, 8. and E. S. Scott to Richard Russell, 27 April 1951, Russell Papers, Box 2.

10. Harris, "The MacArthur Dismissal," 65; J. M. Hiatt to Sen. Richard Russell, Russell Papers, Box 4; for Vaughan, see Nitze, *From Hiroshima to Glasnost*, 108, McCullough, *Truman*, 591–92, and quote from Acheson in Beisner, *Dean Acheson*, 125; for Rhee and South Korea, see Truman, *Memoirs*, 2:329, 402; William S. White, "Acheson's Stock Shows No Appreciable Change," *NYT*, 17 June 1951, 4:6.

11. Report by the 8 Taft Republicans, ca. August 1951, in *MacArthur Hearings*, 3588; Thomas Eaton to Sen. Richard Russell, 16 May 1951, Russell Papers, Box 3.

12. Harris, "MacArthur Dismissal—Study In Political Mail," 195, 198, 201, 217, 261, 282; Eben Ayers Diary, 16 April 1951, Ayers Papers, TPL; Halford Ross Ryan, "Harry S. Truman: A Misdirected Defense for MacArthur's Dismissal," *Presidential Studies Quarterly* 9 (Fall 1981): 576–79; "Radio Report to the American People on Korea and the Far East," 11 April 1951, *PPOPT*, 226; Bradley and Blair, *General's Life*, 637.

13. "Remarks at West Point," 20 May 1952, and Press Conferences, 3 May 1951, 21 June 1951, 26 July 1951, and 11 December 1952: all in *PPOPT*, 1951, 263, 346, 425, and 1952, 347, 1074; Truman in Eben Ayers Diary, 3 Nov. 1951, Ayers Papers, TPL; for quote on Lee, see Hillman, *Mr. President*, 101; on unsent letters, see Elsy, *Unplanned Life*, 209.

14. John E. Mueller, *War, Presidents, and Public Opinion* (New York: John Wiley's Sons, 1973), 229; W. H. Lawrence, "Truman Indicates He May Run Again to Assure Peace," *NYT*, 13 Feb. 1952, 1; Truman to Arthur Schlesinger, Jr., 5 Nov. 1951, Merrill, ed., *Documentary History of Truman Presidency*, 20:400, and Rovere and Schlesinger, *General and the President*, 27; Kenneth Heckler, memo for John A. Carroll, 17 April 1951, and memorandum for Mr. Murphy, 7 May 1951: both in Averell Harriman Papers, Box 304, Library of Congress; Pearson, "Secret MacArthur Data Cited," *WP*, 4 May 1951, 9; Report of Congressman Charles B. Deane, ca. Oct. 1949, President's Secretary's File, Foreign Affairs, Far East, Box 177, TPL; Elsey, *An Unplanned Life*, 207.

15. Robert Caro, *The Years of Lyndon Johnson: Master of the Senate* (New York: Knopf, 2002), 372; Ayers, *Diary*, 241, 295, 328; Richard M. Fried, *Men against McCarthy* (New York: Columbia University Press, 1976), 86, 136.

16. Gilbert C. Fite, *Richard B. Russell, Jr., Senator from Georgia* (Chapel Hill: University of North Carolina Press, 1991), 194–97, 251–52, 281, 436–46; Caroline Ziemke, "Senator Richard Russell and the 'Lost Cause' in Vietnam, 1954–1968," *Georgia Historical Quarterly* 72 (Spring 1988), quote on 42.

17. Fite, *Russell*, 224, 259; Robert Mann, *The Walls of Jericho: Johnson, Humphrey, Russell, and Civil Rights* (New York: Harcourt, Brace, 1996), 69; Caro, *Years of Johnson*, 464–70.

18. "Compared with Tydings," *WP*, 6 May 1951, 2:1; "Memorandum on MacArthur Hearings," n.d., Russell Papers, Box. 6; Caro, *Years of Johnson*, xiv, 202, 218, 222, 372; Mann, *Walls of Jericho*, 38; quotes in Fite, *Russell*, 137, 235; Harold Martin, "The Man Behind the Brass," *Saturday Evening Post*, 233 (June 2, 1951): 22–23.

19. Sen. Russell Long, LBJ, and reporter William S. White quoted in Mann, *Walls of Jericho*, 76, 109, 110; Eric F. Goldman, *The Tragedy of Lyndon Johnson* (New York: Knopf, 1969), 90, 119; Caro, *Years of Johnson*, 207; George E. Reedy, *The Twilight of the Presidency* (New York: World Publishing, 1970), 44–45.

20. "Analysis of May 21 Testimony," "Public Relations Analysis of MacArthur Testimony and Effects," n.d. and "Revised Memorandum on the MacArthur Investigation," n.d., all in Russell Papers, Box 6.

21. Johnson, 5 May 1951, at *MacArthur Hearings*, 214; Sen. Johnson quoted in Col. Willis S, Mathews, "Memorandum for Gen. Collins," 23 May 1951, JCS, GF, 1951–53, RG 218, Box 4, NA.

22. Incident told and Johnson and MacArthur quoted in Robert Dallek, *Lone Star Rising: Lyndon Johnson and His Times, 1908–1960* (New York: Oxford University Press, 1991), 236–41; for Johnson's private statement to MacArthur, see George Reedy, "Oral History," 21 May 1982, 4:8, Lyndon Johnson Presidential Library [hereafter JPL], Austin Texas.

23. Texas newspaperman Ronnie Duggar quoted and Johnson's questioning discussed in Dallek, *Lone Star Rising*, 241, 400; Sam Huston Johnson, "Oral History," 23 June 1976, 5:38, JPL; Johnson and MacArthur at *MacArthur Hearings*, 206–207.

24. Johnson, 12 Dec. 1950, in *Congressional Record*, 81st, Cong., 2nd. Sess., 16458–59; Johnson quoted in Mann, *Walls of Jericho*, 86; "Senators in poll 23–22 for General," *NYT*, 29 April 1951, 37; Russell to R. A. Caldwell, 26 May 1951, and Fred Moss to Russell, 30 Nov. 1950, Boxes 1 and 6, Russell Papers; untitled notes of conversation with Hoover, n.d., Fellers Papers, MMFL; James, *Years of MacArthur*, 1:353, 3:616; for Hoover's private misgivings, see "Memo. of Conference with Hoover," 14 April 1951, H. Alexander Smith Papers, Box 106, Mudd Manuscript Library, Princeton University.

25. Hanson Baldwin, "The Magic of MacArthur," *NYT*, 23 April 1951, 6. "Report from the Nation: The Reactions To General MacArthur's Week," and "How Congress Reacted to General M'Arthur's Address—An Applause Chart," *NYT*, 22 April 1951, E:2 and 5; Pentagon statement in *NYT*, 20 April 1951, 8.

26. "MacArthur Is Loaded with Documents . . . ," *Newsweek* 37 (7 May 1951), 23; MacArthur, 3 May 1951, *MacArthur Hearings*, 38, 48.

27. Pace, "Oral History," 14, MMFL; James, *Years of MacArthur*, 1:288–89.

28. Collins, *War In Peacetime*, 232; quotation from Arthur Krock, "Administration's Turn To Take The Offensive," *NYT*, 10 June 1951, 4:3; also see "Joint Chiefs vs. MacArthur," *WP*, 3 June 1951, 4B.

29. Hunt, *Untold Story of MacArthur*, 26–31; MacArthur, *Reminiscences*, 26; "Bradley Comments," *NYT*, 20 April 1951, 8; "Congress to Get Pentagon Side of Asian Story," *WP*, 22 April 1951, 1 and 4.

30. Pearson, *Pearson Diaries*, 157, 159; Cabinet Meeting, 16 April 1951, Connelly Papers, Box 1, TPL; Marshall at *MacArthur Hearings*, 323.

31. Marshall and subsequently Gen. Collins at *MacArthur Hearings*, 323, 351, 1239, 1248–49, 1266; Marshall as a witness described in "350,000 Words," *NYT*, 13 May 1951, 4:1; "Memo re MacArthur Hearings," 15 May 1951; "Public Relations Analysis of MacArthur Testimony and Its Effects," n.d.; both in Russell Papers, Box 5.

32. "350,000 Words," *NYT*,13 May 1951, 4:1; Truman Diary, 14 Sept. 1950, in Truman, *Off the Record*, 192; "Questions To Be Asked To General Bradley," 15 May 1951, Russell Papers, Box 5.

33. James Tobin, *Ernie Pyle's War: America's Eyewitness to World War II* (New York: Free Press, 1997), 110; David Nichols, ed., *Ernie's War: The Best of Ernie Pyle's World War II Dispatches* (New York: Random House, 1986), 357–58; for one (of the many) revisionist assessments of Bradley's generalship, see Martin Blumenson, *The Battle of the Generals: The Untold Story of the Falaise Pocket—The Campaign that Should Have Won World War II* (New York: William Morrow, 1993), esp. 268; Russell at *MacArthur Hearings*, 726; Marshall, n.d., quoted in D'Este, *Eisenhower: Soldier's Life*, 404; Adrian Fisher, "Oral History," 30 Oct. 1969, 16, JPL.

34. Russell, *MacArthur Hearings*, 726; Col. Marshall Carter to Bradley, 23 April 1951, JCS, GF, 1951–53, RG 218, Box 4; Bradley Calendar, 24 April 1951, Bradley Papers,

USMHI; Sec. of the Air Force Thomas Finletter, 21 May 1951, quoted in Pearson, *Pearson Diaries*, 162.

35. Bradley, statement at *MacArthur Hearings*, 727, 732; Gallup poll in *WP*, 10 June 1951, 8M; drafts of statement, n.d., MacArthur File, Bradley Papers, USMHI; Bradley to Sen. Bourke Hickenlooper, 21 May 1951, *MacArthur Hearings*, 943.

36. "Analysis of May 21 Testimony," Box 6, Russell Papers; Senator Brien McMahon quoted in Matthews, "Memorandum for General Bradley," 15 May 1951, JCS, GF, 1951–53, RG 218,Box 4; for the Taft-Russell coalition, see Caro, *Years of Johnson*, 200, 216; Fite, *Russell*, 250.

37. William S. White, "GOP Is Badly Split Over Inquiry Tactics," *NYT*, 21 May 1951, 4:7; Taft in *Congressional Record*, 81st Cong., 2nd Sess., 4474.

38. *Gallup Poll*, 2:994; Bradley interview, 30 March 1955, Post-Presidential Papers, Box 641, TPL; Lippmann, "The Constitutional Crisis," *WP*, 21 May 1951, 7; Reston, *Deadline*, 137, 142.

39. Wiley and Russell, 23 May 1951, *MacArthur Hearings*, 1017, 1030; William S. White, "GOP Is Badly Split Over Inquiry Tactics," *NYT*, 21 May 1951, 4:7; "Wiley Rebuked by Russell On Reference to 'Whitewash'," *WP*, 23 May 1951, 12; Bradley, memoranda for record, 24 and 25 April 1951, MacArthur folders, Bradley Papers, U. S. Military Academy and USMHI, respectively; "Questions to be asked to General Bradley," 15 May 1951, Russell Papers, Box 5.

40. "McCarthy Bids Johnson Tell Why He Was Broken," *NYT* 25 May 1951, 17; *Life*, 24 March 1952, quoted in Caro, *Years of Johnson*, 378, 381. This writer counted over 200 letters of praise sent to Russell; the first two quoted were written on 17 and 22 May 1951. Roger Schindler to Russell, 11 May 1951; "Public Relations Analysis of MacArthur Testimony and Its Effects," n.d., all in Russell Papers, Boxes 3, 4, and 5; Marquis Childs, "Is GOP Strategy Backfiring?" *WP*, 19 May 1951, 7.

41. Bradley and Collins at *MacArthur Hearings*, 740, 747, 748, 1196, 1200, 1202, 1216, 1264, 1266; Memorandum for Record, 25 April 1951, Bradley Papers, MacArthur File, USMHI; Smith, "Oral History," 13.

42. *Time*, 4 June 1951, and *Time* reporter memo per Russell on Johnson, ca. Dec. 1951 quoted in Caro, *Years of Johnson*, 379, 382, also see 222; Harriman, "Oral History," 19–20, MMFL; L. J. Sverdrup [St. Louis public works construction entrepreneur and WWII brigadier general in MacArthur's corps of engineers] to Truman, 17 Nov. 1964, RG 15, Box 12, MMFL; Russell in 1953 quoted in Mann, *Walls of Jericho*, 131; Truman to MacArthur, 2 April 1964, RG 13a, Papers of Jean MacArthur, Sympathy and Condolences VIP File; MMFL; MacArthur quoted in Dr. Norman M. Scott, "General of the Army Douglas MacArthur and me," *Bohemian Club Literary Notes* (Winter 1997–98): 6.

43. *MacArthur Hearings*, 13; MacArthur, 20 Jan. 1954, quoted in *NYT*, 9 April 1964, 16; MacArthur, December 1952 and not dated, quoted in Blaik, *Red Blaik Story*, 493, 502, 506; Hunt, *Untold Story of MacArthur*, 181–82, 451, 458; Saltzman, "Oral History," 5–7.

44. Saltzman, "Oral History," 6; James, *Years of MacArthur*, 1:436; Acheson to Hickenlooper, n.d., in Abramson, *Spanning the Century*, 442; Rusk quoted in McGlothlen, *Controlling the Waves*, 20.

45. Unidentified observer quoted in "Policy," *NYT*, 3 June 1951, 4:1; "Acheson, 'Iron Man' Witness," *WP*, 10 June 1951, 6M; "Acheson and Politics," *NYT*, 3 June 1951, 4:1; numerous memorandum in Acheson Papers, Box 63, for example, "Meeting with Secretary on MacArthur Hearings," 17 May 1951, TPL.

46. William S. White, "M'Arthur Case A Political Tally," *NYT*, 3 June 1951, 4:6; Stewart Alsop, "Acheson: Not Whether, But When," *WP*, 2 June 1951, 7; Truman's letters in Acheson, *Present at Creation*, 114, 237.

47. News Conference, 13 Sept. 1951, *PPOPT*, 519; Acheson, *Present at Creation*, 495, 526, untitled report on committee members, n.d., Theodore Tannenwald Papers, Box 4, TPL; for Taft, see William S. White, "M'Arthur Case A Political Tally," *NYT*, 3 June 1951, 4:6.

48. Quotation in Chace, *Acheson*, 322.

49. Acheson's wife cited in Clark Clifford, *Counsel to the President: A Memoir* (New York: Random House, 1991), 142; Acheson quoted in Alsop, "Not Whether, But When," *WP*, 2 June 1951, 7; White, *In Search of History*, 343–46; Collins, *War in Peacetime*, 289.

50. State Department, "Special Guidance," 23 Dec. 1949, and Acheson: both in *MacArthur Hearings*, 1667–69, 1673–74; Reston "Issue Now Is Truce in Korea," *NYT*, 10 June 1951, 4:3.

51. Acheson, "Memo of Conversation on Formosa Problem with Senators Knowland and Smith," 5 Jan. 1951, *FRUS*, 6:260; Acheson, 6 and 7 June 1951, at *MacArthur Hearings*, 2001, 2125; MacArthur, 23 July 1951, MacArthur, *Speeches and Reports*, 181.

52. Kusnitz, *Public Opinion and Foreign Policy*, 24, 31, 34; *Gallup Poll*, 2:932, 962; Howard to MacArthur, 5 Dec. 1950, RG 5, Box 28, MMFL.

53. "United States Delegations Minutes of Second Meeting of President Truman and Prime Minister Attlee," 4 and 5 Dec. 1950, *FRUS*, 7:1368–69, 1401–1402; Truman on Howard quoted in Hamby, *Man of the People*, 485; for Marshall in 1946, see Macdonald, *Adventures in Chaos*, 81; Jim Lucas column from Korea in *Washington Daily News*, 24 Jan. 1951, 1.

54. "Memorandum of Conversation by Secretary of State," 29 December 1949; *FRUS*, 9:466–67; *Gallup Poll*, 2:954–55; Acheson, 5 Dec. 1950, *FRUS*, 7:1402.

55. Fraser J. Harbutt, *The Iron Curtain: Churchill, America, and the Origins of the Cold War* (New York: Oxford University Press, 1986), esp. 130–33, 150; James Reston, "Issue Is Not M'Arthur Or Acheson," *NYT*, 3 June 1951, 4:3. Acheson, 5 Dec. 1950, *FRUS*, 7:1401–1402.

56. "Question of Chiang," *NYT*, 10 June 1951, 4:3; Hanson Baldwin, "M'Arthur's Strategy," *NYT*, 13 May 1951, 4:4; Steven Rearden, *History of the Office of the Secretary of Defense: The Formative Years, 1947–1950* (Washington: Historical Office of Secretary of Defense, 1984), 218–19; Collins, "Memorandum for Secretary, JCS," 2 March 1951, JCS, GF, 1951–53, RG 218, Box 17.

57. Duffy and Carpenter, *MacArthur: Warrior as Wordsmith*, 65–68; Marquis Childs, "Martyrdom vs. War with China," *WP*, 12 April 1951, 11.

58. "Memorandum for the President about 114th NSC Meeting," 3 April 1952, PSF file, Box 220, TPL; Rankin, *China Assignment*, 141; Truman, 9 and 11 Sept. 1952, in Truman, *Off the Record*, 269, 271.

59. Livingston Merchant, 18 July 1951, quoted in Finkelstein, *Taiwan Dilemma*, 243; CIA report, 14 Sept. 1954, quoted in Chiang, *Friends and Enemies*, 144; for opinions and the other quotation from American diplomats and military officers, see Tucker, ed., *China Confidential*, 76–77, 134–35.

60. Macdonald, *Adventures in Chaos*, esp. 93–102; Acheson in 1949 quoted in Beisner, *Dean Acheson*, 175; Fenby, *Chiang Kai-shek*, 184, 232, 240, 403, 409; Chiang quoted in Ned Almond, "Oral History," 37, MMFL.

61. Thomas Gold, *State and Society in the Taiwan Miracle* (Amonk, NY: M. E. Sharpe, 1986), chapter 5; Howard Boorman, ed., *Biographical Dictionary of Republican China* (New York: Columbia University Press, 1967), 2:206–207; Donald Gillin, "Problems of Centralization in Republican China: The Case of Ch'en Ch'eng and the Kuomintang," *Journal of Asian Studies* 29 (Aug. 1970): 846–50.

62. Joe Collins at JCS meeting with State Dep't, 29 Dec. 1949, quoted in Finkelstein, *Taiwan Dilemma*, 246; Kurt M. Campbell and Derek J. Mitchell, "Crisis in the Taiwan Strait?," *Foreign Affairs* 80 (July–August 2001): 14–25.

63. Acheson, March 1950, quoted in Gardner, "Korean Borderlands," 133; CCP, 1 Aug 1950, quoted and issued discussed in Gittings, *Role of Chinese Army*, 121, 129, 130; Mao quoted in William Taubman, *Khrushchev: The Man and His Era* (New York: Norton, 2003), 342.

64. Stalin to Soviet Military Advisor, Beijing, in *CWIHPB*, Winter 1995–96, 60.

65. Nitze, interview for BBC documentary on Korea, Box 130, Nitze Papers.

66. McMahon described in James R. Newman and Bryon S. Miller, *The Control of Atomic Energy* (New York: McGraw-Hill, 1948), x; *MacArthur Hearings*, 74–75, 80, 98, 101.

67. Reston, "MacArthur Offers Congress Policy Basis on Hard Facts," *NYT*, 4 May 1951, 13; McMahon quoted in Ferrell, *Truman: A Life*, 335; *MacArthur Hearings*, 288; for isolationists and MacArthur, see Justus D. Doenecke, *Not to the Swift: The Old Isolationists in the Cold War Era* (Lewisburg: Bucknell University Press, 1979), 10, 216; 220; Lippmann, "The Question of American Destiny," *WP*, 8 May 1951, 13.

68. D. V. Jones to Russell, 26 April and Russell to Jones, 2 May 1951, Russell Papers, Box 2; Moore, *Kefauver Committee*, 145–71, 195–203; David Lawrence, "Secret MacArthur Hearings Called Democratic Cover-Up," *NYHT*, 1 May 1951, 8; Vice President Alben Barkley quoted in Cabinet Meeting, 14 May 1951, Connelly Papers, Box 1, TPL.

69. Robert Lovett quoted in Cabinet Meeting, 14 May 1951, Connelly Papers, Box 1; Bradley at *MacArthur Hearings*, 953. Manning to Russell, 24 May 1951, Russell Papers, Box 3.

70. Bradley and Vandenberg at *MacArthur Hearings*, 732, 1393; Cave Brown, *Treason in the Blood*, 400–405, 423–24; *New Yorker* 27 (26 May 1951): 22.

71. MacArthur, *Speeches and Reports*, 173–74; Tobey, Marshall, and JCS in *MacArthur Hearings*, 741, 946–47, 1220, 1262.

72. Letter to Joe Martin, 20 March 1951, James, *Years of MacArthur*, 3:590; CINCFE to DA, 10 March 1951, RG 16a, Box 5, MMFL; MacArthur at *MacArthur Hearings*, 5–9, 77–78.

73. National Intelligence Estimate, "Relations Between Chinese Communist Regime and USSR," 10 Sept. 1952, *FRUS, 1952–1954*, 14:101; MacArthur to Marshall, 8 Nov. 1950, RG 16a, Box 5, MMFL; LTG. W. E. Todd, ca. 1 July 1949, quoted in McGlothlen, *Controlling the Waves*, 71–72.

74. "The MacArthur Proposition" and "The Initiative in Korea," *NYT*, 22 April 1951, E:10, 18 April 1951, 30, and 19 April 1951, 30; Acheson, 1 June 1951, *MacArthur Hearings*, 1719.

75. E. T. Woolridge to Admiral [A. C.] Davis, 21 December 1950, JCS, GF, 1951–53, RG 218, Box 14; Linsey Parrott, "M'Arthur Aims Weighed in Korean And Far East," *NYT*, 1 April 1951, 4:1; MacArthur and Acheson at *MacArthur Hearings*, 300, 1719, 1776, 1946; Sen. Homer Ferguson (Rep.-Mich.) cited in Caridi, *Korean War and American Politics*, 157.

76. MacArthur at *MacArthur Hearings*, 274–75; Lester H. Brune, "The Soviet Union and the Korean War," in Brune, ed., *The Korean War: Handbook of the Literature and Research* (Westport, Conn.: Greenwood, 1996), 215; Stalin to Mao, 5 June 1951, *CWIHPB*, Winter 1995–96, 13.

77. Schecter, ed., *Khrushchev Remembers: Glasnost Tapes*, 101; Michael McCarthy, "Uncertain Enemies: Soviet Pilots in the Korean War," *Air Force History* 44 (Spring

1997): 36–39; General Al Guenther, 9 May 1952, quoted in Sulzberger, *Long Row of Candles*, 751.

78. Acheson, 1 June 1951, at *MacArthur Hearings*, 1719; situation described, U.S. government officials Paul Nitze and Herbert Brownell quoted, and Soviet general quoted in Jon Halliday, "Air Operations in Korea: The Soviet Side of the Story," in William J. Williams, ed., *A Revolutionary War: Korea and the Transformation of the Postwar World* (Chicago: Imprint Publications, 1993), 158–60; Stalin, 20 Aug. 1952, quoted in Bajanov and Bajanova, *Korean Conflict*, 180.

79. Marshall quoted in John Wiltz, "The MacArthur Hearings of 1951: The Secret Testimony," *Military Affairs* 39 (Dec. 1979): 168; Soviet general quoted Halliday, "Air Operations in Korea," 159; intelligence report cited in Roy K. Flint, "The Truman-MacArthur Conflict: Dilemmas of Civil-Military Relations in the Nuclear Age," in Richard H. Kohn, ed., *The United States Military under the Constitution of the United States, 1789–1991* (New York: New York University Press, 1991), 235, 264; for actual capacity see, Holloway, *Stalin and the Bomb*, 243, 332.

80. Mao to Stalin, 3 July, Stalin to Mao, 29 May, and Peng to Mao, 4 June 1951: all in Bajanov and Bajanova, *Korean Conflict*, 128–30, 140–41; for Stalin's fear that Truman would unleash nuclear weapons on Russia, see Talbott, ed., *Khrushchev Remembers*, 1:361, 2:356, and Gen. Dmitry Volkognov, 22 June 1993, in Foreign Broadcast Information Service, *Russian International Affairs*, 11–12. JCS quoted in Wiltz, "MacArthur Hearings," 168.

81. "Memorandum for Mr. Harriman, Mr. Murphy, and Company," 29 May 1951, Merrill, ed., *Documentary History of Truman Presidency*, 20:246.

82. MacArthur at *MacArthur Hearings*, 39–40; "Memo Re Marshall Testimony," n.d., Russell Papers, Box 6.

83. David Lawrence, "Prolonging Korea Stalemate Laid to Democratic Leaders," *NYHT*, 27 April 1951, 12; statistics in Xu Yan, "Chinese Forces and Casualties," 49–50; for battlefield data, see Billy C. Mossman, *Ebb and Flow: November 1950–July 1951* (Washington: U.S. Army Center of Military History, 1990), chapters 19–22; PFC Paul Martin, 29 1951, in Knox, *Korean War: Oral History*, 2:210.

84. Johnson and Collins in *MacArthur Hearings*, 1275; MacArthur statement of 7 March 1951, and JCS testimony reprinted in ibid., 363, 379, 416, 430, 755, 968, 1226, 1244, 3540.

85. Truman at 74th Meeting of the NSC, 11 Dec. 1950, PSF, Box 210, TPL; Marshall, 25 July 1949, quoted in Maurice Matloff, *Strategic Planning for Coalition Warfare, 1943–1944* (Washington: Center of Military History, 1959), 4; Marshall, April 1951, quoted in Frank Pace, "Oral History," 17, MMFL; McMahon quoted in *NYT*, 21 May 1951, 4.

86. "Memo Re Second Day of Marshall Testimony," n.d., and "Analysis of May 21 Testimony," Russell Papers; Boxes 5 and 6; Marshall at *MacArthur Hearings*, 363; see for example, CJ Moran to Russell, 15 May 1951; "housewife" to Russell, 12 May, and Mrs. Chauncey Hawkins to Russell, 14 May 1951: all in Russell Papers, Box 4; Bradley at *MacArthur Hearings*, 756, 937.

87. Anthony Leverino, "Wanted By The GOP—The Man," *NYT*, 13 May 1951, 4:5; Marshall, *Interviews and Reminiscences*, 4:487–88; "Korean Visit Just Routine, Marshall Says," *NYT*, 9 June 1951, 1; 3; "Marshall Asserts Foe Is Badly Hurt," *NYT*, 13 June 1951, 7.

88. Quirk, *Wars and Peace*, 236–41.

89. Rosemary Foot, *A Substitute for Victory: The Politics of Peacemaking at the Korean Armistice Talks* (Ithaca: Cornell University Press, 1990), 17; Ridgway, *Korean War*, 183; Jian, *Mao's China and Cold War*, 100; "Memorandum of telephone conversation

between Acheson and Senator Robert Kerr," 29 June 1951, Acheson Papers, Box 68, TPL; *Gallup Poll*, June and July 1951, 2:993 and 998; News Conference, 28 June 1951, *PPOPT*, 365.

90. *Reminiscences*, 407.

91. Raymond Daniel, "Britain Jubilant at M'Arthur Shift," NYT, 12 April 1951, 16; Rusk, 24 March 1951, quoted in Belmonte, "Anglo-American Relations and Dismissal of MacArthur," 659; Gallup Poll in WP, 20 May 1951, 5B; radio address (12 April) quoted in Marvin E. Stromer, *The Making of a Political Leader: Kenneth S. Wherry and the United States Senate* (Lincoln: University of Nebraska Press, 1969), 64; for the Democrats following the path of Labour and the quote, by Joe Martin, 15 April 1950, see Hasenfus, "Managing Partner: Martin," 250–53, 263–64.

92. Raymond Daniel, "British Fear U.S. Heads Down 'M'Arthur Road'," NYT 27 May 1951, 4:6; Acheson to Embassy, 17 April 1951, FRUS, 7:352. "Memorandum of Conversation by the Deputy to the Consultant," 5 April 1951, FRUS, 6:966.

93. Acheson at Meeting on North Atlantic Union and Other Matters, 14 Aug. 1950, Acheson Papers, Box 67, TPL; Edmonds, *Setting the Mould*, 198–200; Bullock, *Bevin*, 821; Truman to Attlee on 7 Dec. 1950 in FRUS, 7:1451–52; Truman, *Memoirs*, 2:409–10.

94. Howard K. Smith comment in *Nation* 171 (9 Dec. 1950): 520–21; Michael Foot, *Aneurin Bevan: A Biography* (London: Macgibbon and Kee, 1962–73), 2:309–10, 327, 343; left-wing press quoted in Clifton Daniel, "Anti-U.S. Talk Persists in Britain," NYT, 29 Dec. 1950, 6; Kenneth O. Morgan. *Labour In Power, 1945–1951* (Oxford: Clarendon Press, 1984), 430–31, 448, 454.

95. Bevan quoted in NYT, 17 March 1952, 2; Alfred Landon and Senator William Knowland, 31 Jan. and 2 Feb. 1951, respectively, quoted in Donald Mrozek, "Progressive Dissenter: Herbert Hoover's Opposition to Truman's Overseas Military Policy," *Annals of Iowa* 42 (Summer 1976): 284–85; "Heroism in Korea," WP, 15 May 1951, 14; Carl Zeiss of Woodsctock, Ill. to Richard Russell, Russell Papers, Box 4; Acheson, 2 June 1951, *MacArthur Hearings*, 1772.

96. "Moves by Britain," NYT, 13 Aug. 1951, 4:2; Prime Minister Attlee, 18 April 1951, quoted in Foot, *Bevan*, 320; Wherry, 12 April 1951, quoted in Stromer, *Making of a Political Leader*, 64; Raymond Daniel, "British Drop Formosa Issue For Duration of Korea War," NYT, 13 Aug. 1951, 1; *Manchester Guardian* quoted in Howard K. Smith, "Thou Art Soldier Only," *Nation* 172 (21 April 1951): 363.

97. Sen. Alexander Wiley and Marshall, 9 May 1951, *MacArthur Hearings*, 417; Truman, 6 Jan. 1951, quoted in Hersey, "Profiles: The President," 21 April 1951, 37; "Annual Message to Congress," 8 Jan. 1951, *PPOPT*, 9.

98. Bradley, 5 April 1949, quoted in Escott Reid, *Time of Fear and Hope: The Making of the North Atlantic Treaty, 1947–1949* (Toronto: McClelland and Stewart, 1977), 123; MacArthur and Bradley, *MacArthur Hearings*, 104, 730–31.

99. Carlo D'Este, *Bitter Victory: The Battle for Sicily, 1943* (New York: Dutton, 1988), 330–32, and D'Este, *Eisenhower: Soldier's life*, 647–49; "Questions to be Directed to General Marshall and/or Other Remaining Witnesses," n.d., Russell Papers, Box 6.

100. Bradley at *MacArthur Hearings*, 753; Bess, "Are Generals in Politics a Menace?" 136.

Ending the War without Truman or MacArthur

1. Eisenhower to Clifford Roberts, 19 June 1952, in *Eisenhower Papers*, 13:1251.

2. *FRUS*, 7:718.

3. Walter G. Hermes, *Truce Tent And Fighting Front* (Washington: Center of Military History, 1966), 16–36, 155–66.

4. Ibid., 122, 153–55; Chou En-lai to ambassador, 2 July 1950, in Xiaobing Li, et. al, ed., *Mao's Generals Remember Korea* (Lawrence: University Press of Kansas, 2001), 247n12; Chou En-lai telegram to UN secretary general, 24 Aug. 1950, in *Documents Concerning Taiwan*, 21.

5. Mao to Kim, 13 June 1951, CWIHPB, Winter 1995–96, 61–62; Pingchao Zhu, "The Road to an Armistice: An Examination of the Chinese and American Diplomacy during the Korean War Cease-Fire Negotiations, 1950–1953" (Ph.D. diss, Miami University, 1998), 127–28; Collins, *War in Peacetime*, 366.

6. Mao to Stalin, 21 June 1951, and Stalin to Mao, 13 June 1951, in Bajanov and Bajanova, *The Korean Conflict*, 132, 136; Chang and Halliday, *Mao: Untold Story*, 362–63, 374; Stalin conversation with Chou En-lai, 20 Aug. 1952, CWIHPB, Winter 1995–96, 116.

7. Yan, "Chinese Forces and Casualties: Facts and Statistics," 51, 53; Hermes, *Truce Tent and Fighting Front*, 170, 486, 495–96.

8. Nitze and Lovett, 2 and 16 March 1950, quoted in Cumings, *Origins of Korean War*, 2:178–79; Alfred H. Paddock, Jr., *U.S. Army Special Warfare: Its Origins* (Washington: National Defense University Press, 1982), 84–86; Eisenhower to Robert Stevens, Sec. of the Army, 2 April 1954, *Eisenhower Papers*, 15:999–1000; McClure to Eisenhower, June 1947, in Alfred H. Paddock, Jr., "Robert Alexis McClure: Forgotten Father of Army Special Warfare," *Special Warfare* 12 (Fall 1999): 5.

9. Mark Elliot, *Pawns of Yalta: Soviet Refugees and America's Role in Their Repatriation* (Urbana: University of Illinois Press, 1982), 37, 40–42, 112; interview with Bradley, 29 March 1955, Post-Presidential Papers, Box 641, TPL.

10. Elliot, *Pawns of Yalta* 102, 121, 135–36; for Kremlin propaganda on race, see Thomas Borstelmann, *The Cold War and the Color Line: American Race Relations in the Global Arena* (Cambridge: Harvard University Press, 2001), 75.

11. Bradley to Marshall, 15 Jan. 1951, and other documents in Mitrovich, *Undermining the Kremlin*, 58, 67, 97, 187; McClure to Collins, 5 July 1951, quoted in Barton J. Bernstein, "The Struggle over the Korean Armistice: Prisoner of Repatriation," in Bruce Cummings, ed., *Child of Conflict: The Korean-American Relationship, 1943–1953* (Seattle: University of Washington Press, 1983), 276; Bradley to SecDef., 8 August 1951, Psychological Strategy Board Files, Box 32, TPL; Bradley speech, 17 April 1951, in NYT, 10; SecDef to JCS, 25 Sept. 1951, quoted in Schnabel and Watson, *History of JCS: Korean War*, 1:681.

12. Gittings, *Role of Chinese Army*, 110–11; 117; Hanson W. Baldwin, "Chinese Captives Talk," NYT, 1 June 1951, 3.

13. Samuel M. Meyers and Albert D. Biderman, ed., *Mass Behavior in Battle and Captivity: The Communist Soldier in the Korean War* (Chicago: University of Chicago Press, 1968), 55, 78, 82; Ridgway, "Oral History," 61–62; Hermes, *Truce Tent And Fighting Front*, 170; Elliot, *Pawns of Yalta*, 139.

14. Patrick Dolan, n.d., quoted in Anthony Cave Brown, *The Last Hero, Wild Bill Donovan* (New York: Vintage Books, 1984), 552; McClure to Collins, 5 July 1951, in Bernstein, "Struggle over Korean Armistice," 276; Stueck, *Korean War: International History*, 266, 270, 279; Mao, 15 July 1952, quoted in Zhihua, "Sino-North Korean Conflict," CWIHPB, Winter 2003–Spring 2004, 20.

15. Mao, 2 Oct. 1950, in "Mao's Dispatch of Chinese Troops," 1:68; Jian, *Mao's China and Cold War*, 320n74; Hong Xuezhi, "Adopting an 'Active Defense' Strategy" in

"Chinese Generals Recall the Korean War," *Chinese Historian* 7 (Summer 1994): 147; Zhang, *Mao's Military Romanticism*, 154–55; Chinese negotiator, 15 Jan. 1952, quoted in Stueck, *Korean War: International History*, 252.

16. Ambassador Alan Kirk, 28 May 1951, cited in Sulzberger, *Long Row of Candles*, 636; Chai Chengwen, "Preparing for the Truce Talks in July 1951" in "Chinese Generals Recall the Korean War," 150; "Statement on Ridgway's Korean Armistice Proposal," 7 May 1952, *PPOPT*, 121.

17. Marshall quoted in Pace, "Oral History," 17, MMFL; Truman Diary, 9 Sept. 1952, in Truman, *Off the Record*, 270.

18. Marshall Schulman, 15 May 1951, quoted in Steven Casey, "White House Publicity Operations during the Korean War, June 1950–1951," *Presidential Studies Quarterly* 35 (Dec. 2005): 700; Patterson, *Mr. Republican*, 492; Martin, broadcast on 13 April 1951, in *Congressional Record*, 81st Cong., 1st Sess., A2110; Truman, *Memoirs*, 2:106; Miscamble, *Kennan and Foreign Policy*, 107; George Morgan, 1 July 1952, quoted in Mitrovich, *Undermining the Kremlin*, 95.

19. Truman, 4 Dec. 1950, during meeting with Prime Minister Atlee, *FRUS*, 7:1368; "Radio Report on Far East," 11 April 1951, *PPOPT*, 226–27; Ridgway quoted in *WP*, 10 May 1951, 13, and cited in Bohlen, *Eyewitness to History*, 298–300.

20. Truman Diary, 27 Jan. 1952, in PSF, Box 333, TPL; "M'Arthur Denies Truman Charge," *NYT*, 23 Dec. 1960, 1.

21. James Van Fleet, commanding general Eighth Army, 27 Nov. 1951 quoted in Hermes, *Truce Tent and Fighting Front*, 177; Ridgway to JCS, 1 March 1952, Ridgway Papers, Box 20; "Acheson Would Accept 38th . . . ," and "Taft Blasts 'Compromise' Korean Peace," in *WP*, 3 June 1951, 1 and 10 June 1951, 6M; "Report of certain members . . . ," *MacArthur Hearings*, 3605; Harris, "MacArthur Dismissal—Study in Political Mail," 275–76; public opinion polls in Scott and Withey, *United States and United Nations*, 84–86; Marquis Childs, "Korean War: Americans Still Don't Understand It," *WP*, 30 May 1951, 9.

22. Foot, *Substitute for Victory*, 88–92.

23. Stalin, 20 August 1952, *CWIHPB*, Issues 6–7, 12; Acheson to Truman, 8 Feb. 1952, *FRUS, 1952–1954*, 15:44; State Department position paper, 20 May 1952, quoted and Acheson discussed in Foot, *Substitute for Victory*, 88, 91, 127.

24. MacArthur and Marshall at *MacArthur Hearings*, 72, 363; CNO W. H. Fechteler to Secretary of Defense. 15 Oct. 1951, Psychological Strategy Board Files, Box 32, TPL.

25. Lippmann, "What The Generals Told Us," *WP*, 4 June 1951, 7; Elliot, *Pawns of Yalta*, 43, 110, 113; Eden, ca. Sept. 1952, quoted in Victor S. Kaufman, *Confronting Communism: U.S. and British Policies toward China* (Columbia University of Missouri Press, 2001), 59.

26. Mao, 18 July 1952 and 5 Sept. 1950, quoted in *CWIHPB*, Winter 1995/1996, 78, and Zhang, *Mao's Military Romanticism*, 189, respectively; Acheson to Truman, 15 Nov. 1952, Acheson Papers, Box 71; Acheson at 74th Meeting of NSC, 11 Dec. 1950, PSF, Box 210, both in TPL.

27. Adm. Leslie Stevens, 21 Dec. 1950, quoted and others cited in Mitrovich, *Undermining the Kremlin*, 71, 101, 150; Acheson to Lester Pearson, 29 July 1950, quoted in Stueck, *Rethinking Korean War*, 222; Acheson to Canadian Cabinet, 22 Nov. 1952, and to Anthony Eden, 19 Dec. 1952 quoted in Bernstein, "Struggle over Korean Armistice," 305, and Stueck, *Korean War: International History*, 299; Eden's private secretary, Evelyn Shuckburgh, quoted in Beisner, *Dean Acheson*, 442; Acheson to Truman, 15 Nov. 1952, Acheson Papers, Box 71, TPL; Hillman, *Mr. President*, 101.

28. Quote in Virgil Pinkley with James F. Scheer, *Eisenhower Declassified* (Old Tappan, N.J.: Fleming H. Revell Comp., 1979), 241.

29. Eisenhower, May 1951 and March and May 1952, quoted and paraphrased in Sulzberger, *Long Row of Candles*, 635. 738, 752; Eisenhower, *Diaries* (ed. Ferrell), 204; White, *In Search of History*, 348–51; final quote, 2 June 1952, in Paul David, ed., *Presidential Nominating Politics in 1952* (Baltimore: Johns Hopkins Press, 1954), 1:52.

30. Hermes, *Truce Tent and Fighting Front*, chapter 13; conversation between Stalin and Chou, 20 Aug. 1952, quoted in Bajanov and Bajanova, *The Korean Conflict*, 181; meeting of Stalin and Kim, 4 Sept. 1952, *CWIHPB*, Winter 2003–Spring 2004, 379; Conrad C. Crane, "Raiding the Beggar's Pantry" The Search for Airpower Strategy in the Korean War," *Journal of Military History* 63 (Oct. 1999): 913–19, quote from air force planner on 915.

31. Alsop columns in *WP*, 18 May 1951, 21 and 24 Aug. 1952, 58; army position paper, 15 Sept. 1952, quoted in Max Hastings, *The Korean War* (New York: Simon and Schuster, 1987), 314; *Gallup Poll*, 2:932, 988–89; Harris, *Is There a Republican Majority?* 26; Roper Poll, July 1952, cited in Haynes, *Awesome Power*, 237. Lyndon Johnson's approval rating sank to 28 percent in the fall of 1968, Richard Nixon's to 25 percent in the summer of 1974.

32. Gallup polls in *WP*, 10 June 1951, 8M and *Gallup Poll*, 2:1038, 1062; Beisner, *Dean Acheson*, 440.

33. Eisenhower to Julius Earl Schaefer, 27 Dec. 1951, and to Edward Everett Hazlett, 21 June 1951, *Eisenhower Papers*, 12:819 and 368, respectively; Gallup Polls published in *WP*, 15 April 1951, 2:1, and cited in David, ed., *Nominating Politics in 1952*, 1:33.

34. Quotations in Neal, *Harry and Ike*, 142, 157, 188; Eisenhower, *At Ease*, 370–72; Anthony Leviero, "Wanted By The GOP—The Man," *NYT*, 13 May 1951, 4:5; Milton Eisenhower cited in Smith, *Dewey*, 579.

35. Eisenhower, Jan. and Feb. 1948, quoted in Howard Schonberger, "The General and the Presidency: Douglas MacArthur and the Election of 1948," *Wisconsin Magazine of History* 57 (Spring 1974): 209; Eisenhower, Dec. 1944, quoted in D'Este, *Eisenhower: Soldier's Life*, 655; on NATO, Nov. 1950, quoted in Condit, *Test of War*, 361; Eisenhower discussed and quoted on MacArthur in Ambrose, *Eisenhower*, 1:443, 478, 548–49.

36. MacArthur describing Taft to British diplomat in Dec. 1947 quoted in Schaller, *American Occupation of Japan*, 116; Taft, 25 July 1950 and 31 July 1951, in Patterson, *Mr. Republican*, 455, 491; Taft in *NYT*, 2 June 1951, 15, and *NYHT*, 10 January 1951, 1.

37. "Revised Memorandum on the MacArthur Investigation," n.d., Russell Papers, Box 6; Taft in *NYT*, 2 June 1951, 15, and *NYHT*, 10 January 1951, 1; Marshall in "Prepare For 10 Years of Tension," 29; Taft in *NYHT*, 8 April 1951, 4, and in *WP*, 6 May 1951, 1; MacArthur, *Speeches and Reports*, 181; Taft in Patterson, *Mr. Republican*, 487; Stewart Alsop, "MacArthur, Taft, And Eisenhower," *WP*, 2 May 1951, 15.

38. Letter to Dewey, 24 May 1951, in Patterson, *Mr. Republican*, 491; Caridi, *Korean War and American Politics*, 160, 195; for attacks on Stimson, see Westerfield, *Foreign Policy and Party Politics*, 154.

39. Eisenhower to Sulzberger, 29 Dec. 1951, with accompanying editorial footnotes, *Eisenhower Papers*, 12:825–26; Eisenhower quoted and his behavior in 1948 described in Pickett, *Eisenhower Decides To Run*, 41, 174; Smith, *Dewey*, 582; Steven Neal, *Dark Horse: A Biography of Wendell Willkie* (Garden City: Doubleday and Comp. 1984), 52, 86–87, 119–22; Robert McCormick quoted on pulling "a Willkie" in Vaughan, "Oral History," 119; Notes of Bonner Fellers, 13 and 14 April 1951, Fellers Papers, MMFL.

40. Caridi, *Korean War and American Politics*, 215–16; Homer Ferguson (Rep.-Mich.) to Herbert Hoover, 8 May 1952, quoted in Mrozek, "Progressive Dissenter: Hoover," 288–89; Eisenhower, 30 Oct. 1951, cited in Sulzberger, *Long Row of Candles*, 685; MacArthur, *Speeches and Reports*, 202, 204; MacArthurites cited in Marquis Childs, "Eisenhower on the Spot," *WP*, 11 May 1951, 20; MacArthur quoted in "The General vs. Generals," *Time*, 59 (26 May 1952): 24.

41. Taft quoted in William S. White, *The Taft Story* (New York: Harper and Brothers, 1954), 90; for quotations about "deputy commander," see Goulden, *Korea*, 608, and Pinkley, *Eisenhower Declassified*, 251; quotes from 1944 in James, *Years of MacArthur*, 2:423; report by Republican minority on the Russell Committee, ca. August 1951, in *MacArthur Hearings*, 3590.

42. Eisenhower quoted in *NYT*, 6 and 19 June 1952, 10 and 14, and in Robert A. Divine, *Foreign Policy and U.S. Presidential Elections: 1952–1960* (New York: New Viewpoints, 1974), 46; for public opinion polls on prospective candidates, see David, ed., *Nominating Politics in 1952*, 1:40–41, 54. In November 1951, when the Gallup poll asked Republican country chairmen which man "do you personally prefer as Republican candidate for President in 1952," 1.027 said Taft, 375 said Eisenhower, and 83 said MacArthur, see *Gallup Poll*, 2:1021.

43. For Eisenhower's staff, see Hasenfus, "Managing Partner: Martin," 292–93; News Conference, 12 June 1952, *PPOPT*, 416, 418; Truman on Taft, 11 July 1952, in Truman, *Off the Record*, 249.

44. W. H. Lawrence, "White House Sticks To Its Guns," *NYT*, 20 May 1951, 4:6; James, *Years of MacArthur*, 3:648–52; MacArthur, *Speeches and Reports*, 211, 213.

45. Adlai Stevenson, 12 Aug. 1952, quoted in McCullough, *Truman*, 907.

46. John Hersey, "Profiles: Mr. President," 14 April 1951, 42, 54; for quote on Bradley, see Hillman, *Mr. President*, 103; Bradley and Blair, *General's Life*, 653–57, for Bradley's fury in late 1944, see D'Este, *Eisenhower, Soldier's Life*, 647–49, 668, 671.

47. Truman on Russell in Mann, *Walls of Jericho*, 123; Truman on Russell and Harriman in Neal, *Harry and Ike*, 252; Gallup Poll, April 1952, cited in Fite, *Russell*, 277; for Kefauver, see David, et. al., *Nominating Politics in 1952*, 1:63–64.

48. McCullough, *Truman*, 889; Eisenhower quoted in Neal, *Harry and Ike*, 254; Truman at convention quoted in Divine, *Foreign Policy and Elections: 1952–60*, 39–40.

49. Reporter quoted in McCullough, *Truman*, 912; Truman describing his activities, 25 Sept. 1947, in Forrestal, *Diaries*, 319; Eisenhower, n.d., quoted in Pickett, *Eisenhower Decides to Run*, 47; Truman campaign speeches, Oct. 1952, *PPOPT*, 727, 737; Dewey quoted in *NYT*, 22 Oct. 1952, 14.

50. George Ball quoted in McCullough, *Truman*, 906; Stevenson, "Korea in Perspective," *Foreign Affairs* 30 (April 1952): 354; Eisenhower and Stevenson quoted in Divine, *Foreign Policy and Elections, 1952–60*, 71, 73, and John Barlow Martin, *The Life of Adlai E. Stevenson* (Garden City, N.Y.: Doubleday, 1976–77), 1:733–34.

51. Hazel Erskine, "The Polls: Is War A Mistake?," *Public Opinion Quarterly* 34 (Spring 1970): 138, and *Gallup Poll*, 2:1102, 1106; for voter interviews, see Samuel Lubell, *Revolt of the Moderates* (New York: Harper and Brothers, 1956), 39–43; Harris, *Is There a Republican Majority*, 27; Caridi, *Korean War and American Politics*, 224, 232, 235; Eisenhower to Clifford Roberts, 9 June 1952, *Eisenhower Papers*, 13:1251.

52. Poll and final quote from Eisenhower in Caridi, *Korean War and American Politics*, 212, 235; Divine, *Foreign Policy and Elections, 1952–60*, 69–75; Bradley and Blair, *General's Life*, 656; *Gallup Poll*, 2:1106.

53. MacArthur quoted in Ambrose, *Eisenhower*, 2:32; "MacArthur: Prefers Taft, Likes Ike, Hates Harry," *Newsweek* 39 (25 Feb. 1952), 23; D'Este, *Eisenhower: Soldier's Life*, 488; Truman quoted in Nixon, *Memoirs*, 378; Truman in 1959 quoted in Neal, *Harry and Ike*, 305.

54. Eisenhower quoted on "barnstorming" in Smith, *Dewey*, 606; Eisenhower described and quoted in Nixon, *Memoirs*, 379.

55. Truman campaign speech, 7 Oct. 1952, *PPOPT*, 282; T. Harry Williams, "The Macs and the Ikes: America's Two Military Traditions," *American Mercury* 75 (Oct. 1952): 32–39. Some embittered soldiers on Bataan called MacArthur "dugout Doug" but that nickname did not make it to the nation at large.

56. Truman, ed., *Where Buck Stops*, 56; Arnold Saltzman, "Oral History," 9–10, MMFL; Eisenhower described and quoted, 1967, in D'Este, *Eisenhower: Soldier's Life*, 45, 542.

57. Taylor quoted in Holman Hamilton, *Zachary Taylor: Soldier in the White House* (Indianapolis: Bobbs-Merrill, 1951), 134; editor of *The Springfield [Mass.] Republican*, ca. Nov. 1867, quoted in Brooks D. Simpson, *Let Us Have Peace: Ulysses S. Grant and the Politics of War and Reconstruction, 1861–1868* (Chapel Hill: University of North Carolina Press, 1981), 219; Eisenhower quoted in Goldman, *Crucial Decade*, 219; Congressman Carroll Reece quoted in David, ed., *Nominating Politics in 1952*, 1:52. I am only comparing Scott to Taylor as candidates for president. After Taylor became president, he was outspoken and unyielding on slavery and secession.

58. Discussion at 145th Meeting of NSC, 20 May 1953, in Ann Whitman File, 1953–61, NSC Series, Box 4, EPL.

59. Paul Nitze, "Interview given for BBC Documentary, 'Korea'," ca. Nov. 1986, Nitze Papers, Box 130; Eisenhower, *Diaries* (ed. Ferrell), 30 June 1950, 17; Eisenhower paraphrased in Adm. Forrest Sherman to Adm. Chester Nimitz, 6 July 1950, JCS, CF, RG 218, Box 232, NA.

60. Eisenhower, *Diaries* (ed. Ferrell), 30 June 1950, 17; Taft wing Republicans quoted in Goulden, *Korea*, 608–609; questions at the MacArthur hearings and the subsequent report by the 8 Taft Republicans, ca. August 1951, in *MacArthur Hearings*, 1225, 1258, 3575; European opinion discussed in Foot, *Substitute for Victory*, 172.

61. MacArthur to Eisenhower, 17 Dec. 1952, quoted in *NYT*, 9 April 1964, 16. According to a Roper Poll, 53 percent of the public wanted to "knock-out" the communists, 22 percent wanted to continue negotiations, and 12 percent wanted to pull out of Korea with or without a settlement, see *Time Magazine*, 22 Sept. 1952, 26; Walter Bedell Smith, 19 May 1953, in *FRUS, 1952–1954*, 15:1053.

62. Jason Kendall Moore, "Between Expediency and Principle: U.S. Repatriation Policy towards Russian Nationals, 1944–1949," *Diplomatic History* 24 (Summer 2000): 385–87, 389–92; Eisenhower on Zhukov in 1945 described in Harriman interview, 8 Dec. 1954, Post-Presidential Papers, Box 641, TPL; "Memorandum of Conversation with Zhukov," 20 and 23 July 1955, *FRUS, 1955–1957*, 5:410, 413–15,417, 490–91; Eisenhower Diary, 14 July 1955, *Eisenhower Papers*, 16:1779.

63. Kenneth A. Osgood, "Form before Substance: Eisenhower's Commitment to Psychological Warfare and Negotiations with the Enemy," *Diplomatic History* 24 (Summer 2000): 412–17; Theoharis, *Yalta Myths*, 28, 52–54, 138; Mitrovich, *Undermining the Kremlin*, 104, 108, 114, 120.

64. Rosemary Foot, *The Wrong War, American Policy and the Dimensions of the Korean War, 1950–1953* (Ithaca: Cornell University Press, 1985), chapter 7; Bradley to Secretary of Defense, "U.S. Courses of Action in Korea," 3 Nov. 1951, JCS, CF, RG 218, Box 233, NA.

65. JCS to Secretary of Defense, 19 May 1953, and NSC Meetings, 13 and 20 May 1953: all in *FRUS, 1952–1954*, 15:1012–17, 1060–65.

66. Bradley, 6 Feb. 1953, quoted and issues discussed in Accinelli, *Crisis and Commitment*, 114–17; "State of the Union," 8 Feb. 1953, *Public Papers of the Presidents of the United States: Dwight D. Eisenhower* (Washington: U.S. Government Printing Office, 1958–61), 16–17 [hereafter *PPOPE*] "Formosan Decision First Step 'Asian Fight Asian' Policy," *Newsweek* 41 (9 Feb. 1953): 50.

67. Dulles quoted and issue discussed in Chang, *Friends and Enemies*, 81–83, 194; "Chiang Almost Ready," *Newsweek* 41 (9 Feb. 1953): 34; Accinelli, *Crisis and Commitment*, 91, 94–95.

68. For NSC director and Eisenhower quoted, see "Brief of Conversation between Generals Matthews and General Cutler, "5 Feb. 1953, and Bradley to Chase (Personal), 5 Feb. 1953: both in JCS, GF, 1951–53, RG 218, Box 7; "Memorandum of State Dep't-JCS Staff Meeting," 9 April 1952, *FRUS, 1952–54*, 14:34–40.

69. "M'Arthur Denies Truman Charge," *NYT*, 23 Dec. 1960, 1; "Truman on MacArthur: 'I Expressed an Opinion'," *NYHT*, and "HST Has 'No Proof' of MacBomb Charge," *New York Daily News:* both 24 Dec. 1960, 1. MacArthur made the invasion of the mainland his priority when getting Ridgway to take his case to the army chief of staff. After his dismissal, he made statements about using nuclear weapons to Eisenhower and selected newspapermen, see memo to Eisenhower, 14 Dec. 1952, in MacArthur, *Reminiscences*, 411, and interview with Bob Considine on 27 Jan. 1954, in *NYT*, 9 April 1964, 16.

70. Major General Charles L. Bolte to MacArthur, 21 Dec. 1950, RG 9, Box 121, MMFL; Eisenhower in Dec. 1952 quoted in Foot, *Wrong War*, 205. In 1948, Eisenhower described the atomic bomb as "horrible and destructive," see *Crusade in Europe*, 443.

71. Secretary of State John Foster Dulles, n.d. and 21 May 1953, quoted respectively in Rosemary Foot, "Nuclear Coercion and the Ending of the Korean Conflict," *International Security* 13 (Winter 1988–89): 92, and Edward C. Keefer, "President Dwight D. Eisenhower and the End of the Korean War," *Diplomatic History* 10 (Summer 1986): 280; Eisenhower quoted, mid-1948, in Borowski, *Hollow Threat*, 117; for Eisenhower's chronic ambiguity on nuclear weapons, see Campbell Craig, *Destroying the Village: Eisenhower and Thermonuclear War* (New York: Columbia University Press, 1998), 57–60, 99–102.

72. Marshall, 9 May 1951, *MacArthur Hearings*, 415; Eisenhower to John Cowles, 3 Oct. 1951, *Eisenhower Papers*, 12:603; Dwight D. Eisenhower, *The White House Years: Mandate for Change, 1953–1956* (Garden City, N.Y.: Doubleday, 1963), 179–80.

73. News Conference, 28 May 1953, *PPOPE*, 335; Eisenhower, 30 May 1953, quoted in Richard Leighton, *Strategy, Money, and the New Look, 1953–1956* (Washington: Historical Office of the Secretary of Defense, 2001), 4.

74. Gittings, *Role of Chinese Army*, 121, 135; Stalin to Mao, 5 June 1951, quoted in Bajanov and Bajanova, *Korean Conflict*, 172; Yan, "Chinese Forces and Casualties: Facts and Statistics," 58; Stalin to Chou En-lai, 3 Sept. 1952, quoted in *CWIHPB*, Winter 1995–96, 16.

75. Payne, *Spanish Civil War, Soviet Union, and Communism*, 157, 243–44; Chester Bowles, *Ambassador's Report* (NY: Harper and Brothers, 1954), 242–43; Lindesay Parrott, "Question In Korea Is: Does Foe Want A Truce?," *NYT*, 2 March 1952, E:3; speech of 7 Feb. 1953 in Michael Y. H. Kau and John K. Leung, eds., *The Writings of Mao Zedong, 1949–1976* (Armonk, N.Y.: M. E. Sharpe, 1986), 1:317.

76. Heinzig, *Soviet Union and Communist China*, 93–106; for fear of Truman using nuclear weapons, see Schecter, ed., *Khrushchev Remembers: Glasnost Tapes*, 100–101, and Strobe ed., *Khrushchev Remembers*, 1:361, 2:356; Brent and Naumov, *Stalin's Last Crime*, esp. 7, 211, 237–40, 284–85; Yoram Gorlizki and Oleg Khlevniuk, *Cold Peace:*

Stalin and the Soviet Ruling Circle, 1945–1953 (New York: Oxford University Press, 2004), 87, 97–98, 156–57, 167.

77. Gorlizki and Khlevniuk, *Cold Peace*, 152–54, 157–60; Brent and Naumov, *Stalin's Last Crime*, 284–92; Payne, *Spanish Civil War, Soviet Union, and Communism*, 190, 197, 242–43.

78. Bohlen, *Witness to History*, 347, 359, 363–64; Brent and Naumov, *Stalin's Last Crime*, 332–33; Gorlizki and Khlevniuk, *Cold Peace*, 100, 132–34, 167.

79. Schecter, *ed.*, *Khrushchev Remembers: Glasnost Tapes*, 100; Eisenhower quoted in Sherman Adams, *Firsthand Report: The Inside Story of the Eisenhower Administration* (London: Hutchinson, 1962), 102; messages quoted in Bajanov and Bajanova, *Korean Conflict*, 190–93; Foreign Minister Molotov, 4 July 1953, in *CWIHPB*, Winter 2003–Spring 2004, 382; Dulles quoted in McGeorge Bundy, *Danger and Survival: Choices About the Bomb in the First Fifty Years* (N.Y.: Random House, 1988), 243; Acheson, 19 Dec. 1967, McClellan and Acheson, ed., *Among Friends: Personal Letters*, 287; Acheson quoted in Reston, *Deadline*, 153.

80. Hermes, *Truce Tent and Fighting Front*, 431–32, 527; Truman, 1956 and 1958, quoted in Neal, *Harry and Ike*, 299, 305; Zhang, *Mao's Military Romanticism*, 245.

81. Pingchao Zhu "Road to Armistice," 218–19, 258, 263; Zhang, *Deterrence and Strategic Culture*, 139–40; "Our Great Victory in the War to Resist U.S. Aggression," 12 Sept. 1953, *Selected Works of Mao Zedong* (Peking: Foreign Language Press, 1977), 5:115–16; Xiaobing Li, *Mao's Generals Remember*, 227; Jian, *Mao's China and the Cold War*, 15, 51; Heinzig, *The Soviet Union and Communist China*, 259–61.

82. Di "Last Campaign To Unify China," 58; Truman, ed., *Where the Buck Stops*, 192–93; Truman, 13 Sept. 1951, quoted in Miscamble, *Kennan and Foreign Policy*, 246.

83. Mark W. Clark, *From the Danube to the Yalu* (New York: Harper, 1954), 1.

84. Letter reprinted in Ridgeway, *Soldier*, 327.

85. Reston in *NYT*, 27 July 1953, A3; *U.S. News and World Report*, 7 Aug. 1995, 14. Rhee to Ridgway, 17 July 1951, Ridgway Papers, Box 20;

86. Report of 16 July 1953 quoted in Chang, *Friends and Enemies*, 90; Mao, late May 1958, quoted in Zhang, *Deterrence and Strategic Culture*, 229; Eisenhower quoted in Neal, *Harry and Ike*, 147–48; Ridgway quoted in Murray Schumach, "The Education of Matthew Ridgway," *NYT Magazine*, May 6, 1952, 63.

87. Quotes from Craig, *Destroying the Village*, 66, 94.

88. Eisenhower in *NYT*, 24 June 1952, 20; Patterson, *Mr. Republican*, 592, 596, 600, 609, 612; Ridgway, "Memorandum for Record: Guidance to MG. G. H. Davidson," 19 Oct. 1953, Ridgway Papers, Box 28.

89. Eisenhower quoted and issue discussed in Soffer, *Ridgway*, 182–83, 188; Ridgway, *Soldier*, 286; Ridgway quoted and described in Leighton, *Strategy, Money, and the New Look*, 367, 371, 621; Eisenhower quoted in Ambrose, *Eisenhower*, 2:592.

90. Ambrose, *Eisenhower*, 2.234; Rusk quoted in Chang, *Friends and Enemies*, 260; "Battle of Indo-China," *Time* 51 (23 Oct. 1950): 30; for Wake Island and subsequent quote on 4 Dec. 1950, see *FRUS*, 7:957, 1368.

91. "Memorandum of conversation between MacArthur and Robert Murphy," 30 April 1952, Acheson Papers, Box 63; Sams, "Oral History," 25; MacArthur quoted in *NYT*, 9 April 1964, 16; Chace, *Acheson*, 389, 394, 406; James, *Days of MacArthur*, 3:672, 681; MacArthur quoted in Scott, "General of the Army Douglas MacArthur and me," 5.

92. "Radio Report to the American People on Korea and the Far East," 11 April 1951, *PPOPT*, 225; McCullough, *Truman*, 985; Truman, ed., *Where Buck Stops*, 69; George

Elsey Notes, 27 June 1950 published in Library of Congress Congressional Research Service, *The U.S. Government and the Vietnam War* (1984–), 1:75.

93. For positions of the military see *U.S. Government and Vietnam War*, 1:82–83, 106, 109, quote on page 95; Acheson quoted in Robert J. McMahon, "Harry S. Truman and the Roots of U.S. Involvement in Indochina, 1945–1953," in David L. Anderson, *Shadow on the White House: Presidents and the Vietnam War, 1945–1975* (Lawrence: University Press of Kansas, 1993), 36–37; Chace, *Acheson*, 350; intelligence agencies cited, Paul Nitze in 1952 quoted, and issue discussed in Leffler, *Preponderance of Power*, 473–74, 488.

94. Johnson in David Halberstam, *The Best and the Brightest* (New York: Random House, 1972), 120, 298, and George Mc. T. Kahin, *Intervention: How America Became Involved in Vietnam* (New York: Knopf, 1986), 339; Secretary of Defense Robert McNamara to Johnson, 20 July 1965, *FRUS*, 3:171.

Truman and MacArthur

1. Truman, *Memoirs*, 2:385, 387, 392; MacArthur, *Reminiscences*, 391; MacArthur, 22 Nov. 1944, quoted in Forrestal, *Diaries*, 18.

2. News Conference, 5 Jan. 1950, *Truman Public Papers*, 11.

3. Truman Diary, 14 May 1934, PSF, Box 334, TPL; Truman, 1959, in Weber, ed., *Talking with Harry*, 246–47.

4. MacArthur quoted in Perret, *Old Soldiers Never Die*, 356; MacArthur to Carlos Romulo, 26 Dec. 1950, quoted in Gaddis, "Defense Perimeter Concept," 113–114n150; Truman, 28 Nov. 1950, in *FRUS*, 7:1247.

5. "Waging Modern War: An Interview with General Wesley K. Clark," *Royal United Service Journal* 146 (Dec. 2001): 6, 11; JCS chairman quoted in Wesley K. Clark, *Waging Modern War: Bosnia, Kosovo, and the Future of Combat* (New York: Public Affairs, 2001), 273.

6. Michael Ignatieff, "The Virtual Commander," *New Yorker* 75 (2 Aug. 1999): 32; unnamed four-star general quoted in Vernon Loeb, "Fast Climber Who Has Made Some Enemies," *Washington Post*, 17 Sept. 2003, 1. Clark described by an aide, Margaret Sullivan, in article by *Lost Angles Times* reporter Ralph Varabedian, n.d., found in www.rapidfire-silverbullets.com/Clark's%20Ret; accessed on 3 January 2007. An army officer told me of hearing General Clark, shortly before he retired, speak for two hours about all the people and obstructions he faced over Kosovo. I asked, "Who were the people that caused him the problems?" and was told, "It seemed to be almost everyone."

7. Alexander M. Haig, Jr., *Caveat: Realism, Reagan and Foreign Policy* (New York: Macmillan, 1984), 119, 122–30; Haig's private remarks at government meetings quoted in Lou Cannon, *President Reagan: The Role of a Lifetime* (New York: Simon and Schuster, 1991), 196, 345; Haig, *Inner Circles*, 26, 36, 546.

8. Haig, *Inner Circles*, 546–49, 561–62; Evan Thomas, "The Water Walker," *Newsweek* 142 (29 Sept. 2003): 29.

9. Mort Kondracke and Maria Liasson on *Fox TV News*, 21 Jan. 2004; Edward Wyatt, "Clark Ending His Campaign after Poor Showing in the South," *NYT*, 11 Feb. 2004, 1; pollster Andrew Kohut on National Public Radio, *Morning Edition*, 29 Jan. 2004; Louis Menand, "Permanent Fatal Errors," *New Yorker*, 6 Dec. 2004, 60; Bush described and quoted, 23 Sept. 2004, in Bob Woodward, *State of Denial: Bush at War, Part III* (New York: Simon and Schuster, 2006), 325–26, 336, 339.

Selected Bibliography

Manuscript and Archival Material

Acheson, Dean. Papers, Harry S. Truman Presidential Library, Independence, Missouri.

Ayers, Eben. Papers, Truman Presidential Library.

Bradley, Omar N. Papers, United States Military Academy, West Point, New York.

———. Papers, United States Military History Institute, Army War College, Carlisle Barracks, Pennsylvania.

Byers, Clovis. Papers, Douglas MacArthur Memorial Foundation Library, Norfolk, Virginia.

Connelly, Mathew. Papers, Truman Presidential Library.

Dennison, Robert. Papers, Truman Presidential Library.

Douglas, Paul. Papers, Chicago Historical Society.

Early, Stephen. Papers, Franklin Roosevelt Presidential Library, Hyde Park, New York.

Eisenhower, Dwight D. Papers. Pre-Presidential Files, Ann Whitman File, Dwight D. Eisenhower Presidential Library, Abilene, Kansas.

Elsey, George M. Papers, Truman Presidential Library.

Fellers, Bonners. Papers, MacArthur Memorial Foundation Library.

Freeman, Douglas Southall. Papers, Library of Congress, Washington, D.C.

Harriman, Averell. Papers, Library of Congress.

Joint Chiefs of Staff. Chairman's File; Geographical Files, 1948–1950 and 1951–1953, National Archives and Records Administration, College Park, Maryland.

Lowe, Frank. Papers. MacArthur Memorial Foundation Library.

MacArthur, Douglas. Military Correspondence; Personal Correspondence, MacArthur Memorial Foundation Library.

Miller, Merle. Papers, Truman Presidential Library.

Nitze, Paul. Papers, Library of Congress.

Princeton University Seminar Meeting of Truman Administration Officials, 1953–1954, copy in Truman Presidential Library.

Quirk, James. Papers, Truman Presidential Library.

Ridgway, Matthew. Papers, United States Military History Institute.

Rusk, Dean. Papers, University of Georgia, Athens, Georgia.

Russell, Richard. Papers, University of Georgia.

Smith, H. Alexander. Papers, Mudd Library, Princeton University, Princeton, New Jersey.

State Department. Central Files, National Archives and Records Administration.

———. Selected Records Relating to the Korean War, Truman Presidential Library.

Stimson, Henry. Diary, Yale University Library, New Haven, Connecticut.

Tannenwald, Theodore, Jr. Papers, Truman Presidential Library.

Truman, Harry S. Military Records File; Central File; President's Personal File; President's Secretary's File; Post-Presidential File, Truman Presidential Library.

United States Government Psychological Strategy Board Files, Truman Presidential Library.
War Department. War Plans Division, National Archives and Records Administration.
Whitney, Courtney. Papers, MacArthur Memorial Foundation Library.

Oral Histories

Acheson, Dean. Truman Presidential Library.
Almond, Ned. MacArthur Memorial Foundation Library.
———. United States Military History Institute, Army War College, Carlisle Barracks, Pennsylvania.
Dennison, Robert. Truman Presidential Library.
Egeberg, Roger. MacArthur Memorial Library.
Eisenhower, Dwight D. MacArthur Memorial Foundation Library.
Elsey, George M. Truman Presidential Library.
Feller, Bonner. MacArthur Memorial Foundation Library.
Harriman, Averell. MacArthur Memorial Foundation Library.
———. Truman Presidential Library.
Hull, John E. United States Military History Institute.
Jessup, Philip. MacArthur Memorial Foundation Library.
Johnson, Harold K. United States Military History Institute.
Mansfield, Mike. MacArthur Memorial Foundation Library.
Michaelis, John H. MacArthur Memorial Foundation Library.
Mildren, Frank T. MacArthur Memorial Foundation Library.
Muccio, John J. Truman Presidential Library.
Mydans, Carl. MacArthur Memorial Library.
Pace, Frank. MacArthur Memorial Foundation Library
———. Truman Presidential Library.
———. United States Military History Institute.
Polk, James H. United States Military History Institute.
Reedy, George. Lyndon Johnson Presidential Library, Austin, Texas.
Renfro, Louis H. Truman Presidential Library.
Rusk, Dean. University of Georgia, Rusk Papers.
Saltzman, Arnold A. MacArthur Memorial Foundation Library.
Sams, Crawford. MacArthur Memorial Foundation Library.
Sebald, William. MacArthur Memorial Foundation Library.
Smith, Oliver P. MacArthur Memorial Foundation Library.
Tubby, Roger. Truman Presidential Library.
Vaughan, Harry. Truman Presidential Library.
West, Charles J. MacArthur Memorial Foundation Library.
Willoughby, Charles A. MacArthur Memorial Foundation Library.
Wright, Edwin K. MacArthur Memorial Foundation Library.

Published Papers, Diaries, Letters, Speeches, and Government Records

Acheson, Dean. *Among Friends: Personal Letters of Dean Acheson.* Ed. David S. McLellan and David C. Acheson. New York: Dodd, Mead, 1980.
Ayers, Eben A. *Truman in the White House: The Diary of Eben A. Ayers.* Ed. Robert H. Ferrell. Columbia: University of Missouri Press, 1991.

Eisenhower, Dwight David. *The Papers of Dwight David Eisenhower*. Ed. Alfred Chandler. Baltimore: Johns Hopkins Press, 1970–.

———. *The Eisenhower Diaries*. Ed. Robert H. Ferrell. New York: Penguin Books, 1981.

———. *Eisenhower: The Prewar Diaries and Selected Papers, 1905–1941*. Ed. Daniel D. Holt and James W. Leyerzapf. Baltimore: Johns Hopkins University Press, 1998.

Forrestal, James. *The Forrestal Diaries*. Ed. Walter Millis. New York: Viking, 1951.

Hillman, William. *Mr. President: Personal Diaries, Private Letters, and Revealing Interviews of Harry S. Truman*. New York: Farrar, Straus and Young, 1952.

Huston, John W. *American Airpower Comes of Age: General Henry H. "Hap" Arnold's World War II Diaries*. Maxwell Air Force Base: Air University Press, 2002.

Important Documents Concerning the Question of Taiwan. Peking: Foreign Languages Press, 1956.

MacArthur, Douglas. *General MacArthur: Speeches and Reports, 1908–1964*. Ed. Edward T. Imparato. Paducah: Turner Publishing, 2000.

———. *A Soldier Speaks: Public Papers and Speeches of General of the Army Douglas MacArthur*. Ed. Vorin Whan. New York: Praeger, 1965.

Marshall, George Catlett. *George C. Marshall Interviews and Reminiscences for Forrest C. Pogue: Transcripts and Notes, 1956–1958*. Lexington: George C. Marshall Research Foundation, 1986.

———. *The Papers of George Catlett Marshall*. Ed. Larry Bland. Baltimore: Johns Hopkins University Press, 1982–.

Merrill, Dennis, ed. *Documentary History of Truman Presidency*. Vols. 18, 19, and 20. Washington: University Publications of America, 1997.

Pearson, Drew. *Drew Pearson Diaries: 1949–1959*. Ed. Tyler Abell. New York: Holt, Reinhart, and Winston, 1974.

Public Papers of the Presidents of the United States: Dwight D. Eisenhower, 1953–1961. Washington: U.S. Government Printing Office, 1958–1961.

Public Papers of the Presidents of the United States: Harry S. Truman, 1945–1953. Washington: Government Printing Office, 1961–1966.

Stilwell, Joseph. *The Stilwell Papers*. Ed. Theodore White. New York: William Sloane, 1948.

Truman, Harry. *Dear Bess: The Letters of Harry to Bess Truman, 1910–1959*. Ed. Robert H. Ferrell. New York: Norton, 1983.

———. *Off the Record: The Private Papers of Harry S. Truman*. Ed. Robert H. Ferrell. New York: Penguin Books, 1982.

———. *Strictly Personal and Confidential: The Letters Harry Truman Never Mailed*. Ed. Monte M. Poen. Boston: Little Brown, 1982.

U.S. Department of State. *Foreign Relations of the United States, 1945*, Vols. 6 and 7; *1947*, Vol. 7; *1948*, Vols. 6 and 9; *1949*, Vols. 5, 7, 8, and 9; *1950*, Vols. 1, 6, and 7; *1951*, Vols. 4, 6, and 7; *1952–1954*, Vol. 14; *1955–1957*, Vol. 5; *1965*, Vol. 3.

———. *United States Relations with China, with Special References to the Period 1944–1949 [China White Paper]*. Washington: U.S. Government Printing Office, 1949.

U.S. Senate. *Final Report of the Select Committee to Study Government Operations with Respect to Intelligence Activities*. Washington: U.S. Government Printing Office, 1976.

U.S. Senate Committees on Armed Services and Foreign Relations. *Hearings to Conduct an Inquiry into the Military Situation in the Far East and the Facts Surrounding the Relief of General of the Army Douglas MacArthur from His Assignments in That Area [MacArthur Hearings]*. 82d Congress, 1st Session, 1951.

Vandenberg, Arthur H., Jr. *The Private Papers of Senator Vandenberg*. Boston: Houghton, Mifflin, 1952.

Weber, Ralph, ed. *Talking with Harry: Candid Conversations with President Harry S. Truman*. Wilmington: Scholarly Resources, 2001.

Books, Studies, and Memoirs

Abramson, Rudy. *Spanning the Century: The Life of W. Averell Harriman, 1891–1986*. New York: William Morrow, 1992.

Accinelli, Robert. *Crisis and Commitment: United States Policy toward Taiwan, 1950–1955*. Chapel Hill: University of North Carolina Press, 1996.

Acheson, Dean. *Present at the Creation: My Years in the State Department*. New York: Norton, 1969.

Ambrose, Stephen E. *Eisenhower*. Vols. 1 and 2. New York: Simon and Schuster, 1983–1984.

Appleman, Roy. *Disaster in Korea: The Chinese Confront MacArthur*. College Station: Texas A and M University Press, 1989.

———. *Ridgway Duels For Korea*. College Station: Texas A and M University Press, 1990.

———. *South to the Naktong, North to the Yalu*. Washington: U.S. Army Center of Military History, 1992; originally published, 1961.

Armstrong, Charles. *The North Korean Revolution, 1945–1950*. Ithaca: Cornell University Press, 2003.

Bajanov, Evgeniy, and Natalia Bajanova. *The Korean Conflict, 1950–1953: The Most Mysterious War of the 20th Century—Based on Secret Soviet Archives*. Moscow: Institute for Contemporary International Problems, Russian Foreign Ministry, 1998.

Barber, James David. *The Presidential Character: Predicting Performance in the White House*. Englewood Cliffs, N.J.: Prentice-Hall, 1977.

Beisner, Robert L. *Dean Acheson: A Life in the Cold War*. New York: Oxford University Press, 2006.

Bird, Kai. *The Chairman: John J. McCloy, The Making of the American Establishment*. New York: Simon and Schuster, 1992.

Bix, Herbert P. *Hirohito and the Making of Modern Japan*. New York: Harper Collins, 2000.

Blaik, Earl. *The Red Blaik Story*. New Rochelle: Arlington House, 1974.

Blair, Clay. *The Forgotten War: America in Korea, 1950–1953*. New York: Times Books, 1987.

Blum, Robert. *Drawing the Line: The Origin of the American Containment Policy in East Asia*. New York: Norton, 1982.

Bohlen, Charles E. *Witness to History, 1929–1969*. New York: Norton, 1973.

Borowski, Harry R. *A Hollow Threat: Strategic Air Power and Containment before Korea*. Westport, Conn.: Greenwood, 1982.

Bradley, Omar N., and Clay Blair. *A General's Life*. New York: Simon and Schuster, 1983.

Braim, Paul F. *The Will to Win: Life of General James A. Van Fleet*. Annapolis: Naval Institute Press, 2001.

Brent, Jonathan, and Vladmir Naumov. *Stalin's Last Crime: The Plot against Jewish Doctors, 1948–1953*. New York: Harper Collins, 2003.

Brines, Russell. *MacArthur's Japan*. Philadelphia: J. B. Lippincott, 1948.

Brown, Anthony Cave. *Treason in the Blood: H. St. John Philby, Kim Philby, and the Spy Case of the Century.* Boston: Houghton Mifflin, 1994.

Bullock, Alan. *Ernest Bevin: Foreign Secretary, 1945–1951.* London: Heinemann, 1983.

Caridi, Ronald J. *The Korean War and American Politics: The Republican Party as a Case Study.* Philadelphia: University of Pennsylvania Press, 1968.

Caro, Robert. *The Years of Lyndon Johnson: Master of the Senate.* New York: Knopf, 2002.

Chace, James. *Acheson: The Secretary of State Who Created the American World.* New York: Simon and Schuster, 1998.

Chang, Gordon. *Friends and Enemies: The United States, China, and the Soviet Union, 1948–1972.* Stanford, Calif.: Stanford University Press, 1990.

Chen Jian. *Mao's China and the Cold War.* Chapel Hill: University of North Carolina Press, 2001.

Collins, J. Lawton. *Lightning Joe: An Autobiography.* Baton Rouge: Louisiana State University, 1979.

———. *War in Peacetime: The History and Lessons of Korea.* Boston: Houghton Mifflin, 1969.

Condit, Doris M. *The History of the Office of the Secretary of Defense: The Test of War, 1950–1953.* Washington: Office of the Secretary of Defense, 1988.

Connaughton, Richard. *MacArthur and Defeat in the Philippines.* Woodstock: Overlook Press, 2001.

Craig, Campbell. *Destroying the Village: Eisenhower and Thermonuclear War.* New York: Columbia University Press, 1998.

Cumings, Bruce. *The Origins of the Korean War.* Vols. 1 and 2. Princeton: Princeton University Press, 1981–1990.

Dallek, Robert. *Lone Star Rising: Lyndon Johnson and His Times, 1908–1960.* New York: Oxford University Press, 1991.

David, Paul, ed. *Presidential Nominating Politics in 1952.* Baltimore: Johns Hopkins University Press, 1954.

Davies, John Patton. *Dragon by the Tail: American, British, Japanese, and Russian Encounters.* New York: Norton, 1972.

Davis, Burke. *Marine! The Life of Chesty Puller.* New York: Bantam, 1964.

D'Este, Carlo. *Eisenhower: A Soldier's Life.* New York: Henry Holt, 2002.

Divine, Robert A. *Foreign Policy and U.S. Presidential Elections: 1952–1960.* New York: New Viewpoints, 1974.

Donovan, Robert J. *The Presidency of Harry S. Truman.* Vols. 1 and 2. New York: Norton, 1977–1982.

Drea, Edward J. *MacArthur's Ultra: Codebreaking and the War against Japan, 1942–1945.* Lawrence: University Press of Kansas, 1992.

Duffy, Bernard K., and Ronald H. Carpenter. *Douglas MacArthur: Warrior and Wordsmith.* Westport, Conn.: Greenwood, 1997.

Edmonds, Robin. *Setting the Mould: The United States and Britain, 1945–1950.* New York: Norton, 1986.

Egeberg, Roger Olaf, M.D. *The General: MacArthur and the Man He Called "Doc."* New York: Hippocrene Books, 1983.

Eisenhower, Dwight D. *At Ease: Stories I Tell to Friends.* Garden City, N.Y.: Doubleday, 1967.

———. *Crusade in Europe.* Garden City: Doubleday, 1948.

Elliot, Mark. *Pawns of Yalta: Soviet Refugees and America's Role in Their Repatriation.* Urbana: University of Illinois Press, 1982.

Elsey, George M. *An Unplanned Life: A Memoir.* Columbia: University of Missouri Press, 2005.

Fehrenbach, T. R. *This Kind of War: A Study in Unpreparedness.* New York: Macmillan, 1964.

Feis, Herbert. *The China Tangle: American Effort in China from Pearl Harbor to the Marshall Mission.* New York: Antheneum, 1965.

Fenby, Jonathon. *Chiang Kai-Shek: China's Generalissimo and the Nation He Lost.* New York: Carroll and Graf, 2003.

Ferrell, Robert H. *Collapse at Meuse-Argonne: The Failure of the Missouri-Kansas Division.* Columbia: University of Missouri Press, 2004.

———. *Harry S. Truman: A Life.* Columbia: University of Missouri Press, 1994.

Field, James A., Jr. *History of United States Naval Operations: Korea.* Washington: U.S. Govt. Printing Office, 1962.

Finkelstein, David. *Washington's Taiwan Dilemma, 1949–1950: From Abandonment to Salvation.* Fairfax, Va.: George Mason University Press, 1993.

Fite, Gilbert C. *Richard B. Russell, Jr., Senator from Georgia.* Chapel Hill: University of North Carolina Press, 1991.

Foot, Rosemary. *A Substitute for Victory: The Politics of Peacemaking at the Korean Armistice Talks.* Ithaca: Cornell University Press, 1990.

———. *The Wrong War, American Policy and the Dimensions of the Korean War, 1950–1953.* Ithaca: Cornell University Press, 1985.

Freeman, Douglas Southall. *R. E. Lee: A Biography.* Vols. 2 and 4. New York: Scribner's, 1934–1935.

Gittings, John. *The Role of the Chinese Army.* New York: Oxford University Press, 1967.

Goncharov, Sergi N., John W. Lewis, and Xue Litai. *Uncertain Partners: Stalin, Mao, and the Korean War.* Stanford: Stanford University Press, 1993.

Gorlizki, Yoram, and Oleg Khlevniuk. *Cold Peace: Stalin and the Soviet Ruling Circle, 1945–1953.* New York: Oxford University Press, 2004.

Goulden, Joseph C. *Korea: The Untold Story of the War.* New York: McGraw-Hill, 1982.

Grasso, June. *Truman's Two-China Policy, 1948–1950.* Armonk, N.Y.: M. E. Sharp, 1987.

Haig, Alexander. *Inner Circles: How America Changed the World, A Memoir.* New York: Warner Books, 1992.

Hamby, Alonzo L. *Man of the People: A Life of Harry S. Truman.* New York: Oxford University Press, 1998.

Harris, Louis. *Is There a Republican Majority: Political Trends, 1952–1956.* New York: Harper and Brothers, 1954.

Harris, Mene Arthur. "The MacArthur Dismissal—A Study in Political Mail." Ph.D. diss., University of Iowa, 1966.

Hasenfus, William Albert. "Managing Partner: Joseph W. Martin, Jr., Republican Leaders of the United States House of Representatives, 1939–1959." Ph.D. diss., Boston College, 1986.

Haynes, Richard F. *The Awesome Power: Harry S. Truman as Commander in Chief.* Baton Rouge: Louisiana State University, 1973.

Heefner, Wilson A. *Patton's Bulldog: The Life and Service of General Walton H. Walker.* Shippensburg, Pa.: White Maine, 2001.

Heinl, Robert Debs. *Victory at High Tide: The Inchon-Seoul Campaign.* Philadelphia: J. B. Lippincott, 1968.

Heinzig, Dieter. *The Soviet Union and Communist China 1945–1950: The Arduous Road to the Alliance.* London: M. E. Sharpe, 2004.

Heller, Francis, ed. *The Korean War: A 25 Year Perspective.* Lawrence: Regents Press of Kansas, 1977.

———. *The Truman White House, The Administration of the Presidency, 1945 to 1953.* Lawrence: Regents Press of Kansas, 1980.

Hermes, Walter G. *Truce Tent and Fighting Front.* Washington: Center of Military History, 1966.

Hersey, John. *Men on Bataan.* New York: Knopf, 1942.

Holloway, David. *Stalin and the Bomb: The Soviet Union and Atomic Energy, 1939–1956.* New Haven: Yale University Press, 1994.

Holober, Frank. *Raiders of the China Coast: CIA Covert Operations during the Korean War.* Annapolis: Naval Institute Press, 1999.

Isaacson, Walter, and Evan Thomas. *The Wise Men: Six Friends and the World They Made.* New York: Touchstone, 1988.

James, D. Clayton. *The Years of MacArthur.* Vols. 1–3. Boston: Houghton Mifflin, 1970–1985.

Johnson, David E. *Douglas Southall Freeman.* Gretna, La.: Pelican, 2002.

Jung Chang, and Jon Halliday. *Mao: The Unknown Story.* New York: Knopf, 2005.

Kennan, George F. *Memoirs, 1925–1950.* New York: Bantam, 1969.

Khrushchev, Nikita Sergeevich. *Khrushchev Remembers.* Vols. 1 and 2. Ed. Strobe Talbott. Boston: Little Brown, 1970–1974.

Kiernan, V. G. *Colonial Empires and Armies: 1815–1960.* Great Britain: Sutton, 1998.

Knox, Donald. *The Korean War: An Oral History.* Vols. 1 and 2. New York: Harcourt, Brace, Jovanovich, 1983–1988.

Kusnitz, Leonard A. *Public Opinion and Foreign Policy: America's China Policy, 1949–1979.* Westport, Conn.: Greenwood, 1984.

La Bree, Clifton. *The Gentle Warrior: General Oliver Prince Smith, USMC.* Kent, Ohio: Kent State University Press, 2001.

Leahy, William. *I Was There.* New York: McGraw Hill, 1950.

Leary, William M., ed. *We Shall Return! MacArthur's Commanders and the Defeat of Japan 1942–1945.* Lexington: University of Kentucky Press, 1988.

Lee, Clark, and Richard Henschel. *Douglas MacArthur.* New York: Henry Holt, 1952.

Leffler, Melvyn P. *A Preponderance of Power: National Security, the Truman Administration, and the Cold War.* Stanford: Stanford University Press, 1992.

Leighton, Richard. *Strategy, Money, and the New Look, 1953–1956.* Washington: Historical Office of the Secretary of Defense, 2001.

Linn, Brian McAllister. *Guardians of Empire: The U.S. Army and the Pacific, 1902–1940.* Chapel Hill: University of North Carolina Press, 1997.

MacArthur, Douglas. *Reminiscences.* New York: McGraw-Hill, 1964.

Macdonald, Douglas. *Adventures in Chaos: American Intervention for Reform in the Third World.* Cambridge: Harvard University Press, 1992.

Mann, Robert. *The Walls of Jericho: Johnson, Humphrey, Russell, and Civil Rights.* New York: Harcourt, Brace, 1996.

Mansourov, Alexandre Y. "Communist War Coalition Formation and the Origins of the Korean War." Ph.D. diss., Columbia University, 1997.

Marshall, S. L. A. *Infantry Operations and Weapons Usage in Korea, Winter of 1950–51*. Operations Research Office, Johns Hopkins University, n.d.

Martin, Joseph W., Jr., as told to Robert J. Donovan. *My First Fifty Years in Politics*. New York: McGraw-Hill, 1960.

McCullough, David. *Truman*. New York: Touchstone, 1992.

McFarland, Keith D., and David L. Roll. *Louis Johnson and the Arming of America: The Roosevelt and Truman Years*. Bloomington: Indiana University Press, 2005.

McGlothlen, Ronald. *Controlling the Waves: Dean Acheson and U.S. Foreign Policy in Asia*. New York: Norton, 1993.

Meilinger, Phillip S. *Hoyt S. Vandenberg: The Life of a General*. Bloomington: Indiana University Press, 1989.

Merry, Robert W. *Taking on the World: Joseph and Stewart Alsop — Guardians of the American Century*. New York: Viking, 1996.

Miller, Edward. *War Plan Orange: U.S. Strategy to Defeat Japan*. Annapolis: Naval Institute Press, 1991.

Miller, Merle. *Plain Speaking: An Oral Biography of Harry S. Truman*. New York: G. P. Putnam's Sons, 1974.

Millett, Allan R. *The War for Korea, 1945–1950: A House Burning*. Lawrence: University Press of Kansas, 2006.

Miscamble, Wilson D. *George F. Kennan and the Making of American Foreign Policy, 1947–1950*. Princeton, N.J.: Princeton University Press, 1992.

Mitrovich, Gregory. *Undermining the Kremlin: America's Strategy to Subvert the Soviet Bloc, 1947–1956*. Ithaca: Cornell University Press, 2000.

Moore, William Howard. *The Kefauver Committee and the Politics of Crime: 1950–1952*. Columbia: University of Missouri Press, 1974.

Morton, Louis. *The Fall of the Philippines*. Washington: Office of the Chief of Military History, 1953.

Mueller, John E. *War, Presidents, and Public Opinion*. New York: John Wiley's Sons, 1973.

Murphy, Robert. *Diplomat among Warriors*. New York: Pyramid Books, 1965.

Neal, Steven. *Harry and Ike: The Partnership That Remade the Postwar World*. New York: Scribner, 2001.

Neustadt, Richard E. *Presidential Power: The Politics of Leadership*. New York: Signet Book, 1964.

Nitze, Paul H. *From Hiroshima to Glasnost: At the Center of Decision, a Memoir*. New York: Grove Weidenfeld, 1989.

Nixon, Richard. *RN: The Memoirs of Richard Nixon*. New York: Grosset and Dunlap, 1978.

Offner, Arnold A. *Another Such Victory: President Truman and the Cold War, 1945–1953*. Stanford: Stanford University Press, 2002.

Paige, Glenn D. *The Korean Decision: June 24–30, 1950*. New York: Free Press, 1968.

Pash, Boris T. *The Alsos Mission*. New York: Award House, 1969.

Patterson, James T. *Mr. Republican: A Biography of Robert A. Taft* Boston: Houghton Mifflin, 1972.

Payne, Stanley G. *The Spanish Civil War, the Soviet Union, and Communism*. New Haven: Yale University Press, 2004.

Pearson, Lester B. *Mike: The Memoirs of Lester Pearson*. Vol. 2. New York: Quadrangle, 1975.

Perret, Geoffrey. *Old Soldiers Never Die: The Life of Douglas MacArthur.* Holbrook, Mass.: Adams Media, 1986.

Petillo, Carol Morris. *Douglas MacArthur: The Philippine Years.* Bloomington: Indiana University Press, 1981.

Pingchao Zhu. "The Road to an Armistice: An Examination of the Chinese and American Diplomacy during the Korean War Cease-Fire Negotiations, 1950–1953," Ph.D. diss., Miami University of Ohio, 1998.

Pinkley, Virgil, with James F. Scheer. *Eisenhower Declassified.* Old Tappan, N.J.: Fleming H. Revell, 1979.

Pogue, Forrest C. *George C. Marshal.* Vols. 2–4. New York: Viking Press, 1963–1987.

Potter, E. B. *Admiral Arleigh Burke.* New York: Random House, 1990.

Quirk, Rory. *Wars and Peace: The Memoir of an American Family.* Novato, Calif.: Presidio Press, 1999.

Rankin, Karl Lott. *China Assignment.* Seattle: University of Washington Press, 1964.

Reston, James. *Deadline: A Memoir.* New York: Random House, 1991.

Rickenbacker, Edward V. *Rickenbacker.* Englewood Cliffs, N.J: Prentice-Hall, 1967.

Ridgway, Matthew B. *The Korean War.* New York: Doubleday, 1967.

———. *Soldier: The Memoirs of Matthew B. Ridgway.* New York: Harper and Brothers, 1956.

Roe, Patrick C. *The Dragon Strikes: China and the Korean War, June–December 1950.* Novato: Presidio, 2000.

Rogers, Paul P. *The Bitter Years: MacArthur and Sutherland.* New York: Praeger, 1991.

———. *The Good Years: MacArthur and Sutherland.* New York: Praeger, 1990.

Rovere, Richard, and Arthur Schlesinger, Jr. *The General and the President: The Future of American Foreign Policy.* New York: Farrar, Straus and Young, 1951.

Rusk, Dean. *As I Saw It: Dean Rusk as told to Richard Rusk.* Ed. Daniel S. Papp. New York: Norton, 1990.

Schaller, Michael. *The American Occupation of Japan: The Origins of the Cold War in Asia.* New York: Oxford University Press, 1985.

———. *Douglas MacArthur: The Far Eastern General.* New York: Oxford University Press, 1989.

Schecter, Jerrold, ed. *Khrushchev Remembers: The Glasnost Tapes.* Boston: Little, Brown, 1990.

Schoenbaum, Thomas J. *Waging Peace and War: Dean Rusk in the Truman, Kennedy, and Johnson Years.* New York: Simon and Schuster, 1988.

Schnabel, James F., and Robert J. Watson. *The History of the Joint Chiefs of Staff: The Korean War.* Wilmington, Del.: Michael Glasner, 1979.

Schnabel, James F. *Policy and Direction: The First Year.* Washington: Office of the Chief of Military History, 1972.

Scott, William A., and Stephen B. Withey. *The United States and the United Nations: The Public View, 1945–1955.* New York: Manhattan Publishing, 1958.

Sebald, William J., and Russell Brinan. *With MacArthur in Japan: A Personal History of the Occupation.* New York: Norton, 1965.

Sheng, Michael. *Battling Western Imperialism: Mao, Stalin, and the United States.* Princeton, N.J.: Princeton University Press, 1997.

Short, Philip. *Mao: A Life.* New York: Henry Holt, 2000.

Shu Guang Zhang. *Deterrence and Strategic Culture: Chinese-American Confrontations, 1949–1958.* Ithaca: Cornell University Press, 1992.

————. *Mao's Military Romanticism: China and the Korean War, 1950–1953.* Lawrence: University Press of Kansas, 1995.

Smith, Richard Norton. *Thomas E. Dewey and His Times.* New York: Simon and Schuster, 1982.

Soffer, Jonathan M. *General Matthew Bunker Ridgway: From Progressivism to Reaganism, 1895–1993.* Westport: Praeger, 1998.

Sorley, Lewis. *Honorable Warrior: General Harold K. Johnson and the Ethics of Command.* Lawrence: University Press of Kansas, 1998.

Spanier, John W. *The Truman-MacArthur Controversy and the Korean War.* New York: Norton, 1965.

Spurr, Russell. *Enter the Dragon: China's Undeclared War against the U.S. in Korea, 1950–1951.* New York: Henry Holt, 1988.

Steinberg, Alfred. *The Man from Missouri: The Life and Times of Harry S. Truman.* New York: G. P. Putnam's Sons, 1962.

Stimson, Henry, and McGeorge Bundy. *On Active Service in Peace and War.* New York: Harper and Brothers, 1948.

Stueck, William, Jr. *The Korean War: An International History.* Princeton: Princeton University Press, 1995.

————, ed. *The Korean War in World History.* Lexington: University of Kentucky Press, 2004.

————. *Rethinking the Korean War.* Princeton, N.J.: Princeton University Press, 2002.

————. *Road to Confrontation: American Policy towards China and Korea, 1947–1950.* Chapel Hill: University of North Carolina Press, 1981.

Sulzberger, C. L. *A Long Row of Candles: Memories and Diaries, 1934–1954.* New York: Macmillan, 1969.

Theoharis, Athan G. *The Yalta Myths: An Issue in U.S. Politics, 1945–1955.* Columbia: University of Missouri Press, 1970.

Toland, John. *In Mortal Combat: Korea, 1950–1953.* New York: William Morrow, 1991.

Truman, Harry S. *Memoirs.* Vols. 1 and 2. New York: Doubleday, 1955–1956.

————. *Mr. Citizen.* New York: Bernard Geis, 1960.

Truman, Margaret, ed. *Where the Buck Stops: The Personal and Private Writings of Harry S. Truman.* New York: Warner, 1989.

Tuchman, Barbara W. *Stilwell and the American Experience in China, 1911–1945.* New York: Macmillan, 1970.

Tucker, Nancy Bernkopf, ed. *China Confidential: American Diplomats and Sino-American Relations, 1945–1996.* New York: Columbia University Press, 2001.

Stromer, Marvin E. *The Making of a Political Leader: Kenneth S. Wherry and the United States Senate.* Lincoln: University of Nebraska Press, 1969.

Understanding and Remembering: 50th Anniversary of the Korean War International Symposium. General Douglas MacArthur Memorial Foundation, 2003.

Ulam, Adam. *Titoism and the Cominform.* Cambridge: Harvard University Press, 1952.

Wainwright, Jonathan. *General Wainwright's Story.* New York: Bantam, 1986.

Weintraub, Stanley. *MacArthur's War: Korea and the Undoing of an American Hero.* New York: Free Press, 2000.

Westad, Odd Arne. *Decisive Encounters: The Chinese Civil War, 1946–1950.* Stanford: Stanford University Press, 2003.

Westerfield, H. Bradford. *Foreign Policy and Party Politics: Pearl Harbor to Korea.* New Haven: Yale University Press, 1955.

White, Theodore H. *In Search of History: A Personal Adventure.* New York: Harper and Row, 1978.

Whiting, Allen S. *China Crosses the Yalu: The Decision to Enter the Korean War.* Stanford: Stanford University Press, 1968.

Whitney, Courtney. *MacArthur: His Rendezvous with History.* New York: Knopf, 1956.

Willoughby, Major General Charles A., and John Chamberlain. *MacArthur, 1941–1951.* New York: McGraw-Hill, 1954.

Xiamong Zhang. *Red Wings over the Yalu.* College Station: Texas A and M Press, 2002.

Xiaobing Li, Allan R. Millett, and Bin Yu, ed. *Mao's Generals Remember Korea.* Lawrence: University Press of Kansas, 2001.

Young, Kenneth Ray. *The General's General: The Life and Times of Arthur MacArthur.* Boulder, Colo.: Westview, 1994.

Zubok, Vladislav, and Constantine Pleshakov. *Inside the Kremlin's Cold War.* Cambridge, Mass.: Harvard University Press, 1996.

Articles

Aurthur, Robert Alan. "Harry Truman Chuckles Dryly." *Esquire* 76 (Sept. 1971).

Belmonte, Laura. "Anglo-American Relations and the Dismissal of MacArthur." *Diplomatic History* 19 (Fall 1995).

Bernstein, Barton J. "The Struggle over the Korean Armistice: Prisoner of Repatriation." In Bruce Cummings, ed., *Child of Conflict: The Korean-American Relationship, 1943–1953.* Seattle: University of Washington Press, 1983.

Bess, DeMaree. "Are Generals in Politics a Menace?" *Saturday Evening Post* 224 (April 26, 1952).

Blum, Robert. "Surprised by Tito: The Anatomy of an Intelligence Failure." *Diplomatic History* 12 (Winter 1988).

Bowers, Faubion. "The Late General MacArthur, Warts and All," reprinted in William M. Leary, ed., *MacArthur and the American Century: A Reader.* Lincoln: University of Nebraska Press, 2001.

"Burke Speaks Out on Korea." *Proceedings of the United States Naval Institute* 126 (May 2000).

Casey, Steven. "White House Publicity Operations during the Korean War, June 1950–June 1951." *Presidential Studies Quarterly* 35 (Dec. 2005).

Chen Jian. "The Ward Case and the Emergence of Sino-American Confrontation, 1948–1950." *Australian Journal of Chinese Affairs* 30 (July 1993).

"Chinese Generals Recall the Korean War." *Chinese Historian* 7 (Summer 1994).

Chisholm, David. "Negotiated Joint Command Relationships." *Naval War College Review* 53 (Spring 2000).

Cohen, Warren. "Acheson, His Advisers, and China, 1949–1950." In Dorothy Borg and Waldo Heinrichs, ed., *Uncertain Years: Chinese-American Relations, 1947–1950.* New York: Columbia University Press, 1980.

CSI Report, No. 5, Conversations with General J. Lawton Collins. Combat Studies Institute, U.S. Army Command and General Staff College, n.d.

Dickson, Bruce. "The Lessons of Defeat: The Reorganization of the Kuomintang on Taiwan, 1950–52." *China Quarterly* 133 (March 1993).

Eastman, Lloyd. "Who Lost China? Chiang Kai-shek Testifies." *China Quarterly* 88 (Dec. 1981).

Farrar, Peter N. "Britain's Proposal for a Buffer Zone South of the Yalu in November 1950: Was It a Neglected Opportunity to End the Fighting in Korea?" *Journal of Contemporary History* 18 (Fall 1983).

"Friendship Racket." *Life* 27 (Aug. 1, 1949).

Gaddis, John Lewis. "The Rise and Fall of the 'Defense Perimeter' Concept, 1946–1951." In Dorothy Borg and Waldo Heinrichs, ed., *Uncertain Years: Chinese-American Relations, 1947–1950*. New York: Columbia University Press, 1980.

Gardner, Lloyd C. "Korean Borderlands." In William Stueck, Jr., ed., *The Korean War in World History*. Lexington: University of Kentucky Press, 2004.

Giangreco, Dennis. "The Soldier from Independence: Harry S. Truman and the Great War." *Journal of the Royal Artillery* 130 (Autumn 2003).

Halliday, Jon. "Air Operations in Korea: The Soviet Side of the Story." In William J. Williams, ed., *A Revolutionary War: Korea and the Transformation of the Postwar World*. Chicago: Imprint Publications, 1993.

He Di. "The Last Campaign to Unify China." *Chinese Historians* 5 (Spring 1992).

Hemingway, Al. "The Real MacArthur." www.the historynet.com/WorldWarII/articles/ 2000.

Hersey, John. "Profiles: Mr. President." *New Yorker*, 7 April, 14 April, and 5 May 1951.

Karber, Phillip A., and Jerald A. Combs, "The United States, NATO, and the Soviet Threat to Western Europe: Military Estimates and Policy Options, 1945–1963." *Diplomatic History* 22 (Summer 1998).

La Follette, Philip F. "With MacArthur in the Pacific: A Memoir." *Wisconsin Magazine of History* 60 (Autumn, 1980).

Lees, Lorraine M. "The American Decision to Assist Tito, 1948–1949." *Diplomatic History* 2 (Fall 1978).

MacArthur, Douglas. "Formosa Must Be Defended." *U.S. News and World Report* 32 (1 Sept. 1950).

———. "Mr. Truman Yielded to Councils of Fear." *U.S. News and World Report* 40 (17 Feb. 1956).

"Mao's Dispatch of Chinese Forces to Korea, July–October 1950." *Chinese Historians* 5 (Spring 1992).

"Mao's Telegrams during the Korean War, October–December 1950." *Chinese Historians* 5 (Summer 1992).

Marshall, Charles Burton. "The Very Image of a General." *Washington Post Book World*, 11 Oct. 1970.

Matray, James I. "Ensuring Korea's Freedom: The Decision to Cross the 38th Parallel." *Journal of American History* 66 (Sept. 1979).

Meixsel, Richard Bruce. "Manuel L. Quezon, Douglas MacArthur and the Significance of the Military Mission to the Philippine Commonwealth." *Pacific Historical Review* 70 (May 2001).

Mitchell, Franklin. "An Act of Presidential Indiscretion: Harry S. Truman, Congressman McDonough and the Marine Corps Incident of 1950." *Presidential Studies Quarterly* 11 (Feb. 1981).

Mrozek, Donald. "Progressive Dissenter: Herbert Hoover's Opposition to Truman's Overseas Military Policy." *Annals of Iowa* 42 (Summer 1976).

Nowowiejski, Dean. "Comrades in Arms: The Influence of George S. Patton on Walton H. Walker's Pusan Perimeter Defense." Unpublished paper, United States Military History Institute, 2001.

Paddock, Alfred H., Jr. "Robert Alexis McClure: Forgotten Father of Army Special Warfare." *Special Warfare* 12 (Fall 1999).

"'Prepare for 10 Years of Tension:' Interview with George C. Marshall." *U.S. News and World Report* 30 (April 13, 1951).

"Russian Documents on the Korean War, 1950–53." *Cold War International History Project Bulletin* 14/15 (Winter 2003–Spring 2003).

Schaller, Michael. "MacArthur's Japan: The View from Washington." In William M. Leary, ed., *MacArthur and the American Century: A Reader.* Lincoln: University of Nebraska Press, 2001.

Scott, Dr. Norman M. "General of the Army Douglas MacArthur and Me." *Bohemian Club Literary Notes* (Winter 1997–1998).

Shen Zhihua. "Sino-North Korean Conflict and its Resolution during the Korean War." *Cold War International History Project Bulletin* 14/15 (Winter 2003–Spring 2004).

———. "Sino-Soviet Relations and the Origins of the Korean War: Stalin's Strategic Goals in the Far East." *Journal of Cold War Studies* 2 (Spring 2000).

Sheng, Michael M. "Beijing's Decision to Enter the Korean War." *Korea and World Affairs* 19 (Summer 1995).

Sutherland, John P. "The Story General Marshall Told Me." *U.S. News and World Report* 47 (Nov. 2, 1959).

Weathersby, Kathryn. "'Should We Fear This?' Stalin and the Danger of War with America." Woodrow Wilson International Center, Cold War History Project, Working Paper No. 39 (July 2002).

"'Why I Won'—'Why I Lost.'" *U.S. News and World Report* 29 (17 Nov. 1950).

Wiltz, John Edward. "The MacArthur Hearings of 1951: The Secret Testimony." *Military Affairs* 39 (Dec. 1979).

———. "Truman and MacArthur: The Wake Island Meeting." *Military Affairs* 42 (Dec. 1978).

Xu Yan. "The Chinese Forces and Their Casualties in the Korean War: Facts and Statistics." *Chinese Historians* 6 (Fall 1993).

Index

Italicized page numbers indicate illustrations.

Michael D. Pearlman retired in 2006 as a professor of history at the United States Army Command and General Staff College, Fort Leavenworth. He is author of *Warmaking and American Democracy: The Struggle over Military Strategy, 1700 to the Present* and *To Make Democracy Safe for America: Patricians and Preparedness in the Progressive Era.*